Natural Law

Natural Law: Historical, Systematic and Juridical Approaches

Edited by

Alejandro N. García, Mario Šilar and José M. Torralba

Cambridge Scholars Publishing

Natural Law: Historical, Systematic and Juridical Approaches,
Edited by Alejandro N. García, Mario Šilar and José M. Torralba

This book first published 2008 by

Cambridge Scholars Publishing

12 Back Chapman Street, Newcastle upon Tyne, NE6 2XX, UK

British Library Cataloguing in Publication Data
A catalogue record for this book is available from the British Library

ISBN (10): 1-84718-643-2, ISBN (13): 9781847186430

TABLE OF CONTENTS

Part III: Systematic Approaches

Part IV: Juridical Approaches

ACKNOWLEDGEMENTS

Most of the chapters in this book were originally delivered as papers at the XLIV Reuniones Filosóficas (Philosophical Meetings) on Natural Law held at the University of Navarra from the 27th to the 29th March, 2006, organised by the Department of Philosophy in conjunction with the School of Humanities and Social Sciences and the Institute for Business and Humanism. We would like to thank Prof. Ana Marta González for her support and help in the preparation of this volume.

INTRODUCTION

The theory of natural law has become the focus of renewed interest in recent years, which is not limited only to academic reflection on moral issues. Indeed, the age-old question of a universal and abiding law has been revisited by anthropologists, sociologists, jurists, economists and psychologists, as well as by a large number of philosophers. In their re-examination of natural law, the purpose of these thinkers is marked by an attempt to address some of the most controversial questions facing contemporary multicultural societies. To a significant extent, therefore, renewed interest in the theory of natural law may be attributed to the fact that it is both convincing in itself and capable of shedding light on the cultural differences that criss-cross contemporary society.

The question of natural law is not a minor one. Multicultural societies are defined as such by the prevalence of a wide range of values, normative frameworks, and modes of behaviour, relationship and social life. The need to shape a common, normative framework that can encompass and respect difference may imply the recognition of a single human nature and of moral criteria whose validity is not merely conventional. In short, such a project requires that the theory of natural law be taken seriously.

To acknowledge natural law is to concede the existence of a basic common denominator shared with the other, who can no longer be regarded as absolutely alien, and instead becomes part of a more fundamental "we". This "we" encompasses every individual as a human being, and is prior to any convention, specific cultural phenomenon or political system. The grounds on which recognition of the other and a shared framework for social life may be articulated in a complete and reasoned way are based on this nature.

It is clear that this project calls for refined analysis and closely developed conceptualisation. Moreover, the approach ought to be interdisciplinary and kaleidoscopic. The purpose of this volume of papers, which presents the reflections on natural law of philosophers, theologians, anthropologists, sociologists and jurists in four themed sections, is to respond to these requirements.

The articles that comprise the first section provide an overview of the major thinkers and concepts in the history of the theory of natural law. Laura Corso de Estrada offers a starting-point for this historical impetus through her study of the Stoic vision reflected in the work of Cicero, which prompts analysis of the concept of "nature" as part of the Stoic articulation of a moral code based on the teleology of nature itself. Thereafter, Juan Luis Caballero's article examines one of the first conceptualisations of natural law in the Christian tradition. His refined and rigorous analysis of a number of extracts from St. Paul's *Letter to the Romans*, in particular, shows the profound implications and significance of his approach.

These articles pave the way for studies of the Middle Ages and the work of Thomas Aquinas. Joaquín García-Huidobro explores the links between practical reason and practical truth in Aquinas's thought, which give rise to a wide-ranging theory of natural law. In her article, María Elton examines Thomist arguments concerning meaning, the extent to which natural reason may err in its concretion of moral norms, and how all of this may be expressed clearly in terms of norms of custom.

The focus of María Idoya Zorroza Huarte's inquiry is Spanish thought in the School of Salamanca. The purpose of the writers in the school of thought associated with Salamanca was to arrive at an understanding of the reality underlying economic issues; in contrast to the voluntarism of nominalist thinkers, their work gave rise to a conception of economics based on natural law. This article is followed by Manfred Svensson's chapter on the reception of the legacy of Aristotelian thought and the idea of natural law in the work of Phillip Melanchthon, one of the most significant and influential thinkers in this regard during the Reformation.

This reflection on the Modern period is further developed by Raquel Lázaro who points out a number of the perhaps less widely acknowledged arguments contained in Cartesian thought: the notes on moral theory in which Descartes declares a debt to Montaigne's thought and sets out a number of interesting conclusions regarding natural law that deny Scholastic conceptions of practical reason and universal law.

In his article, Ángel Beleña offers a critical account of the philosophical naturalism embodied in Hume's moral reflections. The basic theses of Hume's thought are outlined, and the final paradox in which they are left exposed to a divine voluntarism is detailed. Agustín Ignacio Echavarría presents the contribution of Leibniz to the discussion; his analysis of Leibniz's conceptualisation of *universal harmony* and its grounding of *divine justice* prompts a far-reaching account of the idea of natural law and its moral implications.

Ivone Moreira proposes that the work of Edmund Burke be reinterpreted in relation to natural law. Both the most utilitarian views and those which are linked to the idea of natural law in different ways are outlined; the choice of texts and the overview offered in the article enable critical evaluation of the utilitarian perspective which predominates in Burke's thought.

This section on the major figures and topics in the history of natural law theory is brought to a close by José María Torralba whose article addresses Kantian thought. He shows that, in contrast to the established consensus regarding his work, Kant's philosophy is not alien to the tradition of natural law; indeed, his distinctive moral theory can only be understood in the light of natural law theory. Torralba's article focuses on the role of natural law in Kant's theory of moral judgment, as a first step towards the application of moral norms to practical action.

The second section of the book comprises a set of articles on different aspects of the contemporary reception of natural law. The first article, by Encarna Llamas, outlines a number of the most recent phenomenological interpretations. The work of Robert Sokolowski and Charles Taylor acts as a touchstone for understanding the current state-of-play in this line of thought.

In the second chapter in this section, Julia Urabayen explores Hannah Arendt's ideas with regard to human rights. The problems that arise when rights are made relative to citizenship are clearly dealt with; Urabayen goes on to show how rights based on human nature itself can only be safeguarded through an adequate definition of politics based on plurality. Margarita Mauri's article is a study of the work of Alasdair MacIntyre, as one of the contemporary philosophers whose work deals with the idea of natural law from a philosophical perspective in a most consistent way.

The chapter by Tomás Trigo draws this section of the book to a close. Trigo provides an overview of the debate in the 1960s and 1970s concerning the relationship between natural law and the Law of Christ.

The third section of the book comprises systematic and critical interpretations and studies of the issue. The first article, by Héctor Zagal, provides a critical evaluation of the versions of the idea of human nature reflected in the Aristotelian-Thomistic tradition. Zagal's article also points out a number of the significant difficulties involved in the attempt to ground moral law on an inadequate epistemology.

Mario Šilar presents some of the most recent versions and interpretations of the question in current Thomistic thinking. Rhonheimer's study of Thomistic thought regarding natural law discloses a set of refined interpretations of the relationship between natural law and practical reason; at the same time, this approach enables the resolution of a number of the controversial debates raging at the heart of the Thomistic tradition. The article by Teresa Enríquez offers a detailed account of the idea of *imperium*, in which new arguments concerning the fundamental link between natural norms and practical knowledge are advanced.

In a similar vein, and in light of the philosophical perspective of Thomas Aquinas and the anthropology of Leonardo Polo, Juan Fernando Sellés seeks to address the question of why the individual may obey or contravene the natural law; the conceptual distinctions between natural law, essential law and personal law drawn in the article enable a surefooted response to this question.

From a different perspective, José Ignacio Murillo addresses the strict distinction between *is* and *ought to be*, between reality and the moral law, in the work of David Hume; the difficulty implicit in a merely naturalist definition of individual health is invoked in this regard. The health of human being appears to be dependent on a norm that functions as the principle of intelligibility, a view which considerably extends the debate concerning the idea of human nature.

The book's final section focuses on the juridical interpretation and functionality of natural law. The first article, by Ángela Aparisi, outlines the implications of practical reason for moral theory and the juridical practice of prudence; that this type of rationality is necessary to the application of both natural law and juridical praxis to specific cases is explained. In his article, Carlos I. Massini takes the significance of practical reason in the juridical sphere as a keystone of his interpretative framework; Massini's purpose is to bring into clearer focus a range of standard arguments from different perspectives in the debate regarding the status of juridical science.

Pablo Sanchez-Ostiz addresses the distinctions between *conduct rules* and *imputation rules*, and the juridical implications they imply for the idea of natural law. These distinctions, along with further subdivisions, suggest that the attribution of responsibility through the notion of imputation rests on a single conception of rationality as the common basis for the interpretation of human behaviour.

Diego Poole's article is an attempt to redefine the principles of natural law, its links to practical reason and moral virtue, by drawing on classical sources in this area. His approach prompts further reflection on the idea of the common good, enabling a reformulation of the analogical conception of the law as the straightforward arrangement of parts towards the common good as a whole.

Finally, the concluding article in the book, by Caridad Velarde, aims to respond to the question regarding the essential criteria by which the sphere of juridical law may be defined. Given that juridical law may be read both from a normative perspective, as well as in terms of the obligations it entails, Velarde argues that the difference between juridical rules and the normativity involved in the spheres of morality or religion ought to be based on the idea of the *exigibility* of actions.

This book also contains an extensive bibliography of texts on natural law. The aim has been to provide a list of works that encompasses the wide variety of perspectives and debates concerning this issue, which may be of equal value and use to those starting their inquiries in this field and to those who are already expert in the subject.

Part I:

Historical Approaches

CHAPTER ONE

MARCUS TULLIUS CICERO AND THE ROLE OF NATURE IN THE KNOWLEDGE OF MORAL GOOD

LAURA E. CORSO DE ESTRADA

A historico-genetic approach to Marcus Tullius Cicero's more strictly philosophical writings, makes it possible to observe that his speculative efforts to justify the regulating order of practical life are deployed on the ontological, anthropological and moral planes, and at the same time, focus on the sphere that is pertinent to each of them, round the thematic core issue of the notion of "natura". Cicero's task is not without justification, if we consider the express sense that he assigns to his philosophical work—considered as a whole—and, also, to the main influence of his own approach in this respect.

In a recurrent way, Cicero underlines his purpose of attaining a plane of philosophically organic justification of the moral order, and expresses his perception of the epistemological scope and hierarchy that such a task entails. This is revealed, for example, in the passage of *De divinatione*, in which he distinguishes propaedeutic, teleological, cosmic-theological and strictly ethical developments in the course of his writing—at the time in progress—.[1] This obviously responds to the structuring sense that Cicero assigns to the practice of philosophy in the realization of "humanitas",[2]

[1] In Marcus Tullius Cicero, *De divinatione* (Stuttgart: Teubner, 1965), II, 1, 1-2, 3., Cicero expresses his commitment to constitute a corpus of philosophical matter as a contribution to public life. In the same place, he explicates the function that in such class of works have the ones written by himself until that moment, with a comprehensive aim in the domains practical-moral and its foundations.

[2] In his writings Cicero has developed the traits of his conception of humanitas as a paradigm. So, in ———, *De finibus bonorum et malorum* (Paris: Les Belles Lettres, 1961), V, 19, 54., he explains that the "cultivation of the soul" ("animi cultus") needs the cultivation exerted by philosophy in man as "a certain food of

and also—no less important—to the methodological value of moral assumptions from the point of view of justification. Thus, as made patent in the evolution of Cicero's writing, the consideration of existence and of the nature of a prescriptive "natural law" ("lex naturae") for practical life, cannot be autonomous from a philosophy of man and of a comprehensive view of reality. In this sense, it is also necessary to point out that Cicero's express allegiance to the Academy,[3] his frequent resorting to a directly

---

his humanity" ("quidam humanitas cibus"); this is the same that he had supported in ———, *De republica* (Stuttgart: Teubner, 1992), I, 17, 28., where he affirms that the denomination of "men" belongs only to the ones who "have been cultivated by the proper arts of human condition" ("essent politi propriis humanitatis artibus"). See also ———, *De oratore* (Paris: Les Belles Lettres, 1956), III, 15, 58., where we find an exhortation to frequentation of knowledge "as the way to shape the mind of children according to humanity and virtue" ("ut puerorum mentes ad humanitatem fingerentur atque virtutem"), *passim*; see the study of P. Boyancé in his Preface to P. Boyancé, *Études sur l'humanisme cicéronien* (Bruxelles: Latomus, 1970), 7ff.

[3] Cicero defines expressly himself as a disciple of the Academy since his meeting of Philo of Larisa; see Marcus Tullius Cicero, *Brutus* (Paris: Les Belles Lettres, 1966), LXXXIX, 306.; ———, *De natura deorum* (Stuttgart: Teubner, 1961), I, 3, 6, passim. In the development of many of his writings he exposes about the matter, shaping the mode of his adherence to that school and emphasizing the influx that platonic tradition and the positions of the named Philo and Anthiocus of Ascalon have exerted upon his own philosophical elaboration. In the most part of his expositions about this matter, Cicero holds the unity of the Academy as a philosophical movement, beyond differences that could be plead in relation with the teaching of the chiefs of this school; so, he assures the continuity of a dialectic attitude of search of truth that founds its matrix in Socratic and Platonic tradition. Hence, Cicero does not seem to admit distinctions between an "Ancient" and a "New" Academies along the history of the school; see about the matter, among other passages,———, *Academicorum reliquiae cum Lucullo* (Stuttgart: B.G. Teubner, 1961), 12, 46.; *Cicero, De finibus bonorum et malorum, II, 1,1.*; Marcus Tullius Cicero, *Tusculanae disputationes* (Paris: Les Belles Lettres, 1931), II, 3, 9. In relation with interpretation of Academy's history and, particularly, with the role of the New Academy in that process, see, among other various studies: C. Lévy, "Scépticisme et dogmatisme dans l'Academie: l'esoterisme d'Arcesilao," *Revue des Etudes Latines*, no. 56 (1978). Also ———, *Les philosophies hellénistiques* (Paris: Le Livre de Poche, 1997)., particularly pp. 181-212, where Levy considers the problem of interpretative positions about the matter in relation with the masters of the Academy posterior the period of Platonic tradition proper.

Platonic tradition,[4] and his access to testimonies from the (first and middle) Stoa were all constituting parts of a vast whole that he definitely projected on to the features that he assigned to nature, from his re-elaboration of all this as a Latin philosopher and author.

The thesis formulated in his early *De inventione Rhetorica*, subsequently noted by Christianity, in which Cicero pronounces himself in favour of the existence of a "natural right" ("naturae ius"), which constitutes a "certain force sown in nature,"[5] reveals a manifest doctrinal correlation to the notion expressed in that very same work related to the eminence of "virtus", i.e. being "in conformity with nature" ("naturae modo"),[6] given that this connection reveals his purpose of considering aretology as inserted within a conception of reality as a whole.

The first of Cicero's texts that can be regarded as properly philosophical, *De republica*, *De legibus*, develop his views within the context of the teachings of the Greek schools of thought that his analysis documents. Thus, despite its fragmentary preservation, Cicero's speculative effort in *De republica*, concerning political life in Rome—in which his own interests are involved—comprises his elaboration of a way to justify moral order in practical life from the epistemological consideration inherent to a philosophical examination of which may be the best form of government of the *res publica*.

In *De republica* Cicero contrasts two possible models in the moral development of human existence, both depending on a philosophy of man and of reality as a whole. On the one hand, in *De republica* I, he makes Scipio Emilianus[7] assert the existence of a Reason ("mens") that rules the whole world,[8] which he describes as a fully superior and divine, not

---

[4] In this sense we must underline that Cicero had access to platonic dialogues that he translated into latin, as the *Timeo*, of great influence in the cosmic-anthropologic elaboration of ciceronian *De republica* and *De legibus*.

[5] Marcus Tullius Cicero, *De inventione Rhetorica* (Paris: Les Belles Lettres, 1994), II, 53, 161.: "quaedam in natura vis insevit".

[6] Ibid., II, 53, 159.: the complete definition of *virtus* as *animi habitus naturae modo atque rationi consentaneus*.

[7] Recognized later because his services to roman public life, and remembered as the "Second African", or successor of Publio Scipio, the first one with such appellative, who in the context of the "Scipio's dream" in *De republica* VI, prophesies the achievements of his foster son in the course of his life; see Cicero, *De republica*, VI, 11, 11.

[8] So, in Ibid., I, 36, 56., Scipio Emilianus affirms: "Those who have investigated the nature of all things thought that all this world is governed by a Reason" ("Qui natura omnium rerum pervestiganda senserunt omnem hunc mundum mente").

mediated, "nature law" ("lex naturae") universal, absolutely primal, invariable and eternal. It is particularly expressive of that conception the passage of *De republica* I where Scipio discerns, with a literary context of platonic resonance, hierarchical dimensions in the plurality of reality, and the primacy of goodness that must be predicated of all what reveals a modality of being not mutable and, therefore, imperishable, as it is peculiar to a divine nature. Because he says there: "what can be considered as superior among human things for whom has contemplated the divine reigns, or as permanent for whom has knew what is eternal?"[9]

Cicero places the natural order of the world as a whole and the normative order of practical life on this ontic plane, whereas the ruling divine Reason, which is endowed with the primal and proper sense of "Reason" ("Ratio") and of "Right Reason" ("Ratio recta"), is "disseminated" ("diffusa") throughout everything that exists;[10] as explained in the oration in which Lelius, who had close links with Scipio's circle, expands on this view. This explains why, in the same context Cicero should ask rhetorically:

> which superior authority, which magistrate, which kingdom can exceed that of he who, despising all human possessions and considering them to be inferior to wisdom, does not reflect in his soul except about what is perennial and divine?.[11]

In other words, he presents a paradigm of man, that of the virtuous man, that matches the features of the Socratic-Platonic intellectualist tradition taken up again by the Aristotelian and Stoic teachings, and which Cicero receives within the sphere of Latin thinking, re-elaborating a philosophic conception of reality and human nature. In fact, the evolution of Ciceronian thought with shades of Plato differentiates between ontic planes: the one that corresponds to the divine founding rationality, which is the ruler of the sphere of mutability; yet also conceived of within the doctrinal framework of the First Stoa, in terms of the entitative unit that

---

[9] Ibid., I, 17, 26.: "quid porro aut praeclarum putet in rebus humanis, qui haec deorum regna perspexerit, aut diuturnum, qui cognoverit quid sit aeternum"; this text follows with a comparison between particular earthly goods dependent of value judgments limited to a particular an movable reality, and not immediate and imperishable goods.

[10] Cfr. Ibid., III, 22, 33.

[11] Ibid., I, 17, 28.:"quod autem imperium, qui magistratus, quod regnum potest esse praestantius quam despicientem omnia humana et inferiora sapientia ducentem nihil umquam nisi sempiternum et divinum animo volutare?"

defines a "true Law" ("lex vera") and "right Reason" ("recta ratio"), a "sempiternal" ("sempiterna") and "immutable" ("immutabilis"), and which identifies with "God" ("deus"), "Master" ("magister") and "Sovereign" ("imperator") of all,[12] inherent to all beings in the world. This conception of reality bespeaks a teleology constitutive of a natural universal order, in which Cicero has brought about the convergence of two of the most salient teleological theories of Antiquity, namely, Platonism and Stoicism; which, beyond undeniable differences in doctrine, as pointed out by J. Moreau and J. Pepin, share the vision of a cosmos that has been penetrated in its whole and parts by divine rationality.[13] In this sense a thorough analysis of the Ciceronian position reveals the influence of Antiochus of Ascalon, the last scholarch of the Academy, who, in an effort to make the school's approach return to its initial identity, fused together into a common heritage the teachings of Plato with those of Aristotle and the Stoics, as documented by Cicero himself.[14]

From a methodological point of view, it should be noted that in *De republica* Cicero makes an appeal to nature considered as a whole, and to human nature, as part of that whole, in the justificatory way of moral order. In *De republica* VI, in the context of "Scipio's dream", he asserts distinctly the divine origin of the human soul in passages that have particularly intense similarities with Platonic texts, in which he underlines the kinship of man and divinity,[15] by means of which man is destined—ever since he came to be—to live a life inherent to his condition, endowed with the ability to disclose such end . In other words, there is in man himself an inchoate "humanitas" that reveals itself in his specific natural

---

[12] Cfr. Ibid., III, 22, 33.

[13] Cfr. J. Moreau, *L'ame du monde. De Platon aux Stoïciennes* (Paris: Les Belles Lettres, 1939), 2ff., *passim*, and Jean Pepin, *Théologie Cosmique et Théologie Chrétienne (Ambroise, Exam. I, 1, 1-4)* (Paris: Presses Universitaires de France, 1964), 128-30.

[14] Cicero identifies in the teaching of the named Anthiocus some thesis of stoical source; Cicero, *Lucullus* 22, 69 and 70 (in Cicero, *Academicorum reliquiae cum Lucullo*.). But, following Anthiocus, he affirms recurrently in his writings that between the teachings of the academic-peripatetic patrimony and the one of the Stoa there are differences only of linguistic modality; see Marcus Tullius Cicero, *De legibus* (Paris: Les Belles Lettres, 1968), I, 13, 38.; Cicero, *De finibus bonorum et malorum*, III, 3, 10, passim.

[15] Cicero, *De republica*, VI, 17,17.; VI, 24, 26, y *Plato, Timée (Paris: Les Belles Lettres, 1925)*. 69, c, 90 a; ———, *La República* (Madrid: Centro de Estudios Políticos y Constitucionales, 1997). 589 d; ———, *Las Leyes* (Madrid: Centro de Estudios Constitucionales, 1984). 899 a; *passim.*

inclinations. And this becomes manifest, according to Cicero in *De republica*, by the "need for virtue" ("necessitas virtutis") "naturally" (a natura) existing in mankind and "the love" ("amor") to defend the common good,[16] both of which constitute the anthropological foundations on which Cicero builds up the aptitude of humankind to realize its perfective end, which comprises the opening to others under man's natural sociability. This thesis is reinforced by Cicero when he asserts the existence of—also natural—signs, of the natural moral order, such as the spontaneity of shame and the fear of disapproval.[17]

In order to appreciate the organic speculative effort undertaken by Cicero, it may be of interest to contrast the views described above, with respect to which this author expresses his allegiance in *De republica* through the favourable opinion of Scipio Aemilianus, with the views expressed by Lucius Philo (another member of the circle of intellectuals in this dialogue), intended to represent the ongoing discussions at the Academy at the time of Carneades. According to Lucius Philo, who restricts the sphere of the real to the diversity and mutability of events, the variety of conceptions of the law, dispositions, norms and customs existing in different peoples, and even in one same city implies the non existence of one single way of defining what is just or unjust for all men. From this we can surmise that "nature is not the mother of justice,"[18] and that the indigence of the human condition only allows the peoples to make a "pact" ("pactio") in order to attain civic harmony.[19]

In *De legibus* we find that there is a fundamental assertion that can be likened to the central features of Cicero's views in *De republica*, in which the link between divine Reason, cosmic nature and human nature

---

[16] Cicero, *De republica*, I, 1,1.: "hoc definio, tantam esse necessitatem virtutis generi hominum a natura tantumque amorem ad communem salutem defendendam datum".

[17] See Ibid., III, 22, 33.; V, 4, 6. Cicero takes again this thesis which affirms the existence of natural signs of a natural order in other writings; so, in ———, *De legibus*, I, 14, 40., he sustains the existence of "the furies" ("furiae") who disturb the soul of the guilty and, in the same place, the need of justification that the impious has to cover his actions. In this sense, he also exposes in other passages about the external manifestation of internal traits; see Marcus Tullius Cicero, *De officiis* (Paris: Les Belles Lettres, 1965), I, 30, 108., where because of this he transfers terms of corporeal fields to moral fields, as he does in Cicero, *De legibus*, I, 19, 51., where he predicates the "ugliness" ("deformitas") of soul as a consequence of vices.

[18] Cicero, *De republica*, III, 13, 23.: *iustitiae non natura ... mater est.*

[19] Ibid.

constitutes the justificatory way that underpins moral order.[20] If we take a brief look at the main theses in common, we can point out that in *De legibus* Cicero defines the epistemological plane from which it is possible to examine what be the law, as well as the methodological procedure to do so. In fact, following his line of reasoning, we can say with respect to the former issue that its object is to consider the law "from the deepest plane of philosophy;"[21] as for procedure, he suggests starting from the consideration "of the nature of man"[22] in order to arrive at "the Universal reason of being of the law in general and all laws as a whole,"[23] thus making explicit the purpose of his enquiry.

The notion of law that Cicero examines at length in *De legibus* I and II, allows us to perceive the differentiation between the philosophical planes from which he perceives and justifies his conception around nature. As in *De republica*, also in *De legibus,* in its inherent and fully primary sense, the law is predicated from a reality that is not human but divine, identified with "the greatest Reason inherent to nature,"[24] i.e such "force of nature,"[25] "common to all times,"[26] as is the "Reason of the God" ruling above all things,[27] "the heavenly Law,"[28] "right Reason of Supreme Jupiter."[29]

It is on this foundational ontic plane that Cicero places, in this work as well, the intrinsic rationality of the cosmos manifesting its teleological natural order. And he constitutes the genus of mankind as "sown throughout the Earth"[30] and elevated from its origin by the "divine gift" ("munus divinum") of the soul,[31] as the single participant in the cosmic sphere of such "relationships as kinship and family" are to be found together with divine reality on account of their shared nature in rationality.[32] Not disregarding the intense doctrinal and linguistic resonances of the cosmic theological conception of the Stoa and, definitely

[20] See also ———, *De officiis*, III, 5, 23, passim.
[21] ———, *De legibus*, I, 5, 17.: "ex intima philosophia".
[22] Ibid.: "ab hominis ... natura".
[23] Ibid.: "tota causa est universi iuris ac legum".
[24] Ibid., I, 6, 18.: "Ratio summa, insita in natura".
[25] Ibid., I, 6, 19.: "naturae vis".
[26] Ibid.: "saeclis communis omnibus".
[27] Ibid., II, 4, 8.: "mens dei".
[28] Ibid., II, 4, 9.: "caelestis lex".
[29] Ibid., II, 5, 11.: "ratio est recta summi Iovis".
[30] Ibid., I, 7, 24.: "sparsum in terras".
[31] Ibid.
[32] Ibid., I, 7, 23.: "homines deorum agnatione et gente teneantur"

on the teachings of this school about the "lógos spermatikós" spread over everything existing,[33] it is impossible not to pay attention also the presence of features typical of Platonic elaboration on this issue, as P. Festugière, P. Boyancé and later C. Lévy have noted. In this connection, the remarkable influence of *Timaeus* is of particular interest, as revealed by these Ciceronian theses in *De legibus*, and the speculative drift that this contributes with Cicero's elaboration beyond the strict immanence and corporalism of the first Stoa. Thus, Festugière's attention is caught by the passage in Plato's *Timaeus*, in which the creator of the world announces that it will be necessary to "spread" on men the "seed" that will make them sharers of the divine nature.[34]

As can be derived from the theses contained in *De legibus*, Cicero adheres to an invariable methodological position in his appeal to nature as the justificatory way of moral order. This is precisely because the rational participation of human nature in divine Reason enables man, on the basis of the knowledge of his own condition, to become aware of the law, which he himself carries, as the law that rules his own perfective aim. In other words, the appeal to self-knowledge for the realization of moral good, which is characteristic of the Socratico-Platonic tradition and has been clearly accepted by Cicero, finds through him in Rome a justification that is both cosmic-theological and anthropological in his conception of the natural Law as divine rationality, of which human rationality has a share. Cicero points this out expressly and asserts: "he who knows himself, in the first place will perceive that there is in him something divine and will appreciate his reason as a consecrated image existing within him."[35]

So, what does man find within himself? In *De legibus* we find not only the cosmic-theological justification of human connaturality with the natural universal Law, the Right Reason of the cosmos, but also the psychologico-cognoscitive justification of why this law exerts a teleological regulation leading to the knowledge of moral good. Thus, in what follows we shall refer to the Stoic tradition doctrinal framework by means of which Cicero links the inner perception of the human self with

[33] Cfr. Diogene Laerzio, *Vite dei Filosofi* (Bari: Laterza, 1962), 136.

[34] Cfr. Plato, *Timée*. 41, c; and cfr. P. Festugière, *La Révélation d'Hermes Trismègiste* (Paris: Lecoffre, 1950), IV, 430. Boyancé, *Études sur l'humanisme cicéronien*, 295. C. Lévy, *Recherches sur les Académiques et sur la philosophie cicéronienne* (Paris-Rome: Palais Farnèse-École Française de Rome, 1992), 516-17.

[35] Cicero, *De Legibus*, I, 22, 59: "qui se ipse norit primum aliquid se habere sentiet divinum ingeniumque in se suum sicut simulacrum aliquod dicatum putabit".

the tendency projected in practical life. This is particularly relevant because Cicero—among other men in Antiquity—has also realized the existence of the sphere of subjectivity, which R. Mondolfo rightly places among the important contributions to thought made in those times.[36]

When in *De legibus* I Cicero lists the gifts with which nature has endowed man and describes those of a physical nature, on whose aptitude to express psychological features he reflects,[37] he goes into the human aptitudes that divinity has given him so that he can get to know. Thus, he says, on the one hand, that nature "has given him the senses, as assistants and messengers,"[38] but he also adds that within the domain of human reason, nature "has placed some inchoate notions,"[39] which he proceeds to describe as "not clarified and not sufficiently defined."[40] In other subsequent passages, with equivalent formulations, he adds that they are "primal and germinal,"[41] or rather "sketchy notions,"[42] which he also characterizes as being "similarly imprinted on all"[43] and aimed at getting to know "what is honourable in virtue and what is dishonest among vices."[44]

It is in the Hellenistic disputes on truth criteria that we can find the context within which Cicero has elaborated the thesis presented in *De legibus*, i.e. a natural cognoscitive aptitude of human reason, which disposes man towards discerning right in practical and moral matters.

---

[36] R. Mondolfo, *La comprensión del sujeto humano en la cultura antigua* (Buenos Aires: Imán, 1955), 13.

[37] In Cicero, *De legibus*, I, 9, 26 and 27., Cicero describes the congruity of the physical traits of man with those that belong to his specific nature; thus, justifies the fact that nature has done man erect with his rational aptitude for the community with gods, and he detains in some particular notes and, specially, in the expressive of face; see also about the matter ———, *De officiis*, I, 30, 107.

[38] Cicero, *De legibus*, I, 9, 26.: "natura ... sensus tamquam satellites attribuit ac nuntios".

[39] Ibid.: "inchoavit intellegentias". Although the passage cited presents some difficulties related to the use of the Latin term "inchoavit", we have followed the observations of the K. Ziegler, Heildelberg, edition of 1950, and also the doctrinal support offered to this notion by other texts by Cicero from *De legibus,* which we also examine in the present work.

[40] Ibid.: "obscuras nec satis expressas".

[41] Ibid., I, 9, 27. y I, 10, 30: "prima et inchoata intellegentia".

[42] Ibid., I, 22, 59.: "adumbratae intellegentiae".

[43] Ibid., I, 10, 30.: "similiter in omnibus imprimuntur".

[44] Ibid., I, 16, 44.: "Nam, ut communis intellegentia nobis notas res efficit easque in animis nostris inchoavit, honesta in virtute ponuntur, in vitiis turpia".

In line with the Stoic position, Cicero also assigns to knowledge a leading role in relation to practical valuation and the realization of the trend. But also, as already aimed at in the First Stoa, there is an attempt, through this anthropological analysis, to reconcile the cognoscitive connaturality of man with the practical truth.

It was not Cicero's aim to suggest an innatist position, but a conception of human nature which, on the one hand is expressive of the rationality of the whole yet, on the other hand, is the cosmic apex of such rationality, carries within its own self the seeds of its own perfective aim. Thus, the participation of divine "Mens" in that of man implies that it should invest reason itself with the order leading to the disclosing of the truth that constitutes its object. And, as we have seen, following Cicero's views in this connection, this participation of divine Reason in man does not itself consummate man's cognoscitive power, nor does it replace in man the process of pursuit of what is true, since it only bestows the aptitude to attain it, as Cicero makes it clear in his choice of words, when he says that nature has carried out an "inchoate" work in man, which has imprinted on his reason the mere "germ" or "sketch" of knowledge.[45] In this sense, Cicero also makes his position explicit when he says that such germ of knowledge was given to man so that he may be led by nature itself in the pursuit of other knowledge,[46] or rather, that these notions that are merely outlined in him by nature should be clarified by the cultivation of wisdom.[47] In other words, and as already mentioned before, would be a natural *primal* disposition.

Already in the first Stoa, in connection with his conception of the "comprehensive represention" entailing the guarantee of their truth in their being accepted by the "logos,"[48] it is possible to distinguish certain "notions" ("énnoiai"), that are "natural" ("émphytoi") in terms of the

---

[45] See *supra* notes: 38-41.

[46] Cicero, *De legibus*, I, 9, 27.: "It results manifest …that human nature proceeds by its own in an ascending way, and even without any guide, starting from what has knew across that first and germinal knowledge, nature reinforces reason by itself and perfects it" ("perspicuum fit ... ipsam per se naturam longius progredi, quae etiam nullo docente, profecta ab iis quorum ex prima et inchoata intellegentia genera cognovit, confirmat ipsa per se rationem et perficit").

[47] Ibid., I, 22, 59.: "he perceived in his soul and in his knowledge in the manner of certain inchoated notions of all things that, when they have been clarified by the guide of wisdom, allows him to understand that he will be a good man" ("adumbratas intelligentias animo ac mente conceperit, quibus inlustratis sapientia duce bonum virum")

[48] Laerzio, *Vite dei Filosofi.*, 54, *passim.*

human dispositions to get to know them which, for this reason, are described as "pre-notions" or "anticipations" ("prólepseis"), which are "common" ("koinnai") to all men.[49] As pointed out, among others by R. Mondolfo[50] and A. Voelke,[51] Stoicism makes a doctrinal effort to link the cognoscitive sphere, and more precisely, that of internal perception, with that of the expressive force of a preceding practico-moral value judgement. This accounts for his assertion of the existence of "pre-notions" or "anticipations" ("prólepseis") concerning a guiding knowledge in matters moral, i.e. in relation with the good and the bad, the just and the unjust, the honourable and the dishonourable.[52] It is these pre-notions, both among the Stoics and in Cicero's re-elaboration, that were later extended to theological matters[53] and, in the case of Cicero in particular, to speculative matters.[54]

In a period that followed *De legibus*, in *De Finibus,* Cicero resorts to the Stoic theory of "oikeíosis"[55] in his writing and includes in his study a particularly analytic consideration of the inter-relation between knowledge and trend, asserting the existence of a primary ruling impulse of human life that impels towards love and self-knowledge, according to which self-

---

[49] Cicero, *Academicorum reliquiae cum Lucullo*, 11, 41.; *Lucullus* 6, 18; 47, 145; Laerzio, *Vite dei Filosofi*., 54, *passim.* See among other studies: F. Sandbach, "Ennoia and prólepsis in the Stoic Theory of Knowledge," in *Problems in stoicism*, ed. A. Long (London: The Athlone Press, 1971), 30-31.

[50] Cfr. Mondolfo, *La comprensión del sujeto humano en la cultura antigua*, 518.

[51] Cfr. A. Voelke, *L'idée de volonté dans le stoïcisme* (Paris: Presses Universitaires de France, 1973), 50ff.

[52] Cfr. Hans Friedrich August von Arnim, *Stoicorum Veterum Fragmenta* (Stuttgart: Stoicorum Veterum Fragmenta, 1964), 128; Laerzio, *Vite dei Filosofi*, 53.; and the study of Sandbach, "Ennoia and prólepsis in the Stoic Theory of Knowledge," 30-31.

[53] Cfr. Ibid., 69, and Cicero, *De natura deorum*, II, 5, 13 and ff., *passim.*

[54] Cicero, *De finibus bonorum et malorum*, III, 6, 20., *passim.*

[55] Cicero's development in Ibid., III, 4, 16. about the stoic doctrine of "oikeiosis", is presented in this passage as: "ipsum sibi conciliari" ("to attracted to himself") and "commendari ad se conservandum" ("to be conducted to the conservation of himself") as a consequence of the first inclination of nature, constitutes one of the main texts for the reconstruction of the named teaching of the school, as also the exposition of Laerzio, *Vite dei Filosofi*, 85. See in Cicero, *De finibus bonorum et malorum*, IV, 10, 24-26.; *Lucullus* 12, 38; ———, *De officiis*, I, 4, 11. In this sense, see among other studies: S. Pembroke, "Oikeiosis," in *Problems in stoicism*, ed. A. Long (London: The Athlone Press, 1971), 114-49. See also J. Annas, *The morality of Happiness* (New York: Oxford University Press, 1993), 264, 87 passim.

appetition as the object of such primary love becomes the natural way to self-knowledge and the process of disclosure of the human condition. In this sense we can realize the continuity of the appellation to nature in order to reach the human perfection. Natural inclinations of man dispose him to find in himself and in the progressive development of his specific condition a paradigm in germen. Cicero sustains that "the first inclinations of nature" ("initiis") are sources of knowledge of "duties" ("officia"), because natural ends are invested of moral finalities. As he says, in the measure in which this natural aptitude of knowing and wishing the own condition is accomplished, man chooses for himself that which is "in accordance with nature" and rejects what is its contrary;[56] when this way of living gets continuous and stable , human life affirms in knowledge and in love of what properly constitutes its good.[57]

Cicero examines carefully how the field of natural inclinations doesn't fit man to his own individuality, because the perception of human condition in itself constitutes the source of his opening to others with whom participates of rational nature and with whom conforms a primary community. Cicero sustains this expressly in *De legibus* when he affirms: "there is nothing superior to reason, and, so reason is present in man and in the god, there is a primary association of man and the god because of reason. But, among these ones in whom reason is common, also is common the right reason, which, because it is law, must make us think that we, men, are associated with gods precisely in virtue of that law. Those who have this things in common must be considered as belonging to the same city."[58] About this position Cicero also exposes in the named *De finibus*, in an open convergence with stoic tradition: "the world…is as the great and common city of men and gods…Each one of us is part of that world, hence we must put common benefit before that ours...[59] We have been born to get together with the other men and for association and

[56] Cicero, *De finibus bonorum et malorum*, III, 6, 20.: "ea quae secundum naturam sunt ipsa propter se sumenda sint contrariaque reicienda".

[57] Cfr. Ibid., III, 6, 20-21.

[58] ———, *De legibus*, I, 7, 23.: "nihil est ratione melius, eaque est et in homine et in deo, prima homini cum deo rationis societas. Inter quos autem ratio, inter eosdem etiam recta ratio communis est: quae cum sit lex, lege quoque consociati homines cum dis putandi sumus ... Quibus autem haec sunt inter eos communia, ei civitatis eiusdem habendi sunt".

[59] ———, *De finibus bonorum et malorum*, III, 19, 64.: "Mundum ... quasi communem urbem et civitatem hominum et deorum ... unum quemque nostrum eius mundi esse partem; ex quo illud natura consequi, ut communem utilitatem nostrae anteponamus".

community of mankind."[60] Cicero takes again this thesis with continuity in his writings, as in *De officiis*: "Nature, by force of reason, links man with man, for the communication with words and for life in society."[61]

From the above, it may be pertinent to conclude that Cicero's philosophical aim in elaborating his cosmic-theological and anthropological assumptions of the moral order enabled him to establish that virtue consists "in conforming" to nature as a seminal principle of moral life, in line with the Socratico-Platonic tradition as forged by the Stoic doctrine. Cicero identifies expressly this thesis with the teaching of the Stoa when sustains: "That what stoics call 'homology', we will denominate—if it seems appropriate—'convenientia'."[62] Because human condition carries inborn in its rational nature the aptitude "for a certain way of living"[63] not "for anyone".[64]

Works Cited

Arnim, Hans Friedrich August von. *Stoicorum Veterum Fragmenta*. Stuttgart: Stoicorum Veterum Fragmenta, 1964.

Annas, J. *The Morality of Happiness*. New York: Oxford University Press, 1993.

Boyancé, P. *Études Sur L'humanisme Cicéronien*. Bruxelles: Latomus, 1970.

Cicero, Marcus Tullius. *Academicorum Reliquiae Cum Lucullo*. Stuttgart: B.G. Teubner, 1961.

—. *Brutus*. Paris: Les Belles Lettres, 1966.

—. *De Divinatione*. Stuttgart: Teubner, 1965.

—. *De Finibus Bonorum Et Malorum*. Paris: Les Belles Lettres, 1961.

—. *De Inventione Rhetorica*. Paris: Les Belles Lettres, 1994.

—. *De Legibus*. Paris: Les Belles Lettres, 1968.

—. *De Natura Deorum*. Stuttgart: Teubner, 1961.

—. *De Officiis*. Paris: Les Belles Lettres, 1965.

—. *De Oratore*. Paris: Les Belles Lettres, 1956.

---

[60] Ibid., IV, 2, 4.: "viderent ... natosque esse ad congregationem hominum et ad societatem communitatemque generis humani"; *passim*.

[61] ———, *De officiis*, I, 4, 12.: "natura vi rationis homini conciliat homini et ad orationis et ad vitae societatem".

[62] ———, *De finibus bonorum et malorum*, III, 6, 21.: "quod 'homologia' Stoici, nos appellemus 'convenientiam', si placet".

[63] Ibid., III, 7, 23.: "ad quandam formam vivendi".

[64] Ibid.: "non ad quodvis".

—. *De Republica*. Stuttgart: Teubner, 1992.
—. *Tusculanae Disputationes*. Paris: Les Belles Lettres, 1931.
Festugière, P. *La Révélation D'Hermes Trismègiste*. Paris: Lecoffre, 1950.
Laerzio, Diogene. *Vite Dei Filosofi*. Bari: Laterza, 1962.
Lévy, C. *Recherches sur les académiques et sur la philosophie cicéronienne*. Paris-Rome: Palais Farnèse-École Française de Rome, 1992.
—. *Les Philosophies Hellénistiques*. Paris: Le Livre de Poche, 1997.
—. "Scépticisme Et Dogmatisme Dans L'academie: L'esoterisme D'arcesilao." *Revue des Etudes Latines*, no. 56 (1978): 335-48.
Mondolfo, R. *La comprensión del sujeto humano en la cultura antigua*. Buenos Aires: Imán, 1955.
Moreau, J. *L'Ame Du Monde. De Platon aux Stoïciennes*. Paris: Les Belles Lettres, 1939.
Pembroke, S. "Oikeiosis." In *Problems in Stoicism*, edited by A. Long, 114-49. London: The Athlone Press, 1971.
Pepin, J. *Théologie cosmique et théologie chrétienne (Ambroise, Exam. I, 1, 1-4)*. Paris: Presses Universitaires de France, 1964.
Plato. *La República*. Madrid: Centro de Estudios Políticos y Constitucionales, 1997.
—. *Las Leyes*. Madrid: Centro de Estudios Constitucionales, 1984.
—. *Timée*. Paris: Les Belles Lettres, 1925.
Sandbach, F. "Ennoia and Prólepsis in the Stoic Theory of Knowledge." In *Problems in Stoicism*, edited by A. Long, 22-37. London: The Athlone Press, 1971.
Voelke, A. *L'Idée De volonté dans le Stoïcisme*. Paris: Presses Universitaires de France, 1973.
Von Arnim, I. *Stoicorum Veterum Fragmenta*. Stuttgart, 1964.

CHAPTER TWO

ROM 1:18–2:16 AND NATURAL LAW: A RHETORICAL APPROACH

JUAN-LUIS CABALLERO

The word "nomos", law, appears quite frequently in the *Letter to the Romans*; in this work of St. Paul this word plays a leading role in the history of the salvation of mankind. Nevertheless, throughout the writings of Paul the word law is used with great ambivalence, and its exact meaning is not always clearly pinpointed: it may be the Mosaic Law, the law of Christ, law in a much more generic sense, etc.

Specifically, in the first two chapters of the *Letter to the Romans*, an unwritten law is referred to, engraved on the hearts of men[1]:

"So, when gentiles, not having the Law, still through their own innate sense behave as the Law commands, then, even though they have no Law, they are a law for themselves. They can demonstrate the effect of the Law engraved on their hearts, to which their own conscience bears witness; since they are aware of various considerations, some of which accuse them, while others provide them with a defense" (Rom 2:14-15).

What is Paul talking about in these verses? Just how useful would this text be in the scope of things that we consider when reflecting on what we call natural law?

In this study we will focus on two passages from the *Letter to the Romans*: Rom 1:18-32 and Rom 2:14-16. The intent of the following considerations is to situate these two sets of verses in the general context of the *Letter to the Romans*.[2] To this effect we will approach the texts from a rhetorical point of view, in order to best determine their function and

---

[1] The translation of the Bible quoted in this study is that of the *New Jerusalem Bible* (New York: Doubleday, 1985).

[2] We leave aside other Pauline texts that may be of interest when dealing with natural law and conscience, such as Rom 7:14-25 or 1 Cor 8.

sense in the Letter as a whole. The recourse to the rhetorical aspect is founded on the chiefly argumentative nature of the document in question.

Some initial considerations

Due to the absolutely singular nature of the writings of the New Testament, part of which is formed by the individual characteristics of the Pauline letters, a few things must be considered in order to set the scene:

a) The *Letter to the Romans* is not a Letter that can be understood straight away. Leaving aside other aspects that can make its sense dark and distant, this Letter, especially in Chapters 1-8, is of a profoundly argumentative nature. This implies that for its correct understanding, an approach that allows for a personalization of the theses purported by Paul—the propositions—is needed; not to mention the necessity of the classification, according to importance, of the reasons and proofs that he gives to support them. The latter are given in favor of the former, and are not what the Letter directly deals with.[3]

b) We must take into account its historical context, both cultural and religious, as well as the exact sense that Paul gives each term he uses, which confers a concrete and meaningful orientation to the comparisons, the paradoxes, and the antitheses, all of which he so frequently puts into use.

c) It is necessary, and on occasion crucial—in reference to the understanding of the text—, to define who the speaker or speakers are, in the "dialogue" that the Apostle presents: the pious Jew; the Christian of Jewish origin; the Christian of a gentile origin; the gentile, or the non-Jew, i.e., the nations: the setting in which St. Paul finds himself is the Judaism of his time.[4]

d) Even though it may seem a somewhat generic piece of input if not illustrated with examples, it is important to keep in mind that Paul very frequently uses implications in his reasoning that derive from statements in Holy Scripture, and yet do not appear explicitly in the Biblical text.

---

[3] Cf. George A. Kennedy, *New Testament Interpretation through Rhetorical Criticism*, Studies in Religion (Chapel Hill/London: The University of North Carolina Press, 1984), 9.

[4] Cf. Jean-Noël Aletti, *Comment Dieu est-il juste? Clefs pour interpréter l'épître aux Romains* (Paris: Seuil, 1991).

The viewpoint of the Letter to the Romans

The Letter to the Romans reflects on the Gospel of Christ, more specifically on his saving power that is for everyone, Jews and non-Jews; Jew being the person who accepts the Mosaic Law and puts it into practice. The Letter moves on, to considering life according to the Gospel. The following scheme of the Letter may be helpful for us to see its contents at a glance[5]:

Greetings (1:1-7)
Exordium (1:8-17)
Proofs:
    I (A) 1:18-4:25: Jews and Greeks justified by faith alone
    I (B) 5-8: the new life and hope of the baptized
    II 9-11: Israel and other nations: the future of Israel
Exhortations (12:1–15:13)
Peroration (15:14-21)
News and Final Greeting (15:22-16:27)

The text that we are going to study, Rom 1-2, is in the first part of the argumentation found in Rom 1-8. In order to situate its rhetorical role in the most exact way possible, we must pay attention to the development and key points of the discursive train of thought, even if only roughly.

Rom 1-2 in the context of the Rom 1-8 discourse

In a much more detailed manner, here is the division of the discourse found in Rom 1-8:

1:16-17 proposition or principal thesis of the Letter
1:18-8:39 first proof
    a) 1:18-4:25 Jews and Greeks justified by faith alone
        1:18-3:20 reasoning following the Jewish principles

[5] This division was proposed by ———, "Romanos," in *Comentario Bíblico Internacional. Comentario católico y ecuménico para el siglo XXI*, ed. William R. Farmer, et al. (Estella: Verbo Divino, 1999), 1417. Other modern and interesting commentaries on the Letter to the Romans are: Joseph A. Fitzmyer, *Romans*, The Anchor Bible (New York: Doubleday, 1993); Douglas J. Moo, *The Epistle to the Romans* (NICNT, Grand Rapids: Eerdmans, 1996); Antonio Pitta, *Lettera ai Romani* (Milano: Paoline, 2001).

3:21-4:25 Christian reasoning
b) 5:1-8:39 the new life and the hope of the baptized

Rom 1:16-17. The proposition or fundamental thesis of the Letter is contained in these verses, in such a way that they are a summary of everything to come:

"For I see no reason to be ashamed of the gospel; it is God's power for the salvation of everyone who has faith—Jews first, but Greeks as well—for in it is revealed the saving justice of God: a justice based on faith and addressed to faith. As it says in scripture: *Anyone who is upright through faith will live*".

Chapters 1-8 give, in an argumentative layout, the reasons and proofs that back the thesis of the Letter. Paul's logic is not easy to follow if we do not take into consideration both the literary devices that he uses, as well as the addressees to whom he is writing. In reality it is all about showing the saving power of the Gospel; a force that affects everyone, Jews and non-Jews alike. The factors that come into play are the Gospel: its content, effects, finality, addressees, etc.; sin and divine justice; that which the believer is and does: justification, salvation, behavior, etc.; the Mosaic Law: its function and its relationship with previous factors.

In the discourse, chapters 1-4 tell us about salvation for all, Jews and gentiles, through faith in Jesus Christ, about the source of this justification, and about how this justification is brought about: everyone, without exception, has been justified in the same way: either everything is done by way of the Law, or by way of Jesus Christ. Thus, these chapters refer to the manifestation of divine justice and its different modalities.

The conclusion to chapters 1-4 is based on what is expressed in chapters 1-2: all are justified in the same way because everyone is a sinner. In effect, everyone, Jews and Gentiles alike, is a sinner before God due to the fact that, one way or another, they have decided not to pay homage to Him or do His will. This is why, in the past, God has dispensed negative retribution: He cannot stand sin. Nevertheless, God's justice is mercy. Which is why everyone has access—and after the coming of Christ there are no special privileges: the justice of God is impartial—to the salvation that God has offered us through our faith in Jesus Christ—which is exactly what the Gospel tells us—.

We are interested in studying why Saint Paul speaks about an universal guilt and with what choice of words; this we will see when commenting Rom 1:18-32.

The Jewish principles used in Rom 1:18-3:20

In 1:18-3:20 Paul bases his argument on the Jewish principles of the time: not that he accepts them. What he does is analyze the situation of man according to these principles and the biblical ideas about the retributive justice of God in order to reach a number of consequences that could be accepted by pious Jews: it is all about demonstrating that the fulfillment of the Law is not exclusively theirs and, therefore, it is not a private criteria of retribution used only for them. Further on, beginning at 3:21, he analyzes this situation according to Christian principles. The Jewish ideas on which Paul bases his argument are:

a) A reflection on the issue of the suffering of the People, of the just man, and of someone chosen by God. The question is: Why does God allow suffering? The biblical texts already delve into the infidelity of the Chosen People, sin, and eschatological retribution: God, Who is just, will reward once and for all, at the end of times, each according to his works: then all the evil-doers will be punished.

b) The Jew, who structures life according to the Law (i.e. the Mosaic Law),[6] expects his retribution to be in line with his acceptance and completion of said Law: Jews await justice in a particular manner, which will be used with them in a different way, according to their methods of repentance and justification, as dictated by their religious creed. A Jew is he who has the Law, a subject of the Law; without which a Jew looses his identity—what saves him—; he plummets: "For the ones that God will justify are not those who have heard the Law but those who have kept the Law" (Rom 2:13).[7] The Law is what decides the positive or negative divine retribution for the Jews.

Nevertheless, Paul does not agree with this principle: it is in the Gospel where we find the revelation of final retributive justice. Christ suffices. The Letter to the Romans is intended to remove set external categories that do not "work": good/not good, Jew/non-Jew. The path to justification is faith in Jesus Christ and not the fulfillment of the external works prescribed by Law. Only the first of the two is universal and life-giving.

c) We are dealing, in the end, with the Jewish categories of "sinning" and "being a sinner". According to religion, the world is divided into Jews and non-Jews or gentiles. The former are characterized by their living of

---

[6] "Hence you will keep my laws and my customs. Whoever complies with them will find life in them. I am Yahweh" (Lev 18:5).

[7] Cf. Romano Penna, *Lettera ai Romani. I. Rm. 1-5. Introduzione, versione, commento* (Bologna: EDB, 2004), 232-34.

the (Mosaic) Law. The Law is the instance that makes way for the heritage promised by God to Abraham, that is, the blessings. But Jews believe that being an heir of Abraham depends both on the faith that he had when he believed in God as well as the fulfillment of the (Mosaic) Law, primarily the precept of circumcision: faith and Law go together. A Jew is no longer a sinner, however he still may sin, for which he must make amends; he is already removed from the category of condemnation.

Rom 1:18 - 2:16 and the retributive justice of God

Keeping in line with Rom 1:18–4:25, we can further divide the block formed by Rom 1-2, according to St. Paul's reasoning:

Rom 1:18-32: the situation of those who have turned down God and his justice.
Rom 2:1-16: circumcision of the heart vs. the external categories.
Rom 2:17-24: the situation of the Jew that lives opposed to the Law.
Rom 2:25-29: inquiring of the boundaries.

The main theme of Rom 1:18-2:16 is the retributive justice of God, in two moments:

a) Rom 1:18-32: justice (final, negative retributive justice) as anger that resorts to chastisement;

b) Rom 2:1-16: justice as the working of God's impartiality based on everyone's works, indiscriminately, and the equality of Jew and Greek when facing it.

The reasoning is as follows: man needs to be saved because he is a sinner, a condition that closes the doors for everlasting life. At the beginning of this process is the justice of God that is directly applied to the problem of sin as the disobedience to the will of God. God rewards according to each person's deeds, but his justice is not comparable to that of humans, and it is directed neither towards the punishment nor towards the death of the sinner, but towards the necessary correction for man to convert and be saved. This punishment is pedagogical, at the same time that it is just: God punishes, but He does not annihilate; He wants to justify. God's justice is, essentially, His divine mercy.

We must also take into account that the penalty of death rules according to a law. God, however, does not bind himself to a law. The form of punishment He applies is letting the world go its merry way; a situation which takes the world to insanity. It is a fact that God has practiced negative retribution in the past: He cannot put up with sin. The depravation and dissoluteness of the gentiles come from here, and the fault is not God's, but the sinners'.

The path to salvation passes, first and foremost, through the justification of the sinner. However, who is the sinner? Paul opens his discourse stating that, before the redeeming action of Christ, all men are sinners; Jew and gentile alike. Thus, each and every person is subject to the wrath of God, and all need to be justified: pagans, idolaters of Israel, etc.

It is here when another vital topic comes onto the scene: the paths to justification, and whether or not there are relevant privileges for anyone to this respect. The divine principles of retribution begin in Chapter 2. It is in this context that the so-called "rule of the Law", proper of the Jews, will appear, to be evaluated afterwards by Paul. In the end, the bottom line is that there is only one criterion for retribution: faith in Jesus Christ.

The argumentation unfolds in a progressive manner. Paul wants to show why justification must take place for everyone in the same way, and he does this by retaking the biblical and Jewish ideas on the retributive justice of God. First he explains the case of those who do evil (1:19-31) and approve of it (1:32). He moves on to talk about, in second place, those who criticize and judge the former and yet act in the same way (2:1-5). Lastly, in 2:17-24, he deals with those who preach of goodness and do evil. These categories do not include all men; neither do they include all pagans, nor all Jews. In the first two groups (which are the ones that interest us here and now), we can find both Jews and gentiles. To be more specific, pagans that do evil, as well as idolatrous Jews belong to the first group.

So, it is not an external category that is important, even though it has its use. What is important is doing good or evil. The Mosaic Law points to the good that should be done. However, that very same good deed can also be done by a pagan who is guided by what is engraved in their hearts. The point is that there are no differences as far as retribution goes, and for this very reason, neither are there for justification: divine justice reaches every human being through grace in the same way, only by way of faith.[8] The impartial criterion used by God is the circumcision of the heart, which is not exclusive of the Jews.

[8] Cf. Aletti, "Romanos," 1420-22.

Rom 1:18-32 and natural Revelation

> The retribution of God from heaven is being revealed against the ungodliness and injustice of human beings who in their injustice hold back the truth. For what can be known about God is perfectly plain to them, since God has made it plain to them: ever since the creation of the world, the invisible existence of God and his everlasting power have been clearly seen by the mind's understanding of created things. And so these people have no excuse: they knew God and yet they did not honour him as God or give thanks to him, but their arguments became futile and their uncomprehending minds were darkened (…). That is why God abandoned them in their inmost cravings to filthy practices of dishonouring their own bodies (…). They are well aware of God's ordinance: that those who behave like this deserve to die -yet they not only do it, but even applaud others who do the same (Rom 1:18-21.24.32).

Some men are guilty of not knowing God, and for not having paid Him homage, even though they had the ability to do so; their errors went side-by-side with sufficient knowledge of God, of His will (v.19), and of the divine decree according to which those who do such things (the aforesaid vices) deserve death.[9] This guilt makes itself manifest in different ways: for the Jews, when they do not fulfill the Mosaic Law—one should listen to a series of norms that imply their being put into action—; for the rest, when they have chosen not to know God through natural revelation. This sin, that can affect Jews and non-Jews alike, provides for an erroneous relationship between God and man; disobedience to His divine will.

Paul establishes the starting line, for retribution, making use of accepted ideas, expectations and categories, of the Judaism and stoicism of the era: those who had had the opportunity to know the God and His will, and did not, however, follow it, are guilty and have no excuse. This is what happened to the "first" sinner, Adam, as told by the Book of Genesis: having known God, he chose not to be faithful to Him. The peak of the evil of these people is described in verse 32: "They are well aware of

[9] Alessandro Sacchi, "La legge naturale nella Bibbia," in *La legge naturale* (Bologna: EDB, 1970), 52. See also: André Feuillet, "La connaissance naturelle de Dieu par les hommes d'après Rom 1,18-23," *Lumière et Vie*, no. 14 (1954); Giuseppe Segalla, "L'empietà come rifuto della verità di Dio in Romani 1,18-28," *Studia Patavina*, no. 34 (1987); Stanislas Lyonnet, "La connaissance naturelle de Dieu," in *Études sur l'Épître aux Romains* (Roma: PIB, 1989); Antonio Pitta, "Soltanto I pagani oggetto dell'ira di Dio (Rm 1,18-32)," *Parola Spirito e Vita*, no. 26 (1992); Alessandro Sacchi, "Ira di Dio e salvezza dei gentili," in *Lettere Paoline e altre lettere* (Leumann, Torino: ElleDiCi, 1995).

God's ordinance that those who behave like this deserve to die—yet they not only do it, but even applaud others who do the same—". Human evil is the effect, and not the cause of sin.

The argumentation should sprout from the fact that humanity is totally responsible for its actions—and thus inexcusable—, in order for divine retribution to be totally just. In Rom 1:19-32 this idea is repeated once and again in a construction that goes back and forth between human action and Divine reaction.

a) Human action:

For what can be known about God is perfectly plain to them, since God has made it plain to them: ever since the creation of the world, the invisible existence of God and his everlasting power have been clearly seen by the mind's understanding of created things. And so these people have no excuse: they knew God and yet they did not honour him as God or give thanks to him, but their arguments became futile and their uncomprehending minds were darkened. While they claimed to be wise, in fact they were growing so stupid that they exchanged the glory of the immortal God for an imitation, for the image of a mortal human being, or of birds, or animals, or crawling things (19-23).

Divine reaction:

That is why God abandoned them in their inmost cravings to filthy practices of dishonouring their own bodies (24).

b) Human action:

Because they exchanged God's truth for a lie and have worshipped and served the creature instead of the Creator, who is blessed for ever. Amen (25).

Divine reaction:

That is why God abandoned them to degrading passions: why their women have exchanged natural intercourse for unnatural practices; and the men, in a similar fashion, too, giving up normal relations with women, are consumed with passion for each other, men doing shameful things with men and receiving in themselves due reward for their perversion (26-27).

c) Human action:

In other words, since they would not consent to acknowledge God (28a).

Divine reaction:

> God abandoned them to their unacceptable thoughts and indecent behaviour. And so now they are steeped in all sorts of injustice, rottenness, greed and malice; full of envy, murder, wrangling, treachery and spite, libelers, slanderers, enemies of God, rude, arrogant and boastful, enterprising in evil, rebellious to parents, without brains, honour, love or pity (28b-31).

This consideration about the relationship between human actions and Divine reaction is only possible because the human beings depicted in 1:19-31 are inexcusable. If not, divine retribution would be a flagrant injustice.

What is it that pagans could have come to know, that formed part of the divine will? The contrary to the vices that Paul confronts them with, which consists in the precepts of the Decalogue and culminates in the love of one's neighbor, which is exemplified by mercy; the opposite virtue of the last vice on the list that sums up the rest. This will coincides with the one concerning the Jews, found in the Mosaic Law; the Jews that will be condemned will be treated so for having committed these very same vices (cf. Rom 2:17-24).[10]

Rom 2:1-16: keys for comprehension

Before moving on to the text of Rom 2:14-15, let us take a look at the keys needed to understand the passage in which we find these verses.[11] Rom 2:1-16 is in the chapter in which we find the principles of divine retribution: what God has said. God is impartial, and the Gospel is the absolute manifestation of this impartiality. From Rom 2:9 on, we find the relationship between the Jews and the Greeks. This chapter prepares the way for the subject of the universality of divine justice.

a) In Rom 2:1-6 Paul invokes those who are in contradiction with themselves, ably using the categories *say/do.* This is why his discourse is now directed at the heart; it is where contradiction and lack of circumcision are found, and here is where God enlightens us with the precise meaning of circumcision of the heart.

b) The reason for these verses is to enunciate the criteria by which divine justice will be founded on, and later dissipate, in verses 17-29, the

---

[10] Sacchi, "La legge naturale nella Bibbia," 53.

[11] Aletti, "Romanos," 1424.

boundaries between Jew and non-Jew in virtue of this same divine retribution, that is based on works (Rom 2:6-10.13.15a) and is impartial (cf. Rom 2:11).

c) Paul somehow levels things out: it is not true that there is a distinction such as, on the one hand those who know the will of God—because they possess the Mosaic Law—and on the other, those who do not know it. Thanks to their conscience, human beings can have an idea of justice. This fact is important in Paul's argumentation; it will allow him to establish that circumcision of the heart is not of Jewish inheritance, and that in this way the boundary between Jew and non-Jew is thinner than it may seem.

d) The axiom of divine impartiality is not incompatible, in itself, with a separate and distinct retribution for the Jew on one hand, and the non-Jew on the other. However, the Apostle places as the decisive element the inmost religious identity, i.e. the circumcision of the heart. The impartiality and the knowledge of the heart—that which cannot be seen-go together—(cf. Rom 2:11.16); God sees both the inner sanctity and evil.

Let us insist upon the fact that it is not divine impartiality that abolishes the distinction between Jew and Greek; God has made a choice—Israel—and both should be treated in a different way. The contrary would be unjust. Rom 2:1-8 clearly states that God will punish; Rom 2:9-16 says that there will be retribution for Jews and Greeks alike, however not according to what they say, but what they do: if the Jews have the Torah, they will be judged according to whether or not they fulfill what it requires of them.

e) The group of "everyone who does good" is one of the essential factors for the discourse in Rom 1:18-3:20. It allows for the comparison and questioning of identities, and, thus, of the corresponding retribution. If God is a just judge, He must not be biased by statute or privileges and advantages derived from it. For, He knows the interior of each and every person, and is aware that even though one does not belong to the People of the Covenant, circumcision of the heart is a possibility.

Rom 2:14-15 and the Law Written in the Heart

These verses express, succinctly, various central aspects of Paul's reasoning; each and every one is of great interest for Theological study. The text reads as follows:

"12All those who have sinned without the Law will perish without the Law; and those under the Law who have sinned will be judged by the Law. 13For the ones that God will justify are not those who have heard the

Law but those who have kept the Law. [14]So, when gentiles, not having the Law, still through their own innate sense behave as the Law commands, then, even though they have no Law, they are a law for themselves. [15]They can demonstrate the effect of the Law engraved on their hearts, to which their own conscience bears witness; since they are aware of various considerations, some of which accuse them, while others provide them with a defense... [16]on the day when, according to the gospel that I preach, God, through Jesus Christ, judges all human secrets" (Rom 2:12-16).

Here we add the Greek text, because in it we find key expressions that are necessary in order to discover the correct interpretation:

> [12] ὅσοι γὰρ ἀνόμως ἥμαρτον, ἀνόμως καὶ ἀπολοῦνται· καὶ ὅσοι ἐν νόμῳ ἥμαρτον, διὰ νόμου κριθήσονται· [13] οὐ γὰρ οἱ ἀκροαταὶ νόμου δίκαιοι παρὰ τῷ θεῷ, ἀλλ' οἱ ποιηταὶ νόμου δικαιωθήσονται. [14] ὅταν γὰρ ἔθνη τὰ μὴ νόμον ἔχοντα φύσει τὰ τοῦ νόμου ποιῶσιν, οὗτοι νόμον μὴ ἔχοντες ἑαυτοῖς εἰσιν νόμος· [15] οἵτινες ἐνδείκνυνται τὸ ἔργον τοῦ νόμου γραπτὸν ἐν ταῖς καρδίαις αὐτῶν, συμμαρτυρούσης αὐτῶν τῆς συνειδήσεως καὶ μεταξὺ ἀλλήλων τῶν λογισμῶν κατηγορούντων ἢ καὶ ἀπολογουμένων, [16] ἐν ᾗ ἡμέρᾳ κρίνει ὁ θεὸς τὰ κρυπτὰ τῶν ἀνθρώπων κατὰ τὸ εὐαγγέλιόν μου διὰ Ἰησοῦ Χριστοῦ.

a) As we have already said, verse 13 establishes a fundamental Jewish principle upon which Paul bases his argument; further on he will let us know that he himself does not side with it. This principle is that of the inseparability of *listening* and *doing* or *putting into practice*. By stating this, Paul is referring to the comprehension of justice as the *completion of that which is established by law*, i.e. the justice of the Law.[12]

b) Verse 14 poses various grammatical, translational, and theological problems. First of all, the use of the expression ὅταν, *when*, expresses something real, and not something hypothetical: some Greeks actually do fulfill what the Law requires.

Secondly, we must see if the expression φύσει, *by nature*, falls upon the preceding word—the subject "gentiles"—, or the following one—"fulfills"—. The closest translation is this: "when (…) acting according to nature, they fulfill the precepts of the Law".

The theological complication derives from the Pelagian dispute. In this theological controversy, so that it could not be concluded that grace is not

---

[12] This is how St. Thomas explains it. Cf. Juan Larrú, *Cristo en la acción humana según los Comentarios al Nuevo Testamento de Santo Tomás de Aquino* (Roma: Lateran University Press, 2003), 312.

necessary (φύσει = without the grace of Christ), Augustine[13] identified the pagans of verse 14, ἔθνη, as Christians of pagan origin that do good with the help of grace (φύσει = human nature reformed by grace),[14] and he identified the law they fulfill as the Law of the New Covenant. Nevertheless, φύσει does not indicate the absence of grace, but only the absence of the written Law which is a privilege of the Jews. Here we have one of the key points of the Pauline argument.[15]

c) How is it possible that, albeit not knowing the precepts of the Law, some pagans fulfill what it requires? It is clear that those who live righteously[16] do that which the Jewish Law asks of them—not each and every precept—.[17] The gentile who does not have the Torah, is able to live by the fundamental moral principles, without the necessity of a hard copy of the law like that of Moses (cf. 1 Tim 1:8-9):

"In every person there is an innate moral demand, even though it is not always followed; in detail, it is more precise to say that it is not the law of God that is innate in man, but an intuitive faculty that enables him to apprehend and know some of the demands or first moral principles".[18]

d) What does it mean that these pagans are law for themselves (= *auto-nomos*)? It means that pagans who act with rectitude have something inside themselves that shows them right and wrong (at least the general guidelines), in the same way the Jews have the Law. As verse 15 states, they are law for themselves because they auto-instruct and auto-induce themselves towards that which is good, either due to their own conscience or to arguments between one another, based on logical reasoning, about what is right and what is wrong. This "autonomy", consequently, is neither independence of, nor opposition between, person and human nature.[19]

---

13 Augustine of Hippo, *De spiritu et littera*, vol. 60, xxvii, 47 (Viena: Corpus scriptorum ecclesiasticorum latinorum, 1913), 201.

14 Cf. Stanislas Lyonnet, "Lex naturalis et iustificatio Gentilium," *Verbum Domini*, no. 41 (1963).

15 Sacchi, "La legge naturale nella Bibbia," 53-54.

16 According conscience and reason, says John Chrysostom, when commenting this passage: John Chrysostom, *Homilias in Epistolam ad Romanos*, Patrologiae cursus completus, series Graeca, 60 (Paris: J.P. Migne, 1862), 429.

17 They fulfill the moral mandates of the Law, which emerge from the judgment of natural reasoning. Cf. Larrú, *Cristo en la acción humana según los Comentarios al Nuevo Testamento de Santo Tomás de Aquino*, 314.

18 Penna, *Lettera ai Romani. I. Rm. 1-5. Introduzione, versione, commento*, 237. The translation is ours.

19 Larrú, *Cristo en la acción humana según los Comentarios al Nuevo Testamento de Santo Tomás de Aquino*, 322.

e) Verse 15 considers the law written in the hearts of men; an idea that is somehow taken up again in verses 25-29 where the topic is the circumcision of the heart:

> Being a Jew is not only having the outward appearance of a Jew, and circumcision is not only a visible physical operation. The real Jew is the one who is inwardly a Jew, and real circumcision is in the heart, a thing not of the letter but of the spirit. He may not be praised by any human being, but he will be praised by God (Rom 2:28-29).

This circumcision is the gift that characterizes the People of God in eschatological times:

> Yahweh your god will circumcise your heart and the heart of your descendants, so that you will love Yahweh your god with all your heart and soul, and so will live. (…)For this Law which I am laying down for you today is neither obscure for you nor beyond your reach. It is not in heaven, so that you need to wonder, *Who will go up to heaven for us and bring it down to us, so that we can hear and practice it?* Nor is it beyond the seas, so that you need to wonder, *Who will cross the seas for us and bring it back to us, so that we can hear and practice it?* No, the word is very near to you, it is in your mouth and in your heart for you to put into practice (Deut 30:6.11-14).

> I shall pour clean water over you and you will be cleansed; I shall cleanse you of all your filth and of all your foul idols. I shall give you a new heart, and put a new spirit in you; I shall remove the heart of stone from your bodies and give you a heart of flesh instead. I shall put my spirit in you, and make you keep my laws, and respect and practice my judgments (Ezek 36:25-27).

The fact that the pagans who act with rectitude will be the ones to achieve it, and not the Jews, to whom it corresponds by right, is in itself a profound condemnation of those Jews who have transgressed the Law.[20] This is the idea that verse 15 expresses when it says that pagans already have what the Law prescribes written in their hearts, and for this reason they are able to know it just as well as those who have the written Law; as well as *some* capacity to fulfill it, i.e. to direct their actions towards the true good. A prophecy, analogous to the one given for the Jews in the texts we have seen, is brought about in the pagans. The Pauline expression calls to mind that of Jer 31:33, however the meaning does not seem to be

[20] Sacchi, "La legge naturale nella Bibbia," 54.

identical: in the Letter to the Romans the setting is not that of a miraculous and eschatological intervention of God, but of duties, capacities, and abilities of man as such[21]:

> Look, the days are coming, Yahweh declares, when I shall make a new covenant with the House of Israel (and the House of Judah), but not like the covenant I made with their ancestors the day I took them by the hand to bring them out of Egypt, a covenant which they broke, even though I was their Master, Yahweh declares. No, this is the covenant I shall make with the House of Israel when those days have come, Yahweh declares. Within them I shall plant my Law, writing it on their hearts. Then I shall be their God and they will be my people. There will be no further need for everyone to teach neighbour or brother, saying, *Learn to know Yahweh!* No, they will all know me, from the least to the greatest, Yahweh declares, since I shall forgive their guilt and never more call their sin to mind (Jer 31:31-34).

The Law written in the hearts or souls of man is a subject well-known to stoicism and Neo-Platonism. In the writings of rabbis, however, there is no mention of a law written in the hearts of pagans, but in that of the Israelites, according to the promise of Jer 31:33. As we read in some commentators, Deut 30:14 makes up the background of Rom 2:14-15: this would mean its origin is not Greek, but from the Old Testament.[22]

f) What does "They have *what the Law prescribes* written in their hearts" mean, τὸ ἔργον τοῦ νόμου γραπτὸν ἐν ταῖς καρδίαις αὐτῶν? Paul usually speaks of the precepts or works of the Law, in plural, with a negative connotation. Here, in singular, it points to a more positive meaning, and it does not make any reference to the fulfillment of the Law on the part of pagans; it does mention, in general terms, what the Law demands, that, as we have already mentioned, makes reference to the commandment of love: both natural law and the Mosaic Law are directed towards the same end. A long time ago, Philo, a contemporary of Paul, expressed in his works the Jewish conviction, of Hellenistic times, that some of the key people previous to Moses, like Abraham, who were not in possession of the Law, nonetheless fulfilled its demands.

> About all of these topics, let it suffice what we have said; but Moses, to top it all off, adds, to so abundant and great praise of the wise man, the following statement: "this man fulfilled the Divine Law and all the

[21] Cf. Otto Kuss, *La Lettera ai Romani* (Brescia: Morcelliana, 1962).
[22] Aletti, "Romanos," 1425.

> commandments of God" (Gen 26:5), not indoctrinated by writings, but propelled by unwritten nature to seek healthy and wholesome impulses. And having to do with what God promises, what else is it up to man to do if not trust with the most steadfast trust he can muster? In this consisted the life of the first one, the founder of the nation, who, more than a man obedient to laws, as some say, was himself an unwritten law and norm, as our explanation shows.[23]

Philo united the stoic sense of "nature" with the understanding of God as creator and legislator. And, in order to overcome the contingency of the Law of Moses, he identified it with the law of nature by which the universe was created and is sustained. In this way, this divine creation of the world points to the possibility for humans, leaving aside positive revelation, to discern and comply with God's will for human life, which is expressed in another way in the Jewish Law.[24]

What Philo says is important, due to the fact that Abraham represents the gentile archetype, i.e. the man who is not subject to the Law, which was made known long after his death. Paul's word choice brings us to the conclusion that the Apostle admits the same possibility for the gentiles as Philo did for Abraham.

g) Verse 15 reads: "to which their own conscience bears witness; since they are aware of various considerations, some of which accuse them, while others provide them with a defense". The word *syneidesis*,[25] which

---

[23] Philo of Alexandria, *Abraham* 275-276; see also *De specialibus legibus* 2,42-53. Cf. Philon d'Alexandrie, *Les oeuvres de Philon d'Alexandrie*, vol. 20: De Abrahamo (Paris: Cerf, 1966), ———, *Les oeuvres de Philon d'Alexandrie*, vol. 24: De specialibus legibus (I-II) (Paris: Cerf, 1975). Cf. Also Hindy Najman, "The Law of Nature and the Authority of Mosaic Law," *Studia Philonica Annual*, no. 11 (1999).

[24] Brendan Byrne, *Romans*, Sacra Pagina Series 6 (Collegeville, Minnesota: The Liturgical Press, 1996), 92.

[25] Cf. Ceslas Spicq, "La conscience dans le Nouveau Testament," *Revue biblique*, no. 47 (1938); Jacques Dupont, *Syneidesis. Aux origines de la notion chrétienne de conscience morale* (Louvain: 1948); Claude Anthony Pierce, *Conscience in the New Testament. A study of syneidesis in the New Testament, in the light of its sources and with particular reference to St. Paul, with some observations regarding its pastoral relevance today* (London: SCM Press, 1958); Margaret E. Thrall, "The Pauline Use of Syneudhesis," *New Testament Studies*, no. 14 (1967-68); Robert Jewett, *Paul's Anthropological Terms: A Study of Their Use in Conflict Settings* (Leiden Brill, 1971); Ugo Vanni, "La coscienza (syneidesis): una novità antropologica-teologica di Paolo?," in *Atti del III Simposio di Tarso su San Paolo Apostolo*, ed. Luigi Padovese (Roma: Pontificio Ateneo Antoniano, 1995).

appears fourteen times in Paul's writings, is applied here to pagan morality: conscience is the common denominator among all men, regardless of religious identity.

As Ceslas Spicq explains, conscience, συνείδησις, is based on knowledge; a knowledge that the knower shares (συν-εἰδέναι = to know) with himself—one is conscience of one's self—or with others, at a psychological level as well as an ethical one. For Paul conscience is the interior faculty for personal discernment between good and evil, i.e. the practical guide for behavior and motive for action.[26]

In Rom 2:15, conscience represents the possibility of verifying, for the gentiles, not only the possibility for them of the Law, but also, and above all else, the correspondence between human behavior and the dictates of the Law: the fact that the gentiles, reflecting upon their behavior, can feel remorse or even feel that what they have done is defendable, is a final testimony of an existent law written in their hearts.[27]

This brings us to another, more ample and controversial, present-day problem, which Benedict XVI has frequently addressed in his theological work: the question on truth. In the case at hand, the frame is that of religions, moral conscience, and the ability of man to know that which is true. The excerpt from Rom 2:14-15 indicates the importance of this passage of Paul:

> There is an organ in man that gives unity to him: the moral conscience. The Pauline proposition that the possibility to listen to the moral conscience exists in every man was a brave assertion. Thus, the separation of the idea of salvation from that of knowledge and observance of the Torah, and its relation to the generic demands of the moral conscience, in which the one and only God speaks, which tells each and every person the essentials of the Torah: "So when the gentiles, not having the Law, still through their own innate sense behave as the Law commands, then, even though they have no Law, they are a law for themselves. They can demonstrate the effect of the Law engraved on their hearts, to which their own conscience bears witness..." (Rom 2:14ss). Paul does not say: when pagans observe what their religion states, it is good according to divine judgment. On the contrary, Paul condemns most of the religious practices of the time. He recurs to a different source, that which is written in

[26] Ceslas Spicq, "συνείδησις," in *Theological Lexicon of the New Testament* (Peabody: Hendrickson, 1994), 335.

[27] Byrne, *Romans*, 89.

everyone's heart, that which is uniquely good because it comes from the only God.[28]

h) This is not the end of it. How should we understand the expression, "*of various considerations, some of which accuse them, while others provide them with a defense*", καὶ μεταξὺ ἀλλήλων τῶν λογισμῶν κατηγορούντων ἢ καὶ ἀπολογουμένων? Now it is all about a second testimony; one between human beings, on a collective level, along side the conscience, which is internal: the verdicts that men pronounce about the actions of others, accusing and defending "one another" also serves the purpose of discovering this law written on the hearts of men[29]: this auto-criticism, said out loud by one's conscience and personal reflection is preparation for divine judgment, of which it will even form part.

Thus, we may say that verses 14-15 consider a natural revelation of an ethical sort, even though the topic as such is not originally of St. Paul, who makes the ideas expressed in the Judaism of his time his own. Moreover, these verses are the normal consequence of Rom 1:20 ff : if we are able to know God, why not His will as well?

Works Cited

Aletti, Jean-Noël. *Comment Dieu est-il juste? Clefs pour interpréter L'épître aux Romains*. Paris: Seuil, 1991.

—. "Romanos." In *Comentario Bíblico Internacional. Comentario Católico y Ecuménico para el Siglo XXI*, edited by William R. Farmer, Armando J. Levoratti, Sean McEvenue and David L. Dungan. Estella: Verbo Divino, 1999.

Byrne, Brendan. *Romans*, Sacra Pagina Series 6. Collegeville, Minnesota: The Liturgical Press, 1996.

Chrysostom, John. *Homilias in Epistolam ad Romanos*, Patrologiae Cursus Completus, Series Graeca, 60. Paris: J.P. Migne, 1862.

d'Alexandrie, Philon. *Les oeuvres de Philon d'Alexandrie*. Vol. 20: De Abrahamo. Paris: Cerf, 1966.

—. *Les oeuvres de Philon d'Alexandrie*. Vol. 24: De specialibus legibus (I-II). Paris: Cerf, 1975.

---

[28] Joseph Ratzinger, *Fe, verdad y tolerancia. El cristianismo y las religiones del mundo* (Salamanca: Sígueme, 2005), 179. The translation is ours. The original German is: ———, *Glaube, Wahrheit, Toleranz. Das Christentum und die Weltreligionen* (Freiburg im Breisgau: Herder, 2003).

[29] Kuss, *La Lettera ai Romani*, 101.

Dupont, Jacques. *Syneidesis. Aux origines de la notion chrétienne de conscience morale*. Louvain, 1948.

Feuillet, André. "La connaissance naturelle de Dieu par les hommes d'après Rom 1,18-23." *Lumière et Vie*, no. 14 (1954): 63-80.

Fitzmyer, Joseph A. *Romans*, The Anchor Bible. New York: Doubleday, 1993.

Hippo, Augustine of. *De Spiritu et Littera*. Vol. 60, xxvii, 47. Viena: Corpus scriptorum ecclesiasticorum latinorum, 1913.

Jewett, Robert. *Paul's Anthropological Terms: A Study of Their Use in Conflict Settings*. Leiden Brill, 1971.

Kennedy, George A. *New Testament Interpretation through Rhetorical Criticism*, Studies in Religion. Chapel Hill/London: The University of North Carolina Press, 1984.

Kuss, Otto. *La Lettera ai Romani*. Brescia: Morcelliana, 1962.

Larrú, Juan. *Cristo en la acción humana según los Comentarios al Nuevo Testamento de Santo Tomás de Aquino*. Roma: Lateran University Press, 2003.

Lyonnet, Stanislas. "La connaissance naturelle de Dieu." In *Études sur L'épître aux Romains*, 45-47. Roma: PIB, 1989.

—. "Lex naturalis et iustificatio gentilium." *Verbum Domini*, no. 41 (1963): 238-42.

Moo, Douglas J. *The Epistle to the Romans*. NICNT, Grand Rapids: Eerdmans, 1996.

Najman, Hindy. "The Law of Nature and the Authority of Mosaic Law." *Studia Philonica Annual*, no. 11 (1999): 55-73.

New Jerusalem Bible. New York: Doubleday, 1985.

Penna, Romano. *Lettera ai Romani. I. Rm. 1-5. Introduzione, Versione, Commento*. Bologna: EDB, 2004.

Pierce, Claude Anthony. *Conscience in the New Testament. A Study of Syneidesis in the New Testament, in the Light of Its Sources and with Particular Reference to St. Paul, with Some Observations Regarding Its Pastoral Relevance Today*. London: SCM Press, 1958.

Pitta, Antonio. *Lettera ai Romani*. Milano: Paoline, 2001.

—. "Soltanto i pagani oggetto dell'ira di Dio (Rm 1,18-32)." *Parola Spirito e Vita*, no. 26 (1992): 175-88.

Ratzinger, Joseph. *Fe, verdad y tolerancia. El cristianismo y las religiones del mundo*. Salamanca: Sígueme, 2005.

—. *Glaube, Wahrheit, Toleranz. Das Christentum und die Weltreligionen*. Freiburg im Breisgau: Herder, 2003.

Sacchi, Alessandro. “Ira Di Dio E Salvezza Dei Gentili.” In *Lettere Paoline E Altre Lettere, Logos 6*, 421-42. Leumann (Torino): ElleDiCi, 1995.

—. “La Legge Naturale Nella Bibbia.” In *La Legge Naturale. Studi E Ricerche 4*. Bologna: EDB, 1970.

Segalla, Giuseppe. “L’empietà Come Rifuto Della Verità Di Dio in Romani 1,18-28.” *Studia Patavina*, no. 34 (1987): 275-96.

Spicq, Ceslas. “La Conscience Dans Le Nouveau Testament.” *Revue biblique*, no. 47 (1938): 50-80.

—. “Συνείδησις.” In *Theological Lexicon of the New Testament*. Peabody: Hendrickson, 1994.

Thrall, Margaret E. “The Pauline Use of Syneudhesis.” *New Testament Studies*, no. 14 (1967-68): 117-25.

Vanni, Ugo. “La Coscienza (Syneidesis): Una Novità Antropologica-Teologica Di Paolo?” In *Atti Del III Simposio Di Tarso Su San Paolo Apostolo*, edited by Luigi Padovese, 5-25. Roma Pontificio Ateneo Antoniano, 1995.

CHAPTER THREE

PRACTICAL TRUTH AND PRACTICAL FALSEHOOD IN THOMAS AQUINAS

JOAQUÍN GARCÍA-HUIDOBRO*

Not only Marx complained about the theoretical nature of philosophy in his famous *Thesis on Feuerbach*.[1] Also the German romantics of the nineteenth century, like Novalis, directed their critique at the same aspect when they indicated that "we only know in so far as we make."[2] Although the manner of criticism was diverse, both expressions of disappointment show that in the nineteenth century, there were many voices which advocated the need for philosophical enquiries oriented towards the transformation of the world, rather than simple contemplation.

Fortunately, the current state of affairs is rather different from that of the nineteenth century. The rehabilitation of practical philosophy by Gadamer, Ritter, and others, on the continent and a similar movement in the English speaking tradition have witnessed in the last century a renaissance of studies such as ethics, political philosophy and other branches of what Aristotle called the philosophy of human matters. Studies on practical rationality have thus multiplied, although it is still necessary to devote similar attention to another concept which was treated by Aristotle and his medieval followers but was later obscured in modern times: practical truth.

The following study will attempt to demonstrate the importance of such a notion in the philosophy of Aquinas to arrive then at a characterization of this practical truth and practical falsehood, its opposite.

---

* This paper was written with the support of "Fondecyt-Chile" (Projects No. 920474 and No. 1040343).

[1] See Karl Marx, *Thesen über Feuerbach*, ed. Marx/Engels, *Werke*, Bd. 3 (Berlin: Dietz-Verlag), 5-7.

[2] See Walter Rehm, ed., *Novalis. Fragmente* (Frankfurt/Main: Fischer Bücherei, 1956), 167.

We will afterwards discuss the ideas of some authors who understand practical truth as the truth of actions.

Widening the definition of truth

Aquinas dealt with truth in several instances.[3] In these writings, he recognizes the well-known characterization of truth as "a conformity (*adequatio*) of the intellect and the thing,"[4] and explains that, in its proper sense, truth takes place in the human intellect when it composing and dividing ("judgment").[5] In a general sense, we can also speak of the truth of things in so far as they are the cause of the truth of judgement.[6] When making reference to truth, Aquinas has in mind theoretical truth. However, his interest is also directed at practical matters, whose importance is decisive for the eternal destiny of the human being. Nevertheless, this is by no means a simple task. Let us study two pertinent examples. In the first place, if truth is the result of a conformation, it is important to determine the elements to conform. In effect, here it is not possible to speak of conformation of the intellect and the thing, because there is no external thing for the intellect to conform with. In the practical field, the aim is to introduce a new order of things by means of human activity, rather than contemplating existing things. The thing does not yet exist and ought to be realised. This occurs both in the production of objects, proper of technical activity, as much as in that of actions.

There is another difficulty in speaking of truth of practical character. In the speculative field, things can be better apprehended because of their stable character, whereas practical matters are characterized by contingency. The task of guiding the action with rationality is rendered enormously difficult by his variability. Aristotle had already gathered the opinion of the sophists, who denied the existence of naturally just things precisely because human mores were characterized by variation.[7]

---

[3] See Thomas Aquinas, *Summa Theologiae* (Roma: Marietti, 1952), I q. 16; ———, *Quaestiones Disputatae I: De Veritate* (Taurini-Romae: Marietti, 1964), 1, 2; ———, *In Aristotelis Libros Perihermeneias Expositio* (Roma: Marietti, 1955), I, 3.

[4] *De Ver.* 1, 1c.

[5] See Thomas Aquinas, *Summa contra Gentiles* (Taurini-Romae: Marietti, 1961), I, 59; *S. Th.*, I, 16, 2c; *In Periherm.*, III 1, n. 31.

[6] See *De Ver.*, 1, 2c.

[7] See Aristotle, *The Nicomachean Ethics*, trans. David Ross (Oxford: Oxford University Press, 1989), V 7, 1134b18-35a5.

On the contrary, Thomas Aquinas faces such problems by showing how can the praxis be guided by rationality, and his explanation is at least twofold. On the one hand, he develops a theory of virtues, clearly inspired by Aristotelian ideas. They constitute stable ways of acting which respond to the demands of reason. On the other, he adds a theory of natural law that, in spite of being of stoic influence has special features.

Some of these principles have primal character and are evident to all those who have reached the use of reason and understand the meaning of the terms employed.[8] Others, on the contrary, derive from these primary principles. They are, therefore, not evident, and can only be known after some intellectual effort, in some cases a considerable one.[9] These principles move man to acting in accordance with the different virtues.[10] In other words, they move the person to respond in agreement with reason in the face of the requirements imposed by the different contexts surrounding human acts. That the virtuous act can be justified rationally does not mean that it is deduced simply from the conjunction of certain theoretical premises, because in the praxis the aim is not deduce but to introduce a new order into the surrounding world.

The contingency of the praxis is, therefore, not an obstacle for its rational guidance. Aquinas asserts the existence of a practical use of reason which refers precisely to things that could be one way or another, like actions for example.[11] At the same time, he acknowledges a form of truth of this type. He refers to it in the *Summa Theologica* when responding to an objection which assumes that the contingency of human things renders a rational treatment of these matters impossible.[12]

In answer to this objection, Aquinas introduces the notion of practical truth into the very core of his theory of virtues, thus becoming one of the pillars of our approach to the subject:

> As stated in Ethic. vi, 2, truth is not the same for the practical as for the speculative intellect. Because the truth of the speculative intellect depends on conformity between the intellect and the thing. And since the intellect

---

[8] See *S. Th.*, I-II q. 94 a. 2c.

[9] See Ibid., I-II q. 100 a. 3c.

[10] See Ibid., I-II q. 96 a. 3.

[11] See Ibid., I q. 79 a. 11.

[12] "It is not human never to err in taking counsel about what is to be done; since human actions are about things that may be otherwise than they are." *S. Th.,* I-II q. 57 a 5 obi. 3a. I follow the translation in Thomas Aquinas, *The Summa theologiae*, trans. Fathers of the English Dominican Province, 2 ed. (New York: Benziger Brothers, 1947-1948).

> cannot be infallibly in conformity with things in contingent matters, but only in necessary matters, therefore no speculative habit about contingent things is an intellectual virtue, but only such as is about necessary things. On the other hand, the truth of the practical intellect depends on conformity with right appetite. This conformity has no place in necessary matters, which are not affected by the human will; but only in contingent matters which can be effected by us, whether they be matters of interior action, or the products of external work. Hence it is only about contingent matters that an intellectual virtue is assigned to the practical intellect, viz. art, as regards things to be made, and prudence, as regards things to be done.[13]

This is a truth which is only possible in the field of contingency. The correspondence or conformity does take place, but results from the interaction between the practical intellect and the right appetite, which are the terms to be adjusted. Let us now analyze each one of these elements with some detail.

The elements of practical truth

The first of these elements is the right appetite. Concerning it we can ask two questions: what kind of appetite is, and what is the measure of its rectitude.

The appetite which must be correct is, in the first place, the will, which is the intellectual appetite. If the will is torn by vices, the human being will seek goods which are only apparent and choices will led not to human excellence, but corruption. But the will is not the only appetite, because in humans we also find a concupiscible appetite that desires the delectable, and an irascible appetite which is directed towards goods difficult to obtain. As these do not necessarily follow reason, they are always in risk of avoiding its demands. [14]

In order for the sensitive appetites to be amenable to the voice of reason, it is necessary that they be modeled upon certain virtues.[15] This possibility of the sensitive powers to be in this way perfected or directed by reason is in agreement with the distinction which Aristotle makes and which signals that in the human soul there is a rational part and another irrational part (for example, the vegetative functions) and another which is

---

[13] *S. Th.*, I-II q. 57 a. 5 ad 3.

[14] See Ibid., I-II q. 17 a. 7 c.

[15] See Ibid., I-II q. 58 a. 2 c.; I-II q. 56 a. 4 ad 4.

capable of obeying reason.[16] This latter part is comprised of the concupiscible and the irascible appetites in the measure which, by means of exercise, they acquire the virtues of temperance and courage. When it is said that "they are able" to obey reason, it is recognized that in many cases they do not do so. These, then, are the men who have a sub-human existence that is merely animal,[17] and "follow the inclinations of the sensitive nature against the order of reason."[18] The good moral disposition is thus indispensable for praxis. Without it, one cannot have a good life nor can one conduct oneself in accordance with the noblest which is to be found in man. One the other hand, moral virtue is decisive neither in the domain of the technical nor in the realm of the merely speculative.[19]

In so far as it determines the rectitude of the appetite, the answer of Aquinas is clear: the orientation toward the end. But while the end is given to us by nature,[20] this orientation could be ignored, as it is in the case of the vicious person, who is badly disposed to it, or is at least looking for it through a wrong path (albeit the human person never ceases to pursue goodness). The appetite will be right if it follows the end given by nature. But such an end ought to be known, and the knowledge of natural ends is treated by St Thomas in the *Summa Theologica*, for example, when he refers to natural law. As previously mentioned, St Thomas thinks that the human intellect naturally or spontaneously knows certain primary principles,[21] such as "goodness is to be pursued and practiced and evil is to be avoided" or that "we ought to act rationally." These principles indicate the ends which an author has called "basic"[22] in human action (the ends function as principles in the practical order), which knows the *synderesis* or habit of first principles.

The intellect infallibly knows these ends[23] and it presents them to the will; but the will may refuse to follow them, in which case it ceases to be right. The *intellectus*, which provides the will with the ends, is accordingly

---

[16] See *NE*, I 13, 1102b30-32.

[17] See Thomas Aquinas, *Sententia libri Ethicorum: Opera omnia iussu Leonis XIII P. M. edita*, t. 47 (Romae: Ad Sanctae Sabinae, 1969), *In I Ethic.*, lect 5. [Spiazzi] n. 60.

[18] *S. Th.*, I-II q. 71 a. 2 ad 3.

[19] See Ibid., I-II q. 57 a. 3c.

[20] See *In VI Ethic.*, lect 2, n. 1131.

[21] See *S. Th.*, I-II q. 94, a. 2c.

[22] See John Finnis, *Natural Law and Natural Rights* (Oxford: Oxford University Press, 1980), chapter 2, *passim*.

[23] See *S. Th.*, I-II q. 100, a. 11c.

the first measure of rectitude, because it is always right.[24] Following this layout, then, the *voluntas recta* is the measure for reason to be true and successful in the search for means in the attainment of the end. The idea of an end provided by nature is a controversial suggestion these days, and so it was in the time of Aristotle.[25]

The second element of practical truth is true reason. The word "reason" is here employed in a restricted sense: it includes only the faculty of knowing discursively (*ratio*), and does not refer to the intuitive use of intellectual capacity (*intellectus*), because according to Aquinas, the latter knows infallibly in such a way that it cannot be false when judging about its own object.[26] That reason which must be true is that which is threatened by the possibility of error. Therefore, the expression "recta ratio" is not redundant. Thus, not simply any reason can be true reason in the thought of Aquinas. In the first place, because human reason is fallible and could lack the necessary information or be influenced by the passions, given that practical knowledge is directly affected by the dispositions of the agent. These passions can have an influence so great on man such that they impede the proper functioning of reasoning about practical matters. And, lastly, because there are certain forms of "diminished" rationality which, though they do not commit logical errors in reasoning, they nonetheless suffer from a fundamental deviance.[27] Habitual language itself expresses this possibility of bad reasoning by distinguishing between the "rational" and the "reasonable". Human reason is not merely calculative or strategic reason, but rather that which orients itself toward the achievement of the good life of man.

It remains to be seen which are the criteria for the truth of reason, namely, what measures exist for determining when we are or are not in the presence of true reason. To resolve this, Aquinas makes an analogy: first between the intellectual powers and the appetitive powers,[28] and then between the speculative and practical orders.[29]

---

[24] It should noted that what we have suggested appears to be contradicted by Aquinas, who indicates in *Scriptum Super Libros Sententiarum* (Paris: Lethielleax, 1929-1947), *In II Sent.*, d. 39, q. 2, a. 2, ad 2 that there is always a right will, that which is called *voluntas ut natura*. However, this will desires happiness generally, that is without specifications. What is relevant for us here is that the will may stray from the path to the fundamental ends, which are referred to by the first principles

[25] See *NE*, III 5, 1114b 12ss.; *In III Ethic.*, lect 13, n. 525.

[26] See *S. Th.*, I q. 85 a. 6.

[27] See Ibid., III q. 55 a. 2.

[28] See *In VI Ethic.*, lect. 2, nn. 1128-1129.

[29] See Ibid., lect. 2, n. 1130.

Concerning the relationship between the intellect and the appetitive powers as given by the parallel which exists between the affirmation of a property (in the intellectual operation of judgment) and the pursuit of the good (on the part of appetite) and, on the other hand, the resemblance which we correlatively recognize between the judgment which negates and the flight of evil. Thus, that "in judging, the intellect has two actions, viz., affirmation by which it assents to what is true, and negation by which it dissents from what is false. To these two correspond proportionately to two acts in the appetitive faculty, namely, pursuit by which the appetitive faculty tends and adheres to good, and flight by which it withdraws and dissents from evil." Here we see that those acts of intellect and of appetite "can harmonize one with the other."[30]

In the virtuous man there is a harmony between that which the intellect says and that which the appetites seeks: "In this manner the intellect and the appetitive faculty can be brought into harmony inasmuch as what the intellect declares good, and what the intellect denies to be good the appetitive faculty seeks to avoid."[31] For the incontinent man, by contrast, this equilibrium is not to be found, such that many times he does something different from that which he recognizes as being the authentic good and is instead carried along by his senses or by whim. This interior harmony or agreement of the virtuous subject is given the name of practical truth:

> If choice ought to be good [...] the reason must be true and the appetitive faculty right, so that the same thing which reason declares or affirms, the appetitive faculty pursues (In order that there be perfection in action it is necessary that none of its principles be imperfect). But this intellect or reason which harmonizes in this way with the right appetitive faculty and its truth are practical.[32]

The above discussion has already revealed to us some of elements necessary for determining what is the measure which makes reason true. The following discussion will permit us to view the subject in greater detail.

Aquinas says that that which goodness is in the order of the will, that is what truth is in the realm of the intellect, while falsehood is equivalent to

---

[30] Ibid., lect. 2, n. 1128. I follow the translation of Thomas Aquinas, *Commentary on Aristotle's Nicomachean Ethics*, trans. C. I. Litzinger (Notre Dame, Indiana: Dumb Ox Books, 1993).

[31] Ibid., lect. 2, n. 1128.

[32] Ibid., lect. 2, n. 1129.

evil. In case of speculative intellect, "the absolutely truth is its good," namely, the true independent of circumstances and of the subject, while "the absolutely false is its evil."[33] In case of practical intellect, truth and falsehood continue constituting their own environment, yet even here "the good of the practical intellect is not absolute truth, but the 'conformable' truth (*veritas confesse se habens*), i.e., corresponding to a right appetitive faculty, as has been shown, because on the point the moral virtues are united."[34] When Aquinas, following the Latin translation of Aristotle's text, speaks of "the 'conformable' truth", he is referring to the truth possessed by the virtuous man which lives in harmony with himself because he desires that which the intellect designates and rejects that which is irrational. True reason, then, is that which adjusts itself to the right appetite.

The problem here is that it seems that this circular thinking because "the truth of the practical intellect is determined by means of comparison with the right appetite, (and) the rectitude of the appetite is determined because it is in agreement with true reason, as has been said; from this it follows that there is ascertain circularity is such determinations."[35] To solve this paradox, Aquinas advances the distinction which, despite having an Aristotelian inspiration, is not employed by Aristotle in the passage which is the specific object of the commentary: appetite can just as readily refer to an end as to a means, and that one or the other can determine or be determined differently:

> Given this, it must be said that the appetite is of the ends and of that which is for the ends. But the end is determined in man by nature, as was shown in the third book, but that which is for an end is not determined in us by nature; rather, it must be acquired by means of reason. Furthermore, in this way is made manifest the fact that the rectitude of the appetite with respect to an end is the measure of the truth in practical reason. And, according to this, the truth of practical reason is determined according to its concordance with the correct appetite. But the truth of practical reason is the rule of rectitude of the appetite in relation to that which is for an end. And, for this in accord with that, the appetite is called correct which pursues those things which the true reason indicates.[36]

---

[33] Ibid., lect. 2, n. 1130.
[34] Ibid.
[35] Ibid., lect. 2, n. 1131.
[36] Ibid.

While the end is given by nature, finding the means is often an arduous task ever threatened with the possibility of error. Only the prudent man can succeed in the attempt. Here reason can be either true or false according to whether those means which it seeks are or are not conducive to the end which nature gives and which the appetite desires. For this reason, an appetite oriented toward an end is the rule for knowing if the reason which seeks the means is true or false. But, once reason has become truthful, namely, once it has determined those means which are reasonable for achieving the good end, then the appetite must desire these means. If the appetite desires something other than that which reason has determined, then it is not right appetite, as it is in the case of the incontinent. By contrast, if "the appetite follows that which reason affirms as a good, and flees from that which understanding denies as being such,"[37] then the appetite will be correct. Here, the reason which determines adequately the means (true reason) is the measure for establishing whether the appetite (of the means) is correct.

We can affirm, therefore, that no circular reasoning occurs because the appetite correctly oriented toward an end (the right appetite) determines reason while reason searches for means and thus qualifies reason as either true or false; and once it finds the means, the true reason determines whether the appetite of those means is correct. How can it happen in certain cases that the will does not follow that which reason has indicated? Because of the merely relative control which the will has over the sensitive powers, for what might very well happen if the man in question is neither temperate nor valiant, his gluttony or cowardice has influence over the will, and thus does not choose that which the intelligence demonstrates to it as the good. In this way Aquinas moves partly away from the Socratic idea that evil is the fruit of ignorance.[38]

It has been shown that practical truth requires the concurrence of a desiderative element and one of cognitive character. Only when both are present and fulfill certain conditions we are in the presence of that truth, which is the origin of good actions. But if the conditions of rectitude and truth are not present, there will still be action, although it will be deficient. The intervention of desire is what explains the movement which originates the action, because the intellect alone is incapable of moving, unless it is faced with an end that is presented by desire. Conversely, desire alone is

---

[37] Ibid., lect. 2, n. 1128.

[38] See *S. Th.*, I-II q. 58 a. 2.

also unable to move if it is not accompanied by the cognitive capacity which informs that object X could satisfy its desire.[39]

Therefore, intellectual thinking alone is not enough to act: without the intervention of desire, human action would be impossible. This explains, therefore, why people who have suffered certain injuries in the frontal lobule of the brain, where the organic support of the emotions is located, are unable to make decisions, in spite of having their reason functioning perfectly and being also able to describe in detail the courses of action they have in hand. Their inability to get emotionally involved with one of the alternatives they have prompts perplexity or the adoption of clearly absurd decisions.[40] But the desire of a virtuous and healthy man is not just any desire, but one that is directed and accompanied by the intellect. There are rational and irrational types of desire. The realm of praxis, then, is not foreign to rationality and that is why Aristotle can characterize man's choice as a "desiderative reason or ratiocinative desire."[41]

Practical falsehood

What we have reviewed concerning practical truth allows us to enter into discussion concerning the question of falsehood in the practical domain, a theme which is implicit in Aquinas' reflections on practical truth as well as in his teachings about error.

If practical truth consists of a concordance between true reason and the right appetite, then the source of falsehood can be ascribed to either a lack of rectitude of the appetite or to the fact that reason is not true. In the following we will consider both of these cases.

Human appetite can deviate from its end. As, for example, here on earth, where "the will does not necessarily adhere to God nor to that which is of God."[42] Aquinas shows that certain moral failings are comprised in such a way that they signify a rejection, implicit or explicit, of those ends which are given to us through nature.[43] That there are ends given to us through nature does not means that the will necessarily desires them in each and every one of its acts. By nature, the will is necessarily directed in

---

[39] See Alejandro Vigo, *Estudios Aristotélicos* (Pamplona: Eunsa, 2006), 287-91.
[40] See Antonio Damasio, *Descartes' Error: Emotion, Reason, and the Human Brain* (New York: Putnam, 1994), *passim*.
[41] *EN* VI 2, 1139b4. See Vigo, *Estudios Aristotélicos*, 291.
[42] *S. Th.*, I q. 82 a. 2c.
[43] See, for example, *S. Th.*, I-II q. 154 a. 12.

the pursuit of the good or, in other words, of happiness.[44] But this tension of the spiritual appetite is toward the good in general inasmuch as it could be directed towards very diverse ends,[45] many of which, although from a certain perspective could be considered good they are not anything more than apparent goods. For this reason, although it is possible to perpetuate evil willfully, that is, by refusing to take in those ends which nature presents as those most appropriate for man, this happens precisely because the inevitable pursuit of the good bequeaths to the will the force necessary to pursue partial goods.

The same that happens concerning the appetite of the end occurs to that appetite of that which conducts it to its ends. A wrong orientation toward an end causes reason to err, or, something else which is possible, because it does not desire those goods which reason shows as means for arriving at the good end. A lack of those virtues necessary for habituating the sensitive appetites in following the voice of reason can all cause the appetite to go wrong and thus not produce the concordance in which practical truth consists.

The origins of a false judgment of reason are diverse, one of them is an error of fact. Also, it is possible to fall into errors of practical reasoning, and it could even seem that the error is consubstantial with the same form of acquiring those virtues whose existence in the subject is decisive for the configuration of practical truth. We shall look at each one of these causes in more detail.

In the first place, a speculative error about the act with which it is concerned or its circumstances can cause an error in practical judgment. It is not that practical judgment is deduced from realizing a certain state of things, rather that this judgment many times presumes upon certain previous pieces of knowledge which function as conditions of the judgment's healthy existence. It can, starting from false facts, induce incorrectly[46] or err concerning the end or those means necessary to achieve the end.[47] In short, without adequate knowledge we cannot have true reason.

Moreover, there can be an error in reasoning. Although the *synderesis* does not fail, and the first principles are known in the necessary form,[48] the practical conclusions derived from these principles require a certain

[44] See *S. Th.*, I q. 82 a. 1 ad 3; *In III Ethic.*, lect. 5, n. 446.
[45] See Ibid., I q. 82 a. 2 ad 1.
[46] See Ibid., II-II q. 55 a. 3c.
[47] See *In III Sent.*, dist. 36 q. 1 a. 1c.
[48] See *In II Ethic.*, lect. 4, n. 286.

reflection, in which factors such as haste, the influence of education, and of momentary passions and of vices,[49] can cause it to miscarry. Even so Aquinas indicates that there are certainly more complex ethical principles that are only within the reach of wise men;[50] not in the absolute sense of this expression but rather in the sense of "the prudent man who is wise concerning human things."[51] From this it seems clear that Aquinas is very conscious of the complexity which surrounds ethical questions. Additionally, given that praxis deals with that which can be done in other ways, many times it is not clearly known, for example, what precisely will be the consequences of our acts (from this, the attempt to establish morality as the calculus of the good and the bad consequences of our acts becomes readily questionable).

Third, it happens that according Aquinas, moral life does not consist in applying rules or methods to pre-established cases, but rather in the acquisition and practice of virtues. No moral technique allows one to decide well in a consistent way through time and in the midst of unforeseen situations which is almost always the actual case in the praxis of most men. Consider, for example, economic and political praxis whose variability is so wide-ranging that it cannot be easy to always have a rule at hand in order to solve each new problem as it presents itself. Without virtue, then, it is not possible to live well, because only the virtuous is capable of acting correctly in various circumstances. But virtues are not innate,[52] even though there may be certain natural predispositions according to character for the practice of certain virtues;[53] rather, they must be acquired by means of their exercise. In recent decades, attention has been called to what appears to be a cornerstone of Aristotelian ethics,[54] namely, that principle which says: "For the things we have to learn before we can do them, we learn by doing them."[55] Obviously, we are not virtuous by nature nor for having learned theoretically in what virtue consists. Rather, that "by means of the operation we come to be virtuous."[56] If this is the case, if it is true that virtue, just like walking,

---

[49] See *In III Ethic.*, lect. 13, n. 520.
[50] See *S. Th.,* I-II q. 100 a. 1c & 3c.
[51] *In II Ethic.*, lect. 7, n. 323.
[52] See Ibid., lect 1, nn. 248ss.
[53] See *In VI Ethic.*, lect. 13 and *In II Ethic.*, lect. 11, n. 374.
[54] See Fernando Inciarte, *El reto del positivismo lógico* (Madrid: Rialp, 1974), chapters VI & VII.
[55] *EN*, II, 1, 1103 a 32-35.
[56] *In II Ethic.*, lect. 1, n. 251.

learning to play the zither, or learning to talk, is acquired by means of exercise,[57] then the possibility of error—just like falling, playing a wrong note, or misusing words—will be present in each one of the stages of this process. In this sense, Fernando Inciarte has emphasized the role or error in the make up of practical truth;[58] an idea that is in harmony with the precepts of both Aristotle and Aquinas, given, for example, the necessity of experience in moral life.[59] And what, primarily, is experience if not those lessons that are garnered from the errors of ourselves and others?

In the process of rectifying the appetites there is a true retro-alignment. The *recta ratio* is, in fact, according to Inciarte, *correcta ratio*,[60] because during the exercise of those acts which contribute to the formation of virtue there is a continual process of adjustment, in which the subject becomes progressively more aware of his capacities as well as increasingly developing them.[61] But also the subject perceives his limitations and becomes aware of the measure in which, by means of his own action, it is possible to change his surroundings.[62]

The process of acquiring virtues is, moreover, slow and painful. The best manifestation that one possesses a certain virtue is not to be found in this or that isolated action but rather in the peaceful way in which one possesses such an habit. Virtues are not to be obtained naturally,[63] but once they have been acquired they allow action to proceed easily, in a fashion similar to how the natural powers act.[64]

Aquinas recognizes the difficulty in discovering the just mean in which virtue consists, and he recommends that anyone who wants to acquire a virtue that he at least stay away from the most dangerous extremes[65] or, knowing to what sort of actions he is inclined, that he instead act in the opposite direction just like someone bending the branch of a tree in the opposite direction in order to straighten out its habitual disposition.[66]

Making reference to the Aristotelian text commented by Aquinas, Vigo thinks that this way of proceeding occurs in cases in which determining

---

[57] See Ibid., lect. 1, n. 250.
[58] See Inciarte, *El reto del positivismo lógico*, 203.
[59] See *S. Th.*, I-II q. 40 a. 5 ad 1.
[60] See Inciarte, *El reto del positivismo lógico*, 183.
[61] See *S. Th.*, I-II q. 40 a. 5c.
[62] See Ibid., I-II q. 40 a. 5c. See II-II q. 47 a. 3 ad 2.
[63] See *In II Ethic.,* lect. 1, nn. 248-251.
[64] See Ibid., lect. 3, n. 265. See n. 266.
[65] See Ibid., lect. 11, n. 371.
[66] See Ibid., lect. 11, n. 375.

the middle is very difficult, if not impossible.[67] In any case, it is a very adequate criterion for whom is just beginning to exercise the acquisition of virtue. Accordingly, Aquinas also suggests that one abstains, as much as possible, from those corporal pleasures whose pursuit tends to cloud one's judgment.[68]

The aforementioned points which Inciarte makes regarding the role of error in the constitution of true reason appear to point in the same direction that the analysis of Aquinas took in the preceding paragraphs.

The factors are sufficiently legion which increase the difficulty of this process of reason's coming to full conformity with the right appetite such that the lack of truth caused by a deficiency from the rational side of the relation of concordance appears more excusable than the lack of rectitude of the appetite. So much so that some authors seem to think that this deficiency does not impede the formation of practical truth, but rather the only thing this demands is a subjective coherence between the well-ordered will and the judgment of reason; although the latter, for lack of knowledge of reality, may be erroneous.[69] Such an interpretation cannot be reconciled with the thought of Aquinas, for whom the "practical intellect knows truth as the speculative, but ordains to action knowable truth."[70] Nevertheless, these interpretation puts into relief the necessity for prudence to always conform to the right appetite. Aquinas, meanwhile, proceeds even farther afield. On the one hand, mere good will is not enough to be a complete man, whose understanding grasps the truth, but, on the other hand, he teaches that the conscience could be insurmountably erroneous, and that he whose conscience fails does not act morally badly when he decides something distinct from that which the reality of things indicates.[71] Nonetheless, Aquinas' complete and virtuous man it not simply someone who does not commit moral faults of consideration. His ethics, like all virtue ethics, is not content with the observance of negative

---

[67] See Alejandro Vigo, *Zeit und Praxis bei Aristoteles. Die Nikomachische Ethik und die zeit-ontologischen Voraussetzungen des vernunftgesteuerten Handelns* (Freiburg-München: Karl Albe, 1996), 83 nt. 64.

[68] See *In II Ethic.*, lect. 11, n. 377.

[69] See Thomas Deman, "Renseignements techniques au traité de la Prudence," in *Saint Thomas d'Aquin. Somme théologique* (Paris: éd. de la Revue des Jeunes, 1949), 458-78. For a criticism of Deman's position, see Carlos Ignacio Massini, "Reflexiones sobre un texto de Santo Tomás acerca de la verdad práctica," *Philosophica* 7 (1984): 148-54.

[70] *S. Th.*, I q. 79 a. 11 ad 2.

[71] See Ibid., *S. Th.*, I-II q. 19 aa. 5 & 6.

precepts of law; rather, it points to the complete development of human potentialities.

Truth in actions

Although the notion of truth does not play the same role in the practical realm which it plays in the theoretical domain, this does not mean that practical truth does not occupy a place in intellect, as does all truth in the proper sense. In fact, we have shown the diverse conformities that occur between the appetite and reason in the task of originating a good action. These are: first, the conformity of the appetite with those ends given naturally by the intellect; second, the conformity of that reason which searches for means with the correct appetite of the end; and third, the conformity of the appetite which desires means to that reason which has known which of those means are appropriate for obtaining the end in question. Of all the conformities that are possible between the appetite and the intellect, practical truth is found, properly speaking, in that very reason which, by judging the means, conforms to the correct appetite for the end. In the weakest sense, one can also speak of practical truth in order to refer to all the other conformity relations which take hold in a man whose heart and head move in harmony. Truth, however, remains in the domain of judgment. Actions, in contrast, must be called either good or bad, more than true or false.

Does this mean that we cannot recognize a truth of or in actions? Since the text of Saint Paul which spoke of doing the truth[72] until the theses of Marx concerning Feuerbach, diverse texts have attempted to link truth and action. Recently, perhaps one of the authors who has most strongly insisted upon the theme of the truth of action is the above-mentioned Fernando Inciarte:

> By 'practical truth' I mean not the true of propositions about actions (for example the truth of moral judgments). By "practical truth" I understand rather the truth of actions themselves. True moral judgments are still theoretical.[73]

---

[72] See *Ephesians* 4, 15.

[73] Fernando Inciarte, "Practical Truth," in *Persona, verità e morale. Atti del Congresso Internazionale di Teologia Morale (Roma, 7-12 aprile 1986)* (Roma: Città Nuova Editrice, 1986), 201.

Anyway, that the truth is properly in the intellect does not impede our recognizing other analogical conceptions of truth among which one must include truth within the actions themselves. This for at least three reasons.

Firstly, because actions are an effect of practical truth, and it is not arbitrary to indicate the effect by its cause.[74] A good action, then, comes about as the fruit of the concordance between the right appetite and true reason. Again, we see the difference between the speculative and practical truth. In the domain of the speculative, things are not—in the proper sense—the truth, but are the cause of the truth which exists in the intellect. In the practical domain, by contrast, there is nothing external to which the reason must conform itself, but reason harmonizes with something interior to the subject, the right appetite. If it is about something external that we are talking, it ought to be constituted by the actions which must be done in the here and now. The goodness of an action is a fruit of the truth of an intellect oriented toward praxis. On the practical level, then, it can be said that the thing is not the cause, but rather an effect of the truth. This is clearly established when observing the analysis that Aristotle and Thomas Aquinas make of the practical syllogism, whose conclusion is not a theoretical premise, but an action,[75] which in an analogical sense could be called true or false. Both refer to this matter, among other points, when they deal with the incontinent case, where the action, in sum, does not correspond with their beliefs, because their will is weak and is not able to resist passions when they push in a direction contrary to that indicated by reason. It is important to distinguish the practical syllogism for that identified as deontic. As Skarica says:

> The last one is characterized for not being ordered directly to the action, but to establishing a conclusion directive of action, for example, a law or norm. […] It is easy to confuse one syllogism with the other, because they

[74] See *S. Th.*, I q. 79 a. 13c.

[75] This is clearly established in Aristotelian thinking (*De motu animalium* 7, 701a32-33). Within the philosophy of Aquinas (*S. Th.*, I-II q. 13 a. 1 ad 2m), it could be thought that only analogically, the conclusion of the practical syllogism consists in an action: "Conclusio etiam syllogismi qui fit in operabilibus, ad rationem pertinet; et dicitur sententia vel iudicium, quam sequitur electio. Et ob hoc ipsa conclusio pertinere videtur ad electionem, tanquam ad consequens". In other texts, however, Aquinas also appears to assert that, to some extent, an action could be the conclusion of this syllogism. "Conferens enim de agendis, utitur quodam syllogismo, cuius conclusio est iudicium seu electio vel operatio." *S. Th.*, I-II q. 76 a. 1c; see I-II q. 13 a.3c.

> are both in some way ordered to the action, but one is in a direct way, and the other in an indirect way.[76]

Second, because in practical truth it seems to be that—strictly speaking—conformity is only produced in the singular case of the subject's being oriented toward praxis. The moral propositions which a prudent man in Australia espouses, when preoccupied about the welfare of the nations, do concern matters of profound ethical relevance, but because these matters do not bear down upon him there and then, they are not considered as within practical truth. Judgments like "it is good that in Red China a political regime is implemented which assures the liberty of its citizens" may be true or false, but, although such judgments refer to practical matters, one cannot say that in the subject who pronounces them there is practical truth. Namely, that they achieve a concordance between the right appetite and true reason. It is not in vain that Aquinas insists that such a concordance is really only taking into consideration *contingent things that can be done by us*, and not necessary things which are not dependent upon our will.[77] It is in front of these things which appetite "awakens", thus leading to choice which is an "intellective appetite".[78] In this sense, it is said that

> although the mind is the initiator of acts, nonetheless, the mind, considered by itself, or rather, speculative reason, nothing moves because nothing designates the pursuit or aversion [...] and thus it is not the principle of any act, rather only that which is by reason of something, namely, which is ordered toward some particular operable like an end. And this is reason or the practical mind.[79]

A change in a Chinese regime is, effectively, something contingent, but it does not depend on the will—neither ours nor that of the aforementioned Australian—to achieve it. This shows the importance of facticity in praxis: it is not enough to say that the matter being deliberated is contingent, rather one has also to include that as well as the contingent it must also deal with something that is in the reach of whomever is acting, given the circumstances in which he finds himself. That is why Aquinas says that "not only do men not deliberate with regard to necessary things,

---

[76] Mirko Skarica, "La verdad práctica en santo Tomás de Aquino," *Anuario Filosófico* 32 (1999): 309-10.
[77] See *S. Th.*, I-II q. 57 a. 6 ad 3um.
[78] *In VI Ethic.*, lect. 2, n. 1137.
[79] Ibid., lect. 2, n. 1135.

natural things and fortuitous things, they moreover do not do it with regard to all things human, as the Lacedaemonians do not deliberate concerning how the Scythians—who are very far from them—must agree in the best manner one with the others";[80] by contrast "we deliberate concerning the operable, of that which is to be found within us, or rather, about that which is in our own power."[81]

Thus, it is not merely that actions have a great deal to do with the idea of truth inasmuch as they are an effect of practical reason, rather that a second, much more powerful, reason exists, and this is that practical truth can only arise when the subject is confronted with having to decide whether to commit or omit something and how to go about doing so. "It is not merely any relation to action that makes the understanding a practical one [...], rather that in order for the understanding be practical it is necessary that it be *regulating the action directly.*"[82]

Finally, the very use of language itself permits us to speak analogically of true and false actions. Aquinas advances this in various senses:

a) In the case of a theatric representation, it can be said that the (true) actor who is playing a part is a "false Hector."[83] By this he is not indicating that an actor is either bad or false player, rather he may even be trying to say the complete opposite: "This man acts so well that he can make us believe that he is, in fact, the true Hector of an obviously ancient, ancient story; but let us be honest: he is a man just as real as we are; although you do not believe it, he is a false Hector." To continue with the example, it might be that the leading actor gets sick and is replaced by an amateur, for whom a prompter must provide the significant part of the lines. In this case, we can talk about a false actor whose acting is so deficient that he is even incapable of playing a false Hector.

b) Another thing that is spoken about is a "false man": someone whose conduct does not correspond to his words.[84] Falsity, hypocrisy, inauthenticity are more or less contemporary adjectives based upon that analogical employment of the word "truth" which allows us to speak of a truth within one's actions.[85] In the case of language, something similar can be seen. To tell a lie is an action which could be qualified as a false one. In the lie, the words which are offered are true words but they do not mean

---

[80] *In III Ethic.*, lect. 7, n. 464.
[81] Ibid., lect. 7, n. 465.
[82] *De Ver.*, q. 14 a. 4c.
[83] *S. Th.*, I q. 17 a. 1c & ad 1.
[84] *In I Sent.* dist. 19 q. 5 a. 1c.
[85] See *S. Th.*, I q. 17 a. 2c *in fine*.

what they say and for this reason are deceptive, and the cause of someone's mistake in a judgment of something.[86] Aquinas also resorts to a scriptural form of speaking where "falsehoods" refers to moral failings inasmuch as those who commit them deviate from the order mandated by divine intellect, which is the ultimate measure of truth.[87]

c) Thirdly, a special case is that of technique or art, which will not be the subject of the present study. One can call a work false that does not correspond with the idea of the agent, or more specifically, with the artifice.[88] This is an interesting theme, because while in the speculative field it is the thing that measures the intellect and determines its veracity or falsity, in the technical, on the contrary, it is the intellect which measures the thing produced, which is said to be true or false whether corresponds or not to the reason of art. Following this criterion, nothing impedes us in the field of the praxis to identify as false a work which does not correspond with what we intended to produce, and as true that which does correspond with our intention, albeit this is not the principal sense of the practical truth.[89]

It is appropriate to consider that to which Aquinas alludes concerning art in one of the principal texts in which practical truth is mentioned:

> The truth of the practical intellect depends on the conformity with right appetite. This conformity has no place in necessary matters, which are not affected by the human will; but only in contingent matters which can be effected by us, whether they be matters of interior action, or the products of external work. Hence it is only about contingent matters that an intellectual virtue is assigned to the practical intellect, viz. art, as regards things to be made, and prudence, as regards things to be done.[90]

At first glance, there seems to be a contradiction between this passage in the *Summa teologiæ* and another very well know one that also pertains to the same question, in which, in order to show the difference which obtains between prudence and art, Aquinas indicates that

---

[86] See *In Peri hermen.*, lect. 3, n. 31 *in fine*.
[87] See *S. Th.*, I q. 17 a. 1c.
[88] *In Peri hermen.*, lect. 3, n. 29.
[89] For an analysis of this sense of practical truth, based on the *Expositio* of Saint Thomas about the Aristotelian *Peri hermeneias*: Skarica, "La verdad práctica en santo Tomás de Aquino," 291-314.
[90] *S. Th.,* I-II q. 57 a. 5 ad 3.

> consequently, it is requisite for prudence, which is right reason about things to be done, that man be well disposed with regard to the ends: and this depends on the rectitude of his appetite. Wherefore, for prudence there is need of a moral virtue, which rectifies the appetite. On the other hand the good things made by art is not the good of man's appetite, but the good of those things themselves: wherefore art does not presuppose rectitude of the appetite. The consequence is that *more praise is given to a craftsman who is at fault willingly, than to one who is unwillingly*; whereas it is more contrary to prudence to sin willingly than unwillingly, *since rectitude of the will is essential to prudence, but not to art.*[91]

The contradiction apparently resides in the fact that the first of these texts seems to demand a concordance between the right appetite and true reason also in the realm of art in order for practical truth to exist, while the second text frees art from the question of rectitude of appetite, resorting to the classic example in art that it is better that one should fail desiring to do so than that the one should succeed inadvertently. The basic thing, then, in the technical is true reason. A good will is not relevant for the technician *qu*a technician. But the classic example ought not to be absolutized, because the technician is additionally a man. It is certain that it is the better doctor or artisan who commits an error desiring to do so than he who makes a mistake through ignorance. But, from this can it necessarily be deduced that they are both equally good technicians, he who makes a mistake desiring to do so and he who completes the same task well and with cheerful good will?

By freeing *techné* from the rectitude of appetite, the second text is concerned only with the conceptual distinction between art and prudence. The first, by contrast, presents a broader context in which prudence is necessary in order to "live well".[92] And in this sense, inasmuch as the technician is a man, there is no doubt that he needs to have a good will or, in other words, a right appetite. On the other hand, the consideration of technical activity within the entire collectivity of human life appears to permit us to speak of practical truth also in the domain of making, because, although taken separately in abstract analysis, each one of these activities only seems to perfect produced works, which are "external to man".[93] Nevertheless, in this particular case, the subject which accomplishes them may or may not be disposed with respect to

[91] Ibid., I-II q. 57 a. 4c.
[92] Ibid., I-II q. 57 a. 5.
[93] Ibid., I-II q. 57 a. 4 ad 1.

fundamental good and his technical activity may or may not be a contribution for which his own life will be successful.[94]

The existence of practical truth permits us to glimpse the fact that another use of reason exists beyond the theoretical. Human reason is not limited to contemplating the reality of things or to carrying out deductions given certain truths possessed in a more or less serene manner. That one can thus speak of a practical use of reason, makes us see that human reason is not merely constatative, but also perceptive, and, moreover, that it can constitute itself in a form capable of guiding human action. The fact that praxis has as its object things which can be of very different kinds, while perhaps making it easy to dismiss all of ethics as a realm of absolute certainties, offered by a system of pre-existing norms, should not however lead one to the despair of a non-cognitive emotivism. If we are confronted by having to decide, and if this decision takes place in the realm of the variable, then reason can give us inestimable aid, as long as it is a modest reason which takes into account experience and is in tune with the circumstances. A reason that knows how to listen to others and is capable of discovering in very diverse situations what is just towards man and what degrades him. In order to be able to complete a task such as this, there is no other solution for reason than to become practical.

Works Cited

Aquinas, Thomas. *In Aristotelis Libros Perihermeneias Expositio*. Roma: Marietti, 1955.

—. *Quaestiones Disputatae I: De Veritate*. Taurini-Romae: Marietti, 1964.

—. *Scriptum Super Libros Sententiarum* Paris: Lethielleax, 1929-1947.

—. *Sententia libri Ethicorum: Opera omnia iussu Leonis XIII P. M. edita, t. 47*. Romae: Ad Sanctae Sabinae, 1969.

—. *Summa contra Gentiles*. Taurini-Romae: Marietti, 1961.

—. *Summa Theologiae*. Roma: Marietti, 1952.

—. *The Summa theologiae* Translated by Fathers of the English Dominican Province. 2 ed. New York: Benziger Brothers, 1947-1948.

—. *Commentary on Aristotle's Nicomachean Ethics* Translated by C. I. Litzinger. Notre Dame, Indiana: Dumb Ox Books, 1993.

Aristotle. *The Nicomachean Ethics* Translated by David Ross. Oxford: Oxford University Press, 1989.

[94] See Ibid., I-II q. 18, a. 9c.

Damasio, Antonio. *Descartes' Error: Emotion, Reason, and the Human Brain*. New York: Putnam, 1994.
Deman, Thomas. "Renseignements techniques au traité de la Prudence." In *Saint Thomas d'Aquin. Somme théologique* 458-78. Paris: éd. de la Revue des Jeunes, 1949.
Finnis, John. *Natural Law and Natural Rights*. Oxford: Oxford University Press, 1980.
Inciarte, Fernando. *El reto del positivismo lógico*. Madrid: Rialp, 1974.
—. "Practical Truth." In *Persona, verità e morale. Atti del Congresso Internazionale di Teologia Morale (Roma, 7-12 aprile 1986)*, 201-15. Roma: Città Nuova Editrice, 1986.
Marx, Karl. *Thesen über Feuerbach*. Edited by Marx/Engels, *Werke, Bd. 3*. Berlin: Dietz-Verlag.
Massini, Carlos Ignacio. "Reflexiones sobre un texto de Santo Tomás acerca de la verdad práctica." *Philosophica* 7 (1984): 148-54.
Rehm, Walter, ed. *Novalis. Fragmente*. Frankfurt/Main: Fischer Bücherei, 1956.
Skarica, Mirko. "La verdad práctica en santo Tomás de Aquino." *Anuario Filosófico* 32 (1999): 291-314.
Vigo, Alejandro. *Estudios Aristotélicos*. Pamplona: Eunsa, 2006.
—. *Zeit und Praxis bei Aristoteles. Die Nikomachische Ethik und die zeit-ontologischen Voraussetzungen des vernunftgesteuerten Handelns*. Freiburg-München: Karl Albe, 1996.

CHAPTER FOUR

THE DARKENING OF NATURAL REASON AND THE FORCE OF LAW AND CUSTOM

MARÍA ELTON

1. The variations of moral law in different circumstances are explained by Thomas Aquinas in the following text:

> The natural law, as to general principles, is the same for all, both as to rectitude and as to knowledge. But as to certain matters of detail, which are conclusions, as it were, of those general principles, it is the same for all in the majority of cases, both as to rectitude and as to knowledge; and yet in some few cases it may fail, both as to rectitude, by reason of certain obstacles (just as natures subject to generation and corruption fail in some few cases on account of some obstacle), and as to knowledge, since in some the reason is perverted by passion, or evil habit, or an evil disposition of nature.[1]

These matters of detail constitute particular precepts,[2] which can vary according to the text cited above. Such change may occur for two different reasons: a) because their rectitude is not fitting to the case to which they are to be applied; or b) because their rectitude is not known by some, whose reason is darkened. An analysis of the latter point—the darkening of natural reason—is the focus of this article. Individual ignorance of the particular precepts of natural law is frequent in a social order in which some customs render the apprehension of the right discourse of reason concerning the moral good man must carry out difficult.

Aquinas cited the Germans as a useful example of the darkening of natural reason due to bad customs, in line with the description provided by Julius Caesar in his historical account, *De Bello Gallias*. He says that

[1] *S. Th.* I-II, q. 94, a. 4.

[2] See *S. Th.* I-II, q. 100, a. 11.

"theft, although it is expressly contrary to the natural law, was not considered wrong among the Germans."[3] The Germans are a good example of darkened reason: they were ignorant of the natural law because of their evil habits.

In the same text, Thomas Aquinas notes that everything to which man feels naturally inclined belongs within natural law, including man's most specific natural inclination: to act in accordance with reason. The way in which reason proceeds from common principles to particular ones is different in theoretical reason and practical reason. Theoretical reason allows of no exceptions to its conclusions because it knows necessary things. In contrast, practical reason comes to know human acts that are contingent, so it can recognize necessity only in its common principle. Thus, as it moves to more particular principles, it discovers exceptions.[4]

Practical reason proceeds from common to particular principles as new conditions of the reality surrounding actions arise. In such circumstances, practical reason may be darkened on account of bad customs or a deformed natural disposition.[5] Thus, two different historical phenomena in this darkening of natural reason may be discerned: a) the first phenomenon, which occurs among people who lack the necessary historical experience to know certain principles they never have seen practiced in other communities or by exemplary persons;[6] and b) the second, which is prompted by a perversion of certain previously established customs, a corruption that is allowed by the society and the ruler.

---

[3] *S. Th.* I-II, q. 94, a. 4.

[4] See *S. Th.* I-II, q. 94, a. 4.

[5] See Ibid.

[6] Thomas Aquinas teaches that science in general, and moral science in particular, may be acquired by an inward principle (one who investigates for himself) or by an outward principle (one who is taught). By the light of the active intellect, every man has access to the principle of science by which he may know the universal principles common to every science. When man applies these universal principles to particular cases whose recollection or experience is provided by the senses, he acquires by his own inquiry the science of things about which he was ignorant. However, when man is taught, he is led by the teacher from known things to other things of which he was unaware. Aquinas quoted Aristotle in this regard: "All teaching and all learning proceed from previous knowledge"(See *S. Th.* I, q.117, a.1). From this point of view, the need for a certain degree of moral practice—whether personal or other—if knowledge of moral science is to progress through teaching, becomes clear; the peoples who lack this experience and must acquire it by their own investigation make very slow progress in this knowledge.

Point a) above would appear to be the case of the Germans who, according to Julius Caesar, regarded theft as legitimate when it was carried out outside their territory, and resorted to it in order to give the young something to do and thus avoid idleness.[7] Julius Caesar's account goes into some detail about the Germans; the difference between his narrative and the brief reference made by Thomas Aquinas yields a significant point for the present line of argument.[8] The Germans did not engage in theft in every circumstance, but only in the case of the property of those living outside their territory. Amongst themselves, they did not steal from one another. Therefore, it may be said that the Germans acknowledged, at least, that man is a social animal who is not self-sufficient in the acquisition of everything necessary to human life. In order to ensure that society was preserved, the Germans did not take what did not belong to them and abstained from causing injury inside their own territory.[9]

This form of conduct, which became customary, reflects a principle of moral rectitude that is distorted in some practices. In other words, theft is morally evil; but it is morally acceptable if it is committed against people living outside one's own territory. The nature of this principle of rectitude and its deviations are examined in the next section.

2. Thomas Aquinas asserts that it is fitting that there be a permanent principle of rectitude in man, namely synderesis, which involves avoiding every evil and pursuing every good, so that human actions may be right.[10] This principle is founded on the notion of good. He formulates it as follows: "good is that which all things seek after"; thus, the first precept of the natural law is that: "good is to be done and pursued, and evil is to be avoided".[11] Synderesis is not a logical principle or statement, but a light of the active intellect pertaining to the nature of the soul itself.[12]

---

[7] See Julius Caesar, *The Gallic War*, trans. Carolyn Hammond, *Oxford World's Classics* (Oxford: Oxford University Press, 1999), 161.

[8] I share the position articulated by Crowe that Caesar's opinion about the morality of the Germans was not quite as harsh as Saint Thomas assumed it to be—which is why Caesar explains the special circumstances in which the Germans considered theft to be legitimate (M. B. Crowe, "The Natural Law Before St. Thomas," *Irish Ecclesiastical Record* 76 (1951): 208. Quoted by R. A. Armstrong, *Primary and Secondary Precepts in Thomistic Natural Law Teaching* (The Hague: Martinus Nijhoff, 1966), 150.

[9] See *SCG*, III, 129.

[10] See *De Veritate*, q. 16.

[11] *S. Th.* I-II, q. 94, a. 2.

[12] See *De Veritate*, q. 16, a. 3.

The active intellect is the natural reason[13] which, in the practical order, and because it is a light, makes the ends of the natural inclinations of man visible. Natural reason apprehends these ends as good, and thus to be sought, and the opposite as bad, and thus to be avoided.[14] That what the intellect discovers is not the result of a process of logic—the ends of the natural inclinations of man—should be noted. The intellect is not abstract; it has personal significance. The human intellect participates in the divine intellect because it is its image and because it is a second cause. Given that it is an image of the divine intellect, the human intellect is not merely the capacity of thought, but contains to a certain extent the truth about man. This does not mean that it has innate ideas, but that it participates in the divine light, wherein is contained every truth about created things.[15]

Nevertheless, the human intellect is imperfect, and thus is endowed with a dual form of knowledge: the first is strictly natural, and the other discursive. Synderesis is the natural habit of the intellect; it urges what is good and condemns what is evil, insofar as the first principles prompt human inquiry and govern the judgment passed on its findings,[16] so that particular and concrete principles, which are closer to action, may be established. These secondary principles are derived from and implicit in the light of synderesis: they make what must be done concrete, and thus depend closely on moral dispositions. The dependence of the discourse of practical reason on affects is one of the principal causes of its darkening.

However, the clouding of practical reason does not mean the extinction of synderesis, which is impossible because the soul cannot be deprived of the active intellect. Nevertheless, the light of synderesis may be deflected to its opposite in the discursive process of natural reason. The individual's failure to apply rightly the universal judgment of synderesis to the particular[17] at the moment of choice does not destroy synderesis altogether, only to a certain extent. Practical reason establishes a precept about the goodness of an action when it chooses what must be done in relation to a particular end.[18] This precept is derived from synderesis, which moves man to do good acts. However, when man loves the lesser good more, the aforementioned precept fails to effect its due orientation. Man may love wealth or pleasure more than the order of reason or Divine

[13] See *S. Th.* II-II, q. 9, a. 1.
[14] See *S. Th.* I-II, q. 94, a. 2.
[15] See *S. Th.* I, q. 88, a. 3, ad. 1.
[16] See *S. Th.* I, q.79, a. 13.
[17] See *De Veritate*, q. 16, a. 3.
[18] See *S. Th.* I-II, q. 47, a. 8.

law or Divine charity, or some such thing, because he has an unruly appetite and prefers to be deprived of a spiritual good in order to possess a temporal good.[19]

Man acquires a vicious habit through the practice of inappropriate conduct. This vice incites him to follow false and corrupt operable principles, rather than universal ones, in his deliberations; i.e. not synderesis, but concrete precepts wrongly derived from it.[20] These principles should be established by moral science and moral wisdom[21]: intellectual habits which contain the secondary precepts by means of which—if rightly formed—the moral conscience must be directed. Moral science and wisdom cannot develop in men who have bad moral dispositions; in which case reason is diminished in its capacity for moral explanation. Reason is rendered defective[22] and loses its correctness,[23] even though synderesis retains its integrity. Thomas Aquinas holds that, unlike the conscience, synderesis never acts recklessly.[24] Moral conscience is the act by which the universal judgment of synderesis is applied to a particular act, through the discourse of reason;[25] it may omit the consideration of certain realities that ought to guide human acts when it establishes a secondary precept.[26]

The light of synderesis is not corrupted in this defective rational process, but it is concealed. Man continues to be the image of God through his intellect, although his reason may in fact be faulty.[27] Thus, it may be concluded that the Germans did not regard theft as legitimate absolutely, but granted it legitimacy when certain circumstances obtained: specifically, when the victims of theft are those living outside one's own

[19] See *S. Th.* I-II, q. 78, a. 1.

[20] See *De Veritate*, q. 16, a. 3, ad. 3.

[21] See *De Veritate*, q. 15, a. 3, ad. 2.

[22] See *De Malo*, q. 7, a. 5, ad. 6.

[23] See *De Veritate*, q. 15, a. 3, ad. 1.

[24] See *De Veritate*, q. 17, a. 2, ad. 1.

[25] See *De Veritate*, q. 17, a. 2.

[26] See *De Veritate*, q. 15, a. 3.

[27] There is a fundamental contrast on this point between Thomas Aquinas and the original reformers, such as Luther and Calvin. The reformers, along with some modern iusnaturalists, argued against the scholastic *imago Dei* doctrine—that is, they rejected the possibility that man could have any rational knowledge of God's nature, on the basis of which he might draw moral lessons for himself. They denied that the natural law could be known as a participation in the eternal law. See Knud Haakonssen, *Natural law and Moral Philosophy: from Grotius to the Scottish Enlightenment* (Cambridge: Cambridge University Press, 1996), 36.

territory, and when the action is carried out with a good end in mind—that is, to engage the young in exercise and avoid idleness.

3. The weakness of human nature predisposes human reason to the darkening of the particular precepts of natural law. Having lost the rectitude of its primitive state,[28] human nature collapsed upon itself and fell to its own deficiency as a mental-corporal nature. Man was left exposed to the rebellion of the will and, in particular, sensibility, against reason. This weakness of reason cannot be ignored by moral philosophy. Man in his present state may fall short of moral understanding. Therefore, "spoiled reason" is not a reason that is "inaccurately made use of" in man. This distinction is a subtle one but it points out that human reason itself cannot be wrongly used; it may, however, be carried away by unreasonable tendencies.[29] Aquinas asserts that "corrupt reason is not reason".[30]

Instances of "spoiled reason" may be discerned in an individual, and at a social level in the bad customs of a people. In the first case, there is the man with vicious habits, who regards as lovable anything opposed to spiritual good, which is excluded from his reasoning in a connatural way.[31] The vicious person is different from the incontinent person, who has moral science but does not apply it to his acts because the disorder of his passions makes it difficult. Quoting Aristotle, Thomas Aquinas compares the vicious person to the chronically ill, and the incontinent person to the occasionally ill. He who sins by vice is ill-disposed to the principles of practical things, and his fault is the more dangerous. Although his purpose may be temporarily disrupted by passion, he who sins because of a momentary passion tends toward the good end.[32]The latter sinner is more capable of repentance and his act is less harmful.

The chronic illness of reason may also be the origin of the bad customs of a people, which may sometimes be permitted by law. Thomas Aquinas thought that the Germans were an example of this perversion, since theft was a law and custom of their social organization. As has already been pointed out, however, the Germans allowed theft only in special circumstances. They lived in families and groups whose magistrates and

---

[28] See *S. Th.* I, q. 95, a. 3.

[29] See Martin Rhonheimer, *La perspectiva de la moral. Fundamentos de la Ética Filosófica*, trans. José Carlos Mardomingo (Madrid: Rialp, 2000), 174.

[30] "*...ratio corrupta non est ratio*" (*In II Sent.*, d. 24, q. 3, a. 3, ad. 3).

[31] See *S. Th.* I-II, q. 78, a. 2.

[32] See Ibid.

leaders were elected by the people every year, and who governed their respective groups. The Germans carried out hunting and military exercises, and from childhood were accustomed to hard work and weary effort. Chastity was valued and practiced among the young. Farming was not a priority and their land was unfenced, nor were there individually-owned allotments, as the magistrates stipulated. Every year, the people were allocated different plots in order to prevent their being tempted by the sedentary life and to abandon war, or to enlarge the plot of land they had been assigned with a corresponding increase in inequality among them. This type of sedentary life might provoke greed for money, which is the breeding ground of disagreement and dissension, and the urge to build to escape heat and cold. The Germans gloried most in life in great lonely expanses of land, and for this reason the magistrates of justice sanctioned theft outside their territory.[33]

On the basis of Caesar's account, the Germans may be described as barbarian and primitive—a people who had many virtues, but a defective moral conscience in relation to the right to property. Jacques Maritain pointed out that the moral conscience of men and nations has been progressing throughout history through increased differentiation from the "fundamental dynamic schemes" of natural law. This progress presupposes some moral practices which constitute the historical experience of mankind.[34] These "schemes" may be identified with synderesis, whose content is made more and more explicit by moral experience. The Germans had no knowledge of the more developed moral practices of other peoples when Julius Caesar wrote his account. As a result, a very limited state of development of their knowledge of the particular precepts of natural law may be assumed. At the same time, the state of their moral conscience was explicitly expressed in their customs and laws.

4. The repetition of outward acts by an individual or a people reflects the inclination of the will and of certain concepts of reason. When acts are carried out repeatedly, when man falls back on them as a matter of course, such acts may be read as proceeding from a deliberate rational judgment. Thus, customs have the force of law, and laws are abolished and

---

[33] See Caesar, *The Gallic War*, 21-23.

[34] See Jacques Maritain, "Pour une philosophie de l'histoire," in *Oeuvres Completes. Volume X* (Fribourg: Éditions Universitaires Fribourg Suizze, 1985), 699-705.

interpreted in accordance with custom.[35] If the community is free, the consent of the whole people, expressed in common custom, has greater value than the authority of the ruler when it comes to the establishment of a law. The power of the ruler in framing laws resides only in his being a representative of the people.[36]

A significant question arises in this context: what can the ruler do when the customs of the community do not conform to the common good? Any response to this question depends on whether or not the ruler is aware of this error. Therefore, the answer will be different depending on whether we relate it to the Germans at the beginning of the Christian era or to the moral conscience of a people undergoing a moral crisis.

The Germans, whose customs were described by Julius Caesar, lived in hard and primitive conditions during the first century, totally cut off from other more learned and civilized human groups. The conclusion that they lacked the necessary experience to have a more developed conscience in relation to the right to property comes easily. According to Thomas Aquinas, moral precepts acquire obligatory force from natural reason itself, regardless of whether or not they have been established by law. Yet only the first of these moral precepts, which is the end of the others, is so certain and evident as to be in no need of promulgation, i.e. love of God and of one's neighbor. Given that human judgment may be led astray in certain instances, there are some more detailed precepts, the reasons for which even an uneducated man may easily grasp, that must nonetheless be promulgated. Among these is the prohibition on theft in its different forms, such as larceny,[37] with which the Germans did not comply.

The first principles are known immediately, and the second principles by simple reasoning. Although, as has been noted already above, it may err through a bad personal moral disposition, natural reason, as an active power, is sufficient unto itself to perform a perfect act. It arrives at the knowledge of the unknown through its own *discovery* or by *learning by instruction.* In the latter case, however, one person is said to teach another insofar as he shows the other person, by means of signs, the reasoning process he himself may follow in his own natural reason until he arrives at a knowledge of the things which he did not know.[38]

---

[35] See *S. Th.* I-II, q. 97, a. 3.
[36] See *S. Th.* I-II, q. 97, a.3, ad. 3.
[37] See *S. Th.* q. 100, a. 11.
[38] See *De Veritate*, q. 11, a. 1.

As Maritain pointed out, the process of discovery in man is very slow, because of the weakness of his reason[39] and the fact that certain customs contrary to natural law may prevail for long periods of time.[40] This would appear to have been the situation of the German people in the first century. They were a primitive people; through lack of contact with more developed cultures, they lacked the opportunity to be taught by others and to receive divine revelation.

5. A distinction between two historical phenomena in which natural reason may be darkened was drawn at the beginning of this article. One of them is inherent to peoples who lack the historical and moral experience required for the knowledge of certain principles. This phenomenon appears to be sufficiently exemplified by the Germans as cited by Aquinas. The other phenomenon arises as a result of the perversion of previously established good customs, and is the focus of the following discussion. Its interest lies in the fact that it is the situation obtaining at present. The Christian *ethos*, which enabled the predominance of a moral standard that grounded a great culture and civilization, now appears to be darkened to a significant extent among the peoples who were once nurtured by that *ethos*.

For some thinkers, the crisis of the Christian *ethos* has prompted the need to offer a speculative foundation of the natural law. However, the argument here is that an exclusively theoretical foundation for moral rules is not sufficient for moral practices. The principal failing in the current

---

[39] Reference to *S. Th.* I, q. 95, a. 3 may be of interest in this regard. Aquinas holds that the weakness of reason is a consequence of original sin. Man lost the state of innocence because of his guilt; in a certain sense, however, he possessed all the virtues because reason was subject to God, and the lower powers to reason. The natural law had full efficacy in this state. The loss of this preternatural gift did not involve the destruction or corruption of human nature; rather, man in his present state acquires moral virtue only with difficulty. Reason can know natural law in the state of fallen nature, but this knowledge may be clouded by disorder in the passions and the will. This doctrine is entirely different from the Protestant tradition of natural law, found in Luther, for whom natural reason is entirely blind and ignorant, and cannot order the will correctly in any way. Thus, man can neither intend nor do any good, since he always errs [*De servo arbitrio,* WA, XVIII, 712, 31-37; cited by Javier Hervada, *Historia de la ciencia del derecho natural* (Pamplona: Eunsa, 1987), 200. The will, in turn, is also corrupted—"bad and useless" [*De servo arbitrio,* 762, 5-7 and 11-12, cited by Hervada, *Historia de la ciencia del derecho natural*, 200.].

[40] See Maritain, "Pour une philosophie de l'histoire," 699-705.

situation lies with the spontaneous knowledge of natural law. The pervasiveness of bad customs has provoked the decadence of spontaneous moral knowledge as a consequence, and has given rise to a new, erroneous social *ethos*.

The following question arises in this context: what caused the decadence of a mature *ethos* which had been in accord with the right development of natural reason? The response suggested here is that this decline was enabled through the influence of bad moral customs acquired little by little, which cloud the application of synderesis to the most concrete precepts. The most general principles of natural law cannot be blotted out from men's hearts. However, secondary precepts may be effaced in the human heart either through evil persuasion, as in speculative matters when errors occur in relation to necessary conclusions, or through vicious customs and corrupt habits.[41] The Germans are an example of the gap between the first universal principles and concrete precepts. For them, theft was not legitimate in universal terms, but only in some particular cases: they could steal from their neighbors, in order to keep them at a distance from their own territory, and so that the young might acquire practical experience in certain skills.

In addition, given that the customs prevailing in a society are key to the acknowledgement or disavowal of the secondary precepts of natural law, these rules become the expression of the general assent of the people in a free community.[42] It seems that this social phenomenon existed without conflict among the Germans—a free society that chose its magistrates every year, yet who did not know better rules in relation to property, nor the full perversity of theft. Given their historical situation, they were also unable to get information on morally superior customs. Christianity afforded them this opportunity in the fifth century, when the Germans invaded the Roman Empire, and they themselves came to be leaders of a new, more Christian and very much more humane culture.

Nevertheless, the phenomenon of the darkening of man's natural reason, as a consequence of the decadence of customs, has provoked conflict. In such cases, a partial consensus of the community seems to hold to the belief that the positive law—which is an expression of natural law—should change according to the historical circumstances of society. Two questions may be posed to Thomas Aquinas in the face of this

---

[41] See *S. Th.* I-II, q. 97, a. 6.

[42] See *S. Th.*, q. 97, a. 3, ad. 3.

conflict: a) is natural law changeable according to the social structure; and b) can positive law prevent the decadence of customs?

With respect to question a), in his renowned study on natural law, R. A. Armstrong points out that there are hundreds of texts in the work of Thomas Aquinas where human nature is held to be immutable. However, in addition to these, there are three apparently contradictory texts which seem to articulate the mutability of human nature.[43] Two of these three texts are related to the contingency of the matter of the law, and the other is related to the influence of the passions on reason and the irregular development of knowledge of natural law among men. Although only the last text is directly pertinent to the subject of the darkening of natural reason, the other two are also referred to in order to discount entirely the notion that Thomas Aquinas may have asserted that human nature is mutable according to historical circumstances. (Such an assertion would wholly undermine the argument outlined here.)

In a significant passage in *De Malo,* with regard to the need that good and just things be determined by law, Thomas Aquinas notes:

> We can consider just and good things in two ways: in one way, formally, and then they are always and everywhere the same, since the principles of justice in the natural power of reason do not change; in the second way materially, and then just and good things are not everywhere and among all peoples the same, and such things need to be determined by law. And the latter happens because of mutability of human nature and because of the different conditions of human beings at different times and in different places. For example, justice always requires that there be an equal exchange in buying and selling, but justice requires that so much given for a measure of grain in a certain place or at a certain time, and that more or less given in another place or at another time.[44]

This statement may seem to suggest that Thomas Aquinas makes the morality of actions entirely dependent on human law, which, in turn, may change according to circumstances of place and time. However, this is not in fact the case. Firstly, because, as is made clear in the text itself, some things are moral by nature: in a purchase and sale, the transaction is ordered by equivalence, which is formal and known to natural reason; and secondly, some things are accidental to nature, such as the amount involved in these transactions according to time and place, and constitute

---

[43] See Armstrong, *Primary and Secondary Precepts in Thomistic Natural Law Teaching*, 174.

[44] *De Malo,* q. 2, a. 4, ad. 13.

the materiality to which formal reason is applied. The latter must be established by human law; the essential reasons of human nature are always to be borne in mind in this regard.

Actions are good or bad according to their object. As the species of natural things is determined by their form, so objects shape the species of actions. The objects are not the things in themselves; rather, they are the relation of actions to things, constituted as a form established by reason. The goodness of an action is understood in light of its appropriate object.[45] For example, natural reason ordains that parents must take care of their children before they have the power of reason,[46] and afterwards educate them.[47] This is a relation between certain actions and persons, established as a form constituted by reason. However, the way in which this guardianship is put into practice is naturally different according to time and place and also depends on the development of the society and its educational institutions. Human law changes according to these different circumstances. Thus, natural law has different applications because of the variability of the matter in which it is embodied; natural law itself, however, does not change.

In any case, the objection to nothing being immutable in human nature is also addressed by Thomas Aquinas himself in a dialogue wherein he discusses whether right may be conveniently divided into natural right and positive right. He answers that although it is always immutable, human nature may sometimes fail; and human nature may be described as mutable in this sense.[48] For example, although natural equality implies that a loan be repaid to the creditor, it need not be paid back if the creditor is a traitor to his country.[49]

According to Thomas Aquinas, the secondary precepts of natural law may fail not only in relation to knowledge, as happened among the Germans, but also "as to rectitude, by reason of certain obstacles, just as natures subject to generation and corruption fail in some few cases on account of some obstacle."[50] The obstacle in the previous example is the will of the traitor.

---

[45] See *S. Th.* I-II, q. 18, aa. 1 and 2.
[46] See *S. Th.* II-II, q. 10, a. 12.
[47] See *SCG*, III, 122; *Supl.*, q. 41, a. 1.
[48] See S.Th., II-II, q. 57, a. 2, ad. 1.
[49] See S.Th., I-II, q. 97, a. 4, ad. 3.
[50] *S. Th.* I-II, q. 94, a. 4.

> This lack of reliability should not be attributed so much to the precept in itself as to the precept seen through its application to action. This variation has taken place in its turn only because, in the action which that precept was designed to regulate, a "circumstance" has been introduced that notably modifies the object of the action itself, to the extent that this action can no longer be regarded in the first instance or exclusively as yet another case of the same precept, at least as long as the "disturbing" circumstances are present.[51]

A circumstance that is the principal condition of the object that determines the action's species[52] must be distinguished from a circumstance added to the object that makes a moral action better or worse without changing its species.[53] The first is exemplified in the case referred to above in which the creditor is a traitor to his country;[54] and thus the object of the action to pay back the loan would not be to return the loan, but to put the country in danger.

Given that these rules may be wrongly applied in some cases, when the circumstances that determine the species of the action change, the secondary precepts of natural law cannot be reduced to a compilation of regulations. Beyond positive knowledge of the rule, which secondary precept of natural law is to be applied in each case would also have to be known in line with prudence.[55]

> Consequently he who is placed over a community is empowered to dispense in a human law that rests upon his authority, so that, when the law fails in its application to persons or circumstances, he may allow the precept of the law not to be observed [...] if however he grants this permission without any such reason, and of his mere will, he will be an unfaithful or an imprudent dispenser: unfaithful, if he has not the common good in view; imprudent, if he ignores the reasons for granting dispensations.[56]

---

[51] Ana Marta González, "*Depositum Gladius non debet restitui furioso:* Precepts, synderesis and virtues in Saint Thomas Aquinas," *The Thomist* 62, no. 2 (1999): 222.

[52] See *S. Th.* I-II, q. 18, a. 10.

[53] See, *S. Th.* I-II, q. 18, a. 11.

[54] See *S. Th.* I-II, q. 97, a. 4, ad. 3.

[55] See González, "*Depositum Gladius non debet restitui furioso:* Precepts, synderesis and virtues in Saint Thomas Aquinas," 222.

[56] *S. Th.* I-II, q. 97, a. 4.

Thus, two of the texts in which Thomas Aquinas seems to point out that human nature is mutable in a certain sense are refuted by arguments advanced by Aquinas himself. Hence, the present decadence of the Christian *ethos* cannot be attributed to certain changes in human nature due to circumstances of time and place. Although the third text suggests a certain adaptability of law to the circumstances in which man finds himself, it does so in the context of a clear assertion regarding those things that are immutable by nature.

In this third text, Aquinas addresses the question of whether or not marriage comes within the remit of natural law. In the body of this piece of writing, he argues that it does so, as an end toward which nature is inclined; but it should be adopted by man's free will, as are acts of virtue. This inclination is a dual one: the first element concerns the principal end of matrimony, namely the good of the offspring, who are not only begotten but are also to be educated by their parents until they reach the state of virtue, which is only possible when the children know for certain who their parents are. The second element concerns the second end of matrimony, namely the mutual services that married persons render each other in household matters.[57] One of the objections to this position is that natural things are the same for all, but matrimony is not the same for all because its practice varies according to different laws.[58] Aquinas cites Aristotle in his response to this objection: human nature is not immutable as Divine nature is. Hence, what pertains to natural law may vary in accordance with the various states and conditions of men.[59]

This response to the third objection and the line of argument in this article are not contradictory; however, for the purposes of the current debate about the subject, a more detailed interpretation of Aquinas's succinct explanation is required. At the beginning of his text, Aquinas states that something is natural in two ways: first, as the necessary result of principles of nature, as upward movement is natural to fire; and second, as something to which nature is inclined although it may come to pass through the intervention of free will. Matrimony is natural in the second way[60] and is an example of how human nature is not immutable: its ends may not be attained by some men, because of the failure of free will, due

[57] See *Supl.*, q. 41, a. 1.

[58] See *Supl.*, q. 41, a. 1, obj. 3.

[59] See *Supl.*, q. 41, a. 1, ad. 3.

[60] See *Supl.*, q. 41, a.1.

to the influence of the passions on reason, or because natural reason may only have arrived at a basic stage of development in some societies.[61]

Natural reason may be darkened and fail to respond to the demands of the ends of human nature at any moment in history, even when a society may have attained an advanced knowledge of natural law. The latter case is facilitated by the spread of vicious customs which prevent the universal knowledge of synderesis from shedding its light on the objects of action. The question addressed in the final section of this article is as follows: Can human and positive law, both of which are derived from natural law,[62] prevent this deformation?

6. Like Aristotle, Thomas Aquinas holds that positive law has educational value.[63] Thus, its establishment may prevent the darkening of natural reason to a considerable extent. Such significant aspects as the following may be discerned in this statement: a) the need for law among the young and adults; b) the different reception of the law among those who have good customs and those who have bad customs; c) the importance of obliging the latter to comply with the law by means of punishment; and d), in what sense this force of law is educational and underwrites the preceptive capacity of natural reason.

In relation to point a), Aquinas argues that man should not only be reared under good laws and well cared for when he is young. Adults, too, must discover and become accustomed to honorable ways of acting in accordance with the law.[64] Although, in the context of the Aristotelian tradition, men may come to know the moral law by natural reason and act according to it, Aquinas takes into account the notion of fallen human nature, whereby men do not follow this norm without difficulty; the following quotation makes his position clear:

> to live a temperate and a hard life by refraining from pleasures and by not abandoning the good on account of labors and pain is unattractive to many, specially to young men who are prone to pleasures [...] For this reason the rearing of children and their activities must be regulated by good laws.[65]

---

[61] See Armstrong, *Primary and Secondary Precepts in Thomistic Natural Law Teaching*, 175.

[62] See *S. Th.* I-II, q. 95, a. 4.

[63] See *In X Ethicorum*.

[64] See *In X Ethicorum* 1180 a 1.

[65] *In X Ethicorum* 1179 b 31, 155-160.

That the people's acknowledgment of natural law depends on the moral quality of their customs is asserted in point b). As has already been explained above, natural reason, as an active faculty, can pass, through teaching, to its perfect act, i.e. knowledge of the particular precepts that are potentially in synderesis. However, good customs are also required if this is to occur. Teaching is a form of persuasion which may challenge and move to do good generous youths who are not enslaved to vice and passion and who have refined natural dispositions inasmuch as they are inclined to virtuous deeds.[66] Aquinas stated that virtue is not only knowledge, as Socrates held; it also involves rectitude of the appetitive faculty, which may be attained through the customs that incline this faculty to good.[67] Nevertheless, the natural inclinations to temperance and bravery with which some have been endowed by God are not in themselves sufficient because they are imperfect virtues that require the perfection of the intellect or reason.[68] Those who truly love what is good must also be disposed to the perfection of virtue through the good advice of reason.[69]

However, Aquinas takes into account the fallen condition of human nature and holds that many men cannot be induced to lead virtuous lives by persuasive words because they are not subject to the fear of disgrace or shame. Given that their lives are ruled by passion rather than reason, these men do not refrain from evil because of fear of disgrace but because of fear of punishment. They seek only to experience pleasure and avoid pain, without ever knowing what is truly good and pleasant, nor ever tasting its delights. These men are only restrained by fear of punishment.[70]

Thus, the importance of positive law as an expression of natural law in the formation of good customs which help men to know the natural law through natural reason is considered in point c). "Generally speaking, passion that—when firmly rooted by habituation—masters man does not yield to argument but must be attacked by violence to compel men to good."[71] Many obey by necessity or force, rather than by persuasion. They pay more attention to the hurt they might suffer in punishment than to

---

[66] See *In X Ethicorum* 1179 b 4, 50-55.
[67] See Ibid., 1179 b 18, 105-110.
[68] See Ibid., 1179 b 18, 95-100
[69] See Ibid., 1179 b 4, 55.
[70] See Ibid., 1179 b 4, 60.
[71] Ibid., 1179 b 18, 130-135.

what is honorable.[72] Insofar as it is promulgated by the ruler, the law has power.[73]

Nevertheless, the coercion of law does not deprive those subdued by its force of freedom, despite their bad habits. With respect to point d), the obligation of the law is educational and, in a certain sense, sets natural reason free to know according to its potential. Actions carried out through fear are mixed: they are involuntary, insofar as no one absolutely wishes to do them; and voluntary, insofar as a sensible man wishes to do them for his own safety.[74] In the case at issue here, to perform a good action which is not the fruit of passion or a cause of delight is involuntary. On the other hand, to avoid the pain of punishment, as the end of what is being done, is voluntary. There is no necessity in what is done because the end of action is sought. Thus, the ruler, by establishing natural law as a positive law and the corresponding punishment in the case of failure to comply, plays on the concupiscence of people of bad disposition. These people carry out (materially, not formally) virtuous actions in order to comply with the law, and to avoid pain. However, the repetition of these imperfect actions may lead to a more delightful and less difficult fulfillment of what is good and, should it be chosen, enable its practice for its own sake.[75]

Hence, promulgated natural law has an educational value that the political authority must take into account. Should the ruler fail to endorse this important aspect of the common good, the private individual ought to be able to establish among his children and friends, thus contributing to their virtuous lives. Strict supervision of the education of children and the virtuous activities of citizens is of principal concern to the public authority; and, in the absence of such authority, to every private person.[76] "In fact, public laws and customs introduced by rulers hold the same place in states as do paternal precepts and customs introduced by parents in families."[77]

---

[72] See Ibid., 1179 b 31, 175.
[73] See Ibid., 1180 a 14, 215-220.
[74] See *In III Ethicorum* 1110 a 11, 125-150.
[75] Antonio Millán Puelles, *La formación de la personalidad humana* (Madrid: Rialp, 1963), 207-10.
[76] See *In X Ethicorum* 1180 a 24.
[77] Ibid., 1180 a 34, 50-55.

Works Cited

Primary Sources

Abbreviations and references of the works of Thomas Aquinas quoted

De Malo	*Quaestiones Disputatae De Malo*
De Veritate	*Quaestiones Disputatae De Veritate*
S.C.G.	*Summa Contra Gentiles*
In Ethicorum	*Sententia Libri Ethicorum*
S.Th.	*Summae Theologiae*

The references follow the divisions of Thomas Aquinas, *Opera omnia*. Roma: Commissio Leonina; Paris: Librairie Philosophique J. Vein, 1882.

The following translations have been consulted:

(De Malo)
Aquinas, Thomas. *On Evil* Translated by Richard Regan. Oxford: Oxford University Press, 2003.

(De Veritate)
Aquinas, Thomas. *Truth* Translated by James V. McGlynn, S.J. Indianaplis/Cambridge, Hackett Publishing Company, Inc. 1954.

(In Ethicorum)
Aquinas, Thomas. *Commentary on Aristotle's Nicomachean Ethics* Translated by C.I. Litzinger. Chicago: Henry Regnery Co. 1964.

(S.Th.)
Aquinas, Thomas. *Summa Theologica* Translated by the Fathers of the English Dominican Province. New York: Benzinger Bros., 1947.

Secondary Sources

Armstrong, R. A. *Primary and Secondary Precepts in Thomistic Natural Law Teaching*. The Hague: Martinus Nijhoff, 1966.

Caesar, Julius. *The Gallic War* Translated by Carolyn Hammond, *Oxford World's Classics*. Oxford: Oxford University Press, 1999.

Crowe, M. B. "The Natural Law Before St. Thomas." *Irish Ecclesiastical Record* 76 (1951): 193-204.

González, Ana Marta. "*Depositum Gladius non debet restitui furioso:* Precepts, synderesis and virtues in Saint Thomas Aquinas." *The Thomist* 62, no. 2 (1999): 217-40.

Haakonssen, Knud. *Natural law and Moral Philosophy: from Grotius to the Scottish Enlightenment*. Cambridge: Cambridge University Press, 1996.

Hervada, Javier. *Historia de la ciencia del derecho natural*. Pamplona: Eunsa, 1987.

Maritain, Jacques. "Pour une philosophie de l'histoire." In *Oeuvres Completes. Volume X*, 607-761. Fribourg: Éditions Universitaires Fribourg Suizze, 1985.

Millán Puelles, Antonio. *La formación de la personalidad humana*. Madrid: Rialp, 1963.

Rhonheimer, Martin. *La perspectiva de la moral. Fundamentos de la Ética Filosófica* Translated by José Carlos Mardomingo. Madrid: Rialp, 2000.

CHAPTER FIVE

SOME REFLECTIONS ON ETHICAL RATIONALITY IN THE ECONOMIC THEORY OF THE SCHOOL OF SALAMANCA

MARIA IDOYA ZORROZA

In the writings of the School of Salamanca (Francisco de Vitoria, Domingo de Soto, et al.) we encounter an interesting reflection on the economic practices which, already in the 16th century, prefigured the commercial and economic reality of the modern era. Nevertheless, the intention of these thinkers was not to write treatises on economics, but rather to understand the reality of economic issues, in order to encounter the elements which would permit them to make an adequate ethical evaluation of economic activity. The anthropological thesis that underlies this analysis (in Francisco de Vitoria as well as in the other thinkers of this School) consisted in understanding economy reality as *action*, indeed as *human* action in society. The rational understanding of ethics in these authors is particularly notable, for instance, in their determination of the criteria of evaluation. Indeed, such criteria for evaluating economic activity might be produced, in the absence of norms or custom, through the deliberation of a prudent man or a group of such men. The anthropological implications of this connection to ethical rationality provides a renewed basis for a conception of economics based on the natural law, as opposed to the voluntarism of nominalist thinkers.

Introduction

Important contemporary scholars have shown a renewed interest in the thought that was developed in the School of Salamanca in the 16th century; this interest is not merely historical (in order to fill in an unjustly neglected chapter in the *history of thought*). Without a doubt, in a period characterized by important cultural and social changes, Salamanca signified a point of intellectual irradiation in diverse areas,[1] including, among others, anthropology, metaphysics, international law and economic theory.[2]

The theologians who studied and taught in this University, in particular the group that came to be called the "School of Salamanca," made a genuine effort to illuminate human action—in its social, economic and political dimension—in the light of the thought of St. Thomas Aquinas, believing that in Aquinas's thought one encounters the highest expression of Christian humanism. In the Thomist synthesis, the Classical traditional of philosophical reflection (in particular the Aristotelian tradition) is joined to the Scriptural and Patristic tradition, in the framework of an ordered system of thought through which reality is interpreted in a profound way (the theologians of the School of Salamanca took as their basic text the *Summa Theologiae,* which gradually took the place of the medieval commentaries on the *Sentences*).[3]

It is this integrated vision (in which the individual perspectives of the various human sciences—of economics, law, etc—complement each other through being integrated within a solid—Thomist—anthropology) which today is the object of a "rediscovery" and renewed research.[4] Through

---

[1] Cf., for example, Juan Belda Plans, *La Escuela de Salamanca y la renovación de la teología en el siglo XVI* (Madrid: Biblioteca de Autores Cristianos, 2000), 147ff.

[2] The 16th century, and particularly in Spain, presents an enormously complex historical situation (socially, culturally, economically and politically): it was the nexus of the various circumstances that produced the birth of the modern era; in the economic realm, there is a revitalization of economic, productive and commercial activity (the massive arrival of precious metals that followed the discovery of America, the opening of new markets, the development of banking activities, growing capitalization, commercial speculation, intensification of credits, insurance, loans, high finance, etc.); in addition to all of this, there was also the fact that the economy became internationalized. This new economic reality required, therefore, understanding and moral evaluation.

[3] The change began in Paris, with Peter Crockaert; and it was Francisco de Vitoria who achieved its gradual incorporation into Spanish university instruction. Cf. Ricardo García Villoslada, *La Universidad de París durante los estudios de Francisco de Vitoria O.P. 1507-1522*, vol. XIV (Roma: Analecta Gregoriana, Universitatis Gregorianae, 1938), 308-19.

[4] There are numerous studies on the economic reality of this era, including: J. Carrera Pujal, *Historia de la economía española* (Barcelona: Bosch, 1943); Ramón Carande Thovar, *Carlos V y sus banqueros. La hacienda real de Castilla* (Madrid: Sociedad de Estudios y Publicaciones, 1949); Abelardo Del Vigo Gutiérrez, *Cambistas, mercaderes y banqueros en el Siglo de Oro español* (Madrid: Biblioteca de Autores Cristianos, 1997); ———, *Economía y ética en el siglo XVI*

these efforts—if we focus on the area of economic morality—while much still needs to be done (both at the level of the manuscripts and texts, as well as research on the doctrines contained therein[5]), there has nevertheless been a major advance in the recuperation of the historical value and the intellectual contribution of the economic thought of the authors of Spain's 16th century in general, and of the School of Salamanca in particular. Indeed, some of the authors who have led this "rediscovery" have been particularly clear concerning the lasting value of this tradition of thought:

> The 'pure' economics which they also handed down to those laical successors was, practically in its entirety, their own creation. It is within their systems of moral theology and law that economics gained definite if not separate existence, and it is they who come nearer than does any other group to having been the 'founders' of scientific economics. And not only that: it will appear, even, that the bases they laid for a serviceable and well-integrated body of analytic tools and propositions were sounder than was much subsequent work, in the sense that a considerable part of the economics of the later nineteenth century might have been developed from those bases more quickly and with less trouble than it actually cost to develop it, and that some of that subsequent work was therefore in the nature of a time—and labor—consuming detour.[6]

> The high level of Spanish sixteenth-century economics... was largely the achievement of the late scholastics—the School of Salamanca—. Spanish writers, building on the work of their predecessors, made what proved to be the last great attempt to tackle the problem of usury, and in so doing developed various concepts that have passed into modern economic theory.[7]

(Madrid: Biblioteca de Autores Cristianos, 2006); H. Kamen, *Spain, 1469-1714: A Society of Conflict* (London: Longman, 1991); J. Larraz, *La época del mercantilismo en Castilla* (Madrid: Aguilar, 1943); J. Lynch, *España bajo los Austrias* (Barcelona: Península, 1975); P. Vilar, *Oro y moneda en la Historia, 1450-1920* (Barcelona: Ariel, 1969); V. Vázquez de Prada, *Historia económica y social de España* (Madrid: Ariel, 1978).

[5] Cf., instance, Laurence S. Moss, "Introduction," in *Economic Thought in Spain*, ed. M. Grice-Hutchinson (Aldershot: Edward Elgar, 1994), x, ff.

[6] Joseph Alois Schumpeter, *History of Economic Analysis* (New Cork: Oxford University Press, 1966), 97.

[7] M. Grice-Hutchinson, *Early Economic Thought in Spain, 1177-1740* (London: Allen & Unwin, 1978), 81.

The names of such authors as J. A. Schumpeter,[8] Marjorie Grice-Hutchinson,[9] Alejandro A. Chafuen,[10] Raymond De Roover, among others[11] indicate the importance of the subject area and the importance of recuperating these conclusions concerning economic reality. The thinkers of the School of Salamanca undertook their reflections on economic issues within the general framework of treatises on the virtue of *justice*, understanding that whatever harms this virtue should be rejected, not only because it produces damage to the person who acts or suffers the action, but also because it produces a harm that affects society as a whole and the individuals that make it up: the uncontrolled search for profit, monopolistic practices, inequality or coercion in contractual relations. This contextualization of their economic thought was a result of their clear understanding that commercial activity is not an independent and self-justifying activity, but rather is undertaken within a broader framework that gives it justification and meaning:

> What the Scholastics were intending to do—and, concretely, the theologians of the School of Salamanca—was to form the Christian conscience, and in this case the conscience of those participating in

---

[8] Schumpeter, *History of Economic Analysis*; Joseph Alois Schumpeter, *The Theory of Economic Development* (Cambridge: Harvard University Press, 1961).

[9] Grice-Hutchinson, *Early Economic Thought in Spain, 1177-1740*, Marjorie Grice-Hutchinson, *Economic Thought in Spain. Selected Essays* (Aldershot: Edward Elgar, 1994), ———, *The School of Salamanca: Readings in Spanish Monetary Theory, 1544-1605* (Oxford: Clarendon Press, 1952).

[10] A. Chafuen, *Christians for Freedom: Late-Scholastic Economics* (San Francisco: Ignatius Press, 1986).

[11] José Barrientos, *Un siglo de moral económica en Salamanca (1526-1629)* (Salamanca: Ediciones Universidad de Salamanca, 1985); F. Gómez Camacho, *Economía y filosofía moral: la formación del pensamiento económico europeo en la escolástica española* (Madrid: Síntesis, 1998), ———, *El pensamiento económico en la Escuela de Salamanca. Una visión multidisciplinar* (Salamanca: Ediciones Universidad de Salamanca, 1998); D. Iparraguirre, "Las fuentes del pensamiento económico en España en los siglos XIII al XVI," *Estudios de Deusto* 2, 2nd period (1954), ———, "Historiografía del pensamiento económico español," *Anales de economía*, no. 25-26 (1975); O. Langholm, *Price and Value in the Aristotelian Tradition: A Study in Scholastic Economic Sources* (Bergen: Universitetsforlaget, 1979); J. T. Noonan, *The Scholastic Analysis of Usury* (Cambridge: Harvard University Press, 1957); R. Sierra Bravo, *El pensamiento social y económico de la escolástica* (Madrid: CSIC, 1975); Stephen T. Worland, *Scholasticism and Welfare Economics* (Notre Dame (Indiana): University of Notre Dame Press, 1967).

economic activity, in order that these persons might know which practices were correct from the moral point of view, and which were disordered. The value of reference is always the same: justice; the danger which is constantly present to those involved in commercial activities is well identified: usury. It is almost always the case, therefore, that the discussion revolves around the same issue: to judge whether the various commercial and financial activities give rise to the vice of usury.[12]

Therefore, one must always bear in mind that while economic historians encounter in the School of Salamanca important achievements later rediscovered by posterior economic theory (such as the quantitative theory of money, the valuation of gain lost *lucrum cessans* in calculating the benefit to be received from money lent, the law of supply and demand in the setting of prices, etc.), these economic mechanisms were discovered in the course of an attempt to understand economic action (going beyond mere casuistry), focusing primarily on the *individual behavior* of the agent involved in these activities, their social repercussions and their moral evaluation. They were not intending to develop a theory of macroeconomics, nor were they defending a radical economic liberalism as the engine of the economy.[13] These authors were aware that economic activity is *action*, in the first place, with a *moral* character. Thus, the Salamantine thinkers did not have their primary interest in exploring in exhaustive and detailed fashion the reality of the exchanges, transactions and other economic practices involved in commercial activity, but rather to investigate the moral value and justice (or lack thereof) implicit in them, and in particular, those activities which could be difficult to evaluate from a moral perspective[14]:

---

[12] Teodoro López, "Mercado, justicia y bien común," "Carranza y su tiempo". *Congreso Internacional V Centenario del nacimiento del Arzobispo Bartolomé Carranza de Miranda* (in press).

[13] Cf. A. García Sanz, "El contexto económico del pensamiento escolástico," in *El pensamiento económico en la Escuela de Salamanca*, ed. F. Gómez Camacho and R. Robledo (Salamanca: Ediciones Universidad de Salamanca, 1998), 20.

[14] For example, in Luciano Pereña, "La Escuela de Salamanca. Notas de identidad," in *El pensamiento económico en la Escuela de Salamanca: una visión multidisciplinar*, ed. Ricardo Robledo Hernández and Francisco Gómez Camacho (Salamanca: Ediciones Universidad de Salamanca, 1998), 62-64; Barrientos, *Un siglo de moral económica en Salamanca (1526-1629)*, 12. R. Sierra Bravo (Sierra Bravo, *El pensamiento social y económico de la escolástica*, 112.) states that "the Scholastic economic order is, thus, an order which is subordinated to the requirements of morality, and therefore it is not only subordinated to man, who is a being superior to all wealth—which has its purpose in service to human persons,

> The motive of scholastic analysis was manifestly not pure scientific curiosity but the desire to understand what they were called upon to judge from a moral standpoint... They were directors of individual consciences or, rather, teachers of directors of individual consciences.[15]

Therefore, Francisco de Vitoria, Domingo de Soto, Mancio de Corpus Christi, Martín de Azpilcueta, Domingo Báñez and the other authors of this School, "explain, clarify, make explicit and extend that which is either implicit or merely stated without explanation in St. Thomas, and also introduce new questions and problems which had not been studied earlier."[16] At the same time, they remained faithful to the anthropology and ethics that underlies the Thomistic framework; nevertheless, they "demonstrate their independence of criteria" by distancing themselves from Aquinas in particular issues, while adopting his basic anthropology to the new economic reality (such as the consideration of '*lucrum cessans*' and material damages as factors to be taken into account in the evaluation of the mutual obligations that are contracted upon making a loan).

The Framework for Understanding Economic Activity

That which both Francisco de Vitoria and the other authors of the School of Salamanca conceived of as "economic reality" was not seen as a reality *abstracted and apart from* the actions of individuals, of persons, and thus with independence from those elements which make economic activity a kind of *human* activity (given that it involves the elements proper to that which is human: reason and freedom). Thus, the economic dynamisms which are brought to light demonstrate that the economic order is a *rational ordering* in the order of the *practical* reason, and not a spontaneous, mechanical or "natural" ordering.

A case which exemplifies this rationality, and which is taken up by Vitoria and by other authors of the School of Salamanca, is that of the law of supply and demand in the establishing of the *current* or *market price.*

---

and thus has the character of a means or instrument for use by persons—but is also subordinated to the rules of justice." Cf. Francisco de Vitoria, *Contratos y usura* (Pamplona: Eunsa, 2006), 129-30.

[15] Schumpeter, *History of Economic Analysis*, 102.

[16] José Barrientos, "El pensamiento económico en la perspectiva filosófico-teológica," en (eds.), ," in *El pensamiento económico en la Escuela de Salamanca*, ed. F. Gómez Camacho and R. Robledo (Salamanca: Ediciones Universidad de Salamanca, 1998), 95ff.

They indicated that this price can be a just price, insofar as there is just competition as well as freedom among the agents involved, and there is no *urgent necessity* that provokes an imbalance in this free competition, there exists no monopoly, and there are many buyers and sellers.[17] But the recognition of this market law goes hand-in-hand with the recognition that, in the first place, this commercial activity must, like all *human* activity, be undertaken in conditions of freedom, responsibility and utility; in the second place, they recognize that this dynamic can be corrupted when free competition is not present, or there does not exist sufficient abundance of merchandise, buyers, sellers, etc.—i.e, when either the circumstances, or an express desire to enrich oneself at the expense of the common good, change the framework for interpreting the action.

Therefore, all economic action, as *human* action, involves: a) *an objective* sought by the subject that performs the action, as Vitoria notes; b) the *intention* of the agent (in terms such as the following: whether the agent wishes to loan to or associate him or herself with the other person; whether he wishes to sell his merchandise more rapidly, or instead wishes to prejudice another person, etc.). Along with the intention, there is the object, i.e. the action itself, with its objectivity and corresponding value (this objectivity would permit, at the end of the 16th century, a complete *systematic treatment of contracts*);[18] finally, the circumstances must be taken into consideration, since they can change the quality of the concrete action.

The purpose of economic reality—proper to the human being, *qua* corporeal-spiritual reality as well as necessarily social reality—is the acquisition of those goods necessary for human life (both individual and collective) and their correct distribution. This action should be guided by *justice,* i.e. it must preserve the required *equality,* an equality or proportion that must be maintained in all commercial or economic relations, since economic mediations must respect this equality, because these mediations:

---

[17] Cf., Vitoria, *Contratos y usura*, 89; or for example, Francisco de Vitoria, *Comentarios a la Secunda Secundae de Santo Tomás* (Salamanca: Biblioteca de Teólogos españoles, 1935)., II-II, q77, a1 n4; a4 n3, etc.and the Carta de Francisco de Vitoria a Miguel Arcos of 1546 (Vitoria, *Contratos y usura*, 265ff.)

[18] Bartolomé de Albornoz, *Arte de los contractos* (Valencia: Pedro de Huete, 1573); and the most complete systematic treatise on the topic: Francisco García, *El Tratado utilísimo y muy general de todos los contratos, cuantos en los negocios y comercios humanos se suelen ofrecer* (Valencia: Ioan Navarro, 1583).

> have been introduced [in this case, purchase agreements] for a common utility, and must not be more prejudicial to one party than to the other.[19]

All these factors of economic behavior fall within the ambit of the *practical* reason, and are not a spontaneous, mechanical or "natural" ordering. Therefore, it becomes especially important to discuss *prudence,* not only in regards to the subject who acts, but also in regards to those who manage this kind of action and who establish the norms for its practice.

The Recourse to the Prudent Man

It is paradigmatic, it would appear, to make use of the "prudent man" not only as a criterion for judgment, but also as a factor for determining economic values (when the two standard determining factors are not present) in a given situation. That is to say, the good and prudent man—or several virtuous men—represents that person who, not being blocked in his understanding of the natural law as a result of vices or selfish distortions, but rather maintaining a correct and upright moral judgment, is thus able to weigh the various elements present in an economic action and provide a correct moral evaluation (or, in what amounts to the same thing, is capable of judging the justice or injustice inherent in the action). In short, the judgment of the prudent expert indicates to us the *rationality* and *objectivity* present in a reality which is complex, changing and individualized.

In the framework of providing evaluation and ethical guidance in the economic realm, the various authors of the School of Salamanca, following the text and the spirit of Thomas Aquinas, observe three general criteria: conformity with applicable law—taking into account that all law, in order to be law, must be just[20]—or with the norms of the community in question; and if these fail to resolve the question, there remains an appeal

---

[19] Vitoria, *Contratos y usura*, 83..

[20] In addition, prudence is the virtue most proper to the "good man and good ruler" according to Aristotle (Politics, III, 1127a 20); Aquinas states in *Summa Theologiae*, II-II, q47 a11 ob2, that "virtue is the same in a good man and in a good ruler."

to *custom* or *communis opinio* or *aestimatio,*[21] or to an evaluation by one or more *prudent, honest* and *just* men.

In order to be able to judge and evaluate economic actions, it is not sufficient to be an expert; in addition, one must be an *honest and prudent* man.[22] This prudent or honest man is not a theoretical fiction, or an abstract or ideal subject. Rather, the term refers to a person who, having sufficient knowledge of the reality which is being evaluated—i.e. is an expert whose prudence has been demonstrated, who has practice in the virtues, and is able to weigh the pertaining circumstances in a rational and correctly adjusted manner, without his judgment being distorted by personal inclinations, desires or selfishness—is able to provide a *just* and objective solution which is good for all those concerned, not just for himself. And, insofar as the solution is just, it will have taken into account the intention, action, circumstances and distinct variables which affect the situations being judged, and will thus be a particular, non-universalizable solution not deducible simply from abstract norms.

In this way, Vitoria—and with him, the School of Salamanca as a whole—is appealing to human reason, *qua* practical, as a normative model. Human reason can guide action in a manner properly adjusted to its particularity and contingency, and can be a norm for this action, insofar as it has attained to *seeing* the *objective truth of the action.*

Let us look at those texts which, in regards to decisions or judgments in the economic realm, illustrate this point.

Francisco de Vitoria states: "The price of salable goods of this type is that which a *prudent man* would give in exchange for said goods"; or the same text: "In the same way, in a situation where there are many sellers and few buyers, the price of the good should not be determined by the common estimation of the persons involved in the market, but rather there must also be taken into consideration the reasonable causes by means of which the price of the thing is obtained. […] The price must be established according to the judgment of an honest man"; and even: "pricing

[21] Cf. Eduardo Moore, *La moral en el siglo XVI y primera mitad del XVII. Ensayo de síntesis histórica y estudio de algunos autores* (Granada: School of Theology of the Company of Jesus, 1956), 9.

[22] Cf. the difference between an immanent action (*agere*) and transitive action (*facere*, or *production*), present in the Nichomachean Ethics VI, and later in Thomas Aquinas, *Summa Theologiae*, I-II, q57, a4, c.; *In Ethica*, (ed. Eunsa, Pamplona, 2001), VI, lect. 3, p. 356.

merchandise now according to what it will be worth in August, since the price can be established now via the judgment of honest men."[23]

Domingo de Soto makes a similar point: "There is no science concerning these particular cases, but instead there is the judgment and counsel of prudent men"; "Concerning this issue, no absolute rule can be given. Rather, in this regards, it is sufficient to rely upon the judgments of prudent men."[24] "Restitution need not be made at the same price for which the thing was bought, but rather in accordance with the judgment of a good man"; "In judging things of this type, one should not base a decision on the conditions holding for the individuals involved, but rather the conditions that hold in the majority of the cases among prudent men."[25] "The natural price is not determined by the judgment of the individual merchant, but by the opinion of prudent and fair-minded men"; "Such things [jewels and other precious objects] are least necessary to the republic and may be sold for whatever price a prudent and well-informed purchaser may care to pay."[26]

In a decision by professors of the University of Paris it was decided that "this must be measured according custom and according to the judgment of good and prudent men," that "the profit [*el cuánto más*] must be decided upon according to custom and the judgment of good and prudent men," and "in many things a prudent man may make a decision, despite not being learned, just as a learned man might."[27]

Martín de Azpilcueta writes in a similar vein: "taking from him what prudent men would take, according to the *pacto de retrovendendo*". "And everything must be down according to the judgment of the good man"; "So that in the promissory note or obligation, it is made clearly manifest (if possible) the amount that is owed, and if not, it will be up to the decision of the good man."[28]

---

[23] This is how it is interpreted in Vitoria, *Contratos y usura*, 225, 89.

[24] Domingo de Soto, "De dubio et opinione, In STh, I-II, 96v," (Berlin manuscript), ———, "Tratado de justicia, Ms. Ott. Lat. 781," (Vatican Library)., 18r; also 19v.

[25] de Soto, "Tratado de justicia, Ms. Ott. Lat. 781," 49r and 113r.

[26] Domingo de Soto, *De iustitia et iure* (Salamanca: Andreas a Portonariis, 1556)., VI, q2, a3, pp. 546-549; translation by M. Grice Hutchinson in: Grice-Hutchinson, *The School of Salamanca: Readings in Spanish Monetary Theory, 1544-1605*, 86-88.

[27] Cf. Vitoria, *Contratos y usura.*, 272-273, 278.

[28] Cf. Martín de Azpilcueta, *Comentario resolutorio de usuras* (Salamanca: Andrea de Portonariis, 1556)., n. 246, p. 286; n. 251, p. 289; n. 279, p. 303.

Another example: "Whatever may be, nevertheless, the just price of this office, it is not established by the law, but rather it must be determined by the judgment of prudent men"; "This exchange consists truly in an exchange of monies whose just price is set in accordance with prudent merchants."[29]

Pedro Fernández affirms: "[He] is obliged to provide restitution according to that which a prudent man would decide"; "I call a just price… that which, in brief, an honest man would set": "according to the judgment of an honest man."[30]

Finally, one of the best-known and most cited authors, Tomás de Mercado, insists that the determination of interest, i.e. the restitution that one party is obligated to give to another in a concrete situation, must be determined according to the decision of a *prudent* person: "The determination of any moderated interest [*interés moderado*] is to be performed according to the decision of a prudent man"; "[He] must be given that [amount] which prudent persons would judge [as correct]"; "It is necessary to remit [the issue] to the judgment and decision of two or three persons who, in addition to being virtuous, are prudent and experts in the area of business in question."[31]

The ultimate basis that justifies the incorporation of this criterion, i.e. appealing to the evaluation or decision of the prudent or honest man, when there exists no just law or custom concerning a given practice—in our case—in the realm of economic morality, can be found in the text of the *Summa* in which Aquinas states: if all human law derives from the natural law, it is therefore the case that the laws and norms of action which regulate human life must be particular determinations of the natural law, which are binding as common principles. In addition, he notes that these common principles are known by "subjects who are expert and prudent, since they immediately see how the issue needs to be decided,"[32] with the

---

[29] Cf. Mancio del Corpus Christi and Bartolomé Medina, *Expositio in Secundam Secundae. Tratado sobre la usura y los cambios*, trans. Teodoro López (Pamplona: Eunsa, 1998)., 175, 159.

[30] Cf. Pedro Fernández, *La justicia en los contratos (Ms. Ottob. Lat. 1039)* trans. Teodoro López and Maria Idoya Zorroza (Pamplona: Eunsa, 2007)., 235v, 236r, 242v, etc. We could also add texts by Bartolomé Carranza, *Tratado sobre la justicia*, Teodoro López ed. (Pamplona: Eunsa, 2003)., 203v, 204r, etc.

[31] Tomás de Mercado, *Tratos y contratos de mercaderes* (Salamanca: Mathias Gast, 1569)., III, ch. 2; VI, ch. 3.

[32] Thomas Aquinas, *Summa Theologiae*, I-II, q95, a2, ad4: "These words of the jurist are to be understood as referring to decisions of rulers in determining particular points of the natural law: on which determinations the judgement of

result that *prudence* has a decisive role in discovering *practical truth*, the truth in the action. In support of his position, and in the same text, Aquinas cites the testimony of Aristotle, who, in the *Nichomachean Ethics,* affirms that "in this class of things it is necessary to pay attention to the judgment or opinion of the experts and elders, or those who are prudent, with no less firmness than to that which is known by demonstration."

The Implications of Reliance on the "Prudent Man"

In appealing to a good, honest or prudent man[33] as a criterion of determination or evaluation, the Salamantine authors are proposing an anthropological conception that views all economic action as *human action* [*agere,* as well as a *facere*] which cannot be understood outside of the context of its moral value; in addition, in all action, however limited it might be, one can find a *practical truth.* In virtue of this *truth,* we have access to an arena of objectivity and rationality which will indicate its *moral value,* and the correctness (or lack therefore) of its being realized, *above and beyond the utility or practicality* that it might have, either for the individual(s) involved or for the community in which they are inscribed.

On the one hand, it is clear that economic action, *qua* action, is not the product so much of a *knowing* (understanding the universal and necessary principles of the practical subject matter) but rather of a *knowing-how* (practical reason, not a mere *application* of theoretical reason); therefore, the Salamantine authors appeal not only to someone who possesses prudence, but who additionally has sufficient knowledge of the subject area to make judgments, and *in addition* acts with prudence. On the other hand, the exercise of judgment aims for the determination of a reality or

---

expert and prudent men is based as on its principles. In so far, to wit, as they see at once what is the best thing to decide"

33 Despite this plurality of terms, we will take them here as synonyms for "prudent" insofar as "only the prudent man can be just" (Joseph Pieper, *Prudencia y templanza* (Madrid: Rialp, 1969), 18.); "if the good man is indeed good, he is so thanks to his prudence" (p. 40), and Thomas Aquinas underlines this by interpreting prudence, on the one hand, as requiring the other virtues, and on the other, as being the basis for their acqusition. Prudence, in sum, is the virtue of knowing how to act (agere); the prudent man is the one who is wise in moral matters. Therefore, the modern conception must be put to one side, since it interprets the prudent man in a distorted manner, as the person who is a calculator of minimums.

criterion on the part of those who are able to *see* and *demonstrate* with objectivity the elements of just and fair action, once all of the circumstances have been weighed. We might say that the prudent man is able to discover the *practical truth* (and, *qua* true, objective) which is involved in the concrete circumstances, while not considering the circumstances as *particular and contingent*.

It is clear that in regards to these issues, the Salamantine authors assert that we cannot encounter universal and necessary affirmations.[34] Nevertheless, there is in these cases an objectivity which is neither *deduced* nor *produced* (which would confuse action with technique, in the manner of casuistry), but rather is *discovered.* Thus, such actions contain within them a *truth* and a *rationality* which is not extrinsic to them,[35] but rather *intrinsic* and *essential,* and is not produced by an adequation with an abstract end or truth. On the contrary, these authors defend that there is genuine truth *in the action*: "The proper meaning of prudence is, strictly speaking, that not only the goal of human actions, but also the means which lead to the goal, must be in conformity with the truth of real things."[36]

The subject matter concerning which the authors of the School of Salamanca are writing is the *correct* manner of acting in a determined community; this leads us to the need to define how these authors seeks 'that which is correct.'

These authors are not looking to discover techniques for optimizing these economic activities and practices; the motive for which Vitoria, Soto and other authors study economic issues is quite distinct. When they are determining whether it is licit to charge for exchanging different monies, the differences of prices in seasonal markets according to supply and demand, the practice of resale, defects in salable goods and calculation of their cost, or non-homogeneous mercantile societies, etc., they are not looking for ways to optimize commerce, productivity or economic liquidity, but rather they are considering whether these actions—which are performed for the benefit of the agent(s) and of the republic (i.e. the community which hosts the commercial actors)—are correct actions. That

---

[34] Vitoria, *Contratos y usura*, 142.

[35] As B. Häring and L. Vereecke summarize, if moral action is unlinked from its component of virtue, there remains a direct relationship between action and law, with the latter being understood as having an extrinsic and imposed character. Cf. B. Häring and L. Vereecke, "La théologie morale de S. Thomas d'Aquin à S. Alphonse de Liguori," *Nouvelle Revue Theologique* 77, no. 7 (1955): 680-83.

[36] Pieper, *Prudencia y templanza*, 66.

is to say, they wish to know whether these actions, in addition to attaining their economic object, are appropriate for a rational and moral subject, being good for him as well as for the community in which he lives, and that they respect the common good and justice.

It is certainly the case that each action has its own proper reality, i.e. a consistency and objectivity of its own which are independent of the decision of the actor, and which should be known. But the actions of which we are speaking are susceptible of a *rational* ordering (not a spontaneous, mechanical or "natural" ordering). For example, both Vitoria as well as the other authors of the School of Salamanca understand the law of supply and demand in the context of the establishment of the *current* price, but while they recognize that these economic mechanisms establish a just price under certain conditions (there being just competition and freedom amongst buyers and sellers),[37] they also recognize that underlying and comprising this mechanism, there exists human action which can distort its functioning, and that all action, *qua human* action, must be undertaken in a context of freedom, responsibility and utility. Therefore, this mechanism can be, and indeed is, corrupted when there is a lack of the conditions of free competition, abundance of goods, buyers and sellers, etc.; in other words, when the conditions themselves, or the express desire for profit at the expense of the common good, change the framework of the action.[38] Therefore, their attitude in regards to commercial activity is one of *vigilance,* so that selfishness or vicious desire for wealth, etc. do not break the delicate equilibrium of justice.

In this context, to speak of *practical truth* and of *practical reason* implies that the reason of which we are speaking is not the theoretical reason of science or speculative wisdom, nor of an abstracted theoretical reason that is applied later to the activity or action itself. And given that the object of which we are treating is *human acting* per se, the search for the *right reason* of the activity [*recta ratio agibilium*][39] is a matter of

---

[37] Cf., Vitoria, *Contratos y usura*., p. 89; p. 265ff.; In ———, *Comentarios a la Secunda Secundae de Santo Tomás*., II-II q77 a1 n4; a4 n3, etc.

[38] D. Iparraguirre states that "the observations of economic phenomena that the Scholastics have bequeathed to us are generally directed towards discovering which obstacles are created by the passions and wrongly-used human freedom, blocking the realization of the natural (rational) order which was intended,": D. Iparraguirre, *Francisco de Vitoria: una teoría social del valor económico* (Bilbao: Mensajero del Corazón de Jesús, 1957), 18.

[39] Joseph Pieper, *Las virtudes fundamentales* (Madrid: Rialp, 1998)., emphasizing that, as opposed to modern morality, which centers itself on the concept of the conscience, Thomistic morality considers prudence to be central. Cf. J. F. Sellés,

prudence. Prudence is the virtue that shapes human *doing* in accordance with the rule of *right reason,* which is the measure of human acting.[40]

Human acting does not follow *right reason* as though the latter were an *application* or translation of abstract contents to a concrete reality. Therefore, it would be an error—in my opinion—to read the texts and the distinct cases that are discussed by the authors of the School of Salamanca (in these cases, treating of economic realities) as though they were a kind of casuistry; this would mean not only ignoring the anthropological bases upon which these authors base their arguments (and which are clearly stated in the same text which serves as the interpretative basis for their expositions: the *Summa Theologiae*), but also would mean applying an interpretation to them which is alien to their basic principles.

On the one hand, practical reason is not an application of an abstract and generic principle to a concrete reality. The *distance* which separates *intellection* from *action* makes necessary the virtue and practice of prudence, which is an *intellective-practical habit.* Insofar as it is intellective, it grasps the good which must be performed, and the good which is found in that concrete possible action, *qua* practical, *illuminates, directs and regulates the acts* of operations and even of tendencies. This ordering is neither spontaneous nor natural, but rather requires *training*, which is nothing other than the acquisition of positive habits (moral virtues). "In concrete moral action, knowing and desiring are profoundly intertwined. They are like two spools which bear a single thread, and whose initial extremes begin beyond the limits of the narrow confines of rational evidence."[41]

Prudence, says Thomas Aquinas, *presupposes the rectitude of the will,*[42] a *rightly ordered will*[43] which follows the direction of that which is

---

La virtud de la prudencia según Tomás de Aquino, Cuadernos de Anuario Filosófico, Serie Universitaria (Pamplona: Servicio de Publicaciones de la Universidad de Navarra, 1999).

[40] Thomas Aquinas, De virtutis cardinalibus, a2. "Human actions are good when they are in conformity with their rule. But this rule is twofold: there is a rule which is, as it were, inherent in and proper to man, which is right reason. The other has the character of primary and transcendent measure, and this is God. The human being attains to right reason thanks to produce, which is the norm of the doable."

[41] Pieper, *Prudencia y templanza*, 98-99.

[42] Thomas Aquinas, *Summa Theologiae*, I-II, q56 a2 ad3: "Prudence is really rooted in reason: but it presupposes in principle the rectitude of the will."

[43] "The uprightness of the will for the end clears the way to the truth, so that this latter can stamp a just conformity to being upon desiring and acting. For the unjust

presented as good; in addition, an *ordering* of the distinct ends of human inclinations and tendencies (regulating and directing them, since each of them presents as good that which fulfills its own particular end) in order to achieve that which is presented as the proper end of the acting in question (and not in order to subordinate the common good to that of one of its parts). An upright *action* requires a *correct manner of performing it:* the *ordering* of the faculties of *desiring* and of *enjoying* towards that which the reason indicates as *good.*[44]

In addition, one of the most important issues (as St. Thomas notes) is that the *rectitude* of the *judgment of conscience*—which is what impels the action—is harmed when there is a disordered structure in the harmonization of these operative impetuses. The passions can produce obstacles for proper deliberation (by the practical judgment or by prudence) concerning what must be done,[45] which indicates a defect in the *rational acting* of the human being.

> Consequently, as by the habit of natural understanding or of science, man is made to be rightly disposed in regard to the universal principles of action; so, in order that he be rightly disposed with regard to the particular principles of action, viz. the ends, he needs to be perfected by certain habits, whereby it becomes connatural, as it were, to man to judge aright to the end. This is done by moral virtue: for the virtuous man judges aright of the end of virtue, because 'such a man is, such does the end seem to him' (Ethics, III, 5). Consequently the right reason about things to be done, viz. prudence, requires man to have moral virtue. As to universal principles of action, man is rightly disposed by the natural understanding of principles, whereby he understands that he should do no evil; or again by some practical science. But this is not enough in order that man may reason aright about particular cases. For it happens sometimes that the aforesaid universal principle, known by means of understanding or science, is destroyed in a particular case by a passion: thus to one who is swayed by concupiscence, when he is overcome thereby, the object of his desire seems good, although it is opposed to the universal judgment of his reason. Consequently, as by the habit of natural understanding or of science, man is made to be rightly disposed in regard to the universal principles of action; so, in order that he be *rightly disposed with regard to the particular principles of action, viz. the ends, he needs to be perfected by certain*

will thoroughly prevents that the truth of real things may come to be the measure of human action"; Pieper, *Prudencia y templanza*, 100.

[44] Thomas Aquinas, *Summa Theologiae*, I-II, q57, a5.

[45] Ibid., I-II, q59, a2.

habits, whereby it becomes connatural, as it were, to man to *judge aright to the end*. This is done by moral virtue.[46]

The acting subject must be able to *see* the truth which is proper to the effective or possible action. And this capacity to see must be *objective*; the person who does not have a correct intention, or who allows himself to be dominated by one or another of his passions, distorts the truth of the action which presents itself to him. On the other hand, "the prudent man does not muddy his vision of reality via the yes or no of the will, but rather makes it depend on the yes or no of the truth of the things," such that he is able to assure that "the 'selfish interests of the subject' are called to be silent, so that the actor can perceive the voice of the truth of the real things."[47]

Therefore, the *prudent man* is that person who is able to grasp the moral truth which is present in a concrete action—a truth which must be the rule and measure of the action itself—and is able to perceive the truth value inherent in the action itself, its correspondence with the truth, because he can make an objective judgment concerning the acting. This is because he knows the end which must be attained, and his faculty of judgment is not disturbed nor compromised by disorder in the passions[48] or tendencies, and thus *this objective judgment* of the prudent man is the *norm of action* for human acting in the given situation and circumstances.

It is clear that the questions that the authors of the School of Salamanca discuss in particular detail in their writings are those which treat of *difficult or doubtful situations* (where the norms of a just law or established custom fail to produce just action). For these situations, the Salamantine authors seek to introduce *rationality* into the action. It must be clarified *which reality* is being discussed (it is not the same thing to make evaluations when the issue in question is a purchase agreement or when it is a loan or monetary exchange) and what the intentions and circumstances are. Further, the correct *intention* of the person who acts must be indicated, along with the circumstances which must be taken into account, prior to indicating the action which must be performed or prior to

---

[46] Ibid., I-II, q58, a5; I-II, q65, a4, co.

[47] Pieper, *Prudencia y templanza*, 10, 66.

[48] Cf. Ana Marta González, *Moral, razón y naturaleza. Una investigación sobre Tomás de Aquino*, 2 ed. (Pamplona: Eunsa, 2006), 197-229. Also in Thomas Aquinas, In *Ethica*, VI, lect4, p. 360.

judging an action that has already been performed. This process[49] is the same as that which the *prudent man* performs.

> The objective knowledge of reality is, thus, decisive in order to act with prudence. The prudent man contemplates, on the one hand, the objective reality of the things involved, and on the other, the *wanting* and the *doing*.[50]

It is worth underlining that while in the ambit of the concrete moral action there are no necessary and universal truths, nevertheless there is a *truth* and an *objectivity* in the action, by means of which the action may be evaluated. It is possible to encounter a *measure for the action*, and this measure is that which makes the action transcend pure particularity—despite its facticity and conditioning—and which makes it *rational.* We can speak of truths even in cases where there is no *generalization* or mere *concretizing* of an abstract universal, either when we can encounter a *constant* in the distinct particularities, or when we can apply a general norm to a series of deeds or facts. In general, there exists (practical) truth because, whatever the variable circumstances there may be in all human action, there is something *constant:* the human being and the necessities of his realization. Thus, the criteria of acting are achieved when the subject acts *rationally,* in conformity with that which is most proper to him, but without marginalizing the richness of dimensions of the human person and his action. Josef Pieper says:

> The only immediate measure of a concrete action is the act of self-command [*imperium*] of the prudent man who decides to act. This measure can in no way be reconstructed via abstraction [...] nor can it be calculated beforehand. The command of prudence is necessarily and constitutively the resolution and decision to execute an action "here and now."[51]

---

[49] These levels are not only found in regards to the action of the concrete subject, but also especially in regards to the legislator as orderer of the community, establishing common laws.

[50] Pieper, *Prudencia y templanza*, 15.

[51] Ibid., 83. "The judgments of moral doctrine, as well as those of casuistry, remain necessarily in the plane of the non-concrete; they can never express the totality of an effective 'here and now,' since only the person who in fact decides—and no-one else—experiences (or at least can experience) the concrete situation in which an action is performed [...]. The truly concrete, nevertheless, is only accessible to a more immediate experience"; pp. 83-84.

It is the prudent man who is able to judge the truth of a concrete and particular action (that which is *doable*) based on its connection with the first principles of the natural law,[52] which are the first principle of acting. He is such not only because he has developed the intellectual acts and habits which are necessary in order to make the required judgments in order to understand and determine the concrete action, but also because he has been able to harmonize—in conformity with the proper nature of men, as rational beings—the distinct inclinations and tendencies which may distort the objectivity of the faculty of judgment. Thus, it can be said that it is only in prudent men that their judgments attain *objectivity,* since they have been purified of selfish or particular intentions and inclinations, and can be considered as criteria of action and standards of judgment of what is upright and correct in that which is undertaken.

We cannot derive the same universality and certainty as is available in theoretical or speculative judgments, since we are moving within the ambit of the practical reason, which does not consider that which is universal and necessary, but rather considers the concrete and determinate action of an equally concrete and determined subject. Nevertheless, it is possible (to the degree in which the action is characterized by being within an essentially—and not merely complementarily—rational ambit) to establish criteria and norms for the action in question, which is exemplified in the reliance upon the *prudent man* as standard of judgment of a concrete action. In other words, the good or prudent man, or a group of such men, represent that person who—lacking obstacles to his understanding of the natural law due to vices or selfish distortions, and maintaining a moral judgment which is upright and correct—is able to weigh the various elements present in an economic action and discern its moral value. Or, stated equivalently, he is able to judge the justice or injustice present in the action, and is able to provide a *just* solution, not merely a solution which is useful to himself. And insofar as his solution is just, it will take into account the action, the circumstances and the distinct variables which affect that concerning which is being judged.[53]

---

[52] There is also a source of rectitude which impregnates the acting of the reason; this is synderesis or natural reason understood as the habit of the first practical principles; on this subject, see F. Molina, *La sindéresis*, Cuadernos de Anuario Filosófico, Serie Universitaria, n. 82 (Pamplona: Servicio de Publicaciones de la Universidad de Navarra, 1999), 8ff.

[53] J. R. Junges, "Conciencia y discernimiento: Investigación histórico-descriptiva y crítico-reinterpretativa sobre las posiciones de algunos autores neo-tomistas de lengua francesa" (Pontificia Università Gregoriana, 1986), 77-78, Thomas

Prudence is not a *criterion for determining objectivity, but rather is at the service of objectivity (which is expressed in the law, and receives from the law its force of obligation).* It does not eliminate the effects of the contingency that affects the action, but rather makes possible a certainty which is *adequate to* the contingent reality of human action. Experience and the *wisdom* which comes from it, even though they arise from that which is particular, are not something singular and unrepeatable, as the *effective human act* is. This resulting generality (which can hold in *ut in pluribus*, in the majority of the cases) must be taken into account.[54]

Works Cited

Azpilcueta, Martín de. *Comentario Resolutorio de Usuras*. Salamanca: Andrea de Portonariis, 1556.

Barrientos, José. *Un Siglo de moral económica en Salamanca (1526-1629)*. Salamanca: Ediciones Universidad de Salamanca, 1985.

—. "El pensamiento económico en la Perspectiva Filosófico-Teológica," In *El pensamiento económico en la Escuela de Salamanca*, edited by F. Gómez Camacho and R. Robledo. Salamanca: Ediciones Universidad de Salamanca, 1998.

Belda Plans, Juan. *La Escuela de Salamanca y La renovación de la Teología en el Siglo XVI*. Madrid: Biblioteca de Autores Cristianos, 2000.

Carande, R. *Carlos V Y Sus Banqueros. La Hacienda Real De Castilla*. Madrid: Sociedad de Estudios y Publicaciones, 1949.

Carranza, Bartolomé. *Tratado sobre la Justicia*. Teodoro López ed. Pamplona: Eunsa, 2003.

Carrera Pujal, J. *Historia de la economía española*. Barcelona: Bosch, 1943.

Corpus Christi, Mancio del, and Bartolomé Medina. *Expositio in Secundam Secundae. Tratado sobre la Usura y los Cambios*. Translated by Teodoro López. Pamplona: Eunsa, 1998.

Chafuen, A. *Christians for Freedom: Late-Scholastic Economics*. San Francisco: Ignatius Press, 1986.

de Albornoz, Bartolomé. *Arte de los Contractos*. Valencia: Pedro de Huete, 1573.

Demand, "Probabilism," in *Dictionnaire de Théologie Catholique*, ed. A. Vacant and E. Mangenot (Paris: Letouzey et Ané, 1909-1953), 435-36.

54 Cf. Thomas Aquinas, in *Summa Theologiae*, II-II, q47, a9, ad2, and Aristotle, Nichomachean Ethics, I, 1094b 12.

de Mercado, Tomás. *Tratos y Contratos de Mercaderes*. Salamanca: Mathias Gast, 1569.

de Soto, Domingo. "De Dubio Et Opinione, in S.Th, I-II, 96v." Berlin manuscript.

—. *De Iustitia Et Iure*. Salamanca: Andreas a Portonariis, 1556.

—. "Tratado De Justicia, Ms. Ott. Lat. 781." Vatican Library.

Del Vigo Gutiérrez, Abelardo. *Cambistas, Mercaderes y Banqueros en El Siglo de Oro Español*. Madrid: Biblioteca de Autores Cristianos, 1997.

—. *Economía y Ética en el Siglo XVI*. Madrid: Biblioteca de Autores Cristianos, 2006.

Deman, Th. "Probabilism." In *Dictionnaire de Théologie Catholique*, edited by A. Vacant and E. Mangenot. Paris: Letouzey et Ané, 1909-1953.

Fernández, Pedro. *La Justicia en los contratos (Ms. Ottob. Lat. 1039)* Translated by Teodoro López and Maria Idoya Zorroza. Pamplona: Eunsa, 2007.

García, Francisco. *El tratado utilísimo y muy general de todos los contratos, cuantos en los negocios y comercios humanos se suelen ofrecer*. Valencia: Ioan Navarro, 1583.

García Sanz, A. "El Contexto Económico Del Pensamiento Escolástico." In *El pensamiento económico en la Escuela de Salamanca*, edited by F. Gómez Camacho and R. Robledo. Salamanca: Ediciones Universidad de Salamanca, 1998.

García Villoslada, Ricardo. *La Universidad de París durante los estudios de Francisco de Vitoria O.P. 1507-1522*. Vol. XIV. Roma: Analecta Gregoriana, Universitatis Gregorianae, 1938.

Gómez Camacho, F. *Economía y Filosofía Moral: La formación del pensamiento económico europeo en la escolástica española*. Madrid: Síntesis, 1998.

—. *El pensamiento económico en la escuela de Salamanca. Una visión multidisciplinar*. Salamanca: Ediciones Universidad de Salamanca, 1998.

González, Ana Marta. *Moral, razón y naturaleza. Una investigación sobre Tomás de Aquino*. 2 ed. Pamplona: Eunsa, 2006.

Grice-Hutchinson, M. *Early Economic Thought in Spain, 1177-1740*. London: Allen & Unwin, 1978.

Grice-Hutchinson, Marjorie. *Economic Thought in Spain. Selected Essays*. Aldershot: Edward Elgar, 1994.

—. *The School of Salamanca: Readings in Spanish Monetary Theory, 1544-1605*. Oxford: Clarendon Press, 1952.

Häring, B., and L. Vereecke. "La Théologie Morale de S. Thomas d'Aquin à S. Alphonse de Liguori." *Nouvelle Revue Theologique* 77, no. 7 (1955): 680-83.

Iparraguirre, D. *Francisco de Vitoria: Una teoría social del valor económico*. Bilbao: Mensajero del Corazón de Jesús, 1957.

—. "Historiografía del pensamiento económico español." *Anales de economía*, no. 25-26 (1975).

—. "Las fuentes del pensamiento económico en España en los siglos XIII al XVI." *Estudios de Deusto* 2, 2nd period (1954).

Junges, J. R. "Conciencia y discernimiento: Investigación histórico-descriptiva y crítico-reinterpretativa sobre las posiciones de algunos autores neo-tomistas de lengua francesa." Pontificia Università Gregoriana, 1986.

Kamen, H. *Spain, 1469-1714: A Society of Conflict*. London: Longman, 1991.

Langholm, O. *Price and Value in the Aristotelian Tradition: A Study in Scholastic Economic Sources*. Bergen: Universitetsforlaget, 1979.

Larraz, J. *La Época del mercantilismo en Castilla*. Madrid: Aguilar, 1943.

Lynch, J. *España bajo Los Austrias*. Barcelona: Península, 1975.

Molina, Francisco. *La sindéresis*, Cuadernos de Anuario Filosófico, Serie Universitaria, N. 82. Pamplona: Servicio de Publicaciones de la Universidad de Navarra, 1999.

Moore, Eduardo. *La moral en el Siglo XVI y primera mitad del XVII. Ensayo de síntesis histórica y estudio de algunos autores*. Granada: School of Theology of the Company of Jesus, 1956.

Moss, Laurence S. "Introduction." In *Economic Thought in Spain*, edited by M. Grice-Hutchinson. Aldershot: Edward Elgar, 1994.

Noonan, J. T. *The Scholastic Analysis of Usury*. Cambridge: Harvard University Press, 1957.

Pereña, L. "La Escuela de Salamanca. Notas de identidad." In *El pensamiento económico en la Escuela de Salamanca: Una visión multidisciplinar*, edited by R. Robledo Hernández and F. Gómez Camacho. Salamanca: Ediciones Universidad de Salamanca, 1998.

Pieper, Josef. *Las virtudes fundamentales*. Madrid: Rialp, 1998.

—. *Prudencia Y Templanza*. Madrid: Rialp, 1969.

Schumpeter, Joseph Alois. *History of Economic Analysis*. New Cork: Oxford University Press, 1966.

—. *The Theory of Economic Development*. Cambridge: Harvard University Press, 1961.

Sellés, J. F. *La virtud de la prudencia según Tomás de Aquino*, Cuadernos De Anuario Filosófico, Serie Universitaria. Pamplona: Servicio de Publicaciones de la Universidad de Navarra, 1999.

Sierra Bravo, R. *El pensamiento social y económico de la Escolástica*. Madrid: CSIC, 1975.

Vázquez de Prada, V. *Historia económica y social de España*. Madrid: Ariel, 1978.

Vilar, P. *Oro y Moneda en la Historia, 1450-1920*. Barcelona: Ariel, 1969.

Vitoria, Francisco de. *Comentarios a La Secunda Secundae De Santo Tomás*. Salamanca: Biblioteca de Teólogos españoles, 1935.

—. *Contratos Y Usura*. Pamplona: Eunsa, 2006.

Worland, Stephen T. *Scholasticism and Welfare Economics*. Notre Dame (Indiana): University of Notre Dame Press, 1967.

CHAPTER SIX

PHILLIP MELANCHTHON AND THE RECEPTION OF ARISTOTELIAN NATURAL LAW THEORY IN THE EUROPEAN REFORMATION

MANFRED SVENSSON

Introduction

During the past decades there has been a growing interest in Phillip Melanchthon, Luther's most important colleague in Wittenberg. This interest is not limited to his work as a theologian and reformer, but it extends to his philosophical work as well.[1] One may of course be sceptical regarding Melanchthon's relevance as a philosopher. But although he is not a philosopher of first rank, he is certainly the single most important author for the transmission of the classical philosophical tradition, specially in its Aristotelian form, in the European Reformation. Understanding the way in which Melanchthon transmitted this heritage is thus a key step if we wish to understand how Aristotle was read and commented on during the following decades, during the formation period of the modern mind.

A frequently discussed topic in recent Melanchthon-research has been natural law theory. This attention given to natural law is easy to understand. For the question has often been raised, whether the Protestant emphasis on the corruption of men and on justification by faith alone makes any consideration of philosophical ethics possible or even desirable. And this seems particularly acute in regard to the part of ethics dealing

[1] Heartfelt thanks go to David Marshall, Sven Grosse and to my wife Carolina for helping to improve the contents and the English version of this paper.

with natural law.[2] However, the subject does not seem to have been so problematic for the sixteenth-century Reformers. Now, while the discussion of concrete ethical problems led all of them to use the expression "natural law", none of them possessed anything resembling a natural law *theory*. Their references to "natural law" are thus references to a common possession of humanity which, because of its universality, does not seem to demand a supporting theory: their references to natural law resemble thus our own daily references to human rights. In this regard Melanchthon, the ethicist of the Reformation, is an exception: in his case we not only find casual references to natural law, but even detailed reflection that leads to a clear development of his position. In this way the study of his reflection on natural law opens the way for a better understanding of the nascent Protestant mind, of the tradition of natural law ethics, and of the transmission of the Aristotelian legacy in general.

Melanchthon discusses aspects of natural law ethics in various contexts. In the first place, we can mention his own work on dogmatics. Melanchthon is the author of the first Protestant systematic theology, the *Loci Communes* of 1521. In each of the successive revisions and editions of this work the discussion of natural law is more extensive. In the second place, we should mention Melanchthon's ethical works. He is the only Protestant Reformer to have published a treatise on ethics, the *epitome philosophiae moralis*, fruit of his teaching on the *Nicomachean Ethics*. In fact, more than once the *epitome* was published with Melanchthon's commentary on the *Nicomachean Ethics* as an appendix. In the third place, we have to mention Melanchthon's commentaries on classical works. For his work in organizing German universities he is known as the *praeceptor Germaniae*. Part of this work as organizer was the writing of a large number of commentaries on classical works, commentaries which served as handbooks for newly reformed universities. In regard to our subject the most relevant of those commentaries are those on Cicero's *de officiis*[3] and

---

[2] See, for instance, Haakonssen: "For Protestant thinkers the starting point was the complete discontinuity between God and man, a discontinuity which made it impossible to give a rational account of human morality by reference to God and his eternal law. Only faith could bridge the gulf between humanity and its Creator." Knud Haakonssen, *Natural law and moral philosophy from Grotius to the Scottish Enlightenment* (Cambridge: Cambridge University Press, 1996), 25.

[3] His commentaries on *de officiis* are put together in Phillip Melanchthon, *Opera quae supersunt omnia*, ed. C.B. Brettschneider and H.E Bindseil, *Corpus Reformatorum* 1-28 (Halle-Braunschweig: C.A. Schwetschke, 1834-1860), 16, 539-680. (Cited as *CR*).

on the *Nicomachean Ethics*, the *Enarrationes aliquot librorum ethicorum Aristotelis*.

These *Enarrationes* are the subject matter of the present study. The studies hitherto dedicated to Melanchthon and natural law have rather ignored it, probably because of it being "merely" a commentary and not Melanchthon's own work.[4] But those acquainted with the tradition of commentaries on Aristotle's work know, on the one hand, that these commentaries have always been ground for the development of highly creative theories and, on the other hand, that they are texts well suited to make a careful inspection of continuity and rupture with tradition possible. With this in mind, we will first focus on Melanchthon's interest in natural law, and the causes for his growing discussion of the subject. Second, we will turn to the foundation of natural law where Melanchthon, though writing a commentary on Aristotle, rather takes a stand for the Stoic tradition. Third we will discuss matters regarding the promulgation of positive law and Melanchthon's apparent restriction of philosophical ethics to external actions. On the whole we will see how his theological background led him to a partly problematic version of natural law, but to some interesting insights and emphases as well.

The *Enarrationes* ant the *utilitas* of Natural Law

The text of the *Enarrationes* was edited many times, this meaning not only slight and major changes in the text, but in some editions a complete rewriting of the text—nothing uncommon in Melanchthon's work—. Nevertheless one aspect remains constant: Melanchthon's commentaries are selective. Though possessing the whole work, he only comments on

---

4 The most important hitherto published papers are Christoph Strohm, "Zugänge zum Naturrecht bei Melanchthon," in *Der Theologe Melanchthon (Melanchthon-Schriften der Stadt Bretten, Band 5)*, ed. Günter Frank (Stuttgart: Thorbecke, 2000); Charlotte Methuen, "Lex Naturae and Ordo Naturae in the Thought of Philip Melanchthon," *Reformation and Renaissance Review* 3 (2000); Lars Klinnert, "Verheißung und Verantwortung. Die Entwicklung der Naturrechtslehre Philip Melanchthons zwischen 1521 und 1535," *Kerygma und Dogma* 50 (2004); and part of Clemens Bauer, *Gesammelte Aufsätze zur Wirtschafts- und Sozialgeschichte* (Freiburg: Herder, 1965). Frank takes the commentary into account, but his paper is not principally focused on natural law: Günter Frank, "The Reason of Acting: Melanchthon's Concept of Practical Philosophy and the Question of the Unity and Consistency of his Philosophy," in *Moral Philosophy on the Threshold of Modernity*, ed. J. Kraye and R. Saarinen (Dordrecht: Springer, 2005).

some books of the *Nicomachean Ethics*, namely I, II, III and V. Some topics of philosophical relevance are thus necessarily omitted: on the one hand the final discussion about the highest good, specially on the superiority of the contemplative life over the active one in book X; on the other hand, the discussion of book VI about the different intellectual virtues, specially the detailed treatment of practical reason—a relevant omission, considering the relation between natural law and practical reason in previous thinkers—. This is revealing in regard not only to Melanchthon's limitations as a philosopher, but also to his intentions, in which he is truly an Aristotelian: his work as a moral philosopher is practical. He tries to correct the habits of his time and uses the commentary on Aristotle as his tool.[5] The books which he selects are simply those which are the most easy to use with this intention (one will hardly reform the habits of a generation with, say, a reading of book VI of the *Nicomachean Ethics*).

In June 1528 we find the first reference to the project of a commentary on the *Ethics*. The reference is to be found in a letter to Joachim Camerarius, who after the death of Melanchthon would be the first Protestant to write a commentary on the whole of the *Ethics*.[6] After mentioning his idea of publishing an amended version of the Greek text of Aristotle's *Ethics*, Melanchthon writes: "To this I will add some annotations that might help the readers in such an obscure and enigmatical disputation."[7] This first attempt only touched on books I and II of the *Ethics*. Adding books III and V four years later, he again writes to Camerarius: "With huge effort I have translated book five and added a commentary. […] I implore that you send me your judgement once you have read it."[8] A month later he insists:

> I send you the fifth of the *Ethics*, so that you can read it and, I implore you, show me if something has to be rendered in some other way. You know

---

[5] See Phillip Melanchthon, *Melanchthons Briefwechsel*, ed. Heinz Scheible (Stuttgart-Bad Cannstatt: frommann-holzboog, 1977-), 580, 5. (Cited as *MBW*) It is a letter to Justus Jonas, where, after a long listing of the calamities of his times, and thinking specially about the education of his own and Jonas' children, he concludes: "Ego enarro sententias Salomonis et *ton logon peri stephanou*. Quo absoluto decrevi interpretari Aristotelis' *Ethika*".

[6] Joachim Camerarius, *Ethicorum Aristotelis Nichomachiorum Explicatio Acuratissima* (Frankfurt: 1578).

[7] *MBW*, 693, 3 (*CR*, 1, 983).

[8] Ibid., 1241, 1. (*CR*, 2, 585).

how little idle time I have and how much one must guess in Aristotle because of his brevity.[9]

After translating and commenting on four books of the *Ethics*, all of Melanchthon's calls for help refer to book V, the one with the relevant natural law-passage;[10] and this fifth book is the one he reedited most and the only one with substantive corrections up to the last version published by Melanchthon[11]—a clear sign of his never diminishing interest in the subject of this book—.

Melanchthon's vivid interest in the fifth book of the *Ethics* and the problem of natural law is not only attested to in the mentioned letters, but also in his introduction to the commentary. This small introduction, "On the Utility of Moral Philosophy," precedes the text of the version of 1560, which we will follow here. In this brief introduction Melanchthon gives thirteen reasons for the study of moral philosophy. But most of them don't refer to this discipline in general, but only to natural law theory, which for Melanchthon seems to be *the* subject matter of ethics. Some of these reasons for the study of moral philosophy are of political nature, for instance, the following very simple argument: "Since God wishes public ethics [*civiles mores*] to be ruled by the laws of the magistrates, he approves of this discipline as well, which is source of those laws."[12] This is the kind of argument that could come from the non-Christian philosopher as well. But most of the arguments of this brief introduction are not directed to philosophers in general, but address another question: how is the treatment of natural law justified for the Christian theologian? In fact, the first of the *utilitates* of moral philosophy is the way it teaches the difference between Law and Gospel: it "makes the kind of doctrine

---

[9] Ibid., 1240, 2. (*CR*, 2, 589). He insists in *MBW*, 1253 (*CR*, 2, 595).

[10] See Aristotle, *Ethica Nicomachea*, ed. J. Bywater (Oxford: Clarendon Press, 1894), V, 7, 1134b. (Cited as *EN*).

[11] The first edition of the commentary, published in 1529, only included books I and II. After 1532 he includes books III and V, giving special attention to V. In 1535 Melanchthon published the commentary on the four books together with a commentary on the *Politics*, and in 1545 a completely new version of the four books. In 1546 he wrote the definitive edition of the commentary on I, II and III, while book V retained his attention up to a final revision in 1560 – the year of his death. A description of the main editions can be found in *CR*, 16, 1-10 and the complete catalogue in *CR*, 16, 277-78.

[12] Ibid., 16, 279, third utilitas.

clear."[13] So natural law is treated as a part of divine law, which is in turn distinguished from the Gospel. In this way Melanchthon is above all opposing those who, being theologians, despise moral *philosophy*. His strategy in this and other texts is to argue identifying "law" and "philosophy"—both must be known by the theologian, at least with the purpose of distinguishing them form the gospel—. This distinction being, according to Luther, "the most elevated art in Christendom," that which makes a good theologian, Melanchthon's identification of law and philosophy amounts to a defence of philosophy which leaves it in a status similar to the law of the Old Covenant—a theologically altogether respectable status—.[14]

Melanchthon's arguments thus point mainly in one direction: he is not appealing to natural law in order to criticize a positivistic adversary. On the contrary, he is rather opposing an adversary which we could call antiphilosophical: the Radical Reformation. The opposition to the Biblicism he finds in its different currents leads him to a defence of natural law which at the same time is a defence of philosophy in general, inasmuch as "there are some illiterates that yell about philosophical precepts opposing piety—and so they condemn philosophy as a whole—."[15] So he is not arguing against a relativistic opposition to natural law, but against the direct appeal to divine law in political matters, without mediation of human rationality. A symptomatic example of such an appeal can be found in the Peasant's War. In the historiography of the war there is usually a distinction between two groups: an earlier one, characterized by a traditional appeal to the "Old Law" (*Altes Recht*), and a later group appealing to "divine law" (*Göttliches Recht*).[16] The major uprising of 1525, against which Melanchthon and the other Reformers reacted, is in fact characterized by this direct foundation in divine law, which lent it the supraregional and apocalyptic character previously made impossible by

[13] Ibid., 16, 277, first utilitas: "Utilis est collatio cum Evangelio et lege Dei, ac illustrat genera doctrinae".

[14] In this regard I disagree with Frank, "The Reason of Acting," 230-32. Because of Melanchthon's embedding of natural law in divine law, Frank interprets his position as ultimately theological. Against this I would not only point to the arguments just presented, but also to the fact that divine law is as philosophical a notion as natural law.

[15] *CR*, 16, 280. "Sunt alii quidam illiterati, qui vociferantur praecepta philosophica cum pietate pugnare, eaque simpliciter damnant."

[16] See Peter Bierbrauer, "Das Göttliche Recht und die naturrechtliche Tradition," in *Bauer, Reich und Reformation*, ed. Peter Blickle (Stuttgart: Ulmer, 1982), 210-34.

the merely local validity of the "Old Law". Appealing to natural law in such a situation means trying to make politics possible again, giving rationality the possibility to act in the public discourse. It means being a moderating factor, mediating in the oscillation between the legalism and antinomianism characteristic of the radicals.[17]

It is also this discussion with the radicals that allows for Melanchthon's even insisting upon the role of natural law in the settlement of ethical discussions *inside the church*: "Even in the church, in the discussions about our civil duties and our morals, many things are taken from this doctrine, from natural law."[18] Not even between believers does Melanchthon look for *merely* biblical discussions. On the other hand, "confirmation" is all he expects in this point: the reflection about natural law "*confirms* the opinion of those who have been rightly instructed"[19] (*instituti sunt*)—i.e. rightly instructed in Christian doctrine—. Philosophical knowledge does not add anything to what we know, but "those who have been instructed in this philosophy explain these questions with greater mastery."[20] Together with the *utilitas* of this confirmation, Melanchthon also seems to think of an apologetic function of natural law theory. This is due to the easier recognition of the limits of philosophy in this branch of philosophical reflection. Inasmuch as moral philosophy can point to actions that men should do and which they nevertheless do not,

> it gives witness in favour of the doctrine of religion, since philosophy sees this weakness in the nature of man, but confesses that it cannot find the cause for such a great calamity.[21]

---

[17] See George Williams, *The Radical Reformation* (Michigan: Truman State Universtiy Press, 2000), *passim* and above all 228. This is no isolated evolution, but a movement of the whole of Melanchthon's thought between 1521 and 1525, after his encounter with the radicals. See Hermann Pfister, *Die Entwicklung der Theologie Melanchthons unter dem Einfluß der Auseinandersetzung mit Schwarmgeistern und Wiedertäufern* (Freiburg i. Br.: Deutsche Pax-Christi Bewegung, 1968); and Klinnert, "Verheißung und Verantwortung." I have tried to show the same kind of evolution in Melanchthon's view of history in Manfred Svensson, "Felipe Melanchthon y la teoría de la primera historiografía protestante," in *Historia: el sentido humano del tiempo*, ed. Paola Corti, Rodrigo Moreno, and José Luis Widow (Viña del Mar: Ediciones Altazor, 2005).

[18] *CR*, 16, 279; a similar assertion in *CR*, 16, 364.

[19] Ibid., 280, eleventh utilitas.

[20] Ibid., 16, 279.

[21] Ibid., 16, 280, twelfth utilitas.

Thus, while in another sense natural law theory is a confirmation of certain things already known by the Christian, and so stands after Christian doctrine, in this regard it rather opens the way for Christianity, standing before it.

On the other hand, although he explicitly writes about the relevance of natural law for theology, he carefully dissociates the subject from the contemporary theological controversy about Law and Gospel. The *iustitia Dei* being the great controversial issue of the century, Melanchthon writes that in his commentary he will only touch on universal and particular justice, "and not on reconciliation, which means divine acceptance, imputation of justice."[22] One may ask if this separation of the two senses of *iustitia* is as unproblematic as Melanchthon seems to think. But at least his intention in separating the two senses seems to be clear: in midst of the controversy about the divine justice, he is trying to save natural law theory as a part of justice not affected by this controversy and thus still common to Catholics and Protestants, indeed to all of Humanity.

Notitiae and hearts that do not obey

Together with the tradition Melanchthon speaks of natural law as a source of positive law, or rather, of the knowledge of human nature as a source of justice. The source of law, Melanchthon writes, must be sought in "the true philosophy, i.e. taking into account human nature, the creation of man."[23] But if creation is introduced, the next step must be taken into account as well: the fall of man. Does anything which man can know as normative remain after the fall? Melanchthon gives a positive answer to this question. But he reaches his positive answer notoriously departing from the Aristotelian position. He writes that the foundation of natural law sought for in human nature is not to be found in some inclinations or purposes, but in some *notitiae*, some innate notions, given to human nature by God in the moment of creation and, though obscured, not deleted by sin.

He is talking about first principles. In fact he begins his commentary on the fifth book of the *Ethics* with an exposition of the difference between practical and theoretical principles. But even though he refers to both kinds of principles, appealing to the fact that they are known as evident, he does not refer to the different access we have to those

---

[22] Ibid., 16, 364-5.
[23] Ibid., 16, 383.

principles, nor to the different methods required by these different areas of rationality. What he is doing is simply to use the force of the evidence of theoretical principles in order to show the necessity of something analogous in practical life. His argument can thus be summed up in the following statement: since it seems to be true that we need the principles x and y (say non-contradiction and excluded middle) for a right use of theoretical reason, it seems equally probable that we need some principles a and b for the right use of practical reason. This appears to be a fairly reasonable and traditional argument.[24] In one aspect Melanchthon departs however from the tradition, inasmuch as his reference to a highest practical principle is not a reference to the traditional "do good, avoid evil". His first practical principle includes a knowledge of the difference between good and evil, but it becomes imperative not in the self-evident manner of the traditional first practical principle, but only because it includes a knowledge of the obedience due unto God as well.[25]

We have pointed to the fact that Melanchthon deviates from Aristotle in this point, since he sees the foundation of natural law *only* in this kind of principle. In fact he thinks that one must choose between those innate notions and the inclinations of human nature, and thus concludes that

> it is more accurate to see a law in the notions impressed by God, rather than in the affections (like those who, in an all too vague description, consider the inclinations that we have in common with the beasts to be natural law). (…) Not the affections, but the notions constitute rules.[26]

It is hard to know with whom Melanchthon is engaging in controversy, since his description of the rival position is rather coarse and would hardly fit some of the main philosophical theories on the subject.[27] It is clear

[24] It is explicit in Ibid., 16, 286. Aquinas argues in a very similar way in Thomas Aquinas, *Summa theologica*, ed. Leonina, *Opera omnia*, vols. 4-12 (Vatican City: Vatican Polyglot Press, 1888-1906), I-II, q. 94, a. 2. (Cited as *S.Th.*)

[25] "Principia practica sunt notitiae a Deo mentibus insitae, ut monstrent obedientiam Deo debitam, et discrimen honestorum et turpium, et regant mores." *CR*, 16, 384.

[26] Ibid., 16, 385.

[27] In this regard one should compare *S.Th.* I-II, q. 94, a. 2, and its gradual description of the inclinations that we have in common and those we do not have in common with other beings, with Ulpianus, *Digest* 1, 1, 1, 3 (Ulp., 1 inst.). Ius naturale est, quod natura omnia animalia docuit: nam ius istud non humani generis proprium, sed omnium animalium. It seems to be highly probable that Melanchthon has a text like this in mind. A century later, in his very

however, that he sees the question as an either/or, and thus arrives at his foundation of natural law in mere innate notions. On the other hand, one may in part be thankful for Melanchthon's occasional departing from tradition. For he does not define natural law, like Aquinas, as "participation of the eternal law in the rational creature,"[28] but as a "divinely impressed notion in regard to practical principles *and to the conclusions necessarily drawn from those principles*."[29] The fact that he intermingles first principles and conclusions derived from those principles, is an attenuating factor of his intellectualism: for in those conclusions the appeal to certain inclinations of man have already been integrated, showing them to be an unavoidable part of moral reflection.

However this may be, Melanchthon's dissociation of natural law and human inclinations seems to be related to the effort of "saving" the access to natural law in the postlapsarian world, without putting the "total depravity" of man into question. In this way he writes about the *notitiae* that "they are obscured, but they remain; and they give witness [to the truth] […], even though the hearts don't obey."[30] The fact that we still have the knowledge of the *notitiae*, of the practical principles, is not problematic inasmuch as the "disobedience" of the affections suffices to ascertain the gravity of the fall: so he seems to be making place for a natural law theory in nascent Protestant theology. Whatever one thinks of this kind of foundation for natural law, the fact that Melanchthon stands for it corrects part of the *opinio communis* in regard to rationality and law in the Reformation. The familiar interpretation differs from the one given here. The doctrine of sin of the Protestant reformers, so we are told, leads them to deny the possibility of our reason's coming to know our nature;[31] thus, if we ever find an appeal to natural law in their writings, it will be a voluntaristic species of natural law, or at least it will prepare the way for a voluntaristic foundation of natural law. In Melanchthon, a Reformer of the first generation and close associate of Luther, we have found rather the

---

Melanchthonian *Epitomes theologiae moralis*, Georg Calixt criticizes the same position as Melanchthon, expressly referring to Ulpianus. See Georg Calixt, *Epitomes theologiae moralis*, ed. Inge Mager, Georg Calixt. Werke in Auswahl, Band 3 (Göttingen: Vandenhoeck & Ruprecht, 1970-1982), 69.

[28] *S.Th.* I-II, q. 91, a. 2 c.

[29] *CR*, 16, 384 (My italics). His position is however still problematic, since he takes the conclusions to be impressed by God as well.

[30] Ibid., 16, 279.

[31] So for example the treatment of Melanchthon in Harold Berman, *Law and Revolution II. The Impact of the Protestant Reformations on the Western Legal Tradition* (Cambridge, (Mass.): Harvard University Press, 2003), 77-87.

opposite: he seems to have no doubt as to the capacity of our reason to reach the knowledge necessary for founding a natural law theory; but the doctrine of sin finds, so to speak, its revenge in the dissociation of natural law from the inclinations of man.

On the other hand, the passage is symptomatic in regard to Melanchthon's commentary on Aristotle in general. He is not writing a commentary *ad litteram*. He doesn't seem to be primarily interested in exposing or even getting to know Aristotle's position. He rather follows the text of Aristotle in order to let him raise subject matters and questions. But when Melanchthon himself departs from Aristotle or the Aristotelian tradition, as in his dissociation of natural law and inclinations, he is either not conscious of this parting of ways, or he doesn't find it worth mentioning: while presenting himself a rather Stoic doctrine of natural law founded on the *koinai ennoiai*, he still has only words of praise for Aristotle. However, he does not seem to be fully unconscious of this point, for the praise given refers, above all, to the pedagogical usefulness of Aristotle's text, while the highest praise is reserved for Plato.[32]

Positive law and interiority

If we put aside the foundation of natural law, a look at its content will shed further light on Melanchthon's position. A good starting point is the already mentioned definition of this law:

> Natural law is a divinely impressed notion in regard to practical principles and to the conclusions necessarily drawn from those principles, not only in regard to the public morals, but primarily in regard to the knowledge of God and to the obedience that we owe Him; then to public morals, which must be referred to the following end: that God be praised. And the summary we propose is to be found in the Decalogue.[33]

Let us pay attention to some aspects of this definition, starting with the last sentence, the reference to the Decalogue as a summary of natural law. The idea of the Decalogue as a summary, or as the best summary, of natural law, is of course a common place of the tradition. The relevant

---

[32] "Plato altius fuit exorsus, consideravit enim, qui sit ordo homini ad suas vires, sed Aristotelica definitio facilius intelligi potest." *CR*, 16, 365. However, while I agree with Frank, "The Reason of Acting" as to the intellectualism of Melanchthon's position, I take it to be of a more Stoic than Platonic nature.

[33] *CR*, 16, 384.

point to notice is the fact that Melanchthon holds the whole of the Decalogue to be *natural* law: one can *argue* in favour of every one of the commandments.[34] This is a second point in which he departs from a voluntaristic approach to our subject: he is clearly rejecting the idea that some of the ten commandments are natural law and some merely divine positive law, an idea which is to be found in some late medieval authors. We do not know about the extent of Melanchthon's knowledge of those authors. In any case, he doesn't join this position, but only accepts the idea that there is a *gradual* difference between the different commandments. Thus he, for example, believes that commandments about marriage and sexual life appear more often than others in the Bible, since this part of our knowledge is, he assumes, more seriously obscured than others: an emphatic promulgation is then needed.[35]

Returning to the definition of natural law, we can see that he refers not only to the first practical principles, but, as we have mentioned before, to the conclusions necessarily derived from those principles. The process by which one advances to those conclusions which are necessarily drawn, he regards as *demonstratio*. But these conclusions—e.g. the prohibition of murder or theft— are still of a general kind. Positive law arises through the applying of these conclusions to a concrete situation. This application however has no longer the status of a *demonstratio*, but of a *ratio probabilis*. Positive law is "the application (*determinatio*) of these general conclusions to a certain circumstance, according to some probable reason."[36] Thus, while practical reason as distinct from theoretical seemed to be absent from the way Melanchthon presents our access to natural law, it is not absent from the promulgation of positive law. In fact, probably the theological controversies after the Augsburg and Leipzig Interims played a role in the development of his position, making him more sensible to gradual phenomena in ethics. Melanchthon was among those theologians who held certain Roman Catholic practices to be indifferent matters (*adiaphora*), tolerable for the sake of church unity. There seem to be some echoes of the adiaphorist controversy in the commentary on the *Ethics*. So

---

34 As he does in Ibid., 16, 385-89.

35 "Nec dubium est magno consilio Dei hanc legem ante caeteras clara voce promulgatam esse, quia post lapsum, notitia naturalis de hoc ordine coniugii futura erat obscurior." *CR*, 16, 387.

36 "Sicut autem supra dixi, ius naturale esse principia practica, et conclusiones ex illis ductas *per demonstrationem*, ita hic observandum est, ius positivum esse determinationem talium conclusionum generalium ad certam circunstantiam, *propter probabilem aliquam rationem*." *CR*, 16, 393 (My italics).

he writes that not everything derived from natural law has the same strength:

> There are degrees in those things which we call natural law. For some have necessary causes and are altogether immutable, while for other things we find causes that are not necessary, though they are of some weight.[37]

Among those laws that are mutable, on the other hand, some belong to natural law, while others are in force only through the authority of positive law.[38] So there are degrees as well among those things that are mutable,

> since some are altogether *adiaphora*, while others are only partially *adiaphora*, with some probable causes in nature. These causes incline us rather in one direction than in the other. But the second option may be followed as well, without a serious corruption of our nature as a consequence.[39]

Whatever one may think of Melanchthon's position in the adiaphorist controversy, we can at least for a second time verify that what some would consider an unfruitful theological controversy in fact played an important role in his way to an ever more realist theory of law.

The reference to the positive role played by his theology in this point of his philosophy leads us to a further point where his theology is at work, namely the fact that Melanchthon emphatically restricts the validity of natural law to "external actions": Natural law, he tells us, "contains nothing but precepts regarding external actions."[40] This is indeed a curious affirmation, limiting the application of moral philosophy to an area exactly the opposite of that to which Kant would limit it 200 years later. Specially among Lutheran theologians critical of their own doctrine of the two kingdoms, this assertion seems to confirm the suspicion that thus the Gospel has nothing to say about outer actions: that it is restricted to interiority, leaving the world in the hands of naked law.[41] This however

---

[37] Ibid., 16, 393.

[38] "Quae vero in his, quae mutari possunt, naturalia sunt, quae autem non naturalia, sed lege tantum veleant." *CR*, 16, 394.

[39] Ibid., 16, 393.

[40] "Nam Philosophia tota nihil continet nisi praecepta de externa actione." *CR*, 16, 280.

[41] This is for example the criticism of Frey: "Das Gesetz wird in die civitas terrena hineingenommen, das eigentliche Gottesreich auf Erden jedoch gänzlich in die

doesn't seem to be a necessary conclusion. A good starting point is to search for the origin of this idea of Melanchthon in Luther's *Von der Freiheit eines Christenmenschen.* There the necessity of good works makes its appearance thanks to this distinction between the inner and the outer man. The doctrine that everything depends on faith would lead to a kind of quietism, Luther allows, if we were only an "inner man". But what does "inner man" mean in this text? Luther's text seems ambiguous to me. In his first approach Luther is not referring to our spirit in contradistinction to our bodily existence. We are an "inner man" to the extent that we have been transformed by grace; we remain an "outer man" to the extent that we are still sinners.[42] In the next paragraph however, the notion of the "outer man" is used to designate not our existence as sinners, but our existence as bodily creatures that live in society.[43] Surely the first meaning must be the most relevant for Luther. But we should perhaps take both meanings into account: inasmuch as we have not been completely and definitively transformed, and inasmuch as we live with others, we remain an "outer man" and need works (Luther), and thus philosophical ethics as well (Melanchthon). This seems to be the main point in the link between natural law and the external: the recognition not only of our political life, but of our being not yet completely transformed, of our yet being in need of counsel—and thus it would be an "antiradical" argument again—.

The disjunction between the external and the internal is thus less pronounced than the impression given by the limitation of natural law to external actions. In fact, Melanchthon seems to think of a rather mobile frontier, where natural law, more than a source for ruling the outer in contradistinction to the inner, is the bridge which allows for a crossing from philosophy to theology. In fact, Melanchthon not only views natural law as the summit of moral philosophy, but as the summit of philosophy in general. Philosophy "is no other thing than the explanation of these matters."[44] One could argue that Melanchthon holds this belief not because the actions of men are a more noble subject matter than the subject matters of other philosophical disciplines—which they very probably are not—, but precisely because of natural law's constituting an adequate passage to

---

Innerlichkeit verdrängt." Christofer Frey, *Die Ethik des Protestantismus von der Reformation bis zur Gegenwart* (Gütersloh: Gütersloher Verlagshaus, 1989), 52.

[42] See Martin Luther, *Werke. Weimarer Ausgabe* (Weimar: Böhlau, 1883-), VII, 30, 3-5. (Cited as *WA*).

[43] Ibid., VII, 30, 14-15.

[44] "Nec aliud est philosophia, quam harum sententiarum quaedam explicatio et enarratio." *CR*, 16, 281.

theology.[45] The exposition of the fifth book of the *Ethics* begins in fact with an allusion to the incompleteness of philosophy: *philosophica sunt manca*.[46] Natural law thus might be in some sense restricted to "outer actions", but at the same time it points to its own perfection in the inner justice. In being a measure for the outer and pointing to the inner, natural law already contributes to the transformation of men. So it is by no means restricted to securing the minimal conditions of outer justice, merely refraining evil. Melanchthon here rather holds the Aristotelian position: ethics exists to make us better persons. But he is as moderate as Aristotle in his expectations as well: philosophical ethics can make nothing out of a moral idiot, but "it makes the soul of the best of men even more moderate."[47]

Conclusion

The commentary on Aristotle's *Ethics* that we have thus far surveyed left a trace in Melanchthon's work in dogmatics as well. In the *Loci Communes* of 1521 he had presented natural law only in a brief introduction to the law. Many of the ideas we have found in the *Enarrationes* are already present here, such as the reference to theoretical and practical principles, or the distinction between the innate notions and the inclinations we have in common with the beasts. But he was then sceptical about the cognoscibility of natural law through human reason and thus about the property of calling it natural.[48] In fact, in this work he assumed that natural law was rather a knowledge we have received from Adam through tradition. But in the *Loci secundae aetatis*, the completely new version of 1535, we already find a doctrine that in its main lines adopts the positions we have found in the commentary on Aristotle.[49] As to this position, it may be criticized on many grounds: because of the limited

---

[45] That Melanchthon thought of natural law as the point of distinction and contact between philosophy and theology can be confirmed through another fact: instead of the introduction regarding the utility of moral philosophy, to which we have already referred, the editions of 1530, 1532 and 1535 had an introduction "about the difference between Christian and philosophical doctrine." About this subject Melanchthon often writes; but this is the right place to do it: hic locus proprie id poscit (*CR*, 16, 280).

[46] Ibid., 16, 364.

[47] Ibid., 16, 385. Similar in Ibid., 16, 279. For Aristotle see *EN*, I, 2.

[48] See *CR*, 21, 116-120.

[49] See Ibid., 21, 398-405.

philosophical apparatus of Melanchthon, because of an undue emphasis on natural law as the heart of ethics, or because of founding natural law only in the *notitiae*, apart from the inclinations of men. But we have seen as well, that some important criticisms that might be levelled against his position can be contested. And above all, he is a good witness to the survival of a natural law theory in first generation Protestantism, and of the fact that the appeal to natural law in this case wasn't directed against a relativist position, but rather against the sectarianism that can arise from the direct appeal to divine law in political life. And far from being an isolated case, Melanchthon's discussion of natural law proved to be one of the areas where his writings were the most influential.[50]

Works Cited

Aquinas, Thomas. *Summa theologica.* Edited by C. Leonina, *Opera omnia*, vols. 4-12. Vatican City: Vatican Polyglot Press, 1888-1906.

Aristotle. *Ethica Nicomachea.* Edited by J. Bywater. Oxford: Clarendon Press, 1894.

Bauer, Clemens. *Gesammelte Aufsätze zur Wirtschafts- und Sozialgeschichte*. Freiburg: Herder, 1965.

Berman, Harold. *Law and Revolution II. The Impact of the Protestant Reformations on the Western Legal Tradition*. Cambridge, (Mass.): Harvard University Press, 2003.

Bierbrauer, Peter. "Das Göttliche Recht und die naturrechtliche Tradition." In *Bauer, Reich und Reformation*, edited by Peter Blickle, 210-34. Stuttgart: Ulmer, 1982.

Calixt, Georg. *Epitomes theologiae moralis*. Edited by Inge Mager, *Georg Calixt. Werke in Auswahl*, Band 3. Göttingen: Vandenhoeck & Ruprecht, 1970-1982.

Camerarius, Joachim. *Ethicorum Aristotelis Nichomachiorum Explicatio Acuratissima*. Frankfurt, 1578.

Frank, Günter. "The Reason of Acting: Melanchthon's Concept of Practical Philosophy and the Question of the Unity and Consistency of his Philosophy." In *Moral Philosophy on the Threshold of Modernity*, edited by J. Kraye and R. Saarinen, 217-33. Dordrecht: Springer, 2005.

Frey, Christofer. *Die Ethik des Protestantismus von der Reformation bis zur Gegenwart*. Gütersloh: Gütersloher Verlagshaus, 1989.

---

[50] For his influence, see Inge Mager, *Georg Calixts theologische Ethik und ihre Nachwirkungen* (Göttingen: Vandenhoeck & Ruprecht, 1969); and Strohm, "Zugänge zum Naturrecht bei Melanchthon."

Haakonssen, Knud. *Natural law and moral philosophy from Grotius to the Scottish Enlightenment*. Cambridge: Cambridge University Press, 1996.

Klinnert, Lars. "Verheißung und Verantwortung. Die Entwicklung der Naturrechtslehre Philip Melanchthons zwischen 1521 und 1535." *Kerygma und Dogma* 50 (2004): 25-56.

Luther, Martin. *Werke. Weimarer Ausgabe* Weimar: Böhlau, 1883-.

Mager, Inge. *Georg Calixts theologische Ethik und ihre Nachwirkungen*. Göttingen: Vandenhoeck & Ruprecht, 1969.

Melanchthon, Phillip. *Melanchthons Briefwechsel*. Edited by Heinz Scheible. Stuttgart-Bad Cannstatt: frommann-holzboog, 1977-.

—. *Opera quae supersunt omnia*. Edited by C.B. Brettschneider and H.E Bindseil, *Corpus Reformatorum*, 1-28. Halle-Braunschweig: C.A. Schwetschke, 1834-1860.

Methuen, Charlotte. "Lex Naturae and Ordo Naturae in the Thought of Philip Melanchthon." *Reformation and Renaissance Review* 3 (2000): 110-25.

Pfister, Hermann. *Die Entwicklung der Theologie Melanchthons unter dem Einfluß der Auseinandersetzung mit Schwarmgeistern und Wiedertäufern*. Freiburg i. Br.: Deutsche Pax-Christi Bewegung, 1968.

Strohm, Christoph. "Zugänge zum Naturrecht bei Melanchthon." In *Der Theologe Melanchthon (Melanchthon-Schriften der Stadt Bretten, Band 5)*, edited by Günter Frank, 339-56. Stuttgart: Thorbecke, 2000.

Svensson, Manfred. "Felipe Melanchthon y la teoría de la primera historiografía protestante." In *Historia: el sentido humano del tiempo*, edited by Paola Corti, Rodrigo Moreno and José Luis Widow, 283-94. Viña del Mar: Ediciones Altazor, 2005.

Williams, George. *The Radical Reformation*. Michigan: Truman State University Press, 2000.

CHAPTER SEVEN

MONTAIGNE AND DESCARTES: A DIALOGUE ON MORALS

RAQUEL LÁZARO

The opening pages of the *Discourse on the Method* disclose the practical impetus of Descartes' philosophy: "It was always my most earnest desire to learn to distinguish the true from the false in order to see clearly into my own actions and to proceed with confidence in this life."[1] A few brief paragraphs prior to this declaration Descartes tells his readers that he chose to study the humanities precisely because he had been assured that a rounded education in the arts would provide him with all the useful knowledge necessary to live a good life.[2] From the very beginning, therefore, a primary intention at the heart of Cartesian philosophy is the desire to learn to guide and govern one's own actions. This moral concern was not alien to Descartes' life and times: the morality of human behaviour became a matter of pressing interest during a historical era marked by the fragmentation of religious authority, bitter political disputes and the pre-eminence of various forms of scepticism in intellectual circles.

In the first part of the *Discourse*, the touchstone of moral concern is articulated in the term *certainty*. In itself, the word is striking: if the hallmarks of human behaviour are open-endedness and contingency, the actions of men in particular situations are inherently uncertain, dependent

---

[1] René Descartes, *Discourse on the Method*, trans. John Cottingham, Robert Stoothoff, and Dugald Murdoch, The Philosophical Writings of Descartes, vol. I (Cambridge: Cambridge University Press, 1995), 115. Nicolas Grimaldi has carried out valuable work on this aspect of Cartesian thought. See Nicolas Grimaldi, *Six études sur la volonté et la liberté chez Descartes* (Paris: Vrin, 1988). This article draws on Grimaldi's scholarship in significant ways, as well as on the content of a long conversation with him in relation to the questions addressed here.

[2] See Descartes, *Discourse on the Method*, 113.

upon given circumstances to be taken into account, intentions to be discerned, doubts to be resolved, etc. Even if it were to be argued that the universal, theoretical principles which govern human behaviour are certain, such certainty cannot be attributed as a matter of course to human actions in particular situations. Thus, in classical moral thought, given that an exact moral science could not be derived from the contingency of human behaviour, the wisdom of prudence always had the final say in discussions about morals. Nevertheless, Descartes centres his philosophical project not on prudence but on certainty—that is, the absence of doubt or hesitation, error or uncertainty—. Descartes' position prompts two fundamental questions: Why is certainty given such central significance, and how may a philosophical and moral project be carried out on such a basis?

The *Discourse on the Method* (1637) is the cornerstone of Cartesian philosophy; the text is a compendium of the questions which animated Descartes' philosophical interest and study: how is life to be lived in the light of reason—the faculty of reason, common to all men, the key to all human understanding and knowledge of the truth—. Although the *Discourse* does not take the form of a dialogue, it is worth reflecting on the question of to whom Descartes was responding in his work. Descartes makes explicit reference to scholastic and stoic philosophers, but a significant number of scholars and commentators have argued that Michel de Montaigne was to the forefront of Descartes' mind as the principal intended interlocutor.[3] Cartesian thought was the dominant philosophical

[3] See J-R. Armogathe, "La première crise de la conscience européenne," in *Gènese de la raison classique de Charron à Descartes*, ed. T. Gregory (Paris: PUF, 2000), 1 ; S. Toulmin, *Cosmópolis. El trasfondo de la Modernidad* (Barcelona: Península, 2001), 75; Jacques Lemaire, ed., *Montaigne et la Révolution philosophique du XVI siècle* (Bruxelles: Éditions de l'Université de Bruxelles, 1992), 7 ; Hasan Melehy, *Writing Cogito. Montaigne, Descartes and the Institution of the Modern Subject* (Albany, N.Y.: State University of New York Press, 1997), 96; Léon Brunschvicg, *Descartes et Pascal, lecteurs de Montaigne* (Neuchatel: De la Baconnière, 1945), 97, 106, 08 ; Genevieve Rodis-Lewis, *Descartes. Biographie* (Paris: Calmann-Lévy, 1995), 71-76. Vivien Thweatt also argues that Charron's work had a considerable influence on Descartes' thought; although Descartes rejected some of the positions adopted by Charron, a number of key Cartesian ideas such as will, reason, "bons sens", etc. are to be found in *La Sagesse*. See Vivien Thweatt, *La Rochefoucauld and the Seventeenth Century. Concept of the self.* (Genève: Librairie Droz, 1980), 19; G. Gadofre, "La chronologie des six parties," in *Le Discours et sa Méthode*, ed. Nicolas Grimaldi and Jean-Luc Marion

position until 1660, but a reading of texts from the period shows that a number of parties played a role in philosophical debate at the time: the new Cartesian philosophy, the by-then discredited scholasticism and the scepticism of Montaigne and Charron.[4]

Montaigne's description of man in the *Essays* is marked by a profound pessimism: man is a contradiction in terms of judgment and action; an imperfect spiritual and corporeal being; a relentless seeker after a truth that always lies beyond his reach; one who must content himself with the appearances discerned by his senses because he can gain no purchase on the reality of being and beings. Man does not see or experience reality as it is; his perception is subjective and, as a consequence, the judgments and conclusions he reaches are questionable and uncertain.[5] Reason cannot determine or universalize the essence of contingent realities; rather, it is subject to the whims of changing opinion and judgement. All of reality, man himself included, is change and movement; and because he is susceptible to illness, tiredness, age and, above all, his passions, man cannot gain adequate or objective access to reality. Nothing can grant man certain knowledge of the truth: his fallibility is intrinsic to his nature and irremediable.

Montaigne writes with the explicit intention of bruising man's pride, of wounding the unjustified pride men take in their lives. Montaigne reflects on man in the light of nature alone, as, for Montaigne, both theoretical and practical reason are bankrupt; moreover, he seeks a moral law that depends upon neither revelation nor supernatural grace. Thus, to Montaigne's mind, the fundamental moral act is man's recognition of his own fallibility and frailty. Each man may impose order on his disordered life, which is plagued by contradictions, only once this principle of fallibility has been accepted; that order is to come from taking the lives of the great men of history as his example.

Since reason is without meaning or use or value, the exercise of reason is a process of invention and fantasy that yields only doubt and opinion. Any philosophy based on reason, according to Montaigne, is a dream that promises man possession of knowledge—the false promise of science, the

---

(Paris: PUF, 1987), 27; Anthony Grafton, *Bring Out Your Dead. The past as revelation* (Cambridge (Mass.): Harvard University Press, 2001), 254.

[4] See Antony Mckenna, *Entre Descartes et Gassendi: la première édition des Pensées de Pascal* (Paris – Oxford: Universitas – Voltaire Foundation, 1993), 9.

[5] See Michel de Montaigne, *Essays*, ed. Mortimer J. Adler et al., *Great Books of the Western World*, Volume 23: *Erasmus and Montaigne* (Chicago: Encyclopaedia Britannica Inc., 1993), Book II, chapter 16, 344.

promise to make man master of the universe when, in truth, he is not wholly in possession of himself—. Man is not the measure of all things; rather, it is he who is measured by things beyond himself: the fame, honour and glory which others bestow upon him. Hence, for Montaigne, the pressing urgency of the moral project, and his definition of the fundamental moral principle of man's existence: the recognition of his fallibility, his nothingness.

Philosophy must teach man how to live: that is, how to live a life of virtue, how not to live in fear of death. Only scepticism and the sense of bewilderment at his own real condition can lead man to true wisdom, the absolute truth—that is, God, who can only be found in faith—. For Montaigne, no true knowledge is possible beyond the confines of the fideistic scepticism that he himself proposes and defends.

In light of this account of the keynotes to the *Essays*, the *Discourse on the Method* begins to read more and more as though it were a direct response to Montaigne's line of argument; but does Descartes in fact reject Montaigne's philosophy in its entirety or may some traces of Montaigne's philosophy still be discerned in Cartesian moral thought? The purpose of this article is to read Descartes' *Discourse on the Method* in the light of Montaigne's *Essays*.

The style of the *Discourse* is similar to that of the *Essays*: both are rooted in the genre of biography, both are written in French. Accounts of life experience prompt philosophical reflection and speculation; ideas arise in the context of the search upon which each author is engaged. Descartes' development as a philosopher saw him spend time as a pupil in Montaigne's school of thought, from which he later moved on to leave that phase of his thinking behind; nevertheless, Montaigne's preoccupations are also Cartesian concerns.

Descartes' stated purpose does not encompass a desire to instruct others: "My present aim, then, is not to teach the method which everyone must follow in order to direct his reason correctly, but only to reveal how I have tried to direct my own".[6] Montaigne had said the same: he wrote of his "opinions and beliefs" in order to come to a greater knowledge of himself; his essays were written, he remarks, "as children set forth their essays to be instructed, not to instruct".[7]

Descartes tells of the books and texts that he had read, and how all his study had only lead him into doubt and error: "I had gained nothing from my attempts to become educated but increasing recognition of my

---

[6] Descartes, *Discourse on the Method*, 112.
[7] Montaigne, *Essays*, I, chapter 56, 195.

ignorance."[8] In this belief and sentiment, Descartes is a faithful disciple of Montaigne, for whom the heart of wisdom is recognition of one's own ignorance. Moreover, Descartes is also of follower of Montaigne in another form of learning: travel, one of the best schools of knowledge and understanding;[9] "I spent the rest of my youth travelling…"[10] Nevertheless, the only fruit of books and travel and philosophical dialogue for Descartes and Montaigne was a diversity of judgements, opinions and beliefs. Descartes wrote

> I found hardly any reason for confidence, for I observed in [the customs of other men] almost as much diversity as I had found previously in the opinions of philosophers.[11]

As Montaigne before him, Descartes came face to face with the dilemma of diversity, a lack of coherence and unity, and the focus of his philosophical interest began to mirror that of the older author's. He too turned back towards the self, and the pre-eminence of the self, the subject, as the principal object of philosophical thought gained new impetus.

Montaigne's *Essays* are a study of the self,[12] but he does not write of origins and ends: his is not a metaphysical project. The purpose of Montaigne's epistemology is to determine the limits of ethics, to address the question of how man ought to live. In that sense, his approach is more psychological than speculative. The self of Descartes' philosophy, however, is not the empirical, perceiving self of Montaigne's thought; rather, it is the thinking self which discovers itself through the application of the Cartesian method. The Cartesian self becomes a knowing subject and a known subject in the light of reason, and the faculty of reason develops in every human being from the philosophical starting point which Descartes sets out to define.[13] While *The Passions of the Soul* makes clear that his work also has a psychological dimension, Descartes' primary purpose was to provide the metaphysical basis for the *res extensa* and the *res cogitans*, a project which had very little in common with Montaigne's.

---

[8] Descartes, *Discourse on the Method*, 113.

[9] See Montaigne, *Essays*, I, chapter 17, 80.

[10] Descartes, *Discourse on the Method*, 115.

[11] Ibid.

[12] Friedrich defined Montaigne's project as descriptive anthropology in order to deflect a strong element of the criticism levelled against it: that Montaigne's work is Christian anthropology in a radically secular form. See Hugo Friedrich, *Montaigne* (Paris: Gallimard, 1968), 156.

[13] See Melehy, *Writing Cogito*, 11.

A further distinction between the two philosophers: unlike Montaigne, Descartes holds that man can tell the difference between what is true and what is false, that man may seek and find the truth by the light of reason. Man's failure to find the truth stems from his failure to use the faculty of reason as he ought; the diversity of judgments and opinions is not the consequence of a fatal flaw in reason, nor proof that the truth can never be established; rather, the dilemma of diversity shows that until now "we direct our thoughts along different paths and do not attend to the same things"[14]: men have not been addressing the same question. Given an adequate method, we would come to the knowledge of the truth, in spite of "the mediocrity of [my] mind and the short duration of [my] life."[15] This last remark is an example of Cartesian irony: death and the misery of man's condition are the keynotes of Montaigne's work.

The fundamental problem of knowledge of reality is defined by Montaigne in the twelfth chapter of the second volume of his *Essays*: reality is not given to us in form and essence according to its own power and authority; if that were the case, all men would perceive and know the same things in the same way. Thus, subjectivity must play a role in objective knowledge of reality. Montaigne argues that the knowing subject compromises the objectivity of knowledge. There are no objective modes of understanding common to all men which might allow certain knowledge of the truth: "Our natural judgement does not grasp very clearly what it grasps."[16] The conclusion Montaigne draws from the dilemma of diversity is that men arrive at their beliefs and opinions by different means of understanding and judgement: thus, if there is one reality given to all, the problem of diversity must be attributed to the knowing subject in itself; and specifically, to man's bodily condition and the senses: "It is certain that our apprehension, our judgment, and the faculties of our soul in general, suffer according to the movements and alterations of the body, which alterations are continual."[17] Diversity of judgement provokes uncertainty and doubt.[18]

---

[14] Descartes, *Discourse on the Method*, 111.

[15] Ibid., 112.

[16] Montaigne, *Essays*, II, chapter 12, 312.

[17] Ibid., 313.

[18] Pascal was to defer later to Montaigne's position rather than Descartes', insofar as he too maintained that man, the knowing subject, is the union of a body and a soul. On that basis, Pascal argued that man comes to knowledge of the truth not only as a *res cogitans*, but also in his heart, a synthesis of will, feeling and subjective certainty that is not in itself rational. For Pascal, intellectual intuition is

The following question arises as a consequence of Montaigne's position: what if it were possible to avoid the pitfall of the senses? What if a way were to be found that made reality intelligible without recourse to the senses? If the faculty of reason is the same for all men, what form of knowledge might it disclose? This is the question to which Cartesian thought is intended to respond.

Before going on to describe the particular characteristics of his method, Descartes writes:

> I learned not to believe too firmly anything of which I had been persuaded only by example and custom. Thus I gradually freed myself from many errors which may obscure our natural light and make us less capable of heeding reason.[19]

Montaigne's profound love of history was rooted in his respect for custom and example, the last bastions of defence against the force of the radical scepticism that he himself articulated and maintained. Given that all is changing and diverse, that man can be certain of nothing, every man may defer to the customs of his people and the example of the great men of history in order to impose some form of order on his disordered life. Descartes, on the other hand, before entering into the exact detail of his own method, reiterates what he had already argued in *Rules for the Direction of the Mind*: "All forms of knowledge are merely probable must be rejected". Custom and example—and, by extension, everything that is probable or contingent—may be the ground of error and doubt, and therefore false.

Descartes sets out to tell what is true from what is false, and to define the method by which such a clear distinction might be made. To do so, he drew on the science of mathematics for his philosophical work, and found the criteria for truth in the idea of self-evidence. Self-evidence does not allow of contradiction, it is beyond probability; to Descartes' mind, therefore, self-evidence overcomes the force of scepticism in a definitive way. In mathematical terms, self-evident truth is immediate; it bypasses the senses, and thus lays down the line which philosophical thought must follow. There is no scale of knowledge in Cartesian philosophy: there is no middle ground between absolute certainty and utter ignorance.

---

the mode of knowledge and understanding proper to the union of body and soul in man. See Mckenna, *Entre Descartes et Gassendi*, 24.

[19] Descartes, *Discourse on the Method*, 116.

The exercise of reason with certainty is the touchstone of Descartes' conviction concerning the method he outlines: man may advance with certainty towards the truth, and thus come to possess a universal and infallible form of knowledge. What Descartes demands of mathematics provide is what Montaigne had argued was impossible: "A solid, well-grounded building, everything in its proper place, every door its proper frame". However, the building Montaigne describes must meet two key criteria: to be founded on clear grounds, and built (by Descartes) in the light of reason and his own experience.[20] In Cartesian thought, objective proof becomes subjective certainty in the experience of the knowing subject.

The first self-evident truths are theoretical truths: the *cogito* and God. These remain when all else has been called into question and doubt. In this regard, however, Descartes' approach is not wholly original, for Montaigne had already wondered: "Why do we not consider the possibility that our thinking, our acting, may be another sort of dreaming, and our waking another kind of sleep?"[21] Descartes is prepared to call everything into question and doubt in order to find out if anything will remain to his mind in a clear and distinct way. Thus, he discovers that he himself is a thinking thing, which is the self-evident truth on which his philosophical project would be based. The question arises, however: what is the *cogito*?

The *cogito* is an immaterial substance, which has no need of matter in order to exist; it can be known more readily than the body itself because it is known in an immediate way and with certainty. Through acknowledgement of its limitations and frailty, moreover, the *cogito* is led to certain knowledge of the existence of a Perfect Being from which derive the first self-evident truths in the *cogito* itself, whose existence guarantees the possibility of certain knowledge of the reality and truth of the *res extensa*.

A number of objections might be made to the position adopted by Descartes as outlined in the previous paragraph, but the focus of interest for this article is the moral dimension of Cartesian philosophy: what bearing does Descartes' epistemology have on the moral concerns that he himself articulated so clearly in the opening part of the *Discourse on the Method*?

In the fifth part of the *Discourse on the Method*, Descartes re-opens his dialogue with Montaigne, albeit without making explicit reference to the

[20] See Brunschvicg, *Descartes et Pascal, lecteurs de Montaigne*, 102.
[21] Montaigne, *Essays*, II, chapter 12, 330.

latter's name or work. Descartes argues that for all the labour to survive that may be observed in the lives of animals, animals show no signs of the powers of speech or communication. Thus, animals lack both intelligence and reason, and the souls of animals are in no way like the souls of men. The soul of man is immortal and independent of the body; Descartes sounds a note of warning in this regard:

> There is [no error] that leads weak souls further from the straight path of virtue than that of imagining that the souls of the beasts are of the same nature as our own.[22]

The fact that Montaigne, in his desire to puncture man's unjustified pride and vanity and to highlight his nothingness, frequently compared the life of man to the lives of animals, and concluded that there was little evidence to support the idea that man is superior to animals, is of note in this context. However, Montaigne's position must be read in terms of his moral concerns: it was not his intention to provide a new ontological classification of beings. The substance of Montaigne's argument was to show that in moral terms man was not intrinsically superior to animals: in fact, provoked by his passions—and, above all, by his capacity for cruelty[23]—man might commit acts that no animal could ever carry out.

Descartes withheld his definitive blow against the edifice of Montaigne's thought until the final moment of his argument, when he asserts that through the method he defines: "[We could] make ourselves, as it were, the lord and masters of nature."[24] This statement is not only a firm defence of the value of science, an idea that was anathema to Montaigne, another figment of man's delusion of grandeur; it also amounts to a promise of salvation for all mankind: through science, all the diseases that afflict man might be cured,[25] and death itself conquered. The science of medicine, the use and value of which had also been dismissed by Montaigne, might also form part of man's moral project as more

---

[22] Descartes, *Discourse on the Method*, 141. This statement is complemented by Descartes' remarks in a letter to Mersenne concerning the same question on 23 November 1646.

[23] Human cruelty was a matter of particular concern in Montaigne's moral project; lengthy passages of his work are given over to condemnation of the cruelty of men, especially in the context of the religious wars in which France was then involved. See Emmanuel Faye, *Philosophie et perfection de l'homme. De la Renaissance à Descartes* (Paris: Vrin, 1998), 195.

[24] Descartes, *Discourse on the Method*, 142.

[25] Ibid., 143.

science would make men more wise. For Montaigne, however, disease and death were the hallmarks of man's fallibility and frailty, his nothingness; as such, within the framework of his thought, they were also man's ultimate grounds of hope. If man were to believe that disease and death might be overcome, could that belief in victory be anything more than another sign of his crippling pride?

In the *Discourse on the Method*, Descartes adopts positions and advances arguments that go against the grain of Montaigne's thought. These may be summarised as follows:

1. Descartes dismisses probable knowledge as merely another form of false knowledge.
2. In response to the dilemma of diversity in judgements and opinions, Descartes argues that the unity derived from the knowing subject offers a sure path to knowledge of the truth.
3. In contrast to Montaigne's total rejection of science, Descartes takes science as the template for his philosophical project, and attributes the discovery of what is most useful and necessary to human life to the progress of science.
4. Descartes rejects Montaigne's definition of wisdom based on ignorance as the most certain and universal principle of knowledge; in its stead, he proposes the one science of knowledge open to all by the power of reason.
5. In contrast to Montaigne's description of the 'I' as the human subject which sees itself in terms of endless contradiction, Descartes argues proof of the existence of the *cogito*, the knowledge of which is clear and distinct.
6. The *cogito*'s rational knowledge of God replaces Montaigne's radical fideism.
7. Descartes argues that rational intelligibility, rather than dependence on the workings of the senses, is the ground of knowledge.
8. Montaigne holds that man's first knowledge is bodily: he feels the power of his passions, the force of frailty in his flesh; thus far in the *Method*, however, Descartes has argued that the *cogito* is the core of man's being, and his first knowledge is that which the *cogito* discloses—the innate ideas—.
9. Reason, described by Montaigne as weak or bankrupt, is replaced in Cartesian thought by reason defined in bold terms of power and potential.
10. Montaigne's conception of reason as engaged upon a restless and endless search for the truth yields to Descartes' notion of reason

as the ground of certainty which works its way from truth to truth in order to encompass all that may be of use and value to it.

The account of the *Discourse on the Method* provided in this article has not yet touched upon what Descartes refers to as a "provisional moral code". Descartes devotes the third part of the *Discourse* to reflections on this question; an exploration of the origin of Descartes' thinking in this regard is of significant interest.

The first version of the *Discourse* was composed of five parts; there was no section which dealt exclusively with morality or moral concerns. Before the text was published, however, given the heated debates then raging about religious and moral questions, the publisher suggested that Descartes ought to supply some commentary on the uses of doubt because of the centrality of the idea to his work and in order to pre-empt any charges of scepticism that might be made against him. In his response to the publisher's advice, Descartes turned to the idea of human freedom, a turn which threatened to rock the foundations of the philosophical edifice he had so carefully constructed: human freedom opens the door to contingency and probability, both of which Descartes had previously identified with what is false. Descartes had set out to overcome all forms of scepticism forever by means of *a priori*, deductive science: what foundations would he have to lay in order to fulfil his objective?

The cornerstone of Cartesian philosophy is divine truth. God may create beings in one form or another; once created, however, that form is immutable. According to Descartes, there are two forms of created being: *res extensa* and *res cogitans*, each utterly distinct and separate from the other. God ordained, however, that they be perfectly joined *a priori*, as both are subject to the divine design and plan. God has given man the fundamental ideas he needs in order to understand the world; by deduction from these innate ideas, man may come to understand all other ideas and knowledge by the light of reason. Intuition is the perception of these clear and distinct ideas which accurately reflect reality because they are given by God to that end. Ideas are true not because they are true to reality; rather, reality cannot fail to be true to the ideas seeded in man's mind by God; thus, the ideas in themselves are true. Ideas are not the fruit of the judgments man may make on the basis of the experience of his senses; rather, man's ideas are prior to all experience, although they are not wholly unrelated to it.

These are the foundations on which Descartes bases his immutable, determinist scientific project. This is the context in which the proposition that to do what is right requires right judgement ought to be understood: to do right is to act in relation to the *res extensa*, an utterly distinct and separate substance linked to the *res cogitans* through the innate ideas given to man by God.

Grimaldi argues that there are three orders of reality in Cartesian thought: the order of truth, the order of science and the order of happiness. The order of truth is linked to the reality and potential of the innate ideas which are self-evident and of divine origin: this is the order of metaphysics, mathematics and the first principles of physics. The second order comprises all that is scientific and technical, ideas and designs that mirror the workings of the natural world; their similarity to nature is a function of their usefulness; they need not, in themselves, accurately reflect reality as it is. The third order is the order of morals, to which Descartes also responds in line with the criteria of his scientific approach: use or usefulness. The moral order is the order of happiness and is primarily concerned with the will, which defines the moral agent as such and may act independently of the understanding.

Perfect morality would enable effective action on the basis of the knowledge of the truth disclosed by the one, certain reason of science. The form of morality discussed in the *Discourse on the Method* is a "provisional"—that is to say, incomplete—morality; it is not made clear, however, if this provisional moral code may ever be brought to completion. The purpose of this provisional morality is to guide man's actions while he is immersed in the process of doubt, the search for evident truths which the *Discourse* describes.

In the third part of the book, therefore, a breach is opened in Descartes' argument. Given that the will may act independently of the understanding, it may come to desire what it does not know in a clear and distinct way; that is, it may desire what is merely probable. If the will may act in a way that is wholly independent of the understanding, its action is spontaneous; it determines itself in absolute terms. As a consequence, in other words, the idea of truth advanced by Descartes is a form of theoretical knowledge which may have no bearing on practical knowledge. Such unbridgeable divisions between the faculties of the mind mark the great divide between Cartesian and classical thought.

When Descartes found himself forced to take human freedom into account, he quickly discovered that man cannot always wait for clear and distinct knowledge of the truth in order to begin to act. Descartes had sketched the outline of his method, although he had not yet entered into significant detail with regard to its content: he had given no indication of the ideas that lie beyond all doubt; nor is it clear how long the process of the method of doubt might last—centuries perhaps—. Hence the need to establish some norms to guide and govern the lives of men for however long reason's search for self-evident truths might last: "Lest I should remain indecisive in my actions while reason obliged me to be so in my judgements, and in order to live as happily as I could during this time, I formed for myself a provisional moral code consisting of just three or four maxims, which I should like to tell you about."[26] The maxims proposed by Descartes are the following:

> The first was to obey the laws and customs of my country, holding constantly to the religion in which by God's grace I had been instructed from my childhood, and governing myself in all other matters according to the most moderate and least extreme opinions; the opinions commonly accepted in practice by the most sensible of those with whom I should have to live.[27]
>
> My second maxim was to be as firm and decisive in my actions as I could and to follow even the most doubtful opinions, once I had adopted them, with no less constancy that if they had been certain.[28]
>
> My third maxim was to try always to master myself rather than fortune, and to change my desires rather than the order of the world. In general I would become accustomed to believing that nothing lies entirely within our power except our thoughts, so that after doing our best in matters external to us, whatever we fail to achieve is absolutely impossible so far as we are concerned.[29]

The transition from the second to the third part of the *Discourse on the Method* provokes considerable surprise in the reader; the third part addresses ideas that Descartes had sought to discount from the start: custom and diversity, probability and uncertainty. More striking still is the discovery that the norms of provisional morality proposed by Descartes had already been articulated by Montaigne,[30] although he had framed them

---

[26] Ibid., 122.
[27] Ibid.
[28] Ibid., 123.
[29] Ibid.
[30] According to Rodis-Lewis, Descartes derived his first norm of provisional morality from Charron's thought. A statement pertinent to this point is to be found in chapter VIII of the second book of *La Sagesse*. See Pierre Charron, *De la Sagesse* (Paris: Fayard, 1986). Rodis-Lewis's argument is accepted in this article; however, the emphasis here is on the fact that Charron's thought is faithful to the position first articulated by Montaigne. The third norm of provisional morality also reflects the influence of Charron. See Rodis-Lewis, *Descartes. Biographie*, 74-75.

in different terms and to a different end. Descartes' purpose extends beyond Montaigne's more limited objective, and was to be completed in the writing of *The Passions of the Soul* and the *Correspondence*. However, if the provisional moral code is in effect the definitive account of morals, as many scholars and commentators have argued, and there is little significant difference between the norms of provisional morality as expressed by Descartes and Montaigne, the following question arises: what specific contribution is made by the author of the new method to an understanding of morality in practical terms? As a partial response to this question, it might be said that whereas Descartes' account of reason and science marks a radical break with prior philosophical tradition, his approach to morals is more conservative:[31] in a certain sense, therefore, Cartesian moral thought is a continuity of what had come before, with a number of specific nuances and emphases of its own.

Like Descartes, Montaigne paid tribute to the religion into which he had been born, the faith in which he had been raised and instructed, and in which he intended to remain a firm believer. Like Descartes, too, Montaigne did not doubt that understanding the dogmas and mysteries of religion lay beyond the power of reason. The division between faith and reason is clear to both philosophers; hence the fideistic response to questions of faith.[32]

Man's practical need to act, even before self-evident truths have been established in the light of reason, forced the hand of Cartesian moral thought. The fundamental principle of Montaigne's understanding of morals, however, was man's recognition of his fallibility and frailty. As a consequence, man ought to be faithful to the beliefs in which he had been raised; hold reasonable, conservative opinions; hate pride and learn to distrust his own inclinations; spurn any radically new positions; be content to suffer what he cannot change; and cling to the customs of his people. In other words, if he were attentive to Montaigne's fundamental moral principle, man would be lead to fulfil the norms of provisional morality laid down by Descartes.

What follows is a brief exploration of the norms of provisional morality advanced by Descartes. The first states that something other than personal opinion should act as guide to human behaviour in practice. The

---

[31] See Faye, *Philosophie et perfection de l'homme. De la Renaissance à Descartes*, 295.

[32] See Anthony Levi, *French moralists, the theory of the passions, 1585 to 1649* (Oxford: Clarendon Press, 1964), 325.

criteria Descartes proposes in this regard flies in the face of that which he suggested in relation to the search for theoretical truth. A rule to govern human behaviour in practice had already been set out in the *Essays*, derived as a logical consequence from a form of scepticism that belongs firmly to the tradition established by Pyrrho: man should follow the path laid down by law and custom; obedience to civil, political and religious authority was to be the key to order and moderation in the lives of individuals. Montaigne argued that there were few men ordered and strong enough to establish their own criteria for action by themselves, beyond the basic rules of common sense.[33]

Descartes' second norm of provisional morality comprises his theory of virtue. Virtue is neither an edifying habit of human nature nor the fulfilment of what is good once what is good has been discerned by reason; rather, to Descartes' mind, virtue is the appropriate exercise of the will, which freely and spontaneously makes a choice and thereafter acts in a way consistent with its decision. Although Montaigne's account of human virtue is closer to classical philosophical thinking than Descartes' theory, he too points to constancy of choice and determination in action as the hallmarks of virtue: only the man who is constant and consistent in the exercise of the will is a virtuous man.[34] The source for Descartes' second norm of provisional morality is the work of Montaigne's disciple, Charron.[35]

The final chapter of the *Essays* contains a sentence which encapsulates the third Cartesian norm of provisional morality: "We must learn to endure what we cannot avoid".[36] To acknowledge one's condition, to faithfully rejoice in one's own being is the path to absolute perfection, is to become like God.[37] What cannot be avoided or changed is synonymous with what man cannot do: that is, what lies beyond man's power, beyond his will. Neither Montaigne nor Descartes propose an ideal of perfection to be striven for in moral terms on the basis of human nature, however human nature might be defined; for both philosophers, to become like God is understood in terms of what man can or cannot do by the power of the will.

Montaigne says that man ought to rejoice in his own being as God rejoices in his divinity, but without losing sight of the truth of his

---

[33] See Montaigne, *Essays*, II, chapter 12, 311.
[34] See Ibid., II, chapter 1, 199.
[35] See Charron, *De la Sagesse*, II, chapter 3, art. 12.
[36] Montaigne, *Essays*, III, chapter 13, 572.
[37] See ———, *Essays*, III, chapter 13, 587.

condition. Given that the human condition is imperfect, man must acknowledge his imperfection and limitations; to act in the light of this clear understanding is an exercise of power (in a negative sense) which allows man to be lord and master of his own action.[38] In the opening pages of the *Essays*, Montaigne wrote that man's power depends on his will, which acts in accordance with what is probable or changing,[39] and sometimes at the prompting of his passions. Descartes' understanding of the will is similar, although the reach of the will in Cartesian thought is open to the infinite.

For Montaigne, the will is in a certain sense synonymous with desire: it is the imprint of God on man. For Descartes, the will is free will, and the seal of divinity on the human soul; as the divine will is infinite, so too the human. Given this description, how is the faculty of will to be exercised? The practical necessities of human life require that the will act before reason has established the self-evident truths of knowledge. Thus, the will guides and governs human action in the face of absolute contingency, as what reason cannot grasp lies beyond the power of man to determine. Grimaldi notes, however, the importance in this context of Descartes' assertion that the will respond to absolute contingency by opting for what is necessary.

Descartes' position marks a radical departure from classical philosophical thought. In the classical philosophical tradition, the higher faculties of understanding and will, acting in unison, constituted the imprint of God on man. The intellect was the spark of Divine Intelligence in man, which enabled him to grasp the real in an intentional way, to begin to understand the mystery of reality without ever fully plumbing to its depths. The will was defined as the faculty which spurred the intellect to understanding, which desired what the intellect came to know as good and determined what would not be good for man through the otherness and distance from the self that mark its object and its action.

In Descartes' philosophy, however, as in Montaigne's, the intellect is no longer the seal of the divine on the human soul. For Montaigne, the intellect is so tainted, so wholly a sign of human fallibility, that it may not even serve to seek out knowledge of the Creator of the world. For

---

[38] "La sagesse de l'humble acceptation de la realité terrestre, et la joie de découvrir notre finitude assez inépuisable pour nous assurer le bonheur de sa mouvante profusion". Friedrich, *Montaigne*, 40.

[39] See Montaigne, *Essays*, I, chapter 7, 61. This idea is adopted and repeated by Charron. See Charron, *De la Sagesse*, Book I, chapter 17, p. 151. See also Levi, *French Moralists, the Theory of the Passions, 1585 to 1649*, 102.

Descartes, reason is the repository of the innate ideas that God implants in the human mind, a source of material from which man may deduce all the knowledge that is useful to him in accordance with the appropriate method. In neither school of thought, however, is reason a light that illumines the action of the will, a guide to what ought to be chosen or done in the here and now, nor to where the sympathies of the will should lie. Given the radical separation of will from reason, what governs the desire of the will? What is its inspiration, what its object?

The object of reason is necessary, infallible truth—that is, metaphysical truth. Given that only such clear and distinct truth could force the will to action, the desire of the will may, in practice, tend towards any object. Ideas of good and evil have no fixed meaning in this context: there is no order prior to man's understanding that might define the perfect goal of the will or determine its action. By the power of the faculty of reason, knowledge may advance to new discovery through deduction from theoretical ideas and truths; at the same time, the faculty of the will is radically free and open to the infinite. Virtue is a function of consistency and constancy in the determination of the will; the virtuous man is not a good man but a wise man, the man who chooses what he believes to be best and acts in a consistent and constant way on that basis.[40]

Probability is the keynote of Cartesian moral thought as it is of Montaigne's account of morals. Descartes, however, has taken a further step: given that the will may act without the guidance of the self-evident truths of reason, its autonomy is absolute; the truths of faith constitute the only guide to the action of the will, and these lie beyond the scope of philosophical enquiry. The Cartesian account of the radical division between the faculties of the mind, and thus between theory and practice, gives rise to a conception of man who is simultaneously powerful by virtue of the will and "blind to the truth" in practice: open to the infinite, a wholly autonomous will acts without illumination from the light of a reason to which it is in no way linked and which can supply no self-evident truths by which it might be guided. Either the unpredictable, and perhaps perverse, consequences of this description of man in moral terms are accepted for whatever they may be, or some form of self-control in the exercise of the will is called for. The meaning of the proposition that to do what is right requires right judgement, therefore, amounts to nothing more

[40] See René Descartes, *The Passions of the Soul*, trans. John Cottingham, Robert Stoothoff, and Dugald Murdoch, *The Philosophical Writings of Descartes*, vol. I (Cambridge: Cambridge University Press, 1995), art. 153, 384.

than a statement of pragmatism based on use or usefulness, although Descartes attempts to disguise this fact by arguing that once the will has determined what is probably the case, it must act as though that knowledge were certain and true. In the end, Descartes is force to conclude that man must "judge as well as we can in order to do what to do what is best". The question remains as to whether any limit may be placed on the infinite will of Cartesian thought. In other words, in light of the contingency of the human condition, absolute freedom has replaced truth as the substance of the *cogito*,[41] a conclusion which, as Grimaldi notes, Descartes himself may never have intended to reach.

In his account of the will, Montaigne had circumscribed its power within the limits of the finite and retained several key elements of classical philosophical thought concerning morals: the classical definition of virtue and the three basic parameters of moral judgement—the intention, circumstances and end of action—. Given the much diminished role of reason in his scheme of things, it might be argued that Montaigne's philosophy of morals is incoherent; in some defence of his position, however, and in line with his insistence on abiding by the established laws and customs of the people, Montaigne's moral discourse reflects the tradition of his time.

In the *Essays*, Montaigne asks how man ought to live in light of his fallible, imperfect nature—not in the light of reason—. Descartes too was intent on discovering how man may live a good life; indeed, his preoccupation with morals led him to abandon his study of mathematics and physics in order to devote his time to questions of morality.[42] His attitude at this point, it would appear, was to regard philosophy as a path to spiritual perfection;[43] and it was because he felt certain that man must judge rightly in order to do right that he embarked on his search for unquestionable truth. This search led him to assert the existence of the *res cogitans*, which is capable of knowing truth once it has been furnished with innate ideas by God.

The radical separation of reason from will, however, provoked a contradiction: reason seeks out the truth in a scientific sense, while the will determines how man ought to act according to an equation of contingency and probability. There were few with the talent and time and dedication to

[41] See Grimaldi, *Six études sur la volonté et la liberté chez Descartes*, 22.

[42] See Adrien Baillet, *La vie de Monsieur Des-Cartes, vol. II* (Paris: Chez Daniel Horthemels, 1691), 111.

[43] See Pierre Mesnard, *Essai sur la Morale de Descartes* (Paris: Boivin & Cie, 1936), 13.

carry out the task entrusted to the faculty of reason—Descartes himself, perhaps, and one or two others—; to guide the decisions and actions of everyday life were of more pressing concern to most men.[44] Thus, the only recourse available to most ordinary men (that is, *not* men of science) who sought to heed his philosophy was Descartes' provisional moral code, a pragmatism of use and usefulness. In other words, man would have to make do with a theory of morals that was in almost every significant sense indistinguishable to that which had already been proposed by Montaigne—with this one difference: that morality had been wholly divorced from the truth—.

The consequences of Descartes' radical break with classical philosophical tradition continue to reverberate in our own time: science and ethics are considered to be wholly separate, autonomous spheres of interest and influence. Scientific progress is measured in terms of the usefulness of new discoveries, especially in the field of medicine, the concerns of which are inextricably linked to the great mysteries—the beginning and the end—of human life. In modern conceptions of ethics, the only limits on the absolute autonomy of the will are those imposed by civil law. Truth, the fundamental link between science and ethics, has been discarded. Modern philosophical thought, shaped to so great an extent as it has been by Descartes' philosophy, dismisses natural law, the reflection of this truth in reality, which is given as it is sought, as the arrogant dogmatism of an illusory supra-individual reason which lays claim to an unjustified and totalizing vision of reality and seeks thereby to impose its laws and customs on others.

Nevertheless, given the experience of new forms of violence in social life and the manipulation of human life with respect only to its usefulness or as part of man's will to dominate (perspectives which are neither explicit nor implicit in Descartes' work), debate in philosophical circles has begun to centre on the ethical and juridical limits on a conception of the human will defined as of limitless potential and radically separate from the truth. Philosophical thought is turning once again towards reason as ground and guide to the principles of practical life, a position which the dominant current in modern thought has long sought to deny.

---

[44] See Ibid., 161.

Works Cited

Armogathe, J-R. “La première crise de la conscience européenne.” In *Gènese de la raison classique de Charron à Descartes*, edited by T. Gregory. Paris: PUF, 2000.

Baillet, Adrien. *La vie de Monsieur Des-Cartes, vol. II*. Paris: Chez Daniel Horthemels, 1691.

Brunschvicg, Léon. *Descartes et Pascal, lecteurs de Montaigne*. Neuchatel: De la Baconnière, 1945.

Charron, Pierre. *De la Sagesse*. Paris: Fayard, 1986.

Descartes, René. *Discourse on the Method* Translated by John Cottingham, Robert Stoothoff and Dugald Murdoch, *The Philosophical Writings of Descartes*, vol. I. Cambridge: Cambridge University Press, 1995.

—. *The Passions of the Soul* Translated by John Cottingham, Robert Stoothoff and Dugald Murdoch, *The Philosophical Writings of Descartes*, vol. I. Cambridge: Cambridge University Press, 1995.

Faye, Emmanuel. *Philosophie et perfection de l'homme. De la Renaissance à Descartes*. Paris: Vrin, 1998.

Friedrich, Hugo. *Montaigne*. Paris: Gallimard, 1968.

Gadofre, G. “La chronologie des six parties.” In *Le Discours et sa Méthode*, edited by Nicolas Grimaldi and Jean-Luc Marion. Paris: PUF, 1987.

Grafton, Anthony. *Bring Out Your Dead. The past as revelation*. Cambridge, (Mass.): Harvard University Press, 2001.

Grimaldi, Nicolas. *Six études sur la volonté et la liberté chez Descartes*. Paris: Vrin, 1988.

Lemaire, Jacques, ed. *Montaigne et la Révolution philosophique du XVI siècle*. Bruxelles: Éditions de l'Université de Bruxelles, 1992.

Levi, Anthony. *French Moralists, the Theory of the Passions, 1585 to 1649*. Oxford: Clarendon Press, 1964.

McKenna, Anthony. *Entre Descartes et Gassendi: la première édition des Pensées de Pascal*. Paris – Oxford: Universitas – Voltaire Foundation, 1993.

Melehy, Hasan. *Writing Cogito. Montaigne, Descartes and the Institution of the Modern Subject*. Albany, N.Y.: State University of New York Press, 1997.

Mesnard, Pierre. *Essai sur la Morale de Descartes*. Paris: Boivin & Cie, 1936.

Montaigne, Michel de. *Essays*. Edited by Mortimer J. Adler et al., *Great Books of the Western World*, Volume 23: *Erasmus and Montaigne*. Chicago: Encyclopaedia Britannica Inc., 1993.

Rodis-Lewis, Genevieve. *Descartes. Biographie*. Paris: Calmann-Lévy, 1995.

Thweatt, Vivien. *La Rochefoucauld and the Seventeenth Century. Concept of the self.* Genève: Librairie Droz, 1980.

Toulmin, S. *Cosmópolis. El trasfondo de la modernidad*. Barcelona: Península, 2001.

CHAPTER EIGHT

NATURAL LAW IN HUME: AN IMITATION OF DIVINE VOLUNTARISM?

ÁNGEL BELEÑA LÓPEZ

If by *natural law* we mean a set of regulations which, we could say, derive from the very nature of things (ignoring their origin for the moment), and indicate the morality that is required in human action, then there is no doubt that David Hume is one of the fiercest enemies of this traditional concept of natural law. Thus his alleged indictment is frequently considered the key reference point for rejecting natural law as the basis for moral obligations.

However, from a different standpoint, Hume may be considered to be of the main defenders of ethical theories based on nature; to such an extent that I believe the Scottish philosopher to be, if not the greatest, one of the original sources of modern naturalism.

We immediately see that, in the modern cultural context, we have a problem of terminology on the concepts of "nature", "natural", "naturalism" which, consequently, must affect our reflections on this so-called "natural law." This confusion also affects controversies about the presence of "moral realism" in several ethical theories: Hume's and also those of other authors in the same cultural and philosophical field.[1]

For Hume what does "natural law" mean? He does not seem to interpret it literally. However, it is obvious that this concept and its meaning are present to a certain extent in his thinking on morals. There are many examples. His discourse in Book III of *A Treatise on Human Nature*, and particularly his lengthy explanation on the origin of moral obligation, can be seen as an implicit allegation against the traditional

---

[1] "Moral realism" in this context at least, is taken to mean the defense of the existence of moral values independently of a law. In other words, our moral obligations exist whether or not they were established by external orders.

concept of "moral law", or rather, what was understood by this term in his times.[2]

This latter point is important when evaluating *which* concept of natural law is opposed in Hume's ethics. Like his predecessors Shaftesbury and Hutcheson, he opposes the conception of morals as a set of burdensome, often useless practices, presented in unpleasant, unfriendly tones, which rarely attract the support of humankind. As he asks in his *An Enquiry Concerning Principles of Morals*,

> what hopes can we ever have of engaging mankind to a practice which we confess full of austerity and rigour? Or what theory of morals can ever serve any useful purpose, unless it can show, by a particular detail, that all the duties which it recommends, are also the true interest of each individual?[3]

We could then say that he rejects the moral theories of natural law, not so much because our moral obligations stem from them naturally (this would be the naturalistic fallacy), but rather, to my mind, because they are not sufficiently based on what is natural. But in order to understand this properly, we must be clear about the meaning of "natural".

"Naturalism" in Shaftesbury and Hutcheson

The desire to keep ethics within the area of what is natural is a phenomenon with different meanings depending on context. In the field of British philosophy, which was more or less empiricist, at least from the second half of the XVII century, until Hume himself, the idea that moral obligation would not have a solid basis if it simply depended on a law imposed by the Will of the Legislator was gaining strength. The prevailing voluntarist conception of natural law (which could be found in Pufendorf, Locke, and even, to a lesser degree, in Grotius) provoked a reaction in many authors. So, Cumberland wanted to base the obligatory character of

---

[2] We can find a study of how Hume's criticism of the traditional idea of natural law was conditioned by earlier concepts in David Saith Morrice, *A comparative study of the position of St. Thomas Aquinas, John Locke and David Hume relating to the problem of natural law* (Boston Spa, West Yorkshire: British Library, c.1990; Thesis University of Aberdeen, 1979).

[3] David Hume, *Enquiry concerning the Principles of Morals* in *Enquiries Concerning the Human Understanding and Concerning the Principles of Morals*, ed. L. A. Selby-Bigge (Oxford: Clarendon Press, 1975), § 228. Author's italics. All other quotes from this work will be marked with the initials *EM*.

natural law on the *naturally*—empirically—good consequences of virtue and the evil consequences of vice, without resorting to rewards and eternal punishment.[4] Shaftesbury wished to avoid divine voluntarism and the legalistic character of ethics by referring to a "*natural* moral sense" which gives us moral knowledge.[5] Hutcheson, again, spoke of a universal *natural* benevolence connected with that "moral sense."[6]

This field was part of the "breeding ground" which led to Hume. At the beginning of the *Enquiry*, Hume complains that

> our modern enquirers, though they also talk much of the beauty of virtue, and deformity of vice, yet have commonly endeavoured to account for

---

4 In his treatise on natural law he writes: "In the following treatise (…) I have endeavour'd to prove the law of nature, only from that reason we find ourselves at present possess'd of, and from experience". And he adds: "We therefore believe the sacred Scriptures to be the Word of God, the Author of nature, because they every where illustrate, confirm, and promote the law of nature." R. Cumberland, *A Treatise of the Laws of Nature* [*De Legibus Naturae disquisitio philosophica*, 1672], trans. John Maxwell, London, 1727 ed. (New York: Garland, 1978), § XXVII, p. 34.

5 Because "if the mere will, decree, or law of God be said absolutely to constitute right and wrong, then are these latter words of no significancy at all" (*Inquiry concerning Virtue or Merit*, I, 3, 2, in Anthony Ashley Cooper Shaftesbury, 3rd Count, *Characteristics of Men, Manners, Opinions, Times, etc.*, ed. John M. Robertson, reprint of the 1900 ed., 2 vols. (Bristol: Thoemmes Press, 1997), 263. (All other quotes from this work will be marked with *Char.*). He believes that, with Locke's Divine voluntarism, God would be free to do anything, even evil "for if He wills it, it will be made good; virtue may be vice, and vice virtue in its turn, if he pleases. And thus neither right nor wrong, virtue nor vice, are anything in themselves; nor is there any trace or idea of them naturally imprinted on human minds. Experience and our catechism teach us all!" ———, *The Life, Unpublished Letters, and Philosophical Regimen of Earl of Shaftesbury*, ed. Benjamin Rand, reprint of London, Swan Sonnenschein, 1900 ed. (Bristol: Thoemmes Press, 1995), 404.

6 I quote the following from among his arguments against voluntarism: "Human laws may be call'd good, because of their conformity to the Divine. But to call the laws of the supreme Deity good, or holy, or just, if all Goodness, Holiness, and Justice be constituted by Laws, or the Will of a Superior any way reveal'd, must be an insignificant tautology, amounting to no more than this, 'that God wills what He wills'." Francis Hutcheson, *An inquiry into the original of our ideas of beauty and virtue in two treatises: I. Concerning beauty, order, harmony, design. II. Concerning moral good and evil*, London, 1738, 4th ed. (Farnborough, Hants: Gregg International, 1969), VII, v, 275.

> these distinctions by metaphysical reasonings, and by deductions from the most abstract principles of the understanding.[7]

And he makes a clear reference to Shaftesbury, who did, in fact, compare ethics with our ability to notice esthetic beauty. Certainly, Shaftesbury, wishing to keep away from a legalist and extrinsic conception of morality (natural law) and keep it in harmony with our nature, advances positions which Hume would later radicalize:

> If there be no real amiableness or deformity in moral acts, there is at least an imaginary one of full force. Tho perhaps the thing itself shou'd not be allow'd in Nature, the imagination or fancy of it must be allow'd to be from Nature alone. Nor can any thing besides art and strong endeavour, with long practice and meditation, overcome such a natural prevention or prepossession of the mind, in favour of this moral distinction.[8]

This is exactly what Hume did: he presumed that in moral acts there was no true amiableness or deformity, that the thing itself did not exist in Nature (in the traditional sense), but that such a "moral quality" is an "imaginary quality of full force," which comes from Nature itself (from our natural perception). Although Shaftesbury seems to trust that our mental powers connect us "with the eternal nature of the universe," the tone of several of his expressions is immanentist.[9]

Both Hutcheson and Hume refer, in much the same way, to the *factual makeup of our nature.* Thus Hutcheson, when referring to the perception of beauty, considers that this is part of our mind as are all other senses, so "were there no mind with a sense of beauty to contemplate objects, I see not how they could be call'd beautiful."[10] In keeping with his empiricist

---

[7] *EM*, § 134.

[8] *Char.*, I, 260. Author's Italics.

[9] Another quote with the same meaning: "Is there then, said he, a natural beauty of figures? And is there not as natural a one of Actions? No sooner the eye opens upon figures, the ear to sounds, than straight the beautiful results, and grace and harmony are known and acknowledg'd. No sooner are Actions view'd, no sooner the human affections and passions discern'd (and they are most of 'em as soon discern'd as felt) than straight an inward Eye distinguishes, and sees the fair and shapely, the amiable and admirable, apart from the deform'd, the foul, the odious, or the despicable. How is it possible therefore not to own, That as these distinctions have their foundation in Nature, the discernment it-self is natural, and from Nature alone?" *Char.*, II, 137. Author's italics.

[10] Hutcheson, *An inquiry into the original of our ideas of beauty and virtue*, I, XVI, 14-5. Significantly, he claims that if we do not find beauty through our senses, it

psychology, he states that the "ideas" received by the internal senses, including the "moral sense", are the same as those of "colors, sounds, tastes, smells, pleasure, pain," that is, "only Perceptions in our Minds, and not Images of any like external Quality."[11] Hutcheson can still be considered a "moral realist" in as far as he is concerned with the possibility that moral good is a property of natural order, not in an arbitrary but in an objective way; however, as has been said, the fact that the appearance of objects [in both the essence of morality and beauty] does not depend on the exercise of the will, but rather is determined by causes which are external to us or implanted in our nature guarantees the *universality*, but not the *reality* of moral good and evil.[12] Now let us see the case of Hume.

What is "natural" in Hume

When considering the origin of our moral differences, and tackling the possibility of finding this origin in nature, Hume himself confesses "that our answer to this question depends upon the definition of the word, Nature, than which there is none more ambiguous and equivocal."[13] He then revises the definitions of the term "natural" which may throw some light on the matter: the opposite of miraculous (what may be called supernatural); the opposite of "uncommon"; or the opposite of "artificial". On the basis of these three definitions, he criticizes those who claim that virtue is *natural* and vice *unnatural*, because none of these differentiate between virtue and vice. Indeed, both virtue and vice belong to nature (they are not miraculous), they are both usual or common (though virtue is less so), and equally artificial (in as far as they are added to nature by decisions).

---

does not mean that this does not exist: animals may find beauty in a different way because their senses are different. See Ibid., II, I, 16.

[11] Hutcheson, Francis, *Illustrations on the moral sense*, IV, 285, in Francis Hutcheson, *Essay on the Nature and Conduct of the Passions and Affections, with Illustrations on the moral sense*, ed. Paul McReynolds, 1742, 3rd ed. (Gainesville, Florida: Scholars' Facsimiles & Reprints, 1969). This "immanency" of the moral perception —already implicit in Shaftesbury— reappears almost literally in Hume. See *infra*, note 16.

[12] D. D. Raphael, *The Moral Sense* (Oxford: Oxford University Press, 1947), 19.

[13] David Hume, *Treatise of Human Nature*, ed. L. A. Selby-Bigge (Oxford: Clarendon Press, 1978), 474. (All other quotes from this work will be marked with *THN*).

These differences of Hume's, may, perhaps intentionally, confuse more than clarify, particularly when he makes a note stating that it may mean the opposite of "civil" and also of "moral". Whatever the case may be, it is interesting to note his scorn, "nothing can be more unphilosophical," he says, "than those systems, which assert, that virtue is the same with what is natural, and vice with what is unnatural." To make the matter absolutely clear, a few lines further on he repeats "'tis impossible, therefore, that the character of natural and unnatural can ever, in any sense, mark the boundaries of vice and virtue."[14] A fragment of his letter to Hutcheson thanking him for his reflections on Book III of the *Treatise* may help us to understand Hume's aversion to the idea of "natural":

> I cannot agree to your sense of 'natural'. 'Tis founded on final causes, which is a consideration that appears to me pretty uncertain and unphilosophical. For, pray, what is the end of man? Is he created for happiness, or for virtue? for this life, or for the next? for himself, or for his Maker? Your definition of natural depends on solving these questions, which are endless and quite wide of my purpose. I have never called justice unnatural, but only artificial. Atque ipsa utilitas, justi prope mater et aequi, says one of the best moralists of antiquity. Grotius and Pufendorf, to be consistent, must assert the same.[15]

Hume agreed with Hutcheson—and with Shaftesbury—that moral distinctions do not stem from reason, but from a moral sense. His disagreement comes from the fact that, having admitted the former point, he could not (unlike his predecessors) support the belief in a true "*is-ought*" that stated reason could have its roots in knowledge of nature. Hutcheson's idea of "natural" is of no use to Hume because it maintains the possibility that our knowledge may reach level of reality which would correspond to an unchanging, eternal law ("natural law"), which would go beyond our mere natural observations and motivations. Thus the "*is-ought passage*" is misunderstood when, as the standard interpretation states, it refers to the possibility of making moral judgments from factual ones, or is used in the controversy between naturalists and no-naturalists with Hume as one of the latter. Moreover, the "*is-ought passage*" is part of a declaration of naturalistic intentions, if we take *naturalism*, in its most basic sense, to be a philosophical attitude or doctrine which states that Nature and its spontaneous processes (natural facts) are the only authentic

---

[14] Ibid., 475.

[15] David Hume, Letter 17.9.1739, in David Hume, *The Letters of David Hume*, ed. J. Y. T. Greig (Oxford: Clarendon Press, 1932), I, 33. The moralist is Horace.

reality. What Hume proposes is giving up the traditional idea of what Ethics itself is, in harmony with his Newtonian project of considering Ethics as one more natural science. The text that precedes the "*is-ought passage*" is clear:

> When you pronounce any action or character to be vicious, you mean nothing, but that from the constitution of your nature you have a feeling or sentiment of blame from the contemplation of it. Vice and virtue, therefore, may be compar'd to sounds, colours, heat and cold, which, according to modern philosophy, are not qualities in objects, but perceptions in mind. And this discovery in morals, like that other in physics, is to be regarded as a considerable advancement of the speculative sciences.[16]

If ethics can be taken as another natural science, its aim will be to *explain*—as a fact, therefore—the (natural) reason for our moral judgments, given our (natural) feelings. So we can conclude, as Kemp Smith has already stated, that "moral judgments, in marking out the good and the evil, have their source not in the eternal nature of any independent reality, but solely in the particular fabric and constitution of the human species."[17] And in this sense, it is obvious that for Hume "*ought* derives from *is*"; this is precisely what he demonstrates in the *Treatise* itself, after the "*is-ought passage*", by basing *moral* obligation on *natural* obligation. But we must not forget that when Hume used expressions such as "moral obligation" and "ought", they meant something completely different from their usual meanings. It is not simply that Hume understood the knowledge of moral obligation differently, and so came to different moral conclusions from those of any other moral philosopher. He really does mean something completely different.

The Humean confusion in the use of the terms "natural" and "moral" is particularly significant in his obscure presentation of *moral* obligation as opposed to *natural* obligation. Certainly neither is easy to understand. In short: why does he need to explain to Hutcheson that justice is not unnatural, but merely artificial? Because he needed to justify the idea of *moral* obligation as a result of an artifice. By considering the virtue of justice as artificial he differentiates it from the natural virtues, which are mere natural skills which do not demand thought to be put into effect. Justice and moral obligations in general demand the exercise of reason in

---

[16] *THN*, 469. Author's italics.

[17] Norman Kemp Smith, *The Philosophy of David Hume* (London: Macmillan, 1964), 199.

order to find the general natural good which follows from their observance. However, the idea that moral obligations can become artificial is simply a question of immediacy, not of their ultimate meaning. Then, finally, morals are reduced to a natural reason: it is the very makeup of our nature that leads us to moral assessment. How? By making us approve of actions (or rather, the results of actions) because of their utility.[18] Thus there is a natural empirical explanation for the existence of what we call morals.[19] And in this way, I believe, Hume does not achieve a true statute for ethics like that which his predecessors sought, but rather deprives ethics of authentic entity.

Conclusion: Hume and the Divine Moral Voluntarism

So Hume's final position is curious when we consider it within the framework of a philosophical movement inspired by the wish to avoid a concept of natural law based on the will. Morals are a contingent fact which we cannot explain and must simply take as fact. It is the case that

> a convenient house, and a virtuous character, cause not the same feeling of approbation (…). There is something very inexplicable in this variation of our feelings; but 'tis what we have experience of with regard to all our passions and sentiments.[20]

And looking back at Hutcheson, who referred to God for the foundations of our moral feelings, Hume states that the criterion which guides this feeling of approval "arising from the eternal frame and constitution of animals, is ultimately derived from that Supreme Will,

---

[18] "In all determinations of morality, this circumstance of public utility is ever principally in view; and wherever disputes arise, either in philosophy or common life, concerning the bounds of duty, the question cannot, by any means, be decided with greater certainty, than by ascertaining, on any side, the true interests of mankind." *EM*, § 143. Author's italics. "I am also of opinion, that reflexions on the tendencies of actions have by far the greatest influence, and determine all the great lines of our duty." *THN*, 590. Author's italics.

[19] As Wand has argued, "moral obligation on this view has no distinctively moral function. It comes into play, according to Hume, only because men have not sufficient insight into the consequences of their unjust actions in a relatively large society." Wand, "Hume's Account of Obligation," in *Hume*, ed. V. C. Chappell (London: Macmillan, 1968), 325.

[20] *THN*, 617. Author's italics.

which bestowed on each being its peculiar nature, and arranged the several classes and orders of existence."[21]

Thus, by basing morals on the true, contingent make-up of our nature, his proposal is also a clear imitation of "voluntarist positivism": "Nature is thus, but could be otherwise." In accordance with this nature, we can but say that "utility is the mother of the just," and in this context perhaps "Grotius and Pufendorf, to be consistent, must assert the same." And just as Pufendorf could find no better reason than the imposition of Divine Will to explain why certain actions are prohibited to humans but may be carried out by animals without fault or sin,[22] nor did Hume find any reason except a real sentiment of disapproval in our nature to explain why certain "actions" of irrational beings (e.g. the "parricide" of a tree by its seed, or incest) should be immoral for humankind.[23]

Works Cited

Cumberland, R. *A Treatise of the Laws of Nature [De Legibus Naturae disquisitio philosophica, 1672]* Translated by John Maxwell. London, 1727 ed. New York: Garland, 1978.

Haakonssen, Knud. "The Character and Obligation of Natural Law according to Richard Cumberland." In *English philosophy in the age of Locke*, edited by M. A. Stewart, 29-47. Oxford: Clarendon Press, 2000.

Hume, David. *Enquiries concerning the human understanding and concerning the principles of morals*. Edited by L. A. Selby-Bigge. Oxford: Clarendon Press, 1975.

—. *The Letters of David Hume*. Edited by J. Y. T. Greig. Oxford: Clarendon Press, 1932.

---

[21] *EM*, § 246. Author's Italics.

[22] "We see beasts every day doing such things without fault or sin, in committing which, men would have been guilty of the highest wickedness. Yet are not the natural motions of men and of the beasts in themselves different, but some actions of men are by the authority of a Law invested with a moral quality, which does not at all touch or affect the proceedings of brutes." Samuel Pufendorf, *Of the law of nature and nations* [*De iure naturae et gentium, 1672*], trans. Basil Kennet, with notes by Mr. Barbeyrac London, 1749, 5th ed., I, 2, vi. As Haakonssen has stated, Pufendorf's voluntarism must be understood in the sense that natural law is a necessary character *due to human nature*, but the choice, by God, of human nature continues to be free. See Knud Haakonssen, "The Character and Obligation of Natural Law according to Richard Cumberland," in *English philosophy in the age of Locke*, ed. M. A. Stewart (Oxford: Clarendon Press, 2000), 40.

[23] See *THN*, 466-8.

—. *Treatise of Human Nature*. Edited by L. A. Selby-Bigge. Oxford: Clarendon Press, 1978.

Hutcheson, Francis. *Essay on the Nature and Conduct of the Passions and Affections, with Illustrations on the moral sense*. Edited by Paul McReynolds. 1742, 3rd ed. Gainesville, Florida: Scholars' Facsimiles & Reprints, 1969.

—. *An inquiry into the original of our ideas of beauty and virtue in two treatises: I. Concerning beauty, order, harmony, design. II. Concerning moral good and evil*. London, 1738, 4th ed. Farnborough, Hants: Gregg International, 1969.

Morrice, David Saith. *A comparative study of the position of St. Thomas Aquinas, John Locke and David Hume relating to the problem of natural law*. Boston Spa, West Yorkshire: British Library, c.1990.

Pufendorf, Samuel. *Of the law of nature and nations [De iure naturae et gentium, 1672]* Translated by Basil Kennet. with notes by Mr. Barbeyrac London, 1749, 5th ed.

Raphael, D. Daiches. *The Moral Sense*. Oxford: Oxford University Press, 1947.

Shaftesbury, Anthony Ashley Cooper, 3rd Count. *Characteristics of Men, Manners, Opinions, Times, etc.* Edited by John M. Robertson. reprint of the 1900 ed. 2 vols. Bristol: Thoemmes Press, 1997.

—. *The Life, Unpublished Letters, and Philosophical Regimen of Earl of Shaftesbury*. Edited by Benjamin Rand. reprint of London, Swan Sonnenschein, 1900 ed. Bristol: Thoemmes Press, 1995.

Smith, Norman Kemp. *The Philosophy of David Hume*. London: Macmillan, 1964.

Wand, Bernard. "Hume's Account of Obligation." In *Hume*, edited by V. C. Chappell. London: Macmillan, 1968.

CHAPTER NINE

THE METAPHYSICAL FOUNDATIONS OF NATURAL LAW IN THE EARLY WRITINGS OF LEIBNIZ

AGUSTÍN ECHAVARRÍA[*]

Divine justice, natural law and voluntarism

As Gaston Grua has stated,[1] the evolution of Leibniz's thought may be interpreted as a sustained and progressive clarification of a single, originary intuition. The early emergence of his major doctrines and their later coherent unfolding is a distinctive characteristic of his thought. In principle, his doctrine concerning the natural law need not be regarded as an exception to this rule, given that it is intimately linked to the central theme of his thought: the bases of divine justice. Indeed, Leibniz's

---

[*] The following abbreviations are used in the footnotes: A = G. W. Leibniz, *Sämtliche Schriften und Briefe*, series I-VII, ed. Preussische (later: Deutsche) Akademie der Wissenschaften zu Berlin (Darmstad (later: Leipzig; now: Berlin): 1923 ff.); Dutens = *Gothofredi Guillelmi Leibnitii, Opera omnia, nunc prima collecta*, vols. I-VI, ed. L. Dutens, I-VI vols. (Geneva: 1768); Mollat = *Mittheilungen aus Leibnizens ungedruckten Schriften*, ed. Georg Mollat (Leipzig: Haessel, 1893). Translations from Leibniz's texts are mine, unless otherwise stated. I would like to thank Prof. Martin Schneider, Director of the Leibniz-Forschungsstelle (Münster), where I completed the bibliography of this article. I also would like to thank Prof. Philip Beeley for his comments on the central topic of this paper, and Prof. Francesco Piro for sending me his article, which I have quoted above. This research was supported by grants from the Friends of the University of Navarra, Inc. and the Deutsche Akademische Austauschdienst.

[1] See Gaston Grua, *Jurisprudence universelle et Théodicée selon Leibniz* (Paris: PUF, 1953), 19-20; ———, "Optimisme et piété leibnizienne avant 1686, avec des textes inédits," *Revue Philosophique de la France et de l'Étranger* 37 (1946): 410.

theodicy, i.e. his doctrine of divine justice, originates in the context of his legal philosophy; it is nothing other than a certain "universal jurisprudence," arising from the application to the case of God of a common definition of justice, which in turn is a product of his "combinatorial art."[2]

The fundamental outlines of Leibniz's doctrine on natural law, articulated in a paradigmatic way in his mature short work entitled *Méditation sur la notion commune de la justice*,[3] may be summarized as follows: a) justice and goodness do not depend on the choice of the divine will; rather, "they belong to the necessary and eternal truths about the nature of things, as do numbers and proportions;"[4] b) the contrary principle, postulating the will as the ultimate justification of law (*stat pro ratione voluntas*) and defining justice as that which is useful to the most powerful—a definition Plato voices through Thrasymachus, and which coincides with Hobbes's position concerning divine omnipotence as the source of law[5]—is "the motto of a tyrant," because it completely confuses "right" and "fact;"[6] c) there is a "formal reason" of justice, common to God, angels and men, which allows for the determination of whether an action is just or unjust, so that the difference between human and divine justice is only a matter "of degree;"[7] d) given that there is an intelligible definition which corresponds to the formal reason of justice, certain conclusions may be derived by means of the laws of logic, wherein jurisprudence becomes a necessary and demonstrative science, independent of facts, and dependent only on reason, as metaphysics, arithmetic and geometry;[8] e) justice consists in the "charity of the wise,"[9]

---

[2] See Grua, *Jurisprudence universelle et Théodicée selon Leibniz*, 20; Patrick Riley, *Leibniz's Universal Jurisprudence. Justice as the Charity of the Wise* (Cambridge, London: Harvard University Press, 1996); Simone Goyard-Fabre, "La Jurisprudence Universelle selon Leibniz," in *Perspectives sur Leibniz*, ed. Renée Bouveresse (Paris: Vrin, 1999).

[3] See Mollat, 41-70. Translations from this short work are taken from G. W. Leibniz, *The Political Writings of Leibniz*, ed. Patrick Riley (Cambridge: Cambridge University Press, 1972), 45-64.

[4] Ibid., 41.

[5] "In *regno naturali*, regnandi et puniendi eos, qui leges suas violant, jus Deo est a sola *potentia irresistibili.*" Thomas Hobbes, *Opera philosophica quae latina scripsit omnia in unum corpus nunc primum collecta* (London, 1839-1845), ed. William Molesworth (Aalen: 1961), II, *De cive*, 15, §5, 334.

[6] See Mollat, 41.

[7] Ibid., 45.

[8] See Ibid., 47.

[9] Ibid., 54.

i.e. in the union of "wisdom" and "goodness," where "good" signifies all that "serves in the perfection of intelligent substances;"[10] f) spiritual beings are "the substances more resembling God, because they are capable of recognizing and of producing order and craftsmanship,"[11] and God takes special care of them; g) as "perfectly just monarch" of the most perfect State, God permits the good fortune of the evil and the wretchedness of the good, because according to the rule of His perfect governance, this apparent injustice will receive its recompense in the next life, when rewards and punishments will be distributed accordingly,[12] such that the maximum happiness of His creatures coincides with the harmony and beauty of the universe.

If Grua's continuist thesis is to hold true, this metaphysical position, falling clearly within the tradition of Christian Platonism,[13] ought to appear in Leibniz's earliest writings, albeit only in a roughly sketched way. Nevertheless, in line with a long-standing interpretation, in the first years of his philosophical project (1663-1670), Leibniz—influenced by the ideas of Hobbes—is said to have deferred to a voluntarist and utilitarian basis for justice, based solely on divine omnipotence and the will.[14] This voluntarism is seen as clearly evidenced by Leibniz's adherence to the definition of justice proffered by Thrasymachus, i.e. as that which is *potentiori utile*; this position is textually verifiable in at least three places in his early philosophical writings.[15] Many authors have rejected this thesis for convincing reasons, and have highlighted the continuity in the development of Leibniz's juridical doctrine by refining the true meaning of his adhesion to Thrasymachus's definition.[16]

---

[10] Ibid., 48.

[11] Ibid., 50.

[12] See Ibid., 49.

[13] See Patrick Riley, "Leibniz's Méditation sur la notion commune de la justice, 1703-2003," *The Leibniz Review* 13 (2003): 67-78.

[14] This thesis had already been the subject of discussion in Gottschalk Guhrauer, *Gottfried Wilhelm Freiherr von Leibniz, Eine Biographie* (Breslau: 1842), I, 227 ff.; Robert Zimmermann, *Das Rechtprinzip bei Leibniz. Ein Beitrag zur Geschichte der Rechtphilosophie* (Wien: Braumüller, 1852), 8-11 and 30-32; Erwin Ruck, *Die Leibniz'sche Staatsidee* (Tübingen: Mohr, 1909), 20-25.

[15] In *Dissertatio de arte combinatoria* (1666), A, VI, 1, 230; *Nova methodus discendae docendaeque jurisprudentiae* (1667), A, VI, 1, 344; and *Specimen demonstrationum politicarum* (1669), A, IV, 1, 10.

[16] See Vittorio Mathieu in G. W. Leibniz, *Scriti politici e di diritto naturale*, ed. Vittorio Mathieu (Torino: Unione Tipografico-Editrice Torinese, 1951), 18-19; Tullio Ascarelli in Thomas Hobbes and G. W. Leibniz, *Thomas Hobbes, A*

Nevertheless, over the last 45 years, the "early voluntarism" thesis appears to have re-emerged in a strong way, attracting favorable support in the secondary literature, and indeed without almost any further discussion.[17] This position has been described in different ways. Commentators occasionally speak of a "dramatic" change or "radical change of heart" on Leibniz's part around 1670,[18] of a "crisis" that prompted an "inversion" of the equation between wisdom and power;[19] there have even been claims that Leibniz's first theodicy is "anti-metaphysical."[20] In other cases, the authors argue positively for the thesis of an initial voluntarism and a later rupture;[21] finally, the idea is assumed

---

Dialogue between a Philosopher and a Student of the Common Laws of England - G. W. Leibniz, Specimen quaestionum philosophicarum ex iure collectarum. De casibus perplexis. Doctrina conditionum. De legume interpretatione, ed. Tullio Ascarelli (Milano Giufrè, 1960), 50-51; Émilianne Naert, *La pensée politique de Leibniz* (Paris: PUF, 1964), 12-13; Werner Schneiders, "Naturrecht und Gerechtigkeit bei Leibniz," *Zeitschrift für philosophische Forschung* 20 (1996): 609-10; ———, "Leibniz und die Frage nach dem Grund des Guten und Gerechten," *Studia Leibnitiana. Supplementa* 4 (1969): 89-90; Hans-Peter Schneider, *Justitia Universalis. Quellenstudien zur Geschichte des "Christlichen Naturrrechts" bei Gottfried Wilhelm Leibniz* (Frankfurt am Main: Klostermann, 1967), 354-55; Hartmut Schiedermair, *Das Phänomen der Macht und die Idee des Rechts bei Gottfried Wilhelm Leibniz*, Studia Leibnitiana. Supplementa (Wiesbaden: Franz Steiner Verlag, 1970), 60-65; Francesco Piro, "Jus-Justum-Justitia. Etica e diritto nel giovane Leibniz," *Annali dell'Istituto Italiano per gli Studi Storici* 7 (1987): 21-22; Hubertus Busche, *Leibniz' Weg ins perspektivische Universum. Eine Harmonie im Zeitalter der Berechnung* (Hamburg: Meiner, 1997), 212-13.

[17] This thesis was re-introduced to critical debate by Hans Welzel, *Naturrecht und materiale Gerechtigkeit* (Göttingen: Vandenhoeck & Ruprecht, 1962), 146.

[18] See Robert J. Mulvaney, "The Early Development of Leibniz's Concept of Justice," *Journal of the History of the Ideas* 29 (1968): 54, 72. Despite these expressions, and his explicit rejection of Grua's continuist thesis, Mulvaney proposes a moderate interpretation of Leibniz's reversal.

[19] See André Robinet, *Le meilleur des mondes par la balance de l'Europe* (Paris: PUF, 1994), 3-4 ; ———, "Loi naturelle et loi positive dans l'arquitectonique archaïque de l'ouvre de Leibniz," in *La notion de nature chez Leibniz*, ed. Martine de Gaudemar, *Studia Leibnitiana. Sonderheft* (Stuttgart: Franz Steiner Verlag, 1995), 159-70.

[20] Gianfranco Mormino, "La teodicea antimetafisica del giovane Leibniz," *Rivista di Storia della Filosofia* 58 (2003): 49.

[21] See Wolfgang Röd, *Geometrischer Geist und Naturrecht. Methodengeschichte Untersuchungen zur Staatsphilosophie im 17. Und 18. Jahrhundert* (München: Bayerische Akademie der Wissenschaften, 1970), 108; Jean-Louis Gardies, "La

uncritically in some accounts[22] and some discussions of[23] Leibniz's juridical thought.

In addition to his adherence to Thrasymachus's definition, another point adduced in favor of the voluntarist thesis is the existence of an "initial relative positivism" in Leibniz's works, reflected in the "inductive" and "encyclopedic" conception of rationality present in his *Nova methodus discendae docendaque jurisprudentia* (1667), which contrasts "law and mathematics" in a radical way.[24] Moreover, according to this interpretation, in the first years of his philosophical career Leibniz was quite far from having a harmonious concept of a universal jurisprudence common to God and men,[25] and from a harmonious conception of the divine perfections.[26] Finally, the immortality of the soul and the existence of God are interpreted as being mere postulates of practical reason, and incapable of providing jurisprudence and law with a foundation of full theoretical rationality.[27]

The aim of the present article is to show that a close analysis of Leibniz's early writings does not prompt an unequivocal conclusion of a voluntarist conception of justice. Rather, I argue that the foundations for the later development of a metaphysical basis for natural law are present, *in nuce*, in these writings, grounded in the idea of the universe as a *Respublica optima* governed by God, who continually keeps in mind the laws of "universal harmony" and attains the greatest good possible in the kingdom of spiritual beings.

---

rationalité du droit chez Leibniz," *Archives de Philosophie du Droit* 23 (1978): 117.

[22] See Charles Yves Zarka, "Le droit naturel selon Leibniz," in *La notion de nature*, ed. Martine de Gaudemar, *Studia Leibnitiana. Sonderheft* (Stuttgart: Franz Steiner Verlag, 1995), 96-97.

[23] See Patrick Riley, "Leibniz's Meditation sur la notion commune de la justice: A Reply to Andreas Blank," *The Leibniz Review* 15 (2003): 203. Riley alludes to the supposed voluntarism of the *Nova methodus*, in order to reply to Blank that Leibniz's youthful writings cannot be considered "the relevant background" to an interpretation of the *Méditation*. Blank concedes this point in his response to Riley: Andreas Blank, "Leibniz on Justice as a Common Concept: A Rejoinder to Patrick Riley," *The Leibniz Review* 16 (2006): 205.

[24] See Gardies, "La rationalité du droit chez Leibniz," 117-19.

[25] See Robinet, *Le meilleur des mondes par la balance de l'Europe*, 11, 23.

[26] See Ibid., 28.

[27] See Ibid., 33-34.

First outlines of Leibniz's doctrine of natural law

There are very few texts which could inspire a voluntarist interpretation in the writings and notes written by Leibniz prior to his *Dissertatio de arte combinatoria*. The claim in the notes to the *Tabellae* of Stahl, which states that God cannot be the "moral cause" of sin because He is not subject to any law,[28] does not provide sufficient evidence to conclude that God is, by virtue of his omnipotence, completely beyond all objective norms of action.[29] The affirmation is formulated in the context of Leibniz's adherence to the Scholastic doctrine concerning the "physical", not "moral", concurrence of God in sin. According to this doctrine, all created freedom is fallible because it is not the norm of its own action.[30] God, as Creator, does not receive the law from another; rather, by His essence, He is the ultimate source and "author" of the law; this is a thesis which continues in Leibniz's later thought[31] and shows no trace of arbitrarianism.[32]

Certain statements in these early works point in a direction quite different from voluntarism. The strong influence of the Scholastic and Aristotelian-Platonic conception of J. Thomasius is noteworthy.[33] In his

---

[28] "1. causa moralis est solùm in actibus moralibus, s. in ordinem ad Legem; 2. is demum causa moralis est cui lex data est. Ex hoc patet Deum causam moralem esse non posse, qvia Deo Lex data non est." A, VI, 1, 27.

[29] The questionable interpretation articulated by Robinet, *Le meilleur des mondes par la balance de l'Europe*, 9.

[30] A classical thesis of the Thomist school. "Solum autem illum actum a rectitudine declinare non contingit, cuius regula est ipsa virtus agentis. [...] Divina autem voluntas sola est regula sui actus: quia non ad superiorem finem ordinatur." Thomas Aquinas, *Summa Theologiae*, I, q. 63, a. 2.

[31] See *Observationes de principio juris* (1699), Dutens IV, III, 273: "Deum esse omnis naturalis juris auctorem (quod ait §. 41.) verissimum est, at non voluntate, sed ipsa essentia sua, qua ratione etiem auctor est veritatis."

[32] On Creation as a "legislative act" in Leibniz, see Albert Heinekamp, *Das Problem des Guten bei Leibniz*, Kantstudien Ergänzungshefte (Bonn: Bouvier, 1969), 108-09; Claudio Tommasi, *La ragione prudente. Pace e riordino dell'Europa moderna nel pensiero di Leibniz* (Il Mulino: Bologna, 2006), 90-91.

[33] See Guido Aceti, "Jakob Thomasius ed il pensiero filosofico-giuridico di Godoffredo Guglielmo Leibniz," *Jus. Rivista di scienze giuridiche* 8 (1957): 259-319; Christia Mercer, *Leibniz's Metaphysics. Its Origins and Development* (Cambridge: Cambridge University Press, 2001), 32 ff.; ———, "Leibniz and His Master: The Correspondence with Jakob Thomasius," in *Leibniz and His Correspondents*, ed. Paul Lodge (Cambridge: Cambridge University Press, 2004), 10-46.

notes on the *Opera philosophica* of his master (1663-1664?), it is clear that Leibniz knew of his conception of the "natural law" as the "dictamen of right reason", as an "internal and immutable obligation" which has its origin in "God and nature", is "the same for the entire world", "obliges all men", and is accessible by natural *notitias*; positive or "legitime" law would be, for its part, an "external and modifiable" obligation based on the will of men, different in each republic, and knowable by promulgation.[34] Leibniz adopts this distinction between natural and positive law in his *Specimen quaestionum philosophicarum ex jure collectarum* (1664),[35] where he refers to "law" as a "certain dictamen of the reason", and as a "certain supreme *ratio* existing in God,"[36] and to natural law as a "dictamen" or "proposition of the soul" in those beings endowed with spirit.[37]

In the same work, Leibniz makes reference for the first time to the principle of the choice of the best and divine wisdom as the norm of

---

[34] A, VI, 1, 52. A. Robinet interprets a note Leibniz introduces in the same place—in which he explains that God could change that which is not of absolute necessity ("aut est necessitas absoluta aut hypoth. non si haec omne Ius voluntarium est. Si absoluta, at nulla contradictio")—as an explicit rejection of the distinction between natural and positive law: see Robinet, *Le meilleur des mondes par la balance de l'Europe*, 10. H.-P. Schneider's interpretation appears to be closer to the mark, wherein Leibniz's adherence to this distinction is maintained: see Schneider, *Justitia Universalis*, 343.

[35] A, VI, 1, 83.

[36] Ibid., 83-84. Although he traces this position to the Stoics, he subscribes to it in the context of attributing, by analogy, a certain kind of justice to animals. See Busche, *Leibniz' Weg ins perspektivische Universum*, 97-9.

[37] See Ibid., 84. Here, Leibniz attacks Hobbes' opinion, which claims that the human soul is naturally corporeal and mortal, and only immortal by virtue of divine omnipotence. Leibniz notes that the "vestiges of reason" in men constitute evidence that we differ "substantially" from animals. His anthropological conception is in clear contrast to the Hobbesian vision of the law of the strongest, which lowers man to the level of beasts. Therefore, despite the resemblance with Leibniz's expressions, Hobbes has in mind the conservation of natural life: "Est igitur lex naturalis, ut eam definiam, dictamen recatae rationis circa ea, quae agenda vel omittenda sunt ad vitae membrorumque conservationem, quantum fieri potest, diuturnam." Hobbes, *Opera philosophica* (London, 1839-1845), II, *De cive*, 2, §1, 169-70. Accordingly, Philip Beeley shows that the different ways in which Leibniz and Hobbes understand *recta ratio* and apply the Euclidean method to jurisprudence lead to antagonistic conceptions of natural law: Philip Beeley, "Right Reason and Natural Law in Hobbes and Leibniz," *Synthesis philosophica* 24 (1997): 445-59.

action: God could not have created a world different from the one which He did create, not because this would be impossible *per se*, but because such a world, "because of the wisdom of the Creator, who chooses the best, was not to be."[38] In the last two chapters of the *Specimen*, Leibniz addresses the problem of the essence and foundation of "relations", paying special attention to the ontological status of juridical relations.[39] While "weak", these beings are nevertheless "real", and are founded on the substances in which they immediately inhere.[40]

All these fragmentary elements do not constitute a solid metaphysical foundation for natural law, but they are evidence of Leibniz's early interest in finding a rational norm of action, an objective measure of justice—for both divine and human action—and his desire to develop an ontology of juridical relations based not on the will, but on the nature of things.[41] Through his readings of Johann Heinrich Bisterfeld, Leibniz discovered a metaphysical foundation appropriate for these purposes: the Pythagorean-Platonic idea of "universal harmony."[42]

Indeed, in his notes on Bisterfeld (1666), Leibniz emphasizes and subscribes to the thesis of the *immeatio*[43] or co-presence of all things in all by means of the "concurrence," "combination" and "complication" of their relations.[44] This "panharmony of all things" forms a "society of relations," which has its ultimate basis in the Holy Trinity, "source of all order, norms and ends."[45] In this context, the "relations" are no longer the "weakest" entities, but the "most effective,"[46] because they are intrinsically constitutive of the reality of substances. Logic is thus a "mirror of

---

[38] A, VI, 1, 86. "Uti, cum negatur, potuisse mundum à Deo aliter, quàm factus est, creari, non quòd impossibile sit, sed quia ob sapientiam Conditoris, qui optimum eligit, non erat futurum." That A. Robinet sees a voluntaristic necessitarianism which eliminates the notion of "possible worlds" in this passage, where there is an implicit distinction between absolute and hypothetical necessity, is disconcerting. See Robinet, *Le meilleur des mondes par la balance de l'Europe*, 13.

[39] See A, VI, 1, 93-94.

[40] See Ibid., 95.

[41] See Ibid., 95.

[42] See Leroy E. Loemker, "Leibniz and the Herborn Encyclopedists," *Journal of the History of Ideas* 22 (1961): 323-38.

[43] See Maria Rosa Antognazza, "Immeatio and Emperichoresis. The Theological Roots of Harmony in Bisterfeld and Leibniz," in *The Young Leibniz and His Philosophy*, ed. Stuart Brown (Dordrecht, Boston, London: Kluwer, 1999), 41-64.

[44] See A, VI, 1, 159.

[45] Ibid., 158.

[46] Ibid., 159.

relations", since every argument expresses relations of "convenience" and "disconvenience."[47]

These elements contribute in a decisive way to forging the Leibnizian idea of the order of the universe as an expression of divine wisdom, which governs all things according to the rules of compensation and proportion between variety and identity. In line with this position, when commenting on Bisterfeld, Leibniz holds that the goodness of a being consists in its "congruence" with its "office in the Republic of the Universe;"[48] that the metaphysical ideas mentioned above are implicated in his concept of universal justice is, therefore, obvious. These ideas would be of fundamental importance both for his development of a general scientific methodology (the *ars combinatoria*),[49] as well as its particular application to jurisprudence.

The metaphysical foundations of the *ars combinatoria* and its application to legal science

In the *Dissertatio de arte combinatoria* (1666), Leibniz develops his inventive logic on the basis of the idea of a "universal characteristic", a rational and objective method of calculation that would allow for the combination of all subjects with their possible predicates. The method consists in the analysis and reduction of all notions—on the basis of their definitions—to their primary concepts or elements, which would be absolutely simple and indefinable; by virtue of their combinations, one may derive, by deduction, all possible propositions, both universal and singular.[50]

Leibniz proposes the use of this method to achieve demonstrative certainty in legal science,[51] establishing an analogy between geometry and jurisprudence: both are sciences in which one can arrive at simple terms,

---

[47] Ibid. See Maria Rosa Antognazza, "Debilissimae Entitates? Bisterfeld and Leibniz's Ontology of Relations," *The Leibniz Review* 11 (2001): 1-13.

[48] A, VI, 1, 156.

[49] The importance of Bisterfeld's idea of universal harmony for the development of Leibniz's logical calculus was highlighted by Willy Kabitz, *Die Philospohie des jungen Leibniz. Untersuchungen zur Entwicklungsgeschichte seines Systems* (Heidelberg: Carl Winter, 1909) and later by Massimo Mugnai, "Der Begriff der Harmonie als metaphysische Grundlage der Logik und Kombinatorik bei Johann Heinrich Bisterfeld und Leibniz," *Studia Leibnitiana* 5 (1973): 43-73.

[50] See A, VI, 1, 194-195.

[51] "Usus est in casibus apud Jureconsultos formandis." Ibid., 189.

through the combination of which one may derive all possible cases.[52] Hobbes—to whom Leibniz himself attributes the origin of his idea of thought understood as "calculus"[53]—had already suggested the use of the "geometric method" in legal science.[54] Nevertheless, the similarity between these authors is only superficial, because the ontology which underwrites the *Dissertatio* is completely incompatible with Hobbesian extreme nominalism.[55]

Indeed, the "universal characteristic," as Leibniz himself notes, is intended to find theorems which depend on the "eternal truths," founded on the divine understanding, not on the choice of the will.[56] In addition, Leibniz explicitly links the metaphysical foundation of the *ars combinatoria*—which lays bare the constitution of reality, through reason—to the intrinsic connection of all things by virtue of the "universal harmony,"[57] and to the relations of similarity and dissimilarity between beings by virtue of *immeatio*.[58]

---

[52] "Jurisprudentia enim cum aliis Geometriae similis est, tum in hoc quod utraque habet Elementa, utraque casus. [...] Termini quorum complicatione oritur in Jure diversitas casuum sunt: Personae, Res, Actus, Jura." Ibid.

[53] "Profundissimus principiorum in omnibus rebus scrutator Th. Hobbes meritò posuit omne opus mentis nostrae esse *computationem*, sed hac vel summam *addendo* vel *substrahendo* differentiam colligi." Ibid., 194.

[54] See Thomas Hobbes, *Critique du "De mundo" de Thomas White*, ed. Jean Jacquot and Harold Whitmore Jones (Paris: Vrin, 1973), XXXIII, § 1, 269-70.

[55] Although George MacDonald Ross has recently refined Couturat's critique of Tönnies, my view is that Couturat is right in denying that Leibniz neither adopted nor could have adopted Hobbes' radical nominalism: Louis Couturat, *La logique de Leibniz, d'après des documents inédits* (Paris: Alcan, 1901), 466; Ferdinand Tönnies, "Leibniz und Hobbes," *Philosophische Monatshefte* 23 (1987): 566-67; George MacDonald Ross, "Leibniz's Debt to Hobbes," in *Leibniz and the English-speaking World*, ed. Pauline Phemister and Stuart Brown (Dordrecht: Springer, 2007, 2007), 21-22.

[56] "Admonendum denique est, totam hanc artem complicatoriam directam esse ad theoremata, seu propositiones quae sunt eternae veritates, seu non arbitrio DEI sed natura constant." A, VI, 1, 199.

[57] "Ab instituto autem abiisse nemo nos dicet, qui omnia ex intima Variationum doctrina erui viderit: quae sola propè per omne infinitum obsequentem sibi ducit animum; et harmoniam mundi, et intimas constructiones rerum, seriemque formarum una complectitur." Ibid. 187.

[58] "Uno saltem verbo indigitabimus omnia ex doctrina metaphysica relationum Entis ad Ens repetenda esse, sic ut ex generibus quidem relationum Loci, ex theorematis autem singulorum maximae efformentur. Hoc vidisse arbitror, praeter morem compendiographum solidissimum Joh. Henr. Bisterfeld in Phosphoro

The application of the combinatorial art to juridical concepts discloses the "simple terms" which enable the articulation of the general principles of legal science. When applied to the realm of divine governance, which rules the "universal republic" of men, these common terms and principles give rise to a "special" jurisprudence—which is nothing other than theology.[59] Thus, by virtue of the existence of certain common rational principles of the law in force in the different realms of reality, the basic outlines of Leibniz's idea of universal jurisprudence become clear.

In the context of this speculative framework, it would appear to be rash to attribute a crassly voluntaristic sense to Leibniz's formulation of Thrasymachus's definition of justice towards the end of the *Dissertatio*:

> Thrasymachus well says, in Plato's *Republic*, Book I, that *justice* is what is useful to the more powerful. For in a proper and simple sense, God is more powerful than others [...]. Besides, usefulness to God is not a matter of profit but of honor. Therefore *the glory of God is obviously the measure of all law.*[60]

On the one hand, by distinguishing between "profit" and "honor", Leibniz shows that what is "useful" for the powerful should not be read in an utilitarian way, as a particular interest of God's, stripped of all care for the good of His creatures; some years earlier, Leibniz had rejected the

Catholico, seu Epitome artis meditandi ed. Lugd. Bat. anno 1657, quae tota fundatur in immeatione et περιχωρήσει, universali omnium in ómnibus, similitudinem item et dissimilitudine omnium cum omnibus, quarum principia: Relationes. Eum libellum qui legerit, usum artis complicatoriae magis magisque perspiciet." Ibid., 199.

59 "Theologia autem quasi species est Jurisprudentiae, de Jure nempe Publico in Republica DEI super homines" Ibid., 168 ; and : "Par in theologia terminorum ratio est, quae est quasi Jurisprudentia specialis, sed eadem, fundamentalis ratione caeterarum. Est enim velut doctrina quaedam de Jure publico quod obtinet in Republica DEI in homines; [...]" Ibid., 190. A. Robinet sees a "purely external" parallelism between human and divine politics in this passage: see Robinet, *Le meilleur des mondes par la balance de l'Europe*, 22. In contrast, W. Schneiders proposes that this passage be read in line with later texts from the *Nova methodus* in which Leibniz sketches the idea of a universal republic: see Werner Schneiders, "Respublica optima. Zur metaphysischen und moralischen Fundierung der Politik bei Leibniz," *Studia Leibnitiana* 9 (1977): 7.

60 A, VI, 1, p. 230. The quotation here is from G. W. Leibniz, *Philosophical Papers and Letters*, ed. Leroy E. Loemker (Dordrecht: Reidel, 1969), 76.

despotic Hobbesian concept of "utility" as the source of law.[61] On the other hand, however confused and obscure the concept of the "glory of God" may appear to us, it cannot be identified *simpliciter* with naked will or power or deprived of any connection to the idea of "universal harmony;"[62] less still if, as is detailed in the following section, the metaphysical context of the *Dissertatio* and Leibniz's significant transformation of Thrasymachus's definition in the *Nova methodus* the following year are taken into account.

The metamorphosis of Thrasymachus in the *Nova methodus*

In his *Nova methodus discendae doquendaque jurisprudentiae* (1667), Leibniz aims to carry out a methodical reform of the science of law in order to elevate it to the status of a demonstrative science,[63] thereby re-founding natural law on a basis which would surpass the inadequate proposals of Hobbes, Grotius and Pufendorf.[64] The importance attributed to the *ratio studiorum* (*didactica*, *polemica*, *historica*, and *exegetica*)[65] in this work, i.e the inductive and encyclopedic methods of compilation and interpretation of the law in force, in no way corresponds to a "legal positivism". The distinction between immutable natural law as the ultimate

---

[61] See his letter to J. Thomasius (September 1663), A, II, 1, 5: "Demum vivus aut Hobbes aut Hobbesianus elucet, cum enim utilitatem aequi matrem habeat, igitur prout illi velificabitur jus omne, stabit cadetque: [...] Haec in Hobbesio saepe reprehendentem V.E. audivi."

[62] I agree with the interpretation of Piro: "Bisogna però súbito chiarire che l'*utilitas* divina consiste nella 'gloria' e che non vi è un'utilità *privata* di Dio, la cui potenza è incontradittoria con l'utilità delle menti da lui create. La giustizia è dunque, nella sua divina essenza, armonía dell'Uno e dei Molti." Piro, "Jus-Justum-Justitia," 21. W. Schneiders discusses this passage from the same perspective in Schneiders, "Leibniz und die Frage nach dem Grund des Guten und Gerechten," 89; and ———, "Naturrecht und Gerechtigkeit bei Leibniz," 610.

[63] For a detailed analysis of this work, see Cesare Vasoli, "Enciclopedismo, pansofia e riforma 'metodica' del diritto nella 'Nova methodus' di Leibniz," *Quaderni Fiorentini per la storia del pensiero giuridico moderno* 2 (1973): 37-107.

[64] On Leibniz and the school of natural law, see Rene Sève, *Leibniz et l'école moderne du droit naturel* (Paris: PUF, 1989).

[65] For a detailed analysis of this issue, see Guido Aceti, "Sulla 'Nova Methodus discendae docendaque jurisprudentiae' di Leibniz," *Jus. Rivista di scienze giuridiche* 8 (1957): 1-41.

norm of justice, which is demonstrable on the basis of the nature of things,[66] and a positive (or civil) law which is more "fact" than "law"[67]—since it depends on the will of the legislator[68]—is very clear in this work. The inductive procedures have a propaedeutic function in Leibniz's ambitious project to find a method enabling rational demonstration that the contents of Roman law coincide for the most part with natural law.[69]

The doctrine developed in this work is in perfect continuity with the outline of universal jurisprudence sketched in the *Dissertatio.*[70] Jurisprudence is the "science of actions insofar as these are said to be just or unjust."[71] The subject of these morally qualifiable actions is the "person" or "rational substance", be it a man, an angel or God himself.[72] A common definition of justice is applied to all these subjects: "The just or unjust is all that which is publicly useful or pernicious."[73] It is important to

---

[66] "Ideò totius arbitror, referre se ad merum immutabileque Jus Naturae." *Nova methodus discendae docendaeque jurisprudentiae* [1667], A, VI, 1, 341.

[67] "Nam si accuratè rem consideremus, omne Jus Civile magis facti est quàm Juris: Quia probandum est non ex natura rerum, sed ex historia seu facto." Ibid.

[68] Leibniz is clearly referring to positive law and not to natural law when he attributes the principle *stat pro ratione voluntas* to divine and human law in this work: "[...] *Euclidi* non creditur quia dicit, sed quia probat, quod secus est in Legibus Divinis Humanisque, ubi stat pro ratione voluntas." Ibid., 294. Leibniz takes the idea of a "divine will-based law" or "positive law" knowable only via revelation and distinct from the natural law of J. Thomasius: see Ibid., 52.

[69] See his letter to T. Hobbes (1670): "[...] igitur cum primum in jurisprudentia pedem posui jam a quadriennio circiter consilia agitavi, qua rationepaucissimis verbis (ad modum *Edicti perpetui*) Elementa Juris ejus quod Romano Corpore continetur condi possint, ex quibus deinde liceat *legis ejus universas* velut demonstrare. [...] Praesertim cum asserere ausim dimidiam Juris Romani meri juris naturalis esse, [...]" A, II, 1, 91-92; and also, A, VI, 4B, 2872-73.

[70] "Nec mirum est, quod in Jurisprudentia, item et in Theologia usu venire, quia Theologia species quaedam est Jurisprudentiae universim sumtae, agit enim de Jure et Legibus obtinentibus in Republicâ aut potius regno DEI super homines; [...] Breviter tota fere Theologia magnam partem ex Jurisprudentia pendet." A, VI, 1, 294-295.

[71] Ibid., 300.

[72] Ibid., 301.

[73] Ibid., 300-301. Leibniz attributes this definition to Plato: "*Plato* passim Juris fundamentum statuit, τὸ κοινῇ συμφέρον, publicam utilitatem" Ibid., 342, which will coexist later in his work with the other definition of justice as *caritas sapientis*. "Justum esse quod publice utile est, quae propositio non potest accurate demonstrari, nisi supposito Deo." A, VI, 4C, 2797.

clarify that "public utility" is understood here in the sense of the ancient doctrine of the common good,[74] which Leibniz translates in terms of the "maximum possible happiness" in the kingdom of spiritual beings.

This common definition is applied in different ways, according to the different hierarchically subordinated levels by which actions may be publicly useful or prejudicial, and thus gives rise to the different types of jurisprudence: "Divine Jurisprudence" rules in the world; "Human Jurisprudence" is in force for the human race; and there is "Civil Jurisprudence" for each republic.[75] At the same time, these types of jurisprudence correspond inversely to the "three grades of natural law," namely, "mere law" or *jus strictum*, which is the law of "war and peace," governed by the principle of *naeminem laedere*; "equity," consisting in "harmony or congruence" between two or more individuals, and whose precept is *suum cuique tribuere*; and "piety," or universal justice, whose precept is *honeste vivere.*[76]

Leibniz holds that if each is correctly placed at its corresponding grade of the natural law, the heterogeneous definitions of Plato, Thrasymachus, Aristotle, Epicurus, Cicero, Grotius, Pallavicino, Hobbes and Sharrok may be reconciled in line with the abovementioned common definition of justice.[77] Only in the case of the third grade of law, whose principle is the superior will of God, does Leibniz admit Thrasymachus's definition of justice as *potentiori utile.*[78]

A close analysis of what Leibniz says in this regard is rewarding: the third grade of natural law, piety, confers their perfection and force on the other two,[79] "since God, being omniscient and wise, assures *jus strictum*

---

[74] This is noted by Gioele Solari, "Metafisica e diritto in Leibniz," *Rivista di Filosofia* 38 (1947): 35-65. See also Schneiders, "Naturrecht und Gerechtigkeit bei Leibniz," 609.

[75] See A, VI, 1, 301.

[76] See Ibid., 343. As Grua notes—Gaston Grua, *La justice humaine selon Leibniz* (Paris: PUF, 1956), 85—Leibniz fundamentally holds to this framework of the degrees of natural law in his later works, identifying *jus strictum* with commutative justice, equity with distributive justice, and piety with universal justice. See A, VI, 4C, 2780; A, VI, 4C, 2858-2859; Mollat, 63-64.

[77] See A, VI, 1, 342-343.

[78] "Tertium Juris principium est voluntas Superioris. Et huc quae Trasymachus apud *Platonem* suprà dicebat: Justum esse potentiori utile." Ibid., 344.

[79] "Pietas igitur tertius est gradus Juris Naturae, tribuitque caeteris perfectionem et efectum." Ibid. This entire sequence, in which Leibniz establishes universal justice as the fundamental basis of the other grades of justice, is closely paralleled by what he says 35 years later in the *Méditation*, Mollat, 60-64.

and equity; because He is omnipotent, he carries them out."[80] That the wisdom of God is the formal reason which sustains the other grades of natural law, whereas power merely plays the role of executing the dictamen of His wisdom, should be noted. "From here on", continues Leibniz, "the utility of the human race, or better, the beauty and harmony of the world, coincides with the divine will."[81] That is to say, the divine will is not a blind power divested of rationality; rather, the "harmony of the world," which is identified with the common good of rational creatures, is its norm of action.

In line with the discussion thus far, Leibniz explains that the precept *honeste vivere* must be followed, and the abuse of any creature and of ourselves avoided;[82] since *jus strictum* and equity lack a link which would effectively guarantee the observance of justice, God himself makes this link effective, "thus what is publicly useful, i.e. for the human race and the world, will also be useful for individuals; and that in this way all that which is honest will be useful, and all that which is disgraceful will be pernicious."[83] Indeed, God's "wisdom" in His providence rewards the just and punishes the unjust, and with His "omnipotence" He executes His judgments.[84]

The conclusion of the passage as a whole is categorical: "The existence of a totally wise and powerful being, namely God, is the ultimate basis of the natural law [...]."[85] Far from being a mere postulate of practical reason, the existence of God—which can be demonstrated with "mathematical certainty"—and personal immortality are metaphysical requirements of the universal order on which natural law depends. Veiled criticism—to be made more explicit later[86]—of Grotius's proposal of a natural sustainable *etiam si nullus esset Deus* may be discerned in this passage.

---

[80] A, VI, 1, 344.

[81] Ibid.

[82] "Ex hoc fundamento, ne se ipso quidem abuti licet, quia nos ipsimet sumus Dei, cui omnipotentia tribuit Jus in omnia. Hinc illud praeceptum: *Honestè vivere.*" Ibid.

[83] Ibid. Note the clear parallel with the *Méditation*, Mollat, 61-62: "[...] la justice est quelque chose de coïncident avec le bon plaisir de Dieu et que jamais il ne peut arriver un divorce entre l'honnête el l'utile."

[84] "Quia Deum justis praemia, injustis poenas destinâsse ex ejus sapientia constat: Et quae destinavit perfecturum omnipotentia ratio evincit." A, VI, 1, 344.

[85] Ibid., 344-345.

[86] See Ibid., 431.

Thus, it is eminently clear that the voluntarist potential of Thrasymachus's definition has been neutralized by its absorption into the Platonic definition of justice as "public utility,"[87] which reconciles individual virtue with the universal good. If the will and power of God are the measure of law, it is because they make the norms of an infinite wisdom which precedes them and is their ground effective in the world; they compensate for the elements of disorder by redirecting them to the "beauty" and "harmony" of the whole. The metaphysical path traced here receives its definitive confirmation a short time later in the *Elementa juris naturalis* (1669-1671), where Leibniz makes explicit the idea of "universal harmony" —"diversity compensated with identity"—as the norm of the divine justice,[88] by virtue of which rational creatures, as "mirrors" of the divine harmony,[89] are the object of a special providence.[90] By introducing modal concepts (*modalia juris*)[91] in this work, Leibniz arrives at a conceptual framework that enables him to provide a systematic foundation for the "universal harmony," setting it in the Absolute Understanding as the "see" of the infinite combinations among possible essences.

---

[87] The very same transformation is carried out in the final place where Leibniz subscribes to Thrasymachus's definition. There, the common good of the universe is also the rule of the will and power of God: "Quod universo utile, id Deus vult. Quod Deus vult, id omnipotens vult. Omnipotens habet ius in omnia, *per demonstrata Hobbesii in Elementis de cive*. Quod is vult, qui in omnia jus habet, id justum est." *Specimen demonstrationum politicarum* (1669), A, IV, 1, 10. Also: "*Utilissimum* cuiqve est, quod Deo gratissimum. [...] Deo autem *gratissimum* est, qvicqvid facit ad perfectionem universi. Ad perfectionem universi facit, qvicqvid facit ad perfectionem generis humani, [...]. Perfectio humani generis in eo consistit, ut sit qvoad eius fieri potest et sapientissimum et potentissimum." *Societas philadelphica* (1669?), A, VI, 1, 552-553.

[88] "DEUS justus est, etsi nullas harum regularum observet, [...] habet enim aliud principium harmoniam universalem." Ibid., 434.

[89] "Unde DEI sapientia exigebat Creaturas rationales, in qvibus res se multiplicarent. Ut una mens esset qvasi mundus qvidam in speculo, aut dioptra, vel qvolibet puncto radiorum visualium colectivo." Ibid., 438.

[90] "De DEO admirabile est, qvod solus nulla cautione indiget, sed cavet nobis ipsa natura sua. Cùm enim sapiens velit, et omnipotens possit nos, si velimus, facere felices." Ibid., 444.

[91] See Ibid., 465 ff.

Conclusion

The purpose of this article has been to reaffirm the thesis of continuity already defended by many other authors, rather than to advance a novel interpretation of Leibniz's theory of natural law. That Leibniz modified various partial aspects of his conception of law and justice, in particular during the first years of his philosophical project, is undeniable. However, there is a fundamental continuity at the metaphysical core of his argument, which is reflected in the progressive clarification of certain principles implicit from the beginning.

The focus has been on showing the weakness of the thesis which suggests the existence of a radical change in Leibniz's thought around 1670, from a position of extreme voluntarism to its extreme intellectualist opposite. In my view, this mistaken interpretation originates in a misapplication of the opinion that Leibniz held about Thrasymachus's definition many years later to his early works. Since Leibniz, in his maturity, judged this definition to be tyrannical and voluntarist, it is concluded that he had always thought it to be so and simply changed his judgment of this definition from positive to negative. On the basis of this equivocal reading, a global interpretation of Leibniz's first works is developed *a posteriori*, emphasizing all the expressions that might be cognate with a voluntarist interpretation, and ignoring the explicit references to divine wisdom and universal harmony.

Nevertheless, the fact that Leibniz rejected Thrasymachus's definition later in his philosophical career does not mean that he regarded it as essentially voluntaristic during the period when he held to it. This is a typical approach used by Leibniz as he developed his philosophy through continuous dialogue: adopting as his own the formulations of others, and redefining their contents in order to reconcile them with his own system.[92] All the evidence implies that in this early stage of development in his thought Leibniz intended to rescue Thrasymachus's definition in a non-voluntaristic sense; and that, later on, he became progressively aware of the impossibility of saving this definition.[93] Several reasons may be given

[92] "Nè può stupirci il ritrovare, nei casi sopra citati, quello que è un método comunissimo nel Leibniz: il riprendere da altri una proposizione e, lasciandone aparentemente intata la forma, svilupparla, dándole un senso affato nuovo e talora rovesciato." V. Mathieu in Leibniz, *Scriti politici e di diritto naturale*, 18-19.

[93] In his revisions to the *Nova methodus* after 1690, Leibniz corrected only the "formula" of Thrasymachus, without modifying the content of the passage: "Z. 11 D: [Tertium Juris] principium est Bonum generale ejusque custus Deus praebet.

to explain why, over the years, Leibniz took an even more hostile position towards Thrasymachus's definition;[94] on the other hand, a fundamental weak point in the thesis of an early voluntarism consists in the absence of sufficient and significant reasons for explaining why such a profound change would have occurred in Leibniz's thought in the years around 1670. As V. Mathieu states: "*Leibnitius non facit saltus.*"[95]

Leibniz's philosophical speculation has a primary object which orients and internally configures the system in all of its determinations as its central axis. This keystone or *leitmotiv* of his philosophy is a totalizing ontological principle (which is therefore, at the same time, theological, ethical and gnoseological) that "makes possible all being and thought"[96]: universal harmony. From this, it follows that understanding Leibniz's philosophy "harmoniouslly" and centring our attention on the points of continuity is the infallible hermeneutic principle that enables an understanding of his system, in relation to both its historical development and its internal unity.

Works Cited

Aceti, Guido. "Jakob Thomasius ed il pensiero filosofico-giuridico di Godoffredo Guglielmo Leibniz." *Jus. Rivista di scienze giuridiche* 8 (1957): 259-319.

—. "Sulla 'Nova Methodus discendae docendaque jurisprudentiae' di Leibniz." *Jus. Rivista di scienze giuridiche* 8 (1957): 1-41.

Antognazza, Maria Rosa. "Debilissimae Entitates? Bisterfeld and Leibniz's Ontology of Relations." *The Leibniz Review* 11 (2001): 1-13.

—. "Immeatio and Emperichoresis. The Theological Roots of Harmony in Bisterfeld and Leibniz." In *The Young Leibniz and His Philosophy*, edited by Stuart Brown. Dordrecht, Boston, London: Kluwer, 1999.

Aquinas, Thomas. *Summa Theologiae*.

Beeley, Philip. "Right Reason and Natural Law in Hobbes and Leibniz." *Synthesis philosophica* 24 (1997): 445-59.

Eqvidem Thrasimacus. Z. 12 D: Justum esse qvod potentiori convenit." A, VI, 1, 344.

[94] V. Mathieu—in Leibniz, *Scriti politici e di diritto naturale*, 19-20—attributes the harshness of Leibniz's judgment concerning Thrasymachus's definition in the *Méditation* to his growing dissension from the voluntarism sustained by Coccej, Groening and Pufendorf.

[95] Ibid., 19.

[96] Werner Schneiders, "Harmonia universalis," *Studia Leibnitiana* 16 (1984): 44.

Blank, Andreas. "Leibniz on Justice as a Common Concept: A Rejoinder to Patrick Riley." *The Leibniz Review* 16 (2006): 205-14.

Busche, Hubertus. *Leibniz' Weg ins perspektivische Universum. Eine Harmonie im Zeitalter der Berechnung*. Hamburg: Meiner, 1997.

Couturat, Louis. *La logique de Leibniz, d'après des documents inédits*. Paris: Alcan, 1901.

Gardies, Jean-Louis. "La rationalité du droit chez Leibniz." *Archives de Philosophie du Droit* 23 (1978): 115-29.

Goyard-Fabre, Simone. "La Jurisprudence Universelle selon Leibniz." In *Perspectives sur Leibniz*, edited by Renée Bouveresse, 133-49. Paris: Vrin, 1999.

Grua, Gaston. *Jurisprudence universelle et Théodicée selon Leibniz*. Paris: PUF, 1953.

—. *La justice humaine selon Leibniz*. Paris: PUF, 1956.

—. "Optimisme et piété leibnizienne avant 1686, avec des textes inédits." *Revue Philosophique de la France et de l'Étranger* 37 (1946): 410-28.

Guhrauer, Gottschalk. *Gottfried Wilhelm Freiherr von Leibniz, Eine Biographie*. Breslau, 1842.

Heinekamp, Albert. *Das Problem des Guten bei Leibniz, Kantstudien Ergänzungshefte* Bonn: Bouvier, 1969.

Hobbes, Thomas. *Critique du "De mundo" de Thomas White*. Edited by Jean Jacquot and Harold Whitmore Jones. Paris: Vrin, 1973.

—. *Opera philosophica quae latina scripsit omnia in unum corpus nunc primum collecta* (London, 1839-1845). Edited by William Molesworth. Aalen, 1961.

Hobbes, Thomas, and G. W. Leibniz. *Thomas Hobbes, A Dialogue between a Philosopher and a Student of the Common Laws of England - G. W. Leibniz, Specimen quaestionum philosophicarum ex iure collectarum. De casibus perplexis. Doctrina conditionum. De legume interpretatione*. Edited by Tullio Ascarelli. Milano Giufrè, 1960.

Kabitz, Willy. *Die Philospohie des jungen Leibniz. Untersuchungen zur Entwicklungsgeschichte seines Systems*. Heidelberg: Carl Winter, 1909.

Leibniz, G. W. *Gothofredi Guillelmi Leibnitii, Opera omnia, nunc prima collecta,* vols. I-VI. Edited by L. Dutens. I-VI vols. Geneva, 1768.

—. *Mittheilungen aus Leibnizens ungedruckten Schriften*. Edited by Georg Mollat. Leipzig: Haessel, 1893.

—. *Philosophical Papers and Letters*. Edited by Leroy E. Loemker. Dordrecht: Reidel, 1969.

—. *The Political Writings of Leibniz*. Edited by Patrick Riley. Cambridge: Cambridge University Press, 1972.

—. *Scriti politici e di diritto naturale*. Edited by Vittorio Mathieu. Torino: Unione Tipografico-Editrice Torinese, 1951.

—. *Sämtliche Schriften und Briefe*, series I-VII. Edited by Preussische (later: Deutsche) Akademie der Wissenschaften zu Berlin. Darmstad (later: Leipzig; now: Berlin), 1923 ff.

Loemker, Leroy E. "Leibniz and the Herborn Encyclopedists." *Journal of the History of Ideas* 22 (1961): 323-38.

Mercer, Christia. "Leibniz and His Master: The Correspondence with Jakob Thomasius." In *Leibniz and His Correspondents*, edited by Paul Lodge. Cambridge: Cambridge University Press, 2004.

—. *Leibniz's Metaphysics. Its Origins and Development*. Cambridge: Cambridge University Press, 2001.

Mormino, Gianfranco. "La teodicea antimetafisica del giovane Leibniz." *Rivista di Storia della Filosofia* 58 (2003): 45-75.

Mugnai, Massimo. "Der Begriff der Harmonie als metaphysische Grundlage der Logik und Kombinatorik bei Johann Heinrich Bisterfeld und Leibniz." *Studia Leibnitiana* 5 (1973): 43-73.

Mulvaney, Robert J. "The Early Development of Leibniz's Concept of Justice." *Journal of the History of the Ideas* 29 (1968): 53-72.

Naert, Émilianne. *La pensée politique de Leibniz*. Paris: PUF, 1964.

Piro, Francesco. "Jus-Justum-Justitia. Etica e diritto nel giovane Leibniz." *Annali dell'Istituto Italiano per gli Studi Storici* 7 (1987): 1-54.

Riley, P. "Leibniz's Meditation sur la notion commune de la justice: A Reply to Andreas Blank." *The Leibniz Review* 15 (2003): 185-216.

—. "Leibniz's Méditation sur la notion commune de la justice, 1703-2003." *The Leibniz Review* 13 (2003): 67-78.

—. *Leibniz's Universal Jurisprudence. Justice as the Charity of the Wise*. Cambridge, London: Harvard University Press, 1996.

Robinet, André. *Le meilleur des mondes par la balance de l'Europe*. Paris: PUF, 1994.

—. "Loi naturelle et loi positive dans l'arquitectonique archaïque de l'ouvre de Leibniz." In *La notion de nature chez Leibniz*, edited by Martine de Gaudemar. Stuttgart: Franz Steiner Verlag, 1995.

Röd, Wolfgang. *Geometrischer Geist und Naturrecht. Methodengeschichte Untersuchungen zur Staatsphilosophie im 17. Und 18. Jahrhundert*. München: Bayerische Akademie der Wissenschaften, 1970.

Ross, George MacDonald. "Leibniz's Debt to Hobbes." In *Leibniz and the English-speaking World*, edited by Pauline Phemister and Stuart Brown, 19-33. Dordrecht: Springer, 2007, 2007.

Ruck, Erwin. *Die Leibniz'sche Staatsidee*. Tübingen: Mohr, 1909.

Schiedermair, Hartmut. *Das Phänomen der Macht und die Idee des Rechts bei Gottfried Wilhelm Leibniz, Studia Leibnitiana. Supplementa.* Wiesbaden: Franz Steiner Verlag, 1970.

Schneider, Hans-Peter. *Justitia Universalis. Quellenstudien zur Geschichte des "Christlichen Naturrrechts" bei Gottfried Wilhelm Leibniz.* Frankfurt am Main: Klostermann, 1967.

Schneiders, Werner. "Harmonia universalis." *Studia Leibnitiana* 16 (1984): 27-44.

—. "Leibniz und die Frage nach dem Grund des Guten und Gerechten." *Studia Leibnitiana. Supplementa* 4 (1969): 85-111.

—. "Naturrecht und Gerechtigkeit bei Leibniz." *Zeitschrift für philosophische Forschung* 20 (1996): 607-50.

—. "Respublica optima. Zur metaphysischen und moralischen Fundierung der Politik bei Leibniz." *Studia Leibnitiana* 9 (1977): 1-26.

Sève, Rene. *Leibniz et l'école moderne du droit naturel*. Paris: PUF, 1989.

Solari, Gioele. "Metafisica e diritto in Leibniz." *Rivista di Filosofia* 38 (1947): 35-65.

Tommasi, Claudio. *La ragione prudente. Pace e riordino dell'Europa moderna nel pensiero di Leibniz*. Il Mulino: Bologna, 2006.

Tönnies, Ferdinand. "Leibniz und Hobbes." *Philosophische Monatshefte* 23 (1987): 557-73.

Vasoli, Cesare. "Enciclopedismo, pansofia e riforma 'metodica' del diritto nella "Nova methodus" di Leibniz." *Quaderni Fiorentini per la storia del pensiero giuridico moderno* 2 (1973): 37-107.

Welzel, Hans. *Naturrecht und materiale Gerechtigkeit.* Göttingen: Vandenhoeck & Ruprecht, 1962.

Zarka, Charles Yves. "Le droit naturel selon Leibniz." In *La notion de nature*, edited by Martine de Gaudemar, 181-92. Stuttgart: Franz Steiner Verlag, 1995.

Zimmermann, Robert. *Das Rechtprinzip bei Leibniz. Ein Beitrag zur Geschichte der Rechtphilosophie*. Wien: Braumüller, 1852.

CHAPTER TEN

EDMUND BURKE AND THE NATURAL LAW

IVONE MOREIRA

One very prominent way of interpreting Edmund Burke's thought is to take his criticism of the abstract Rights of Man as a criticism of and distancing from natural law. Such interpretations also read Burke's remarks about the necessity of prudence in political decision-making—for he often criticised the straightforward application of abstract principles of government or claims of human abstract rights—as though he were merely advocating utilitarian principles.[1] Contrarily of those of Burke's interpreters who read him as a utilitarian, there are other who, in various ways, ally his thoughts to natural law, although not always to the same kind of natural law or to the same aspects of it.[2] In this paper we will follow our own way in order to decide which we find to be more plausible.[3]

---

[1] This interpretation of Burke's thought appeared first in Buckle's *The History of Civilization in England* and later, at the end of the 19th Century, was more forcefully put forth in John Morley's first book about Burke: *Edmund Burke- A Historical Study*. Morley consolidated the utilitarian interpretation of Burke's work, which proved to be very influential, and Burke continued to be portrayed as a utilitarian in the work of many writers, such as William Lecky, Charles Vaughan, George Sabine, Plamenatz, and, in a certain way, F. P. Lock among others.

[2] This group include authors such as Peter Stanlis, Russel Kirk, Strauss, Francis Canavan, Harvey Mansfield, Burleigh Wilkins, Michel Ganzin, Joseph Pappin and Norbert Col, among others.

[3] Wilkins observes that Burke's interpretation has been a function of the dominant ideologies of different periods: "In the nineteenth and early twentieth centuries when utilitarianism was a vital force Burke was depicted as being by and large a utilitarian and a foe of the natural law; more recently, in conjunction with the revival of interest in the natural law, there has emerged a much revised portrait of Burke in which he now figures as a foe of utilitarianism and a champion of the natural law". B. T. Wilkins, *The Problem of Burke's Political Philosophy* (Oxford:

One of the most well-justified utilitarian interpretations of Burke is that of John Plamenatz. In the mid 20th century, at the end of the 1940s, in his book *English Utilitarians,* Plamenatz states that Burke's utilitarian leanings can be identified in three fundamental aspects of this thought:

a) First, in the fact that he only endorses moderate and cautious reform, arguing that the prolonged existence institutions shows them to have successfully resisted the forces of disintegration that touch all human institutions, and thus proves their utility and their capacity to bring about happiness;[4]

b) Second, in his argument in favour of prescription: one of the most heartfelt experiences of man are his hopes; all men hope to maintain their property, and the longer they have had this property, the greater their frustration will be should they loose it. Aside from this, the expectation of preserving something that one already has is even stronger than the enthusiasm for acquiring something new;[5]

c) Third and finally, in his defence of prejudice. Plamenatz maintains that prejudice derives from the former aspect of this thought: that which values prescription, for no possession is as important to man as his convictions. According to Plamenatz, all of the great prejudices upon which Burke places the stability of society are, for him, verifiable and can be shown to be true. They are useful and provide comfort precisely because they are true. Because moral laws and religions were for so long the patrimony of humanity, to criticise them cannot be good, since they cannot be improved, and Burke sees it as dangerous to put this matter to the test.[6]

It is appropriate, at this point, to introduce some reservations to Plamenatz's utilitarian classification of Burke. Burke esteems institutions that prove their quality and operability by withstanding the disintegrating forces of time not only because this is the easiest way to keep men happy, but because these institutions have in their favour the fact that they were constructed upon ample wisdom, which has belonged to society

---

Clarendon Press, 1967), 12. This interpretation of Burke's studies is very accurate to explain the intellectual dominion of the utilitarian interpretation for nearly a century and the emergence of the later significant current that interprets his thought as founded on natural law. But nowadays we can find both interpretations, and the fact that both find arguments in its favour on the texts of Burke, justifies the actuality of the debate.

[4] John Plamenatz, *The English Utilitarians* (Oxford: Basil Blackwell, 1949), 56.

[5] Ibid., 56-57.

[6] Ibid., 57-58.

throughout the course of many generations and which has been perfected as they confronted various difficulties over time. It is for this reason, that they can make men happy and can have a much more enlarged meaning for society, allowing for its development, and being a guarantee of its improvement. That's why Burke, with a humble and prudent attitude, values them. If a utilitarian can defend these ancient institutions, then so can a wise, humble and prudent man who esteemed the values that these institutions were able to defend.

Burke's criticism of Jacobinism and his view that Jacobins were designing reality as French gardeners design their gardens,[7] are clearly aimed at the Jacobin audacity and the way in which they considered their individual decisions and knowledge to be superior to those of others, especially to that knowledge which has been crystallised in the creations of society throughout time. In his criticism, Burke often emphasises this arrogant preference for individual and abstract knowledge, contrasting it with the wisdom of time and of generations.

As for Plamenatz's second argument about prescription, Burke considers property to be at the base of a society's constitution, and government to exist precisely for its protection. One facet of property is learning how to acquire and to defend it and, connected to this, being able to continue refining nature and to perfecting society. Up until here, utilitarians could use this argument too. However, Burke's prescription does not concern property only, but is also a protection to people, being a security against despotic government[8]:

> The strong struggle in every individual to preserve possession of what he has found to belong to him (...) is one of the securities against injustice and despotism implanted in our nature.[9]

This possession of property naturally and organically produces a ruling class, an aristocracy, "a true natural aristocracy is not a separate interest in

---

[7] Edmund Burke, *Reflections on the Revolution in France, The Works of the Right Honorable Edmund Burke*, vol. III (Boston: Little, Brown, and Company, 1865), 461.

[8] A very good analysis of Burke's prescription can be read in Francis Canavan, *Edmund Burke: Prescription and Providence* (Durham, N.C.: Carolina Academic Press and The Claremont Institute for the Study of Statesmanship and Political Philosophy, 1987)., specially pages 113 to 135. Canavan held that 'prescription (...) gave 'right and title' not only to real property, but to inherited liberties, religion, and political authority", p. 115.

[9] Burke, *Reflections*, 415.

the state or separable from it."[10] Now, says Burke, do not think that this aristocracy is only that of birth, name and titles; Burke in fact was a critic of feudal aristocracy, and maintained that the only qualifications for government were moral ones. The aristocracy who matters here would thus be a moral aristocracy. His preoccupation with the consolidation of society is also a preoccupation with the survival and perfection of its moral heritage, which is what man creates with the patrimony of a nature capable of virtue that has been given to him by God and in which God has inscribed His laws.

So, the defence of prescription is much more than a defence of property, because with property, comes government, and with government comes the stability of society which is a vital condition for moral progress. The concern showed by Burke with prescription is not merely about the frustration of loosing property for a long time in our hands; rather, it is a much more enlarged concept of *property*—the moral one—which is at risk of being lost when people don't respect prescription.

As for the third argument, the defence of prejudice, we think that any utility that prejudice may have is only one of the reasons for its preservation, and we do not identify Burke's defence of prejudice as much with its material utility as with his prudential and humble attitude. We also think that prejudice is far from having been "proved" by Burke, as Plamenatz has argued. Just Prejudice, as Burke calls it, is seen as a crystallisation of a kind of knowledge that is not entirely understood by, or even entirely intelligible for, the present generation. *Just prejudice* gives to reason a reason and motive to act more readily in harmony with the knowledge that has been accumulated by generations. In this way, it is a sort of shortcut for practical reason.[11]

---

[10] ———, *Appeal from the New to the Old Whigs, The Works of the Right Honorable Edmund Burke*, vol. IV (Boston: Little, Brown, and Company, 1866), 175.

[11] "In this enlightened age I am bold enough to confess that we are generally man of untaught feelings: that, instead of casting away all our old prejudices, we cherish them because to a very considerable degree; and to take more shame to ourselves, we cherish them because they are prejudices; and the longer they have lasted, and the more generally they have prevailed, the more we cherish them. We are afraid to put man to live and trade each on his own private stock of reason; because we suspect that the stock in each men is small, and that the individuals would do better to avail themselves of the general bank and capital of nations and ages (...) Prejudice is of ready application in the emergency; it previously engages the mind in a steady course of wisdom and virtue, and does not leave the man

The prudential attitude, which Burke espoused, endorsed various practical recommendations, and it is necessary to qualify and discern between a criteria of operability, and a attitude which give privilege to the application of purely utilitarian principles. The application of the prudential attitude requires that the happiness of the governed and the utility of the measures under consideration be taken into account. This can also be a test for a political measure that is being tried out if its application turns out to be successful. However, the principle that underlies the prudential decision is not necessarily that of the happiness of the governed, although it is certainly that of their good, or their *happiness* while living according to virtue. As regards the application of utilitarian principles, by applying the precept of "the greater happiness for the greatest number", the very principle that will underlie the decision will be the happiness of the majority and the utility of the means adopted to serve this end. The problem here is defining the kind of happiness and the kind of utility that we are dealing with. If, as in the Aristotelian tradition, happiness is identified with wisdom, and utility is what best becomes a certain order, then there would be nothing to fear in this principle, and utility would be transfigured into intrinsic goodness. But it is not clear that this is the meaning which utilitarians give to the "greatest happiness for the greatest number", or to utility.

With these distinctions in mind, we would like to analyse a few aspects of Burke's thought, trying to identify the principles he consider should govern practical politics, and bearing in mind his own political battles, the principles he defended in them and the extent to which he was or was not attached to Cicero's and Aquinas's conceptions of natural law.[12] With this aim, we will gather some of Burke's observations about the nature of the law, the condition of government and the correlate nature of political power, and we will analyse these observations.

---

hesitating in the moment of decision, skeptical, puzzled, and unresolved." ———, *Reflections*, 346-47.

[12] On the one hand the choice of Cicero and Aquinas comes from the fact that Burke explicitly refers to Cicero, on the other hand, because we have found a great similarity between St. Thomas's conception of natural law and the same conception on Burke.

Of the nature of the law and the discrimination and hierarchy of its principles

In this section we have chosen aspects in which prudential attitudes and the defence of principles can both be found:

> All human laws are, properly speaking, only declaratory; they may alter the mode and application, but have no power over the substance of original justice. The other foundation of law, which is utility, must be understood not of partial or limited, but of general and public utility, connected in the same manner with, and derived directly from, our rational nature: for any other utility may be the utility of a robber, but cannot be that of a citizen; the interest of the domestic enemy, and not of a member of the commonwealth.[13]

We can see here that all human laws have, as one of their principles, the substance of original justice and that its role is only declaratory. We can also see that the other guiding point of the law, utility, is a general kind of utility but, as we can attest, the first allegiance of law is its connection to that which Burke calls original justice and, more importantly still, this utility is a utility derived from our rational nature and connected to it. If we bear in mind that Burke considered humanity to be a rational nature[14] and human society to be destined to develop that very nature, we can understand how the utility of the law can be the strengthening of this rational dimension, which is necessary for complete human accomplishment.

> They have no right to make a law prejudicial to the whole community, even thought the delinquents in making such an act should be themselves the chief sufferers by it; because it would be made against the principle of a superior law, which it is not in the power of a community, or the whole human race to alter; I mean the will of Him who gave us our nature, and in giving impressed an invariable law upon it. It would be hard to point out any error more truly subversive of all the order and beauty of all the peace

[13] ———, *Tract on the Popery Laws, The Works of the Right Honorable Edmund Burke*, vol. IV (Boston, Little, Brown, and Company, 1866), 323.

[14] Though Burke admits that the rational dimension of the human nature is not the only one we should consider he says also: "The state of civil society (...) is a state of Nature, - and much more truly so than a savage and incoherent mode of life. For man is by nature reasonable; and he is never perfectly in his natural state, but when he is placed where reason may be best cultivated and most predominates. Art is mans nature" ———, *Appeal from the New to the Old Whigs*, 176.

> and happiness of human society, than the position, that any body of men have a right to make what laws they please. (...) Cicero exclaims with the utmost indignation and contempt against such a notion (...) [*De Legibus* I, XIV, XV, XVI] [15]

We can get a better understanding of what he means by the concept of Law by referring to the context from which Burke took this Cicero's quote:

> "those of us who are not influenced by virtue itself to be good men, but by some consideration of utility and profit, are merely shrewd, not good. For to what lengths will that man go who fears nothing but a witness and a judge? What will he do if, in some desolate spot, he meets a helpless man, unattended, whom he can robe of a fortune? Our virtuous man, who is just and good by nature, will talk with such a person, help him, and guide him on his way (…) But if the principles of justice were founded on the decrees of peoples, the edicts of princes, or the decisions of judges, then Justice would sanction robbery and adultery and forgery of wills, in case these acts were approved by the votes or decrees of the populace. But if so great a power belongs to the decision and decrees of fools that the laws of Nature can be changed by their votes, then why do they not ordain that what is bad and baneful shall be considered good and salutary?(…) But in fact we can perceive the difference between good laws and bad by referring them to no other standard than nature."[16]

For Burke too, what he is concerned with in the above observation on the law is not only the consequences of such a law and its arguable utility; it is primarily that this law meets the primordial requisites that it needs to

---

15 ———, *Tract on the Popery Laws*, 322-23.

16 'Tum autem, qui non ipso honesto movemur ut boni viri simus, sed utilitate aliqua atque fructu, callidi sumus, non boni; nam quid faciet is homo in tenebris, qui nihil timet nisi testem et iudicem? quid in deserto loco nactus, quem multo auro spoliare possit, imbecillum atque solum? noster quidem hic natura iustus vir ac bonus, etiam conloquetur, iuvabit, in viam deducet; (...) quodsi populorum iussis, si principum decretis, si sententiis iudicum iura constituerentur, ius esset latrocinari, ius adulterare, ius testamenta falsa supponere, si haec suffragiis aut scitis multitudinis probarentur. quae si tanta potestas est stultorum sententiis atque iussis, ut eorum suffragiis rerum natura vertatur, cur non sanciunt, ut, quae mala perniciosaque sunt, habeantur pro bonis et salutaribus? (...) atqui nos legem bonam a mala nulla alia nisi naturae norma dividere possumus'. Cicero, *De Re Publica, De Legibus*, trans. C.W. Keyes, The Loeb Classical Library (London/Cambridge: William Heinemann/Harvard University Press, 1959), L. I, XIV and XVI, pp. 342-6.

be called law, which is to be in accordance with the principles of a superior law: the will of God impressed on our nature in our creation, and later recognised by human reason.

> We are all born—high as well as low—governors as well as governed in subjection to one great, immutable, pre-existing law, a law prior to all our devices and all our conspiracies, paramount to our feelings, by which we are connected in the eternal frame of the universe, and out of which we cannot stir. This great law does not arise from our combinations and compacts: on the contrary, it gives to them all the sanction they can have.[17]

Still in agreement with Cicero, this definition of the law that Burke formulates in the *Impeachment of Warren Hastings* explains the type of subordination that all of us, without exception, have in relation to this law. He also explains the reason why it serves as a pattern: it is eternal law, prior to all formulations derived from it and invented by us, and it is it—eternal law—that sanctions us in our use of law.

Of the competency of the Governor and the nature of political power

This concept of law that Burke upholds has implications for his concept of what it means to be a governor and of what power must be in order to be legitimate. Burke maintains that human nature, because it is a rational nature, is only fully realised in society. God, who created it like this, did not spare man any of the means for him to be able to realise himself. It is thus clear that God wanted political society, and that all power comes from God:

> Every good and perfect gift is of God: all power is of God; and He who has given the power, and from whom alone it originates, will never suffer it to be corrupted.[18]

Thus, the governors must be aware that the authority they use is entrusted to them by delegation and that they have to be accountable to it:

---

[17] ———, "Impeachment of Warren Hastings", 16 February, 1788, in: Edmund Burke, *Speeches of the Right Honourable Edmund Burke in the House of Commons and in Westminster Hall*, vol. IV (London/Longman: Hurst/Rees, Orme and Brown, 1816), 358.

[18] Ibid.

> All persons possessing any portion of power ought to be strongly and awfully impressed with an idea that they act in trust, and that they are to account for their conduct on that trust to the one great Master, Author and Founder of Society.[19]

And it is thus that according to Burke, the principles that govern politics are, as he himself says, those of morality. History and circumstances teach us prudence, but not principles: "History is a preceptor of prudence, not of principles. The principles of true politics are those of morality enlarged, and I neither now do or ever will admit of any other"[20] and, later, "I (...) declare therefore (...) that the laws of morality are the same everywhere."[21] Nonetheless, history and circumstances are preceptors of prudence to be applied to each concrete case. "But as no moral questions are ever abstract questions, this, before I judge upon any abstract proposition must be embodied in circumstances,"[22] it is by this same connection to circumstances that he also affirms that:

> Nothing universal can be rationally affirmed on any moral or any political subject. Pure metaphysical abstraction does not belong to those matters. The lines of morality are not like the ideal lines of mathematics they are broad and deep as well as long. They admit of exceptions; they demand modifications: These exceptions and modifications are not made by the process of logic but by the rules of prudence.[23]

This proposition, which seems to be in clear contradiction to the universal principles of morality he mentioned before, is often used by critics of Burke in order to illustrate his utilitarianism. However, we interpret the above quote as being concerned with the impossibility of formulating an abstract proposition, which follows from the logical use of reason, trying to synthesise the understanding of the same types of moral issues into a universal formula, or into a derived principle that would have universal application. For circumstances are fundamental in the classification of every moral issue, such that all issues cannot all be encapsulated by one universal category. It is because of this that moral deliberations were entrusted to prudence. We understand that it is not the

---

[19] Burke, *Reflections*, 354.

[20] ———, *The Correspondence of Edmund Burke*, vol. II (Cambridge/Chicago: University of Chicago Press, 1958-1978), 282.

[21] ———, *Speeches*, vol. IV, 354.

[22] Ibid., 66.

[23] Burke, *Appeal from the New to the Old Whigs*, 80-81.

existence of universal moral principles that is being questioned here, but instead the possibility of universally "cataloguing" moral *issues*. We could run the risk of raising the objection that, if this were truth, moral laws would not be used to apply to facts, but this is not the issue; the problem is that the uniqueness and complexity of a fact means that various laws of morality should be applied to it, and that it is necessary to prudently determine how to apply them.

If we compare the Burke's statements with those of Aquinas in S.T. I-II, Question 94, Art 4 we see an undeniable similarity[24]:

> The process of reason is from the common to the proper, as stated in Phys. i. The speculative reason, however, is differently situated in this matter, from the practical reason. For, since the speculative reason is busied chiefly with the necessary things, which cannot be otherwise than they are, its proper conclusions, like the universal principles, contain the truth without fail. The practical reason, on the other hand, is busied with contingent matters, about which human actions are concerned: and consequently, although there is necessity in the general principles, the more we descend to matters of detail, the more frequently we encounter defects. Accordingly then in speculative matters truth is the same in all men, both as to principles and as to conclusions (…) But in matters of action, truth or practical rectitude is not the same for all, as to matters of detail, but only as to the general principles: and where there is the same rectitude in matters of detail, it is not equally known to all.[25]

---

[24] As far as we know, there isn't any direct reference to St. Thomas on the texts of Burke, and the sales Catalogue of his library doesn't include works of Aquinas. But it is almost sure that he had indirectly been in contact with the philosophy of Aquinas. Father Canavan, this time on an appendices to his book, *The Political Reason of Edmund Burke,* has done an excellent job of studying the text books that were in use at Trinity College when Burke studied there. From this investigation he arrived to the conclusion that Burke had studied at Trinity authors that were, in varying degrees, representative of the scholastic tradition, such as: Burgersdijck, Smiglecki, Baron, Eustache de St. Paul, and Sanderson. Francis Canavan, *The Political Reason of Edmund Burke* (Durham, N.C.: Duke University Press, 1960), 202. Sir Ernest Barker thought that Burke always had been a Thomist "even if unconsciously". Cf. Ernest Barker, *Essays on Government* (Oxford: Clarendon Press, 1946), 222.

[25] "Ad rationem autem pertinet ex communibus ad propria procedere, ut patet ex I *Physic*.. Aliter tamen circa hoc se habet ratio speculativa, et aliter ratio practica. Quia enim ratio speculativa praecipue negociatur circa necessaria, quae impossibile est aliter se habere, absque aliquo defectu invenitur veritas in conclusionibus propriis, sicut et in principiis communibus. Sed ratio practica negociatur circa contingentia, in quibus sunt operationes humanae: et ideo etsi in

In order to demonstrate the similarity between Burke and Aquinas on this particular point, we will present another statement which help us to prove it: on one hand, it shows the repeated awareness that concrete moral issues are governed by prudence in the application of the principles that become them and, on the other hand, it also demonstrates Burke's recognition of the existence of a general moral necessities in all things. His refusal is not of the universal law, and its necessity, but of its abstract applicability to moral issues, without tending to their specificities:

> as human affairs and human actions are not of a metaphysical nature, but the subject is concrete, complex, and moral, they cannot be subjected (without exceptions which reduce it almost to nothing) to any certain rule (...) such is the genius of the law of England, that these two principles, of the general moral necessities of things, and the nature of the case, overrule every other principle.[26]

The advantage that Burke sees in the Common Law is precisely that it can unite two fundamental principles and superimpose them upon any others: the principle of general moral necessity, and the regulation of its application by attending to the nature of each particular subject.

Of Government

To conclude we shall look at how Burke envisioned government:

> He had arbitrary power! My lords, the East India Company have not arbitrary power to give him. The King has no arbitrary power to give him. Neither your Lordships, nor the Commons, nor the whole legislature, have arbitrary power to give. Arbitrary power is a thing which no man can give. My Lords no man can govern himself by his own will; much less can he be governed by the will of others.[27]

---

communibus sit aliqua necessitas, quanto magis invenitur defectus. Sic igitur in speculativis est eadem veritas apud omnes tam in principiis quam in conclusionibus (...) In operativis autem non est eadem veritas vel rectitudo practica apud omnes quantum ad propria, sed solum quantum ad communia : et apud illos apud quos est eadem rectitudo in propriis, non est aequaliter omnibus nota." Aquinatis, *Summa Theologiae* II, Prima Secundae, Quaestio XCIV, Articulus 4 (Roma: Marietti, 1950), 428; trans. the Fathers of the English Dominican Province (New York: Benzinger Bros., 1947), I-II, q. 94, a. 4 c.

[26] Burke, Speeches, vol. IV, 224, 235.

[27] Ibid., 357-58.

It is clear that we are governed by a will, and it is clear that this can be the will of another as long as this will is in accordance with the principles of the law:

> will you ever hear the rights of mankind made subservient to the practice of government? It will be your Lordships duty and joy; it will be your pride and triumph to teach men, that they are to conform their practice to principles, and not to drive their principles from the wicked, corrupt, and abominable practice of any man whatever.[28]

Burke criticised and negated the abstract concept of human rights, arguing that it is only possible for these rights to be claimed in political society. And because of this, in this society rights are circumscribed and not abstract. Claiming rights in the abstract, as though they issued from a state of nature prior to the creation of society, is attempting to reap the benefits of the state of political society as well as of the state of nature, and this is not possible. Which are the rights of humanity that the government cannot override? They are those which are consecrated by the scholastic tradition of natural law[29] conceptions, the blatant disrespect of which can un-root the government and society from their foundations:

> The rights of men—that is to say, the natural rights of mankind—are indeed sacred things; and if any public measure is proved mischievously to affect them, the objection ought to be fatal to that measure, even if no charter at all could be set up against it.(...) Indeed, this formal recognition, by the sovereign power, of an original right in the subject can never be subverted, but by rooting up the holding radical principles of government and even of society itself. [30]

Having read and examined these extracts from Burke's work it seems prudent to us not to accept as unequivocal the classification of Burke as a utilitarian and also that the interpretations that connect his thought to natural law are well justified.

---

[28] Ibid., 356-57.

[29] Burke refers to Suarez in his analysis of the criteria for the legitimacy of the law and for the confirmation of his statement that 'partiality and law are contradictory terms', Burke, *Tract on the Popery Laws*, 325.

[30] ———, Speeches, vol II, 409-10.

Works Cited

Aquinas, Thomas, *Summa Theologica,* (New York: Benzinger Bros., 1947)

Barker, Ernest. *Essays on Government*. Oxford: Clarendon Press, 1946.

Burke, Edmund. *Appeal from the New to the Old Whigs, the Works of the Right Honorable Edmund Burke*. Vol. IV. Boston: Little, Brown, and Company, 1866.

—. *The Correspondence of Edmund Burke*. Vol. II. Cambridge/Chicago: University of Chicago Press, 1958-1978.

—. *Reflections on the Revolution in France, the Works of the Right Honorable Edmund Burke*. Vol. III. Boston: Little, Brown, and Company, 1865.

—. *Speeches of the Right Honourable Edmund Burke in the House of Commons and in Westminster Hall*. Vol. IV. London/Longman: Hurst/Rees, Orme and Brown, 1816.

—. *Tract on the Popery Laws, the Works of the Right Honorable Edmund Burke*. Vol. VI. Boston: Little, Brown, and Company, 1866.

Canavan, Francis. *Edmund Burke: Prescription and Providence*. Durham, N.C.: Carolina Academic Press and The Claremont Institute for the Study of Statesmanship and Political Philosophy, 1987.

—. *The Political Reason of Edmund Burke*. Durham, N.C.: Duke University Press, 1960.

Cicero. *De Re Publica, De Legibus*. Translated by C.W. Keyes, The Loeb Classical Library. London/Cambridge: William Heinemann/Harvard University Press, 1959.

Plamenatz, John. *The English Utilitarians*. Oxford: Basil Blackwell, 1949.

Wilkins, B. T. *The Problem of Burke's Political Philosophy*. Oxford: Clarendon Press, 1967.

CHAPTER ELEVEN

KANT ON THE LAW OF NATURE AS THE TYPE OF MORAL LAW: ON THE "TYPIC OF THE FACULTY OF PURE PRACTICAL JUDGMENT" AND THE GOOD AS THE OBJECT OF PRACTICAL REASON

JOSÉ M. TORRALBA

1. Introduction. Natural law and natural right in Kant's philosophy

Kant is not remembered in the history of philosophy as a theorist of natural law. However, as some recent studies have shown, this fact need not inevitably prompt the conclusion that the concept of natural law is alien to Kantian philosophy, nor that Kant himself ignored the specific problems of iusnaturalism.[1] In my view, there are at least three areas in

---

* Publication of this article is part of the Research Project on "Practical Reason and the Social Sciences", Ministerio de Educación y Ciencia (Ref. HUM2006-07605/FISO).

Quotation from Kant's works —Immanuel Kant, *Kant's gesammelte Schriften*, ed. Akademie der Wissenschaften (Berlin: 1902 ff.)— follows the standard format: the Berlin Academy, volume and page number (for example: *KpV*, 5:69), with the exception of the *Critique of Pure Reason* —Immanuel Kant, *Kritik der reinen Vernunft*, ed. Jens Timmermann, nach der 1. und 2. Orig.-Ausg. ed. (Hamburg: Felix Meiner, 1998)—, cited by first (A) and second (B) editions, and the *Lecture on Ethics* —Immanuel Kant, *Vorlesung zur Moralphilosophie*, ed. Werner Stark (Berlin – New York: Walter de Gruyter, 2004)—, which reproduces the original page-numbering of Kaehler's manuscript. The following abbreviations have been adopted: *KrV* (*Critique of Pure Reason*), *KpV* (*Critique of Practical Reason*), *GMS* (*Groundwork of the Metaphysics of Morals*), *MS* (*The Metaphysics of Morals*) and

which the concepts and problems of (classical and modern) iusnaturalism as a whole play a key role in the Kantian ethical and juridical systems.

The first of these areas is the general framework that shapes Kantian ethics, which may only be understood in the context of the debates between intellectualists—such as Leibniz, Wolff and Baumgarten—and voluntarists—such as Pufendorf and Crusius—.[2] The key distinction between conditioned and absolute necessity,[3] on which the idea of the categorical imperative depends, is a valuable example in this regard; the distinction is rooted in Crusius's critique of the Wolffian idea of perfection.[4] The acknowledgement that the principles by which the will is

---

VzM (*Lecture on Ethics*). Unless otherwise stated, English translations are taken from Immanuel Kant, *Practical philosophy*, ed. Mary J. Gregor, trans. Mary J. Gregor (Cambridge: Cambridge University Press, 1996).

[1] See Alejandro G. Vigo, "Kant's Conception of Natural Right," in *Contemporary Perspectives on Natural Law. Natural Law as a Limiting Concept*, ed. Ana Marta González (Aldershot: Ashgate, 2008), 121-40.

[2] Schneewind's work on modern moral philosophy is an invaluable contribution to discussion of these questions. See Jerome B. Schneewind, "Pufendorf's Place in the History of Ethics," *Synthese* 72 (1987): 123-55; ———, "Kant and the Natural Law Ethics," *Ethics* 104 (1993). Schneewind, "Kant and the Natural Law Ethics," 53-74; ———, *The invention of autonomy. A history of modern moral philosophy* (Cambridge: Cambridge University Press, 1998). Henrich and Schmucker's studies of the origin and development of Kantian philosophy are also of fundamental significance. See Joseph Schmucker, *Die Ursprünge der Ethik Kants in seinen vorkritischen Schriften und Reflexionen* (Meisenheim: Hain, 1961); Dieter Henrich, "Der Begriff der sittlichen Einsicht und Kants Lehre vom Faktum der Vernunft," in *Die Gegenwart der Griechen im neueren Denken. Festschrift für Hans-Georg Gadamer zum 60. Geburtstag*, ed. D. Henrich, W. Schulz, and K.-H. Volkmann-Schluck (Tübingen: Mohr – Siebeck, 1960), 404-31; ———, "Über Kants früheste Ethik. Versuch einer Rekonstruktion," *Kant-Studien* 54 (1963): 404-31; ———, "Hutcheson und Kant," *Kant-Studien* 49 (1957): 49-69.

[3] Kant articulates the distinction in the *Preisschrift* (1762): "Wer einem andern vorschreibt, welche Handlungen er ausüben oder unterlassen müsse, wenn er seine Glückseligkeit befördern wollte, der könnte wohl zwar vielleicht alle Lehren der Moral darunter bringen, aber sie sind alsdann nicht mehr Verbindlichkeiten, sondern etwa so, wie es eine Verbindlichkeit wäre, zwei Kreuzbogen zu machen, wenn ich eine gerade Linie in zwei gleiche Theile zerfällen will, d.i. es sind gar nicht Verbindlichkeiten, sondern nur Anweisungen eines geschickten Verhaltens, wenn man einen Zweck erreichen will." Immanuel Kant, *Untersuchung über die Deutlichkeit der Grundsätze der natürlichen Theologie und der Moral*, 2:298.

[4] "...daraus denn zweyerley moralische Nothwendigkeit entstehet, nemlich die geseztliche Verbindlichkeit, und die Verbindlichkeit der Klugheit. (...) Einige nehmen die moralische Nothwendigkeit in einem andern, nemlich in einem

governed, and on which its corresponding objects depend, cannot be reduced to the principles of the understanding provides a further example; this fundamental thesis of Kant's critical ethics derives from the voluntarist tradition.[5] Similarly, Kant's attitude with regard to the source of normativity—that is, the bindingness (*Verbindlichkeit*)[6]—is of special significance. Kant joins Crusius in asserting that the bindingness is the fundamental moral concept, but their positions diverge when Kant rejects the idea that the source of normativity is either the divine origin of (natural) moral law or man's awareness of his dependence on God.[7] Kant holds that the source and ground of its unconditional exigency pertains to moral good in itself. In contrast to the Woffian conception,[8] moral good is

solchen Verstande, da sie eine Gattung von der *necessitate consecutionis* wird. Nemlich die moralische Nothwendigkeit ist bey ihnen diejenige, da ein vernünftiger Geist durch gewisse Vorstellungen des Guten zu etwas determiniert wird." Christian A. Crusius, *Entwurf der nothwendigen Vernunft-Wahrheiten*, 2. Nachdruck der Ausgabe Leipzig 1745 ed. (Hildesheim – Zürich – New York: Olms, 2006), §131, 213-14.

[5] See Henrich, "Über Kants früheste Ethik," 415. Likewise, Pufendorf's theory of moral entities is relevant to an understanding of the Kantian distinction between theoretical and practical reality; such entities are "realities" independently of the properties of the natural world. See Samuel Pufendorf, *De jure naturae et gentium*, ed. F. Böhling (Berlin: Akademie, 1998), vol. 4.1. §2-20; and Schneewind, *The invention of autonomy*, 138 ff.

[6] "*Verbindlichkeit*" is sometimes translated simply as "obligation" but the preferred translation here is "bindingness", in the sense of "binding force" or "obligatory character", in order to distinguish it clearly from "duty" (*Pflicht*). "*Verbindlichkeit*" is similar in meaning to "*Verpflichtung*". For instance, duties of virtue and legal duties impose different kinds of bindingness. Compare also the contrast between "*Tugendpflicht*" and "*Tugendpverpflichtung*". See *MS*, 6:218, 390, 410.

[7] Kant expresses it as follows in his university lectures: "Crusius meynt, alle Verbindlichkeit beziehe sich auf die Willkür eines andern, nach seiner Meynung wäre also alle obligation eine necessitation per arbitrarium alterius. Es hat zwar den Schein, daß man bey einer obligation necessitirt wird per arbitrarium alterius; allein ich werde necessitirt durch ein arbitrarium internum aber nicht durch ein arbitrarium externum." *VzM*, 43.

[8] "Und hieraus können wir verstehen, wie die sinnliche Begierde und der Wille keine besondere Kraft von der vorstellenden Kraft der Seele erfordern. Nehmlich wir haben oben gesehen, daß die sinnlichen Begierden sowohl als der Wille aus Vorstellungen des Guten entspringen." Christian Wolff, *Vernünftige Gedanken [Deutsche Metaphysik]*, 2. Nachdruck der Ausgabe Halle 1751 ed. (Hildesheim – Zürich – New York: Olms, 1997), §878, 544. Hutcheson's influence was also key

defined as independent of any object or state of the world or state of nature; it is dependent on conformity to the "wanting" of the pure will—that is, conformity to the ends of pure practical reason. The conclusion Kant reaches is that adequate comprehension of the good is independent of any knowledge of the world; rather, it depends on an originary "moral comprehension" (*sittlichen Einsicht*).[9]

Thus, Kantian ethics may be described as a response to the emblematic problems and challenges of the modern theory of natural law.[10] As a response, it is unquestionably original; while it draws on elements of both voluntarism and intellectualism, the whole amounts to more than an exercise in the syncretism of parts: Kant's motive was not merely irenic. What makes Kantian philosophy revolutionary, in fact, is the creative synthesis he forges from different approaches, through which he claims to have resolved once and for all the difficulty involved in wholly accounting for human morality. Kantian philosophy does not emerge from a vacuum; rather, it is the only possible solution that remains after all other moral systems have been ruled out.[11] Neither formalism nor the concept of autonomy is Kant's starting-point; they come as conclusions to his work, after long years of reflection and debate with his contemporaries.

---

to Kant's rejection of Wolff's position. See Schmucker, *Die Ursprünge der Ethik Kants*, 87-95.

[9] See Henrich, "Der Begriff der sittlichen Einsicht und Kants Lehre vom Faktum der Vernunft," 77-122.

[10] Schneewind sums up this perspective as follows: "Kant's relation to the [modern] natural lawyers is thus complex. He is indebted to them for his belief in the importance of the unsocial sociability of our nature, and he accepts the consequent need to build a moral outlook around obligation. Yet he rejects their insistence that morality requires obedience to another. Both aspects of this relation to natural law theory are evident in Kant's distinction between hypothetical and categorical imperatives. He plainly uses it to do the work done by the natural lawyers' distinction between counseling someone and obligating someone. Like them he distinguishes what has to be done for personal reasons from what is socially necessary, and like them he identifies the latter with what is morally significant and of overriding importance. But Kant's way of drawing the distinction quite strikingly omits any place for a counselor or obligator. It is, of course, no small difference." Schneewind, "Kant and the Natural Law Ethics," 64.

[11] See *KpV*, 5:39-41.

The doctrine of right in *MS*,[12] wherein Kant critiques theories of natural law inspired by Aristotelian philosophy because they defer to natural inclinations, is the second area in which the problematic issue of natural law arises. The characteristic method of Kantian practical philosophy, which he himself describes as the "paradox of method" (*Paradoxon der Methode*),[13] is incompatible with any reference to the *sensible* nature of human being.[14] Nevertheless, Kant uses iusnaturalist terminology and adopts the modern conception of natural right to a significant extent.[15] The following two issues exemplify this approach (other examples are also to be found).

First, the contrast between positive law and the right to freedom; given that it is native, and not acquired, the right to freedom is defined as a natural right.[16] As Vigo puts it: "as a native right, freedom belongs to everyone 'by nature' (*von Natur*), independently of any possible juridical act, while all other rights are based on the corresponding juridical acts."[17] Hence, Kant's approach rests on an appeal to nature as the referent by which the rights due to persons are determined, in a way that appears to parallel the iusnaturalist tradition. However, for Kant, the person's appeal to nature has a different meaning: the nature in question is not empirical nature, but rational nature—that is, the defining characteristics of human being as endowed with reason, not as a function of its belonging to a given natural species. This idea is a touchstone of Kantian practical philosophy: the metaphysics of morals cannot be based on anthropology.[18]

---

[12] The manual used in his university lectures is the most direct influence in this regard: Gottfried Achenwall, *Anfangsgründe des Naturrechts – Elementa iuris naturae*, ed. Jan Schröder (Frankfurt am Main: Insel Verlag, 1995), in which the theories of Grotius, Hobbes, Cumberland, Pufendorf, Thomasius and Wolf, among others, are discussed. See Otfried Höffe, ed., *Immanuel Kant. Metaphysische Anfangsgründe der Rechtslehre* (Berlin: Akademie, 1999), 11-16.

[13] See *KpV*, 5:62 ff.

[14] See Friedrich Kaulbach, *Studien zur späten Rechtsphilosophie Kants und ihrer transzendentalen Methode* (Würzburg: Königshausen & Neumann, 1982), 49-54.

[15] The doctrine of right (*Rechstlehre*) addresses the basic elements of all law — natural and positive; thus, it rests on the most fundamental level of natural law. See Peter König, "Episodischer Abschnitt, §§32-40". In *Immanuel Kant. Metaphysische Anfangsgründe der Rechtslehre* (edited by Otfried Höffe), 147-151.

[16] See *MS*, 6:237-238.

[17] Vigo, "Kant's Conception of Natural Right," 133.

[18] See *GMS*, 4:389; *MS*, 6:216-217.

Second, and as a result of the first, for Kant, too, the term "natural law" denotes an external law, but one which is different to "positive law." He explains his position as follows:

> Obligatory laws for which there can be an external lawgiving are called external laws (leges externae) in general. Those among them that can be recognized as obligatory a priori by reason even without external lawgiving are indeed external but natural laws, whereas those that do not bind without actual external lawgiving (and so without it would not be laws) are called positive laws. One [external legislation] can therefore contain only positive laws; but then a natural law would still have to precede it, which would establish the authority of the lawgiver (i.e., his authorization to bind others by his mere choice).[19]

Thus, the realm of natural right corresponds to the pure part of the *Rechtslehre*, which, as Vigo explains,

> includes the system of rights which originate from the native right of a person to freedom, given the conditions laid down by the principle of coexistence of freedoms in the Universal Law of Rights. This then is the subject area of juridical science (*Rechtwissenschaft*, *iurisscientia*), the object of which is none other than the systematic knowledge of the 'doctrine of natural right' (*natürliche Rechtslehre*, *Ius naturae*).[20]

The parallel between the functions of natural right at the heart of the *Rechtslehre* and what is reflected in both classical and modern iusnaturalist tradition is unquestionable. The reason for this is obvious: in both cases, the idea of natural right defers to moral law, and thus serves to establish the relationship that must exist between (positive) law and moral principles.[21] The fact that both juridical duties and moral duties are rooted

---

[19] *MS*, 6:224.

[20] Vigo, "Kant's Conception of Natural Right," 135. See *MS*, 6:229. Vigo also points out that the natural right would also have a "critical and regulatory" function in relation to existing juridical systems.

[21] Kaulbach accounts for the way in which Kant attempts to frame the relationship between law and ethics in the *Rechtslehre* as follows: "Die besondere Metaphysik des Rechts nimmt sich vor, die empirische Ansprüche des positiven Rechts mit den reinen Moralgrundsätzen der praktischen Vernunft zu einem Gesamtsystem zu vermitteln. (...) Die vermittelnde Rolle fällt dabei demjenigen Gezetz zu, welches er als das 'natürliche' bezeichnet hat: also dem kritisch geläuterten Vernunftrecht." Friedrich Kaulbach, *Studien zur späten Rechtsphilosophie Kants und ihrer transzendentalen Methode* (Würzburg: Königshausen & Neumann, 1982), 144-45.

in the same principle should not be forgotten in light of the clear distinction drawn between right and morality in Kantian thought; that principle is moral by nature: the categorical imperative. Legislation depends on the principle of freedom in both the *Rechstlehre* and the *Tugendlehre*, but the difference between them is reflected in the type of coercion (*Zwang*) or constraint (*Nötigung*) involved; that is, depending on whether the bindingness is with respect to the external use of freedom or the free determination of the will.[22]

The third area in Kant's work in which natural law surfaces is the focus of this chapter: the relationship between the legality of nature and the legality of freedom articulated by Kant, in which natural law is framed as the type of moral law. In fact, two formulations of the categorical imperative rest on this relationship: as a universal law and as a law of nature. The meaning of the term "natural law" in this context is different to the normal meaning of the term in iusnaturalism; here it denotes the laws of the natural world—that is, the principles which govern the causal chain of phaenomena. In any case, however, Kant defines the principle of morality (the categorical imperative) in terms of natural legality. Thus, it may be said that Kant addresses one of the characteristic problems faced by theorists of natural law; that is, to determine what the first precept of that law is, by which good may be distinguished from evil, and on the basis of which derived obligations or particular duties rest.[23]

---

[22] See *MS*, 6:381; Schneewind, *The invention of autonomy*, 526.

[23] The difference between modern and classical iusnaturalists becomes evident in this regard; whereas the starting-point for the former (Grotius and Pufendorf, for example) is the need to overcome social conflict, the latter focus to a greater degree on the rational nature of human being. In the well-known Thomist phrase, the first principle of practical reason is: "good is to be done and pursued and evil avoided." The passage from which this axiom is taken reads as follows: "Hoc est ergo primum praeceptum legis, quod bonum est faciendum et prosequendum, et malum vitandum. Et super hoc fundantur omnia alia praecepta legis naturae, ut scilicet omnia illa facienda vel vitanda pertineant ad praecepta legis naturae, quae ratio practica naturaliter apprehendit esse bona humana. Quia vero bonum habet rationem finis, malum autem rationem contrarii, inde est quod omnia illa ad quae homo habet naturalem inclinationem, ratio naturaliter apprehendit ut bona, et per consequens ut opere prosequenda, et contraria eorum ut mala et vitanda. Secundum igitur ordinem inclinationum naturalium, est ordo praeceptorum legis naturae." Thomas Aquinas, *Summa theologica* (Madrid: BAC, 1954), I-II, q. 94, a. 2. The argument posited here — that is, natural law as the type of moral law — does not imply that the positions adopted by Kant and Thomas Aquinas be read as in any way similar, nor that the first practical principle each proposes be taken as

2. The delimitation of the morally possible and the constitution of the object of pure practical reason

2.1. The faculty of judgment and the object of pure practical reason

The argument that the law of nature is a type of the moral law is articulated in an obscure, often overlooked section of the *Critique of Practical Reason*, which comes at the end of the second chapter of the Analytic and is entitled "On the typic [*Typik*] of the faculty of pure practical judgment."[24] This is one of the few places in his work where Kant explicitly addresses the faculty of practical judgment—or, in other words, the judicative function of practical reason.[25] The significance of this position for the current discussion lies in Kant's view that the criterion required to pass moral judgment on actions is conferred on the faculty of judgment by the legality of nature. This criterion is the following "rule" (*Regel*): "Ask yourself whether, if the action you propose were to take place by a law of the nature of which you were yourself a part, you could indeed regard it as morally possible through your will."[26] The rule is clearly one of the formulations of the categorical imperative, to which Kant makes no reference at any point in the section; nor does he refer to the "fundamental law of pure practical reason" which he articulates in §7 of the Analytic.[27] In my view, this omission may be explained by the fact

interchangeable; indeed, the opposite is more likely: the general structures of their ethical systems are very different. Moreover, while it may seem little more than a distinction in terms of detail, the key difference between the two principles proposed is the following: whereas Kant's principle is imperative in form, Aquinas's is articulated in the gerundive, which assigns it to the realm of the veritative (and cognoscitive). See Ana Marta González, *Moral, razón, naturaleza*, 2 ed. (Pamplona: Eunsa, 2006), 126-28, who follows G. Grisez and F. Inciarte in this regard. In any case, the fact that both Thomas Aquinas and Kant were faced with the *same problem* is noteworthy; to which each provided a *different solution* in order to fulfill *similar requirements* — that is, in the final analysis: to enable moral judgment.

[24] See *KpV*, 5:67-71. I translate "*Urteilskraft*" as "faculty of judgment" and "*reine praktische Urteilskraft*" as "faculty of pure practical judgment".

[25] See José M. Torralba, *La facultad del juicio en la filosofía práctica de Kant* (Hildesheim – Zürich – New York: Olms, 2008 (forthcoming)).

[26] *KpV*, 5:69.

[27] "So act that the maxim of your will could always hold at the same time as a principle in a giving of universal law." *KpV*, 5:30.

that Kant's purpose in the section on the typic is to show how the universality of the legality of nature may be used in moral judgment and, as a consequence, enables the formulation of the moral principle (the categorical imperative). To express the same position in different terms, the categorical imperative is here defined as the "canon of moral appraisal [*Beurtheilung*]."[28]

A basic distinction that underwrites clear understanding of the function of the categorical imperative in the Kantian moral system must be addressed at this point. Two complementary functions are ascribed to the categorical imperative: it is the principle of the judgment of actions and the principle of the determination of the will.[29] Strictly speaking, autonomy requires that pure reason be capable of both functions: moral judgment and the determination of the will so that it may act in accordance with that judgment.[30] Given that it enables the reader to distinguish between the points at which Kant refers to moral autonomy as the capacity by which the moral law *immediately* determines the will and those wherein he merely considers the capacity of reason to establish what is morally good, this distinction is of significant methodological import. Kant makes explicit reference to this difference in the section on the typic:

> This comparison of the maxim of his actions with a universal law of nature is also not the determining ground of his will. Such a law is, nevertheless, a type for the appraisal (*Beurtheilung*) of maxims in accordance with moral principles.[31]

The example Kant furnishes in this regard sheds considerable light on the issue: in the case of deception, no-one may hold without contradiction that they would like to see the lie become a universal law; this does not

---

[28] *GMS*, 4:424. Beck translates the term as "estimation" rather than "appraisal". See Immanuel Kant, *Critique of Practical Reason*, ed. L. W. Beck, trans. Lewis W. Beck (Chicago: The University of Chicago Press, 1949).

[29] This distinction holds true in all of Kant's moral writings during the critical period (See *GMS*, 4:407-412; *KpV*, 5:44-45, 78, 159-160; *MS*, 6:375); nevertheless, only rarely does Kant articulate it in an explicit way. In contrast, numerous references are to be found in the university lectures: See, for example, *VzM*, 69 and Henry E. Allison, *Kant's theory of freedom* (Cambridge: Cambridge University Press, 1990), 68 ff.

[30] See Dieter Henrich, "Ethics of Autonomy," in Henrich, Dieter. *The Unity of Reason. Essays on Kant's Philosophy*, ed. Richard L. Velley (Cambridge (Mass.): Harvard University Press, 1994), 89-121.

[31] *KpV*, 5:69.

prevent the subject from regarding his own particular case as exceptional, even though he is aware that his action contravenes the moral law.

In the section, "On the typic of the faculty of pure practical judgment," Kant addresses the moral principle insofar as it is the principle of judgment; its role in the determination of the will is sidelined in the discussion. Given that the principal function of the faculty of pure practical judgment is to constitute the object of practical reason, that is, to establish the object to which a morally determined will corresponds, this clarification is of great significance. Moreover, the second chapter of the Analytic, entitled "On the concept of an object of pure practical reason," which concludes with the section on the typic, explores the relationship between the good and the object of the will. The conclusion reached is well-known: the good is not a property of the object brought about as the result of action; rather, to the extent that the will defers to the moral law as the principle of determination, it is a property of the will.[32] However, there is a corresponding object to every determination of the will—even a pure determination, in which no object is involved. The reason for this is straightforward: there can be no determination of the will, as the faculty that activates the subject's action, without reference to an object, as the result of that determination.[33] This statement may be read as an axiom of the theory of action. Nevertheless, given that determination by the moral law is—in a certain sense—prior to and independent of the objects that may flow from it, the object that corresponds to the pure determination of

---

[32] *KpV*, 5:60-67.

[33] The distinction between two meanings of the object should be noted: the object of the faculty of desire — the effect of action in the world; and the object of practical reason (empirically conditioned or pure) — the maxim in itself. All of this depends on the complex Kantian theory of action. For the purposes of this chapter, the significance of the object of practical reason *qua* maxim, which is the principle of determination of the faculty of desire and gives rise, in turn, to the effect in the world of phaenomena, should be borne in mind. That there are two levels of maxim should also be noted — first order (the principle of determination of the faculty of desire) and second order (the *ground* of determination). That the will's determination by the moral law necessarily connotes an object means that it corresponds to a second order maxim (also known as *Gesinnung*), which is the ground of the faculty of choice (*Willkür*). See Lewis W. Beck, *A Commentary on Kant's Critique of Practical Reason* (Chicago: University of Chicago Press, 1960), 92; Jens Timmermann, *Sittengesetz und Freiheit* (Berlin – New York: W. de Gruyter, 2003), 149-154; Maria Schwartz, *Der Begriff der Maxime bei Kant* (Berlin: Lit, 2006), 19-24.

the will is formal.[34] Thus, the object of pure practical reason sets the limits on the framework in which a will determined by the moral law may 'want'—that is, the framework of the "morally possible—."

2.2. The function of the faculty of judgment in the determination of the modality of the categories of freedom

In the section concerning the faculty of pure practical judgment, Kant makes explicit reference to what has been outlined above:

> The concepts of good and evil first determine an object for the will. They themselves, however, stand under a practical rule of reason which, if it is pure reason, determines the will a priori with respect to its object. (...) A practical rule of pure reason first, as practical, concerns the existence of an object, and second, as a practical rule of pure reason, brings with it necessity.[35]

The practical rule of pure reason by which the good will is determined to act is also the rule that sets limits on the framework of the morally possible; that is, on what the good will may want. The object that corresponds to a morally determined will is constituted by this setting of limits; thus, the integrity of the will determined exclusively by the moral law is guaranteed. Kant addresses this question in the Analytic section of *KpV*: if pure practical reason were incapable of determining its corresponding object *by itself*, autonomy would be nothing more than a pipe-dream. In contrast, Kant holds that the object corresponding to such a determination may be wholly constituted *a priori*. The section on the typic contains his argument in this regard.

The judgment concerning what the good will may want sets the limits on the framework of the morally possible. The formula of the categorical imperative is the criterion of judgment. Kant expresses his position in the following terms: "If the maxim of the action is not so constituted that it can stand the test as to the form of a law of nature in general, then it is

[34] This does not mean that the moral determination of the will is determination in a vacuum; the object of pure practical reason and the object of the faculty of desire (the effect of the action) are related. In fact, the pure determination of the will is the principle on which the *entire* process of action on the subject's part depends.
[35] *KpV*, 5:67.

morally impossible."[36] The possible maxims of the will are judged by the faculty of pure practical judgment so that their modality may be determined. This statement may only be understood if the doctrine concerning the unity of the typic of the faculty of judgment with the "categories of practical reason" or the "categories of freedom"[37] is taken into account; this, too, is an obscure and often overlooked passage which is of great systematic significance in the *Critique of Practical Reason* as a whole.[38]

Kant draws up a table of the categories of freedom, which is similar to the table of categories proposed in the *KrV* and structured according to the same four groups: quantity, quality, relation and modality.[39] These categories comprise an *a priori* synthesis of all the possible forms that the maxims (as practical principles of the determination of the will) may take, encompassing the pure and the empirically conditioned; they sum up the different modes in which the will may be determined.[40] Thus, the table of categories supplies an *a priori* map of the practical sphere.[41] The role of

---

36 *KpV*, 5:69-70.

37 *KpV*, 5:65-67.

38 In my view, the best accounts of this issue are provided by: Claudia Graband, "Das Vermögen der Freiheit: Kants Kategorien der praktischen Vernunft," *Kant-Studien* 96 (2005): 21-65; and Robert J. Benton, "Kant's Categories of Practical Reason as Such," *Kant-Studien* 71 (1980): 181-201. Although I disagree with some of its basic theses, the work of Susanne Bobzien, "Die Kategorien der Freiheit bei Kant," in *Kant. Analysen – Probleme – Kritik*, ed. H. Oberer and G. Seel (Würzburg: Könighausen & Neumann, 1988), 193-220, is both complete and valuable. A more detailed textural analysis of the passage dealing with the categories of freedom is to be found in Torralba, *La facultad del juicio en la filosofía práctica de Kant.*

39 However, the argument here is not that there is an exact parallel, in which each refers to its corresponding theoretical category.

40 The categories are "without exception, *modi* of a single category, namely that of causality, insofar as the determining ground of causality consists in reason's representation of a law of causality which, as the law of freedom, reason gives to itself and thereby proves itself a priori to be practical." *KpV*, 5:65. The category of causality is that of the categories of nature or the understanding. Morality refers to the ground of determination of causality, not to the effects of such causality. From the phaenomenal point of view, good and evil are not properties pertaining to the effects of causality; however, from the noumenal point of view, the subject is capable of altering the ground of determination of causality, thus engaging in action.

41 The kind of relationship that obtains between will and action, or agent and object, is contained in the maxim when it is adopted by the will as the principle of

the faculty of pure practical judgment is to determine the modality of the various maxims presented to it by reason, and which have already been constituted as such in terms of quantity, quality and relation. Thus, all possible objects of the will may be known *a priori* as good or evil.

The question of how the category of modality is determined by the faculty of judgment arises in this context. In my view, the modality of the categories of freedom, like the theoretical categories, defer to possibility, reality and necessity.[42] This three-fold division mirrors the different meanings pertaining to the good: the problematic, pragmatic and moral. Firstly, "problematic good" is that which is *useful* to the attainment of a *possible* end. Secondly, for Kant, *usefulness* is also the criterion of "pragmatic" good; however, the end involved is *real*, not merely possible: the happiness of human beings is a case in point. Finally, moral good is independent of any relation to an end, nor is it grounded on usefulness; its realization is of an unconditional or *necessary* nature.[43]

Given that the most general function of the faculty of judgment is to establish the correspondence between a particular instance and the rule, the kind of good pertaining to the different objects of the will may be known *a priori* by the faculty of pure practical judgment in accordance with the rule or practical principle on which each depends. The parallel between the three-fold meaning of the good and the three kinds of imperative framed by Kant is obvious. The faculty of judgment verifies the correspondence of a given maxim to one or other of these imperatives.[44] The rule by which the morality of a given maxim may be known is expressed by Kant as follows: "Ask yourself whether, if the action you propose were to take place by a law of the nature of which you were yourself a part, you could indeed regard it as morally possible through

---

determination. The key point at issue is whether the relationship is determined by the object (the result of action) or, in contrast, if the agent is capable of imposing his own order, independently of the object. This relationship is that of "wanting" (*das Wollen*) or "desiring" (*das Begehren*). See *MS*, 6:211-213.

[42] See *KrV*, A:80/B:106.

[43] See *GMS*, 4:414-415; *VzM*, 30-31; Beck, *A Commentary on Kant's Critique of Practical Reason*, 131 ff. On the (frequently misunderstood) relationship between duty and the good in Kant's work, see Herbert J. Paton, *The Categorical Imperative. A Study in Kant's Moral Philosophy* (New York – Evaston: Harper Row, 1967), 103-12, 16-17.

[44] See Rainer Enskat, "Autonomie und Humanität. Wie kategorische Imperative die Urteilskraft orientieren," in *Systematische Ethik mit Kant*, ed. H.-U. Baumgarten and C. Held (Freiburg – München: Karl Alber, 2001), 82-123.

your will."[45] The question of what may be known of the modality of maxims by means of this rule—or test—arises in this context. In light of the discussion thus far, it seems clear that the rule distinguishes the "morally possible" from the "impossible."

However, the three categories of modality presented by Kant in the table of the categories of freedom are as follows: (1) the permitted (*das Erlaubte*)—the forbidden (*das Unerlaubte*); (2) duty (*die Pflicht*)—contrary to duty (*das Pflichtwidrige*); and (3) perfect duty (*vollkommene Pflicht*)—imperfect duty (*unvolkommente Pflicht*).[46] A superficial reading suggests that the distinction between possible and impossible corresponds to the first group of categories: the permitted and the forbidden. Nevertheless, this is not in fact the case because the categories of freedom not only defer to the forms of 'wanting' of *pure* reason, but also to those of *empirically conditioned* reason, which involve "a priori the manifold of *desires* to the unity of consciousness of a practical reason commanding in the moral law, or of a pure will."[47] All possible desires are synthesized in the categories. Thus, the modality must encompass all the variables involved in the framing of the principle of determination (the maxim) of the will. As Kant himself noted in the introduction to the *KpV*, these variables may be summarized in terms of the three kinds of imperatives: those concerning skill, the pragmatic, and the categorical—"We have here to do only with the distinction of *imperatives* under *problematic*, *assertoric*, and *apodictic*."[48]

The key to this argument rests on the distinction between physical possibility and moral possibility—or, in other words, between technically-practical principles and morally-practical principles.[49] The categorical imperative is a morally-practical principle of the determination of the will and the ground of moral possibility; problematic and assertoric imperatives, on the other hand, are technically-practical principles which are grounded on physical possibility—that is, the possibility of the will having an effect in the world—that is, to attain an end by means of its action. Thus, moral possibility, to which Kant refers in the section concerning the typic, must not be confused with physical possibility, the realm of technically-practical principles. A refined interpretation of this

---

[45] *KpV*, 5:69.
[46] See *KpV*, 5:66.
[47] *KpV*, 5:65.
[48] *KpV*, 5:11, note.
[49] *KpV*, 5:57-58 and *KU*, Ak 5:171-174.

kind enables a clear understanding of Kant's explanation of the first two categories of modality (the permitted and the forbidden):

> In the table of categories of *practical* reason under the heading Modality, the *permitted* and the *forbidden* (the practically objectively possible and impossible), have almost the same sense in the common use of language as the immediately following categories, *duty* and *contrary to duty*; here, however, the *first* mean that which harmonizes or conflicts with a merely *possible* practical precept (as, say, the solution of all problems of geometry and mechanics), the *second*, that which is similarly related to a law *actually* [*Wirklich*] present in reason as such [*überhaupt*].[50]

Thus, whether or not something is permitted depends on the subject's 'desiring' of a given end. "Thus, for example, it is *forbidden*, to an orator, as such, to forge new words or constructions; this is to some extent *permitted* to a poet; in neither case is there any thought of duty."[51]

Neither do the second categories—duty and contrary to duty—yet refer directly to moral duty; rather, they express what is common to all kinds of imperative: that a given practical principle be made obligatory. This applies to prudential, as well as to moral, imperatives.[52] In the case of the imperative of happiness, the imperative orders the carrying out of an action—that is, it is the cause of an effect in the world—independently of incentive (*Triebfeder*). In contrast, the conformity of the maxim to the moral law is not in itself sufficient in the moral sphere; rather, the incentive for which the maxim is adopted as the principle of determination must also be the moral law itself, not the appeal of the representation of the reality of the object. If this latter condition is not met, one may speak only of legality (*Legalität*). As a consequence, it may be said that the

---

[50] *KpV*, 5:11, note. Bobzien's interpretation of this passage appears to be mistaken; she reads the three categories of modality as referring to the moral law. See Bobzien, "Die Kategorien der Freiheit bei Kant," 213-14. The problem arises because Bobzien draws on a few quotations from the *MS*, in which Kant defines the permitted and the forbidden, rather than deferring to Kant's own explanation, in order to account for this passage in the *KpV*. As is pointed out below, the quotations on which Bobzien draws are relevant to the discussion, but not to an interpretation of the table of the categories of freedom.

[51] *KpV*, 5:11, note.

[52] That the prudential imperatives are also *objective* laws of reason should be borne in mind, given that they give rise to necessary determined actions. See *KrV*, A:548/B:576, *GMS*, 4:399, 412-416; Dieter Schönecker and Allen W. Wood, *Kants "Grundlegung zur Metaphysik der Sitten". Ein einführender Kommentar*, 2 ed. (Paderborn – München: Schöningh, 2004), 101-22.

categories of duty and contrary to duty refer to cases of practical necessity wherein the will is regarded as a natural cause—that is, the will is determined by means of technically-practical principles.

The last two categories—perfect and imperfect duty—are moral categories in the strict sense of the term; that is, the categories in which the concept of duty is read as "morally necessary" or necessary in a morally-practical sense. The question of the typic must be addressed again in this regard. Given that its function is to enable the *moral* judgment of maxims, it seems logical to conclude that Kant's proposed rule serves to distinguish between perfect and imperfect duty. In fact, however, the rule serves only to distinguish the morally possible from the morally impossible; that something is morally possible need not entail that it be obligatory—that is, a duty.[53] In my view, this discrepancy between the classification of the categories of modality and the reflections on the typic may be attributed to two systematic reasons (in addition to a degree of carelessness on Kant's part in the revision of his texts).

The first of these is that the formula of the universal law or of nature is only "*a* type for the appraisal of maxims in accordance with moral principles,"[54] to be complemented by the other formulations if the whole realm of moral normativity is to be encompassed—in particular, that which refers to humanity as an end in itself.[55] In this context, as a result, the formula of natural law would be essentially negative by definition—a permissive law (*Erlaubnisgesetz*)[56]—whereas that referring to humanity

[53] Although it may seem paradoxical, the distinction between perfect and imperfect duty in the table of the categories of freedom is unrelated to Kant's attempt, in the *GMS*, to derive and distinguish between the strict (*eng*) and wider (*weite*) meanings of duty on the basis of the formula of the universal law, through the distinction between "*denken können*" and "*wollen können*". See *GMS*, 4:424. The explanation for this is outlined below.

[54] *KpV*, 5:69. The emphasis is mine.

[55] See Brigitta-Sophie von Wolff-Metternich, "Sobre el papel del juicio práctico en la filosofía moral de Kant," *Anuario Filosófico* 37 (2004): 733-47; Verena Mayer, "Das Paradox des Regelfolgens in Kants Moralphilosophie," *Kant-Studien* 97 (2006): 343-68.

[56] "In seinem Kern has das Sittengesetz daher den Charakter eines Erlaubnisgesetzes, das unmittelbar einen Spielraum für legitimierungsfähige Maximen legitimiert und nicht ohne ihre Hilfe den Raum des von ihnen zu regulierenden konkreten Handelns erreicht." Wolfgang Wieland, *Urteil und Gefühl. Kants Theorie der Urteilskraft* (Göttingen: Vandenhoeck & Ruprecht, 2001), 161.

would prescribe *positive* duties.[57] In any case, given that—in accordance with the fundamental principles of modal logic—the contrary to the forbidden is obligatory,[58] *some* positive duties may be derived from a negative criterion. For example, theft is forbidden; therefore, one is obliged to pay for what one obtains.

Moreover, the distinction between rules of judgment which determine moral obligations in a dual sense (negative and positive) is cognate with the *KpV* as a whole. To set limits on the realm of the morally possible is sufficient for the constitution of the object of pure practical reason, since it is a formal object. The positive prescription of moral duties is the task that Kant sets himself in the *MS*, through reflection on the idea of ends that are duties; this presupposes the application of the moral law—to a certain extent—to rational beings which are, at the same time, sensibly conditioned.[59]

The second systematic reason, which explains the discrepancy between the table of categories and the doctrine of the typic, lies in the fact that the *moral* modalities (the permitted, the forbidden, the obligatory) ought to be included in the third group of the categories of modality; however, in order to do so, Kant would have to split the table of the categories of freedom, which—as has already been discussed above—encompass all the *practical* modalities (both the technically-practical and the morally-practical), not merely the *moral* modalities. It is not clear why Kant did not do so. What is clear, however, is that while the categories of freedom are at the heart of Kant's argument in the *KpV*, no further reference is made to them in his later works.[60] This does not mean that the classification of modalities in the table of categories and the development of the modalities on the basis of the typic are contradictory; rather, they are *complementary* positions. To assign the moral modalities to the third group—that is, the categories of perfect and imperfect duty—is enough.

---

[57] See *MS*, 6:388-389. See Schönecker and Wood, *Kants "Grundlegung zur Metaphysik der Sitten"*, 125 ff.

[58] See Ramón Rodríguez, *La fundamentación formal de la ética* (Madrid: Universidad Complutense, 1982), 172.

[59] The levels of application of the moral law, and their relationship to the different functions of the faculty of judgment are explored in José M. Torralba, "Facultad del juicio y aplicación de la ley moral en la filosofía de Kant," *Methodus* II (2007): 1-30.

[60] Kant intended to develop his metaphysics of morals on the basis of this table; nevertheless, the project was later set aside, without explanation.

In fact, in the *MS*, Kant defines the moral modalities in these exact terms. In the section entitled "Preliminary concepts of the metaphysics of morals," he notes: "According to these [moral] laws,[61] certain actions are *permitted* or *forbidden*, that is, morally possible or impossible, while some of them or their opposites are morally necessary, that is, obligatory;"[62] later, he goes on to define what is morally permitted as follows: "That action is *permitted* (*licitum*) which is not contrary to obligation; and this freedom which is not limited by any opposing imperative, is called an authorization (*facultad moralis*). Hence it is obvious what is meant by *forbidden* (*ilicitum*).[63] Obligation has a strictly moral meaning in this context: "*Obligation* is the necessity of a free action under a categorical imperative of reason."[64]

3. Natural law in moral judgment

The discussion thus far has supplied a description of the place in the system pertaining to the faculty of pure practical judgment in the constitution of the object of pure practical reason, in line with the doctrine of the categories of freedom. That Kant deploys the categorical imperative—in its formulation as the law of nature—as a rule by which the modality of the categories is determined has been noted. Moreover, that Kant does not rely on the doctrine of the categorical imperative articulated in *GMS*, but—at this point in the *KpV*—offers an argument for why the natural law may be put to work in moral judgment, has also been discerned. This final aspect merits further consideration if the argument that natural law is the type of moral law is to be clearly understood.

Kant reads the legality of nature as the type of moral law for the following three reasons (at least). First, this reading enables the establishment of some kind of relationship or reference between the precepts of moral law and actions in the world of phaenomena, which is an indispensable condition for the possibility of moral judgment. Second, it allows Kant to argue that there is a certain degree of continuity between freedom and nature, and thus safeguard the integrity of what has been established by the *Faktum*.[65] Finally, formalism, the touchstone of Kantian morality, finds sure ground in the *form* of the legality of nature (which

---

[61] I have altered Gregor's translation, which reads "categorical imperatives".
[62] *MS*, 6:221.
[63] *MS*, 6:222.
[64] *MS*, 6:222.
[65] See *KpV*, 5:42 ff.

may be understood through the categories of nature); that form—universality and necessity—is the basis of all types of law, theoretical or practical. Each of these reasons is discussed in greater detail below.

At the start of the section concerning the typic, Kant holds that: "whether an action possible for us in sensibility is or is not a case that stands under the rule requires practical judgment, by which what is said in the rule universally (*in abstracto*) is applied to an action *in concreto*.[66] However, such an undertaking would appear to be impossible, given that:

> it seems absurd to want to find in the sensible world a case which, though as such it stands only under the law of nature, yet admits of the application to it of a law of freedom and to which there could be applied the supersensible idea of the morally good, which is to be exhibited in it *in concreto*.[67]

The radical difference between the moral law (the rule) and action (the case) is similar to that between concept and intuition in the theoretical sphere. Nevertheless, the understanding may avail of the schematism which enables the application of the categories to the intuitions. The problem in this regard is that "the morally good as an object is something supersensible, so that nothing corresponding to it can be found in any sensible intuition."[68] No schematism similar to that of theoretical judgment pertains to practical judgment.[69]

However, Kant holds that an advantageous perspective is enabled in this regard: *pure* moral judgment, in the strict sense, does not require that law and case correspond to one another, but the determination of "the

---

[66] *KpV*, 5:67. Although Kant refers to "an action possible for us in sensibility," the term "maxim" ought to have been used: action, in its *phaenomenal aspect*, is never susceptible to *moral* judgment. Kant states as much at a later point in his work: "Subsumption of an action possible to me in the sensible world under a *pure practical law* does not concern the possibility of the *action* as an event in the sensible world." *KpV*, 5:68.

[67] *KpV*, 5:68.

[68] *KpV*, 5:68. Kant regards the attribution of intuitions to the moral good as a form of "mysticism"; the role of the typic is to prevent such mysticism and lead us to the "rationalism of the faculty of judgment". See *KpV*, 5:70-71.

[69] Thus, Silber's interpretation, wherein he holds that time is the schema of practical reason, is mistaken; although his position is innovative, it is not cognate with Kant's thought. See John Silber, "Der Schematismus der praktischen Vernunft," *Kant-Studien* 56 (1966): 261.

schema of a law itself (if the word schema is appropriate here)."[70] This point lies at the heart of the doctrine concerning the typic, which may only be fully understood in light of everything that has been discussed thus far. The moral judgment of actions or of the maxims of actions is not the function of the faculty of *pure* practical judgment; rather, it is to supply the rule by which maxims and actions may *afterwards* be judged.[71] This rule must fulfill two criteria: (a) that it may be applied in some way to objects of nature; and (b) that, as a rule, it be in agreement with the moral law—that is, that it may serve as a principle of the determination of the will. The formula of the law of nature meets these two requirements: (a) because it is a "law, such a law (...) as can be presented *in concreto* in objects of the senses;"[72] and (b) because its legal *form* shares that of the moral law, "for, to this extent, laws as such are the same, no matter from what they derive their determining grounds."[73] This is the sense in which the form of (natural) legality may be read as the type of moral law.

Thus, given that he interprets "the *nature of the sensible world* as the *type* of an *intelligible nature*,"[74] Kant ensures the "use in application for the law of a pure practical reason."[75] In referring to natural legality and, in particular, to the *form* of this legality, Kant has "intelligible nature" in mind, which would arise if the morally determined will "were accompanied with suitable physical power."[76] Strictly speaking, the moral law is the law that governs intelligible nature. Given the imperfection of human nature, this nature never becomes real; however, the *Faktum* of morality implies that "the counterpart of [intelligible nature] is to exist in

[70] *KpV*, 5:68. And he goes on: "since the *determination of the will* (not the action with reference to its result) through the law alone without any other determining ground connects the concept of causality to conditions quite other than those which constitute natural connection."

[71] In line with the distinction between the (reflexive and determining) judicative functions, Wieland has shown that the faculty of pure practical judgment performs a *merely* determining function, which is similar to that of the faculty of transcendental judgment in the *KrV*. See Wieland, *Urteil und Gefühl*, 164-65; Alejandro G. Vigo, "Determinación y reflexión," *Anuario Filosófico* 37 (2004): 749-95.

[72] *KpV*, 5:69.

[73] *KpV*, 5:70.

[74] *KpV*, 5:70. The key here is not to attribute to intelligible nature "intuitions and what depends upon them but refer to it only the *form of lawfulness* in general." *KpV*, 5:70.

[75] *KpV*, 5:70.

[76] *KpV*, 5:43.

the sensible world,"[77] which is the proper task of morality: to give sensible nature the form of intelligible nature without breaking any causal laws.[78] Sensible nature and intelligible nature are not two different *worlds*; rather they are two different spheres (*Gebiet*), each with its own legality. Given that only the *form* of legality is at issue—a form shared both by freedom and nature—it is possible to 'move' from one sphere to the other and to 'apply' moral law to nature.

Intelligible nature acts as a model because it is a nature in which the possible and the impossible are defined by the moral law. Something is morally possible if it may occur in an (*intelligible*) nature of which one is part. Thus, the faculty of judgment may avail of a reference point in its reflection on how the nature in which one lives *ought to be*. Moreover, to read the moral law as a law of a nature prompts its requirements in a concrete way. Moral judgment establishes the possibility or impossibility of a given practical principle; that is, of a *causal* principle in an intelligible nature.

The second reason why the natural law may be read as the type of moral law has also—in part—been explained. To the extent in which causality through freedom "connects the concept of causality to conditions quite other than those which constitute natural connection,"[79] a continuity between sensible and intelligible nature exists. Insofar as all action is governed by the legality of nature, the causality of human being is unique. Nevertheless, different grounds of determination (*Bestimmungsgründe*) may shape the determination of one and the same causality. These grounds may be structured in two classes: appeal in the representation of the object and the moral law in itself. The ground of his causality, not the legality proper to natural causality, is altered when the agent determines to act in a moral way. The 'effect' of causality through freedom is the formation of the ground of determination. Thus, what is prescribed by moral law is

---

[77] *KpV*, 5:43. The reason why the normative nature of the moral law is not primary, but derived, becomes clear in this context: "Primär ist es [das Sittengesetz] ein *Seingesetz*, das Seingesetz des reinen Vernunftwillens als solchen, und folglich ist auch das Sollen in uns eigentlich eigenes notwendiges Wollen, d. h. das Bewußtsein einer Tätigkeit der reinen praktischen Vernunft, die nur deshalb ihre Wirkung nicht in Handlungen äußert, weil subjektive, 'pathologische' Ursachen sie daran hindern." Joseph Schmucker, "Der Formalismus und die materialen Zweckprinzipien in der Ethik Kants," in *Kant. Analysen – Probleme – Kritik*, ed. H. Oberer (Würzburg: Könighausen & Neumann, 1997), 110.

[78] See Alejandro Llano, *Fenómeno y trascendencia en Kant*, 2 ed. (Pamplona: Eunsa, 2002), 264-65.

[79] *KpV*, 5:69.

compatible with natural legality; and the possibility of continuity between both legalities[80] is pointed to by means of the ground of determination of the agent's causality.

The third reason is probably both the most important and the most widely known: Kantian formalism. This final reason rounds out the network of relations between natural law and moral law, and confers full meaning on what has been discussed thus far in this chapter. Given that principles which defer to some content or object are governed by the legality of nature, and thus are subject to pleasure and pain, Kant holds that moral principles must be formal by nature. The freedom of the will requires that the principles by which it is governed not be material. Kant addresses the issue in the second problem of the well-known Theorem III in the Analytic: "Supposing that a will is *free*: to find the law that alone is competent to determine it necessarily." The solution he proposes is as follows:

> Since the matter of a practical law, that is, an object of maxim, can never be given otherwise than empirically whereas a free will, as independent of empirical conditions (...) must nevertheless be determinable, a free will must find a determining ground in the law but independently of the *matter* of the law. But, besides the matter of the law, nothing further is contained in it than the lawgiving form.[81]

Thus, given that Kant holds that any practical principle that defers to an object would as a matter of course have pleasure as the ground of determination, the basis of the Kantian conception of volition may be described as hedonist.[82] Moreover, since pleasure and pain pertain to the

---

80 See *KpV*, 5:48-57. The following quotation from Kant sums up this argument: "Now, however, the concept of an empirically unconditioned causality is indeed theoretically empty (without an intuition appropriate to it) but it is nevertheless possible and refers to an undetermined object; in place of that, however, the concept is given significance in the moral law and consequently in its practical reference; thus I have, indeed, no intuition that would determine its objective theoretical reality for it, but it has nonetheless a real application which is exhibited *in concreto* in dispositions [*Gesinnungen*] or maxims, that is, has practical reality which can be specified." *KpV*, 5:56. The modification of the ground of determination of causality consists in the 'construction' of the maxim that acts as a practical principle. See Allison, *Kant's theory of freedom*, 35-41, 146-52.

81 *KpV*, 5:29; See also *KpV*, 5:21-28.

82 Of course, on the whole Kant is an anti-hedonist (perhaps the most radical), but he nonetheless draws on an hedonist understanding of desire. See Rodríguez, *La fundamentación formal de la ética*, 36 ff.; Markus Willaschek, *Praktische*

subject's sensible nature, they are governed by natural legality, which is incompatible with freedom. Hence, Kant is left with no other option but to assert that the law by which the free will of human being is governed must, necessarily, be formal.[83]

The two other distinctive facets of moral duty also pertain to the form of legality: unconditioned necessity and, therefore, universality.[84] This is the ultimate ground of Kantian ethics: the intrinsic connection between the moral good, the necessity and universality of duty, and the inescapably formal nature of the law by which the freedom of the will is governed. Moreover, Kant regards this connection as a given that imposes its authority on reason:

> When I think of a *hypothetical* imperative in general I do not know beforehand what it will contain; I do not know this until I am given the condition. But when I think of a *Categorical* imperative I know at once what it contains. For, since the imperative contains, beyond the law, only the necessity that the maxim be in conformity with this law, while the law contains no condition to which it would be limited, nothing is left with which the maxim of action is to conform but the universality of a law as such; and this conformity alone is what the imperative properly represents as necessary. There is, therefore, only a single imperative and it is: *act only*

Vernunft. Handlungstheorie und Moralbegründung bei Kant (Stuttgart – Weimar: J. B. Metzler, 1992), 60-81.

83 Two questions, whose import goes beyond the remit of this chapter, surface in this context. The first concerns whether or not the hedonist position, the basis of Kantian formalism, is sufficiently justified; that is, if an idea such as "rational desire" is in fact impossible. In this regard, see Thomas Buchheim, "Wie Vernunft uns handeln macht," in *Die Normativität des Wirklichen. Über die Grenze zwischen Sein und Sollen*, ed. Th. Buchheim, R. Schönberger, and W. Schweidler (Stuttgart: Klett-Cotta, 2002), 381-413. The second question centers on Kant's determinist conception of the sensible world. This conception prompts the doctrine concerning the typic, among others, in order to explain the continuity between freedom and nature. A number of recent studies have shown that Kant's conception defers more to the rationalist philosophical debates of his time than to an inquiry into nature. See Juan Arana, *Los filósofos y la libertad. Necesidad natural y autonomía de la voluntad* (Madrid: Síntesis, 2005), 75-103.

84 See Rainer Enskat, "Universalität, Spontaneität und Solidarität. Formale und prozedurale Grundzüge der Sittlichkeit," in *Prinzip und Applikation in der praktischen Philosophie*, ed. Th. M. Seebohm (Mainz – Stuttgart: Akademie der Wissenschaften und der Literatur – Franz Steiner, 1991), 34-79; Paton, *The Categorical Imperative*, 148-49, 57-64.

> *in accordance with that maxim through which you can at the same time will that it become a universal law.*[85]

In the final analysis, therefore, given that universality is a basic requirement of any practical principle that lays claim to moral goodness, natural law may be described as the type of moral law.

Works Cited

Achenwall, Gottfried. *Anfangsgründe des Naturrechts – Elementa iuris naturae*. Edited by Jan Schröder. Frankfurt am Main: Insel Verlag, 1995.

Allison, Henry E. *Kant's theory of freedom*. Cambridge: Cambridge University Press, 1990.

Aquinas, Thomas. *Summa theologica*. Madrid: BAC, 1954.

Arana, Juan. *Los filósofos y la libertad. Necesidad natural y autonomía de la voluntad*. Madrid: Síntesis, 2005.

Beck, Lewis W. *A Commentary on Kant's Critique of Practical Reason*. Chicago: University of Chicago Press, 1960.

Benton, Robert J. . "Kant's Categories of Practical Reason as Such." *Kant-Studien* 71 (1980): 181-201.

Bobzien, Susanne. "Die Kategorien der Freiheit bei Kant." In *Kant. Analysen – Probleme – Kritik*, edited by H. Oberer and G. Seel, 181-201. Würzburg: Könighausen & Neumann, 1988.

Buchheim, Thomas. "Wie Vernunft uns handeln macht." In *Die Normativität des Wirklichen. Über die Grenze zwischen Sein und Sollen*, edited by Th. Buchheim, R. Schönberger and W. Schweidler, 381-413. Stuttgart: Klett-Cotta, 2002.

Crusius, Christian A. *Entwurf der nothwendigen Vernunft-Wahrheiten*. 2. Nachdruck der Ausgabe Leipzig 1745 ed. Hildesheim – Zürich – New York: Olms, 2006.

---

85 *GMS*, 4:420-421. The discovery of the properties of morality is the principal fruit of the critique of practical reason; and hence, "to prevent empirically conditioned reason from presuming that it, alone and exclusively, furnishes the determining ground of the will." *KpV*, 5:16. In my view, the justification for defining necessity, universality and the absence of conditionality as the properties of morality lie in the nature of the will itself (*Wille*) as a faculty of the mind (*Gemüt*). That the critical method leads to the definition of the principles, concepts and objects corresponding to each of the fundamental faculties (*Grundvermögen*), as well as their valid use, should be borne in mind. See *KpV*, 5:46-47.

Edwards, J., "Natural Law and Obligation in Hutcheson and Kant." In *Contemporary Perspectives on Natural Law. Natural Law as a Limiting Concept*, edited by A. M. González. Aldershot: Ashgate, 2008, pp. 87-103.

Enskat, Rainer. "Autonomie und Humanität. Wie kategorische Imperative die Urteilskraft orientieren." In *Systematische Ethik mit Kant*, edited by H.-U. Baumgarten and C. Held, 82-123. Freiburg – München: Karl Alber, 2001.

—. "Universalität, Spontaneität und Solidarität. Formale und prozedurale Grundzüge der Sittlichkeit." In *Prinzip und Applikation in der praktischen Philosophie*, edited by Th. M. Seebohm, 34-79. Mainz – Stuttgart: Akademie der Wissenschaften und der Literatur – Franz Steiner, 1991.

González, Ana Marta. *Moral, razón, naturaleza*. 2 ed. Pamplona: Eunsa, 2006.

Graband, Claudia. "Das Vermögen der Freiheit: Kants Kategorien der praktischen Vernunft." *Kant-Studien* 96 (2005): 21-65.

Henrich, Dieter. "Der Begriff der sittlichen Einsicht und Kants Lehre vom Faktum der Vernunft." In *Die Gegenwart der Griechen im neueren Denken. Festschrift für Hans-Georg Gadamer zum 60. Geburtstag*, edited by D. Henrich, W. Schulz and K.-H. Volkmann-Schluck, 77-122. Tübingen: Mohr – Siebeck, 1960.

—. "Ethics of Autonomy." In Henrich, Dieter. *The Unity of Reason. Essays on Kant's Philosophy*, edited by Richard L. Velley, 89-121. Cambridge, (Mass.): Harvard University Press, 1994.

—. "Hutcheson und Kant." *Kant-Studien* 49 (1957): 49-69.

—. "Über Kants früheste Ethik. Versuch einer Rekonstruktion." *Kant-Studien* 54 (1963): 404-31.

Höffe, Otfried ed. *Immanuel Kant. Metaphysische Anfangsgründe der Rechtslehre*. Berlin: Akademie, 1999.

Kant, Immanuel. *Critique of Practical Reason* Translated by Lewis W. Beck. Edited by L. W. Beck. Chicago: The University of Chicago Press, 1949.

—. *Kant's gesammelte Schriften*. Edited by Akademie der Wissenschaften. Berlin, 1902 ff.

—. *Kritik der reinen Vernunft*. Edited by Jens Timmermann. nach der 1. und 2. Orig.-Ausg. ed. Hamburg: Felix Meiner, 1998.

—. *Practical philosophy* Translated by Mary J. Gregor. Edited by Mary J. Gregor. Cambridge: Cambridge University Press, 1996.

—. *Vorlesung zur Moralphilosophie*. Edited by Werner Stark. Berlin – New York: Walter de Gruyter, 2004.

Kaulbach, Friedrich. *Studien zur späten Rechtsphilosophie Kants und ihrer transzendentalen Methode*. Würzburg: Königshausen & Neumann, 1982.

Llano, Alejandro. *Fenómeno y trascendencia en Kant*. 2 ed. Pamplona: Eunsa, 2002.

Mayer, Verena. "Das Paradox des Regelfolgens in Kants Moralphilosophie." *Kant-Studien* 97 (2006): 343-68.

Paton, Herbert J. *The Categorical Imperative. A Study in Kant's Moral Philosophy*. New York – Evaston: Harper Row, 1967.

Pufendorf, Samuel. *De jure naturae et gentium*. Edited by F. Böhling. Berlin: Akademie, 1998.

Rodríguez, Ramón. *La fundamentación formal de la ética*. Madrid: Universidad Complutense, 1982.

Schmucker, Joseph. "Der Formalismus und die materialen Zweckprinzipien in der Ethik Kants." In *Kant. Analysen – Probleme – Kritik*, edited by H. Oberer, 99-156. Würzburg: Könighausen & Neumann, 1997.

—. *Die Ursprünge der Ethik Kants in seinen vorkritischen Schriften und Reflexionen*. Meisenheim: Hain, 1961.

Schneewind, Jerome B. *The invention of autonomy. A history of modern moral philosophy*. Cambridge: Cambridge University Press, 1998.

—. "Kant and the Natural Law Ethics." *Ethics* 104 (1993): 53-74.

—. "Pufendorf's Place in the History of Ethics." *Synthese* 72 (1987): 123-55.

Schönecker, Dieter, and Allen W. Wood. *Kants "Grundlegung zur Metaphysik der Sitten". Ein einführender Kommentar*. 2 ed. Paderborn – München: Schöningh, 2004.

Schwartz, Maria. *Der Begriff der Maxime bei Kant. Eine Untersuchung des Maximenbegriffs in Kants praktischer Philosophie*. Berlin: Lit, 2006.

Silber, John. "Der Schematismus der praktischen Vernunft." *Kant-Studien* 56 (1966): 253-73.

Timmermann, Jens. *Sittengesetz und Freiheit. Untersuchungen zu Immanuel Kants Theorie des freien Willens*. Berlin – New York: W. de Gruyter, 2003.

Torralba, José M. "Facultad del juicio y aplicación de la ley moral en la filosofía de Kant." *Methodus* II (2007): 1-30.

—. *La facultad del juicio en la filosofía práctica de Kant*. Hildesheim – Zürich – New York: Olms, 2008 (forthcoming).

Vigo, Alejandro G. "Determinación y reflexión." *Anuario Filosófico* 37 (2004): 749-95.

—. "Kant's Conception of Natural Right." In *Contemporary Perspectives on Natural Law. Natural Law as a Limiting Concept*, edited by Ana Marta González, 121-140. Aldershot: Ashgate, 2008.

von Wolff-Metternich, Brigitta-Sophie. "Sobre el papel del juicio práctico en la filosofía moral de Kant." *Anuario Filosófico* 37 (2004): 733-47.

Wieland, Wolfgang. *Urteil und Gefühl. Kants Theorie der Urteilskraft*. Göttingen: Vandenhoeck & Ruprecht, 2001.

Willaschek, Markus. *Praktische Vernunft. Handlungstheorie und Moralbegründung bei Kant*. Stuttgart – Weimar: J. B. Metzler, 1992.

Wolff, Christian. *Vernünftige Gedanken [Deutsche Metaphysik]*. 2. Nachdruck der Ausgabe Halle 1751 ed. Hildesheim – Zürich – New York: Olms, 1997.

Part II:

Contemporary Reception of Natural Law

CHAPTER TWELVE

PHENOMENOLOGICAL PERSPECTIVES ON NATURAL LAW

ENCARNA LLAMAS

Original and very interesting proposals concerning the discussion about the role of human nature in morality have been recently developed from a phenomenological perspective. In this article the proposals of Charles Taylor and Robert Sokolowski on the knowledge and the achievement of the good for the human being are contrasted. Both proposals coincide in indicating the discovering of the good in concrete action, establishing that moral knowledge takes place in practice: certain goods appeal to the agent, appearing as the proper ends of human beings that are to be realized by means of the good action. Therefore, human nature shows to be normative as teleological, since ethical claims are derived from its complete constitution. According to these authors, the teleological character of the human being, known trough practical reason in action, is fundamental for ethics.

Discussion about natural law and its role in ethics includes multiple aspects. In this paper I will focus on two. First, the thesis that human nature is morally normative as a final cause, in the specific sense that human beings have to achieve the plenitude of their nature precisely in a process of development in which action plays an essential role. Second, and related to this, I will try to show the eminently practical character of the knowledge of the good for human beings, since it appears in practice, in real actions and situations in which the subject must unearth what is to be done. I will first discuss Sokolowski's approach to natural law, to compare it afterwards with Taylor's proposal of nature as one of the moral sources of human identity, in order to establish coincidences and differences between these two phenomenological approaches to the normative character of human nature.

Robert Sokolowski has recently published: "What is Natural Law? Human Purposes and Natural Ends."[1] His main target in this article is to develop a phenomenology of human nature as a source of morality, based upon the assertion of some ends as proper for human beings, which can be perceived as appellative, in such a way that they move us to act as a good human being should do.

The first question Sokolowski raises is the special character of the description of human nature as not yet fulfilled but tending to its completion at the same time. This distinction is the differentiation between what human beings are and what they ought to be, as the author explains:

> The working out of the definition and description of human nature is at the same time the formulation of what we *ought* to be as human beings, because the good or perfected state of man, which is the issue for ethics, is what defines human being. The normative is also the definitional. We cannot describe what man is without specifying the human good, without showing what it is to be a good (and consequently "happy") man.[2]

Who is then the good human being? The one that becomes what he ought to be. The descriptive and the normative aspects are somewhat identified here: the definitional is the normative for a kind of being that is not yet everything he is, but has to become what he is in plenitude. This identification of the definitional with the normative points to human nature as the root for ethics. But not in a naturalistic sense, since human nature does not redeem automatically this role of measurement of the moral, but only once the subject comes to certain knowledge of his own nature, which guides his acts.

Nevertheless, this is precisely the problematic question: how does human nature work as a moral rule? Sokolowski gives a double response: on one hand, the good of the subject appears in the concrete situation; on the other hand, that good is encountered as something to be done, as a claim for the agent as human being. Human nature acts as moral rule precisely because of its teleological character: human beings are not yet what they should be, and what they *ought to be* is recognized in the particular situation, when the individual discover the way of acting that makes him a good human being. In this way, the *telos* discovered in this or

---

[1] Robert Sokolowski, "What is Natural Law? Human Purposes and Natural Ends," in *Christian Faith and Human Understanding* (Washington DC: The Catholic University of America Press, 2006).

[2] Ibid., 214.

that situation—this good recognized as what should be done now—is the moral rule for the human being.

Consequently, Sokolowski defines natural law as "the ontological priority of ends over purposes,"[3] following the distinction between ends and purposes proponed by Slade. Sokolowski sums this distinction up in this way:

> An end, a telos, belongs to a thing in itself, while a purpose arises only when there are human beings. Purposes are intentions, something that we wish for, or are deliberating about or acting to achieve. Ends, in contrast, are there apart from any human wishes and deliberations. They are what the thing is when it has reached its best state, its perfection and completion in and for itself. Ends and purposes are both goods, but goods of different ontological orders.[4]

The difference between ends and purposes arises precisely in the contrast between them that takes place in action:

> The telos and the essence of the thing come to light for us precisely in contrast with our purposes, and our purposes also come to light in contrast with what belongs to the things themselves.[5]

We distinguish them when they are in conflict in a particular situation, when our purposes show to be different from the end of the thing in itself. As Sokolowski shows, before this contrast, those categories are not even available yet. In a phenomenological approach to the topic—coming to the knowledge of the essential doing distinctions[6]—Sokolowski explains how

---

[3] Slade formulated this concept of natural law in conversation and gave permission to Sokolowski to use it in this article. See also Francis Slade, "On the Ontological Priority of Ends and its Relevance to the Narrative Arts," in *Beauty, Art, and the Polis*, ed. Alice Ramos (Washington DC: The Catholic University of America Press, 2000), ———, "Ends and Purposes," in *Final Causality in Nature and Human Affairs*, ed. Richard Hassing (Washington DC: The Catholic University of America Press, 1997).

[4] Sokolowski, "What is Natural Law? Human Purposes and Natural Ends," 215.

[5] Ibid., 219.

[6] Sokolowski propones making distinctions as an essential characteristic of methodology in Phenomenology. Cf. Robert Sokolowski, "Making Distinctions," *The Review of Methaphysics* 32 (1979)., and ———, "Knowing Essentials," *The Review of Methaphysics*, no. 47 (1994); he applies this methodology to natural law in ———, "Knowing Natural Law," *Tijdschrift voor Filosofie* 43 (1981).

> we let the objectivity come into our consciousness, but the objectivity enters there not as a solitary visitor, all by itself; it enters by being differentiated of what we want.[7]

Therefore, ends and purposes could be coincident or not. When it is the case that what we want is not what appears as the proper end for the thing, we have a conflict in human action. However, ends appear like what we should respect, according to which we should act, while our purposes appear like unmotivated, simply as our interest. It is interesting to emphasize that it is not a question of a material but of a formal distinction: the same good could be an end or—and—a purpose, but they are two different forms in which something is good. Therefore, ends are known in contrast with our purposes and with conventions[8] (which would come to be some sort of agreed, common purposes) in which the good at stake becomes manifest as appellative, as obligatory, as a claim for the subject.

When Sokolowski points to the obligatory character of the ends, he implies that the obligation is imposed on the agent *qua human being*. That is precisely the reason why he should give them priority over his preferences. The agent perceives the end as something that should be done if he is to become a good person. A given situation imposes a claim on him not as a particular individual but as a human being. We could say more: he feels an obligation to behave as a human being, in order to become a complete human being. Human nature is then the formal cause, which completion is the final cause. Human nature is a rule for human action *qua* teleological: the concrete rule is given by the fulfillment that is to be achieved. Sokolowski exemplifies it very clearly:

> The precedence of ends over purposes occurs specially in regard to the ends that are proper to human nature and its various powers. For example, the ends built into human nourishment must be seen to govern the way we eat, and the ends that built into human sexuality must be seen to govern the way we live with our sexuality. In both of these powers, we ought not be governed by what we simply want and the purposes we set for ourselves; we must differentiate between what we want and the reality and the telos of the thing we are dealing with. We must have a sense that our purposes must be measured by the way things are, which means that they must be measured by the way things should be. The distinction between purpose an

[7] Sokolowski, "What is Natural Law? Human Purposes and Natural Ends," 219.

[8] Cf. Ibid., 223-26. It would be very interesting to develop this contrast between ends and conventions in order to show the natural character of the telos, but it would exceed the limits of this article.

> end has to dawn on us, and when it does dawn on us, we experience the pressure and the attraction of the way things have to be; we encounter "the natural law".[9]

Consequently, we could say we come to know natural law, the normative character of nature, in practice. The knowledge that corresponds to natural law is practical knowledge: there is a use of reason for recognizing what is good for us in a given situation according to our way of being. Natural law is not a code that we apply in action, a theoretical knowledge applied to practice. Philosophy has a secondary role in this sense: reflection comes afterwards. The original moral knowledge is practical, experiential, and, therefore, concrete and circumstantial. And at the same time, is a source of morality because it appeals to the subject as a human being.

Therefore, natural law is something more complex than a set of norms or principles given beforehand to be applied in action; it is not a code, like some short of instructions for the correct working of the human being. Human nature is not normative as it is a positive law; on the contrary, natural law rules human action as long as human beings have a rational aptitude to recognize in practice those goods—ends—that make them better, fulfilled human beings. Moral knowledge consists in identifying what should be done, what is intrinsically connected to what we ought to be as human. Knowledge of the good for me as a human being arises in the concrete situation that claims a response from me. This is what Sokolowski calls a "sense of the noble"[10] and attributes it to the person capable of recognizing the supremacy of ends over purposes and conventions. That person is not other than the virtuous agent, "who experiences it [the good] not as an imposed duty but as the way he wants to be."[11] We recognize here the Aristotelic good man, who is precisely the paradigm of the virtuous, the one that gives the pattern for action, what allows Sokolowski to establish that the normative character of human nature is not so much a question of natural *law* but rather of natural *decency*.[12] Also, that's why he affirms that a natural visibility pertains to ends: they are revealed for the good agent in his exercise of practical

[9] Ibid., 227.
[10] Ibid., 228.
[11] Ibid.
[12] Cf. Sokolowski, "What is Natural Law? Human Purposes and Natural Ends," 228-29.

reason; they can be known without something like a public promulgation or a previous philosophical reasoning.

There is an interesting parallelism between Sokolowski's proposal and the conception of human nature as a moral source that Charles Taylor explore in *Sources of the Self.* Taylor does not give a systematic description of natural law in his writings. Nevertheless, the role of human nature as a moral source of human identity is a central issue in his work: precisely, the constitution of human identity consists to a great degree—although not only—in the personal and expressive fulfillment of human nature.

In the philosophical anthropology developed by this author, human identity is understood as constituted in a process of leading a life in the context of a sociocultural constitutive framework: by means of the exercise of freedom in action, and so by personal adherence to certain goods, the subject develops his own identity. At the same time, the sociocultural framework provides certain conceptions of the good and of what I should be as a good human being, which are re-examined and assumed or rejected by the subject, giving the background for the constitution of human identity. It is well known the concept of "strong evaluation" Taylor propones: a pre-rational and significative knowledge that is evaluative.[13] The subject carries out evaluations of everything, that will be known at face as good or bad, valuable or despicable, desirable or non attractive, against a background socioculturally constituted: in a horizon of meanings configured simultaneously by language and social practices, in one side, and by personal decisions, reflection and action, in the other. Therefore, the overlapping of the sociocultural and personal factors is complete in the process of constitution of personal identity. Leading a life is precisely what we do when we evaluate and act in order to achieve those ends that are compulsory for us.[14] And in that process we become fulfilled human beings, we realize our human nature in plenitude, in our unique way.

In this context, the key point of self-fulfillment is the articulation of goods in action. Once the subject has made a positive strong evaluation in a given situation, he will perceive the good at stake as something to be prosecuted, and the action that leads to its consecution as the action that should be performed. There is a claim for the subject to act in a specific

---

[13] Cf. Charles Taylor, *Sources of the self: the making of the modern identity* (Cambridge, (Mass.): Harvard University Press, 1989), First Part, Chapters 1-3.

[14] Cf. ———, "Leading a Life," in *Inconmensurability, Incomparability and Practical Reason*, ed. Ruth Chang (Cambridge: Harvard University Press, 1997).

way if he is to behave as a good human being. Because the most interesting point is that he or she perceives the claim as compelling for him or her as a human being, not as a particular self. Taylor talks about subject-referring claims in contrast with self-referring claims.[15] We can see here the same difference Sokolowski establishes between ends and purposes. The moral character of the action is given by a good that is different from a personal interest or purpose.

I would like to go deep on the taylorian notion of *constitutive good*. Taylor identifies some cases in which the attribution of goodness is done "in a fuller sense" to some kind of reality, when "their relation to this is what makes certain of our actions or aspirations good; it is what constitutes the goodness of this actions."[16] A constitutive good "is a moral source in the sense I want to use this term here: that is, it is something the love of which empowers us to do and be good (...) and hence also loving it is to be a good human being."[17] He is referring with these to:

> Features of the universe, or God, or human beings, (i) on which the life goods depend, (ii) which command our moral awe or allegiance, and (iii) the contemplation of or contact with which empowers us to be good. In virtue of (iii) such constitutive goods function as what I call "moral sources".[18]

Something can be known as good in a way that I am good in loving it and prosecuting it. Thus, constitutive goods are ends for action, precisely because the intentional description performed by the subject (what Taylor calls "articulation")[19] shows a feature of a particular reality that constitutes it in good for him as a human being; and at the same time constitutes the subject in a good human being when he acts to promote that good. So, some goods are constitutive for the kind of being that I am: the

---

[15] Taylor developes this contrast in ———, "Self-interpreting Animals," in *Philosophical Papers I. Human Agency and Language* (New York: Cambridge University Press, 1988), 45-76.

[16] Taylor, *Sources of the self: the making of the modern identity*, 92.

[17] Ibid., 93.

[18] Charles Taylor, "Comments and Replies," *Inquiry* 34, no. 2 (1991): 243.

[19] Cf. Taylor, *Sources of the self: the making of the modern identity*, Chapter 2. See also Charles Taylor, "Language and Human Nature," in *Philosophical Papers I. Human Agency and Language* (New York: Cambridge University Press, 1988). Also "Theories of Meaning", Alan B. Plaunt Memorial Lecture, University of Carleton, Ottawa; published in ———, "Theories of Meaning," *Man and World* 13, no. 3-4 (1980).

constitutive good is perceived as according with me, with what I am and with what I ought to be.

Taylor affirms that articulating a constitutive good is making clear what is involved in the life goods one has assumed. This type of articulation is performed by practical reason, and posterior reflection could be done on it, but not necessarily. That is the reason why he adds:

> "Unreflecting people in the culture, who are drawn to certain life goods, may have nothing to offer in the way of description of constitutive good, but that doesn't mean that their sense of what is worth pursuing isn't shaped by some unstructured intuitions about their metaphysical predicament."[20]

This ontological character of the good grants to Taylor's moral theory all its strength: the moral question for Taylor is a question of goods for the subject, which move him because he perceives them as claims in a horizon of meanings, which includes a self-interpretation of himself like a human being, not only as an individual with these or those preferences.[21]

Like Rosen indicates, this affirmation of constitutive goods leads to the thesis that moral order does not depend on the will of the subject, is somewhat external to him. For Taylor, moral order comes into sight as an order given to the subject trough some articulations.[22]

However, Taylor amends the interpretation of Rosen, to insist that the kind of moral realism he propones is not an objectivist universalist one:

> I want to speak of this demand as something that we discover. And so I want to go on thinking of myself as a moral realist, even though I am uncomfortably aware of Rosen's urging that we both occupy a kind of middle ground between the old Platonic model and naturalist projectivism. But this also means that I do not see morality as 'rooted in an intrinsically rational order' of traditional kind. Which is not to say that *articulating* it in terms of order may not be an important goal for us language beings.[23]

Moral knowledge is not to be explained by submitting every case to a rational rule of universal application, or in a deductive reasoning. On the contrary, the articulation of the constitutive goods derives from the experience of the concrete good: experience of this good here and now as

---

[20] Taylor, *Sources of the self: the making of the modern identity*, 307.
[21] Cf. ———, "Self-interpreting Animals," 58.
[22] Cf. M. Rosen, "Must we Return to Moral Realism?," *Inquiry* 34 (1991).
[23] Taylor, "Comments and Replies," 246.

unavoidable, experience of this situation in which there is something that is not like random, but absolute, inalienable to become this person I want to be. The subject experiences that to resign from a certain good is to resign to be human.

The description of the goods as constitutive it is opened, on one side, to a connection with some things in reality, significantly known and valued; and, on the other, to the way in which the subject understands himself as human, going beyond the personal preferences and the cultural conventions. If it is true that the subject perceives certain claims in a given situation as inalienable goods for a human being, if there are in real situations properties regarding the subject as human—not just us a particular self—then, to affirm these goods is to be a good human being; to act so that the goods at stake are achieved is to become a good person.

Taylor's proposal connects inseparably the notion of constitutive goods with the idea of human nature as a moral source. But nature is now internalized and expressed by the subject in a unique and free way, since the knowledge of the good and of what I am as a human being—intrinsically connected as we have seen before—always happen in a particular horizon of meanings, in a concrete background. Humanness admits multiple realizations, the human nature is such that is always and only realized in a personal expression; it is open to infinite developments, so many as human beings could exist, since it is to be expressively fulfilled. It corresponds to any human being as a proper task to discover and to realize its own nature in his own way. And this is precisely to be good. That's why Taylor points to an internalization of the good and the nature as moral sources:

> But unlike previous conceptions of moral sources in nature and God, these modern views give a crucial place to our own inner powers of constructing, or transfiguring or interpreting the world, as essential to the efficacy of the external sources. Our powers must be deployed if these are to empower us. And in this sense the moral sources have been at least partly internalized (...) The internalization is in a sense more complete in the atheist or naturalist theories, more complete for Nietzsche than for Dostoyevski.[24]

To affirm that morality lies in the affirmation and the adherence of the subject to only one human universal good, expressed in the principles of natural law, could be misunderstood as an attempt to reduce the radical capacity of human beings for self-determination, and to annul the

---

24 ———, *Sources of the self: the making of the modern identity*, 455.

relevancy of the personal difference possible—and inevitable, since the subject lives in a significant interpretation of the world—in the configuration of the identity. The affirmation of "nature as a source can't ignore the point that mere sinking into unity with nature would be a negation of human autonomy".[25] Human beings are not completely identical with the species, their fulfillment as human beings is not determined specifically, but it is to be achieved in a personal way. Taylor points to the necessity of taking in account radical autonomy and expressive unity.

You can see therefore an interesting parallelism between the two authors. First, the constitutive goods of which Taylor speaks play the same role in moral action that ends play in Sokolowski's approach: articulated constitutive goods would be parallel to ends as opposite to purposes, in the sense that human nature is given as a moral source trough the articulation of those goods-ends that are proper for human beings.

Second, both Taylor and Sokolowski point to the practical character of human nature as normative: the good that is proper to the kind of being I am is discovered in experience, in the concrete action. And that practical knowledge come to place in the contrast between what one would like to do and what one is appealed to do as a good human being, or—to use Taylor's words—in the contrast between subject-referring and self-referring claims. Our first notice of something like a natural law takes place in concrete actions and situations, in which we experience something like human, like more human than the opposite, or like inhumane.

Third, the moral character of human nature resides in its teleology: is the fulfillment of human nature what makes that specific ends or goods should be prosecuted in action. Both authors insist on the connection between the good that is to be done and the achievement of my own humanness: the individual experiences a demand as human to act in a concrete way, to do this or that because it is what a good person would do. Human nature is normative as a final cause: not just as something given we should obey but as a *telos* to be achieved. The natural law, therefore, has more to do with the human aptitude to discover and to do the good than with a code or law of general principles that only appear in a posterior reflection. Human beings fulfill the law that nature gives to them precisely when they look for their plenitude in accordance with it, that is to say, in a rational and free way. As Taylor puts it, nature continues to be a moral source, but internalized and in an individual unique expression.

---

[25] Ibid., 385.

Works Cited

Rosen, M. "Must We Return to Moral Realism?" *Inquiry* 34 (1991): 183-94.

Slade, Francis. "Ends and Purposes." In *Final Causality in Nature and Human Affairs*, edited by Richard Hassing, 83–85. Washington DC: The Catholic University of America Press, 1997.

—. "On the Ontological Priority of Ends and Its Relevance to the Narrative Arts." In *Beauty, Art, and the Polis*, edited by Alice Ramos, 58–69. Washington DC: The Catholic University of America Press, 2000.

Sokolowski, Robert. "Knowing Essentials." *The Review of Methaphysics*, no. 47 (1994): 691-710.

—. "Knowing Natural Law." *Tijdschrift voor Filosofie* 43 (1981): 625-41.

—. "Making Distinctions." *The Review of Methaphysics* 32 (1979): 639-77.

—. "What Is Natural Law? Human Purposes and Natural Ends." In *Christian Faith and Human Understanding*, 214-33. Washington DC: The Catholic University of America Press, 2006.

Taylor, Charles. "Comments and Replies." *Inquiry* 34, no. 2 (1991): 237-54.

—. "Language and Human Nature." In *Philosophical Papers I. Human Agency and Language*, 215-47. New York: Cambridge University Press, 1988.

—. "Leading a Life." In *Inconmensurability, Incomparability and Practical Reason*, edited by Ruth Chang, 170-83. Cambridge: Harvard University Press, 1997.

—. "Self-Interpreting Animals." In *Philosophical Papers I. Human Agency and Language*, 45-76. New York: Cambridge University Press, 1988.

—. *Sources of the Self: The Making of the Modern Identity*. Cambridge, (Mass.): Harvard University Press, 1989.

—. "Theories of Meaning." *Man and World* 13, no. 3-4 (1980).

CHAPTER THIRTEEN

GUARANTEEING THE RIGHT TO HAVE RIGHTS: HANNAH ARENDT'S THEORY OF POLITICS

JULIA URABAYEN

The work of Hannah Arendt is synonymous with reflections on the meaning of totalitarianism, citizenship, democracy, the public realm and public life. For this reason, Arendt's thinking is often categorised as political philosophy, although Arendt herself defined her work as a political theory, not a philosophy.[1] The primary purpose of this distinction, by which Arendt distances herself from the philosophical tradition in which she was educated, is to highlight her rejection of one approach to philosophy and, in particular, her rejection of a school of political philosophy that begins with the work of Plato and continues into the work of modern and contemporary philosophers whose understanding of politics remains bound by the exacting limitations which that school of thought imposes.

Arendt's aim is to provide an understanding of politics as a form of human activity, spanning from its origins to its ends; a project that she regards as both necessary and urgent. The dual context from which this thinker—a German Jewish woman—derived her sense of purpose was, first, the historical experience of totalitarianism, which has destroyed, literally, the categories of political thought and our criteria for moral judgment,[2] and, second, the experience of "refugees".[3]

---

[1] "I do not belong to the academy of philosophers. [...] In no sense do I regard myself as a philosopher, nor do I think that I would be made welcome in the academy of philosophers"; in a television interview with Günter Gauss, 28 October 1964, later published as the article: Hannah Arendt, "Seule demeure la langue maternelle," *Esprit* IV, no. 6 (1980): 19-38. [Translation to English is mine].

[2] Cfr.———, *Between Past and Future. Eight Exercises in Political Thought* (New York: Penguin Books, 1985), 3-15. As Eslin points out, this radical rejection of previous tradition is based on the assumption that the tradition is bankrupt; it can

History had shown how in certain places, even at the heart of civilized Europe, the totality of the law might be put into abeyance: human beings were stripped of all protection and treated like animals. Given that no conception of human nature appeared to act as any kind of restraint on such barbarity, it seems clear that something more than human nature itself is called for if the humanity of every man and woman is to be respected and guaranteed.[4] A radical break with the philosophical tradition in which her own thought had developed became necessary because

> the national-socialist system marked the first attempt to put into practice what had until then been only a 'dream', the dream of the metaphysical tradition: that man establish himself as the ultimate ground of all things, the master of the universe. Such a project inevitably entails the negation of plurality, of difference, of contingency, and revealed the full force of its nihilistic purpose in the concentration camps.[5]

Totalitarianism had called human nature itself into question.

Arendt drew the same conclusion from her study of the historical experience of refugees: people who fled their native land in order to save their lives—homeless, nation-less, citizens of no state and, consequently,

---

no longer account for historical reality and must therefore be replaced by a new form of political thought. See J.-C. Eslin, "L'événement de penser," *Esprit* IV, no. 6 (1980): 9-10.

[3] To Arendt's mind, the proposition that human rights are natural rights –that is, rights derived from human nature –is problematic because non-citizens, people who have come to live in a particular state having fled their native land(s), do not enjoy the rights which the constitution of that state appears to guarantee on the basis of a theory of natural human rights. See Hannah Arendt, *The Origins of Totalitarism* (New York: Meridian Books, 1960). Specially, chapter two, nine: "The Decline of the Nation-State and the End of the Rights of Man". As a consequence, Arendt argues that the rights of man must depend on citizenship –not only in practice, but also in principle: "eu égard aux droits de l'homme, il suggère qu'ils ne sont pas naturellement humains, implantés dans des individus pré-politiques, mais enracinés dans la citoyenneté"; R. Legros, "Hannah Arendt: une compréhension phénoménologique des droits de l'homme," *Études phénoménologiques*, no. 2 (1985): 35.

[4] In fact, Arendt argues that if a man or a woman finds himself/herself under attack because he/she is a Jew or a Jewess, he/she must respond as a Jew or Jewess –not as a citizen of the world, nor through an appeal to the universal validity of human rights. See Arendt, "Seule demeure la langue maternelle," 28.

[5] S. Forti, *Vida del espíritu y tiempo de la polis. Hannah Arendt entre filosofía y política* (Madrid: Ediciones Cátedra, 2001), 118.

without rights.[6] Arendt's consideration of these two forms of historical experience led her to reflect on the meaning of citizenship, politics, the law and, above all, human nature and the human condition:

> according to Arendt, man is to be regarded as a free being. This idea so determines her way of thinking that it leads Arendt to concede that her theory of politics may be read as an attempt to provide the general framework for a 'philosophical anthropology' capable of accounting for human freedom by exploring all those phenomena that are in any way related to human nature.[7]

The focus of Arendt's interest, then, is the human condition; and her purpose is to provide a phenomenology of the human condition. This purpose presupposes a distinction between human nature and the human condition. Arendt's reflections on this distinction led her to describe human nature as the subject of repeated and cyclical processes of a biological or organic kind—that is, man as a living being; but this dimension of human being—, in which psychology might also be included, responds only to *what* man is, not *who* he is. Only a study of the human condition, which encompasses limits and limitations, promises and forgiveness, laws and institutions, and man's ability to initiate action, can give an account of who man is.

Not only is human nature unable to answer the question of who man is; Arendt also argues that the aspect of the human condition which best defines personal identity is action. More than any other facet of the human condition, action reveals in a definitive way 'who' the human person is. Personal initiative and freedom as the source of new directions and developments in interpersonal relationships are the basis of the drama of public life, the "space of appearance", which is, in turn, the arena of politics.

In this context, Arendt sets out a strong defence of the right to have rights with a keen awareness all the while of the limits of progress.

---

[6] See J.-C. Eslin, "Une loi qui vaille pour l'humanité," *Esprit* IV, no. 6 (1980): 42. "Thus, *displaced persons* are the dispossessed of the earth, for they are welcome neither in their own countries nor in the countries to which they have fled; as a result, charity, rather than an established bill of rights, is the ultimate guarantor of their right to life"; C. Lafer, *La reconstrucción de los derechos humanos. Un diálogo con el pensamiento de Hannah Arendt* (México: Fondo de Cultura Económica, 1991), 167. [Translation to English is mine].

[7] Forti, *Vida del espíritu y tiempo de la polis. Hannah Arendt entre filosofía y política*, 321.

The natural world and the human condition: work, labour and action

Arendt's political thought is based on an analysis of human activity and identifies political action, the forms of initiative and debate that arise from human freedom, as the defining activity of human being—rather than the labour associated with the biological or physical condition of being human or the work necessary in a world of things, the world of artifice. It should also be borne in mind that in her description Arendt recognizes certain conditions to the human person's being in the world: birth, death and plurality.

Arendt first distinguishes between the active and the contemplative life, and points out that while the latter has traditionally been regarded as pre-eminent the active life is vital and makes the contemplative life possible: "it is quite possible for human beings to go through life without ever indulging in contemplation, while, on the other hand, no man can remain in the contemplative state throughout his life. Active life, in other words, is not only what most men are engaged in but even what no man can escape altogether. For it is in the nature of the human condition that contemplation remains dependent upon all sorts of activities—it depends upon labour to produce whatever is necessary to keep the human organism alive, it depends upon work to create whatever is needed to house the human body, and it needs action to organize the living together of many human beings in such a way that peace, the condition for the quiet of contemplation, is assured."[8]

Traditional consideration of this distinction between active and contemplative has tended to overlook or ignore the different value and meanings of the active life. Arendt's work is an attempt to make up for this lack. The active life, she argues, is composed of three basic forms of activity: labour, work and action, which "are fundamental because each corresponds to one of the basis conditions under which life on earth has been given to man."[9] Life is the condition of labour, the activity which corresponds to the biological reality of the human body; worldliness (human being as being in the world) is the condition of work, which comprises all of the non-natural functions and activities by which human beings make artificial things; plurality is the condition of action, the only form of human activity which does not require the mediation of things. All

---

[8] Hannah Arendt, "Labor, Work, Action," in *The Portable Hannah Arendt*, ed. Peter Baehr (New York: Penguin Group, 2000), 167.

[9] ———, *The Human Condition* (Chicago: University of Chicago Press, 1958), 7.

of these, in turn, are ultimately related to the all-encompassing conditions of human existence: birth and death.[10]

Arendt argues that human beings are conditioned, not determined. No human existence would be possible without the existence of things; and without the existence of human beings, things—unrelated and unable to relate to one another—would constitute a non-world. Thus, Arendt accepts the Heideggerian proposition that the world is a network or framework of relations and relationships established by human beings. The human condition, however, is not human nature; it is not the definition of the essence of human being. To be conditioned is part of human nature, but human beings could establish different or new conditions of existence and remain human, in which case

> the only statement we could make regarding their 'nature' is that they are still conditioned beings, even though their condition is now self-made to a considerable extent.[11]

To reflect on the active life is to focus on the human being as an agent that performs activities which do not necessarily flow from human nature. The active life has been regarded as inferior to the contemplative life in the history of philosophy from ancient times to modern. Arendt intends to focus her attention on a form of life that tradition has overlooked or undervalued:

> if, therefore, the use of the term *vita activa*, as I propose it here, is in manifest contradiction to the tradition, it is because I doubt not the validity of the experience underlying the distinction but rather the hierarchical order inherent in it from its inception. This does not mean that I want to contest or even to discuss, for that matter, the traditional concept of truth as

[10] For Arendt, birth, the ability to begin new things, is closely, though not exclusively, linked to political life; this focus distinguishes her thought from the tradition of metaphysical thinking in which death, mortality, is held to be central. See Ibid., 9. In the same way, Arendt's focus marks a point of departure from Heidegger's description of man as a being-towards-death. Nevertheless, Arendt's position is not a vitalist one as she makes clear that the philosophy of life is the last philosophical position of modernity.

[11] Ibid., 10. The context for these considerations was the moon-landing and the possibility it suggested that human beings might leave Earth and thus become non-terrestrial beings. Arendt argues that man cannot know his own essence as he knows the essence of things: to do so, he would have to stand in his own shadow. Only a god would be capable of such a feat, but man would cease in the act to be a 'who' and become a 'what'.

> revelation and therefore something essentially given to man, or that I prefer the modern age's pragmatic assertion that man can only know what he makes himself. My contention is simply that the enormous weight of contemplation in the traditional hierarchy has blurred the distinctions and articulations within the *vita activa* itself.[12]

Thus, to Arendt's mind, a detailed examination of the active life, a study of its different parts and the distinctions between parts never envisaged by thinkers in the classical period or in the modern age, is of vital necessity.

According to Arendt, the hierarchical pre-eminence of the contemplative over the active life was provoked by Platonic experience and thought after the death of Socrates in which politics was abandoned in favour of philosophy:

> the historic breach between philosophy and politics was opened by the trial and execution of Socrates. Socrates' death is a point of reference in the history of philosophy, as the death of Jesus is in the history of religion. The tradition of political philosophy that has come down to us begins with the death of Socrates which led Plato to despair of the life of the *polis* and to call into question some of the fundamental ideas of Socratic thought.[13]

Another factor which may explain, in part, why the parts and relationships between parts in the active life have been overlooked is the distinction made between private and public, given that some of the activities of the active life pertain to the private, non-public realm. Arendt points out that, according to the Greeks, private life is a form of privation: although private life exists of necessity and co-exists with public life, private activity is without meaning or consequence because it lacks meaning and consequence for others. Some commentators have wrongly attributed this position to Arendt herself. For Arendt, however, private activity is of great significance, for it guarantees the human being's sense of belonging in the world.[14] She notes that while knowledge of the private

---

[12] Ibid., 16-17.

[13] ———, *Filosofía y política. Heidegger y el existencialismo* (Bilbao: Besatari, 1997), 11. [Translation to English is mine].

[14] "Si elle rejoint l'idée grecque du 'domestique' comme exclusion, hiérarchie et obscurité où s'abrite tout ce qui relève du biologique en ce qu'il a d'inexorable, elle pourrait aussi soutenir avec J. Boudin: 'il n'y a point de chose publique s'il n'y a quelque chose de propre'. Ainsi, face au totalitarisme, le privé apparaît-il comme une condition essentielle de la liberté politique minimale qui permet au moins

realm of human being is not a given, and thus has never been an object of philosophical reflection, an understanding of private life is vital:

> privacy was like the other, the dark and hidden side of the public realm, and while to be political meant to attain the highest possibility of human existence, to have no private place of one's own […] meant to be no longer human.[15]

As a consequence, Arendt sets herself the goal of carrying out this necessary study of the human being's non-political activity and of defining the difference between labour and work.[16] The purpose of labour is to meet the natural and primitive needs of human life. Labour involves discomfort, tiredness and suffering, and never escapes the cycle of natural life since it is a function of the metabolism which is part of human being as it is of all living beings.[17] Labour, the cycle of production and consumption, is a necessary activity: "by labouring, men produce the vital necessities that must be fed into the life process of the human body. And since this life process, though it leads from birth to death in a rectilinear progress of decay, is in itself circular, the labouring activity itself must follow the cycle of life, the circular movement of our bodily functions, which means that the labouring activity never comes to an end as long as life lasts; it is endlessly repetitive."[18]

The principal problem posed by this process which ends only with death is that

> the mark of all labouring [is] that it leaves nothing behind, that the result of its effort is almost as quickly consumed as the effort is spent. And yet this effort, despite its futility, is born of a great urgency and motivated by a more powerful drive than anything else, because life itself depends upon it.[19]

---

d'échapper à la 'désolation' comme 'expérience d'absolue non-appartenance au monde'(ST 226)"; A. Enegrén, *La pensée politique de Hannah Arendt* (Paris: Presses Universitaires de France, 1984), 70.

[15] Arendt, *The Human Condition*, 64.

[16] In order to carry out this study, Arendt drew on the distinction expressed by Locke, "the labour of our body and the work of our hands", social and historical experience, and the existence in all Indo-European languages of separate words for labour and work.

[17] One of the first steps taken by Arendt as part of her study of the distinction between labour and work was to distance her position from Marxist thought.

[18] Arendt, "Labor, Work, Action," 170-71.

[19] ———, *The Human Condition*, 87. For Arendt, the belief that human need or labour may ever be wholly escaped is a delusion.

Although this form of activity is governed by need, the need for survival, it is also productive, as human being's activity is not reduced to producing only what they need. Man's capacity for labour extends beyond his needs, but what is produced quickly succumbs to the natural cycle of life.

The activity of work, in contrast, has a beginning and an end; it is an autonomous and objective form of production that may serve goals which do not respond to the immediate needs of human life: "the work of our hands, as distinguished from the labour of our bodies [...] fabricates the sheer unending variety of things whose sum total constitutes the human artifice."[20] Work makes the world meaningful, protects human beings from nature, and offers some security for their sense of instability and mortality. What is produced by the activity of work is not permanent or eternal. Nevertheless, while the objects produced by work form part of the cycle of life and return to it, they have an independence and objectivity with respect to their maker which reflects the fact that they could resist to human needs.

Man uses the objects of his work, but he does not consume them; independent of him, they resist assimilation to human being:

> what distinguishes the most flimsy pair of shoes from mere consumer goods is that they do not spoil if I do not wear them, that they have an independence of their own, however modest, which enables them to survive even for a considerable time the changing moods of their owner. Used or unused, they will remain in the world for a certain while unless they are wantonly destroyed.[21]

---

[20] Ibid., 136.

[21] Ibid., 138. Thus, Arendt seeks to justify the distinction she has made between labour and work. The ideas of durability and objectivity are central to her argument. The objectivity and independence of what is produced by human work, with respect to use, is especially noticeable in works of art: "nowhere else does the sheer durability of the world of things appear in such purity and clarity, nowhere else therefore does this thing-world reveal itself so spectacularly as the non-mortal home for mortal beings. It is as though worldly stability had become transparent in the permanence of art, so that a premonition of immortality, not the immortality of the soul or of life but of something immortal achieved by mortal hands, has become tangibly present, to shine and to be seen, to sound and to be heard, to speak and to be read"; ———, *The Human Condition*, 168. Another key difference between labour and work is that the process of work is always carried out – the object of work made – by following a model.

Arendt refers to this process as "reification" and points out that the process by which man removes a part of matter from its rightful place in nature is a process which implies, to a greater or lesser degree, a destruction of nature. It is in the context of this process that human beings face the temptation of Prometheus, the temptation to work towards the domination of the world by unnatural or unwarranted means.[22]

Leaving to one side the question of what degree of control man should seek to exercise over nature, Arendt highlights the fact that these two activities, labour and work, are two forms of being in the world and two ways of understanding the relationship between man and nature. Labour makes man part of the cycle of natural life and relates to his basic needs; at the same time, a balance is struck between use and renewal—when, and only when, labour is not allowed to usurp the other fields of activity, above all, that of work. Given that "it is artifice which brings the world into being and takes possession of it by working against the cycles of nature by violent means,"[23] however, it is work that underlies the durability, stability and objectivity of the world. The key here is man's presence in the world: human being is being in the world, and a stable dwelling-place grounds the stability of human being. It is important to recall in this context the distinction that Arendt makes between living on earth and inhabiting the world. Earth is the natural environment in which each human being lives; the world, on the other hand, is always a shared world, a space of appearance and artifice, an existential and inter-personal reality: *inter est*.[24]

But this, labour and work, does not account for every aspect of human life. Man, as man, expresses himself through action and speech, and "speech is what makes man a political being".[25] If a person were to renounce action or speech, he or she would cease *eo ipso* to live a human

---

[22] In this regard, Arendt highlights the fact that in the Old Testament man is not named lord and master of nature; rather, man is lord of all living creatures, which were made to help and serve him, just as he himself was placed in the Garden of Eden to serve and conserve nature. See Arendt, *The Human Condition*, chapter four, footnote three.

[23] Enegrén, *La pensée politique de Hannah Arendt*, 37.

[24] Levinas also speaks of human interest, and links being in the world to economics, to home, woman and paternity. See E. Levinas, *Totalité et inifini. Essai sur l'extériorité* (La Haye: Nijholf, 1971).

[25] Arendt, *The Human Condition*, 3. According to Arendt, any process of socialization that denigrates politics turns man into an *animal laborans*, a being which simply consumes. Arendt seeks to reclaim the value of the public realm in response to this loss or disregard for important dimensions of human being.

life. Belonging in the world is the fruit of some initiative, a form of re-birth, the beginning of a new someone. These re-born beings come to make their presence felt in the world through their actions and speech with and to others:

> the realm of human affairs, strictly speaking, consists of the web of human relationships which exists wherever men live together. The disclosure of the 'who' through speech, and the setting of a new beginning through action, always fall into an already existing web where the immediate consequences can be felt.[26]

Initiative is the defining characteristic of human action, to begin or put something new in motion in a context of plurality and a shared existence with equals.

The space of plurality and shared existence, the community of human beings, is the field of politics. Action is the defining characteristic of politics: politics is a form of *praxis* carried out among a community of equals gathered together in the public realm, the space of appearance; this praxis becomes *lexis* or word, which is not knowledge but judgement or opinion conditioned by prudence and common sense. *Lexis* tells a story, it makes history—a story which reveals the human being as the agent of history. Action is at the heart of human being, for it involves intersubjectivity, language and the free will of human agents.

Arendt returns again and again to the idea that action is a function of plurality, not the activity of the individual alone. Solitary action is the definition of tyranny: a tyrant does not act, he inflicts violence, and views others as material on and through which he may carry out his work. Authentic action draws on a wealth of diversity and the freedom of human beings, and is performed in the public realm where freedom and diversity are made manifest. The keystone of politics, therefore, is not unity, but plurality, diversity, distinction, difference; and, as a consequence, the purpose of politics can never be to impose uniformity.[27]

In any case, politics is both based on and highlights the fact that human beings have the power to initiate action, to add something new to the world through natality or birth. Man is not born to die; rather, he is born to

---

[26] Ibid., 183-84.

[27] "La cité n'est que la pluralité de ses citoyens qui doit être préservée de toute subordination à un appareil unificateur, défendue jusqu'au bout contre les entreprises théoriques entraînées aux totalisations qui réservent l'efficience à une unité suffisante"; Enegrén, *La pensée politique de Hannah Arendt*, 46.

bring new things into being, things which are born of his individuality. Thus, as a revelation of the individual 'I', the distinguishing feature of human action is its unpredictability.[28]

Arendt does not regard the active life, as expressed in political terms, as the only worthy form of life; she does not disregard or discount the meaning and value of the contemplative life. Nevertheless, the primary focus of her work is to offer an account of the forms of human experience from which political concepts derive and to restore to action the meaning and value it has lost. One of the hallmarks of her thought, therefore, is to examine the links between philosophy and politics, theory and praxis. Arendt's work is anti-Platonic in the following sense: she refuses to define, interpret or evaluate the active life in the terms and categories of the contemplative life.[29]

Human affairs, therefore, cannot be addressed from the perspective of contemplative reason. To do so would be to lose sight of what define human action: contingency, finitude, originality, unpredictability, irreversibility, fragility and vulnerability;[30] in fact, to do so would be to replace action with the tyranny of reason. Equally mistaken and distorting are the many attempts in modern times to interpret politics in terms of work, *praxis* in terms of *poiesis*. In response to these inadequate or erroneous approaches, Arendt proposes to re-establish the true meaning of politics through an

> understanding of the *polis* […] the idea of a civic community brought about by the participation of citizens in public life and based on the firm

---

[28] As it not immediately pertinent to the matter under discussion, the figure of the narrator or historian and his role in the development and interpretation of narrative and history is not addressed here.

[29] Arendt draws on two currents in political thought: the line of thought that begins with Plato and leads to Marx, passing through the work of Hobbes and Locke, which strips politics of meaning and turns instead to philosophy; and the school of thought which might be referred to as "civic republicanism", which includes such thinkers as Machiavelli, Tocqueville and Jefferson among its followers and whose guiding light is Socrates who strove to give an account of real political experience. See C. Sánchez Muñoz, *Hannah Arendt. El espacio de la política* (Madrid: Centro de Estudios Políticos y Constitucionales, 2003), 35-55.

[30] To resist the absolute claims of irreversibility and unpredictability in action, Arendt turns to the human capacity for forgiveness in the case of the former, and the making and keeping of promises in the case of the latter.

commitment to keep the public realm in being as the only space in which mutual recognition is made possible.[31]

In short, Arendt takes it as her purpose to show that politics still has meaning as a human activity.

The realm of politics: action and freedom as the defining characteristics of human being

According to Arendt, plurality is the condition of politics:

> the 'world' in Heidegger's conception of 'being-in-the-world' is modified in order to prove that is a world shared with others, and thus plurality is a fundamental characteristic both of the 'human condition' and political life.[32]

For Arendt, plurality is the human condition itself and the basis of all political life; it is only by means of the key notion of plurality that we can ever come to understand the "public realm", and within the public realm, citizenship and democracy. When plurality is recognised to be an essential characteristic of human being, it becomes clear that politics cannot be a merely banal or secondary activity for a being who is *per se* a being with others:

> action, the only activity that goes on directly between men without the intermediary of things or matter, corresponds to the human condition of plurality, to the fact that men, not Man, live on the earth and inhabit the world. While all aspects of the human condition are somehow related to politics, this plurality is specifically *the* condition—not only the *conditio sine qua non*, but the *conditio per quam*—of all political life.[33]

---

[31] Sánchez Muñoz, *Hannah Arendt. El espacio de la política*, 25. [Translation to English is mine]. This understanding of the *polis* is clearly part both of Arendt's critique of Platonic thought and of the project of deconstruction in which she engages to undo the traditional priority attributed to being at the expense of appearance.

[32] N. Campillo, "'Mundo' y 'pluralidad' en Hannah Arendt," in *Paideia*, ed. Ángel Álvarez Gómez, et al. (Cursos y congresos nº 156: Universidad de Santiago de Compostela Publicatións, 2005), 1104. [Translation to English is mine].

[33] Arendt, *The Human Condition*, 7.

Only plurality or the recognition of what is shared or public makes a diversity of perspectives in judgement and opinion possible—that is, politics in the strict sense of the term. Plurality shapes the world as a "space of appearance", a space inhabited by actors and spectators:

> the world men are born into contains many things, natural and artificial, living and dead, transient and sempiternal, all of which have in common that they *appear* and hence are meant to be seen, heard, touched, tasted, and smelled, to be perceived by sentient creatures endowed with the appropriate sense organs. Nothing could appear, the word 'appearance' would make no sense, if recipients of appearances did not exist—living creatures able to acknowledge, recognize, and react to—in flight or desire, approval or disapproval, blame or praise—what is not merely there but appears to them and is meant for their perception. In this world which we enter, appearing from a nowhere, and from which we disappear into a nowhere, *Being and Appearing coincide*. Dead matter, natural and artificial, changing and unchanging, depends in its beings, that is, in its appearingness, on the presence of living creatures. Nothing and nobody exists in this world whose very being does not presuppose a *spectator*. In other words, nothing that is, insofar as it appears, exists in the singular; everything that is is meant to be perceived by somebody. Not Man but men inhabit this planet. Plurality is the law of the earth.[34]

The political realm as such is both a particular place and the constitutional framework which enables the relationships between the actors who inhabit it—the 'between' or 'among' which underlies the unity and diversity of plurality.[35] The face-to-face relationships in the political realm give rise to forms of mutual understanding where no one is anonymous; thus, the political realm is an almost transcendental realm in which human beings appear to one another and lay down the limits and laws of interaction:

---

[34] Hannah Arendt, *The Life of the Mind (Volume I: Thinking)* (London: Secker & Warburg, 1978), 19. Being and appearance are identified in Arendt's work because of the anti-Platonic approach she adopts and the influence of Heidegger on her thought. Nevertheless, the position she adopts is not a postmodern one: Arendt rejects any conception of pure fluidity and insists on permanence and stability. Her purpose is to highlight the fact that our sense of reality is shared: being-in-the-world is being-in-the-world-with.

[35] In Greek thought, according to Arendt, neither the founding of the city (the development of the physical/geographical living space) nor the drafting of legislation constituted political activity; rather, they were regarded as forms of pre-political activity. See Arendt, *The Human Condition*, 194-95.

> it is the space of appearance in the widest sense of the word, namely, the space where I appear to others as others appear to me, where men exist not merely like other living or inanimate things but make their appearance explicitly.[36]

Arendt's purpose, therefore, is to bring about the restoration of the world by restoring meaning and value to politics and the political realm.[37] The modern world has lost any sense of "being-among" and a return to its senses depends upon recovering the meaning and value of public life. Arendt attributes this loss of meaning to changes which inaugurated the modern age, a great alienation which turned the relationship between the active and the contemplative life upside-down and confused the meanings of the different aspects of the active life:

> we tend to overlook the central importance of this alienation for the modern age because we usually stress its secular character and identify the term secularity with worldliness.[38]

In other words, the original meaning of politics has been lost, *praxis* become *poiesis*, and power, domination.

The authentic meaning of worldliness has been lost in the modern age, the 'I' closed in upon itself has lost the public realm as the political realms; and *homo laborans* has been wrongly identified *homo faber*. Arendt's critique of the modern age and modern thought centres on the idea of the masses and the undoing of the ties that bind in social and community life, both of which lead to atomisation and isolation. The decline and fall of the world as a shared world marks, at the same time, the end of citizenship and the public realm; the nation-state and bureaucracy (or government by no one) take their place. For Arendt, these changes are signs of world alienation and the alienation of man, but they may also be enabling opportunities.[39]

---

[36] Ibid., 198-99.

[37] Arendt points out that the realm of politics has been usurped by economics in the modern age, the *agora* become nothing more than a market-place. This change has stripped man of one of his defining features; moreover, it has robbed him of any form of relationship with nature beyond labour, given that the meaning of work has been reduced to labour as a result of the Industrial Revolution. See Ibid., 159-63.

[38] Ibid., 253.

[39] This argument entails a radical revision of our conception of reality: "only when the *vita activa* had lost its point of reference in the *vita contemplativa* could it become active life in the full sense of the word; and only because this active life

It is in this context that Arendt proposes a paradigm-shift in philosophical thought:

> the utter failure of reason must be read, nevertheless, as a validation of the thought of the world, thought reconciled to the world. The element of surprise from which philosophy first sprang must give way to new reflections from the world on thought. In Arendt's view, the question of the meaning of being has become a question concerning the phenomenal condition of thought, word and action.[40]

The most significant consequence of this change in thinking is that phenomenological analysis, which regards plurality as the condition of action, acquires political meaning. Plurality defines human beings as beings in the world; plurality is also a defining characteristic of politics, the plurality of actors and spectators and the diversity of perspectives in judgement and opinion. To Arendt's mind, the public realm has ontological status: it is the space of appearance, a shared world, and thus

> an *a priori* element of knowledge—that is, it implies the *prior condition* by which the experience of subjects who act in the world of appearance in which they themselves appear as such is made possible.[41]

A key aspect of Arendt's reflection on plurality arises in the context of her consideration of the link between plurality and rights. Arendt contends that although plurality has the two-fold character of equality and distinction, equality itself is not a natural phenomenon; rather, it is the fruit of an artificial institution, the *polis*—the *nomos* of the *polis* make men equal. This equality is political equality, and it is reflected in the fact that all have access to the public realm, and in the law that grants equal participation in the exercise of power to all. This equality is a purely formal equality which coexists with distinction and allows each human being to assert his/her own identity. This conception of equality allows for the existence and adoption of forms of political organization different to the natural structures of home and family. These natural structures respond to the need to survive and pertain to the private sphere of life. Politics, by

---

remained bound to life as its only point of reference could life as such, the labouring metabolism of man with nature, become active and unfold its entire fertility." Ibid., 320.

[40] Campillo, "'Mundo' y 'pluralidad' en Hannah Arendt," 1120-21.

[41] Sánchez Muñoz, *Hannah Arendt. El espacio de la política*, 260.

contrast, is a consequence of freedom, the result of free, willed decisions, and pertains to the public realm.[42]

To Arendt's mind, the natural is what is given to us, the factual; and the human attitude to what is given is gratitude: "there is such a thing as a basic gratitude for eveything that is as it is; for what has been *given* and was not, could not be, *made*."[43] However, the factual does not define man in himself or his identity. Human identity is revealed through interaction with others, in action and speech.[44] Each human being may tell a story or recount history and interact with other human beings. Thus, for Arendt, human identity is formed through the relationships established with others through action and speech. Human identity is narrative identity; hence, Arendt's description of the political character of human being: "wherever the relevance of speech is at stake, matters become political by definition, for speech is what makes man a political being."[45]

The world is a shared and stable world through language and speech; moreover, language reveals who the speaker is, and is the condition by which new things may appear. Politics, in general terms, is reflection and debate about issues in the public realm,[46] which in turn opens up new space for action and the exercise of freedom. In this context, the question of the institutionalization of action arises as a problem: how is action to be made permanent. To Arendt's mind, the true meaning of politics is

---

[42] To make a distinction between politics and social need is to remove any ground for social justice; such a distinction cannot account for the necessity or complexity of the relationships between the political and the social. For Arendt, politics cannot be concerned with social issues because they are not matters of opinion; they are questions to be addressed by experts, with certainty. See Ibid., 288.

[43] Hannah Arendt, "A "Daughter of Our People": A Response to Gershom Scholem," in *The Portable Hannah Arendt*, ed. Peter Baehr (New York: Penguin Group, 2000), 392.

[44] A point to which many studies of this matter have adverted is that Arendt's distinction between action and work is similar to the distinction between *praxis* and *poiesis* in Aristotle's thought. This distinction is also reflected in the work of the Frankfurt School and in the thought of Habermas, a "disciple" of Arendt's.

[45] Arendt, *The Human Condition*, 3.

[46] Political debate and reflection presuppose plurality and the equality of speakers and actors in a shared world. Thus, Arendt may not be regarded as a communitarian because she does not hold with "the idea of community as a community of shared traditions in which speech occurs; rather, Arendt holds that what unites human beings in a common space is the fact of living on earth and inhabiting a shared artificial world composed of objects and institutions"; Sánchez Muñoz, *Hannah Arendt. El espacio de la política*, 181.

inherently unstable, a fact which is amply illustrated by the difference between the French and American Revolutions. According to Arendt, the revolutions which occurred in the modern age have sought to provide politics with a solid foundation, but only the American Revolution succeeded in this purpose and "founded a completely new body politic without violence and with the help of a constitution."[47]

Thus, Arendt contends that politics is rooted in the human condition, not in human nature:

> politics has very little to do with human nature, about which very few valid affirmations may be made [...] [Politics] has a great deal to do with the human condition, with the fact that a great number of human beings live on earth and inhabit the world together—irrespective of how human nature is or should be (or even if human beings have a nature as such), or if man is a sinner or evil. Were it not for human plurality, politics would not be possible, and plurality is not a quality of human 'nature', but the essence of the human condition in the world.[48]

Conclusions

For Arendt, the most important feature of human being is not human nature, but action or freedom:

> action, with all its uncertainties, is like an ever-present reminder that men, though they must die, are not born in order to die, but to begin something new. *Initium ut esse homo creatus est*—'that there be a beginning man was created,' said Augustine. With the creation of man, the principle of beginning came into the world—which, of course, is only another way of saying that with the creation of man, the principle of freedom appeared on earth.[49]

---

[47] Arendt, *Between Past and Future. Eight Exercises in Political Thought*, 140. Other examples of political activity cited by Arendt include the student protest movements, civil disobedience and jury service.

[48] Unpublished text (MSS box 56, 1, 1953), quoted in Sánchez Muñoz, *Hannah Arendt. El espacio de la política*, 137. This argument reveals the difference between the position adopted by Arendt and those of the Neo-Aristotelians and the communitarians. Arendt does not concede the existence of a common *ethos* or subscribe to an ethos defined in communitarian terms (perhaps through the influence of Kant's philosophy on her thought). Arendt holds that the community is artificial, not natural. See Ibid., 126.

[49] Arendt, "Labor, Work, Action," 181.

Freedom, the heart of human identity, is reflected primarily in politics and political life:

> political activity, like all other forms of human activity, is essentially the beginning of something new; thus, to use the terminology of political science, political activity as such is the essence of human freedom. The significance of the ideas of beginning and origin for an understanding of politics began to diminish when concepts and methodologies proper to the study of history were applied in the field of political science. How vital these ideas were to politics in Greek thought is reflected in the fact that the Greek word *arché* means both beginning and government.[50]

Given that her purpose is to lay the foundations for a political realm that guarantees the right to have rights, Arendt's reflections on the distinction between natural and positive law arise as a matter of course.[51] Arendt's conception of nature as a series of natural or biological processes cannot serve as a solid foundation for a theory of natural law:

> in contrast to positive law, which applies in a particular time and space, natural law may be figured as the theoretical Archimedes point that makes meta-juridical thinking possible: natural law is based on the immutability of certain principles, which positions it outside time and history, and the universality of those principles, which positions it beyond space and geography. The principles of natural law allow different forms of human behaviour to be judged good or bad; they are *given*, not established by convention; and they are discernible in the light of human reason, and thus within the reach of understanding of all human beings.[52]

---

[50] Hannah Arendt, "Comprensión y política," in *De la historia a la acción* (Paidós: Barcelona, 1995), 43.

[51] According to Arendt, there is only one, genuine human right: the right to belong to a political community. See ———, "The Rights of Man: What are They?," *Modern Review* III, no. 1 (1949): 24-30. Moreover, Arendt views all solemn declarations of human rights as abstract statements. See Arendt, *The Origins of Totalitarism,* Volume II, chapter two, nine.

[52] Lafer, *La reconstrucción de los derechos humanos. Un diálogo con el pensamiento de Hannah Arendt*, 18. [Translation to English is mine]. According to this theory, natural law is immutable, universal and knowable; and it is the standard by which specific human actions and behaviour may be judged. See ———, *La reconstrucción de los derechos humanos. Un diálogo con el pensamiento de Hannah Arendt*, 40.

In any case, however, Arendt's experience and study of the decline and fall of Western civilization did not inspire much faith in the power or value of natural law.[53] As a consequence, she argues that human rights must be underwritten by politics, through an individual's belonging to a state that regulates and guarantees those rights. The key question, therefore, is what grounds the right to have rights, to which all may lay claim on the basis of citizenship? Arendt did not address this question in a systematic way. Nevertheless, an idea to which Arendt returned again and again is that

> citizenship is the right to have rights: that all human beings have equal rights and dignity is not a given; it is a construct based on the experience of living in a shared world in which all must have access to public life in the public realm. Entry to the public realm allows for the building of a shared world through a process that involves the definition and declaration of human rights.[54]

If there were no political realm, if the world were not a shared world, there would be no reason for human beings to regard one another as equals, and some individuals might come to be regarded as insignificant or superfluous. In a note to the work of Kafka, the range of reference of which may be extended to encompass all human beings, Arendt wrote: "he did not want to be an exception, but a citizen, 'a member of the community'."[55] The terrible experience of naked human existence—to be a no one living in no man's land, in a place where all law has been put into abeyance—became a terrifying reality in the twentieth century: in

[53] Arendt argues that neither an understanding of natural law nor appeals to the universality of human rights could have prevented the rise of Nazism. See Arendt, *The Origins of Totalitarism*, 267-302. As Legros points out, Arendt thought revolves around a paradox: "les droits de l'homme se prétendent antérieurs par nature à l'institution politique, se veulent, en tant que droits naturels, indépendants de la citoyenneté, mais cependant les hommes en sont privés s'ils n'ont pas atteint une certaine forme d'État, celle, selon les Déclarations elles-mêmes, qui fait place à la souveraineté populaire et nationale"; Legros, "Hannah Arendt: une compréhension phénoménologique des droits de l'homme," 30.

[54] See Lafer, *La reconstrucción de los derechos humanos. Un diálogo con el pensamiento de Hannah Arendt*, 24.

[55] F. Kafka, *Obras completas* (Barcelona: Galaxia Gutenberg/Círculo de Lectores, 1999), 192. [Translation to English is mine]. Arendt makes her own Jefferson's remark in his presidential address to Congress in 1801 regarding the right of every man to a place to live.

concentration and internment camps, in the lives of refugees, the dispossessed and displaced.

Thus, in a certain sense, Arendt's work is a further example of how natural law had lost its meaning and power in the modern age. This loss,[56] which was provoked by a combination of different historical factors, led to a gradual blurring of the distinction between natural and positive law. To give an account of the terrible history of the twentieth century is to strive to ensure that it is never repeated: Arendt contends that the most appropriate response must be the definition and development of politics and the political realm as the ground for the right to have rights. To Arendt's mind, it is only in the public realm that the dignity of the individual identity, equality and distinction of every human being may be acknowledged and freed from the threat of violence.[57]

Works Cited

Arendt, Hannah. *Between Past and Future. Eight Exercises in Political Thought*. New York: Penguin Books, 1985.

—. "Comprensión y Política." In *De La Historia a La Acción*, 29-46. Paidós: Barcelona, 1995.

---

[56] "The Rights of Man, supposedly inalienable, proved to be uneforceable –even in countries whose constitutions were based upon them– whenever people appeared who were no longer citizens of any sovereing state. To this fact, disturbing enough in itself, one must add the confusion created by the many recent attemps to frame a new bill of human rights, which have demostrated that no one seems able to define with any assurance what these general human rights, as distingished from the rights of citizens, really are. Although everyone seems to agree that the plight of these people consists precisely in their loss of the Rights of Man, no one seems to know which rights they lost when they lost these human rights"; Arendt, *The Origins of Totalitarism*, 293.

[57] "H. Arendt donne donc à entendre que la perte de la citoyenneté est par principe *une perte des droits de l'homme*, et dès lors que la citoyenneté dans son sens essentiel n'est pas le fait d'êtres humains immergés dans un Esprit collectif, imprégnés d'une sensibilité commune et intégrés dans un État national comme au sein d'une totalité organique, mais tout au contraire le fait d'individus singuliers, distincts les uns des autres et égaux entre eux, vivant dans la pluralité et un monde public –mais aussi dans un monde privé qui échappe à la sphère du politique–, capables dès lors d'exercer les facultés humaines les plus hautes: de pratiquer concrètement les droits de l'homme, les droits dont ils bénéficient en tant qu'êtres proprement humains"; Legros, "Hannah Arendt: une compréhension phénoménologique des droits de l'homme," 49.

—. "A "Daughter of Our People": A Response to Gershom Scholem." In *The Portable Hannah Arendt*, edited by Peter Baehr, 391-96. New York: Penguin Group, 2000.

—. *Filosofía y política. Heidegger y el existencialismo*. Bilbao: Besatari, 1997.

—. *The Human Condition*. Chicago/London: University of Chicago Press, 1958.

—. "Labor, Work, Action." In *The Portable Hannah Arendt*, edited by Peter Baehr, 167-81. New York: Penguin Group, 2000.

—. *The Life of the Mind (Volume I: Thinking)*. London: Secker & Warburg, 1978.

—. *The Origins of Totalitarism*. New York: Meridian Books, 1960.

—. "The Rights of Man: What Are They?" *Modern Review* III, no. 1 (1949): 24-30.

—. "Seule demeure la langue maternelle." *Esprit* IV, no. 6 (1980): 19-38.

Campillo, N. "'Mundo' y 'pluralidad' en Hannah Arendt." In *Paideia*, edited by Ángel Álvarez Gómez, Berta Pérez Rodríguez, Rafael Martínez Castro and Karina Trilles Calvo. Cursos y congresos nº 156: Universidad de Santiago de Compostela Publicatións, 2005.

Enegrén, A. *La Pensée Politique de Hannah Arendt*. Paris: Presses Universitaires de France, 1984.

Eslin, J.-C. "L'événement De Penser." *Esprit* IV, no. 6 (1980): 7-18.

—. "Une Loi Qui Vaille Pour L'humanité." *Esprit* IV, no. 6 (1980): 41-45.

Forti, S. *Vida del espíritu y tiempo de la Polis. Hannah Arendt entre filosofía y política*. Madrid: Ediciones Cátedra, 2001.

Kafka, F. *Obras completas*. Barcelona: Galaxia Gutenberg/Círculo de Lectores, 1999.

Lafer, C. *La reconstrucción de los Derechos Humanos. Un diálogo con el pensamiento de Hannah Arendt*. México: Fondo de Cultura Económica, 1991.

Legros, R. "Hannah Arendt: Une compréhension phénoménologique des droits de l'homme." *Études phénoménologiques*, no. 2 (1985): 27-53.

Levinas, E. *Totalité Et Inifini. Essai Sur L'extériorité*. La Haye: Nijholf, 1971.

Sánchez Muñoz, C. *Hannah Arendt. El espacio de la política*. Madrid: Centro de Estudios Políticos y Constitucionales, 2003.

CHAPTER FOURTEEN

ALASDAIR MACINTYRE: ON NATURAL LAW

MARGARITA MAURI

In line with the theory that the fundamental concepts of a subject are to be reinterpreted in the light of contributions that have established its limits and endowed it with meaning within a given tradition, MacIntyre addresses the theory of natural law articulated by St. Thomas Aquinas, deferring to his own method of rationalizing human morality in terms of the Aristotelian-Augustinian-Thomistic tradition. He holds that this tradition best expresses the moral dimension of human existence. MacIntyre refers to natural law in three ways, offering:

a) criticism of the different contemporary interpretations of natural law;
b) an interpretation of natural law in the work of St. Thomas Aquinas;
c) an explanation of how knowledge of natural law functions in moral life.

MacIntyre singles out thinkers, such as Finnis, who argue that natural law may be explained and understood without reference to nature, the will or the existence of God. The misconceptions in many contemporary readings of natural law derive from the attempt to adapt its explanation to modern culture. As MacIntyre sees it, the problems to which one is seeking a solution and the dialogue with earlier philosophical thought that arises as a matter of course must be taken into account if natural law is to be understood. For this same reason, in any enabling discussion of the subject, natural law must be read in the context of those concepts from which its full meaning is derived. Macintyre's explanations of natural law are brought together in the essay, *Theories of Natural Law in the Culture of Advanced Modernity*:

a) man possesses a rational nature, from which flows a set of principles that must be observed if individual good is to be attained;

b) every legal system must explain its own laws in detail and provide the means by which they may be obeyed.

Although all contemporary explanations of natural law express these two points, they differ in their conception of rationality, nature and the precepts and function of the law. In 1981 MacIntyre published *After Virtue*, the ideas of which were further developed in *Whose Justice? Which Rationality?* (1988) and *Three Rival Versions of Moral Enquiry* (1990), all of which should be considered alongside *Dependent Rational Animals*, published in 1999. The tradition that underpins MacIntyre's ideas is the tradition of virtues, which was first discussed by Aristotle and later taken up by St. Augustine and St. Thomas Aquinas. In stating that this tradition is the ideal framework for the complete fulfilment of human life, MacIntyre touches on the conflict with modernity which, he explains, abandoned the Aristotelian tradition in the sixteenth century and set out on the path towards individualist liberalism. Rationalism, English empiricism, and indeed the Enlightenment itself, were simply natural steps leading to the emotivist moral conceptions that characterize modern society as depicted by MacIntyre in the first chapter of *After Virtue*. The ideological principles inherited from the past that justify and sustain contemporary societies are incompatible with an understanding of virtue as a quality that makes way for the intrinsic good of human life. Virtue, thus understood, can only exist in a certain type of community—a concept of community that is not encompassed by liberalist thought—.

In *After Virtue*, MacIntyre's explanation of virtue unfolds through the concepts of "practice", "narrative order" and "tradition", although the definition of virtue is fundamentally based on "practice".

Practice is described as the *ubi* in which virtues are demonstrated; however, given that they are also necessary in non-cooperative action, they are not exercised solely in the realm of practices. To speak of practices is to speak of human activities performed in cooperation with others; that is, activities set in a social context. These practices generate internal goods and external goods for those participating in them. External goods are contingent goods that are easily recognized by all those external to a given practice. Internal goods, on the other hand, are only obtained through that practice or similar practices, and their recognition is dependent on participation. Goods internal to a practice can only be recognized and attained if the participant in the practice is virtuous. Access to internal and external goods is governed, to a considerable extent, by the attitude of the participants in the practice. In turn, this attitude is determined by the degree of virtue attained. The relationship between each person and other participants in the practice is the key to his relationship with the internal good. Virtue provides the subject with an understanding of others and of himself that is consistent with reality, and ensures that he acts in accordance with this understanding. From this authentic knowledge of the merits of others and one's own shortcomings comes a refined attitude of acceptance of the models of excellence of a practice and of obedience to the particular rules of the practice.

MacIntyre draws on the relationship between "practice" and "virtue" to situate the exercise of virtue in the realm of social interaction, of activities shared with and conditioned by others. However, the concept of "practice" must be completed by that of "narrative order", whereby the role of virtue is analyzed in human life ordered in accordance with a *telos*; that is, virtue is related to personal life and the meaning ascribed to it by man.

For MacIntyre, "narrative order" encompasses a wide-ranging vision of what he understands by the term "self", which should be considered neither as a set of sequences nor as a composite of different roles. The acts performed in this life make sense in a context defined by finalities, beliefs and situations. Thus, MacIntyre claims that the individual plays the main part in his own drama and has a supporting role in the dramas of others. The meaning of human life rests on its conception as a unity with finality, with a *telos*. The notion of personal identity leads to the concepts of "responsibility", "narration" and "intelligibility".

This conception of human life is reflected in the medieval concept of "search" (as MacIntyre states in *After Virtue*[1]); that is, the attempt to give a sense of unity to the events that govern our lives and to determine the acts and situations that draw life towards unity. Only from this unitary conception of human life is it rational to seek to define the exact nature of the good life for man. The search itself shapes the path, and a true search shapes the path to a good life. Virtue underwrites this search for good in three different ways[2]:

a) it helps man to overcome the risks, dangers, temptations and distractions to which he is constantly exposed;
b) it enables increasingly truthful self-knowledge;
c) it provides increasing knowledge of what is good.

[1] Alasdair MacIntyre, *After Virtue*, 2nd ed. (Notre Dame: University of Notre Dame, 1984), 219.
[2] Ibid.

In this vision of human life as a unity ordered by a *telos*, virtue is the quality that gives man true knowledge of his own character, an awareness of what is good for his life, and knowledge of which act ought to be chosen in each situation if the good life is to be attained. The good life is the result of the virtuous action of a "virtuous self". However, both the search for good and the exercise of virtue must be performed within a given community, and the true identity of the self derives from the community.

To consider the importance of virtue in human life understood as a single, whole entity is to disregard the tradition within which each life unfolds. As an individual, says MacIntyre in *After Virtue*, "I am never able to seek for the good or exercise the virtues."[3] Both the internal good of practices and the good sought in individual life are subsumed in the broader context of the community. The concept of community leads to that of "tradition". Tradition characterizes and defines the community. The search for individual good is carried out within a tradition. Cut off from this tradition, the subject would be unable to exercise virtue or attain moral good. In his most recent work, *Dependent Rational Animals*, MacIntyre makes extensive reference to virtue. He defines virtue as a "quality" and distinguishes between two types of quality—of mind and of character—:

> Those qualities of mind and character that enable someone both to recognize the relevant goods and to use the relevant skills in achieving them are the excellences, the virtues, that distinguish or should distinguish teacher from apprentice or student.[4]

The possession of virtues of mind is shown through the ways in which practical reasoning is exercised when the goods of a given situation are recognized. For MacIntyre, these are virtues of knowledge and recognition. The virtues of character, which are virtues of action, are revealed by acts performed in specific situations. Both types of quality are necessary, for three reasons:

a) Moral autonomy depends on the acquisition of certain intellectual and moral virtues, (the purpose of possessing the virtue is personal autonomy);

b) The virtues are necessary to educate others in the attainment of moral autonomy, (the purpose of possessing the virtue is educational);

---

[3] Ibid., 220.
[4] ———, *Dependent Rational Animals* (London: Duckworth, 1999), 92.

c) Certain intellectual and moral virtues are necessary to protect oneself, and others, from the negligence, stupidity, malice, lack of understanding and greed of other people, (the purpose of possessing the virtue is protective).

The first of these three reasons pertains to the personal realm; the other two situate the necessity of the intellectual and moral virtues in the context of one's relationships with others, whether these are relationships established for the benefit of others or for one's own protection from the actions or characters of other people.

The objective is to learn to judge whether it is good to do (x) as a means of achieving (y), whether it is good to do (x) in specific circumstances, and what the best of all possible goods for the individual making the decision in a given situation, which is his own, may be.

MacIntyre argues that the true judgement which should emerge from participation in practices is one that is: (a) linked to the good of each person; (b) characterized by a series of desires; (c) embedded in a situation; and (d) immersed in a specific tradition. MacIntyre's criticism of the thesis that defends the possibility of discussing the good of a person without considering the person himself should be recalled in this context; for MacIntyre, true moral judgement of what is good for a person here and now depends on what that person may be.

In his interpretation of St. Thomas Aquinas's conception of natural law, MacIntyre expresses his agreement with the position adopted by Jacques Maritain. The precepts of natural law, he claims, are rules of reason which the human being obeys without articulating them in explicit formulations. Human beings are essentially social and attain individual good and the common good through close relationships with others; natural law leads man towards the common good, which is inseparable from individual good. The knowledge of natural law is what makes us question ourselves about the exact nature of our individual and common good and prompts us to respond to these questions through our actions, practices and judgements. The social relationships that each person maintains with others, and which forge the framework within which each must learn the nature of his individual good and the common good, are social relationships governed by natural law: "(…) the recognition of natural law is a matter of how such practices are structured."[5]

---

5 ———, "Natural Law as Subversive: The Case of Aquinas," *Journal of Medieval and Early Modern Studies* 26, no. 1 (1996): 80-81.

The exercise of practical reasoning is dependent on the possession of certain virtues and a certain degree of self-knowledge, which originates in and is extended by contact with others. As human beings, our relationships with others reveal facets of our personality that may, on occasion, surprise not only others but also ourselves. In *Dependent Rational Animals*, MacIntyre argues that self-knowledge depends, in part, on what we learn about ourselves from our relationships with others.[6] Other people, when they know us well, judge the opinion that we have of ourselves, thus confirming or negating our own judgement. It is clear that self-knowledge depends on other factors; without a certain capacity for discernment, attention or judgement—qualities that enable us to interpret ourselves through the reactions of others—self-knowledge would not exist, despite daily contact with other people. The development of self-knowledge, concludes MacIntyre, is due, at least in part, to those on whom we depend throughout our lives.

The achievement of moral maturity through education in the daily practice of virtue is conceived as part of a dynamic of social interdependence in which each person gives and receives. Thus, if there are virtues of independence, there are also virtues of dependence. The former enable us *to offer*, the latter *to recognize*, and both enable us to recognize the extent to which our existence, in the broad sense of the word, depends on others. MacIntyre's assertion that "(…) it is nonetheless in virtue of what we have received that we owe"[7] reveals a cooperative conception of human existence, which is sustained in different instances and upon which the good life depends. The activities that enable each person to identify correctly the nature of his individual good and the common good are those activities defined and governed by natural law. Implicit in this statement is an acknowledgement of the difficulty of identifying individual good outside social relationships governed by the precepts of natural law. MacIntyre relates virtue to practice and subordinates both to tradition. However, practice must offer human beings the possibility of enlightening their individual good and the good of others, and this is dependent on the practice being defined and governed by the precepts of natural law. The material framework is thus structured by what is called "natural law", which is the form of our relationships with ourselves and with others. Individual moral development takes place through practices whose meaning derive from tradition. The possibility of education in virtue depends on a social context in which shared activities

[6] MacIntyre, *Dependent Rational Animals*, 94.
[7] Ibid., 101.

are played out. In a number of his works, MacIntyre has discussed the type of society in which education in virtue may be acquired, and has explained why our own society is not one such example.

Life provides knowledge and virtue, and knowledge and virtue furnish those who possess them with a certain type of life. As MacIntyre observes in *Dependent Rational Animals*,

> (…) virtues are indispensable to human flourishing: without developing some range of intellectual and moral virtues we cannot first achieve and then continue in the exercise of practical reasoning.[8]

Works Cited

MacIntyre, Alasdair. *After Virtue*. 2nd ed. Notre Dame: University of Notre Dame, 1984.

—. *Dependent Rational Animals*. London: Duckworth, 1999.

—. "Natural Law as Subversive: The Case of Aquinas." *Journal of Medieval and Early Modern Studies* 26, no. 1 (1996): 61-83.

—. "Theories of Natural Law in the Culture of Advanced Modernity." In *Common Truths: New Perspectives on Natural Law*, edited by E.B. MacLean. Wilmington: Isi Books, 2000.

—. *Three Rival Versions of Moral Enquiry*. London: Duckworth, 1990.

—. *Whose Justice? Which Rationality?* Notre Dame: University of Notre Dame Press, 1988.

[8] Ibid., 97.

CHAPTER FIFTEEN

THE RELATION BETWEEN NATURAL LAW AND THE LAW OF CHRIST IN THE CONTEXT OF THE CURRENT DEBATE ON THE SPECIFICITY OF CHRISTIAN MORALITY

TOMÁS TRIGO

There are two reasons behind this study. One would be to provide a summary of the discussion regarding the relation between Natural Law and the Law of Christ, in the context of a wider debate on the specificity of Christian Morality. This debate began during the 1960s, and reached its peak during the 1970s.[1] And the other reason would be to point out the approach, which in our opinion, expresses this relation in the most correct manner possible.

The problem, as it has been presented by the authors during the first years of the debate, could be formulated in the following manner: Does the Law of Christ add new moral content to the Natural Law? If so, does it only concern general norms, intentions and attitudes? Or does it also include specific contents and behavioral laws?

During the first years of the debate, there have been numerous answers to this issue. We have chosen three which we believe to be the most significant. The answer of J.M. Aubert responds to an ontological model founded on Natural Law; the theory of J. Fuchs, based on the model of moral autonomy; and that of Ph. Delhaye, according to the so-called "Ethic of the Faith".

---

[1] For a detailed study on the matter, cfr. Tomás Trigo, *El debate sobre la especificidad de la moral cristiana* (Pamplona: Eunsa, 2003).

The ontological model founded on Natural Law: Jean Marie Aubert

Aubert's thesis, based on St. Thomas Aquinas, states that from a material point of view, Christian Moral can be identified with the Natural Law: "There is just one common moral code when acting through Faith or in human action as such."[2] The Christian's moral action, excluding the cultural and sacramental dimensions, is not essentially manifested through the acts in themselves: the *materialiter* is the same as that of other men.

Taking into account that man only has a single possible destiny, that which is supernatural, "existentially, there is but a single common moral code possible for both Christians and non-Christians, and this common norm is principally known as reason".[3] However, according to Aubert, reason darkened by sin, should be placed at the service of the supernatural and needs to be enlightened by the Revelation. And it is here where the right of the Church, guardian of the Revelation, lies as it intervenes in human morality. Furthermore, without Grace, natural moral life would not be possible, even among those who do not possess the Faith.

The difference between the Law of Christ and Natural Law can be found in the final, efficient and formal causes of Christian moral action. The final cause is charity, which forms part of the purpose and end of the moral action. The efficient cause is also charity, together with human will. And lastly, the formal cause, where the specificity of Christian action lies, is Faith.

The action of the Holy Spirit, His Grace and the Love-Charity that proceeds from God, communicated through Jesus Christ, turns Ethics into Christian Ethics. However not because of this does a new ethical field, which can be applied exclusively to Christians, appear. Through Grace,

---

[2] Jean-Marie Aubert, "La spécificité de la morale chrétienne selon saint Thomas," *Le Supplément: revue d'éthique et de théologie morale (L'éthique chrétienne à la reserche de son identité)* 23 (1970): 69. In our study, we also take into account the following works: ———, "La morale chrétienne est-elle à la mesure de l'homme?," *Études* 325 (1966): 543-45. ———, "La fonction de la foi dans les décisions éthiques," *Le Supplément: revue d'éthique et de théologie morale (Décision morale et discernement théologique)* 129 (1979): 251-73. ———, "La morale catholique est-elle évangélique?," in *La Loi de la liberté. Evangile et morale*, ed. Christos Yannaras (Maison: Mame, 1972), 119-58. ———, "La morale chrétienne selon saint Thomas," *Seminarium* 3 (1977): 780-811. ———, "Débats autour de la morale fondamentale," *Studia Moralia* 20 (1982): 195-222.

[3] Aubert, "La spécificité de la morale chrétienne selon saint Thomas," 71.

there is simply a transfiguration of the ethical field outlined by God, the Creator, to men. Therefore, and according to the Professor from Strasburg, one may say that in the degree of precepts that are considered with regard to the material object, everything remains in the rational and human order. But at the same time, in the ethical context it is specifically Christian and supernatural, both in its purpose and in the action itself.

This thesis, unlike Naturalism, also possesses the advantage of proving that there is no existing conflict between the Christian message and human reality. And unlike Supernaturalism, which has been exaggerated by some Protestant and Catholic authors, it proves that the New Law is rooted in Natural Law and cannot make do without it.

However, in this thesis, there seems to be more inconveniences than advantages.

On the one hand and most probably due to the abstract character of Aubert's view, one may suppose that the transcendent end of the action (Charity) can be added to an immanent end that is already constituted. But in reality, things do not happen this way. In every choice, the transcendent end is primary for the Christian and thus, determines his specific conduct.

With regard to the efficient cause, Aubert is right when he says that charity supplies greater energy to the will and is therefore, a more perfect type of freedom. But precisely because of this, the Christian may choose his actions, suggested or imparted by the Faith, and its realization is impossible without Grace. Furthermore, this new strength supplied by Charity has consequences in a cognitive context, enlightening the practical reason: that heart in love with God has a greater capacity to discern Moral Truth and can discover, as a result, new manners of action. Because of this, Grace does not only provide more strength and rectitude in the human action, but is also a new source of content within the action.

If one admits the specificity of the final, efficient and formal causes, the non-specificity of the material cause can only be considered from the abstract consideration of Ethics, because a good human act undertaken for the love of God and under the guidance of Grace is specifically different from the act in itself that has been undertaken for different causes. In reality, to claim that there is no difference between Christians and non-Christians from a material point of view is the fruit of an abstraction that allows one to admit that there is no difference between men and other mammals in terms of nutrition and reproduction.

If Aubert applied a concept of Moral Law that is more in accordance with the epistemology of Saint Thomas, he would reach the conclusion from his own proposals that Christian morality is materially different from simple, natural morality. If one takes into account the moral norms expressed in the Decalogue, it is true that these laws constitute the matter for both Christians and non-Christians. But in reality, the person is continuously exercising prudential judgments on the situations he encounters. And these prudential judgments, which constitute the practical norms upon which man bases his behavior, are, for the Christian, radically determined by the doctrine of Christ and the teachings of the Church. In this manner, Christian conduct is not simply a rational conduct *informed* by theological virtues, but a new type of conduct whose sources are in themselves the theological virtues and the Grace from which they emanate.

In fact, after his categorical affirmations of the material identity of Christian Ethics and Natural Law, Aubert seems to have tried to ease them out and finally admits that it is the Law of the Cross that constitutes the typical idea of what is essentially Christian when practicing Moral Law. In Christ's Cross is where that which is specifically Christian lies.[4]

But this Law of the Cross is a specific precept of Christian Moral, and cannot be simply extracted from human nature: it is not anti-natural, but rather surpasses the understanding that nature offers man. As Aubert himself points out, ethical reason is enlightened by Faith. It is there not to make irrational decisions but to follow higher reason: that of Divine Love that knows no limits and of which the Cross of Christ is its greatest exponent. Thus, from this example, is there not a moral conduct that is many times incomprehensible by reason (because it surpasses it) and cannot be explained by the rules of Natural Law?

The model of moral autonomy: Josef Fuchs

Some authors that follow the model of moral autonomy, among them J. Fuchs, manifest the plausible pretension of presenting a Moral Theology made up of natural and supernatural aspects. In this manner, this theory tries to overcome the superposition of both realities into which neo-scholastic Moral Theology has fallen. As opposed to morality centered on Natural Law, these authors wish to elaborate Christian ethics centered on Christ, on Grace, on the theological virtues and on the actions of the Holy Spirit. They wish to call attention to the value of the purpose and to the fundamental norms, and hope to underline the relevance of the transcendental and fundamental option in the person of Christ. In this

[4] See Ibid.: 73.

manner, one may understand Christian life as a whole and not as a series of isolated or unconnected actions.

If man is really the man created in Christ, Natural Law—necessarily—has to be in connection with Christ and His Grace. Specifically in the work of Fuchs entitled *"Moral and Moral Theology according to the Council"*,[5] the author wants to prove that the center of Christian Moral is Christ, that the fundamental category has to be the vocation of the faithful in Christ and that Grace and the actions of the Holy Spirit occupy a primary role in moral life. Christian Morality is manifested above all as the Spirit of Christ that acts within us and, secondly, as the precepts that guide the Christian.

Making Christ the center of Christian Moral brings Fuchs to state that morality in pure Natural Law does not exist for some and Christian Moral for others. If there is only a single vocation that exists for all men, one may conclude that there can only exist a single moral conduct for all men: Christian Morality. As a consequence, the distinction between the Law of Christ and Natural Law should not be understood as if the first was added to the second. When we consider Natural Law first, to which other elements are added, we are proceeding from abstraction because we separate it from the Law of Christ. In reality, Fuchs concludes, *quoad se,* that the first is the Law of Christ which includes or implies Natural Law.

Next, we will try to see if J. Fuchs does indeed achieve this important aim of placing Christ at the center of all Christian Morality.

What is J. Fuchs's response regarding the question on the specificity of Moral Christianity? That is to say, according to his own thesis, what does the Law of Christ add to Natural Law? In order to appreciate the extent of his answer, it is necessary to present a brief summary of his anthropological background.

What is most important to point out is the separation proposed by the anthropology of J. Fuchs between the personal being of man and his manifestation in the essence. Man is a spirit incarnated in a personal dimension that is identified with the spirit and that is manifested, to a certain extent, through the body. Therefore, man can be understood to be in opposition with nature.

It is at this point where the root of the distinction-separation of the two levels of man lies: the transcendental degree—that which is personal, which includes reason and freedom—and the categorical and contingent,

---

[5] Josef Fuchs, *Moral und Moraltheologie nach dem Konzil* (Freiburg [etc.]: Herder, 1967).

which is nature. The second is given to the person and does not depend on his freedom.

The transcendental-categorical distinction implies the existence of two levels both in knowledge and in freedom. The transcendental is the center of the soul, where man is absolutely conscious of himself and his acts, although he is unable to prove and apprehend them in a reflexive manner. It is here where the non-thematic perception of the Absolute lies; it is the region of transcendental freedom—the freedom of that which is absolutely personal. And his actions become a fundamental option: it is a deep attitude that penetrates the particular behavior of the person at each moment and, although it may not determine it, it offers a new value, the moral value. The transcendental horizon is, therefore, that in which man fulfills himself as a person and, finally, with regard to the Absolute.

On the other hand, at the categorical level, man acts with a thematic and explicit conscience, and with a freedom that is merely a sign or manifestation—limited by the contingent—of his transcendental freedom. Therefore, at this degree, the person does not commit himself as such.

From the point of view of theological anthropology, Fuchs claims that Grace is enclosed within the transcendental level. As a consequence, the nature-Grace duality is added to the nature-person duality, which necessarily implies the separation between the structures of Creation and those of Redemption.

We will now analyze Fuchs's answer to the question of the specificity of Christian Moral. According to him, this is undoubtedly a specific Moral. However, this specificity cannot be found in a specific or *categorical* normative order, but in the motivations and intentions—that is to say, in the formal or *transcendental* degree.[6]

That which is properly Christian is in the definitive characteristics presented in the road to Salvation offered by Christ. It is, therefore, based on the act of Revelation and thus, only accessible through the Faith: Faith in the historic event of Salvation, the fundamental option to open oneself to the Divine Requirements.

---

[6] Fuchs's ideas on this issue are dispersed in several publications. The foundations of his answer can be found in his work entitled: ———, *Existe-t-il une "morale chrétienne"?*, coll. "Recherches et Synthèses", section de morale, IX (Gembloux: Éditions J. Duculot, 1973). English version: ———, *Human Values and Christian Morality* (Dublin: Gill and Macmillan, 1970). It constitutes an important landmark of the debate we are studying. Similar positions to those defended by Fuchs are, among others, those defended by B. Schüller, F. Böckle, Ch.E. Curran and A. Auer.

Although Christian intentionality influences categorical behavior, it does not determine its contents. Therefore, if one does not take the transcendental degree into account, "Christian Moral is fundamental and essentially human in its categorical determination and in its matter."[7] The specific Moral behavior of the Christian is not different from that of man, or that of the purest and most noble Moral of true humanity.

The answer of the former professor of the Gregorian University implies that at the level of the contents, in operational norms, the Law of Christ does not add anything new to Natural Morality. In this dimension, Christian Moral is identified with Human Morality. The Law of Grace perfects, completes and upraises Natural Law to a supernatural level, offering new motivations so that an action, which otherwise cannot be—in itself, *materialiter*—differentiated from that of the non-Christian, is instead, transformed into the response to the call of God for Salvation in Christ.[8]

Fuchs also believes that he has found the confirmation of his thesis in Saint Thomas:

> The moral norms of conduct of the new Law of Christ are, according to Aquinas, determined by the *ratio.* They are, therefore, in its materiality, human Morality (Natural Law), and were already contained, to a certain degree, in the *lex vetera*: Christ does not add anything new to Moral Law which, in its material content, is 'specifically' Christian.[9]

With regard to the norms of conduct contained in Sacred Scripture, Fuchs claims that it does not have an absolute validity in the sense of being universally valid, not even the precept regarding the indissolubility of matrimony. The validity of these norms would consist in being models of actions for the Christian, influenced by Faith and Charity.

A result that Fuchs and other defenders of moral autonomy extract from the affirmation that Faith does not modify Human Morality intrinsically, is the following: in order to solve the intermundane problems of Morality, Christians as well as non-Christians only need to turn to experience and reason.

---

[7] Fuchs, *Existe-t-il une "morale chrétienne"?* , 14.

[8] Despite the similarities with the approach of J.M. Aubert, the differences are essential. It is enough to say that moral autonomy assumes a Rahnerian anthropology with its roots in Kant, as well as a formal idea of Natural Law, which would bring one to consequences that Aubert would never accept.

[9] Josef Fuchs, "Esiste una morale non-cristiana?," in *Sussidi 1980 per lo studio della Teologia morale fondamentale* (Roma: P.U.G., 1980), 330-31.

Now, in the measure that one admits that the only valid criteria to discern Moral Good from Evil are those offered by experience and reason, one also tends to affirm that the teachings of the Church are at the same level as that of any other person that makes good use of his reason.

The purpose behind Fuchs's aforementioned Christ-centrism, is also truncated by the transcendental-categorical separation. In fact, the Christological perspective cannot be reconciled with the separation between Christian purpose (transcendental) and human acts (categorical).

As the principle of "theonomous autonomy" states, if the will that God professed during the creation of man is none than the Divine will that man be and live like man, that man create an authentically human behavior through his autonomous use of reason, then it is in man himself where one must find the behavior that is due to him as a being forced by the Absolute, so that his acts go in accordance with the personal dignity of being man. Now, in order to remain coherent with his Christ-centrism, Fuchs should say that according to Divine Will, man must be and live like Christ, and that only Christ represents the project of an authentically—transcendental and categorical—human behavior, because he is authentically Christian. And as a consequence, it is in Christ where man must find the correct behavior in order to act in accordance with the dignity of being a Son of God in Christ. However, this affirmation necessarily denies the autonomy of practical reason in the categorical degree.

On the other hand, Fuchs's proposal easily excludes the relation between Salvation and the world. Reducing the Grace of Salvation to the transcendental degree makes it very difficult to understand that Salvation also concerns the state of the world, and that Christian acts are at the same time, intermundane actions that are both redeemed and co-redemptory. Reducing what is specifically Christian to the transcendental purpose that refers to something that is beyond the world is the same as denying that the Kingdom of God forms part of the world. Moral autonomy seems to forget that

> what is specifically Christian becomes efficient in the intermundane acts precisely because Salvation is, in the end, the salvation of man *and his world,* a restoration in Christ; and because this restoration does not present a promise of the future that is *solely* in the horizon of Hope, but is also an *intermundane* task, both *present and actual,* in the actions of Christian love. And because of this, the reality of human life, the possibilities and obligations that are opened to it, require a Christian interpretation enlightened by Revelation. This is an interpretation that brings about the

formulation of norms of conduct which, if considered exclusively from this context, can never be known in their totality.[10]

The purpose behind the idea of centering Morality in Christ cannot be undertaken with the anthropological proposals of moral autonomy. The only thing that this can offer is a normative code of Ethics that responds to contingent assets and ends, and which will be established by man through autonomous reason. Within this ethical code, the specific moral actions have no value in Salvation, but only in the order of the world. In them, Christian identity is not at risk. Christian specificity is Salvation, which is found in a transcendental level and which can be manifested through any ethical norm established by the use of reason.

The Ethics of the Faith: Philippe Delhaye

For Philippe Delhaye, the foundations of Christian Moral can be found in the Revelation and in the Faith.[11] It is only through Faith and the divinization of man through Christ, that one may understand the sense and the demands of Christian Morality.

The anthropological novelty of the Christian, his new being in Christ, brings him necessarily to new types of actions, not only at the intentional level but as a whole, since the intention is an intrinsic element of the moral act. As a consequence, Christian Morality is something new with respect to Human Morality, both on the transcendental and the categorical levels. These two levels become intimately linked and form a specific unity.

Delhaye proves that in the New Testament there appear novelties in moral regarding the Old Testament as well as other cultures, and even regarding a human morality that is based on metaphysical or on historic nature.

---

[10] Martin Rhonheimer, *Ley natural y razón práctica. Una visión tomista de la autonomía moral* (Eunsa: Pamplona, 2000), 520. For the critics on moral autonomy, we are indebted above all to the work of M. Rhonheimer.

[11] The ideas that we present can be found above all in: Philippe Delhaye, "La mise en cause de la spécificité de la morale chrétienne. Étude de quelques prises de position récentes et réflexions critiques," *Revue Théologique de Louvain* 4 (1973): 308-39.
See also: ———, "Éthique humaine et morale révélée dans l'Épître aux Romains," *Esprit et Vie* 100 (1990): 65-76, 81-92. ———, "La 'loi nouvelle' dans l'enseignement de S. Thomas," *Esprit et Vie* 84 (1974): 33-41, 49-54. Many other authors defend similar positions to those of Delhaye: S. Pinckaers, D. Tettamanzi, J. Ratzinger, A. Feuillet, A. Di Marino, G.B. Guzzetti, B. Stöckle, etc.

Specifically, the "new commandment" of love has a new extension (no one can be excluded) and a new meaning (Christian love is tied to Christ who gives his life for his friends and enemies). This implies that charity does not introduce specificity at a mere transcendental level, but also at the categorical, because one cannot love radically without following the commandments. That is to say, without adopting specific rules of conduct.

The former professor of the School of Theology of Leuven points out that the theological tradition of the textbooks of modern times, centered on the morals of obligation and on natural law, can support the thesis of the material identity of Christian Ethics together with Human Ethics. But he denies that this is so if one takes into account the Holy Scripture in itself, the Patristic tradition, or Saint Thomas Aquinas.

When presenting Moral Theology centered on Natural Law, upon which a spirituality is placed that has its foundations on the theological virtues and on the evangelic advice, an extrinsic conception of the relation between Nature and Grace is at work. But Christian Moral, claims Delhaye, cannot be considered as something juxtaposed on Human Morality, because in the economy of Salvation, purely human morality does not have an end in itself.

The relation between purely human morality and the morality of divinized man is closely tied to the relation between Nature and Grace. Human Morality is neither absorbed nor suppressed. On the contrary, the search for legitimately human values is, instead, reinforced. At the same time, the anthropology upon which Human Morality is founded becomes perfected, because Christ teaches us the whole Truth regarding man. Therefore, the information provided in the Revelation should be placed in relation to—thanks to the use of reason—what one knows about man, his structure and his part in the world, because the use of reason does not introduce a heterogeneous element.

One of the lessons offered by the History of Moral Theology is that when Natural Law plays a principal role, teachings on Morality tend to be based exclusively on the matter of the actions. This is a legitimate point of view. However, it is also incomplete because the moral act has to be considered at the level of the object and of the subject. Furthermore, it tends to forget the essential moral criterion of the Law of Christ: the relation with God.

In Delhaye's study, Natural Law, far from being annulled, is reaffirmed, although it does not possess a preferential position. It is not suppressed but integrated as another element—no longer anthropocentric, but theocentric—of a superior Moral life. In this new life, the primacy in the existential level corresponds to theological life.

Christ, Universal and Personal Law of all moral action

Delhaye's idea, which many authors share and which, to our understanding, is one of the best fruits of the renewal of Moral Theology written during the 20th Century, acquires a new significance thanks to the works presented by H.U. von Balthasar[12] and H. Schürmann in the International Theological Commission—that centered a great deal on the debate regarding specificity. These authors wrote on the sense of Christian Moral and the use of Scripture in Morality. We now focus on the first.

Balthasar summarizes his position in nine theses. The first of these considers Christ as the "specific and complete" norm of moral life:

> Christian ethics should be elaborated from Jesus Christ. He, as the Son of the Father, fulfilled the will of God (everything that should be done) in the world and He did it 'for us'. Thus, we receive from Him, who is the specific and complete norm of all moral activity, the freedom to fulfill the will of God and to live our destiny as free children of the Father.[13]

As a specific, personal norm, Christ makes us capable of fulfilling the will of the Father, with Him. Christ renews the love of the Father, fulfills it completely and makes us capable of fulfilling the Divine Will in two aspects, which are united and inseparable: love and worship.

In his second thesis, Balthasar states the universality of the specific norm:

> The norm that is constituted through the specific existence of Christ, is personal and at the same time, universal, because in Him, the love of the Father for the world is renewed in a total, insuperable and specific manner. This norm is extended to all people and their moral situations, and unites all people, with their uniqueness and their freedom, in the person of Christ. Through the freedom of the Holy Spirit, He reigns over all in order to introduce them to the Kingdom of the Father.[14]

The author wants to state that the specific existence of Christ assumes in itself all other systems of ethical regulation. Christ is the prototype of

---

[12] Hans Urs von Balthasar, "Neuf thèses pour une éthique chrétienne," *Documentation Catholique* 72 (1975): 421-26. We follow the Spanish translation: ———, "Las "nueve tesis" de H.U. von Baltahsar," in *Comisión Teológica Internacional. Documentos 1970-1979* (Madrid: Cete, 1983), 87-103.
[13] von Balthasar, "Las "nueve tesis" de H.U. von Baltahsar," 88.
[14] Ibid., 90-91.

the perfect obedience to God. The synthesis of the complete love for the Father, realized through the person of Christ, is eschatological and insuperable. Therefore, this synthesis is *a priori* a universal norm.

Regarding Natural Law and the Old Law, Balthasar claims that they are elements and fragments contained in the specific universal norm (Thesis 7 to 9).

This presentation seems to be the key in order to overcome the affirmation on heterogeneity between Christ and Natural Law; an affirmation which, according to A. Scola,

> Is the most pernicious for Moral Theology that circulates today. It is responsible, on the one hand, for the rejection of Natural Law on behalf of reference to a Christ that is so generic that it is incapable of founding a specific moral law. And on the other, because of the little care placed on the Christ-like foundation, there exists the conviction that Natural Law is enough to become the basis of the norm in itself.[15]

Balthasar's position has its theological foundations in an objectively Christ-centered vision of man

> Based on the consideration of the predestination of Creation in its relation with Natural Law, upon which moral foundations depend as well as the solution to the *vexata quaestio* on the autonomy or heteronomy of a moral law that is truly in coherence with the freedom of the person. It regards the correct relation between Christian justification and his moral actions, reaching the foundations of what is specifically Christian in moral terms.[16]

The practical dimension of the Trinitarian design of predestination in Creation is Eternal Law. Therefore, Natural Law, which is the participation of the rational creature in the Eternal Law, can no longer be considered as something extrinsic with regard to the Christ-centered point of view. It should be objectively included in it. Christ, the specific and universal Law, becomes the structure that regulates the fragmentary forms of Ethics. This means that one cannot interpret the New Law under the light of the Old one or through Natural Law, but the other way around. Natural Law continues to develop its function as a whole, but without the false distinction between essence—attributed to creation—and history—attributed to the Redemption. On the other hand, the universal and

---

[15] Angelo Scola, *Hans Urs von Balthasar: un estilo teológico* (Madrid: Encuentro, 1997), 118.
[16] Ibid.

necessary character of Natural Law appears to be objectively contained in the universal and immutable properties of predestination in Christ.

Balthasar's proposition does not remove universality from Ethics. On the contrary, it is precisely in its Christ-centered, anthropological and ecclesiastical roots where Ethics finds the universality that is not purely formal. From this point, one can overcome the false conviction that only Natural Ethics can be universal, and that the Christological reference forces Ethics to fragment itself, making it lose its universal characteristic.

Neither is the communicability of Christian morality belittled given that the Natural Law is assumed by the New Law. It is always possible to prove the intrinsic reasonability of a norm that can also be understood naturally, without renouncing to present it as an element of the whole, which receives its complete foundations only through a Christian perspective.

Lastly, the problem from passing from the normative level outlined in the New Testament, to the normative level of specific situations—the *punctum dolens* of the debate on specificity—would lose, according to A. Scola, its most important difficulty. In effect, if Christ is ontologically contemporaneous to every particular historic situation of the believer, without excluding the necessary, hermeneutic mediation, the fundamentals of the problem no longer consist of how to pass from an historic event that took place almost 2,000 years ago to a particular event of today. And, accepting that morality is not reduced to norms, the singularity of Christian Morality consists precisely in the possibility of deducing norms from the Christian event. Furthermore, in order to take the step towards a particular norm, the theologian cannot make do without reference to the apostolic *parenesis*, Tradition, and the Magisterium of the Church, through which Christ continues to instruct man's behavior, so that in the current and specific historic circumstances of each person, His Human and Divine life may be imitated in a true manner.[17]

Christ-like Anthropology

The authors that believe in the full specificity of Moral Christianity base their idea, explicitly or implicitly, on the ontological novelty of man reborn in Christ. The new being of the Christian is defined as being child of God in Christ through the Holy Spirit. To be son of God constitutes a

[17] See ———, *Cuestiones de antropología teológica* (Madrid: BAC, 2000), 134-35.

more fundamental reality, the characteristic that defines him in a definitive manner and the motor of all his moral life: Divine filiation brings one to live the life of Christ, to identify himself with Him, always in search for that which pleases the Father. This is possible through the actions of the Holy Spirit.

In order to found Moral Christianity as something completely specific, it is indispensable to adequately determine the ontological relation between man and Christ and bring it to its final consequences. This relation, which constitutes the key issue in understanding the union between Natural Law and the Law of Christ, between Reason and Faith, and in order to overcome the apparent conflict between autonomy and heteronomy, has not only been misinterpreted by some neo-Thomistic writers and by the dualist anthropology of autonomous moral, but also by some theologians who, like B. Stöckle, defend the Ethics of the Faith.

Among the theologians that believe in the full specificity of Christian morality, we find several that put special interest in correctly establishing the Christological foundations in Moral Theology. One of them is Y. Congar, who underlines that Christ has a decisive, creational and determining anteriority upon which, through grace, we are summoned to fulfill in our actions. From this relation between Christ and the Christian, we can extract the motives of Christian behavior. In this manner, Christian Morality is an expression, at the level of actions, of the ontology of the Christian and this is God's communication in man. As a consequence, the Christian does not exist and does not have to behave exclusively according to the structures of creation, but rather according to the economy of salvation, where he acts as man and as a Christian. And this does not consist on simply living a new intentionality at a transcendental level, but instead it is the expression of a new ontology. Divinization through grace is, therefore, the foundation on which all moral imperatives lie.[18]

R. Tremblay, for his part, insists on the need to be coherent with the essential information of the "primacy" of Christ over man's moral actions, a "primacy" that is established because a relation of effective solidarity exists in the Being of Christ and the being of man. The relation between these two, born from this solidarity, is not of an extrinsic order, but is intrinsic and is interiorized even more through the self-communication of the Being of Christ. In this manner, Christ enters into the deepest ontological stratums of the Christian, transforming him according to his own Being and transforming his conscience as a creature into a filial

[18] See Yves Congar, "Réflexion et propos sur l'originalité éthique chrétienne," *Studia Moralia* 15 (1977): 31-40.

conscience. However, through this ontological union, man does not lose his individual and personal being. Therefore, warns Tremblay, it does not have anything to do with the idea of a philosophical anthropology that is Christianized after, but of a Christ-like anthropology, that admits the Son of God made man as the absolute source of the human being.[19]

The positions of C. Caffarra, A. Scola and I. Biffi run along a similar line. All of them represent an interesting continuation in the moral perspective of the proposals of H.U. von Balthasar, which are summarized in his "Nine Theses." The theological foundation of Balthasar's proposals is precisely a Christ-like anthropology, where he tries to unite, without any possible confusion, what is natural and supernatural, creation and Redemption, essence and history. Quite on the contrary, an anthropology in which nature is seen as separated from Grace seems to have the advantage of offering a neutral terrain upon which universal and immutable contents can be founded. But the inconvenience is that nature then seems to be an *a priori* reality that confronts Redemption, in the sense that while the first offers that which is metaphysical, what is immutable and universal, the second offers the historic, that which can be changed and is contingent.[20] As a consequence, Christian Moral would have no other possibility but to move continuously between these two extreme dangers: the repulse for that which is historic and cultural, in benefit of permanence and universality; and the negation of all timeless certainty as a tribute to the value of the historical dimension.

The articulation of the Christological principle in Moral Law

Taking into account the problems originated from an erroneous conception of the relation between Human Morality and Christian Morality, it seems important to underline that one cannot separate Natural Law from the New Law, reducing the second one to a level of purpose. As the encyclical *Veritatis Splendor* (n.45) states:

> Even if moral-theological reflection usually distinguishes between the positive or revealed law of God and the natural law, and, within the economy of salvation, between the 'old' and the 'new' law, it must not be forgotten that these and other useful distinctions always refer to that law

[19] See Réal Tremblay, "Par-delà de la 'morale autonome' et 'l'éthique de la foi'," *Studia Moralia* 20 (1982): 223-37.
[20] See Scola, *Hans Urs von Balthasar: un estilo teológico*, 119f.

> whose author is the one and the same God and which is always meant for man. The different ways in which God, acting in history, cares for the world and for mankind are not mutually exclusive; on the contrary, they support each other and intersect. They have their origin and goal in the eternal, wise and loving counsel whereby God predestines men and women 'to be conformed to the image of his Son' (*Rom* 8:29).

But, at the same time, it is indispensable to point out a danger which approaches theologians who, reasonably, center moral actions on theological virtues and put the New Law in a preeminent position: the possible disregard for the articulation of the Christological principle with the Moral Law, which would constitute a regress to the dialectic vision of the relation between Reason and Faith.[21]

Ethics that puts the essence and center of morality in Charity, says Rhonheimer in conversation with S. Pinckaers, cannot stop asking itself about the good which is properly human according to the right use of reason, because this good is fulfilled by the Law of the New Testament. It has to be searched according to the criteria of Moral rationality that is specifically human. That is to say, one must proceed using a strictly philosophical methodology.

Although existentially, the order of reason and the order of Charity form a single organic union and work together (like the two natures of Christ), from a cognitive point of view, both levels are different and to a certain extent, independent (as do the two natures of Christ): both have their own intelligibility. But they are not parallel: reason (which concerns the good of man) is an intellectual principle; Charity (that orders us to God) is a principle of inclination, and makes the entire order of moral virtues transform itself towards a single end. From here, one follows that Charity, without the stratum of moral virtues ordered for human good and its corresponding rationality, would be without a basis, without "matter". In effect, in order for Charity to become the "form of the virtues", these should be discernible, independently from the specific demands of Charity, as a "human asset" on the level of a rational morality that is purely natural. In other words, the human level, the life which is *secundum*

[21] This danger has been pointed out by Martin Rhonheimer, "Morale cristiana e ragionevolezza morale: di che cosa è il compimento la legge del Vangelo?," in *Gesù Cristo, legge vivente e personale della Santa Chiesa, Atti del IX Colloquio Internazionale di Teologia di Lugano sul Primo capitolo dell'Enciclica "Veritatis splendor" (Lugano, 15-17 giugno 1995)*, ed. Graziano Borgonovo (Casale Montferrato: Piemme, 1996), 147-68.

rationem (the same *bonum humanum*), is what becomes ordered to the final end, through Charity.

Because of this, Rhonheimer considers the following thesis problematic:

> it would be necessary to begin the moral discourse not at the natural level and its corresponding reasonable demands, but at the level of vertex, that is, of Grace and of Charity.[22]

In his opinion, both levels should be considered like two different fountains, with their own specific intelligibility, which finally converge and enrich each other mutually, forming a moral and specific organism that is new and singular: man in the image of Christ. In any case, he claims that rational moral demands at the natural level can never be deduced or inferred from the supernatural order of Grace and Charity. In the same manner that in Christ the Divine Person has assumed the Human Nature, these demands are also *assumed.* And this is only possible if they possess their own intelligibility and are independent from the essential contents of the New Law. Therefore, there exists a discourse that is specifically philosophical without which Moral Theology may not be able to fulfill its function. Specifically, without this discourse, one would be unable to identify intrinsically evil actions, nor explain why, precisely, Charity (the New Law) is the fulfillment and the perfection of morality.

We believe that Rhonheimer's reflections, which are indispensable in order to avoid an ethereal morality—a morality that could bring one to consider nature as a "pagan" area or a private moral code, against another which is specifically Christian and full of moral significance (an error that autonomous moral commits)—do not really contradict Pinckaers's moral theory as a whole nor other authors with similar ideas. It would probably help to solve this apparent discord to consider that Rhonheimer refers to the necessary conditions for the methodology of the normative, ethical discourse. In effect, if one wants to prove, for example, that to kill an innocent is an intrinsically evil action, it is not enough to say that it is so because it goes against Charity. Other ethical and philosophical reasons must be presented. Now, in order to prove the intrinsic rationality of a norm that is naturally cognitive, one may present it as an element of a whole with its complete foundations through a solely Christian perspective.

[22] This is what S. Pinckaers seems to suggest in Servais Pinckaers, *Ce qu'on ne peut jamais faire. La question des actes intrinsèquement mauvais. Histoire e discussion* (Fribourg-Paris: Ed. Universitaires. - Ed. du Cerf, 1986), 9f.

Works Cited

Aubert, Jean-Marie. "Débats autour de la morale fondamentale." *Studia Moralia* 20 (1982): 195-222.

—. "La fonction de la foi dans les décisions éthiques." *Le Supplément: revue d'éthique et de théologie morale (Décision morale et discernement théologique)* 129 (1979): 251-74.

—. "La morale catholique est-elle évangélique?" In *La Loi de la liberté. Evangile et morale*, edited by Christos Yannaras, 119-58. Maison: Mame, 1972.

—. "La morale chrétienne est-elle à la mesure de l'homme?" *Études* 325 (1966): 529-45.

—. "La morale chrétienne selon saint Thomas." *Seminarium* 3 (1977): 780-811.

—. "La spécificité de la morale chrétienne selon saint Thomas." *Le Supplément: revue d'éthique et de théologie morale (L'éthique chrétienne à la reserche de son identité)* 23 (1970): 55-73.

Congar, Yves. "Réflexion et propos sur l'originalité éthique chrétienne." *Studia Moralia* 15 (1977): 31-40.

Delhaye, Philippe. "Éthique humaine et morale révélée dans l'Épître aux Romains." *Esprit et Vie* 100 (1990).

—. "La "loi nouvelle" dans l'enseignement de S. Thomas." *Esprit et Vie* 84 (1974).

—. "La mise en cause de la spécificité de la morale chrétienne. Étude de quelques prises de position récentes et réflexions critiques." *Revue Théologique de Louvain* 4 (1973): 308-39.

Fuchs, Josef. "Esiste una morale non-cristiana?" In *Sussidi 1980 per lo studio della Teologia morale fondamentale*, 330-1. Roma: P.U.G., 1980.

—. *Existe-t-il une "morale chrétienne"?, coll. "Recherches et Synthèses", section de morale, IX.* Gembloux: Éditions J. Duculot, 1973.

—. *Human Values and Christian Morality*. Dublin: Gill and Macmillan, 1970.

—. *Moral und Moraltheologie nach dem Konzil*. Freiburg [etc.]: Herder, 1967.

Pinckaers, Servais. *Ce qu'on ne peut jamais faire. La question des actes intrinsèquement mauvais. Histoire e discussion*. Fribourg-Paris: Ed. Universitaires. - Ed. du Cerf, 1986.

Rhonheimer, Martin. *Ley natural y razón práctica. Una visión tomista de la autonomía moral*. Pamplona: Eunsa, 2000.

—. "Morale cristiana e ragionevolezza morale: di che cosa è il compimento la legge del Vangelo?" In *Gesù Cristo, legge vivente e personale della Santa Chiesa, Atti del IX Colloquio Internazionale di Teologia di Lugano sul Primo capitolo dell'Enciclica "Veritatis splendor" (Lugano, 15-17 giugno 1995)*, edited by Graziano Borgonovo. Casale Montferrato: Piemme, 1996.

Scola, Angelo. *Cuestiones de antropología teológica*. Madrid: BAC, 2000.

—. *Hans Urs von Balthasar: un estilo teológico*. Madrid: Encuentro, 1997.

Tremblay, Réal. "Par-delà de la "morale autonome" et "l'éthique de la foi"." *Studia Moralia* 20 (1982): 223-37.

Trigo, Tomás. *El debate sobre la especificidad de la moral cristiana*. Pamplona: Eunsa, 2003.

von Balthasar, Hans Urs. "Las "nueve tesis" de H.U. von Baltahsar." In *Comisión Teológica Internacional. Documentos 1970-1979*. Madrid: Cete, 1983.

—. "Neuf thèses pour une éthique chrétienne." *Documentation Catholique* 72 (1975): 421-6.

Part III:

Systematic Approaches

CHAPTER SIXTEEN

NATURALISTIC FALLACY AND ETHICS: PROBLEMS OF THE NORMATIVITY OF NATURE IN ARISTOTELIAN-THOMISTIC PHILOSOPHY

HÉCTOR ZAGAL

The problematic character of human nature

Since G.E. Moore's groundbreaking work *Principia Ethica* appeared in 1902, it has been discussed at length in Aristotelian-Thomistic philosophy how the knowledge of human nature as such is possible. Those serious objections have made clear that the epistemology of nature demands a reformulation. We neoscholastic moral philosophers cannot pretend to speak so carefreely of what is *natural* as we used to do in the past. I will now posit some of the most neglected problems by contemporary critics who appeal to natural law.

1) If we intend to base ethics on nature, we must be able to explain concisely and correctly *what* is nature. It only takes a look to the *Metaphysics* to notice that the notion of *physis* is a very slippery one.

If we examine carefully the arguments to ground an ethics, we will notice very soon the ambiguity of the notion of nature. For instance, let us think about the indulgence of Neo-Theomistic philosophers towards smoking and their rigidity towards drinking alcohol. According to their opinion, smoking is only an artificial activity, whereas being drunk is a state that seriously jeopardizes our health.

2) A second problem is that we lack even a partially scientific method to know what is natural, and more specifically, to know what is natural in the realm of human actions.

In that regard, the case of adultery is a very interesting one. To determine if adultery is or not something natural we have four possibilities:

a) Empirical observation

> One can determine whether adultery is natural or not by observing what happens in the most number of cases. In function of that, one could be able to find out what is natural in human relationships. Although this approach seems promising, let us not disregard the fact that nature, in the empirical world, can only be predicated in hypothetical terms, never in absolute ones. The attributes of human beings are predicated *ut in pluribus* and not *simpliciter*. In other terms: it is natural for dogs to live up to thirteen years, for most of them die at this age. On the contrary, the sum of the internal angles of a triangle is always equal to 180 degrees. Being consequent with this distinction, we could only assert that only what happens in most of the cases is natural. In the case of infidelity, however, how could one deny the observable recurrent tendency among the human race of having more than one sexual partner? The enormous frequency of this would certainly invalidate the argument of the natural wrongness of adultery.[1]

b) *A priori* knowledge

There may be the possibility that we know what is natural independently from experience. Although most couples may be adulterous, it does not follow from this that infidelity is something natural. Whether as a value or as a *telos*, we are able to know by an *a priori* criterion what is natural aside from statistics.

This second methodical posture takes as fact a privileged access to the knowledge of natural laws. To know what is natural independently from statistics presupposes the capacity to distinguish it from what is not: this is a norm that cannot be derived from the same experience with which it enters in conflict. The moral philosopher who defends this position must implicitly hold a rule to pinpoint the imperfections and disorders of human nature. Unfortunately, he cannot make use of the statistics for then he would be doomed. A surprisingly high number of husbands cheat on their spouses and vice versa.

Let us call this individual natural moralist. NM distinguishes subtly between what happens most of the times (*ut in pluribus*) from what is *secundum naturam*. This distinction may be valid if and only if NM can make explicit the criterion by which he makes such a distinction. I insist: this criterion cannot be grounded on an *ut in pluribus* statistical method; therefore, there can only remain a privileged observation of human nature.

---

[1] Recent statistics make known that 45-55% of married women and 50-60% of married men engage in extramarital sex at some time or another during their relationship. Joan Atwood and Limor Schwartz, "Cyber-Sex: The New Affair Treatment Considerations," *Journal of Couple and Relationship* 1, no. 3 (2002): 37.

That is to say, NM would observe Agammenon, Odysseus, Hector and other Homeric heroes in order to evaluate their conduct. In this heterogeneous group, he would recognize in Hector someone that stands out from the others as an exception. The NM observes, analyzes and finally determines that Hector's fidelity to Andromache is a natural behavior, whereas he would regard as blameful the adulterous deeds of Hector's peers. It becomes evident that this kind of arguing would hold implicitly some sort of eidetic intuition.

I am not questioning if Hector's fidelity makes him a better man than Agammenon. I only want to remark that, under this perspective, NM would have to say—without properly demonstrating *how*—that Hector's actions are better than those of Agammenon, because they are more natural.[2]

In other words, NM believes that he has a right reason that allows him to diagnose the actions that are *secundum naturam*. Nevertheless, unless he explains his method, we ought to suppose that he believes himself to have an extraordinary intellectual aptitude to describe human nature.

To escape the statistical fallacy, the scholastic maxim, *operator sequitur esse, et modus operandi sequitur modus essendi*, requires of a round-about interpretation. The *modus essendi* of human beings, their authentic nature, becomes only manifest according to this in some privileged actions executed by right reason. From the wide spectrum of human actions, only a few are considered to be natural. The twisted deeds that are against natural teleology only show a segmented and abnormal side of human nature. In theory, NM would be able to tell the difference between them. In the case of our interest, he would be able to tell that sexual relations outside of marriage, in spite of their frequency, are not *secundum naturam*.

The problem is that in order to consider Hector over Agammenon as a superior moral agent we would necessarily have to know beforehand what is truly natural. NM cannot extract the natural canon from empirical observation, unless he accepts the natural character of some actions that he is not willing to regard as moral. At the end of the day, the difficulty seems still to remain: how does one distinguish the truly natural actions from what is natural *ut in pluribus*, if one lacks a solid and explicit

---

[2] I have made similar approaches in the book of Héctor Zagal and José Galindo, *Ehtik für jungen Menschen* (Ditzingen: Reclam, 2000). But I have acknowledged the problems of Aristotelism in regard of this subject in Héctor Zagal, *Límites de la argumentación ética en Aristóteles* (México D.F.: Publicaciones Cruz O. S.A., 1996).

criterion? Would it be by means of "intuition" or "innate knowledge"? It seems that NM does not contemplate nature *ex nihilo*. He studies it from a highly humanized view of the cosmos.

One could affirm that there exists another path, namely, the distinction between spontaneous and natural. This distinction is, of course, valid, but it lacks the argumentative value which is commonly attributed to it. In the animal kingdom, spontaneous and natural are practically the same; however, that does not occur with us human beings, for we are able to control a considerable amount of our spontaneous movements. Thus, an adult is able to restrain his fear of injections by thinking of the health that this painful means will grant him.

It is evident that a human being cannot be reduced to his spontaneous impulses. The viability of himself and the species are not granted only by means of instinct. In some cases, we need to control our impulses deliberately in order to survive. In the human realm, the spontaneity of an action does not necessarily imply that it is adequate. The problem would be then to determine by which natural guidelines we ought to conduct our natural impulses. The insufficiency of spontaneity to explain human actions does not answer the problem of the knowledge of nature.

The NM would be also obliged to explain why it would be natural to restrain some impulses and not others if his criteria are *a priori.* In short, NM must put in plain words the essence of right reason without recurring to statistics. This explanation should be particularly clear and distinct, for he pretends to establish concrete moral obligations on the basis of this knowledge. NM would be forced to make explicit the knowledge of nature by which he constructs a code of ethics.

If a medical doctor treats a patient without being certain of the course of action he should take, we would certainly have reasons to distrust him. In a like manner, we can distrust NM when he states that human actions must be ordered in function of an obscure concept of nature. We have the right to ask him how he arrives to that conclusion. It would be very distressing if he is unable to explain his reasoning. I fear to say it, but I believe that NM uses unworriedly two very different kinds of arguments. On the one hand, he makes concrete assessments regarding human deeds, as if actions could be empirically classifiable in good and bad ones in terms of to nature. On the other hand, he uses nature as a source of normativity in an *a priori* manner, without recurring to experience.

I give in advance one of my conclusions: Aristotelian-Thomism must revaluate its arguments in order to answer these questions doing justice to its own epistemological grounds. Any attempt to give a solution to these problems shall not lose from sight, for example, that in the *Prior Analytics*

Aristotle denies that we have an apodictic method to know the essence of things, with the exception of mathematical realities. Furthermore, in the *Posterior Analytics* he does not give any precise method to know the essence of any beings, not to mention the essence of human nature.

c) Common sense

To appeal to common sense is far from being a scientific method. It is true that by common sense we can tell that adultery is something wrong, for no one likes to be deceived. Any reasonable person would deny the moral validity of actions such as kidnapping a kid or stealing a purse. Level-headed individuals do not want for others what they do not want for themselves. This attitude certainly resembles to a great extent some of Aristotle's own opinions, like when he says that the person who questions his parent's authority does not need to be given arguments but a punishment.

Unfortunately, NM would be trapped in the same difficulties as before if he follows this line of reasoning. For indeed, by which kind of arguments could he establish common-sense as something natural and normative? Would common-sense be something analogous to nature or something that gives us a privileged access to it? In any case, common sense may be useful for practical life, but only because NM bases his premises on the fact that some actions are common-sensed since no reasonable person would like to suffer them, it does not follow from this that his criterion is reducible to nature itself.

Furthermore, common-sense seems to be insufficient to explain some of the most frequent scenarios with which we have to deal nowadays due to the progress of science. Only by means of common sense it would be extremely difficult to determine the moral validity of cases such as the cultivation of embryos to treat congenital diseases, the practice of euthanasia with terminal patients and the performance of abortion in endangering health conditions for the mother.

d) Tradition and experience

Other possibility would be to recur to traditional values. NM could say that pure and simple empirical observation does not exist, since we always look at things from very specific horizons of comprehension. We do not judge human actions from neutral positions or as impartial spectators. Thus, NM would determine that moral judgments *ex nihilo* are a fiction and that with the passage of time we have gotten more insights of what is truly natural.

I do not deny any of this. It is true that pure empirical observation does not exist, but tradition *per se* is not a guarantee of moral infallibility. To explain the fundament of our ethical judgments on the basis of horizons of culture only transfers the problem to another scenario. It simply presupposes the explanation by placing it in a social instance.

The core of the problem

It may seem that we have forgotten on one of the opening passages of the *Nicomachean Ethics*.[3] Indeed, we cannot demand in the field of human affairs the same exactitude as in mathematics. Frequently, in discussions like these, we ought to be satisfied with mere approaches to the phenomena that we are studying.

Nevertheless, it is also true that we tend to interpret that passage in a very indulgent way. Alongside this thesis, we affirm simultaneously the existence of moral natural laws that are universal and objective. Just like the fire burns here and in Persia, homicide is wrong here and in Sicily.[4] The inexactitude of such kind of judgments, however, lies the imprecision of applying a universal law to a particular situation. In the case of fire, for instance, it may be challenging to determine whether magnesium light would fall under the definition of fire. In the second case, it may be problematic to conclude if Hector's execution in hands of Achilles was a murder or a justifiable crime of war. According to this interpretation, the inexactitude of ethics would derive from *phronesis* and not from ignoring universal laws of behavior. This reading of Aristotle has in its favor several passages of the *Nicomachean Ethics* and of the *Rhetoric* where he affirms the existence of two or three moral absolutes.

Ethics seems to be something inexact at least from two perspectives. On the one hand, we can only assert in few cases that we know the nature of some given object. On the other hand, human nature is particularly complex. Do we truly believe that NM can give us a definite criterion to tell what is natural from what is not? To be sure, our discussion does not have the purpose of denying the existence of human nature. We only reproach NM that his weak demonstrations do not correspond at all with his rigorous exigencies. He is unable to enunciate a precise method to

[3] *Nicomachean Ethics* I, 3, 1904b 13 and I, 4, 1095a 30. Aristotle, *The Complete Works of Aristotle: The Revised Oxford Translation*, ed. Jonathan Barnes (Princeton, NJ: Princeton University Press, 1984).

[4] Ibid., V, 7, 1134 b 18. This is a much more difficult passage than what has been said.

define what is natural and he believes at the same time that he is entitled to determine which ones are morally wrong actions.

Ethics is an inexact science since the distinction of artificial and natural is not as strong as we imagine it to be. In the aftermath, NM cannot satisfactorily explain the relations between these two realities.[5] Let us think, for example, in the cultural dimension of human beings. No one in his five senses would come to the thought that artificial things are *per se* morally wrong. Human beings are cultural animals, and consequently, they construct artifacts. So artificial is the use of the microscope as it is our knowledge and manipulation of the optic laws that allow us to invent microscopes. Human beings are born neither with lens nor with knowledge of physics.

The blurry frontiers of the artificial

The artificial seems to be the field of the physical and mental objects fabricated or elaborated by human beings. Geometric figures of two dimensions and internal combustion engines are artifices. *Prima facie*, artificial is something whose origin resides in intelligence, in contrast to what is completely natural, which is something untouched by the human hand.

The creation of artifacts can easily go from the natural to the unnatural. There are plenty examples that illustrate this. The microscope and the loudspeaker, for instance, are instruments that maximize the capacities of our senses. The lens of a microscope allows us to see beyond what we perceive at first sight. The magnets of the loudspeaker increase the level of our voice far beyond our immediate surroundings.

NM would argue that these artifices give continuity to the *telos* of the sight and the voice respectively. But under this parameter, the use of aphrodisiacs would be something morally correct. There would be no difference in observing protozoa as in extending the duration and intensity of sexual pleasure. The same thing goes with computers. In principle, to realize mathematical operations in five seconds is a potentiation of our intelligence. But does human nature have some limits? If human capacities are naturally limited, are we able to extend them *ad infinitum* or could we commit some unnatural excesses?

[5] The best work I have read related to this subject is that of Robert Spaemann, *Lo natural y lo racional* (Madrid: Rialp, 1989). Cfr., Ana Marta González, *Naturaleza y dignidad* (Pamplona: Eunsa, 1996). González, *Moral, razón y naturaleza* (Pamplona: Eunsa, 2006).

Let us think in another case: the use of parachutes. One would argue again that this artifice is an extension of our locomotive capacities. However, it is obvious that the argument is not flawless, since our extremities are not made for flying. A proof thereof is the high number of accidents that occur in this kind of activities. Traumatologists can make a long list of the severe damages originated by these sports. *Grosso modo*, medicine suggests that we human beings are not made for swimming, running, boxing, or bungee jumping, with the exception of some extraordinary cases.

There is even a more extreme case than those, namely, to fly to outer space. Our metabolism is seriously transformed when we abandon the atmosphere. Our organism needs terrestrial gravity. Flying to outer space implies to translate our body beyond its original physical environment. For the sake of scientific progress, the NASA adds all types of prosthesis to the astronauts in order to fulfill their mission. Little do they care that planet earth is the natural habitat for human beings. On the other hand, NM would not care to disrupt human metabolism as long as machines supply the deficiencies provoked by a voyage like this. Nevertheless, he does not consider such actions to be *contra naturam* but only artificial.

If we understand what is natural as what is given, every artificial object is not-natural. Neoscholasticism indicates, however, that the teleology and not the mere *factum* can be considered natural. Therefore, the machinery of a space shuttle would not attempt against human nature, for it only permits the development of our natural tendencies. I will explore now this solution.

Teleology and nature

The doctrine of natural ends is at the very core of Aristotelism and Thomism. It would not be an exaggeration to suggest the compatibility of teleology and contemporary biology. In the natural world there exist natural functions which imply natural ends. Living creatures are born with some functions that guarantee the viability of the individual and the survival of the species.

If we are honest, we must acknowledge that we infer natural functions from the general use of them by living creatures. Teleology implies serious epistemological difficulties. We affirm that human eyes are meant to see because we use them for that. In the case of moles, on the contrary, eyes do not have the same function they have in other mammals, for moles do not use eyes for seeing. This is something proved by experience.[6] The mole does not "lack" sight. Likewise, the penguin does not lack the capacity of flying, for his wings are not made to fly through the skies. Structures express a function as long as the subjects use them. If a mole with sight was born, it would be regarded as an abnormal mole.

To be sure, the disposition of the physical parts suggests the function of the organ. The parts of an eye such as retina, iris, optic nerve, etc., indicate their *telos*. But in the majority of cases, such taxidermy is too vague and general for the purposes of NM. Only by observing the behavior of animals we are able to know the way they employ sight. Furthermore, in the case of animals, the use comes determined by instinct. No penguin would use a parachute to fly. It follows from this that the analysis of animal parts, aside from their observation, does not explain teleology adequately.[7]

In the case of human beings this is much more complex. Our behavior is not guided only by instincts but also by reason.[8] We are capable of going beyond the limits of what is given to us factically. Our perfection does not reside in limiting ourselves to what we are since our birth. We are able to develop substances to induce or to control appetite, to control our alimentation, to reduce our stomachs.

This rational capacity implies that our natural functions are undetermined to a great extent. *Prima facie*, little would it help us to observe our natural functions in order to elaborate a strict code of conduct. Starting off exclusively with the natural inclination of the rational potencies, we would hardly construct a hard ethics, not to mention a Christian ethics.

It becomes evident the necessity to elaborate a concept of "right reason". Natural rational potencies—as it is pointed out in Thomism—are open to contraries. In other words, natural teleology is insufficient without the concept of rectitude. Rationality as *factum* is not a criterion to orient

---

[6] According to Aristotle, only in a very limited sense does the mole "lack" vision. Despite of it Aristotelian origin, the use of the term privatio tends to be confusing. Cfr. Amalia Quevedo, *La privación según Aristóteles* (Chía: Universidad de la Sabana, 1998), 37-40.

[7] *De partibus animalium* is a clear example of how taxidermy is not a deduction of finalities, but the observation of nature *in situ*. We know finalities by means of observation.

[8] Aquinas, *S. Th. I-IIae*, q. 10, a. 1 and q. 94, a. 2. Cfr. Alfonso Gomez Lobo, "Natural Law and Naturalism," *Proceedings of the American Catholic Philosophical Association* 69 (1984): 264.

our behavior. It is necessary that we ordain it; if we speak of "right reason" it is because there are other uses of reason. Natural finalities, understood as mere spontaneity, do not guarantee moral rectitude. We need more elements to determine what is morally correct.

The Aristotelian solution relies on the qualified "opinion" (*endoxon*). This philosophy adopts the procedure of observing the behavior of those who are acknowledged as virtuous people. Apparently, it is an intermediate posture between apriorism and statistical methods. As it has been pointed out, however, the resort to tradition—the *endoxon* of the righteous—does not give a solution to the core of the problem.

The aporia hunts us. We cannot determine the practical rectitude of reason aside from experience. Our parameter of moral correctness is either *a priori* or derives from experience. Although we can weaken these difficulties to some extent by clarifying the concept of experience, it seems to me that we are facing an unsolvable dilemma. The Aristotelian solution does not seem to be completely adequate, for indeed, how does one know which individuals are "good"?

What is normal?

Another kind of solution that NM could adduce is the following: "the right use of reason is what makes us better individuals." NM could enounce convincing examples: drinking alcohol in excess, consuming drugs or committing felonies are actions that do not perfect us as rational agents. Nevertheless, this exit lacks solidity from an epistemological point of view. If the "right use of reason" makes us morally good, what is then "goodness"? NM would not be able to explain the end without the use and vice versa. The circularity of his argumentation would become manifest.

Let us formulate the question in other terms: how do we know to direct our actions in order to reach rational rectitude? We cannot confide in statistical observation. In the Aristotelian universe—and also in ours—the vicious individuals are many and the virtuous ones stand out as exceptional characters. To top it all, the conditions to be virtuous in an Aristotelian sense are very difficult to acquire. Let us remember that the *spoudaios* for Aristotle is practically never attracted to vice. This problem is analogous to that of hiatus hernia in men. Eight out of ten persons suffer from it. The statistic is so impressive that one would be tempted to think that healthy men are abnormal.

There is indeed a difference between hiatus hernias and vicious behaviors. In the first case, the analysis of the parts and their physical consequences allows us to infer that something wrong occurs in the digestive apparatus. In several moral actions, on the contrary, we lack such empirical indicators. Alcoholism destroys the liver, but what about "white lies"? Vices are not always accompanied by negative external effects.

In the VI book of the *Metaphysics*, Aristotle explores a related subject: the distortion of perception, a phenomenon that was cunningly used by Protagoras.[9] Honey tastes bitter to a sick individual and sweet to a healthy one. The Aristotelian strategy against the arguments of the sophist is based on two principles: (1) the distinction between thought and perception and (2) the concept of normality.

The sick person judges wrongly the taste of honey because his physical constitution is damaged. This argument is solid but its reach is limited. I adduce here again the case of hiatus hernia. It seems that "normal" nature banishes away. Some medical doctors repeat frequently that human beings area always sick, only that some are sicker than others.

To be sincere, we ought to admit that deforms the concept of normality. In Aristotelism and Thomism lies surreptitiously some sort of Platonism behind the idea of a normality that goes beyond particular and factual cases.

Can we still talk of normativity of nature?

The question of the normativity of nature still remains. From the fact that something is as it is, one cannot say that things ought to be like that. From stating the rationality of human beings we cannot posit the limits of reason. This is not a trivial question, especially now that genetic engineering offers us unprecedented technical possibilities that go from the manipulation of genes to human clonation.

The rational order *secundum ordinem rationis* is very weak; it is not easy to transform a natural fact into an unconditioned moral imperative. It is difficult to dissuade a married couple of recurring to artificial insemination using as argument that human reproduction is necessarily bonded by nature to an amorous act. It is not unreasonable to suppose that "natural facts" can be modified, since the technical use of reason is also a natural fact. Let us not loose from sight that NM has desestimated the normative value of spontaneous tendencies. He has diluted the normative value of natural facts to ground moral rules on an ethereal nature *secundum ordinem rationis*.

---

[9] Aristotle, *Metaphysics*, V, 5, 1009a 6.

I believe that any solution to this problem must take all these difficulties into account. In order to give an adequate solution, it is necessary to do a thorough examination of the ambiguities of the concept of nature, without closing the eyes to the challenges now posited by scientific developments. I believe that the Aristotelian-Thomistic philosophy has still a lot to tell us in the field of ethics. However, that does not mean that its whole is perfect and completed. Cases like these only show that some of the principles coined in a tradition need to be reformulated and newly examined.

Works Cited

Aquinas, Thomas. *Summa Theologica* Translated by the Fathers of the English Dominican Province. New York: Benzinger Bros., 1947.

Aristotle. *The Complete Works of Aristotle: The Revised Oxford Translation*. Edited by Jonathan Barnes. Princeton, NJ: Princeton University Press, 1984.

Atwood, Joan, and Limor Schwartz. "Cyber-Sex: The New Affair Treatment Considerations." *Journal of Couple and Relationship* 1, no. 3 (2002): 37-57.

Gomez Lobo, Alfonso. "Natural Law and Naturalism." *Proceedings of the American Catholic Philosophical Association* 69 (1984).

González, Ana Marta. *Moral, razón y naturaleza. Una investigación sobre Tomás de Aquino*. 2 ed. Pamplona: EUNSA, 2006.

—. *Naturaleza y dignidad*. Pamplona: Eunsa, 1996.

Quevedo, Amalia. *La privación según Aristóteles*. Chía: Universidad de la Sabana, 1998.

Spaemann, Robert. *Lo natural y lo racional*. Madrid: Rialp, 1989.

Zagal, Héctor. *Límites de la argumentación ética en Aristóteles*. México D.F.: Publicaciones Cruz O. S.A., 1996.

Zagal, Héctor, and José Galindo. *Ehtik für jungen Menschen*. Ditzingen: Reclam, 2000.

CHAPTER SEVENTEEN

THE PRACTICAL VALUE OF NATURAL LAW THEORY IN THE WORK OF ST THOMAS AQUINAS

MARIO ŠILAR*

Introduction: "Ante scientiam oportet inquirere modum scientiae[1]"

In a recent article, Dr. Alfredo Cruz has rejected the claim that natural law theory (NLT) may have practical value in the realm of moral philosophy. Neither motivation which might infuse human action with a certain force of obligation nor knowledge of natural law (NL) would give NLT practical value.[2]

An alternative conceptual framework for the interpretation of some texts in the work of St Thomas Aquinas, on which Cruz draws in support of his argument, is offered in this paper. In particular, I will argue that the concept of obligation (*vis obligandi*) in Aquinas's work is broader than that deferred to by Cruz in his article. My purpose is to show that NLT has practical significance, at least in a derivative sense.

---

* I would like to express my gratitude to "Friends of the University of Navarra Inc.".

[1] *In Boethium De Trinitate*, pars III, prooemium, prologus.

[2] See Alfredo Cruz, "Natural Law and Practical Philosophy: The Presence of a Theological Concept in Moral Knowledge," in *Contemporary Perspectives on Natural Law. Natural Law as a Limiting Concept*, ed. Ana Marta González (Aldershot: Ashgate, 2008), 161-74. Dr. Cruz kindly commented on an earlier version of this paper and helped me to correct several misinterpretations of his position.

This paper is structured in five sections. The first section examines the relationship, and difference, between theoretical reason (TR) and practical reason (PR). In the second, the meaning of the terms "practical" and "practicable" (*operabile*) in Thomistic moral thinking is explored. The idea of "end" in moral philosophy and virtuous action is analysed in the third section—above all, in light of the *Commentary on the Nicomachean Ethics*. The fourth presents a distinction between the epistemological and real levels in the study of NL. The link between goodness and the obligatory nature of action, the keystone of my argument, is addressed in the fifth section. In this regard, two apparently competing notions surface in Aquinas's writings: self-legislation and the law unto oneself—which should prompt further consideration of the ways in which the concept of law itself is understood.

The potentialities enabled by a wider, analogical interpretation of St Thomas's view of law, as against a limiting, univocal account, are highlighted in the article's concluding section. This broadening of the conceptual framework serves two purposes: it defuses apparent intertextual tensions, and grants NLT a certain degree of practical significance.[3]

"Intellectus speculativus fit practicus per extensionem"[4]

St Thomas adopted the Aristotelian distinction between TR and PR in accordance with the different ends which each may serve in the use of reason.[5] The term *extensionem* denotes the practical realisation of TR,[6]

[3] The first four points do not invalidate Cruz's thesis; in fact, they would appear to be implicit in his line of argument. Nevertheless, a number of specific issues reflected in his position are addressed in the final section and conclusion to this paper.

[4] *In III Sent.*, d. 23, q. 2 a. 3. See *S. Th.* I, q. 79, a. 11. For a detailed analysis of this text, see Georges Cottier OP, "La raison practique chez Thomas d'Aquin," in *Ragione pratica, libertà, normatività* ed. Marcelo Sánchez Sorondo (Roma: Herder - Univeristà Lateranense, 1991), 65-88.

[5] See Aristotle, *De Anima*, ed. Bekker (Berlin: Gigon-Bonitz, 1960-61), L. III, chap. 10, Bk 433a 14-15. *In III de Anima*, chap. 9, no. 35-49 (Leonina), lectio 15, no. 820 (Marietti).

[6] "Similis autem processus esse invenitur rationis practicae et speculativae, utraque enim ex quibusdam principiis ad quasdam conclusiones procedit, ut superius habitum est". *S. Th.* I-II, q. 91, a. 3 c. Rhonheimer holds that the term "extensio" is invoked in order to safeguard the unity of the potency, irrespective of the different acts. See Martin Rhonheimer, *Natural Law and Practical Reason: A Thomist View*

which encompasses both the unity of the potency and the difference between its products—that is, the judgements of reason in their theoretical or practical uses.[7]

Extensio ad opus is made possible by the fact that "truth and good—the objects to which reason is directed—include one another."[8] The difference between TR and PR is expressed as follows:

> it is the speculative intellect which directs what it apprehends, not to operation, but to the consideration of truth; while the practical intellect is that which directs what it apprehends to operation.[9]

Practical intellectual knowledge is enabled by the fact that the "good is something true, otherwise it would not be intelligible."[10] Thus, the following conclusion may be drawn:

> therefore as the object of the appetite may be something true, as having the aspect of good [...]; so the object of the practical intellect is good directed

---

of Moral Autonomy (New York: Fordham University Press, 2000), 24ff. This interpretation seems justified in light of the question addressed in *S. Th.* I, q. 79, a. 11 c. Nevertheless, the idea of *extension* presupposes the possibility that different ends are taken on in that which is *extended.* See also, Ralph McInerny, "Portia's Lament: Reflections on Practical Reason," in *Natural Law and Moral Inquiry. Ethics, Metaphysics, and Politics in the Work of Germain Grisez*, ed. Robert George (Washington D.C.: Georgetown University Press, 1998), 94.

[7] St Thomas refers to *De Anima* (L. III, chap. 10, Bk 433a 14-15) on numerous occasions. The *Commissio Leonina* held that Aquinas, who used the translation by William of Moerbeke, did not read the word "*extensionem*" when he commented on this section [See *In III de Anima*, chap. 9, no. 35-40 (Leonina), lectio 15, no. 820 (Marietti)]. Nevertheless, he refers or alludes to this passage at various points in his work, for instance in: *In III Sent.*, d. 23, q. 2, a. 3, qla. 2 c, *S. Th.* I, q. 79, a. 11 *sed contra*, II-II, q. 4, a. 2 ad 3; *De Veritate*, q. 2 a. 8; q. 14, a. 4 c. The word directs the reader to the *Vetus translatio* by James of Venice, on which St Thomas drew. See "Saint Thomas, utilisateur de la *Vetus* (1247 - vers 1264)," René-A Gauthier, "Préface," in Thomas Aquinas, *Opera omnia iussu Leonis XIII P. M. edita, Sentencia libri De anima*, vol. XLV, 1 (Rome-Paris: Commissio Leonina-J. Vrin, 1984), 267 and ff. Also ———, *Opera omnia iussu Leonis XIII P. M. edita, Quaestiones Disputatae de Veritate* vol. XXII, 1 (Rome: Editori di San Tommaso, 1975), aparatus criticus, 69 (q. 2, a. 8, no. 55). Here the "*per extensionem*" is attributed to *De Anima*, chap. 9, (432b 26 - 433a 1); see also *In III de Anima*, chap. 8, no. 237-298 (Leonina), lectio 14, no. 812-817 (Marietti).

[8] *S. Th.* I, q. 79, a. 11, ad 2.

[9] *S. Th.* I, q. 79, a. 11 c.

[10] *S. Th.* I, q. 79, a. 11 ad 2.

> to the operation, and under the aspect of truth. For the practical intellect knows truth, just as the speculative, but it directs the known truth to operation.[11]

To know the truth directed to operation, the defining function of PR, allows one to speak of the truth—the practical truth—of action, the criteria by which real and apparent goods may be distinguished from one another.[12]

Cruz points out that "the truth of the practical is variable truth, which only exists fully in the particular and the concrete."[13] However, the value of principles, on which the intelligibility of every concrete good depends,[14] should not be ignored on that account. These principles direct and set certain unequivocal limits on meaningful human action.[15] The unity of PR is not undone by the distinction between the first practical principles and the specific judgments of action which comprise the virtue of prudence.[16] In reality, while the acts of PR are directed to action, PR in the perfection of its final concretion is one and the same reason as has such principles for its object. Thus, while the truth of the practical is variable, the fact that the principles are present in every specific judgement of action—in an intentional way, in as particular a form as is required by the need to act in the *hic et nunc*—should also be acknowledged. Moreover, while it is true that contemplation of principles is not in itself sufficient to prompt good action, without those principles, the action would be wholly unintelligible.

---

[11] *S. Th.* I, q. 79, a. 11 ad 2.

[12] See Martin Rhonheimer, *Praktische Vernunft und Vernünftigkeit der Praxis: Handlungstheorie bei Thomas von Aquin in ihrer Entstehung aus dem Problemkontext der aristotelischen Ethik* (Berlin: Akademie Verlag, 1994), 576-92.

[13] Cruz, "Natural Law and Practical Philosophy," 161.

[14] St Thomas holds that those things to which the moral virtues incline, are as the principles of prudence whereas the products of art are not the principles, but the matter of art. See *S. Th.* I-II, q. 65, a. 1 ad 4.

[15] See Ana Marta González, "Natural Law as a Limiting Concept: A Reading of Thomas Aquinas," in *Contemporary Perspectives on Natural Law. Natural Law as a Limiting Concept*, ed. Ana Marta González (Aldershot: Ashgate, 2008), 11-25.

[16] "Etiam cogitatio de eo quod est ad finem, prout consideratur in ordine ad finem, est eadem cum cogitatione finis; non autem cogitatio de eo quod est ad finem ut est res quaedam, et similiter nec voluntas". *In II Sent.*, d. 38, q. 1, a. 4, ad 3. See Martin Rhonheimer, *La perspectiva de la moral: Fundamentos de la Ética Filosófica*, ed. José Carlos Mardomingo (Madrid: Rialp, 2000), 371.

Ethica: scientia practica

The difference between theoretical and practical knowledge lies in the different ends that each serves. The speculative idea is supplemented by the practical with a direction to operation, in the same way as—to defer to the example given by St Thomas—the addition of "rational" to "animal" yields "man" without giving rise in the process to two different things (*res*).[17] This clarification gives an idea of the broader meaning of the concept of "practical truth", which should not be reduced to the agreement of right reason and right desire (appetite);[18] strictly speaking, this refined definition refers only to prudential practical truth.[19] Moreover, this limited understanding may give rise to confusion about the meaning of practical knowledge. In an observation that is as surprising as it is little known, St Thomas holds that the knowledge is not rendered practical by the union between reason and will, but by the direction to operation—to action. Given that the will centres on the end, and the end is to be found in both, the will is common to both speculative and practical understanding.[20] To sum up, therefore, the inclusion of the direction to operation marks the difference between the theoretical and the practical.[21] According to *ST*, I, q. 14, a. 16,[22] three criteria govern this inclusion: object, end and mode.[23]

---

[17] *De Veritate*, q. 3, a. 3 ad 6. Aquinas's view of the unity of the potency, which is consistent with Scholastic tradition, stands in marked contrast to that adopted by his master Albert the Great (Albert the Great, "In VI Ethicorum," in *Opera omnia*, ed. A. Borgnet (Paris: Vivès, 1891), tract. I, c. 3, p. 397a.), who held that TR and PR are two different *powers* of the soul. "While Thomas keeps to the *unity of the power*, at the same time he emphasizes a *fundamental difference between theoretical and practical judgments*, upon which is based the difference between theoretical and practical knowledge" (Rhonheimer, *Natural Law and Practical Reason*, 24.)

[18] See *In VI Ethicorum*, chap. 2, 1139 a27, no. 109-127 (Leonina), lectio 2, no. 1131 (Marietti). See also, Aristotle, *Nicomachean Ethics* (Cambridge: Cambridge University Press, 2000), VI, chap. 2, 1104a-04b.

[19] See *S. Th.* I-II, q. 57, a. 5 ad 3. See Christian Schröer, *Praktische Vernunft bei Thomas von Aquin* (Stuttgart - Berlin - Köhln: Verlag W. Kolhammer, 1995), 196-218.

[20] "Conjunctio intellectus ad voluntatem non facit intellectum practicum, sed ordinatio ejus ad opus: quia voluntas communis est et speculativo et practico voluntas enim est finis; sed finis invenitur in speculativo et practico intellectu". *In III Sent.*, d. 23, q. 2, a. 3, qla. 2 ad 3.

[21] *De Veritate*, q. 3, a. 3, ad 4.

[22] For a more extensive account of the epistemological status of ethics, see Ana Marta González, "Moral, Filosofía Moral y Metafísica en Santo Tomás de

Purely speculative knowledge (object, end and mode of speculation) and purely practical knowledge (object, end and mode in practice) are the extremes on the scale established in accordance with the three-fold criteria. A wide range of intermediate forms of knowledge come between these two extremes, through different possible combinations or by comparison between different types of knowledge.[24] Given that further nuances and new combinations may always arise, the distinction between theoretical and practical resists any reduction to a fixed framework. The practicability of the end may nevertheless be regarded as the determining element in practical knowledge; thus, the more specific the end, the more practical the knowledge. A number of aspects of this position might fruitfully be examined in further detail.

First, St Thomas states explicitly that PR originates in the universal principles of the TR; although its end is the particular and practicable, it is rooted in the same subject as speculative knowledge.[25] It follows that practical knowledge is not perfect unless it attains to the singular;[26] and the closer its consideration of the particular, the more perfect the practical science.[27] However, this "stretching out" (*extensio*) of its speculative act through an "application to task"[28] (*ordinatio ad opus*) is not the sole prerogative of only one habit. Both moral science (the practical science)

Aquino," *Pensamiento* 56, no. 216 (2000): 459-67. Richard Geraghty's dissenting interpretation, which envisages a radical hermeneutics of ethics as an absolutely practical science, should be noted in this context. On the basis of a rather sui generis interpretation of *S. Th.* I, q. 14, a. 16, he concludes that what appears to be a three-fold division is in fact four-fold. See Richard P. Geraghty, *The Object of Moral Philosophy according to St. Thomas Aquinas* (Washington D.C.: University Press of America, 1981), 13-14.

[23] *S. Th.* I, q. 14, a. 16 c.

[24] *In Boethium De Trinitate*, Pars 3, q. 5, a. 1, ad 4. For example, as compared with metaphysics, art—like dialectics—may be regarded as practical knowledge; however, as compared with agriculture, whose object is more practical, it may be regarded as speculative. See William Augustine Wallace, *The Role of Demonstration in Moral Theology: a Study of Methodology in St. Thomas Aquinas* (Washington D.C.: Thomist Press, 1963), 79 and ff.

[25] *In VI Ethicorum*, chap. 2, 1139 a27, no. 128-141 (Leonina), lectio 2, no. 1132 (Marietti).

[26] *SCG*, L. I, c. 65.

[27] "Quod intellectus practicus principium quidem habet in universali consideratione, et secundum hoc est idem subiecto cum speculativo, sed terminatur eius consideratio in particulari operabili [*individual operable things*]". *S. Th.* I, q. 22, a. 3 ad 1.

[28] Rhonheimer, *Natural Law and Practical Reason*, 24.

and prudence involve the application of the universal principles of practice derived from synderesis.[29] This duality is possible because, as is explained below, singular things may be known from two distinct formal perspectives.

Second, St Thomas defines science as *recta ratio scibilium* and prudence as *recta ratio agibilium*.[30] Given that practical knowledge is predicated as much on the *agibile* as the *scibile*, the distinction between *scibile* and *agibile* does not correspond exactly to the difference between theory and practice. This asymmetry shows that the meaning of the "practical" is broader than the meaning of the "practicable". In fact, there are two specifically different ways of knowing the particular and contingent; both are practical, but they defer to different formalities: on the one hand, the practical knowledge of science (*scibilium*), by which singular things are known insofar as they are contained in the universal (theoretical-practical knowledge);[31] on the other hand, singular things are known to prudence (*agibilium*) by virtue of their own particular reasons (practical-practical knowledge). If the object of science is the universal and necessary, rather than singular and contingent things, then that which takes singular and contingent things insofar as they are contained in the universal as its object may be referred to as "practical science". This argument is in line with the dual perspective to which singular things are open alluded to above: 1) *in accordance with their universal reasons*, which are the ground of demonstrations of the contingent (*recta ratio scibilium*); or 2) *in their singularity*, wherein these universal reasons take on extremely variable forms that are not encompassed by immediate intellectual knowledge, but rather, on reflection, by virtue of the role played by the cogitative function in the exercise of prudence (*recta ratio agibilium*).

To sum up, the meaning of what is "practical" involves both a degree of understanding related to the universal and necessary and a specifically practical knowledge of the particular and contingent. In contrast, the

---

[29] In fact, in his commentary on Aristotle, Aquinas holds that the practical science is prudence considered solely insofar as it pertains to reason: "omnia ergo de quibus hic fit mentio, in tantum sunt species prudentiae, inquantum non in ratione sola consistunt, sed habent aliquid in appetitu. Inquantum enim sunt in sola ratione, dicuntur quaedam scientiae practicae, scilicet ethica oeconomica et politica". *In VI Ethicorum*, chap. 7, 1141 b29, no. 90-95 (Leonina), lectio 7, no. 1200 (Marietti). It follows that the practical science corresponds to prudence to a certain extent, without being wholly identical to it.

[30] See *S. Th.* II-II, q. 55, a. 3.

[31] *In II Sent.*, d. 24, q. 2, a. 4 ad 6.

meaning of "practicable" is wholly confined to the context of singular things. St Thomas strengthens the Aristotelian expression[32] "practical science"[33] by means of this refined definition of terms. The analogical meaning of the "practical" must be clearly acknowledged: although they are not predicated on the same ground, both meanings are applied *simpliciter* and *formaliter*, thus preserving the formal character of practical knowledge—its direction to operation,[34] the mode of which (*modus ordinationis*) may be *actual*, in the case of prudence (the *agibile*), or *habitual* in the case of moral science (the *scibile*). Thus, knowledge may be practical as regards its object and mode, and ordered with respect to the end of that action in an actual or virtual way.[35] This duality corresponds to the dual perspective by which contingent things may be known referred to above. Given that direction to operation is deferred to in both moral science and prudence, both forms of knowledge are practical; however, since the mode of direction is different in each case, prudence is practical in an immediate way, while the practicality of the moral science is mediate.

The following conclusions may be drawn from the above discussion: practical knowledge expresses a certain direction to operation; and the judgements of practical knowledge, while universal, comprise an effective norm of moral order, although at the level of concrete good action the exercise of prudence and right reason (*recta ratio*) are also required.[36] The question of the practical value of NLT cannot be adequately addressed if the duality of practical knowledge—actual or habitual—is not taken into account. In fact, the terms of the question demand that the meaning of the "practical"—in St Thomas's definition of the term—mean more than what

---

[32] See Aristotle, *Nicomachean Ethics*, L. I, chap. 2 and 3, Bk 1094a - 94b.

[33] See *S. Th.* I, q. 1, a. 6; q. 14 a. 16; q. 22. a 3 ad 1; I-II, q. 53, a. 4; *In III Sent.*, d. 35, q. 1, a. 3, qla. 2 c., and ad 2; *De Veritate*, q. 2, a. 8; q. 3 a. 3; *In I Post. Anal.*, lect. 41; *In Boethium De Trinitate*, q. 5, a. 1, ad 3, and ad 4; etc. For an historical overview of this question, see Georg Wieland, *Ethica, Scientia Practica. Die Anfänge der philosophischen Ethik im 13. Jahrhundert* (Münster: Aschendorff, 1981).

[34] See John E. Naus, *The Nature of the Practical Intellect according to Saint Thomas Aquinas* (Roma: Libreria Editrice dell'Università Gregoriana, 1959), 200 and ff.

[35] *De Veritate*, q. 3, a. 3.

[36] See Wolfgang Kluxen, *Philosophische Ethik bei Thomas von Aquin* (Mainz: Matthias-Grünewald Verlag, 1964), 44-57. Italian edition: ———, *L'etica filosofica di Tommaso d'Aquino* (Milano: Vita e pensiero, 2006).

is strictly speaking practicable; in the final analysis, the practicable must be read in the context of a full conceptual understanding of the practical.

The "rational demonstrations" of the contingent betoken the presence of universal reasons, recognised by PR as underlying all particular things. Although it may not amount to the highest degree of perfection of practical knowledge, such demonstrative knowledge is a necessary part of all practical sciences in general. The contingent, seen only in the light of its particularity, is undeniably variable; it is the object of intellectual understanding only in a reflected way—that is, by assuming the contribution of the order of appetites, and the involvement of the cogitative power and prudence.[37] Thus, the statement that "the value of knowledge on the practical is the practical value of such knowledge"[38] has true meaning only if the "practical" is not reduced to the "practicable", a reductive reading that collapses the distinction between practical science and prudence.

The idea of "end" in knowledge and action

The discussion thus far enables a more refined understanding of the relationship between knowledge and virtue, in light of St Thomas's account of the requisite attitude for the study of ethics. Man does not inquire into virtue solely in order to know it, but also to become virtuous. Aquinas's commentary on the Aristotelian text highlights the practical commitment implicit in this inquiry, and furnishes a subtle distinction that facilitates a more refined understanding of the scientific nature of this form of knowledge. St Thomas refers to the inexperience of youth in the exercise of knowledge in order to show the duality of ends involved in practical knowledge. Thus, although Aquinas follows the line of argument set out in Aristotelian thought, he offers a more in-depth understanding and more refined definition of the idea of practical knowledge than is reflected in Aristotle's work.

First, Aquinas makes a distinction between two ways of understanding youth: as a function of age (the young man) or of custom (the passionate man); this distinction opens up a dual perspective on the idea of the end. Given that he lacks experience, the young man lacks the requisite aptitude for the end of this science, which is knowledge (*iuvenis aetate deficit a fine huius scientiae, qui est cognitio*). On the other hand, while the

[37] See *S. Th.* I, q. 86, a. 1 ad 2; II-II, q. 47, a. 3 c., and ad 1, q. 49, a. 2 ad 1; *De Veritate*, q. 10, a. 5 c.; ad 2, ad 3, and ad 4.

[38] Cruz, "Natural Law and Practical Philosophy," 161.

passionate man, who is young by virtue of his customs, may acquire a certain degree of knowledge of this science (*finis enim huius scientiae non est sola cognitio, ad quam forte pervenire possent passionum sectatores*), such knowledge may be pointless or useless because the passionate man lives by the drive of his passions, not by the light of reason, and the knowledge acquired might not lead to its proper end, which is action (*ita ille qui est iuvenis moribus deficit a fine, qui est actio*).[39]

Thus, St Thomas simultaneously reaffirms the practical end of this form of knowledge and underscores the significance of the universality of the practical principles for the acquisition and exercise of prudential virtue. The young man (in both senses of the term) is not thwarted by time or age; rather, in both cases the universal principles are impaired, and the passionate man yields to the sway of the particular desires provoked by his passions (*sequitur singula, ad quae passiones inclinant*), while the young man fails to direct action in accordance with the knowledge of moral science he possesses (*qui non sequuntur scientiam, quam de moralibus habent*).[40] The singularity of action and the universality of the principles which direct action and make it meaningful are brought into balance by the duality of ends; and, as a result, the singular is neither subsumed in nor deduced from the universal.

The duality of the end has been systematised in the philosophical tradition in the ideas of *mediate* and *immediate* ends.[41] What is practical is not only a function of what is immediately practical (prudence)—that is, of the final product of PR; rather, it is also a function of the habit of science. Direction to operation safeguards the practical nature of knowledge. Thus, while it may be true to say that practical knowledge is valuable insofar as it enables growth in the exercise of virtue, the view that the content of practical knowledge and the acquisition of virtue are to be regarded as identical does not follow as a matter of course. Everything in the realm of practice is directed towards the final end—that is, to action; however, the meaning of practice encompasses elements beyond those involved in the immediate direction to operation.

---

[39] *In I Ethicorum*, chap. 3, 1095 a4, no. 151-155 (Leonina), lectio 3, no. 40 (Marietti).

[40] *In I Ethicorum*, chap. 3, 1095 a4, no. 155-160 (Leonina), lectio 3, no. 40 (Marietti).

[41] See Santiago Ramírez OP, *Opera omnia. De Hominis beatitudine tractatus theologicus. Tomus 1* (Madrid: Instituto de Filosofía 'Luis Vives', 1972), 107 and ff.

The difference between the *order of action* and the *order of knowledge* should be noted in this context. In each case, the relationship to the mediate-immediate end is effected in a different way: the immediately practical (the exercise of virtue) in the order of action is the mediate or immediate end of moral science; whereas the mediately practical (the habit of science) in the order of action is the immediate end of moral science. In other words, in the order of action, the immediate practical end is the exercise of virtue (prudence), in which case the habit of science is mediately practical because direction to operation depends on the last concretion conferred by the virtue of prudence. In the order of knowledge, the immediate end of moral science is knowledge (*recta ratio scibilium*); hence it is a science. Nevertheless, the mediate end of moral science is direction to operation. If action were taken to be its immediate end, moral science could lay no claim to universality, which is the prerogative of all scientific knowledge. However, given that prudence presupposes the presence of the habit of science, which it encompasses and extends insofar as it also involves the realm of appetite,[42] *recta ratio scibilium* is not merely a remote end with respect to action.

Thus, while St Thomas acknowledges that the disposition prompted by the habit of first principles and science concerning the precepts of the moral order is not sufficient in itself to ensure right judgement with respect to the particular and practicable end, he also clearly states the prior need for this disposition in the perfect development of prudence. This line of argument does not imply that the acquisition and exercise of individual prudence is wholly dependent on the possession of moral science in a systematic way. In fact, one of the defining characteristics of prudence is experiential knowledge;[43] however, some degree of rational or reasoned knowledge, which is connoted by the term "science" in the conceptual framework of Thomistic thought, is required.[44]

It might be argued that while the discussion thus far does broaden the meaning of the "practical" in the context of moral science, it does not provide an adequate response to the question of the "practical value" of a moral doctrine, such as, for example, NLT. A distinction based on the different levels on which the ethical dimension unfolds may be valuable in responding to this objection.

---

[42] *De Virtutibus in communi*, a. 6 ad 1.

[43] "Prudentia est circa singularia, quae fiunt nobis cognita per experientiam". *In VI Ethicorum*, chap. 7, 1142 a11, no. 174-175 (Leonina), lectio 7, no. 1208 (Marietti).

[44] *S. Th.* I-II, q. 6, a. 8; I-II, q. 76, a. 1 c. See Domingo Basso OP, *Las normas de la moralidad* (Buenos Aires: Claretiana, 1994), 254.

Two levels of understanding in the ethical dimension: the case of NL

Rhonheimer frames the ethical dimension on two planes: the Prescriptive-Practical Level (PPL) is the plane of concrete, singular action; the Descriptive-Reflexive Level (DRL) is the plane of reflection and ethical-philosophical thought.[45] It is clear that the scientific nature of the DRL presupposes a higher degree of speculative universality. The difference between the two planes may be illustrated as follows: man, a rational agent committed to action, may discern that specific actions draw him closer to or move him further from his intended end. This experience, as such, pertains to the PPL. However, the structure of rationality implicit in individual human action may also be conceptualized in terms of moral philosophy. This process of conceptualization pertains to the DRL. On this plane of the ethical dimension, the philosopher may discover, for example, that man would not be able to question the rectitude of the action with respect to the end were it not for the fact that he is also aware of the rule and measure which govern action.[46] This conceptualization is not a figment of the moral philosopher's imagination; rather, it is the way in which the phenomenon discerned on the PPL is expressed in conceptual terms. To use the nomenclature of the Scholastic tradition, it is an *in actu signato* explanation of what occurs *in actu exercito*.[47]

Action may be judged in accordance with the rule and measure referred to above, which pertain to both levels of the ethical dimension. St Thomas's thought on this point is consistent: deficiency of the will always originates in a decision to ignore the rule or norm of reason.[48] The fact that, in the order of action, "to distance oneself from the norm of practical reason distances oneself from the end at the same time; in other words, if a man's action moves him further from his end, that is because he has deviated from the norm"[49] should also be noted in this context. NL makes its presence felt at this point: its function as a rule implies that it is constituted by reason (*aliquid per rationem constitutum*) and, thus, a connatural element of the human way of being.

---

[45] See Rhonheimer, *Natural Law and Practical Reason*, 58-61.
[46] *S. Th.* I-II, q. 90, a. 1 ad 1; I-II, q. 91, a. 2 c.
[47] See Cottier OP, "La raison practique chez Thomas d'Aquin," 75-76.
[48] See, for example, *De Malo*, q. 2, a. 1 c.
[49] González, *Moral, razón y naturaleza*, 413. For further discussion of bad action and St Thomas's view that sin consists to a greater degree of distancing oneself from the rule rather than the end, see chap. 5, "La mala acción," 365-466.

My argument is that this interpretative framework enables the fullest understanding of NL. A number of consequences follow from the distinction outlined above. From the PPL perspective, strictly speaking, not even the question of virtue pertains to PR, as such, defined in scientific terms.[50] In fact, virtue is reflected in the action of the virtuous man—not as an explicit conceptual theorisation—on PPL. Thus, any question concerning the practical value of a particular moral doctrine formulated on the basis of PPL would be to all intents and purposes a *contradictio in adiecto*; no doctrine, as such, may be a doctrine on the prescriptive practical level of the ethical dimension. The meaning of the question may be more adequately contextualized in terms of the distinction between the *scibile* (theoretical-practical: science) and the *agibile* (practical-practical: prudence) referred to in some detail above. Given that the idea of value involves a theorisation of the practical, the conceptual content of which pertains to the DRL, not the PPL, the practical value of a moral doctrine is never immediately operative.

As a result, the question concerning the practical value of NLT may only be framed in terms of the DRL; that is, on the plane of philosophical reflection on ethical action. Having established this position, the meaning of the term "practical" as used in the formulation of the question must be analysed. As has already been noted, in order to be authentic theory and genuine practice, a theory of the practical does not require exclusive reference to the practicable or operable. The content of a *theory of the practical* need not be transformed into a *theory of the practicable*, a transformation which would in any case change the meaning of the terms involved.

First, the meaning of "practical" may be read in the strict sense of the term—that is, the practicable or *agibile*; or in a wider sense, such as the *scibile*. In line with both the letter and the spirit of the texts cited thus far, to interpret the term in its strict sense is to deform the meaning of the practical by identifying it with what is practicable. Thus, the issue under discussion should address the "practicable value" rather than the "practical value" of NLT. This question of practicability, however, rests on an extrapolation: it involves an attempt to access the PPL by incorporating categories proper to the DRL. Moreover, any response to such a question that laid claim to the authority of St Thomas's thought would prompt an equivocal position because the interpretation of the term "practical" it contains is different to and more limited than that reflected in Aquinas's work. As has already been discussed above, any response to the question

[50] See Rhonheimer, *Natural Law and Practical Reason*, 22-23.

concerning the practical value of a theory must encompass the inclusion of the plane of universal reasons which underlie singular and contingent actions, which also comprise the meaning of what is "practical".

Second, the term "practical" may be interpreted within the framework of meaning set out by St Thomas. In this context, the universal that underlies singular action must also be regarded as open to "practical evaluation". Thus, the first principles of PR—the content of NL—would have, at least, a mediate practical value. This mediate practical value should not be deferred to either the immediate or remote levels of action.

To sum up, the question concerning the practical value of a moral doctrine requires that the two planes on which ethical issues unfold be taken into consideration. Both planes are practical, but the practical is realised in different ways on each plane. Thus, NL emerges on the PPL, through the various particularizations and concretions of action; while NLT on the DRL articulates conceptual support for the explanation of the reasons that mark the limits of meaningful human action in light of living in accordance with reason.

Good, obligation and NL

NL—to draw on the well-known Thomist definition—is constituted by reason (*aliquid per rationem constitum*).[51] The nature of law contained in NL is underwritten by the link between rationality and legality.[52] Law is a rule and measure of action. Reason is the rule and measure of all man's actions. Reason and law are linked by a common nature: rule and measure.[53] Thus, Aquinas notes on several occasions that the good of man is defined by its conformity to reason.[54]

Not merely by similarity or resemblance is NL ascribed to man, as is the case of irrational beings;[55] the agent who commits himself to action contains within himself a rule which is close-to-hand and homogenous, and constitutes a measure of action: reason.[56] St Thomas also holds that

---

[51] *S. Th.* I-II, q. 94, a. 1 c. See Fulvio Di Blasi, "Law as Act of Reason and Command," *Nova et Vetera. The English Edition of the International Theological Journal* 4, no. 3 (2006): 515-28.

[52] *S. Th.* I-II, q. 91, a. 2 ad 3.

[53] *S. Th.* I-II, q. 90, a. 1 c.

[54] See *S. Th.* I-II, q. 74, a. 4 c.

[55] "In creatura autem irrationali non participatur rationaliter, unde non potest dici lex nisi per similitudinem". *S. Th.* I-II, q. 91, a. 2 ad 3.

[56] *S. Th.* I-II, q. 71, a. 6 c.

knowledge of sinful action depends on the recognition of two factors: the rule or measure, and the end of action.[57] However, distancing oneself from the rule or measure, rather than the end, is the reason *per se* of sin.[58] A reductive and skewed extrinsic reading of the moral rule is deflected by the significance that Aquinas attributes to the rule in determining the morality of action; such a reductive interpretation of moral knowledge could not account for the operative intimacy of human being.[59]

St Thomas holds that "someone who refrains from evil not because it is evil but because there is a divine mandate forbidding it is not free; he who is free refrains from doing evil because it is evil,"[60] and Cruz is right to argue, in the light of this text, that "what God wants, what He seeks through His mandate, is that we should act according to our own good and, moreover, be moved thereto by this good itself, not by divine mandate as such."[61] Aquinas's position is prompted by his commentary on 2 Cor 3:17: *ubi spiritus Domini, ibi libertas*. St Thomas also refers to 1 Tim 1:9 in this regard: the law was not laid down for the just man (*iusto non est lex posita*). The primary purpose of this reference is to point out the error of their ways to those who read the verse as grounds for concluding that the spiritual man is not bound to obey the precepts of divine law (*aliqui erronee dixerunt quod viri spirituales non obligantur praeceptis legis divinae*). This position is erroneous because the precepts of divine law function as a rule for the human will (*sunt regula voluntatis humanae*); the will, as a created faculty, cannot create for itself its own rule of action. To St Thomas's mind, therefore, any state of affairs in which man is not bound by the divine precepts is literally inconceivable. Having addressed

---

[57] *De Malo*, q. 2, a. 1 c.

[58] *De Malo*, q. 2, a. 1 c. This line of argument does not undermine the significance of the end, which is the criterion of the gravity of error. In fact, the higher the end to which human acts are directed, the more serious the sin; See *S. Th.* I-II, q. 73, a. 3 c.

[59] A number of writers point out that this argument rests on the fact that Aquinas does not defer to the modern separation of the good from the norm. See Michel Villey, *La Formation de la Penseé Juridique Moderne* (Paris: Éditions Montchrétien, 1975), Michel Bastit, *Naissance de la loi moderne: La pensée de la loi de saint Thomas à Suarez* (Paris: Presses Universitaires de France, 1990), Brian Tierney, *The Idea of Natural Rights. Studies on Natural Rights, Natural Law and Church Law 1150-1626* (Atlanta: Scholars Press, 1997).

[60] "Ille ergo, qui vitat mala, non quia mala, sed propter mandatum domini, non est liber; sed qui vitat mala, quia mala, est liber." *Super II Cor.*, chap. III, lect. 3, no. 112. [The translation here is from Cruz.]

[61] Cruz, "Natural Law and Practical Philosophy," 169.

this erroneous interpretation, Aquinas goes on to offer a correct reading of the gospel text; that the law was not laid down for the just man should be interpreted in the following way: the just man is moved by an internal habit towards that prescribed by the law (*qui interiori habitu moventur ad ea quae lex Dei praecipit*).

Thus, the reference to 1 Tim 1:9, which might at first glance be read as a refutation of 2 Cor 3:17, in fact provides the ideal conceptual framework for the correct interpretation of the quotation from the letter to the Corinthians. The phrase "where the Spirit of the Lord is, there is freedom," should be read in the sense that the free man is the proper cause (*causa sui*) of his action; in contrast, the servant is moved by the cause of his master. The idea that the free man flees evil because of that evil in itself—rather than because of the existence of a divine command that prohibits it—surfaces in this context. St Thomas goes on to point out that the Holy Spirit perfects the interior of the mind of man by means of good habit so that what is laid down in divine law may be fulfilled. Thus, man is free not because he is bound to obey divine law, but because the inclination of his good habits is to do what he should do—that is, what divine law commands (*non quin subdatur legi divinae, sed quia ex bono habitu inclinatur ad hoc faciendum, quod lex divina ordinat*).

St Thomas addresses this issue once again in his commentary on Gal 5:18: if man is led by the Spirit, he is not bound under the law (*si spiritu ducimini, non estis sub lege*).[62] First, he holds that the phrase "not under the law" (*non estis sub lege*) may be read as referring to the order of judicial, ceremonial or moral precepts, a distinction that Aquinas also invokes in the *Treatise on the Old Law* in the *Summa Theologica*.[63] The expression "to be under the law" (*esse sub lege*) may be read in two ways in the context of moral precepts: in terms of obligation or coercion.[64] All men are subject to the law in the first sense.[65] However, the just man is not subject to the law, read as a form of coercion, because he is moved to action by the Holy Spirit who, through love, inclines him towards doing that which is laid down in the law. The just man has an internal law which leads him to do—in a spontaneous way, not as a consequence of coercion—what the (external) law commands. Thus, the just man is bound

---

[62] *Super ad Gal.*, c. 4, l. 2.
[63] See *S. Th.* I-II, qq. 100-105.
[64] See *S. Th.* I-II, q. 96, a. 5 ad 1.
[65] Mt 5:17 – "Think not that I have come to abolish the law..." —is mentioned in this regard.

by the law, but not coerced by it; whereas the unjust man is not only bound by the law, but also, to a certain extent, coerced by it.

In a further comment on a gospel text, St Thomas goes so far as to say that if all men were just, there would be no need for laws to be laid down (*si omnes essent iusti, nulla necessitas esset dandi legem*). However, rather than reflect on a state of absolute lawlessness, this line of argument leads him to conclude that in such a state of affairs, each man would be a law unto himself (*quia omnes essent sibi lex*).[66] In a strict, univocal interpretation of the idea of law, if each man were a law unto himself, then what is understood by the term "law" would not in fact exist;[67] in a certain sense, the idea that man may be a law unto himself calls the idea of law itself into question. However, in light of the texts and interpretations discussed above, it would appear that St Thomas does not see the obligatory nature of law and the goodness of action as absolutely contradictory.

The vision of a state of affairs in which all men are just, and thus in no need of the prescription of laws, is consonant with St Thomas's thought, albeit as the extreme end-point of his line of argument. Nevertheless, this hypothetical state of harmony need not prompt the conclusion that the idea of law would disappear, or the annulment of the law; rather, that the idea of law becomes particular to the highest degree, that is, to the individual[68]: if the just man is not bound by the law in *vis coactiva*, he is still bound by the law in *vis obligandi*.

The prominence and number of references to the expression *sine lege* throughout the *Corpus* underwrite and reinforce this interpretation. In general, the expression is used to denote the absence of external law, not to deny the subjection of all men in *vis obligandi*; this obligation extends to the just man, who is moved to do what is just even in the absence of law (*inclinatur ex seipsis ad iustitiam faciendam, etiam sine lege*).[69]

For all of the reasons outlined above, Cruz's conclusion that the nature of NL in the field of praxis is somewhat paradoxical seems justified.[70]

---

[66] *Super ad Tim*., I chap. 1, lectio 3.

[67] Given that its end is the common good, Aquinas states explicitly that, at least in the case of human law, the law applies to all men. See *S. Th.* I-II, q. 96, a. 1 c.

[68] The positive argument concerning the fulfilment of the law, rather than the negative view of its annulment, may have been inspired by the gospel (Mt 5:17: "…I have come not to abolish [the law and the prophets] but to fulfil them").

[69] See, for example, *SCG*, III, c. 128, no. 8.

[70] "The expression 'natural law' seems slightly paradoxical taken as the expression of a reality belonging strictly to the sphere of the practical. In this sphere, which is

Nevertheless, in light of the various conceptual nuances reflected in Aquinas's work, to read this paradox within an interpretative framework that suggests that the virtuous man is more or less subject to the law (where the law is not understood as referring to *external* law) seems to follow a truer reading of St Thomas's texts. This does not mean that the virtuous man may conceive of his subjection to the law as a form of coercion. The spirit of the texts cited above implies that the fulfilment of the law for the just or virtuous man does not connote its abolition. To conceive of the just man as an agent who regards himself as not law-governed by any type of law would provoke tension within Thomistic ethical thought and might ultimately undermine the value of NL.

Conclusion: The analogical meaning of law in NL and the interpretation of the practicality of NLT

On the basis of what has been discussed thus far, it would appear that Aquinas concedes a certain experience of obligation which does not necessarily involve a clear "awareness of a law-giver", a position that may only be sustained by an analogous reading of the idea of law, specifically in the case of NL[71]. Thus, NL is different to positive law—human or divine—and remains nonetheless a form of law. As St Thomas himself acknowledges explicitly on several occasions, self-legislation is impossible if NL is conceived of in the same terms as the functioning of positive law.[72] However, if NL is defined as the work of reason itself (*opus rationis*), the conclusion that the good man is a law unto himself (*ipsi sibi sunt lex*)[73] may be stated with equal clarity. Cruz's analysis of the

---

the sphere of action considered from the point of view of the agent, what is connatural is precisely that which is not governed by law. Insofar as we feel that the correctness of an action is self-evident, and right in a practical sense, we do not see the action as governed by a law, nor do we see ourselves as under an obligation and linked to this action by a mandate from our superior. Rather, we perceive such action as an object that fits in with our own inclination and our own character, as a completely intrinsic operative decision, based on an intrinsic principle, not on an extrinsic principle that has been imposed on us". Cruz, "Natural Law and Practical Philosophy," 163-64.

[71] Here I am indebted to very helpful questions raised by Alfredo Cruz. I do not know whether he would agree with my way of answering them.

[72] *S. Th.* I-II, q. 96, a. 5 ad 3. Cruz's argument relies heavily on St Thomas's repeated assertions regarding the impossibility of self-legislation (see *S. Th.* I-II, q. 90, a. 3 c., 93, a. 5 c., *et al.*).

[73] *In III Sent.*, d. 37, a. 1 ad 5; *Super Ep. Ad Romanos*, c. 2, l. 3.

issue in his article suggests that the meaning of the expression that man is a law unto himself is, at best, metaphorical. The argument here is that Aquinas does not express his position in metaphorical terms. Given the radical impossibility of self-legislation, the many points at which reason is compared to a kind of 'ruler' in the realm of human action take on special significance in St Thomas's work; they show that Aquinas attributes a 'legislative' function to natural reason, albeit in an analogous sense. For example, in his account of the distinction between judicial, ceremonial and moral precepts in the Old Law, he writes:

> [Hence] there are no judicial precepts ordaining man in himself. All such precepts are moral, because the reason, which is the principle in moral matters, holds the same position in man, with regard to things that concern him, as a prince or judge holds in the state.[74]

Given the absolute impossibility of self-legislation by *via inventionis* (in the strict sense of the term), and without going so far as to join in Cruz's appeal to principle, that the good man is a law unto himself may be concluded from St Thomas's work (in a broader or derived sense) by *via resolutionis*. While the enlightening and action-guiding power of NL depends on its participation in the light of eternal reason, as a secondary cause in the realm of created things the law is constituted by the work of natural reason—that is, as a regulative judgment or dictate of reason, and the corresponding obligation.[75]

The practical significance of NLT may be illustrated by reference to the meaning of the rules of a competitive game. The purpose of the rules of a game is to make the contest entertaining; the primary purpose of the game's players, however, is to win, not to entertain. For the players, to compete and to be aware of the obligation to obey certain rules are not

[74] *S. Th.* I-II, q. 104, a. 1 ad 3. This reference and interpretation is to be found in Martin Rhonheimer, "Nature as Reason: A Thomistic Theory of the Natural Law," *Studies in Christian Ethics* 19, no. 3 (2006): 372ff.

[75] The nature of law in NL does not depend on its derivation from a *divine legislator*. As Rhonheimer has pointed out, Aquinas never uses the term *legislator* in relation to NL, nor to the Eternal Law; *gubernatio* is the only term used in this regard. "Therefore, according to Aquinas, natural law is not properly dependent on a divine 'legislator' but it is the *participation* of the eternal law and, thus, possessed *as law* by the rational creature (see for this again I-II, q. 91, a. 2 ad 3: 'the participation of the eternal law in the rational creature is properly called a law, since a law is something pertaining to reason, as stated above')". Ibid.: footnote no. 25, 373.

synonymous aims; rather, the players seek to claim the objective of the game—that is, to win the prize—within the framework established by the rules of the game. The practicality of the rules of game in a competition is not primarily 'to have an awareness of the obligation to respect and follow the rules'. The competition is defined by the desire to win through a creative exploitation of the wide range of options enabled by respect for the rules of the game. The content of NLT as the framework that shapes meaningful human action functions in a similar way. In line with the framework established by NLT, man lays claim to specific moral goods; he does so by means of what may be highly creative practices, which at the same time endow action with meaning.

The comparison to the rules of a game sheds light on the degree of practical value pertaining to NLT: NLT has practical value insofar as it is the articulation of the *vis obligandi* of the judgments of PR. This statement is dependent on the extent to which, in the broader conceptual framework set out here, the precepts of PR are—in a derived sense—law; and, to the same extent, on the *vis obligandi* which pertains to them, albeit in an indirect way. To say that no one is obliged to follow a natural inclination is both true and uncontroversial; that is why the term "natural inclinations", rather than "natural obligations", is in common use. Nevertheless, in his pursuit of specific goods, NLT requires that man refrain from acting directly against any of the goods identified as such by reason in accordance with his natural inclinations.[76]

To sum up, the way in which the *vis obligandi* is present in the good of reason—reflected in the precepts of NL—may be conceived of in the same way as the assent of the first speculative principles rests with TR. The first principles play a role in the exercise of TR; the science of metaphysics need not be made explicit in man's every rational practice as a consequence. In a similar way, and insofar as it is committed to action, PR shapes the precepts, and the *vis obligandi*, of NL.[77] Thus, to say that NL is the participation of eternal law in rational creatures is not to define the essence of NL; rather, it is merely to describe the relationship between NL and eternal law.[78] That definition of NL as the participation of eternal law

[76] See John Finnis, *Moral Absolutes. Tradition, Revision and Truth* (Washington D.C.: The Catholic University of America, 1991), 31-83.

[77] See Martin Rhonheimer, "The Cognitive Structure of the Natural Law and the Truth of Subjectivity," *The Thomist* 67, no. 1 (2003): 10-11.

[78] This idea is taken from Rhonheimer: "(as when we say 'man is the image of God in the material world' this is not a definition of the essence of man, but rather a characterisation of the relation of his nature to God's nature; a definition of the

in rational creatures need not be made explicit—in the context of systematic moral science, which pertains to the DRL[79]—for it to have its own prerogative as law.[80] However, a degree of reasoned understanding available to every man (on the PPL), as a result of the exercise of synderesis and the habit of science, is required in relation to the good he ought to pursue.[81] Thus, in line with the argument articulated by Cruz, it may be said that the man's fundamental moral experience is not to obey a law but to work towards the good that he should seek to do (*bonum faciendum*).

The contribution of NL to the practice of good action should be specified in this context; the analysis of the relationship between TR and PR is relevant to this discussion. The judgments of PR are intrinsically oriented to human good, in light of its truth. Like the speculative intellect, the practical intellect comes to know the truth. Good which is known and

---

essence of man would be 'man is a rational animal'). Aquinas's definition of the natural law, which is 'natural law is the light of natural reason, whereby we discern what is good and what is evil' (a definition which exactly evidences what this 'participation in the eternal law' consists in) appears each time he treats the subject, while the characterisation 'rational creature's participation of the eternal law' just appears in the *Summa theologiae* I-II, q. 91, a. 2 to put the doctrine of natural law into the context of the logic of its treatise on law (after the article on 'eternal law'). Notice that according to *S. Th.* I-II, q. 93, a. 3, all laws, including human law, insofar they are true law, derive from the eternal law!" Rhonheimer, "Nature as Reason: A Thomistic Theory of the Natural Law," footnote no. 7, 363.

79 Mark Murphy and Fulvio di Blasi point out the dual reading underlying the account of NLT in Aquinas's work. See Mark Murphy, "The Natural Law Tradition in Ethics," *Standford Encyclopedia of Philosophy* (2002) [electronic document: http:// plato.stanford.edu/ entries/ natural-law-ethics/. Accessed: 23-09-06]. See ———, *Natural Law and Practical Rationality* (Cambridge: Cambridge University Press, 2001), 3-4. See also Fulvio Di Blasi, *God and the Natural Law. A Rereading of Thomas Aquinas*, trans. David Thunder (South Bend, Indiana: St. Augustine's Press, 2006), 30-38.

80 See Rhonheimer, "The Cognitive Structure of the Natural Law and the Truth of Subjectivity," 14.

81 As Llano has pointed out, the "ethical competence of the man on the street" is relevant in this regard. See Alejandro Llano, *Humanismo cívico* (Barcelona: Ariel, 1988). See Ralph McInerny, "Thomistic Natural Law and Aristotelian Philosophy," in *St. Thomas Aquinas and the Natural Law Tradition: Contemporary Perspectives*, ed. John Goyette, Mark S. Latkovic, and Richard S. Myers (Washington D.C.: The Catholic University of America Press, 2004), 38. Also, ———, *Conoscenza morale implicita - Implicit moral knowledge*, trans. Fulvio Di Blasi (Soveria Mannelli (Catanzaro) Rubbettino, 2006).

carried out is 'truth-in-practice'.[82] By its very nature as true, the truth commands the respect of conscience. Thus, the knowing subject is impelled to act by the moral good known to reason to the same extent that the truth once known commands his assent. Therefore, the judgements of PR have the nature of a precept, to which a *vis obligandi*[83] is intrinsic. At the same time, given certain circumstances or in extreme situations, explicit acknowledgement of the participated nature of the precepts of NL may supply the decisive reason for effective obedience to the dictates of NL.

In this context, therefore, it is clear that to include NLT in the structure of PR does not necessarily weaken the only element in the order of practice which has the status of a principle—that is, the good. Given that the good is the principle of action in the order of practice, it is equally clear that the good may appear under numerous and various guises and that man may avail of a variety of mediations to correctly achieve his proper end. The status of the good as a principle is strengthened—not weakened—by the precepts of NL, which function as a protective framework for the realisation of meaningful human action.[84] They frame human action within a structure that puts different goods in order, in accordance with the *bonum rationis* or human good. As has been noted already above, insofar as it furnishes him with a natural inclination towards the appropriate action and end, the rational creature participates in the eternal law (*habet naturalem inclinationem ad debitum actum et finem*).[85] NL comprises the judgements of PR which express the good to be done or the evil to be avoided in a prescriptive or imperative way, in accordance with the order of ends shaped by man's natural inclinations.[86]

---

[82] See Martin Rhonheimer, "Praktische Prinzipien, Naturgesetz und konkrete Handlungsurteile in tugendethischer Perspektive: Zur Diskussion über praktische Vernunft und 'lex naturalis' bei Thomas von Aquin," *Studia Moralia* 39 (2001): 113-58.

[83] See Daniel Westberg, *Right Practical Reason. Aristotle, Action and Prudence in Aquinas* (Oxford: Clarendon Press, 1994), 235.

[84] Martin Rhonheimer, "Practical Reason and the Truth of Subjectivity: The Self-Experience of the Moral Subject at the Roots of Metaphysics and Anthropology," in *The Perspective of the Acting Person. Essays in the Renewal of Thomistic Moral Philosophy*, ed. William Murphy Jr. (Washington D.C.: The Catholic University of America Press, 2008), 95-128.

[85] *S. Th.* I-II, q. 91, a. 2 c.

[86] See Stephen L. Brock, "Natural Inclination and the Intelligibility of the Good in Thomistic Natural Law," *Vera Lex* VI, no. 1-2 (2005): 57-78. Matthew Levering,

To be more specific: NL comprises the judgements of PR which reflect that which it is reasonable, by nature, to do. Thus, the precepts of NL are not an obstacle to the effective execution of moral action; in fact, they are the starting point for all good action. There can be no action without NL: every action is directed towards an end; without an end, no action could ever be undertaken. In Aquinas's words: "the first direction of our acts to their end must needs be in virtue of the natural law;"[87] and, in the order of practice,

> nothing stands firm with regard to the practical reason, unless it be directed to the last end which is the common good: and whatever stands to reason in this sense, has the nature of a law.[88]

From the perspective of the analysis articulated by Cruz in his article, it might be argued that the nature of the law established by PR is subsequent and consequent to a theory that defines human action as rule-governed, to which no practical significance of any kind need be attributed. The argument here is that the issue under discussion is a defining one, and has the potential to enable a more coherent account of the different positions expressed in the *Corpus Thomisticum*, which may appear at times to be opposed or even contradictory. Cruz's article provides a valuable reminder of the fact that Thomist moral theory as a whole cannot be reduced to a 'natural law ethic'; as Aquinas himself observed: "*totam materiam moralem ad considerationem virtutum reducere.*"[89]

Finally, that NLT also encompasses the presence of different levels of perfection in the execution of good action should also be borne in mind. The undue identification of good action with perfectly good action may at times overshadow the moral value of average good action, such as that put into practice by the continent man. The full potential of NL unfolds in the

---

"Natural Law and Natural Inclinations: Rhonheimer, Pinckaers, McAleer," *The Thomist* 70, no. 2 (2006): 155-201.

[87] *S. Th.* I-II, q. 91, a. 2 ad 2.

[88] *S. Th.* I-II, q. 90, a. 2 ad 3.

[89] *S. Th.* II-II, *prologus*. "It is only the virtuous person whose natural reason infallibly illumines and correctly distinguishes good from evil. The possession of moral virtue, to some degree, is thus the condition under which natural law works as it should, though its basic principles are always present in the human mind. Therefore, a truly Thomistic 'natural law morality' at the end must be an ethics of the virtues including a theory of vice and moral evil". Rhonheimer, "Nature as Reason: A Thomistic Theory of the Natural Law," 369-70.

case of the virtuous man—who, at the same time, acts with great naturalness; but this need not prompt the conclusion that NL is not also reflected in the action of, for example, the continent man. Moreover, NL may also be discerned in the action of the incontinent man and the vicious man; in these cases, however, the particular judgment of what is pleasing, rather than the universal judgment of *bonum rationis*, holds sway—with a certain sense of conflict in the case of the former, and no such sense in the latter.[90] The desire to highlight the moral value of the most perfect form of action should not give rise to an underestimation of the value of good action put into practice from a position of perfectible moral goodness. The fundamental nature of the good in moral action is illuminated, not obscured, through practical reflection on NL and theoretical-practical study of NLT.

Works Cited

Primary Sources

Aquinatis, S. Thomae. "<http//www.corpusthomisticum.org/>, Pampilonae, Universitatis Studiorum Navarrensis, 2000. In taenias magneticas a Roberto Busa SJ. denuo recognovit Enrique Alarcón atque instruxit.", 2000.

Aquinas, Thomas. *Summa Theologica* Translated by the Fathers of the English Dominican Province. New York: Benzinger Bros., 1947.

Aristotle. *The Complete Works of Aristotle: The Revised Oxford Translation*. Edited by Jonathan Barnes. Princeton, NJ: Princeton University Press, 1984.

Secondary Sources

Albert the Great. "In VI Ethicorum." In *Opera omnia*, edited by A. Borgnet. Paris: Vivès, 1891.

Aristotle. *De Anima*. Edited by Bekker. Berlin: Gigon-Bonitz, 1960-61.

—. *Nicomachean Ethics* Translated by R. Crisp. Cambridge UK - New York: Cambridge University Press, 2000.

[90] Mark Murphy has carried out a refined analysis of the presence of first principles in NL. See Mark Murphy, "La epistemología de los primeros principios de la ley natural," in *Una ley de libertad para la vida del mundo. Actas del Congreso Internacional sobre Ley Natural*, ed. Juan José Pérez-Soba, Juan de Dios Larrú, and Jaime Ballesteros (Madrid: Collectanae Matritensia, 2007), 111-24.

Basso OP, Domingo. *Las normas de la moralidad*. Buenos Aires: Claretiana, 1994.

Bastit, Michel. *Naissance de la loi moderne: La pensée de la loi de saint Thomas à Suarez*. Paris: Presses Universitaires de France, 1990.

Brock, Stephen L. "Natural Inclination and the Intelligibility of the Good in Thomistic Natural Law." *Vera Lex* VI, no. 1-2 (2005): 57-78.

Cottier OP, Georges. "La raison practique chez Thomas d'Aquin." In *Ragione pratica, libertà, normatività* edited by Marcelo Sánchez Sorondo, 65-88. Roma: Herder - Univeristà Lateranense, 1991.

Cruz, Alfredo. "Natural Law and Practical Philosophy. The Presence of a Theological Concept in Moral Knowledge." In *Contemporary Issues in Natural Law: Natural Law as a Limiting Concept*, edited by Ana Marta González, 161-74. Aldershot: Ashgate, 2008.

Di Blasi, Fulvio. *God and the Natural Law. A Rereading of Thomas Aquinas* Translated by David Thunder. South Bend, Indiana: St. Augustine's Press, 2006.

—. "Law as Act of Reason and Command." *Nova et Vetera. The English Edition of the International Theological Journal* 4, no. 3 (2006): 515-28.

Finnis, John. *Moral Absolutes. Tradition, Revision and Truth*. Washington D.C.: The Catholic University of America, 1991.

Geraghty, Richard P. *The Object of Moral Philosophy according to St. Thomas Aquinas*. Washington D.C.: University Press of America, 1981.

González, Ana Marta. "Moral, Filosofía Moral y Metafísica en Santo Tomás de Aquino." *Pensamiento* 56, no. 216 (2000): 439-467.

—. *Moral, razón y naturaleza. Una investigación sobre Tomás de Aquino*. 2 ed. Pamplona: Eunsa, 2006.

—. "Natural Law as a Limiting Concept: A Reading of Thomas Aquinas." In *Contemporary Perspectives on Natural Law. Natural Law as a Limiting Concept*, edited by Ana Marta González. Aldershot: Ashgate, 2008.

Kluxen, Wolfgang. *L'etica filosofica di Tommaso d'Aquino*. Milano: Vita e pensiero, 2006.

—. *Philosophische Ethik bei Thomas von Aquin*. Mainz: Matthias-Grünewald Verlag, 1964.

Levering, Matthew. "Natural Law and Natural Inclinations: Rhonheimer, Pinckaers, McAleer." *The Thomist* 70, no. 2 (2006): 155-201.

Llano, Alejandro. *Humanismo cívico*. Barcelona: Ariel, 1988.

McInerny, Ralph. *Conoscenza morale implicita – Implicit moral knowledge* Translated by Fulvio Di Blasi. Soveria Mannelli (Catanzaro) Rubbettino, 2006.
—. "Portia's Lament: Reflections on Practical Reason." In *Natural Law and Moral Inquiry. Ethics, Metaphysics, and Politics in the Work of Germain Grisez*, edited by Robert George, 82-103. Washington D.C.: Georgetown University Press, 1998.
—. "Thomistic Natural Law and Aristotelian Philosophy." In *St. Thomas Aquinas and the Natural Law Tradition: Contemporary Perspectives*, edited by John Goyette, Mark S. Latkovic and Richard S. Myers, 23-38. Washington D.C.: The Catholic University of America Press, 2004.
Murphy, Mark. "La epistemología de los primeros principios de la ley natural." In *Una ley de libertad para la vida del mundo. Actas del Congreso Internacional sobre Ley Natural*, edited by Juan José Pérez-Soba, Juan de Dios Larrú and Jaime Ballesteros, 111-24. Madrid: Collectanae Matritensia, 2007.
—. *Natural Law and Practical Rationality*. Cambridge: Cambridge University Press, 2001.
—. "The Natural Law Tradition in Ethics." In *Stanford Encyclopedia of Philosophy*, 2002 [electronic document: http:// plato.stanford.edu/ entries/ natural-law-ethics/. Accessed: 23-09-06].
Naus, John E. *The Nature of the Practical Intellect according to Saint Thomas Aquinas*. Roma: Libreria Editrice dell'Università Gregoriana, 1959.
Ramírez OP, Santiago. *Opera omnia. De Hominis beatitudine tractatus theologicus. Tomus 1*. Madrid: Instituto de Filosofía 'Luis Vives', 1972.
Rhonheimer, Martin. "The Cognitive Structure of the Natural Law and the Truth of Subjectivity." *The Thomist* 67, no. 1 (2003): 1-44.
—. *La perspectiva de la moral: Fundamentos de la Ética Filosófica*. Edited by José Carlos Mardomingo. Madrid: Rialp, 2000.
—. *Natural Law and Practical Reason: A Thomist View of Moral Autonomy*. New York: Fordham University Press, 2000.
—. "Nature as Reason: A Thomistic Theory of the Natural Law." *Studies in Christian Ethics* 19, no. 3 (2006): 357-78.
—. "Practical Reason and the Truth of Subjectivity: The Self-Experience of the Moral Subject at the Roots of Metaphysics and Anthropology." In *The Perspective of the Acting Person. Essays in the Renewal of Thomistic Moral Philosophy*, edited by William Murphy Jr., 250-82. Washington D.C.: The Catholic University of America Press, 2008.

—. "Praktische Prinzipien, Naturgesetz und konkrete Handlungsurteile in tugendethischer Perspektive: Zur Diskussion über praktische Vernunft und 'lex naturalis' bei Thomas von Aquin." *Studia Moralia* 39 (2001): 113-58.

—. *Praktische Vernunft und Vernünftigkeit der Praxis: Handlungstheorie bei Thomas von Aquin in ihrer Entstehung aus dem Problemkontext der aristotelischen Ethik.* Berlin: Akademie Verlag, 1994.

Sancti Thomae de Aquino. *Opera omnia iussu Leonis XIII P. M. edita, Quaestiones Disputatae de Veritate* Vol. XXII, 1. Rome: Editori di San Tommaso, 1975.

—. *Opera omnia iussu Leonis XIII P. M. edita, Sentencia libri De anima.* Vol. XLV, 1. Rome-Paris: Commissio Leonina-J. Vrin, 1984.

Schröer, Christian. *Praktische Vernunft bei Thomas von Aquin.* Stuttgart - Berlin - Köhln: Verlag W. Kolhammer, 1995.

Tierney, Brian. *The Idea of Natural Rights. Studies on Natural Rights, Natural Law and Church Law 1150-1626.* Atlanta: Scholars Press, 1997.

Villey, Michel. *La Formation de la Penseé Juridique Moderne.* Paris: Éditions Montchrétien, 1975.

Wallace, William Augustine. *The Role of Demonstration in Moral Theology: a Study of Methodology in St. Thomas Aquinas.* Washington D.C.: Thomist Press, 1963.

Westberg, Daniel. *Right Practical Reason. Aristotle, Action and Prudence in Aquinas.* Oxford: Clarendon Press, 1994.

Wieland, Georg. *Ethica, Scientia Practica. Die Anfänge der philosophischen Ethik im 13. Jahrhundert.* Münster: Aschendorff, 1981.

CHAPTER EIGHTEEN

IMPERIUM, INSTINCT AND NATURAL LAW

TERESA ENRÍQUEZ

In this article I intend to deal with three concepts drawn up by Aquinas in order to shed light, through them, on how human action is said to be natural. The concepts are *imperium*, *instinctus* and *lex naturalis*. The similarity of these three ideas is based on the subject of form as an operative principle. Indeed, the characterization of these three concepts as principles of the movement of an appetite towards an end is proof of different circumstances of the regulatory character of form.

Taking human action as a movement in a general sense,[1] and the natural action as what derives from the form of the agent,[2] may suggest two main questions on the intervention of natural law on human free will: how far does natural law, like *instinctus*, guide towards an end which is determined by natural form? And how far does it, like *imperium,* guide towards a form which is understood by the intellect? To begin with, the answer would be as follows: the precepts of natural law are similar to instinct in as much as both direct the end determined by natural form, that is, the last end of the human soul; and they are different because natural law does not direct by impulse, but by enlightenment. Thus, the actions directed by the precepts of natural law are not carried out by an instinctive impulse but by imperative acts of intelligence and will.

To examine the links between of the concepts of *imperium*, *instinctus* and *lex naturalis* in depth, the article will be divided into three parts: in the first, I shall present certain similarities and differences between the three concepts; secondly, I shall examine the three concepts with reference to form as the operative principle of the movement of the agent towards an

---

[1] See *S. Th.* I, q. 18, a. 1, co.; *In III De Anima*, lect. 12, n. 765-7; Aristotle, *De Anima* Translated by D. W. Hamlyn (Oxford: Clarendon Press, 1993), L. III, c. 1, n. 1, Bk 431a6.

[2] See *S. Th.* I, q. 71, a. 2, co.

end; and in the third section, I shall focus on the human *imperium*, and its relation with the 'natural movements' found in humankind, in order to clarify the specific character of *ad unum* natural determination which is representative of natural law.

Imperium, instinct and natural law

There is a certain traditional link between *imperium* and *instinctus*. William of Auxerre used the term *imperium* to refer to the *impetus ad operationem,* the Latin expression used by Burgundius of Pisa to translate "ὄρμή" a Greek Stoic term used, in turn, by Saint John Damascene in his analysis of the human act.[3] This analysis was originally elaborated by Saint Maximus the Confessor based on Aristotle and his Stoic commentaries.[4] In 13th century scholasticism, the term *imperium* meant the impulse to free will.[5] In this context, Thomas Aquinas clarifies a certain ambiguity—noted by John Damascene[6]—in the expression *impetus ad operationem*, as this instinct is also present in animals,[7] and resolved this lack of precision by assigning the terms, *imperium* and *instinctus*, to each of the impulses with reference to the order found in humans and animals, respectively. In fact, there is a double component in both the *imperium* and the *instinctus*: one appetitive and one cognitive, that is, one principle that moves and another that commands. Taken as impulses, that is, as movements, *imperium* and *instinctus* are similar; as commands, different.

---

[3] See Odon Lottin, *Psychologie et morale aux XIIe et XIIIe siècles*, 2 vols. (Gembloux (Belgium): J. Duculot, S.A. Editeur, 1948-1057), t. I, 396-97, 405.

[4] See René Antoine Gauthier, "Saint Maxime le Confesseur et la psychologie de l'acte humain," *Recherches de Théologie ancienne et médiévale* 21 (1954): 82-84.

[5] See Thomas Deman, "Le 'précepte' de la prudence chez saint Thomas d'Aquin," *Recherches de Théologie ancienne et médiévale* 20 (1953): 58-59.

[6] "Porro quidem in brutis, protinus ut rei alicujus appetitus nascitur, impulsus ('ὄρμή') quoque ad actionem exsistit. Eorum siquidem appetitus irrationabilis est, soloque naturali appetitu aguntur. Quo fit ut brutorum appetitus, nec voluntas, nec voluntatis actus dici possit. Nam voluntas est appetitus naturalis, rationabilis et liber. At in hominibus, utpote ratione praeditis, naturalis appetitus, non tam ducit, quam ducitur; quippe qui libere et cum ratione movetur, quia facultates cognoscendi et vivendi in homine conjunctae sunt; ac proinde libere appetit, vult, inquirit, considerat, deliberat, judicat, afficitur, eligit, ad agendum prorumpit, agitque in illis rebus quae naturae consentaneae sunt.", S. John Damascene, "De fide orthodoxa," in *Patrologiae cursus completus. T. 94. Series Graeca (MG)*, ed. J.P. Migne (Parisiis: Turnholti (Belgium), 1857-1866), L.II, c. 22; 945 B-C.

[7] See *S. Th.* I-II, q. 17, a. 2, arg. 3.

By ordering, one impels one's own movement; on the other hand, movement carried out by the instinctive impulse is ordered by another[8] as it follows knowledge on what is correct and what is noxious[9] which is not ordering knowledge. While the *imperium* is reason (*ratio*), instinct is only estimation (*estimatio*).[10] Following this distinction, the acts of a human being where an ordering may be found are either commanded or instinctive.

On the other hand, the expression *instinctus naturae* is traditionally linked to *ius* (*lex*) *naturale*. This link comes from Isidore of Seville, who, in the 7th century, added the term *instinctus* to Ulpian's classic definition of *ius natural*.[11] This introduction, according to Greene, resulted in a blurring of the difference between humans and animals, one example of this confusion is: what is natural in humans was reduced to instinct with a completely sensual meaning opposed to reason. Due to this interpretation, in the 12th century, the concept of *synderesis* appeared as the immediate understanding of the first moral principles of natural law. Half a century later, Saint Bonaventure decided that synderesis belonged in the affective area of human nature rather than in the intellectual one. In modern times, the term instinct is used instead of the obsolete synderesis. Francis Hutcheston's theory on the Moral Sense is an example of this semantic legacy.[12] In this context, it is reasonable that Thomas Aquinas, in contrast to Isidore, should prefer the expression *inclinationum naturalium*, which is more generic than that of *instinctus naturae*[13] to refer to humankind; and contrary to Bonaventure, should place synderesis definitely in the intellectual area.

---

[8] See *S. Th.* I-II, q. 17, a. 3, ad 3.

[9] See *In III Sent.,* d. 26, q. 1, a. 1, ad 4.

[10] See *In III Sent.*, d. 26, q. 1, a. 2, co.

[11] "Ius naturale est commune omnium nationum, et quod ubique instinctu naturae, non constitutione aliqua habetur; ut viri et feminae coniuncto, liberorum successio et educatio, communis omnium possessio, et omnium una libertas, adquisitio eorum quae caelo, terra marique capiuntur. Item depositae rei vel commendatae pecuniae restitutio, violentiae per vim repulsio. Nam hoc, aut si quid huic simile est, nunquam injustum, sed naturale, aequumque habetur." Isidore of Seville, *Etymologiarum sive Originum, in Patrologiae cursus completus. T. 81-84. Series Latina (PL)*, ed. J.P. Migne (Parisiis - Turnholti (Belgium): Typographi Brepols Editores Pontificii, 1862-1878), L. V, c. 4. 199 B.

[12] See Robert A. Greene, "Instinct of Nature: Natural Law, Synderesis, and the Moral Sense," *Journal of the History of Ideas* 58, no. 2 (1997): 173-77.

[13] See Ibid.: 180-84.

However, also thanks to Isidore of Seville, Thomas Aquinas realized the philosophical interest of the *Digesto*[14] where, due to Justinian's compilation in the 6th century, the definition of *ius naturale* given by Ulpian was established. There, *ius naturale* is contrary to *ius gentium*: the latter is exclusive to humans; the former is common to humans and animals:

> *Jus naturale* is that which nature has taught to all animals; for it is not a law specific to mankind but is common to all animals—land animals, sea animals, and the birds as well—. Out of this comes the union of man and woman [male and female] which we call marriage, and the procreation of children, and their rearing. So we can see that the other animals, wild beasts included, are rightly understood to be acquainted with this law. Jus gentium, the law of the nations, is that which all human peoples observe. That it is not coextensive with natural law can be grasped easily, since this latter is common to all animals whereas *jus gentium* is common only to human beings among themselves.[15]

In this definition of natural law as a law which is common to humans and animals a certain neo-Platonism[16] can be seen which is similar to that of Porphyry who considered animals to be rational beings.[17] The exclusivity of rationality to humankind belongs rather to a Stoic perspective, such as that of Origen[18] who believed that animals, in contrast to humans, are governed by instinct, as they lack rationality. In the same line, Saint Albertus Magnus rejects the existence of any law in animals because, as they are irrational, they cannot obey any law, not even natural law.[19]

Nevertheless, Thomas Aquinas takes Ulpian's definition of natural law and confirms it as the most exact meaning of *natural law*[20] as compared

---

14 See Antonio Osuna, "Introducción a las cuestiones 90 a 97," in *Suma de Teología* (Madrid: Editorial Católica, 1989), 696.

15 T. Mommsen and P. Krueger, eds., *The Digest of Justinian* (Philadelphia PA: University of Penssylvania Press, 1985), 1 (1.1.1.3).

16 Tony Honoré, *Ulpian* (Oxford: Clarendon Press, 1982), 31.

17 Porphyry, *On Abstinence from Killing Animals*, trans. G. Clark (London: Duckworth, 2000), III.10; II.1-2.

18 Origen, *Contra Celsum*, trans. H. Chadwick (Cambridge: Cambridge Scholar Press, 1980), 4.86.

19 See Lottin, *Psychologie et morale aux XIIe et XIIIe siècles*, t. II, 24.

20 See *In IV Sent.*, d. 33, q. 1, a. 1, ad 4; *S. Th. Suppl. III*, q. 65, a. 1, ad 4.

with those laid down by Cicero[21] or Averrois.[22] The definition of *ius naturale* as 'what nature has taught all animals', unlike the other definitions, pays attention to the object independently of its principle. And this object is composed of those actions of animal kind which are strictly the acts of transmission of the species. The *ius* is *naturale* because it deals with the proper acts of animal kind.[23] As will be seen, the same actions prescribed by natural law proceed from different principles depending on whether they are carried out by an animal or a human being; but in both cases the object of the actions responds to the same description, that is, the union of male and female and the procreation and development of offspring. Thus we can state that the actions prescribed by natural law are the same for animals as for humans, in spite of the fact that they proceed from different commanding principles. In the case of animals, such acts proceed from the instinct; for humans, on the contrary, such actions have their principle in free will mainly.

In his *Sententiae Libri Ethicorum* (*Commentary on the Nicomachean Ethics*), Thomas Aquinas returns to Ulpian's definition and his notion of nature, which he contrasts with that of Aristotle. While the jurist's definition takes what is natural in a restrictive, exclusively animal sense, that of the philosopher deals with what is natural in a wider sense that includes both the generic and the specific. Indeed, in humankind, nature can be considered in two ways: one according to their kind, common to all animals, and another according to their specific difference, that is, rationality.[24] Whatever the case, what is natural always refers to what is one:

> To every nature there is one thing corresponding, proportionate, however, to that nature. For to nature considered as a genus, there corresponds something one generically; and to nature as species there corresponds something one specifically; and to the individualized nature there corresponds some one individual. Since, therefore, the will is an immaterial

---

[21] See *In IV Sent.*, d. 33, q. 1, a. 1, ad 4; *S. Th. Suppl. III*, q. 65, a. 1, ad 4; See M. Tulli Ciceronis, *Rhetorici libri duo qui vocantur de inventione, recognovit E. Stroebel*, vol. 2 (Stuttgart: B.G. Teubner, 1965), L. II, c. 53, 161.

[22] See *In IV Sent.*, d. 33, q. 1, a. 1, ad 4; *S. Th. Suppl.III*, q. 65, a. 1, ad 4; See Averrois Cordubensis, *Commentum magnum super libro De celo et mundo Aristotelis, ex recognitione Francis James Carmody in lucem edidit Rüdiger Arnzen*, ed. G. Endress, 2 vols. (Leuven: Peeters, 2003), L. III, textus 21, comm. 21, 188rb1-188vb65 (Aristotle, De Celo L. III, c. 2, 300b16-23), 528-30.

[23] See *In IV Sent.*, d. 33, q. 1, a. 1, ad 4; *S. Th. Suppl.III*, q. 65, a. 1, ad 4.

[24] See *Sententia Ethic.*, L. 5, lect.12, n.4 (Marietti n.724).

> power like the intellect, some one general thing corresponds to it, naturally which is the good; just as to the intellect there corresponds some one general thing, which is the true, or being, or "what a thing is". And under good in general are included many particular goods, to none of which is the will determined.[25]

So what is natural in will is, definitely, some one thing, but it includes what is diverse. The so-called "one thing" (*ad unum*) which corresponds by nature to specifically human powers contains in itself the opportunity for diversity (*ad opposita*), a strictly rational diversity. Thus, what is natural for humankind is what is rational, that is, something 'non-natural'. Another sense of nature solves the paradox of what is natural as substance.[26] Thus *nature* does not correspond only to natural philosophy, but also to metaphysics.[27] All substance is nature.[28] As Aertsen has stated, the ontological sense of natural law in the human being is reflected in the precepts which emanate from it.[29] Indeed, humankind can, thanks to the nature of their substance, whose shape is the rational soul, aspire to transcendental good, which includes the list of natural good things: being, living and understanding.[30] The first acts ordered towards the achievement of these goods, are also natural. So the intellectual knowledge of the first principles is natural, as are the inclination towards the last end and what belongs to each of the human powers and towards the good of the complete human.[31]

The universality of this concept of nature allows us to draw analogies between such different beings as material things, animals, humans and even God Himself. Thus, Aquinas in his earliest definition of natural law,[32] draws the following analogy: for humans natural law is like instinct for animals, and strictly speaking, like natural shape in inert things. Whatever the case, nature is the essence of the operation in itself.[33] In fact, the natural form is the operative principle in material things because it

---

[25] *S.Th.,* I-II, q. 10, a. 1, ad 3.
[26] See *In V Metaphysic.*, lect.5, n.15 (Marietti, n.822).
[27] See *In V Metaphysic.*, lect. 5, n.1 (Marietti, n.808).
[28] See *In V Metaphysic.*, lect.5, n.16 (Marietti, n.823).
[29] Jan A. Aertsen, "Natural law in the light of the doctrine of trascendentals," in *Lex et libertas: Freedom and Law According to St. Thomas Aquinas*, ed. L. J. Elders and K. Hedwig (Città del Vaticano: Editrice Vaticana, 1987), 99-112.
[30] See, *In III Sent.*, Prooemium.
[31] See *S. Th.* I-II, q. 10, a. 1, co.
[32] *In IV Sent.*, d. 33, q. 1, a. 1, co.; *S. Th. Suppl.III*, q. 65, a. 1, co.
[33] See *De ente et essentia*, c. 1.

decides the movement of these towards their own end according to their genus and species. The magnet is a good example: due to its natural form considering its genus, it falls; and also due to its natural form, but this time considering its species, it attracts. Contrary to the movements of inert objects like the magnet or any other heavy object, the operations of animals and humans, as such, do not come directly from their respective natural forms. Indeed, in the conscious being, natural form is not an operative principle, because conscious agents have two operative principles: knowledge and appetite. For individuals of the animal genus to move in order towards the natural end, in each of their operative principles—knowledge and appetite—there must be a natural act. That natural act in the cognitive power of animals is, precisely, the *estimatio naturalis*, that is, *instinctus*; and in the human being it is what is called *ius naturale* or *lex naturalis*. Then, the natural movement of the appetite follows the respective natural knowledge. Instinct and natural law are knowledge of what is right and what is wrong; both drive the given operation towards the end of its respective agent; but in the animal this act of knowledge is more impulsive than regulatory. In the human, on the contrary, knowledge of what is right and wrong for their human nature is regulatory, and thus is called a law, natural law:

> Therefore the natural law is nothing else than a concept naturally instilled into man, whereby he is guided to act in a befitting manner in his proper actions, whether they are competent to him by virtue of his generic nature, as, for instance, to beget, to eat, and so on, or belong to him by virtue of his specific nature, as, for instance, to reason and so forth. Now whatever renders an action disproportionate to the end which nature intends to obtain by a certain work is said to be contrary to the natural law.[34]

Natural law is analogous to natural form because, in the same way, it is an operative principle that disposes to the proper operation that is appropriate to the corresponding end for the genus and species. Natural law is also analogous to instinct because, like this, it is natural knowledge of the cognitive power which directs to the operation which is suitable for the end of the agent; thus, at times, the judgement of natural reason is also called instinct.[35] But natural law is not only comparable to the inferior rules such as natural form or instinct, but is also similar to the superior

[34] *In IV Sent.*, d. 33, q. 1, a. 1, co.; *S. Th. Suppl.III*, q. 65, a. 1, co.
[35] See *De Veritate*, q. 14, a. 10, arg.7 and ad 7.

rule. In *Summa Theologiae* there is another description of natural law, on this occasion, as part of the act of a superior intellect:

> Wherefore it [the rational creature] has a share of the Eternal Reason, whereby it has a natural inclination to its proper act and end: and this participation of the eternal law in the rational creature is called the natural law. [...] thus implying that the light of natural reason, whereby we discern what is good and what is evil, which is the function of the natural law, is nothing else than an imprint on us of the Divine light.[36]

Due to their rational nature, humankind is subject to eternal law but in a very different way from the other beings in the universe: all are regulated, but only the human being regulates.[37] Certainly, humankind is subject, not by instinct, but by law.[38] Although natural law is, like animal instinct, imposed by another, that is, a superior principle,[39] natural law does not come down to a mere being moved by another. In fact, due to the participation in eternal reason that the free agent enjoys, he directs and orders;[40] therefore the human being does not simply cause his movements but also the order of his movements. This double causality belongs to intellectual nature. Humans do not only act, but also determine their own acts.[41] Natural things only execute those acts that are imposed on the natural form; but the natural form of human beings excludes them from being mere executors of proper operations that are appropriate to the end, that is, of those actions which follow from their natural law. Will is not deprived of a natural tendency which corresponds to its natural form and that tendency is, precisely, natural law, but it is a tendency towards good which must be carried out through free choice.[42] While the natural movements of inert beings or animals are necessary, action following natural law is not; its appetite is free due to its intellectual nature.[43] And it may or may not follow the natural judgement of reason.[44] In this sense, there are two operative principles: nature and will.[45]

---

[36] *S. Th.* I-II, q. 91, a. 2, co.
[37] See *S. Th.* I-II, q. 91, a. 2, co.
[38] See *SCG*, L. 3, c. 75, n. 3.
[39] See *Sententia Ethic.*, L. 7, lect.13 n. 14.
[40] See Primae redactiones *SCG*, L. 3.
[41] See *In II Sent.*, d. 39, q. 1, a. 1, co.
[42] See *In II Sent.*, d. 39, q. 2, a. 2, ad 5.
[43] See *De veritate*, q. 23, a. 1, co.
[44] See Primae redactiones *SCG*, L. 3.
[45] See *SCG*, L.3, c. 85, n. 4.

Nevertheless, in its natural opening to the opposites, not all choices of the will are as natural. Choice following reason is natural; choices against reason, for example, irregular sensual movements, are movements which go against rational nature.[46] On the other hand, proper choice may be made in many ways, which demonstrates the need for prudence. All the many possible inclinations may recognise what is proper, this is why there is unity in natural law.[47] As such, good in humans is universal, not partial, that is, good for the whole human being and not only for some of his parts.[48] But choice in the operation according to natural law is free, that is, of the *imperium* of reason.

Agent, form and end

The *imperium*, the *instinctus* and the *lex naturalis* give rise to teleological movements; to differentiate between the respective movements, attention can be paid to the relationship of the agent and the way it acts, and the end towards which it moves.[49] If the agent moves following a form or an end which are naturally inherent to it, then its movement is that of an instrument, that is, the agent is merely the executor. This is the case in inert things. If the agent understands the form which is its operative principle, even though it cannot propose the end for itself, but this is inherent to its nature, then the agent has instinctive movement. This is the case for the animal genus. If the agent, apart from being capable of understanding the form, can set the end for itself, then it can rule its own movement. Only an intellectual agent can do so, because only reason can know the end, the proportion necessary for the end and rule one over the other. The forms conceived by reason are, in free acts, what natural forms are in natural things;[50] but for the intelligible form to be an operative principle it needs the intervention of will, which moves towards the end.[51] The human act receives its specific being from its corresponding form,[52] and this being reaches its plenitude, that is, its absolute goodness, by fulfilling its proper end.[53] In as far as the specific

[46] See *In II Sent.*, d. 39, q. 2, a. 2, ad 1.
[47] See *S. Th.* I-II, q. 94, a. 4, ad 3.
[48] See *In II Sent.*, d. 39, q. 2, a. 2, co.
[49] See *S. Th.* I, q. 18, a. 3, co.
[50] See *S. Th.* I-II, q. 18, a. 10, co.
[51] See *S. Th.* I, q. 14, a. 8, co.
[52] See *S. Th.* I-II, q. 18, a. 2, co.
[53] See *S. Th.* I-II, q. 18, a. 4, co.

form of the human act is not suitable to its nature, the act will be good or bad.[54] Indeed, a voluntary act against nature is as lacking in its natural specific form as a corpse would be, that is, a body lacking its natural form.[55] From this perspective we see how we can speak of a human act as a compound of form and matter. Reason and will give these same acts a form; and these, the ruled acts, make up the matter of the command; the resulting human act is, thus, like a natural compound.[56]

However, instinct designates a certain operative principle to explain the order of movements which are not directed by human reason. In this sense, animal movements are paradigmatically instinctive: animals do not move like stones, nor like humans, for their movements are impelled by judgement, but this judgement is placed in them by a separate intellect,[57] it is natural judgement and not free.[58] There are also instinctive human behaviours: actions carried out by the human being which are not decided by the human rational command, but by a so-called supernatural instinct: it can be both positive and negative. The so-called inner instinct moves towards good action,[59] and extends to all human powers,[60] and moves humans in the same way as the command of reason moves towards the appetitive powers.[61] Aquinas continues to say that in the same way as the appetitive powers require a special disposition to follow the command of reason, there are also other dispositions to be moved by that principle which is superior to human reason and is called Divine or special instinct.[62] Aristotle also refers to an interior *instinct* as a better principle than human reason.[63] Besides, the negative instinct in humans[64] also has a cognitive character[65] and is also given with a guiding role like that of command.[66] The primary movements of reason and will are not

[54] See *S. Th.* I-II, q. 18, a. 5, co.
[55] See *S. Th.* I-II, q. 18, a. 5, ad 1.
[56] See *S. Th.* I-II, q. 17, a. 4, co.
[57] See *S. Th.* I-II, q. 40, a. 3, co.
[58] See *S. Th.* I, q. 83, a. 1, co.
[59] See *Super Ioannis*, c. 15, lect. 5.
[60] See *S. Th.* I-II, q. 68, a. 4, co.
[61] See *S. Th.* I-II, q. 68, a. 3, co.
[62] See *S. Th.* I-II, q. 68, a. 1, ad 2.
[63] See Aristotle, *The Athenian Constitution. The Eudemian Ethics. On Virtues and Vices*, trans. H. Rackham (London: William Heinemann, 1963), *EE*, L.8, c. 2, n.22-3; Bk 1248 a 32-34. *S. Th.* I-II, q. 68, a. 1, co.
[64] See *Super II Thes.*, c. 2, lect. 2.
[65] See *In II Sent.*, d. 15, q. 1, a. 3, ad 4.
[66] See *Super I Cor.*, c. 12, l.1.

commanded[67]: the inclination of will to the last end comes from a certain natural instinct, not from the command of reason,[68] and the acquiescence to primary principles, such as the first precept of natural law, is carried out naturally not by command,[69] as knowledge of the first principles belongs to the species.[70] Both acts are natural primary movements which, by being natural, are directed towards one thing (*ad unum*). The primary natural acts are inclinations that belong to the natural form.[71]

In the human, we find examples of different movements depending on how the agent relates to the form and the end. The end is determined by will; later, reason commands the movements of the sensitive powers; these, in turn, move the corporal organs which, as they act due to an exterior form, are simply instrumental.[72] The mastery of human beings over their inferior powers is a reflection of mastery over the others creatures of the universe: humans command animals in the same way as they command their sensitive powers, and use inanimate objects as they use their natural powers and their own bodies.[73]

Contemplation of human command of inert beings leads to consideration of God's command of the former. Indeed, natural things, as instruments, are moved by humans, and from humans receive the direction of their movement as a principle which is extrinsic to them; therefore, such movement is not natural.[74] But we will find in these same things a movement that comes from within themselves and manifests a determination towards their own end. But an ordered movement towards an end is, of itself, a commanded movement; thus that movement is both natural and commanded, but not commanded by the human being, but by Divine command.[75] On this issue, we can say that the act of command is prior to the natural act: the imperative act of the Creator permits the natural act of the creature.[76] Thus, the natural act of will is also a commanded act, but not commanded by the will. Except for the voluntary act that consists of the natural inclination to the last end, all other acts

---

67 See *S. Th.* I, q. 18, a. 3, co.
68 See *S. Th.* I-II, q. 17, a. 5, ad 3.
69 See *S. Th.* I-II, q. 17, a. 6, co.
70 See *S. Th.* I, q. 79, a. 5, ad 3.
71 See *De malo*, q. 3, a. 3, co.
72 See *S. Th.* I, q. 18, a. 3, co.
73 See *S. Th.* I, q. 96, a. 2, co.
74 See *S. Th.* I, q. 103, a. 1, ad 3.
75 See *S. Th.* I-II, q. 1, a. 2, ad 3.
76 See *De potentia*, q. 2, a. 6, ad 1.

(through which the will can be ordered to achieve its last end) depend on their own command.[77] Due to the fact that human beings can decide for themselves, the end and the form can rule their own free movement.

The three senses of *imperium*

Given the three elements that make up the definition of *imperium* (command) which correspond to the proper acts of each ruling faculty, it is simpler to understand the three senses of command, and more clearly appreciate the ordering character of both instinct and natural law. The three elements are order, movement and end; thus, respectively, the three senses are ordering, movement and determination of the end; and the corresponding faculties are reason, appetite in general and rational appetite or will.

Reason commands in its own sense because commanding is ordering the movement towards the end.[78] The appetites command because commanding is movement in order towards the end. However, we must differentiate between two kinds of appetite: rational and sensitive. The sensitive appetites command in the widest sense of the word; they are not truly imperative, only in the sense that commanding means moving.[79] The will, taken as an appetite, moves, but in a very different way from that in which the sensitive appetites move. These latter move towards an end given by another; will moves towards an end chosen by itself. Thus, will is an appetite that moves by deciding the principle of the movement, that is, the end. The command exercised by the will acquires a sense that is truly proper to it. Will does not command by *ordering* as reason does; nor does it simply *move*, as the appetites do, it commands by *determining the end*. But the end is the principle both for order and for movement. The end corresponds to whoever commands, as can be seen in the directive arts. This is how the will commands, because the object of the will is, specifically, the end. So the command of the will has a completely particular sense because only the will has the object itself as the end.[80]

Commanding, then, is an act of reason, of will and of the appetites, but in various senses, depending on whether we emphasise the *ordering*, the *end* or *movement*. Despite the diversity of the senses, there is no place for a command in the rational faculty without the presence of the movement

[77] See *De potentia*, q. 2, a. 3, ad 6.
[78] See *S. Th.* I-II, q. 17, a. 1, co.
[79] See *S. Th.* I-II, q. 17, a. 2, ad 1.
[80] See *In IV Sent.*, d. 15, q. 4, a. 1, qc.1, ad 3.

factor. Indeed, a directing faculty cannot command without the intervention of some factor of movement.[81] Thus the ordering act of reason will not be imperative without a prior proper appetitive act,[82] that is, of will.[83] Nor can one call a movement lacking order imperative. We can say that the sensible appetite of the animals commands because they follow an ordering act, namely, the judgement of instinct. This is proven in the fact of the similarity between animal movements and rational works, for example, in anger,[84] hope and despair.[85]

Then again, the command of the rule of reason requires a voluntary act. However, will is not the only driving force for appetite in the human being: the sensitive appetites can also move reason, but their driving power does not contribute to its command, but rather do they restrain it because they move towards a particular end, that is, sensitive good, which cannot be an ordering principle for the whole man. Sensitive appetites can oppose being moved by the command of reason, which, in such a case, fluctuates between being moved by will, or by the sensitive appetite;[86] if these manage to impede the command of reason, then, because of this, they prevent the ordering of human action (commanding is ordering); and as in this case the will does not prevail over the appetites, then nor does reason command. But, as the principle of command is in the will, a defect in the command of reason will be attributed to the will.[87] The operation carried out by the impulse of the sensible appetites when these are no longer subject to rational order, is an operation which can be called disordered. This occurs when human beings no longer act according to their rational form, which disposes them to act following reason (*secundum rationem*), but to act as an irrational subject, and in this way, they act as though driven by some natural instinct, similar to animal instinct.[88] Thus, sensual inclination is opposed to rational instinct.[89] Indeed, by following their sensuality, humans behave like animals; but while animals acting by instinct are following the sense they are given for their specific end, that human action that merely follows the inclination of

[81] See *S. Th.* I-II, q. 17, a. 1, co.
[82] See *S. Th.* I-II, q. 17, a. 1, arg.3 and ad 3.
[83] See *S. Th.* I-II, q. 17, a. 1, co.
[84] See *S. Th.* I-II, q. 46, a. 7, ad 1.
[85] See *S. Th.* I-II, q. 40, a. 3, ad 1.
[86] See *S. Th.* I-II, q. 17, a. 5, ad 1.
[87] See *In II Sent.*, d. 39, q. 1, a. 1, ad 4.
[88] See *SCG*, L.3, c. 85, n.21-22.
[89] See *De veritate*, q. 24, a. 12, co.

the sensitive nature means opposition to reason[90] as this latter has then lost its directive authority and given way to sensuality.[91] Stripped of the reason of their imperative function, humans loose their capacity to command freely, in other words, they lose their natural disposition to freedom, to order their own movement. This turning away is most frequently caused by incentives discovered by human curiosity than by the natural tendencies of sensuality.[92] Nevertheless, humans lose their specific means of being subject to eternal law; they submit to it, certainly, but not in a human way, rather in an animal way, that is, through the sensual impulse.[93] In such cases, the impulse of the operation, which comes from sensual desire, does not have the characteristics of command. The sensitive appetites may move to action, but they cannot order the movement of a whole human because their object is not the end of a complete human being, that is, the last end. A sign of its essentially subordinate character is that this disorder in respect of the last end is out of their reach; for such disorder an act of the rational faculty is necessary.[94]

The phenomenon of subversion of the sensitive appetites against reason, traditionally called incontinence, destroys the imperative authority of reason. From this perspective, another observation on *imperium* that Aquinas finds in Aristotle becomes relevant: "reason exhorts us to do what is best."[95] *Imperium* is a kind of pleading directed towards those faculties which are not wholly subject to it, and can rebel.[96] In continent man, the sensitive appetites obey reason.[97]

Action based on reason is good. To avoid evil, human beings have, amongst other resources, free will and natural law, no matter how limited they are.[98] Natural law taken as a movement which must follow the natural form consists of the execution of the first acts of reason and of will, as only these first acts are commanded by God and not by humans. But natural law also rules on those acts commanded by humans which correspond freely with the rule of reason. From this perspective, natural

---

[90] See *S. Th.* I-II, q. 71, a. 2, ad 3.
[91] See *S. Th.* I-II, q. 91, a. 6, co.
[92] See *S. Th.* II-II, q. 142, a. 2, ad 2.
[93] See *S. Th.* I-II, q. 91, a. 6, co.
[94] See *S. Th.* I-II, q. 74, a. 4, co; Aristotle, *Nicomachean Ethics*, trans. R. Crisp (Cambridge UK - New York: Cambridge University Press, 1957), L. I, c. 13, Bk 1102 b 16.
[95] See *S. Th.* II-II, q. 83, a. 1, co.
[96] See *In IV Sent.*, d. 15, q. 4, a. 1 qc. 1, co.
[97] See *QDL IX*, q. 5, a. 2, arg.
[98] See *S. Th.* I, q. 113, a. 1, ad 1.

law dictates the *imperium* of God and the human *imperium*: the former gives rise to the first natural acts, and the latter to all free acts. The relationship between natural movement and free movement could be compared with the relationship between the heartbeat and the remaining bodily movements.[99] That happiness desired by the will is an act of the natural instinct which is beyond the reach of free will,[100] but the acts carried out by free will have their basis in that first act, which is the desire for happiness, carried out by nature. And just as the properties of the sense of touch are involved in the sense of sight, and the good of animal life is involved in rational good, the voluntary act proper to nature is also involved in the free acts of will.[101] Actually, the natural inclination of will towards the last end does not replace the exercise of human *imperium*, but makes it possible, because due to the fact that it desires the last end it can desire what is necessary to achieve that end. This commensuration of any free act to the last end, depending on the circumstances, is a result of reason, so the natural operation in human beings is action according to reason (*secundum rationem*).[102]

In order to carry out the correct action at any given moment, animals have instinct, but human beings must discern it by reasoning.[103] It is true that natural law guides humans more as an instinct than as a ratified law;[104] but this does not mean that it is something that cannot be taught by the wisest, that is, by those who have the most knowledge of circumstances, or even by God Himself.[105] The teachings of such beings are like conclusions obtained from the first principles of natural law,[106] as Aquinas responds to those who, by drawing a parallel between natural law and instinct, attempt to exclude the moral precepts given by God from natural law.[107]

There is a wonderful example of the need for rational discernment to determine human good based on natural inclination in his arguments on poverty as a virtue.[108] At a first reading this contradicts the natural inclination,[109] common to humans and animals, of having the necessities

---

[99] See *S. Th.* I-II, q. 17, a. 9, ad 2; *S.Th.,* I, q. 60, a. 2, co.
[100] See *S. Th.* I, q. 19, a. 10, co.
[101] See *De veritate*, q. 22, a. 5, co.
[102] See *In II Sent.*, d. 39, q. 2, a. 1, co.
[103] See *Super Iob*, c. 37.
[104] See *Super Gal.*, c. 2, l.4.
[105] See *S. Th.* I-II, q. 100, a. 1, co.
[106] See *S. Th.* I-II, q. 100, a. 1, co.
[107] See *S. Th.* I-II, q. 100, arg. 1.
[108] See *SCG*, L. 3, cc. 131-134.
[109] See *SCG*, L. 3, c. 131, n.4.

of life.[110] Thomas Aquinas does not reject the resemblance to animals in the good that both must find: in order to provide, human beings are organised like bees.[111] Both humans and animals need material resources, but riches are good for humans in as far as indicated by reason.[112] Neither riches nor any particular asset is good for humans if it is not ordered by reason.[113] Reason is to be found both in the use of great riches, stemming from munificence, or from renouncing them all, stemming from poverty.[114] Nor are acts that take from the exercise of reason, such as sleep or the act of copulation, opposed to reason; and the abundant pleasure from this latter is not opposed to virtue if said act has been ordained by honest reason.[115] Indeed,, reason decides the virtue of the act, by attending to the circumstances needed for the act to be in proportion to the correct end. Reason can order the last end according to natural law, that is, the good of what is inferior compared to the good of what is superior; body to soul and the good of the inferior faculties to proper rational good.[116] That natural rectitude that reason recognises is independent of all positive law.[117]

The ordering of action to natural human good is a job for reason. Through the opening of reason to transcendental good, the precepts of natural law direct the operation only to a certain extent. They guide but do not determine what should be done in each case, because the soul is open, in some way, to the infinite (*ad infinitum*). For the human agent neither the natural appetite towards good nor the natural judgement to act according to its nature are enough,[118] because the formal operative principle is the being,[119] and judgement on good is a free judgement. Nor is it determined by the manner of operation: it acts freely and not by instinct. Such lack of determination regarding its natural good is solved by habits, which are determinations that give more ample perfection to the faculties whose acts are free.[120] A form which can act in many ways, such as the human soul,

---

[110] See *SCG*, L. 3, c. 131, n.2.
[111] See *SCG*, L. 3, c. 134, n.2.
[112] See *SCG*, L. 3 c. 134, n.5.
[113] See *SCG*, L. 3, c. 134, n.6.
[114] See *SCG*, L. 3, c. 134, n.7.
[115] See *S. Th.* II-II, q. 153, a. 2, ad 2.
[116] See *SCG*, L. 3, c. 129, n.7.
[117] See *SCG*, L. 3, c. 129, tit.
[118] See *S. Th.* II-II, q. 47, a. 7, ad 3.
[119] See *S. Th.* I-II, q. 9, a. 1, co.
[120] See *In III Sent.*, d. 23, q. 1, a. 1, co.

needs certain habits for its operations.[121] Again, what is natural in the human being is different from what is natural in other creatures. The inert things, whose forms have but one determined operation, are completely determined. For the animals, whose active principle has but a few operations, instinct is enough to determine their operations.[122] But the human being needs something more. The habits that perfect the operation of human beings according to their inclinations are the virtues; amongst which, the foremost must be an ordering virtue, namely, intellectual virtue.[123] The virtue that prepares reason to determine a specific human good, that is, to command according to their nature, is the virtue of prudence.[124] Prudence orders towards the naturally determined last end, but it is not, however, a natural virtue, because what it orders are actions which are not determined by nature. The actions that lead to the natural end of the human being are free, not natural, actions.[125] The so-called animal *prudences* direct operations determined by the nature of each animal. But the attainment of the virtue of prudence in the human being requires great experience and learning, in contrast to what may be called animal *prudences*.[126]

The virtues, which are present wherever there is human *imperium*, are not present in those actions carried out in a natural manner. Indeed, no habit predisposes the will to the last end; nor is there a habit for the exercise of the act of the intelligent agent which allows us to know the first principles.[127] The light of the first naturally known principles, conversely, does produce a habit in the passive intellect, and this is a natural habit.[128] Synderesis is precisely the natural habit of the first practical principles, and its content is natural law.[129] Those acts of will which are not determined by nature, and which may thus be ruled, also require virtues. As the appetitive faculties are not merely executive like the body organs, but also provoke their own movement, they also require virtues that

[121] See *S. Th.* I-II, q. 49, a. 4, ad 1.
[122] See *De virtutibus*, q. 1, a. 6, co.
[123] See *S. Th.* I-II, q. 58, a. 4, ad 1.
[124] See *De virtutibus*, q. 1, a. 6, co.
[125] See *S. Th.* II-II, q. 47, a. 15, co.
[126] See *SCG*, L. 3, c. 122, n.8.
[127] See *In III Sent.*, d. 23, q. 1, a. 1, co.
[128] See *In III Sent.*, d. 23, q. 1, a. 1, co.
[129] "'*Synderesis*' is said to be the law of our mind, because it is a habit containing the precepts of the natural law, which are the first principles of human actions.", *S.Th.,* II-II, q. 94, a. 1, ad 2.

determine their movements consistent with reason.[130] The very virtues of the quick-tempered and of the dissipated perfect their natural disposition to be moved so that they obey, without loathing, the *imperium* of reason.[131] The acts of the sensitive appetites directed by reason are different from their own instinctive acts.[132] But the body, as simple executor, has a natural corporal disposition to be moved as an instrument by reason, as a result of which it does not need virtue to obey reason immediately and without difficulty;[133] nevertheless it does require another type of habit, health, to participate in the disposition of the soul.[134]

Despite the choice of good supplied by the virtues, the will still preserves the possibility of choosing evil,[135] as the condition of its natural form gives it permanent indecision. However, it always has the power, also, of avoiding evil in its acts. In the struggle with the inclination of the sensitive appetites, will is better equipped than reason, as this latter depends on the reserve of sensitive knowledge to execute its own act, and on the contrary, will maintains its power to follow or reject the movement of the sensitive appetites,[136] because only will can freely determine its own act. Moreover, reason has the light of the precept (*praecise-coeptum*[137]) of the Divine law which illuminates and strengthens it in its *imperium*, so it follows natural law.[138] Together with the indication of natural law on what should be done, human beings can rely on assistance to carry it out,[139] as reason can be perfected not only by the instinct of natural reason but also by an even higher instinct.[140]

---

[130] See *In III Sent.*, d. 23, q. 1, a. 1, co.
[131] See *De virtutibus*, q. 1, a. 4. co.
[132] See *S. Th.* I-II, q. 50, a. 3, co.
[133] See *De virtutibus*, q. 1, a. 4, co.
[134] See *In III Sent.*, d. 23, q.1, a. 1, co.
[135] See *In II Sent.*, d. 39, q. 2, a. 1, co.
[136] See *S. Th.* I, q. 115, a. 4, co.
[137] See *Super Psalmo* 18, n.5.
[138] See *SCG*, L. 3, c. 117, n.6.
[139] See *S. Th.* I-II, q. 106, a. 1, ad 2.
[140] See *S. Th.* I-II, q. 68, a. 2, co.

Works Cited

Primary Sources

Aquinatis, S. Thomae. "<http//www.corpusthomisticum.org/>, Pampilonae, Universitatis Studiorum Navarrensis, 2000. In taenias magneticas a Roberto Busa SJ. denuo recognovit Enrique Alarcón atque instruxit.", 2000.

Secondary Sources

Aertsen, Jan A. "Natural law in the light of the doctrine of trascendentals." In *Lex et libertas: Freedom and Law According to St. Thomas Aquinas*, edited by L. J. Elders and K. Hedwig. Città del Vaticano: Editrice Vaticana, 1987.

Aristotle. *The Athenian Constitution. The Eudemian Ethics. On Virtues and Vices* Translated by H. Rackham. London: William Heinemann, 1963.

—. *Nicomachean Ethics* Translated by R. Crisp. Cambridge UK - New York: Cambridge University Press, 1957.

—. *De Anima* Translated by D. W. Hamlyn (Oxford: Clarendon Press, 1993).

Averrois. *Commentum magnum super libro De celo et mundo Aristotelis, ex recognitione Francis James Carmody in lucem edidit Rüdiger Arnzen*. Edited by G. Endress. 2 vols. Leuven: Peeters, 2003.

Ciceronis, M. Tulli. *Rhetorici libri duo qui vocantur de inventione, recognovit E. Stroebel*. Vol. 2. Stuttgart: B.G. Teubner, 1965.

Damascene, S. John. "De fide orthodoxa." In *Patrologiae cursus completus. T. 94. Series Graeca (MG)*, edited by J.P. Migne. Parisiis: Turnholti (Belgium), 1857-1866.

Deman, Thomas. "Le "précepte" de la prudence chez saint Thomas d'Aquin." *Recherches de Théologie ancienne et médiévale* 20 (1953): 40-59.

Gauthier, René Antoine. "Saint Maxime le Confesseur et la psychologie de l'acte humain." *Recherches de Théologie ancienne et médiévale* 21 (1954): 51-100.

Greene, Robert A. "Instinct of Nature: Natural Law, Synderesis, and the Moral Sense." *Journal of the History of Ideas* 58, no. 2 (1997): 173-98.

Honoré, Tony. *Ulpian*. Oxford: Clarendon Press, 1982.

Isidore of Seville. *Etymologiarum sive Originum, in Patrologiae cursus completus. T. 81-84. Series Latina (PL)*. Edited by J.P. Migne. Parisiis

- Turnholti (Belgium): Typographi Brepols Editores Pontificii, 1862-1878.

Lottin, Odon. *Psychologie et morale aux XIIe et XIIIe siècles*. 6 vols. Gembloux (Belgium): J. Duculot, S.A. Editeur, 1948-1960.

Mommsen, T., and P. Krueger, eds. *The Digest of Justinian*. Philadelphia PA: University of Penssylvania Press, 1985.

Origen. *Contra Celsum* Translated by H. Chadwick. Cambridge: Cambridge Scholar Press, 1980.

Osuna, Antonio. "Introducción a las cuestiones 90 a 97." In *Suma de Teología*. Madrid: Editorial Católica, 1989.

Porphyry. *On Abstinence from Killing Animals* Translated by G. Clark. London: Duckworth, 2000.

CHAPTER NINETEEN

NATURAL LAW, ESSENTIAL LAW AND PERSONAL LAW: A STUDY ON THE NATURE, HIERARCHY AND AIM OF THESE HUMAN "LAWS"

JUAN FERNANDO SELLÉS

Approach

If one accepts the real distinction between *the act of being* and *essence* in man, the first question to ask is wherein natural law lies. If the answer is that it lies within the personal *act of being*, then the distinction between each man and humankind will lie in that each one is inferior to humankind, a realisation of the latter, according to the Aristotelian saying: "this flesh and these bones". According to this conception, each person will be according to humankind, and not the other way round. Thus, talking about human dignity would be equivalent to acknowledging the character of human *nature*. Conversely, if we answer that natural law is part of human nature—as its name indicates—and that the latter can be described in relation to the human *essence*, then, as the *essence* is inferior to the personal act of being, we shall have to argue that each person is superior to human nature, to the common in men, and that is why it subordinates the specific in the said nature to his personal requirements. In this case, each person will be seen as superior to the human species, or as its aim. It will also be possible to understand why each person is able to continue natural law and also able to breach it, because the superior governs and directs (for better or for worse) that which is inferior.

This paper accepts the following hierarchy: "natural law", which belongs to human *nature*, is inferior to human *essence*, which it serves and to which it is subordinate. And the latter is inferior to the human personal *act of being*, which it serves and to which it is subject. Why is it possible to continue or to breach natural law? Simply, because each *person* is not reduced to human *nature*.[1] Human nature is not a person (humankind is not a personal subject). To put it another way: no person is reduced to human nature. Human nature is *for* or is dualised with, the human person. The person is *for*, or is dualised with, the personal God. So if the human person without God is incomprehensible, so will human essence and human nature. Therefore, a natural law *etsi Deus non daretur*, is not so.

What is human "natural law"?

For Thomas Aquinas, natural law is the way of being of human nature. The term "nature" indicates the principle of operations. Natural law does not designate human nature statically taken, but rather, its *inclination*,[2] or its performance. It is an *inherent* guideline in human nature,[3] which is considered to be *immutable*[4] because it was *imprinted* on us by God.[5] Through natural law, man can distinguish good from evil, virtue from vice.[6] For Thomas Aquinas, such a law, to which the most common

---

[1] "Because man is a person, he is not subject to the laws of nature, but rather, he stands out among them and enjoys radical freedom. Therefore, his presence in the world through his nature is inventive. Man takes out of himself, he gives, he contributes", Leonardo Polo, *Ética: hacia una versión moderna de temas clásicos* (Madrid: Aedos, 1996), 90.

[2] "Inclinatio naturae pertinet ad praecepta legis naturalis", *S. Th.*, II-II, q. 79, a. 2, ad 2. On this subject and author, see , Carlos Augusto Mesa Posada, *La ley natural en Santo Tomás: fundamentos metafísicos y propiedades* (Chía (Colombia): Universidad de La Sabana, 1998), 154. Sergio Raúl Castaño, "Consideraciones ontológicas sobre la ley natural en Tomás de Aquino," *Sapientia* 54 (1999): 351-66.

[3] "Lex naturalis est lex indita homini", *S. Th.*, I-II, q. 106, a. 1, ad 2.

[4] "Et sic quantum ad prima principia legis naturae, lex naturae est omnino immutabilis", *S. Th.*, I-II, q. 94, a. 5 co. Cf also: *S. Th.* I-II, q. 97, a. 1, ad 1; *S. Th.* I-II, q. 97, a. 3, ad 1.

[5] "Est autem duplex regula humanae vitae; prima quidem est lex naturalis a Deo mentibus hominum impressa, per quam naturaliter homo intelligit quid est bonum ex similitudine divinae bonitatis", *Super Iob*, cap. 23. Cf también: *Super Sent.*, lib. 4, d. 24, q. 1, a. 1, qc. 1 co.

[6] "Lumen rationis naturalis, quo discernimus quid sit bonum et malum, quod pertinet ad naturalem legem, nihil aliud sit quam impressio divini luminis in nobis. Unde patet quod lex naturalis nihil aliud est quam participatio legis aeternae in rationali creatura", *S. Th.*, I-II, q. 91 a. 2 co. Cf. also: *Catena in Lc.*, cap. 6, lec. 7; *Super Rom.*, cap. 7, lec. 2.

precepts belong, is known by all men,[7] and nobody can be mistaken in regard to it.[8] This is why he compares it to the first speculative principles.[9]

But we should not forget that human nature is wounded, right from the beginning, by that reality which the doctrine of the Church calls original sin. In addition, human nature is not immune to personal sins which have occurred profusely throughout the course of history. In this sense, today there is discussion about whether human nature can acquire defects with time[10] and, therefore, whether the said law admits variations or not.[11] For Aquinas, what has changed over the history of humankind (largely for worse) is *knowledge* of natural law, because a progressive obscuring, due to personal guilt, has taken place.[12]

Although we could spend a long time on the issues of natural law dealt with by Thomas Aquinas, we shall now focus on two points which, after Aquinas, are not so clear.

a) Synderesis: the cognitive method of natural law

Thomas Aquinas holds that natural law is not a matter of will, but of reason.[13] However, this is not reason as a power, but as an *innate habit*,[14]

---

[7] "Ad legem naturalem pertinent primo quidem quaedam praecepta communissima, quae sunt omnibus nota", *S. Th.*, I-II, q. 94, a. 6, co.

[8] "Lex naturalis inquantum continet praecepta communia, quae nunquam fallunt, dispensationem recipere non potest", *S. Th.* I-II, q. 97, a. 4, ad 3. Cf. also: *S. Th.*, I-II, q. 94, a. 6, co.

[9] Cf. *S. Th.*, I-II, q. 91 a. 3, co.

[10] "A principio generis humani indita est mentibus hominum lex naturalis, per quam homines Deo subjecti essent: postmodum vero invalescente consuetudine peccatorum, lex naturalis adeo tenebrata est in pluribus, ut iam non videretur ad regimen humani generis sufficere", *Super Sent.*, lib. 3, d. 1, q. 1, a. 4, co.

[11] Cf. Francisco Carpintero Benítez, "La mutabilidad de la ley natural en Tomás de Aquino," *Rivista Internazionale di Filosofia del Diritto* 77 (2000): 470-530. Theo G. Belmans, "L'immutabilité de la loi naturelle selon s. Thomas d'Aquin," *Revue Thomiste* (1987): 23-44. Richard B. Hall, "The Alterability of Natural Law," *The New Scholasticism* 55 (1981): 474-83.

[12] "Lex naturalis obscurari incipiebat propter exuberantiam peccatorum", *S. Th.* I-II, q. 98, a. 6, co. Cf también: *S. Th.*, I-II, q. 100, a. 5, ad 1; *Super Rom.*, cap. 7, lec. 1; *S. Th.* III, q. 61, a. 3, ad 2.

[13] "Lex naturalis est aliquid per rationem constitutum, sicut etiam propositio est quoddam opus rationis", *S. Th.*, I-II, q. 94, a. 1, co.

[14] "Praecepta legis naturalis quandoque considerantur in actu a ratione, quandoque autem sunt in ea habitualiter tantum, secundum hunc modum potest dici quod lex naturalis sit habitus. Sicut etiam principia indemonstrabilia in speculativis non sunt

superior to the reason he calls "natural reason", in other words, *synderesis*,[15] upon which both the operation of will and of intelligence depend.[16] All men have this habit naturally, even if they do not use it.[17] In addition, this habit illuminates and activates human *nature*.[18] As it is innate, it has directly knowledge of the native, natural law.[19] But this does not indicate that it cannot also know what has been acquired by each person in human nature and essence, because it is clear that, while the human person does not invent human powers, their progressive development does depend on the person. To know natural law is to know the way of being of human powers.[20] Indeed, human powers cannot be known by abstraction, because to abstract is to universalise, and no power is known in it concrete disposition by universalising.

Our organic and inorganic powers, in their current, changing, state, are known by synderesis. On the one hand, synderesis knows our body, its

---

ipse habitus principiorum, sed sunt principia quorum est habitus", *S. Th.*, I-II, q. 94, a. 1, co. Cf. also: *Ibid.*, ad 3.

[15] "Synderesis dicitur lex intellectus nostri, inquantum est habitus continens praecepta legis naturalis, quae sunt prima principia operum humanorum", *S. Th.* I-II, q. 94, a. 1, ad 2. Cf also: *Super Sent.*, lib. 2, d. 24, q. 2, a. 4, co. For durrent thinkers "knowledge of natural law is the remit of synderesis", Leonardo Polo, *Antropología trascendental II. La esencia de la persona humana* (Pamplona: Eunsa, 2003), 185. Cf. on this issue: María Elton, "Gnoseología de la ley natural," *Sapientia* 53 (1998): 175-94.

[16] "Omnis operatio, rationis et voluntatis derivatur in nobis ab eo quod est secundum naturam, ut supra habitum est, nam omnis ratiocinatio derivatur a principiis naturaliter notis, et omnis appetitus eorum quae sunt ad finem, derivatur a naturali appetitu ultimi finis. Et sic etiam oportet quod prima directio actuum nostrorum ad finem, fiat per legem naturalem", *S. Th.* I-II, q. 91, a. 2, ad 2.

[17] "Eo quod habitualiter inest, quandoque aliquis uti non potest propter aliquod impedimentum, sicut homo non potest uti habitu scientiae propter somnum. Et similiter puer non potest uti habitu intellectus principiorum, vel etiam lege naturali, quae ei habitualiter inest, propter defectum aetatis", *S. Th.*, I-II, q. 94 a. 1, ad 4.

[18] Cf. Juan Fernando Sellés, "La sindéresis o razón natural como la apertura cognoscitiva de la persona humana a su propia naturaleza. Una propuesta desde Tomás de Aquino," *Revista Española de Filosofía Medieval* 10 (2003): 321-33.

[19] "Homo inter cetera animalia rationem finis cognoscit, et proportionem operis ad finem; ideo naturalis conceptio ei indita, qua dirigatur ad operandum convenienter, lex naturalis vel jus naturale dicitur", *Super Sent.*, lib. 4, d. 33, q. 1, a. 1, co.

[20] "Reliquit enim Deus prius hominem in libertate arbitrii, in lege naturali, ut sic vires naturae suae cognosceret", *S. Th.*, III, q. 1, a. 5, co.

powers or faculties, which make up our *received life* (from our parents).[21] On the other hand, it sheds light on and perfects our intelligence and our will (not received from our parents, because these are spiritual powers, therefore, they depend on each human person); they are initially passive powers, the development of which, through acquired *habits* and *virtues* constitutes our *added life*, which we can call human *essence*. Lack of development constitutes vices. Having said this, since the various human faculties are hierarchically ordered, synderesis does not illuminate all of them equally; it illuminates some more than others. Therefore, we must see which ones it is more difficult to imbue with meaning and also which one is the superior one, which will in turn be the most universal one.

If we achieve this, we will be able to say that natural law is within that faculty to a larger degree than in the others, because natural law is precisely characterised by being universal to human nature.

As to the *powers with an organic medium*, these can be illuminated by synderesis, but only to a certain extent, because their organ sets a limit to their intelligibility, something that does not happen with the two spiritual faculties (*intelligence* and *will*). Therefore, we know more about the active state of sensible faculties than about their organic medium. As has been said, synderesis is not natural law, but rather, it is its cognitive *method*. It is an innate habit that depends on the person. As it is not possible to admit any native defect in the personal *act of being*,[22] we must not accept the existence of lack of knowledge or ignorance in synderesis either. However, synderesis is not a fixed or static habit; it can grow or diminish. Its development or stagnation depends on the person and is therefore free and responsible.

[21] It is impossible to know the human body, its functions and its powers in a rational way, because, in order to know, reason starts out from abstraction, through which one knows what *one* body is, in the universal; but not *my* body concretely, its current state and the state of its functions and faculties. But it is no less clear that we know this *constantly* in a *natural way* and that we act consequently by virtue of this. This knowledge belongs to *synderesis*, whose knowing is not abstractive, universalising, judicative or rationalising, but *direct* on human nature, which is inferior to this knowing.

[22] Remember that original sin is *vulnum naturae*, not *vulnum personae*. The fault of a supposed constituent defect in the human persona *act of being* would be due to the Creator, which is unacceptable.

b) How to discern between natural law and positive laws?

The distinction between *natural law* and *positive laws* lies in that the former is *universal*, whilst the rest are *general*.[23] Generalisation is the proper object of an operative route of reason, with a formal character, which progressively stops seeking to know the content or true nature of intra-worldly realities.[24] This route cannot become saturated.[25] On the other hand, the universal is real. Having said this, there are two possible types of universalisation: those belonging to *physical reality* and those belonging to *human nature*. The former are known by an operative route of reason that discovers the concausal nature of physical reality.[26] The former, as pointed out above, is known by *synderesis*, which—it is convenient to insist—is not an acquired act or habit of reason, but an innate habit, superior to reason and capable of knowing and activating that power.

It is the human *person* who has the said habit at his or her disposal, and, also, human nature and essence. Human *nature* and *essence* are of the sphere of having at one's *disposal*. But it is a having at one's disposal that is *indispensable*.[27] To put it another way: the person must dispose *according* to his or her own essence and nature, not *of* them. One disposes *according* to them insofar as the exercise of one's activity affects them and perfects them. One disposes *of* them if one does not take that perfecting

---

[23] "Laws belong cognitively to the sphere of reason", Polo, *Antropología trascendental II*, 278. And elsewhere he adds: "a law, i.e. any rule, is a homogenising way of thinking",
Leonardo Polo, *Curso de teoría del conocimiento III*, 2nd ed. (Pamplona: Eunsa, 1998), 316. "The discovery of laws is, cognitively speaking, part of the order of reason", Polo, *Curso de teoría del conocimiento III*, 388-89. "Law riles between the general idea and its determination", ———, *Curso de teoría del conocimiento III*, 407. Cf. also: Leonardo Polo, *El orden predicamental*, Cuadernos de Anuario Filosófico n° 182 (Pamplona: Servicio de Publicaciones de la Universidad de Navarra, 2005), 87f.

[24] Cf. Polo, *Curso de teoría del conocimiento III.*

[25] "Generalisation cannot become saturated, so that the formulation of laws cannot be exhausted", ———, *Antropología trascendental II*, 278. Elswhere, he insists; "since generalisation belongs to a non saturable sphere, the possibility of formulating general laws can never be seen as exhausted", ———, *Curso de teoría del conocimiento III*, 389.

[26] The universal is not "logical with a basis *in re*", but real, and it is equivalent to the formal cause, the "unum in multis".

[27] Cf. Julia Urabayen, "La esencia del hombre como disponer indisponible," *Anuario Filosófico* 29, no. 2 (1996): 1051-59.

process into account. Disposing *according to* human nature and essence is ethical. Disposing *of* them is contrary to ethics. Law and cultural customs are external manifestations of human essence. These are ethical if they are forms derived from ethical rules; otherwise, they are not so.

Which is the aim of reason? Truth, in its theoretical use; verisimilitude, in its practical use. Insofar as these aims are achieved, theoretical or practical *habits,* respectively speaking, are acquired, although this is done in different ways: the former, with a single act; the latter, through repetition and rectification.[28] So if synderesis promotes *habits* in intelligence, it disposes *according* to its nature. And the same can be said of the *virtues* regarding the will. Furthermore, the virtues grow insofar as relations with other people are improved. In a parallel way, it can be said that in the other powers of human *nature*, disposing *according to* them will be lawful, and it will not be lawful to dispose *of* them.

What is human "essential law"?

The truth or meaning of the organic and inorganic powers in their state of *nature* is what can be called "natural law". But to progressively illuminate them—especially the inorganic ones—is to favour their *growth* and their aim, which is *perfection* of these powers. It is not convenient to call this new state of the powers a natural state or "natural law", rather, perfective development of natural law or "essential law", because "essence" indicates perfection. Human *essence* is not human *nature*; it is the *perfecting* of it. Since inorganic powers can have unrestricted growth, any moral *determinism* is unacceptable.[29]

If synderesis activates intelligence and will, it will do so in all its uses. Therefore, although it is ordinary to admit that natural law constitutes the north star of *practical reason*,[30] of *will*[31] (especially of its *virtues*[32]), or of

---

[28] Which is why Thomas Aquinas says that natural law has to do with the rectitude of reason: "lex naturalis est secundum quam ratio recta est", *Super Sent.*, lib. 2, d. 42, q. 2, a. 5, co.

[29] "Moral law is not rationally deterministic; if things can only be done as moral law says, the capacity of doing cannot grow", Polo, *Ética*, 120.

[30] Cf. Rhonheimer, *Ley natural y razón práctica. Una visión tomista de la autonomía moral.* Felicien Rousseau, "Loi naturelle et dynamisme de la raison pratique de l'homme," *Laval Théologique et Philosophique* 33 (1976): 165-88.

[31] Cf. Clarke, D. M., "Natural Law and Dynamics of the Will", *Philosophical Studies*, (Ireland) 27 (1980) 40-54.

the conjunction of these elements, i.e. *ethics*,[33] it is clear that the regulative use of the other operative routes of reason will also depend on natural law, whenever one proceeds in the former by acquiring rational habits. In addition—as has been said above—synderesis also knows the organic powers.

As to the inorganic faculties, the most perfectible one is not reason, but the *will*. Indeed, intelligence—according to Thomas Aquinas—is a faculty of means. Rather, it is aimed at knowing intra-worldly realities, because it counts on the cognitive limit it starts out from: *abstraction*. This indicates it is limited in knowing the totality of what is real, because it cannot directly reach that which is not sensible. Conversely, the will is natively open to all good. Indeed, among the classic metaphysical transcendentals (*being, truth, good, beauty*...), synderesis only gets to know one of them, the *good* (the rest are known by habits that are superior to synderesis),[34] and it does so by illuminating the will and noticing that it is open, not only to the medial goods (*voluntas ut ratio*), but also to the ultimate good with no restriction (*voluntas ut natura*).

If synderesis perfects the will more than the reason, we will have to maintain—contrary to the traditional argument—that the highest virtues of this power (*justice and friendship*) are superior to the highest acquired habits of intelligence, both the theoretical ones (*science*), and the practical ones (*prudence*). We will also have to maintain that the will is more universal than intelligence because it is *the intention of another real,* and these other "reals" are of all kinds—sensible and immaterial—. On the other hand, intelligence lacks ideas on the extra-mental realities that cannot be abstracted. If otherness refers to persons, we talk of *justice*; but if instead of as a mere other, we grasp the other as "another me" we talk of

---

[32] "Omnes actus virtutum sunt de lege naturali, dictat enim hoc naturaliter unicuique propria ratio, ut virtuose agat. Sed si loquamur de actibus virtuosis secundum seipsos, prout scilicet in propriis speciebus considerantur, sic non omnes actus virtuosi sunt de lege naturae", *S. Th.*, I-II, q. 94 a. 3, co

[33] Cf. Cvek, P. P., "Thomas Aquinas, Natural Law, and Environmental Ethics", *Vera Lex*, 1 (2000) 5-18; Haakonssen, K., "Divine/Natural Law Theories in Ethics", D. Garber (ed.), *The Cambridge History of Seventeenth Century Philosophy* (Cambridge University Press, New York, 1998); Hall, P. M., *Narrative and the Natural Law: An Interpretation of Thomistic Ethics*, University of Notre Dame Press, Notre Dame [Indiana], 1994, VII; PETERSON, J., "Natural Law, End, and Virtue in Aquinas", *Journal of Philosophical Research*, 24 (1999) 397-413

[34] I hold that the trascendental good is a theme of *synderesis*; the *being*, is of a superior innate habit, the one of the *first principles*; and *truth*, of the highest innate habit, *wisdom*, in the habit of the first principles.

friendship. Neither justice nor friendship are possible without synderesis, but in friendship the activity of this habit is more fully used than in justice, because synderesis can be described as the *I*.[35]

If synderesis is more fully used in the will than in intelligence, why did Thomas Aquinas (among others) teach that our knowing is superior to our willing? In order to answer this question we have to take up what we pointed out earlier: because over and above the two superior powers, there are innate habits that are cognitive, not volitive (in this sense, the *intellectualism* of Thomas Aquinas can be justified). And the human person is above those habits, as it is also cognitive and, furthermore, loving.

What is human "personal law"?

Human nature is universal, common to all men. Human essence is not so common, because it is a perfecting of human nature. It is clear that this perfecting of humanity is superior in some men and inferior in others, depending on the acquired *habits* and *virtues*. This improvement makes up what are usually called human "types", which group together or describe a group of men under a series of common characteristics. However, each human person is not common to any other, but is a radical *novelty*. That is why "personal law" is each one's truth or personal meaning.

Natural law is of the order of *necessity*. Conversely, personal law is of the order of *freedom*. Essential law is the performance human powers achieve in freedom, especially the superior powers, because of the benefit they give the person. Since it is clear that freedom is superior to necessity, the latter must be subordinated to the former. This subordination does not mean infringement or failure to comply with natural law, but favouring it and personal protection of it. Human ethical action is born from personal *freedom* and serves it. Freedom is a transcendental characteristic of the human *act of being*[36] and, as such, it is the root and the aim of *ethics*, which lies in human *essence*. Since ethics is perfective development of

---

[35] Cf. my paper "En torno a la distinción real entre la persona y el yo en el hombre", in Leonardo Polo, *El yo*, Cuadernos de Anuario Filosófico n° 170 (Pamplona: Servicio de Publicaciones de la Universidad de Navarra, 2004), 13-38. Cf also: Francisco Molina, "El yo y la sindéresis," *Studia Poliana* 3 (2001): 35-60.

[36] Cf. Leonardo Polo, *Antropolotía Trascendental I. La persona humana*, 2nd ed. (Pamplona: Eunsa, 2003), 229f. ———, *La libertad trascendental*, Cuadernos de Anuario Filosófico n° 178 (Pamplona: Servicio de Publicaciones de la Universidad de Navarra, 2005).

natural law, this law must be placed at the service of the human person through ethics, not against ethics.[37] At the service of the human person, what for, if the person is superior to human nature and its essential perfecting? So that the personal freedom that each person is does not come across inconveniencies when each person manifests itself through human nature and essence.

Having said this, if that transcendental, active freedom, on which any later activation of human potential depends, were arbitrary, spontaneous, apart from any direction or sense, libertinage would be justified. Nobody is unaware that our culture is full of exquisite discourses defending freedom, but freedom is rarely subordinated to a superior human instance. These are forms of defending freedom by understanding it on its own. However, a personal freedom apart from the truth or personal meaning that each human person is cannot be truly freedom. It cannot be freedom either if it is separated from the human person as a being that gives itself. In other words: a freedom apart from personal knowing and loving, superior to it and characteristic of each human person, is not personal freedom. Neither is it a coexisting freedom, because personal opening up means opening up in regard to different people.

Conclusion. Personal law as the aim of natural and essential law

Personal freedom is the activity of the spirit, or the human, personal *act of being,* but also of human essence and nature. It is a-thematic, not because it lacks a theme in itself, but because its themes are superior to it and are given; i.e. it finds the themes, it does not invent them. Indeed, its themes are truth or human personal meaning and personal loving. But that personal truth and love do not culminate from within, i.e. they are a project, not a personal invention of one's own. To put it another way: rather than saying they *are*, it is better to say that they *will be*, because while we live we are not fully the loving and knowing person we are called to be. The human person exists as a project. The project is not consummate nor is it possible to consummate it from within itself; neither

[37] Therefore moral laws are not empyrical or indifferent for the human person: "These are laws that, if you like, express a must be, because they are not empyrical laws. But this characteristic of moral norms does not lessen their importance. Although they be breached, ethical norms *oblige*. Because they are obligatory, they exist (by no means are they unreal); they rule the finalisation vector of the non-specifically finalised subject". Polo, *Ética*, 58.

can it be consummated from the other created persons, because none of them fully knows the truth of their being. Nobody is, as a person, an invention in their own hands. The key to their personal meaning resides in the Creator.

If the human person did not exist, human natural law would be an aim in itself. But if it exists, the aim of natural law is its *personalisation* by each person, i.e. its *essentialisation*. The key to the personalisation of natural law in each one lies in the discovery by each person of his or her own personal aim. There are no two alike persons, neither are there alike personal aims. If each person does not discover his aim, he will not know how to conduct himself with his human essence and nature. Contrarily, this best disposition depends on their personalisation adjusting to each person's own personal aim. The complete personal aim of the human person, vocation, is only known by the Creator. Orienting the search for one's own personal meaning towards the Creator is the most adequate method not to lose one's personal meaning, and, with it, human nature and essence.

Works Cited

Aquinas, Thomas. *Summa Theologica* Translated by the Fathers of the English Dominican Province. New York: Benzinger Bros., 1947.

—. *Scriptum super Sententiis magistri Petri Lombardi*, 4 t. Parisis: P. Lethellieux, 1929.

—. *Super Epistolas S. Pauli lectura, t. 1: Super Epistolam ad Romanos lectura*. 8th ed. Taurini-Romae: Marietti, 1953.

Belmans, Theo G. "L'immutabilité de la loi naturelle selon s. Thomas d'Aquin." *Revue Thomiste* (1987): 23-44.

Carpintero Benítez, Francisco. "La mutabilidad de la ley natural en Tomás de Aquino." *Rivista Internazionale di Filosofia del Diritto* 77 (2000): 470-530.

Castaño, Sergio Raúl. "Consideraciones ontológicas sobre la ley natural en Tomás de Aquino." *Sapientia* 54 (1999): 351-6.

Elton, María. "Gnoseología de la ley natural." *Sapientia* 53 (1998): 175-94.

Hall, Richard B. "The Alterability of Natural Law." *The New Scholasticism* 55 (1981): 474-83.

Mesa Posada, Carlos Augusto. *La ley natural en Santo Tomás: fundamentos metafísicos y propiedades* Chía (Colombia): Universidad de La Sabana, 1998.

Molina, Francisco. "El yo y la sindéresis." *Studia Poliana* 3 (2001): 35-60.

Polo, Leonardo. *Antropología trascendental II. La esencia de la persona humana*. Pamplona: Eunsa, 2003.

—. *Antropolotía Trascendental I. La persona humana*. 2nd ed. Pamplona: Eunsa, 2003.

—. *Curso de teoría del conocimiento III*. 2nd ed. Pamplona: Eunsa, 1998.

—. *El orden predicamental*, *Cuadernos de Anuario Filosófico n° 182*. Pamplona: Servicio de Publicaciones de la Universidad de Navarra, 2005.

—. *El yo*, *Cuadernos de Anuario Filosófico n° 170*. Pamplona: Servicio de Publicaciones de la Universidad de Navarra, 2004.

—. *Ética: hacia una versión moderna de temas clásicos*. Madrid: Aedos, 1996.

—. *La libertad trascendental*, *Cuadernos de Anuario Filosófico n° 178*. Pamplona: Servicio de Publicaciones de la Universidad de Navarra, 2005.

Rhonheimer, Martin. *Ley natural y razón práctica. Una visión tomista de la autonomía moral*. Pamplona: Eunsa, 2000.

Rousseau, Felicien. "Loi naturelle et dynamisme de la raison pratique de l'homme." *Laval Théologique et Philosophique* 33 (1976): 165-88.

Sellés, Juan Fernando. "La sindéresis o razón natural como la apertura cognoscitiva de la persona humana a su propia naturaleza. Una propuesta desde Tomás de Aquino." *Revista Española de Filosofía Medieval* 10 (2003): 321-33.

Urabayen, Julia. "La esencia del hombre como disponer indisponible." *Anuario Filosófico* 29, no. 2 (1996).

CHAPTER TWENTY

HEALTH AS A NORM AND PRINCIPLE OF INTELLIGIBILITY

JOSÉ IGNACIO MURILLO

Naturalistic fallacy and knowledge of nature

The notion of natural law is not an uncontested one in the history of Western thought. Various philosophical traditions and other currents of opinion raise difficulties and objections against it, or respond to premises that overtly contradict the possibility of its existence.

Ricoeur's position offers an illustration of these difficulties; in *The problem of the foundation of moral philosophy*,[1] he describes this concept as a monstrous idea because it seems to mistake a law of reason for a law of nature. Nonetheless, he is willing to accept it as a limit concept, which can work in three different ways. Firstly, natural law may be invoked as a means of avoiding the identification of moral and positive law. Secondly, in more radical terms, this invocation may be a rejection of convention. Thirdly, the reference to a natural law may imply an attempt to derive the law which governs the life of man from simple knowledge of his nature.

Ricoeur considers the two first ways of speaking of a natural law to be legitimate, although he prefers the first to the second; the third, he regards, on the other hand, as extremely suspicious. "I have many more reservations—he says—when one wants to make the concept of natural law depend on a biological, affective nature; consequently, on anthropological constants that do not appear to me to be discoverable. We do not know for certain what a human being would be exclusive of any and all institutions. Every recourse to a pre-institutional stage can only be deceptive (*un trompe l'oeil*). For what is there about an institution that is

[1] Paul Ricoeur, "The problem of the foundation of moral philosophy," *Philosophy today* 22 (1978): 175-92.

natural? A sort of degradation seems to affect the concept of a natural law when this limit concept moves beyond its functions of protest and of refuge. The limit concept then becomes a screen concept behind which one conceals oneself in order to elude the hazards and the risks of the genesis of meaning that proceeds from freedom's positing of itself, and from the recognition of the other person and the mediation of institutions."[2]

Ricoeur's refusal to accept the invocation of a natural law as anything other than a protest, that is, his rejection of natural law as a criterion from which we may derive positive moral guidelines, is one example among others of a conviction that is widely held in many sectors of our culture: the acceptance of the validity of the accusation referred to as the naturalistic fallacy, in which to move from *being* to *ought to be* is rejected as illegitimate. The classic text where Hume formulates this difficulty is worth recalling in this context:

> In every system of morality, which I have hitherto met with, I have always remark'd, that the author proceeds for some time in the ordinary way of reasoning, and establishes the being of a God, or makes observations concerning human affairs; when of a sudden I am surpriz'd to find, that instead of the usual copulations of propositions, *is*, and *is not*, I meet with no proposition that is not connected with an *ought*, or an *ought not*. This change is imperceptible; but is, however, of the last consequence. For as this *ought*, or *ought not*, expresses some new relation or affirmation, 'tis necessary that it shou'd be observ'd and explain'd; and at the same time that a reason should be given, for what seems altogether inconceivable, how this new relation can be a deduction from others, which are entirely different from it. But as authors do not commonly use this precaution, I shall presume to recommend it to the readers; and am persuaded, that this small attention wou'd subvert all the vulgar systems of morality, and let us see, that the distinction of vice and virtue is not founded merely on the relations of objects, nor is perceiv'd by reason.[3]

It is difficult to deny the force of this observation, which is clearly reflected in its influence throughout history: few thinkers have been able to escape its seductive power. Indeed, it seems as though Hume's argument must be conceded: that no moral command may be deduced from an objective account of reality. The fact that things are in a certain way does not in itself impose any obligation. Even when a description

---

[2] Ibid.: 189.

[3] David Hume, *A Treatise of Human Nature* (Aalen: Scientia Verlag, 1964)., Book III, Section I, Part I, 245-246.

refers to the desires or inclinations of a being, it is not sufficient to impose on us a norm of conduct invested with the unconditional status of a moral duty. In fact, to know what someone or something desires or is prone to do cannot ground a real obligation in an immediate way.

If it is true that any description of reality is deprived of moral power because all knowledge of reality consists of a neutral account of facts, then the moral must defer to a source independent of knowledge which can account for the fact that a person feels an unconditional call to act in a certain way. For Hume, feeling is that source, which is, therefore, divested of any cognitive value. Kant finds it in the *Faktum* of duty, which, when it is perceived, grants us the conviction that we are free, that is, that we can emancipate ourselves from the laws of nature and establish our own law for ourselves. For Kant, moral law is related neither to the nature of beings—where nature is understood as what things are or, at least, the way in which they appear to our knowledge—nor to science, which Kant regards as incapable of providing us with real knowledge of things—but to an experience which, although it is useful in so far as it legitimates our conviction of being free agents, is not in itself the knowledge of anything. Thus, Kant likewise attributes the specific tendency of moral law to a source independent of knowledge of reality. Nor is moral law related to knowledge of reality in the text from Ricoeur cited above; rather, the moral responds to something which seems to be contributed from without: the self-affirmation of freedom and the recognition of the other, which entail, in themselves, a moral demand.

That the rift opened by Hume between knowledge of nature and the moral provokes a certain unease should come as no surprise. This rift seems to preclude the perception of reality as endowed with a moral dimension, and thus prompts the conclusion that such value must be added to our knowledge in one way or another through our subjectivity. In other words, it seems impossible to account for any mediation between our knowledge of the things around us and our obligations in their regard.

If knowledge of things is insufficient to compel us to act, more surprising still is the notion that not even what we know about ourselves can do so. According to this position, and running counter to the whole tradition of wisdom, which underscores the importance of self-knowledge in leading a good life, even knowing who and what I am has no moral relevance.

Having reached a point, therefore, where anthropology and ethics inevitably diverge, it is worth asking whether the conception of knowledge of reality deferred to by this position encompasses all human knowledge, or whether a closer connection between knowledge and moral experience might be discerned in some field.

Science of nature and knowledge of the *télos*

One way to avoid the radical consequences of Hume's position is to claim that it is only valid for one form of knowledge: experimental science. Hence, for example, it is possible to say that the scientific description of reality only takes account of efficient causes, and that, consequently, it is blind to finality, which is the notion that allows us to speak of good and evil, and thus of duty.

According to Kant, this is what occurs in Mechanics, the paradigm of the objective sciences. Mechanics explains everything in terms of causes which do not cause movement in accordance with an end; rather, they comprise the cause of the movement of bodies; this kind of cause is referred to as "force". The notion of force is, in itself, alien to duty. There are stronger or weaker forces, which can be quantified, but, as Nietzsche pointed out, all of them are alien to the moral: they are a mere *factum* from which it is impossible to derive a truly binding norm.

However, the following question arises in this context: is a scientific explanation of reality nothing more than a formulation of efficient causes? Although it is true that the efficient cause is the only type of cause for which Newtonian Mechanics seems able to account—or, to be more precise, a reduced version of it, in combination with inert matter—I am not convinced that knowledge of this type of cause is the defining achievement of this form of science. In my opinion, there is another way of determining the boundaries of Newtonian science. I think that it is more accurate to claim that what Mechanics and related sciences obtain and formulate are the laws which govern the behaviour of a certain kind of beings, laws through which, given some initial conditions, future behaviour may be possible to foresee. The formulation of such laws is the primary objective of this form of science; moreover, a causal explanation has scientific meaning in Mechanics only in this context.

The value of this sort of objectification lies to a significant extent in the possibility of expressing the laws discovered in mathematical terms. Mathematics is of such importance in field of Mechanics that it conditions the object of that science. Thus, Mechanics must frame bodies in line with the possibility of accounting for them in a schema of mathematical objectification. The work of Mechanics is based on the abstract models made possible by Mathematics. This explains why, for example, matter is reduced to mass—that is, a quantifiable magnitude—; space must be homogeneous, because only thus can it be accurately measured; and force allows only of quantitative, not qualitative, differences.

To speak of what is good in this context makes no sense; the old saying, *mathematica non sunt bona*, is pertinent here. Good and evil are not encompassed by the mathematical approach because it objectifies the relations between thought objects (*logos*) without addressing their reality outside the mind. For this reason, Mathematics, as Aristotle reproached Plato,[4] is not capable of explaining movement; it can measure movement, but, in doing so, is unable to account for or explain it as such because all mathematical objects, being mere ideas, cannot be anything other than fixed and motionless. Reality appears in an abstract way in these objectifications, or—to express the same idea in metaphorical terms—in a dissected way: that is, alien to the way in which it really exists.

This form of objective description, which is paradigmatic in Mechanics, may be applied to almost every field of knowledge. At the same time, this kind of objectivity is characteristic of any description that might be referred to as objective or dispassionate. The most terrible crime may be described as though it were merely an act of nature, and the description need not imply any judgement on the acts or agents involved. This approach may also be adopted in the study of history or culture, and is a common strategy in the description of social phenomena in the field of sociology, for example.

If this approach is the only possible way of doing science, Hume's position may be conceded: the valuation or enunciation of duties is absolutely alien to science. Values such as good and evil, moral duty, etc. are not objects; thus, a merely theoretical knowledge cannot encompass them. As has already been mentioned above, Hume himself was aware of this problem and turned to feeling in his search for the source of morality. Although Kant followed in his footsteps, he fled from the danger that this attitude might involve the loss of the unconditional nature of the experience of duty and was forced to locate the origin of the moral in a source that was entirely independent of scientific knowledge. This problem recurs in Scheler's work, where a separate faculty capable of grasping value, distinct from knowledge and the will, is proposed. In the account of the laws of nature as regularities without value offered by Ricoeur to establish normative principles, he too appears to understand the law in the same sense as empirical science.

---

[4] Cfr. Aristotle, *Metaphysics*, I, 9, 980 a 33- 983 a 27; XII, 4-5, 1078 b 7- 1080 a 11.

However, must it be concluded that to speak of good and evil, especially in an absolute sense, always lies beyond the limits of scientific language? And if this conclusion is accepted as inevitable, does this limitation also apply in the case of metaphysics, which would be reduced as a result to describing reality without any reference to finality and therefore without any kind of valuation?

Kant himself acknowledged some difficulties in relation to this position, especially with regard to a specific scientific question: the study of living beings. For Kant, finality is a province open only to rational beings, who can act in line with an objective representation, i.e. an end. This accounts for technical competence, and is concerned above all with the moral. Nonetheless, apart from man, there is another field of being which can neither be understood nor explained using merely mathematical models: organic being, that is, the realm of life.

> No one has doubted the correctness of the fundamental principle that certain things in nature (organized beings) and their possibility must be judged in accordance with the concept of final causes, even if one requires only a **guideline** for coming to know their constitution through observation without rising to the level of an investigation into their ultimate origin.[5]

Kant is perfectly aware that life cannot be accounted for without reference to finality. The study of a living being discloses the parts of which it is composed; these may only be understood as such in relation to the whole of which they are part. The observation is a significant one; indeed, its significance is increased by the fact that is made by someone who regards logic, mathematics and mechanics as paradigmatic of science. Nevertheless, Kant goes on to comment:

> The question can thus be only whether this fundamental principle is merely subjectively valid, i.e., merely a maxim of our power of judgement, or is an objective principle of nature, according to which there would pertain to it, in addition to its mechanism (in accordance with mere laws of motion) yet another kind of causality, namely that of final causes, under which the first kind (that of moving forces) would stand only as intermediate causes.[6]

What response can be made to Kant's statement? Even at the risk of passing too severe a judgement on his work, Kant's a priori commitment

---

[5] I. Kant, *Critique of the Power of Judgement* (Cambridge: Cambridge University Press, 2000), § 72.

[6] Ibid.

to the sciences of his time should be noted. There are, he thinks, only three true sciences—Logic, Mathematics and Mechanics—and only their existence may be accounted for. If that is the case, however, Biology may only be regarded as a science if it is integrated into another true science, such as Mechanics.

Kant is aware that a living being cannot be wholly understood from the point of view of Mechanics. Thus, he is compelled to accept a type of judgement different to what is characteristic of the sciences detailed above. In fact, a living object may only be addressed on the assumption that it was—*as if it were*—produced according to an end. According to Kant, living beings must be regarded as a product of a technique of nature, which does not necessarily entail that its causes were oriented towards a known end. Kant holds that this reservation allows for the possibility of understanding living beings without, at the same time, giving credence to the objective meaning of finality.

To define a problem—how to understand a living being as such—may be a significant contribution in itself, but it is not clear that Kant is able to solve it. In fact, his position falls short because the finality discerned in living beings is not exactly as Kant says it is; nor is it enough to accept finality only in a hypothetical way in order to understand a living being.

On the one hand, as we have seen, Kant accepts that living beings seem to presuppose finality only because they appear to be designed according to a plan. They are machines—very special machines, perhaps, but nothing more—.

On the other, however, finality imbues living beings in such a radical and primary way that it precludes their description as machines produced by some technique. In fact, they are not produced, but generated, which means they never emerge as the result of an activity directed to produce them. At best, it might be possible to accept that a living being might be generated at some point in the future (in the sense that, for instance, it might be possible to establish the conditions in which a very simple unicellular organism could be generated). Nevertheless, that cannot contradict the fact that there is always a discontinuity—a gap—between the emergence of a living being and the process which leads to its appearance. The living being takes care of itself, so to speak, and establishes from itself the rules of its exchange with the environment. In other words, the appearance of a living being allows of only two possible responses: to help it to achieve its goals, or to frustrate them.

Given the distinctive quality of living being, the concept of *nature* should be used in a very qualified sense. Nature may be defined in this context as *the condition of being well or unwell*. To hold that living beings are susceptible to good and evil is to acknowledge the fact that they cannot be understood without reference to an end towards which they themselves, and not only their supposed 'producers', are oriented. The novelty of this position—which is, nonetheless, part of ordinary, prereflexive knowledge—is that even the most elemental and least sensitive living beings are endowed with the power to move themselves towards an internal end, an attribute that most philosophers in the Modern period ascribe only to free subjectivity.

Orientation towards an end prompts consideration of the concept of health, as used in the biological sciences. In line with the argument outlined above, health and illness are two clear consequences of the specific way in which living beings are natural. Strictly speaking, the same cannot be said of minerals or stars, except by analogy to the reality of animals and plants.

However, health and illness are not two equivalent possibilities open to a living being. Thus, to understand a living being as such is not simply to understand it in terms of susceptibility to health and illness (i.e. good and evil), but also to understand the features of the healthy specimen.[7] Moreover, *pace* Kant, the acknowledgement of this finality cannot be merely hypothetical. It is not enough to understand life *as if* it had an internal end: living being may only be grasped if the existence of that end as a present and operative possibility is affirmed.

In addition to its status as a normative ideal, health may also be regarded as a principle of intelligibility of living beings. This approach is confirmed by practice in the field of biology, which takes the healthy specimen as its starting-point. Thus, to return to the discussion in the introduction to this paper, the 'illegitimate' movement from the description of facts (the use of the verb *is*) to the statement of norms (the use of *ought to* forms) is overcome in the realm of life when the living being is recognized as such.

The phrase "when the living being is recognized as such" alludes to something more than knowledge. There are two kinds of recognition. There is the form of recognition that involves recognizing that we are dealing with a living being, which encompasses no moral demand. The second form of recognition, however, does encompass the acceptance of laws imposed by reality from without on the sphere of action. Even in

---

[7] "For what each thing is when fully developed, we call its nature, whether we are speaking of a man, a horse, or a family. Besides, the final cause and end of a thing is its best, and to be self-sufficing is the end and the best". Aristotle, *Politics*, I, 2 (1252a32-35).

acknowledging what is good or bad for an animal, we may treat it simply as a means to our own ends; to recognise that the animal has its own ends (without which it would not be possible to understand it as an animal), to make those ends our own, and to respect them to a certain extent calls for a different type of response.

Only something which has its own proper ends can be respected. However, not all alien ends appear to be inherently worthy of respect. The defining feature of the moral is its unconditional nature. Therefore, the attempt to overcome the naturalistic fallacy by showing that living being cannot be wholly understood without reference to the category of health is not a complete solution to the problem which the fallacy argument decries. However, the category of health limits the extent of the problem by clarifying that knowledge of some aspects of reality requires reference to an intrinsic norm. Thus, the abyss between knowledge and the moral opened in the argument articulated by Hume is narrowed.

Nevertheless, further reflection on knowledge of man is required for a more complete response to the question of the moral.

What is a healthy man?

The importance of health in biology prompts a further question in relation to man. If man is regarded as a living being, he cannot be understood as such without reference to the category of health. However, to determine what constitutes a healthy individual is much more complex in this context because human health resists easy explanation.

The first difficulty lies in the distinction usually made between health, understood as something relating only to biology, and another form of "health", concerning a more "inner" perfection or excellence, which cannot be reduced to the former. This latter perfection is generally understood as being dependent on the free action of each individual and as superior to the organic and sensitive life common to animals as well as human beings. In other words, health, in this second sense, pertains to the moral sphere. According to this distinction, a man may be well in two different and even separable ways. He can be healthy to the degree that he enjoys his natural faculties to perfection, and which reveals him to be similar to other animals; but he can also be well or perfect to the extent that he freely fulfils what he is called to be. This is moral health, which is often referred to as "spiritual health" irrespective of different ontological conceptions of the human spirit. In other words, man can be well and be good.

The existence of these two kinds of perfection highlights the difficulty involved in understanding human being. The same adjective, "human", is used in two different ways. On the one hand, this term, as in the case of other animals, denotes man as a member of a species and is used to describe all the manifestations of that species. On the other, more surprisingly, the word "inhuman" is sometimes used to describe man's behaviour: in some instances, even though he is not ill and his action responds to his specific capacities, man may behave in ways unworthy of his nature and dignity.

A similar phenomenon may be observed in relation to the word "health". Health is the only concept available to describe the perfection of an animal as such. The perfection of a police-dog or a race-horse may of course be spoken about in different terms, but these descriptions defer to ends externally attributed to them, and not included in their nature in itself. "Second-level perfection" may only be attributed to man, not to animals, because it does not refer to nature as given, but to what men have done, to what men do on the basis of their nature.

If this distinctive feature of human being is not merely an intellectual phantom, it poses an epistemological problem. If animals may only be understood by reference to healthy specimens, can biological health alone yield an adequate understanding of what man is?

One possible response is: yes. Thus, there is no essential perfection to be attributed to man beyond his perfection as a biological organism. Any real disorder, therefore, is to be defined as an illness: there is no such thing as inhuman behaviour, strictly speaking, only pathological conduct.

However, this response is complicated by the difficulty involved in defining the meaning of health. The problem of two meanings of perfection is transferred to the concept of health, confusing its sense. This happens in a particular way in the realm of mental disease. Unsatisfactory behaviour is so common that every man might be regarded as an example of one who is ill. As a result, man might be described as an aberration of nature, a merely provisional outcome of evolution; or, if this position is rejected, all man's problems might be attributed to external causes, the influence of civilization, for example, a habitat inhospitable to the characteristics human nature has developed over the course of evolution.

If man is regarded as an aberration of nature, the concept of health must be dispensed with, or, at least, distinguished from the concept of natural perfection, if he is to be understood. An intrinsically erroneous being cannot attain perfection; thus, man may aspire only to an improper form of perfection: the achievement of a state of wellbeing or of ways to mitigate the discomfort inherent in the human condition. In this context, to understand human being is not to understand human nature, but to understand the flaws in man's design; and to know man is simply to describe his behaviour in practice, thus renouncing any claim to a true science of man which might provide him with an appropriate guide to action. From an epistemological point of view, to describe man as an intrinsically imperfect being is to announce the death of man. The difficulty involved in striking a natural balance may prompt man to resign himself to never achieving it, or even to believe that such balance is impossible.

However, human consciousness instinctively rejects this position. The claim that a living being is nothing more than an agglomeration of matter may be made, but man cannot ignore his inner perspective, according to which he is alive and cannot act without aspiring to fulfilment. Moreover, some reference to the self-consciousness of man seems necessary for an adequate understanding of the conception of nature used in biology—albeit in an implicit way—.[8] When a living being is understood as being endowed with certain natural inclinations, man attributes to it, on the basis of its behaviour, something similar to what he knows about himself. This is not anthropomorphism, although it may give rise to it; rather, it is a consequence of the fact that interiority and desire in another person or in an animal can be understood only to the extent that interiority is accessible to the self. Thus, the poverty of the notion of biological health as a category in which a rounded understanding of man might be articulated lends weight to the thesis that there are two meanings of health or human perfection. Nevertheless, this claim may take different forms depending on the way the relation between both is construed.

The idea that there is no connection whatsoever between the two meanings of health, i.e. that human perfection is only a result of freedom and includes no reference to man's perfection as a living being, gives rise to anthropological dualism. This point of view is reflected in some way in the position articulated by Plato, who claims that body and soul have two different natures accidentally bound together.

If, on the other hand, man is held to be a single living being, with a single nature, the relationship between the two types of perfection becomes difficult to explain. One attempt to resolve the problem of the unity of human nature might be to follow the line of argument set out by

---

[8] Cfr. H. Jonas, *El principio vida. Hacia una biología filosófica* (Madrid: Trotta, 2000), 43-59. English version: *The phenomenon of life: toward a philosophical biology,* Northwestern University Press, Evanston (Illinois) 2001.

Aristotle: health is a part of human perfection.[9] Aristotle, however, in accordance with Socratic thought, attributes man's success or failure primarily to the activity which he freely undertakes. In this view, spiritual health is more important than physical health, and the human being may only be destroyed through freely undertaken, improper activity.[10]

Health, happiness and Anthropology

For Aristotle, man's success or failure is linked to the idea of happiness. To speak of happiness in relation to non-human animals is difficult. The correct term might be satisfaction: given that happiness encompasses an understanding of one's life as a whole,[11] of which animals are incapable, happiness cannot be used to describe their state.

The notion of health is connected to the notion of happiness because the latter also connotes perfection, although it adds to it the conscious enjoyment of one's own possibilities and possession of goods without which nature may be healthy and complete but frustrated. The happy man is one who can attain all the goods due to him, and has in fact done so, at least to a certain extent; his life may be said to be fully developed.

The distinction between the notion of health and that of happiness consists in the fact that the healthy man is not necessarily in possession of every good that he desires. Being healthy is not necessarily the same as feeling at ease; one can be healthy in a situation of anxiety or frustration due to external causes. In such cases, health involves, among other things, the capacity to perceive the situation correctly, even if it is painful or distressing, and to react in an adequate way. However, although health is not the same as happiness, perfect happiness encompasses health and does not gainsay it; as the disposition which allows for man's specific activity in accordance with his nature, health is the condition by which the goods that man obtains may be enjoyed. Not only is health a good in itself, it is also a prerequisite for unobstructed action and full enjoyment of what is good. Nobody may be regarded as happy simply because he enjoys good health, but total and perfect happiness includes health.

Fullness of life cannot be equated with health in the case of animals. The idea of fullness of life cannot have practical meaning in the life of an animal; an animal is incapable of acting in the light of an understanding of its own life as a whole. In any case, health is presupposed by any

[9] Aristotle, *Nicomachean Ethics*., I, 8, 1199a25-33; X, 8, 1178b34-36.
[10] "It is better suffering injustice that provoking it". Plato, *Gorgias*, 473a.
[11] Aristotle, *Nicomachean Ethics*., I, 10, 1101a14-21.

definition of fullness of life that might be applied to an animal. It appears that there is no need to define what fullness of life for a dog might be—difficult task in itself—in order to understand the dog for what it is; however, there can be no understanding of the dog as it is without some knowledge of what a healthy dog is.

Thus, the idea that most closely parallels the notion of health in the spiritual order is “virtue”. Virtue is not natural in the same way as health. One may be virtuous or not—and that depends mainly on the way one behaves—. Nevertheless, virtue is natural in the sense that it is the fulfilment of natural possibilities. In fact, nature is to a certain extent a norm for virtue, because the real good of a natural being cannot be attained at the expense of its own destruction, but only by encompassing its aspirations and fulfilling them intrinsically. This is, moreover, the classical definition of virtue.[12]

Another difference between virtue and health lies in the fact that, while biological health appears to be limited, there are conceptions of virtue, such as that in the Christian tradition, which affirm that it is always possible to be more virtuous and deny that man may arrive at definitive fulfilment of virtue in his temporal and mortal state.

In any case, and returning to the argument outlined above, if man cannot be understood without reference to his perfection, and it is agreed that there is a more important and decisive type of health than the merely biological, it follows that no anthropology may be developed independently of an idea of fullness of life.

However, these observations prompt further questions. Biology draws on its analysis of healthy specimens: is it possible to carry out the study of anthropology without making reference to virtuous men? This question, in turn, prompts another, classical concern: can anthropology and ethics be separated? There is a further concern in this regard, above all for the purposes of the objective and supposedly neutral project of modern science: where is the healthy man in this second and more inner way, and what qualities may he have? Moreover, is a hypothetical or ideal model of life sufficient to ground anthropological study, or must such study be based on real life?

Saint Augustine takes as read the existence of a certain previous knowledge about the moral perfection of man in his claim that the mind is understood not by the examination of many minds, but by considering the

[12] Ibid., I, 12, 1102a4ff.

mind in the light of eternal reasons.[13] If everything that is experienced is imperfect, it is difficult to establish in a clear and meaningful way what perfection is; above all, it would be impossible to know whether such perfection may really exist or not.

However, the possibility of achieving such perfection is called into question if this normative knowledge is nothing more than an ideal. It is difficult to accept that a totally unattainable model could move one to aspire to it, even more so given that the attempt to do so might require considerable effort. The conviction that moral goodness is desirable and attainable would appear to be in some way a property of the character of the good man; however, the moral failures of many human beings may cast doubt on this position.

Perhaps this is the reason why anthropology and ethics emerged as scientific (i.e. philosophical) disciplines at the same time, and, from the beginning, drew on the conviction that there is a human model which has real basis.[14] That the schools of thought in anthropology and ethics in ancient times hinge on the work of a number of key figures, especially Socrates, should be noted; but others have followed in their footsteps, with the intention of building on past achievements in this field.[15]

In Christian thought, the notion of personal health is understood in a similar way, although a more nuanced approach is taken. Balanced perfection cannot be fully reached in this life, there can be no complete integration of animal and spiritual health in man, because human nature, affected by sin, is condemned to death, and this mortality, which will not be overcome until the resurrection of the body, entails a degree of incoherence between the two dimensions of man. Nevertheless, Christian anthropology is based on a human model: not only that of Adam, which is

---

[13] "Neque enim oculis corporeis multas mentes videndo, per similitudinem colligimus generalem vel specialem mentis humanae notitiam; sed intuemur inviolabilem veritatem, ex qua perfecte, quantum possumus, definiamus, non qualis sit uniuscuiusque hominis mens, sed qualis esse sempiternis rationibus debeat". *De Trinitate*, IX, 6, 9.

[14] Aristotle is not slow to propose the good man as a criterion of moral goodness: "If this view is right, as it seems to be, and virtue – that is, the good person in so far as he is good – is the measure of each thing, then pleasures will be what appear so to him, and pleasant things will be what he enjoys". Aristotle, *Nicomachean Ethics.*, X, cap. 5 (1176 a 3-1176 a 30), 192. Thus, for Aristotle, the good is more intelligible in the life of the good man than in its reflection in the conscience of one who aspires to goodness.

[15] Cfr. Pierre Hadot, *Qu'est-ce que la philosophie antique?* (Paris: Gallimard, 1996).

beyond us (and relatively unknown), but that of Christ, without whom it is impossible to understand the Christian view of man. In addition, the lives of the saints provide public example of the attempt to put the ideal into practice.

It is clear that the problem of moral health as a guide for action raises new questions that should be dealt with in a considered way. The aim of this paper is not to resolve all the difficulties that arise in the context of the problem it describes, but to point to the fact that the problem must be addressed. The best way to conclude, then, might be offer an overview of the argument that has led to this conclusion in order to frame further discussion. As has been noted, the clear distinction between the scientific description of reality and moral obligation, proposed by Hume and accepted by later thinkers, cannot be applied to knowledge of life. To understand a living being as such, its nature, the criterion of good and evil in its regard, must be acknowledged. Thus, animals are to be understood on the basis of what is known of healthy or fully developed specimens. The problem of defining what constitutes a 'healthy individual' arises in relation to man as a living being, a problem that encompasses moral as well as biological concerns because human perfection connotes man's freedom. In any case, if perfection is a necessary criterion for understanding man as a living being, genuine anthropology must be underwritten by some reference to an exemplary moral norm.

The old conception of natural law, therefore, might also be said to depend on the position adopted in light of what is regarded as the nature and the good of man, and in what way the notion of health may be applied to him.

Works Cited

Aristotle. *Nicomachean Ethics*. Cambridge: Cambridge University Press, 2000.

Hadot, Pierre. *Qu'est-Ce Que La Philosophie Antique?* Paris: Gallimard, 1996.

Hume, David. *A Treatise of Human Nature*. Aalen: Scientia Verlag, 1964.

Jonas, Hans. *El principio vida. Hacia una biología filosófica*. Madrid: Trotta, 2000.

Kant, I. *Critique of the Power of Judgement*. Cambridge: Cambridge University Press, 2000.

Ricoeur, Paul. "The Problem of the Foundation of Moral Philosophy." *Philosophy today*, no. 22 (1978): 175-92.

PART IV:

JURIDICAL APPROACHES

CHAPTER TWENTY ONE

PRACTICAL REASON, MORALITY AND LAW

ANGELA APARISI MIRALLES

1. Theoretical reason and practical reason.

Aristotle clearly demonstrated that the first division of knowledge is that which differentiates it into speculative (or theoretical), and practical.[1] As a result, there are the theoretical or speculative sciences, and the practical sciences. This division, in turn, corresponds to the differentiation that can be established in the activity of human knowledge: we find a speculative or theoretical reason, and a practical reason. The distinction is based on the end or purpose we have in knowing. We can exercise our reason in order to reach the contemplation and comprehension of the truth, or according to action and behaviour itself. Theoretical reason is speculative reason, which seeks knowledge for its own sake, knowledge in itself. Practical reason does not only deal with grasping the truth, but also directing human action according to that known truth.[2] It is for this reason that the aim of practical reason is the orientation of human life in the development of its many facets.

This does not mean, however, that although the intellectual dynamism is different, practical understanding and speculative understanding are two separate faculties. On the contrary, they are one and the same. As Aristotle pointed out, "speculative understanding becomes practical by extension".[3] In the words of Thomas Aquinas, "practical intellect knows truth, just as

---

[1] Aristotle, *De Anima*. III, q. 9, 432 a. 15, cit. in José M. Martínez Doral, *La estructura del conocimiento jurídico* (Pamplona: Universidad de Navarra, 1963), 13.

[2] See Martínez Doral, *La estructura del conocimiento jurídico*, 13f.

[3] Aristotle, *De Anima*. III, q. 10, no. 2, 433 a. 14, in Martínez Doral, *La estructura del conocimiento jurídico*.

the speculative, but it directs the known truth to operation".[4] In this way does Martínez Doral indicate that speculative understanding knows the truth and knows it as theoretical, but if it is oriented to action or to acting, such theoretical reason becomes practical.[5]

1.1. Theoretical reason and legal positivism

In accordance with the aforementioned, legal reasoning as well as morality are logically in the sphere of practical reason. Up until a few years ago, modern mentality and its predominant model of science have blurred this reality. Such mindset tended to place both in the field of theoretical reason, which impeded the adequate comprehension of their nature.[6]

As regards law, detaching legal reasoning (in agreement with the modern parameters of science) from human experience, and requiring absolute geometric exactitude in its conclusions, inevitably led to legal positivism. Actually, this conception would be the result of translating the assumptions of the modern model of science to the very science of law. According to Ballesteros, formalist legal positivism is, to a great extent, the expression of the inferiority complex of law in the face of modern science.[7] Because of this, it will be born out of the attempt to convert its study into an authentic "science" that possesses characteristics proper to new science: permanence, accuracy, universality, etc. The "scientific-ness" or validity of legal knowledge becomes a central question. Based on this, and since what characterises scientific knowledge is precisely that it can be appraised, so it would be with law: if it is to be a science, according to modern parameters, value judgments would have to be excluded.[8] Legal

---

[4] Aquinas, *S. Th.* I, q. 79, a. 11 c.

[5] Martínez Doral, *La estructura del conocimiento jurídico*, 14.

[6] It is interesting to note that modern mentality also changed the way of understanding mathematics for example. For the Greeks, mathematics were relationships existing in reality. Its study revealed the existence of a cosmic order. However, the modern view altered this relation in considering them as constructs of the human mind. So, from Hobbes, the idea of God is lost and the creation of mathematics is exclusively attributed to the human being. (See Jesús Ballesteros, *Sobre el sentido del Derecho: introducción a la filosofía jurídica*, 3rd ed. (Madrid: Tecnos, 2002), 23-24.

[7] Ibid., 19.

[8] See Ángela Aparisi Miralles, "Introducción al concepto de Derecho," in *Introducción a la teoría del Derecho*, ed. Javier De Lucas (Valencia: Tirant lo Blanch, 1994), 33-34.

science, if it is to properly be called science, should refrain from all valuation, as this would precisely be the distinctive seal of scientific knowledge.[9]

As has been previously stated, this led to the presumption neutrality or "valuative asepsis" in the jurist. It is understood therefore that the function of the legal operator does consist of carrying out practical reasoning, but of "describing" and mechanically applying the legality currently in force. In principle, the possibility of the existence of a moral objective cannot be denied. What is being affirmed here is that the work of the jurist, understood as an automatic and self-enclosed process, should avoid any element not strictly positive and descriptive. In short, we are facing an attempt to radically distinguish between law and morality.

As a matter of fact, one of the fundamental postulates of legal positivism is precisely the mentioned demand for separation between law that "is" and law that "should be," between law and morality, with the consequent relegation of the latter to the merely subjective or relative. In this respect, Austin claims, "the existence of law is one thing, its merit or demerit is another."[10] Along this line, Kelsen states:

> Pure theory of law is a theory of positive law. As far as theory (...) it seeks to answer the following question: 'What is law and what is law like?' It is not interested in posing the question around how it should be, according to what criterion must be constructed. It is legal science, not politics of law.[11]

Indeed, while the law represents the objective rule, morality would be nothing more than a subjective authority, and therefore, relative. Just as what happened to philosophy, ethics would be affected by a profound inferiority complex. This conception is closely connected to the ethical emotivism of the empiricists, which reduces morality to a question of taste, a pure subjectivity. Moral principles only express emotions or sentiments, with the intention of influencing the persons involved. As MacIntyre highlighted, as no criteria exists in order to determine what is best, or the least worst, valuative disagreements would be unending.[12]

---

[9] See Ballesteros, *Sobre el sentido del Derecho*, 19f.

[10] Austin, J., *The Province of Jurisprudence Defined*, conf. 5, cit. in H. L. A. Hart, *El concepto de Derecho*, trans. G. Carrió (Buenos Aires: Abeledo-Perrot, 1968), 256.

———, *The Concept of Law* (Oxford: Clarendon Press, 1967).

[11] Hans Kelsen, *La Teoría Pura del Derecho*, trans. L. Legaz y Lacambra (Madrid: Revista de Derecho Privado, 1933), 9.

[12] Alasdir MacIntyre, *After Virtue* (London: Duckworth, 1985), 6f.

Having established these premises, it seems clear that the recovery or "rehabilitation of practical philosophy"[13] that has been taking place mainly in Germany and the USA during the last decades,[14] supposes a reorientation that allows for the establishment of the bases for overcoming the narrow limitations of the positivist method, of positivism itself, and its consequences on the field of ethics and law. Presently, the area of theory of justice also warns of the existence of trends that do not renounce a rational basis, appealing to reasons rather than to emotional questions.[15] This has resulted in a better understanding of the reality of what is moral.[16] This way, it can be noted that perhaps one of the characteristics of current philosophy is the attention paid to human action and its intentional character. This implies a break from the modern way of thinking, since it is impossible to deal with the study of the same resorting only to causal and mechanist assumptions.

2. Practical reason, morality, and law

Practical reason is as opposed to exact reason as it is to arbitrary will. It allows for a search for the truth, which has to be found, and applied, taking into account the circumstances of concrete cases, of reality. Consequently, the most characteristic feature of this knowledge is its "situational" character, although by no means relative. Practical reason applies the first principles to specific and unrepeatable circumstances of reality. It deals with "operables"[17] that have not yet been carried out, such as human actions. For this reason, although its first principles apply to all men (absolutely universal precepts), the more particular it gets the more

---

[13] See Manfred Riedel, ed., *Rehabilitierung der praktischen Philosophie* (Freiburg: Rombach, 1972-1974). Claudio Pacchiani, ed., *Filosofia pratica e scienza politica* (Abano Terme: Francisci, 1980).
[14] See more on this topic: Ballesteros, *Sobre el sentido del Derecho*, 79f. We could cite as representatives of this movement, among others, Joachim Ritther, *"Naturrecht" bei Aristoteles : zum problem einer Erneuerung des Naturrechts* (Stuttgart: W. Kohlhammer, 1961). Robert Spaemann, *Zur Kritik der politischen Utopie* (Stuttgart: Klett-Cotta, 1977). Arendt, *The Human Condition.* Finnis, *Natural Law and Natural Rights.* Et al.
[15] See María Gascón, "Consideraciones sobre el objeto de la filosofía jurídica," *Anuario de Filosofía del Derecho* X (1993): 214.
[16] See Ballesteros, *Sobre el sentido del Derecho*, 77. Ludwig Wittgenstein, *Philosophische Untersuchungen* (Frankfurt: Suhrkamp, 1970).
[17] See Martínez Doral, *La estructura del conocimiento jurídico*, 15.

exceptions we find (relatively universal precepts).[18] In this sense, and with respect to natural law, Thomas Aquinas establishes:

> …natural law, as regards the universal first principles, is the same for all men... as regards certain particular precepts, which are like conclusions derived from universal principles, is also the same... in most cases; but exceptions can happen... be it due to the degree of knowledge, due to the fact that some have their reason clouded by passion, because of a bad habit, or because of a naturally twisted disposition.[19]

With reference to legal reasoning, Thomas Aquinas uses the example of the contract of deposit. Certainly, this type of contract generates, in general, the obligation to return the object deposited to its owner. Nevertheless, this principle is not absolute, since there can be exceptions. For instance, if the object deposited is a weapon and its return could involve serious danger. In his words:

> (...) the proper conclusions of the practical reason, neither is the truth or rectitude the same for all, nor, where it is the same, is it equally known by all. Thus it is right and true for all to act according to reason: and from this principle it follows as a proper conclusion, that goods entrusted to another should be restored to their owner. Now this is true for the majority of cases: but it may happen in a particular case that it would be injurious, and therefore unreasonable, to restore goods held in trust; for instance, if they are claimed for the purpose of fighting against one's country. And this principle will be found to fail the more, accordingly as we descend further into detail (…).[20]

As can be seen in previous texts, Thomas Aquinas also makes note that particular conclusions of practical reason are not equally known by all. Their truth or rectitude is not the same in all on the level of particular knowledge, only on the level of universal knowledge. Even among those who coincide on the practical norm of what is concrete, not everyone knows it equally.

Therefore it can be concluded that in the sphere of practical reason there are universal rules and principles. Notwithstanding, in the particular

---

[18] Javier Hervada, *Introducción crítica al Derecho natural* (Pamplona: Eunsa, 2001), 139f.
[19] Ibid.
[20] Aquinas, *S. Th.* I-II, q. 94, a. 4 c.

conclusions of said principles there can be exceptions, depending on the different circumstances in real life.

2.1. Principles of practical reasoning

Since Plato and Aristotle began studying the contents of practical reasonability more than two thousand years ago, many writers have identified a considerable number of rules in practical reasoning.[21] They can be understood as principles of "practical wisdom" (or, of "vital common sense"), by which not living according to them would be tantamount to acting irrationally. Therefore, these are the requirements that refer to the plenitude of human well-being, to the "achieved life." For Thomas Aquinas, these are requirements not only of intellect and will, but also of human nature.

Its long tradition enables the connection of these principles, using Aristotelian terminology, to the idea of the *phronimos* or the *spoudaios*. The *phronimos* is, for the Greek philosopher, the one who possesses the *phronesis*, or practical wisdom, or full reasonability. The term can also be translated as prudence. According to Aristotle, "Prudence is a way of being rational, true, and practical, with respect to what is good and bad for man."[22] Thomas Aquinas also held prudence in high regard, declaring, "Prudence is a virtue most necessary for human life. For a good life consists in good deeds."[23]

For Finnis,[24] the rules of practical reason establish a "method" or way to elaborate concrete content of natural law from the first principles of the same natural law (principles that, in his opinion, are *pre-moral*.) Such requirements would permit building a framework of guidelines on the basic requisites of moral and legal coexistence. For Cotta these are the "natural conditions of human living."[25] Hervada refers to "natural inclinations whose rational rules form natural law."[26]

---

[21] See Finnis, *Natural Law and Natural Rights*, 100f.

[22] Aristotle, *Nichomachean Ethics*, trans. Terence Irwin (Indianapolis: Hackett, 1987), VI, 5, 1140b.

[23] Aquinas, *S. Th.* I-II, q. 57, a. 5 c.

[24] Finnis, *Natural Law and Natural Rights*, 100f.

[25] Sergio Cotta, *¿Qué es el Derecho?* (Madrid: Rialp, 1993), 54.

[26] The following are mentioned:

"a) the inclination or tendency to preserve the being – life and physical and moral integrity – frequently called instinct of self-preservation;

Among these rules, Finnis highlights the following:

a) The existence of a rational and coherent life plan.[27] Following J. Royce, "a person, an individual "I," can be defined as a human life lived according to a plan.[28] It is about having a harmonious life project, which implies among other things, assuming a vital order, harmonising commitments, knowing how to redirect inclinations, change habits, abandon old projects, et al.

In order to achieve this rational and coherent life plan, it might prove useful to see our own life as if it were a project unfolding within a limited time. Or, as Finnis points out,[29] "Observe life itself from the imaginary point of view of death itself," following the advice of the wise, "in all you do remember the last days." (Ecclesiastes 7:36). Socrates also understood that philosophy is, in a way, the practice of dying.[30]

Adopting this perspective does not imply being aware of the moment of death and the possibility of future existence as it does choosing the most

---

b) the inclination to conjugal union of man and woman, both forming the basic social unit of the human species, ordained at the generation and education of the children;
c) the inclination towards relating to God, as a manifestation of being a *creature*, constitutive dimension of being man;
d) the tendency to work, as an expression of the dominating and transforming nature of man as regards the world around him, and related to this is the tendency to rest and leisure activity;
e) the inclination towards political society and the various forms of association, that come from the social nature of man;
f) the tendency to communicate, expression also of human sociability;
g) the inclination towards knowledge and the different forms of culture and art."
Likewise, it is sustained that together with these natural tendencies, there stand out "lines of strength or basic laws of development of said tendencies:
a) the law of solidarity among men, by virtue of which every man and every collectivity is co-responsible with the rest in the attainment of their ends;
b) the law of perfection and development: each man in particular and the human society in general are called to continuous perfection, material as well as moral and spiritual." Hervada, *Introducción crítica al Derecho natural*, 146.

27 Rawls also refers to this requirement in his work John Rawls, *A Theory of Justice* (Oxford: Clarendon Press, 1971), 407f.

28 Josiah Royce, *The Philosophy of Loyalty* (New York: Hafner Pub. Co., 1908). Cit. in Rawls, *A Theory of Justice*, 408. In the same manner, the phrase appears in Finnis, *Natural Law and Natural Rights*, 129.

29 Finnis, *Natural Law and Natural Rights*, 130.

30 Socrates, *Phaedo*, 64a. cit. in Finnis, *Natural Law and Natural Rights*, 103; 30.

adequate vantage point in order to establish a coherent life project to face the present in a realistic and mature manner.[31]

b) The requirement of not establishing an arbitrary preference among basic human values. For Finnis, such values are self-evident, in the sense that it would be irrational to deny them. They can be concretised in the following:

a. Life
b. Knowledge
c. Play
d. Aesthetic experience (beauty)
e. Sociability (friendship)
f. Practical reasonability
g. Religion

This implies that practical reason, which directs our acting, should not be marginalised, rejected, or that any one of the other values as a unique and exclusive good. On the other hand, this does not mean that some, such as life (presupposed in order that the others be realised) for instance, are more important than others. Certainly, any life project implies a preference for a good or some goods. That does not suppose, since it would be irrational, ignoring the importance and transcendence of the rest. Therefore, independently of the value study might have for a person, they should accept that knowledge is a good in itself, thus it is preferable to ignorance or to error.

c) The non-existence of arbitrary preferences among persons. This is the requirement, expressed in modern philosophical discussion, that moral judgments are can be *made universal*. In the non philosophical field, this principle has been formulated, recalls Finnis, in many different ways:

> Do unto others what you would want done unto you... Do not condemn others for what you yourself desire... Do not hinder others (without due cause) from achieving for themselves what you would want to achieve for yourself.[32]

---

[31] Finnis, *Natural Law and Natural Rights*, 130.
[32] Ibid., 106.

These are reasonable exigencies, in the sense that ignoring them implies partiality and arbitrariness.

d) The requirement of impartiality before one's own life projects. This is about acquiring a certain detachment with respect to personal plans, in the sense that even if the life plan fails, it does not mean that life itself ceases to have meaning. In a way, this principle is a consequence of the previous ones, since it presupposes that the choice of one value or good should not exclude the transcendence and importance of the rest.

e) The need for fidelity in the face of one's own commitments and life project. For Finnis, this requisite not only has a negative dimension (to not frivolously abandon the requirements that derive from one's life plan,) but also a positive one (to seek, in a creative manner, the best way to go ahead with one's own commitments.)

f) To act taking into consideration the consequences of our actions. Nevertheless, this requirement cannot become the exclusive criterion to valuate one's own actions. What this principle establishes is the need to direct actions, to a certain extent, in such a way that they can be effective, that they bring about the desired consequences. This implies finding the best means of achieving the pursued results. However, in accordance with what has been affirmed up to this point, the search for a determined good can never justify the abrogation of the rest of the exigencies of practical reasonability already mentioned.

g) The seventh requirement refers to the need to respect every basic value in each human act. It is closely related to the former. For Finnis, it can be formulated in the following way:

> choosing not to carry out any act which *in itself does nothing more* than damage or impede the realisation or the participation in one or more of the basic forms of human good. The only "reason" for carrying out such an act, other than the wrong of a more or less strong desire, could be the good *consequences* of the act outweigh the damage done in and through that same act...[33]

[33] Ibid., 118.

It is the principle, expressed colloquially, of "the end does not justify the means" or, in other words, "it is not right to do wrong to achieve a good."

Because of this, the requirement establishes that if a determined action directly harms a basic human good, it is unreasonable, no matter how many desirable consequences it may have. The example that Finnis puts forth is the assumption that killing an innocent can obtain the liberation of hostages. In his words, "for example, if the consequentialist reasoning were valid, sometimes one can reasonably kill an innocent person to save the life of some hostages."[34] In this case we find a first action whose end is to directly and definitely harm a basic value. For this reason, the action would not be morally justified.

For Finnis, the strict inviolability of basic (natural) human rights clearly rests upon this requirement of practical reasonability. In the event that this principle is not respected, every human right is jeopardised. No human right will be free from being revoked if the calculation of cost and benefit (or the game of social and personal usefulness) were to be allowed to decide the final solution.[35]

Another question would be the supposition that, upon carrying out a reasonable action a basic good would be harmed. We would face what was traditionally called an "indirect volunteer." In order to adequately valuate these cases it is fundamental to be confined to the intention or the end with which the first action is carried out.

h) The eighth requirement refers to the need to ponder the promotion of the common good in every human action.

i) The last principle refers to the need to act according to one's own conscience, even though this might be invincibly erroneous (since one is not aware of their error and neither do they have the means within their reach to find their way out of their error.)

Apparently, the first to formulate this principle was Thomas Aquinas upon emphasising the significance of the congruence of the will with the intellect, be it right or in error. In his words:

> And since the object of the will is that which is proposed by the reason, from the very fact that a thing is proposed by the reason as being evil, the will by tending thereto becomes evil. And this is the case not only in

---

[34] Ibid.

[35] Ibid., 121.

> indifferent matters, but also in those that are good or evil in themselves. For not only indifferent matters can receive the character of goodness or malice accidentally; but also that which is good, can receive the character of evil, or that which is evil, can receive the character of goodness (...).We must therefore conclude that, absolutely speaking, every will at variance with reason, whether right or erring, is always evil.[36]

For Finnis, the dignity of the conscience, even an erroneous one, has much to do with the idea that the principles of practical reasonability are not merely formal mechanisms to be able to correctly pass judgment on an action, *but are also aspects of personal plenitude* that should be respected in every action.[37]

2.2. Legal reasoning as practical reasoning

It has already been pointed out that legal reasoning, as practical reasoning, is not exclusively logical-deductive. The nature of practical truth admits different ways of comprehending it. As Aristotle indicates, "A man who deliberates rightly can be prudent in general terms. But no one deliberates over what otherwise cannot be, or over what they are not able to do."[38]

On the other hand, legal reasoning does not presuppose a finite, closed, and "mathematical" view of law and reality. In this process different interpretations of law, particular views over the same events—in short, diverse positions and options are compared—. Prudence plays a fundamental role here, which is to *understand* both sides, that is, to deal with *every* point of view. So, a judge who is only preoccupied with only the criminal or the victim would be imprudent (unjust). On the contrary, prudence presupposes capacity for discernment, dealing with all factors and circumstances of reality.

In line with this, neither can the jurist lose sight of the importance of equity. This can never be understood as the negation or the "antithesis" of positive law, but as its completion, its perfection. In the words of Aristotle, "what is equitable is just and better than one kind of justice, not better than absolute justice but better than the error that comes from its absolute character."[39] Certainly, it would have something discretionary, since after

[36] Aquinas, *S. Th.* I-II, q. 19, a. 5 c.
[37] Finnis, *Natural Law and Natural Rights*, 126.
[38] Aristotle, *NE*, VI, 5, 1140a.
[39] Ibid., V, 10, 1137b.

all, it is a decision made by the jurist for which they assume responsibility. In spite of this, it is founded on an argumentation that appears as a result of prudent reasoning, from a comparison among all the points of view, especially taking into account reality, distinct and changing. In the case of the lawyer, as Arbesu states, as they provide legal counsel or defend their client, the lawyer is

> obliged to put into practice prudential knowledge, i.e., to endorse a somewhat uncertain and future practical action... In any case, the lawyer does not exercise any professional function without prudence, therefore, uncertainty and the variety of decisions to be made will always be present (typical of practical action,) as well as the unrepeatable singularity of situations…[40]

We can also affirm from these assumptions that jurisprudence and the work of the jurist involves constant effort and tension towards justice (what is just, legal, and natural,) making sure that *each one receives what they are due*, what corresponds to them by virtue of their nature, the law, or a pact or convention. This is the reason we are faced with a never-ending task in which, much like scientific research that never finishes,[41] there is always room for "improvement." On the other hand, the persistence in the search for the truth occupies an important place in this task. As Villey says, "jurisprudence involves an effort towards the *truth* quite analogous to that of philosophy."[42] Carrying out justice inevitably requires an attempt at the approximation to the truth. In fact, to abdicate from the search for the truth is to ultimately renounce doing justice.[43] In reality, as Aristotle already established, morality and law are, primarily, issues of truth.[44]

The success of a prudential decision would depend not only on technical and professional capacitation, but also especially on the internal dynamism of wanting, and the sincere will, to do justice. Hence, the right

---

[40] C Arbesu Riera, "Excelencia y formación en el ejercicio de la Abogacía," 19. Unedited research.

[41] As Villey points out, we do not find in science only strict and finished reasoning. The real state of science is not that of being finished (Michel Villey, *Compendio de Filosofía del Derecho. Los medios del Derecho* (Pamplona: Eunsa, 1979), 57.

[42] ———, *Compendio de Filosofía del Derecho. Los medios del Derecho* (Pamplona: Eunsa, 1981), 81.

[43] See Carlos Pérez del Valle, *Teoría de la prueba y derecho penal* (Madrid: Dykinson, 1999), 60.

[44] Aristotle, *NE*, VI, 9, 1142b.

intention not only does not contradict the technical-legal requirements, but also strengthens and purifies them. The unity of capacitation and personal virtue positively redounds on knowing how to judge or prudent discernment that should characterise every good jurist. Otherwise, a jurist who is not moved by the virtue of justice, who confuses the common good with personal interests or those of the surrounding persons, would encounter much difficulty in making a prudent and right decision in every case in order to act according to law.[45]

All in all, this corroborates that there exist certain basic structures in human nature, as do certain constant factors in the world around man. Also, that there should be some governing general principles in the field of law with the aim of universality. Notwithstanding, the legal order can never be understood as an enclosed system, allegedly closed and mathematical, applicable without the mediation of a practical reasoning.

Works Cited

Aparisi Miralles, Ángela. "Introducción al concepto de Derecho." In *Introducción a la teoría del Derecho*, edited by Javier De Lucas. Valencia: Tirant lo Blanch, 1994.

Aquinas, Thomas. *Summa Theologica* Translated by the Fathers of the English Dominican Province. New York: Benzinger Bros., 1947.

Arbesu Riera, C. "Excelencia y formación en el ejercicio de la Abogacía."

Arendt, Hannah. *The Human Condition*. Chicago: University of Chicago Press, 1958.

Aristotle. *De Anima*. Edited by Bekker. Berlin: Gigon-Bonitz, 1960-61.

—. *Nichomachean Ethics* Translated by Terence Irwin. Indianapolis: Hackett, 1987.

Ballesteros, Jesús. *Sobre el sentido del Derecho: introducción a la filosofía jurídica*. 3rd ed. Madrid: Tecnos, 2002.

Cotta, Sergio. *¿Qué es el Derecho?* Madrid: Rialp, 1993.

Finnis, John. *Natural Law and Natural Rights*. Edited by H. L. A. Hart, *Clarendon Law Series*. Oxford: Clarendon Press, 1980.

Gascón, María. "Consideraciones sobre el objeto de la filosofía jurídica." *Anuario de Filosofía del Derecho* X (1993): 214.

Hart, H. L. A. *The Concept of Law*. Oxford: Clarendon Press, 1967.

---

[45] See Arbesu Riera, "Excelencia y formación en el ejercicio de la Abogacía," 27-29. Unedited research.

—. *El concepto de Derecho* Translated by G. Carrió. Buenos Aires: Abeledo-Perrot, 1968.
Hervada, Javier. *Introducción crítica al Derecho natural*. Pamplona: Eunsa, 2001.
Kelsen, Hans. *La Teoría Pura del Derecho* Translated by L. Legaz y Lacambra. Madrid: Revista de Derecho Privado, 1933.
MacIntyre, Alasdir. *After Virtue*. London: Duckworth, 1985.
Martínez Doral, José M. *La estructura del conocimiento jurídico*. Pamplona: Universidad de Navarra, 1963.
Pacchiani, Claudio, ed. *Filosofia pratica e scienza politica*. Abano Terme: Francisci, 1980.
Pérez del Valle, Carlos. *Teoría de la prueba y derecho penal*. Madrid: Dykinson, 1999.
Rawls, John. *A Theory of Justice*. Oxford: Clarendon Press, 1971.
Riedel, Manfred, ed. *Rehabilitierung der praktischen Philosophie*. Freiburg: Rombach, 1972-1974.
Ritter, Joachim. *"Naturrecht" bei Aristoteles: zum problem einer Erneuerung des Naturrechts*. Stuttgart: W. Kohlhammer, 1961.
Royce, Josiah. *The Philosophy of Loyalty*. New York: Hafner Pub. Co., 1908.
Socrates. *Phaedo*.
Spaemann, Robert. *Zur Kritik der politischen Utopie*. Stuttgart: Klett-Cotta, 1977.
Villey, Michel. *Compendio de Filosofía del Derecho. Los medios del Derecho*. Pamplona: Eunsa, 1979.
—. *Compendio de Filosofía del Derecho. Los medios del Derecho*. Pamplona: Eunsa, 1981.
Wittgenstein, Ludwig. *Philosophische Untersuchungen*. Frankfurt: Suhrkamp, 1970.

CHAPTER TWENTY TWO

PHILOSOPHICAL HERMENEUTICS AND NATURAL LAW: SOME CRITICAL AND EVALUATIVE CONSIDERATIONS

CARLOS I. MASSINI-CORREAS

Anti-foundationalism and new alternatives

In recent years, the doctrine of natural law has been the object of new critical approaches, some of which differ to some extent to those expressed during the nineteenth century and the first half of the twentieth century in the field of strict legal positivism.[1] These new approaches are framed in the context of various anti-foundationalist schools of thought that assert the radical impossibility of justifying first propositions, i.e. speculative and practical principles that serve as rational grounds for assessments, rules or imperatives. In this regard, Vattimo has written that:

> we must consider the nihilistic meaning of the dissolution of metaphysics in all its reach. This can be done in different ways. The thought that becomes aware of the insuperable lack of foundations that has recently marked the law, making justifying it as "just" useless, can decide that its

[1] For more on this critique, see: Pedro Serna, "Sobre las respuestas al positivimo jurídico," in *Las razones del derecho natural*, ed. Renato Rabbi-Baldi (Buenos Aires: Abaco, 2000), 55-86. See also: Cristóbal Orrego Sánchez, *Analítica del derecho justo. La crisis del positivismo jurídico y la crítica del derecho natural* (México D.F.: UNAM, 2005), 83-140. Gianni Vattimo, "Hacer justicia del derecho," in *Nihilismo y emancipación. Ética, política, derecho* (Barcelona: Paidós, 2004), 161. See also: ———, *Después de la cristiandad. Por un cristianismo no religioso*, trans. C. Revilla (Buenos Aires: Paidós, 2004), 131. On the history and interpretation of contemporary nihilism, see: Franco Volpi, *El nihilismo*, trans. A. Vigo and C.I. del Rosso (Buenos Aires: Biblos, 2005).

> task is that of disclosing this situation, unmasking, at the same time, the falsehood of every foundational attempt.[2]

The anti-foundationalist offensive against any attempt to justify human ethics, the law included, in rational terms is characterized not only by its critique of classical ethics and metaphysics, but also by its desire to undo what remains of the typically modern intention of providing a final rational justification for all kinds of propositions, speculative or practical. In this context, Jorge Vicente Arregui holds that:

> epistemology, at least in its modern approach—which is specific to the seventeenth century and the Enlightenment, extends to the Vienna Circle and has come to be known as foundationalism— [is] the idea of founding our knowledge, of constructing a bombproof building of science, [and] intends to establish an indisputable cornerstone and a rigorous method for this knowledge.[3]

In other words, the main theses of anti-foundationalist thought reject any attempt (classical, modern or late-modern positivist) to find a rational justification for human knowledge and morality, denouncing such attempts as not only false, but also as the 'trojan horses' of unsayable, dark mechanisms and structures of power and domination.[4]

These anti-foundationalist arguments, which draw in general on the ideas articulated by the *unholy trinity*—Marx, Nietzsche and Freud—and

[2] Gianni Vattimo, "Hacer justicia del derecho," in *Nihilismo y emancipación. Ética, política, derecho* (Barcelona: Paidós, 2004), 161. See also: ———, *Después de la cristiandad. Por un cristianismo no religioso*, trans. C. Revilla (Buenos Aires: Paidós, 2004), 131. On the history and interpretation of contemporary nihilism, see: Franco Volpi, *El nihilismo*, trans. A. Vigo and C.I. del Rosso (Buenos Aires: Biblos, 2005).

[3] Jorge V. Arregui, *La pluralidad de la razón* (Madrid: Síntesis, 2004), 18.

[4] It is noteworthy in this regard that most of the authors who argue for absolute anti-foundationalism in ethics and law, and deny any possibility of objectively justifying practical propositions, move from this rejection to an all-encompassing critique of the structures of domination, describing them as unjust, manipulative and degrading, and suggesting that the active work of denunciation and dismantling of these structures be carried out in order to enable human emancipation. In this context, it is clear that the abovementioned structures of domination figure as ethically negative and human emancipation as ethically positive, in an unquestionably objective and "strong" way; see: Carlos I. Massini Correas, "La teoría del derecho natural en el tiempo posmoderno," *Doxa* 21, no. II (1988): 289-303.

Martin Heidegger, have strongly set the tone, subject-matter and style of contemporary philosophy[5] in such a way that it appears to be both almost impossible and irresponsible not to adapt to the frameworks they establish. In this regard, one of the statements read as a given and beyond question is that, after Kant's work, it is impossible to talk in metaphysical terms, a position which takes for granted the truth and definitive nature of Kantian criticism of metaphysical knowledge. In short, it would seem that anti-foundationalism, wherein knowledge lacks metaphysical status and any objective justification of ethics and law is inadmissible, has become a commonplace of philosophical thought, at least from the last third of the twentieth century onwards.

In light of this situation, a number of renowned thinkers involved in the quest for a strong rational—that is, objective— justification of ethics and law[6] have come to regard a frontal attack on nihilistic and anti-foundationalist theses as futile. Hence, they have sought a philosophical alternative that addresses the task of finding a rational justification for statements concerning ethics and law and is capable of withstanding skeptical and anti-foundationalist criticism. The alternative selected in this case is that provided by Philosophical Hermeneutics, primarily in the version articulated by Hans Georg Gadamer. This version is regarded as a postmetaphysical, linguistic and non-realist philosophical project which, at the same time, defers to certain Aristotelian issues and, by virtue of its reference to the prejudices and traditions of thought,[7] rejects the emancipatory hallmark of the standard version. Many scholars have taken on this task, among them Josef Esser, Arthur Kaufmann and Winfried Hassemer in Germany, Francesco Viola, Francesco D'Agostino and Giuseppe Zaccaria in Italy and a number of others in Spain, the United States and Argentina. The iusnaturalist proposals advanced by Viola and

---

[5] See: Giovanni Reale, *La sabiduría antigua*, trans. S. Salvino (Barcelona: Herder, 1996).

[6] In this paper, natural law is understood as the existence of a nucleus of unavailability in law; "the idea of the unavailability of law—Günter Ellscheid has written—has always been considered inherent in the idea of natural law, for nature has always been understood as that not established by human praxis"; Günther Ellscheid, "El problema del derecho natural. Una orientación sistemática," in *El pensamiento jurídico contemporáneo* ed. Arthur Kaufmann and Winfried Hassemer (Madrid: Debate, 1992), 149. See also: Rodolfo Bozzi, *Filosofia del Diritto* (Bari-Roma: Adriatica-Pontificia Università Gregoriana, 1992), 252.

[7] See: Alessandro Argiroffi, *Valori, prassi, ermeneutica: Emilio Betti a confronto con Nicolai Hartmann e Hans Georg Gadamer* (Torino: Giappichelli, 1994).

D'Agostino are analysed below, in order to offer an assessment of their rational integrity and the possibilities they make available.

Hermeneutic iusnaturalism

Prior to analysing the essays of these two writers, the fact that Hans Georg Gadamer, a mentor to both Viola and D'Agostino, has dedicated various passages of his work to articulating his ideas on natural law should be borne in mind. In one of these passages, found in the work entitled "On the possibility of a philosophical ethics," Gadamer writes that:

> undoubtedly, nobody can mention all that is owed to man and his common ways of living; however, this does not mean that everything is possible, that everything can be done, as wanted by him who is in command, arranged and adjusted at his own will and pleasure. There is a natural law. Aristotle balances the conditioning that all moral knowledge is indebted to the moral and political being. He says so with the conviction, shared with Plato, that the being is powerful enough so as to set a limit to all human aberration: "How strong—Plato writes—remains the Polis by virtue of its own nature."[8]

(The interpretation and import of this and other similar passages by Gadamer have been explored in some detail by the present writer elsewhere; for reasons of brevity and relevance these ideas are not rehearsed again here.[9])

To begin the analysis of Francesco D'Agostino's thought, the author's view is that the idea of *nature* lies at the heart of the notion of *natural law*, for

> to make reference to nature is [...] to refer to a dimension that—no matter the sense in which it is understood—constitutes an objective limit to human will, especially to the will of the one who holds power.[10]

---

[8] Hans-Georg Gadamer, "Sur la posibilité d'une éthique philosophique," in *Herméneutique et philosophie* (Paris: Beauchesne, 1999), 126. [Original publication in ———, *Kleine Schriften I. Philosophie, Hermeneutik* (Tübingen: Mohr, 1967). It is the text of a lecture given by Gadamer in 1961.]

[9] Carlos I. Massini Correas, "La filosofía hermenéutica y la indisponibilidad del derecho," *Persona y Derecho* 47 (2002): 257-78.

[10] Francesco D'Agostino, *Filosofia del Diritto* (Torino: Giappichelli, 1993), 75. A few paragraphs before, he writes that "Whatever the meaning one may want to attribute to the idea of 'nature', this is correctly established if it defers to a

Having established the concept of natural law, in an article entitled "*Hermenéutica y derecho natural. Después de la crítica heideggeriana de la metafísica,*" D'Agostino develops what he calls *the new hermeneutic conscience*, holding that

> the critique of metaphysics obliges us to rethink our relationship with being in a radical way, to relinquish the hope of being able to develop a method to comprehends and masters it. It obliges us to admit the impossibility of separating the act of knowledge from the act of interpretion, and commits us to endless reflection on our way of understanding the philosophy of thought and philosophy in general, a process that thus becomes radically hermeneutic by nature.[11]

For D'Agostino, this new hermeneutic conscience encompasses legal thought and the jurist's work, which

> can never be considered passive, that is, merely recognitional of a given law. Being inevitably creative, this activity must be considered normative. Even when the jurist, as his only aim, sets out to clarify the implicit meaning of legislative statements [...], he will inevitably intervene, attributing a meaning to them;

And he concludes with the unequivocal statement that

> the principle from which the jurist shall give hermeneutic life to positive law will be no other than the one that Western tradition denotes in the expression *natural law*.[12]

Later in the discussion, however, D'Agostino makes his own one of the defining statements of hermeneutic philosophy: "there is no one unique true interpretation,"; he acknowledges that this prompts a question—which he refers to as a 'mortal challenge'—regarding the lack of logic in normative interpretation, i.e. "the possibility of emptying the jurist's activity of all objectivity, of weakening it to such an extent that it

---

dimension in which we cannot operate; a dimension that, on the contrary, controls us or, at least, conditions us, and that constitutes for us the horizon of possibility within which justice may be understood"; D'Agostino, *Filosofia del Diritto*, 75.

[11] Francesco D'Agostino, "Hermenéutica y derecho natural. Después de la crítica heideggeriana de la metafísica," in *Las razones del derecho natural: perspectivas teóricas y metodológicas ante la crisis del positivismo jurídico*, ed. Renato Rabbi-Baldi Cabanillas (et al.) (Buenos Aires: Ábaco de Rodolfo Depalma, 2000), 305.

[12] Ibid., 307-08.

becomes, in the end, a game"; all of this in the face of "the challenge of what is referred to, in modern terms, as nihilism."[13] D'Agostino admits that there are gradations to this nihilism, the most mitigated and bourgeois of which is legal relativism, wherein all possible interpretations of a law have the same value, and the jurist is empowered to choose in a decisionist way among them. Notwithstanding what has been outlined thus far, however, D'Agostino maintains that such decisionist relativism is a spurious fruit of hermeneutics, for "if all interpretations have the same value, none has any real meaning: but this is the exact opposite of what hermeneutics proposes."[14]

In this non-relativist sense, as part of a process of interpretation which ascribes a non-arbitrary meaning to normative statements, D'Agostino suggests a number of interpretative canons. One of these interpretative canons, referred to as the "criterion of fidelity", holds that every interpretation must be faithful, primarily, to being: "given that being does not belong to us (on the contrary, we belong to being), we receive more in interpreting than we can possibly give."[15] Above all, however, interpretation must be faithful to the law,

> the law that precedes rules is a law that is not positively formulated, it is *agraphos nomos*, it is an unwritten right [...], not *per accidens*, but on principle. It is, in short, the natural law; not that codified by the iusnaturalism of the modern age, but that envisaged by the classical tradition which appears before our eyes, characteristically, as a law that is accessible only through hermeneutic channels, by means of the creation of rules made by its interpreters.[16]

This passage concludes the brief outline of D'Agostino's formulation of a hermeneutic natural law.

Francesco Viola, a professor of philosophy in Palermo, has systematized a complete legal doctrine that is hermeneutic in nature, on the basis of which he develops a concept of law as social human praxis that is, in itself, interpretative.[17] Further reference to this theory follows; and, in particular, to Viola's arguments concerning natural law. In an

---

[13] Ibid., 308.
[14] Ibid., 310.
[15] Ibid., 313.
[16] Ibid., 313-14.
[17] See Francesco Viola and Giuseppe Zaccaria, *Diritto e interpretazione. Lineamenti di teoria ermeneutica del diritto*, 2nd ed. (Roma-Bari: Laterza-Figlio, 2001).

article published in the *IVR Encyclopaedia of Jurisprudence. Legal Theory and Philosophy of Law*[18] entitled "Positive Law and Natural Law," the author distinguishes between three main sources of validity or 'being in force' of legal rules: their moral value, formal validity and factual existence.

According to Viola,

> the essential requisites of natural law do not include factual existence and so it is not "law" in the narrow sense. However, we may wonder whether effectiveness and moral validity are all that is required for there to be "a legal system" and whether perhaps it is not also necessary a certain correspondence to criteria of justice, at least as regards the legal system as a whole. If it is felt that positive law as a whole, in addition to being effective, must at least satify minimun needs for justice, then the problem of the relation between positive law and natural law really arises, but within positive law itself. Hence the question needs to be formulated as follows: what role is played by values or principles of justice that are not dependent on human will in the concept of positive law?[19]

And later he adds that "we have to go back to the main question: is reference to moral and political values an essential element for identifying positive law?"[20]

To answer this question, Viola maintains that the significance of natural law for positive law may be established in three principal dimensions: (i) the foundation of the obligation to obey legal rules; (ii) the content of legal rules; and (iii) the form of legal rules themselves. With regard to the first point, he criticizes the positivist versions articulated by Kelsen, Hart and Raz, insofar as each concludes by making the obligatoriness of legal rules dependent on mere facts, even when it is the conventions that determine which rules are valid in a given legal system that are the subject of discussion. In relation to Raz's argument that authority would prove superfluous if the law was to be obeyed for reasons other than authority itself, Viola states that

> this argument depends on the role that is assigned to the legal authority, which can have a creative or productive task and/or interpretative task. The

[18] See Viola "Positive Law and Natural Law." In *IVR Encyclopaedia of Jurisprudence, Legal Theory and Philosophy of Law.* <http://www.ivr-enc.info/en/article.php?id=56>, 24 October 2005, 1.

[19] Ibid.

[20] Viola, "Positive Law and Natural Law", 2.

> latter binds the authority to showing that its interpretation of the fundamental values is correct even if it is not the best. This justification implies that the reasons why a norm is issued become part of the essential characteristics of the positive law together with the element of formal validity. Here too one can recognise a certain presence of natural law[21].

The second dimension Viola mentions is that of the content of the norms of positive law, and he makes reference to the question of whether positive law—as such—need be consistent with natural law, i.e. to respect certain minimum ethical requirements in its content. This question is not factual by nature; rather, it is normative, and has been responded to positively in our own time by thinkers such as Hart, Alexy, Finnis, Dworkin and Rawls, to whom Viola refers when dealing with this point. In articulating his own opinion, Viola holds that

> if we consider law as a social practice of an interpretative type and not just a set of rules, then natural law can be present in the judicial process insofar as the judge [...] has the legal and moral obligation to include in the interpretation and argumentation principles and norms that are applicable not because they are legally valid but because they are morally just or fair[22].

Finally, with respect to the formal dimension of positive law, Viola maintains that the question at issue is that of knowing if positive norms—as such—must respect certain formal limits, limits that constitute one of the dimensions of natural law. He makes reference in this context to the morality of law proposed by Lon Fuller in his book *The Morality of Law*,[23] in which a number of formal requirements that law must satisfy in order to constitute law as such are listed.

All these conditions—writes Viola—are formal in a broad sense, but they must be these and no others for the law to perform tasks referring to substantial objectives or values like respect for liberty, equality and people's expectations.

He also recalls, in this regard, that Kelsen expunged the *rule of law* from his theory, regarding it as a mere prejudice linked to the doctrines of natural law. In line with this point, the claim that the formal morality of law is consistent with the conception of law as a hermeneutic practice, in

---

[21] Viola, "Positive Law and Natural Law", 3-4.
[22] Ibid.
[23] See: Lon L. Fuller, *The morality of law* (New Heaven & London: Yale University Press, 1969), 33-94.

which special priority is given to the procedural aspects of legal life,[24] may be acknowledged.

Three critical and evaluative observations

Following this brief discussion of the assertions concerning natural law articulated by two distinguished voices in the hermeneutic understanding of law, a critical revision and evaluation of their central statements may be worthwhile; the focus here is on the analysis of three points: (i) the possibility of a nucleus of ethical unavailability on the basis of the assumptions of hermeneutic philosophy; (ii) the reference in hermeneutic philosophy to Aristotelian practical philosophy and its doctrine of natural law; and (iii) the main characteristics of the hermeneutic philosophy of law and its adaptation to a natural law position.

The first point may be formulated as follows: can natural law be justified rationally, in the sense set out by the abovementioned writers, by reference only to the pragmatic level of language and its interpretations, the level at which hermeneutic philosophy operates? The following quotation from an article by Fernando Inciarte, in which the radical nature of hermeneutic philosophy is succinctly summarized, is apt and relevant:

> the recent metamorphosis of hermeneutic philosophy is due primarily to the fact that the text of which the world consists is no longer considered independent of the interpretation or interpretations to which it may be subjected. In other words, the world, as a text, contains within itself the structure of its interpretation; the one is not separate from the other. In short, the interpreter is now the creator of the text.[25]

---

[24] See: Francesco Viola, "La critica dell'ermeneutica alla filosofia analitica italiana del diritto," in *Ermeneutica e filosofia analitica. Due concezione del diritto a confronto*, ed. Mario Jori Torino (Torino: Giappichelli, 1994), 63-104.

[25] Fernando Inciarte, "Hermenéutica y sistemas filosóficos," in *Tiempo, sustancia, lenguaje. Ensayos de metafísica*, ed. Lourdes Flamarique (Pamplona: Eunsa, 2004), 208.

In a similar sense, Joan Grondin wrote: "What gives hermeneutics the status of *prima philosophia* of our times is, probably, the virtual omnipresence of the interpretative phenomenon, which is the order of the day in philosophy, at least since Nietzsche's reflections on universal perspectivism ('there are no facts, only interpretations'). Nietzsche is probably the first modern philosopher who refined his awareness to perceive the fundamentally interpretative character of our experience of the world." Joan Grondin, *Introducción a la hermenéutica filosófica*, trans. A. Ackermann Pilári (Barcelona: Herder, 1999), 21.

In this world reduced to language—"the being that can be understood is language," wrote Gadamer, and "whatever is the object of knowledge and of its statements, is always taken in by the horizon of language, which coincides with the world"[26]—in which access to natural being is denied *a priori* and where only the uses of language may be known: dialogue, consensus, performative utterances, etc.; the main dimensions of human perfection, what Finnis calls "basic human goods" cannot be known—that is, known in objective terms. Still less is it possible to provide a foundation for human dignity or human rights. In other words, no access to a natural law, which, by definition, must be rooted in a reality—practical reality, but reality nonetheless—independent of the will, dialogue, consensus or human locution, is possible. To be more precise, the radical unavailability typical of natural law, by which it may be rationally justified and command the assent of the intelligence, can only be rooted in something beyond human language and whatever may be designated or referred to by it.[27] Otherwise, it will no longer be, strictly speaking, a natural law and will remain susceptible to manipulative human action, which will establish the (never insurmountable) limits of legal or simply moral praxis through general consensus, dialogue or tradition (the general consensus over time).

To express the argument in different terms: if human experience is reduced to that which has the pragmatic dimensions of language as its object,[28] any reference to a natural law is without foundation and radically weak, weak to a point beyond what is needed to establish an ethical limit that the soaring will to power must (by deontical necessity) respect. The elements of natural reality to which hermeneutic philosophers defer in speaking about natural law—tradition, prejudices, consensus, dialogue (factual or contrafactual)—are valuable instruments for the knowledge of natural law, but they can never constitute or shape it, much less rationally justify it.

Secondly, the dual value of the reference to the use of Aristotelian practical philosophy by many hermeneutic philosophers should be noted: (i) it points to the practical and rational nature of the classical understanding of human activity; and (ii) it prompts a systematic and

---

[26] Hans-Georg Gadamer, *Verdad y método*, trans. A. Agud Aparicio y R. Agapito (Salamanca: Ediciones Sígueme, 1977), 515.

[27] See: George Kalinowski, *Sémiotique et Philosophie* (Paris: Hadès-Benjamins, 1984). See also: Alejandro Llano, "Filosofía del lenguaje y comunicación," in *Sueño y vigilia de la razón* (Pamplona: Eunsa, 2002), 84-85ff.

[28] See: Maurizio Ferraris, *La hermenéutica* (Madrid: Taurus, 2003), 59.

critical alternative to the modern conception of ethics, law and politics, which precludes knowledge of practical knowledge and science.[29] In spite of these positive aspects, however, a number of the ways in which Aristotelian practical philosophy was recovered in philosophical hermeneutics might usefully be called into question. The first of these is the fact that the recovery is effected by removing some of the Aristotelian ethical theses from their metaphysical, and anthropological, contexts. Outside these contexts, and in line with a widely acknowledged hermeneutic thesis, it is almost impossible to understand their full scope and to exploit their full potential.[30]

The aspect of greatest interest here, however, is that which refers to the claim of these authors with regard to important dimensions of practical philosophy (made within the framework of practical philosophy); in particular, in relation to the knowledge of practical principles, whether first or second principles. This has been acknowledged by Giuseppe Abbà, among others, when he speaks about

> those scholars who, in the wake of H. G. Gadamer, have rediscovered Aristotelian *phronesis* as a model of practical knowledge [...] and who, with a markedly anti-theoretical approach, subsume practical philosophy in *phronesis*. Aristotelian practical philosophy cannot be absorbed into *phronesis*; it is a practical science different to *phronesis*.[31]

In fact, as a number of commentators have shown,[32] and as Aristotle himself stated when he wrote that "it is obvious that the *phronesis* is not science,"[33] practical philosophy—*episteme politiké* in Aristotelian language—cannot be reduced to concrete propositions, i.e. completely determined, which pertain to the level of the *phronesis*.

> Even when dealing with a practical science—Ignacio Yarza writes—such as politics, or the legislative science which is part of it, its object must be

---

[29] See Franco Volpi, "Ermeneutica e filosofia pratica," *Ars Interpretandi* 7 (2002): 7.

[30] See Terence H. Irwin, "The Metaphysical and Psychological Basis of Aristotle's Ethics," in *Essays on Aristotle's ethics* ed. Amélie Oksenberg Rorty (Berkeley: University of California Press, 1980), 65.

[31] Giuseppe Abbà, *Quale impostazione per la filosofia morale?* (Roma: LAS, 1996), 39-40.

[32] See, among others: Guido Soaje Ramos, "Filosofía práctica, razón práctica y teleología," *Ethos* 23, no. 25 (1997): 245-59.

[33] Aristotle, *NE*, VI, 1142 to 24.

universal; the ethical philosopher must pursue the knowledge of first principles so that his or her knowledge may be scientific.[34]

Thus, to reduce philosophical consideration of praxis to the mere level of prudence not only involves infidelity to Aristotelian thought, but also a negation of the main level of practical thought and the subsequent renunciation of the most philosophical dimension of practical knowledge.

Finally, with regard to the central characters of hermeneutic iusphilosophy, the fact that interpretative reductionism, i.e. a narrowing or contraction of knowledge and of legal praxis to a merely interpretative task, occurs in almost every case should be noted. In this regard, Francisco Viola sets out a legal theory in which interpretation is not reduced to the determination of the normative meaning of legal texts; rather, it also encompasses legislative activity, the social praxis of which law consists, the assessment of that praxis in terms of justice, and every other dimension of legal reality. The Italian analytical iusphilosopher Riccardo Guastini has challenged Viola's position, describing it as "totally invasive" (*omnipermasiva*),[35] because interpretation pervades all spheres of law, which are, therefore, reduced to different dimensions of interpretative activity. In turn, the Mexican philosopher, Mauricio Beuchot, has described this philosophical approach as "equivocal hermeneutics". This description is based on the fact that, for this hermeneutical approach, absolutely everything is interpretation: thus, it is in the end equivocal, because the same word is used to denote realities that belong to different categories and have different meanings.[36]

To sum up, from this pan-interpretative perspective, everything is interpretation; however, the object of reference of this activity is not clear, i.e. what reality is, in the end, interpreted. Thus, there are interpretations of interpretations, which are, at the same time, interpretations of other interpretations and so on and so forth; a sort of universal and infinite interpretationism which, like any other infinite line of reasoning, ends up justifying nothing rationally. In this regard, as Alejandro Vigo[37] rightly

---

[34] Ignacio Yarza, *La racionalidad de la ética de Aristóteles. Un estudio sobre Ética a Nicómaco I* (Pamplona: Eunsa, 2001), 20-21.

[35] Ricardo Guastini, "Tre domande a Francesco Viola," in *Ermeneutica e filosofia analitica*, ed. Mario Jori (Torino: Giappichelli, 1994), 219-40.

[36] Mauricio Beuchot, *Tratado de hermenéutica analógica*, 2nd ed. (México D.F.: Itaca-UNAM, 2000), 47. Also: ———, *Hermenéutica, analogía y símbolo* (México D.F.: Herder, 2004), 70.

[37] See Alejandro G. Vigo, "La noción de principio desde el punto de vista filosófico. Algunas reflexiones críticas," *Sapientia* 59, no. 215 (2004): 195-221.

points out, even if there are different forms of rational justification that correspond to the different objects, it is clear that, above all, in the order of praxis, some reference to a first principle—and to others close to it, as Thomas Aquinas observed[38]—is required if the order of human legal praxis is to acquire an adequate foundation and a coherent rational justification.

The hermeneutic approach does not seem to provide a justification of this sort; nor, as a consequence, will it be able to support a conception of natural law that might give rise—as the hermeneutic philosophers referred to here assume—to an unavailable, ethical nucleus that is deontically absolute, and thus unexceptionable, by nature.

Conclusion

The following conclusions may be drawn in light of what has been discussed in this paper. Despite the worthy intentions of adherents to hermeneutic iusnaturalism and their laudable aim of proposing a doctrine of natural law that is not susceptible to post-metaphysical and anti-foundationalist critiques, their argument is insufficient and, in the end, fails because of the underlying principles of philosophical hermeneutics itself and the iusphilosophical developments which flow from it follow it. Given this discouraging outcome, it appears that the most suitable and rigorous philosophical approach to the re-foundation and reformulation of natural law would be to reintroduce, once again, the bimillenary tradition of classical realist iusnaturalism.

Clearly, the reintroduction of this "central Western tradition" cannot be reduced to a simple repetition of venerable formulae, nor to an anachronistic exegesis of distinguished texts; rather, it ought to prompt new reflection within the framework of this tradition on the problems that reason must address in relation to the question of legal and ethical limits, (which must at some point be insurmountable), in the context of human praxis and its institutions.[39] The following remark from Gadamer should be recalled in this regard:

---

[38] *S. Th.* I-II, q. 94, a. 6 c. On the problems of the first practical principles in Thomas Aquinas, see: Germain G. Grisez, "The First Principle of Practical Reason. A Commentary on the *Summa theologiae*, 1-2, Question 94, Article 2," *Natural Law Forum* 10 (1965): 168-201.

[39] See: Joseph M. Boyle, "Natural Law and the Ethics of Traditions," in *Natural Law Theory. Contemporary Essays*, ed. Robert George (Oxford: Clarendon Press, 1994), 3-30.

> Aristotle will still be in our conversation a priviledged interlocutor, who, facing the ideal of modernity of a world that can be dominated through knowledge and the capacity of putting it into practice, still represents to us the ideal of reason, the ideal of a world reasonably organized and understandable in which we have to live.[40]

Even though Gadamar excludes Aristotle from the terms of his discussion, his advice on this point deserves particular attention, especially in the task of restoring, reformulating and reinvigorating the philosophy of natural law.

Works Cited

Abbà, Giuseppe. *Quale impostazione per la filosofia morale?* Roma: LAS, 1996.

Argiroffi, Alessandro. *Valori, prassi, ermeneutica: Emilio Betti a confronto con Nicolai Hartmann e Hans Georg Gadamer*. Torino: Giappichelli, 1994.

Aristotle. *Nichomachean Ethics* Translated by Terence Irwin. Indianapolis: Hackett, 1987.

Arregui, Jorge V. *La pluralidad de la razón*. Madrid: Síntesis, 2004.

Beuchot, Mauricio. *Hermenéutica, analogía y símbolo*. México D.F.: Herder, 2004.

—. *Tratado de hermenéutica analógica*. 2nd ed. México D.F.: Itaca-UNAM, 2000.

Boyle, Joseph M. "Natural Law and the Ethics of Traditions." In *Natural Law Theory. Contemporary Essays*, edited by Robert George, 3-30. Oxford: Clarendon Press, 1994.

Bozzi, Rodolfo. *Filosofia del Diritto*. Bari-Roma: Adriatica-Pontificia Università Gregoriana, 1992.

D'Agostino, Francesco. *Filosofia del Diritto*. Torino: Giappichelli, 1993.

—. "Hermenéutica y derecho natural. Después de la crítica heideggeriana de la metafísica." In *Las razones del derecho natural: perspectivas teóricas y metodológicas ante la crisis del positivismo jurídico*, edited by Renato Rabbi-Baldi Cabanillas (et al.). Buenos Aires: Ábaco de Rodolfo Depalma, 2000.

[40] Hans-Georg Gadamer, "La idea de filosofía práctica," in *El giro hermenéutico* (Madrid: Cátedra, 1998), 196.

Ellscheid, Günther. "El problema del derecho natural. Una orientación sistemática." In *El pensamiento jurídico contemporáneo* edited by Arthur Kaufmann and Winfried Hassemer. Madrid: Debate, 1992.

Ferraris, Maurizio. *La hermenéutica*. Madrid: Taurus, 2003.

Fuller, Lon L. *The morality of law*. New Heaven & London: Yale University Press, 1969.

Gadamer, Hans-Georg. *Kleine Schriften I. Philosophie, Hermeneutik*. Tübingen: Mohr, 1967.

—. "La idea de filosofía práctica." In *El giro hermenéutico*. Madrid: Cátedra, 1998.

—. "Sur la posibilité d'une éthique philosophique." In *Herméneutique et philosophie*. Paris: Beauchesne, 1999.

—. *Verdad y método* Translated by A. Agud Aparicio y R. Agapito. Salamanca: Ediciones Sígueme, 1977.

Grisez, Germain G. "The First Principle of Practical Reason. A Commentary on the Summa theologiae, 1-2, Question 94, Article 2." *Natural Law Forum* 10 (1965): 168-201.

Grondin, Jean. *Introducción a la hermenéutica filosófica* Translated by A. Ackermann Pilári. Barcelona: Herder, 1999.

Guastini, Ricardo. "Tre domande a Francesco Viola." In *Ermeneutica e filosofia analitica*, edited by Mario Jori. Torino: Giappichelli, 1994.

Inciarte, Fernando. "Hermenéutica y sistemas filosóficos." In *Tiempo, sustancia, lenguaje. Ensayos de metafísica*, edited by Lourdes Flamarique. Pamplona: Eunsa, 2004.

Irwin, Terence H. "The Metaphysical and Psychological Basis of Aristotle's Ethics." In *Essays on Aristotle's ethics* edited by Amélie Oksenberg Rorty. Berkeley: University of California Press, 1980.

Kalinowski, George. *Sémiotique et Philosophie*. Paris: Hadès-Benjamins, 1984.

Llano, Alejandro. "Filosofía del lenguaje y comunicación." In *Sueño y vigilia de la razón*. Pamplona: Eunsa, 2002.

Massini Correas, Carlos I. "La filosofía hermenéutica y la indisponibilidad del derecho." *Persona y Derecho* 47 (2002).

—. "La teoría del derecho natural en el tiempo posmoderno." *Doxa* 21, no. II (1988): 289-303.

Orrego Sánchez, Cristóbal. *Analítica del derecho justo. La crisis del positivismo jurídico y la crítica del derecho natural*. México D.F.: UNAM, 2005.

Reale, Giovanni. *La sabiduría antigua* Translated by S. Salvino. Barcelona: Herder, 1996.

Serna, Pedro. “Sobre las respuestas al positivimo jurídico.” In *Las razones del derecho natural*, edited by Renato Rabbi-Baldi. Buenos Aires: Abaco, 2000.

Soaje Ramos, Guido. “Filosofía práctica, razón práctica y teleología.” *Ethos* 23, no. 25 (1997): 245-59.

Vattimo, Gianni. *Después de la cristiandad. Por un cristianismo no religioso* Translated by C. Revilla. Buenos Aires: Paidós, 2004.

—. “Hacer justicia del derecho.” In *Nihilismo y emancipación. Ética, política, derecho*. Barcelona: Paidós, 2004.

Vigo, Alejandro G. “La noción de principio desde el punto de vista filosófico. Algunas reflexiones críticas.” *Sapientia* 59, no. 215 (2004): 195-221.

Viola, Francesco. “La critica dell’ermeneutica alla filosofia analitica italiana del diritto.” In *Ermeneutica e filosofia analitica. Due concezione del diritto a confronto*, edited by Mario Jori Torino. Torino: Giappichelli, 1994.

—. “Positive Law and Natural Law.” In *IVR Encyclopaedia of Jurisprudence, Legal Theory and Philosophy of Law*. <http://www.ivr-enc.info/en/article.php?id=56>, 24 October 2005.

Viola, Francesco, and Giuseppe Zaccaria. *Diritto e interpretazione. Lineamenti di teoria ermeneutica del diritto*. 2nd ed. Roma-Bari: Laterza-Figlio, 2001.

Volpi, Franco. *El nihilismo* Translated by A. Vigo and C.I. del Rosso. Buenos Aires: Biblos, 2005.

—. “Ermeneutica e filosofia pratica.” *Ars Interpretandi* 7 (2002).

Yarza, Ignacio. *La racionalidad de la ética de Aristóteles. Un estudio sobre Ética a Nicómaco I*. Pamplona: Eunsa, 2001.

CHAPTER TWENTY THREE

RULES OF IMPUTATION AND HUMAN RATIONALITY

PABLO SANCHEZ-OSTIZ[1]

The concept "law" usually refers to prescriptions, prohibitions, and other regulatory provisions. These are *rules of conduct*, norms that govern conduct and establish whether a specific deed is right or wrong. Even so, in any regulatory model of conduct it is necessary to also have rules that are used to a different end: that of the attribution of responsibility. These are *rules of imputation*. Every regulatory model of conduct has an underlying model of imputation, each coming with its own minimum common elements.[2] Thus, the different regulatory systems of conduct (from spelling to criminal law, all the way to games or etiquette) provide, aside from parameters of conduct, criteria for the attribution of responsibility in the case of violation of the rules of conduct. Any legal regulatory system presupposes that those to whom the system is

---

[1] I would like to express my deep appreciation to J. Hruschka (Professor of Law at Friedrich-Alexander University in Erlangen) for the countless conversations held on the topic of the doctrine of imputation. These pages serve as an insufficient tribute. I would also like to acknowledge the advice and suggestions of B.S. Byrd (Professor of U.S. Law at the School of Law, Friedrich-Schiller University in Jena). I thank you both for your friendship.

[2] This exposition is based in great part on the works of J. Hruschka on the doctrine of imputation. It is about a doctrine which Hruschka did not *invent*, but which he "reveals" (it has been *rediscovered*: "Ich habe dieses System oder diese aufeinander bezogenen Teilsysteme nicht erfunden, sondern vorgefunden. Es ging mir darum, etwas zu *entdecken*, und nicht darum, Produkte meiner Phantasie in die Welt zu setzen." Joachim Hruschka, *Strafrecht nach logisch-analytischer Methode*, 2 ed. (Berlin – New York: Walter de Gruyter, 1988), XX. Concerning the exposition of Hruschka on the doctrine of imputation: cfr. the works at the end of this text.

applicable, firstly, *acted* (*or did not act*), then secondly, acted *wrongly* (or *rightly*, i.e. in accordance with the respective rule of conduct), and finally, are *guilty* (or *praiseworthy*, as the case may be). A body of principles or guiding criteria can be perceived in the rules of imputation that provide a solid basis, far beyond historical conventionalisms and cultural conditioning, to give these rules sense and coherence. This foundation is human rationality.

This work begins with (section 1) the exposition of the concepts that have come to be elaborated and employed in moral doctrine since time immemorial, proceeding to (section 2) a systematic description of the categories used in the operation of imputation. It concludes (section 3) by expounding how human rationality functions as the basis of these rules of imputation.

1. The historical contributions of the doctrine of imputation

In order to synthesize the contributions of the history of thought regarding imputation, three achievements are considered: 1.1) the qualification of conduct as human by virtue of having its *origin* in the agent; 1.2) the differentiation of *two levels* or stages of imputation; and 1.3) the distinction between objects of imputation and rules of imputation. These concepts are interwoven in such a manner that they are very solid as a whole, without losing their simplicity.

1.1. The agent as source of the "deed"[3]

The mere causation of an effect does not necessarily result in imputation of this effect to an agent. History is replete with experiences of objective liability based on merely causing a result, although advances in moral philosophy make it possible to overcome this *modus mechanicus*. Moral philosophers prior to the nineteenth century seemed aware of this. It is accepted that to impute responsibility to a subject is warranted, precisely when the subject *gives rise* to an effect. Imputation is possible insofar as the analysis of the process is dissociated from mechanistic causation. Otherwise, since every effect derives from a cause, the process of mere causation would go back to infinity. Instead, imputation supposes the interruption of this regress in the causal chain. This interruption does not

[3] In this contribution "deed" includes both action and omission.

happen arbitrarily choosing one in a great variety of causes, but precisely addresses the cause that *brings about* a determined causal process. Freedom is necessary for imputation, "originating" freedom, a freedom that causes, which is concisely summarised in the expression *causa libera*. It would not make sense to assert that a cause is what "*gives rise to*" an effect if that cause is taken as any other cause and not as a cause with a different meaning. Imputation is not about the mere specification of causality (*causa libera*), but about specifying one particular cause that makes imputation possible. Indeed, it is the freedom of the *author*[4] that makes it possible to affirm, from the process in which he finds himself involved, what an action is (or an omission, as the case may be).

The link between imputation and the idea of source is clearly found in Kant: "Imputation (*imputatio*) in the moral sense is the *judgment* by which someone is regarded as the author (*causa libera*) of an action, which is then called a *deed* (*factum*) and stands under laws."[5] Still, this notion dates back earlier than Kant. What is more, considering the author[6] as source, inasmuch as he is *causa libera*, is definitely not exclusively Kant, nor is it exclusively Kant to regard imputation as a judgment. What is Kant, properly speaking, lies, *inter alia*, in the positive character of freedom understood as the capacity of pure reason to be practical for itself, that is, in the idea of autonomy. Its study would require more extensive elaboration than the confines of this paper permit. Nonetheless, the idea of freedom as source, and even the very expression *causa libera*, is found in the doctrine of imputation prior to Kant. Samuel Pufendorf uses it in this sense, and after him Christian Wolff and others. Moreover, some writers, as is the case of Pufendorf for instance, have the sense of causal source

---

[4] The term *author* here is used as the translation of the German expression *Urheber* that includes the idea of the creative, originating aspect of the subject. The agent is *author* provided he gives rise to a new process, his deed, and as long as this action or omission is based on his freedom (*causa libera*). These nuances of the meaning of "author" are referred to in a work not yet translated into English: Pablo Sanchez-Ostiz, *La noción de imputación ["The Notion of Imputation"]* (2007, in press), II.3.1.

[5] "*Zurechnung* (imputatio) in moralischer Bedeutung ist das Urtheil, wodurch jemand als Urheber (causa libera) einer Handlung, die alsdann *That* (factum) heißt und unter Gesetzen steht, angesehen wird." Immanuel Kant, *Die Metaphysik der Sitten*, ed. Akademie der Wissenschaften, *Kant's gesammelte Schriften*, vol. VI (Berlin: 1902 ff.), 227 (21-24). English translations are taken from: Immanuel Kant, *Practical philosophy*, ed. Mary J. Gregor, trans. Mary J. Gregor (Cambridge: Cambridge University Press, 1996).

[6] Cfr. footnote 4, on the meaning of *author*.

that derives from freedom, and not from mere causation. The idea of *causa libera* was also used before Pufendorf.

In fact, Aristotle understood "voluntary" action as that which had its *source* in the agent: "in addition to this *man* alone of animals is also the source of certain actions; for no other animal would be said to act;"[7] and "the acts whose moving principles are in us must themselves also be in our power and voluntary."[8] The agent is not answerable for what he has not done voluntarily, and cannot be said to have had its source in him. More precisely, Aristotle states: "the voluntary would seem to be that of which the moving principle is in the agent himself, he being aware of the particular circumstances of the action."[9] This idea is taken up by Thomas Aquinas to refer to voluntary human action: a voluntary act "is moved by an intrinsic principle which includes some knowledge of an end. The agent, therefore, is the source of his act not only with respect to acting but to acting towards an end."[10] The source of an act, "principium intrinsecum," is defined by knowledge of an end and acting for the sake of that end. Note that the original sense of action has a double meaning: knowledge of an end, and acting because of that end.

Imputation relates to a subject who is seen as the source of an event. Imputation is the "identification" of that source.[11] The idea that imputation requires identifying the agent as source is seen in the tradition of ideas dating back to the eighteenth century. It is the first step in the development of doctrines of imputation: the identification of the agent as *radical* source. Specifically, the identification of that source is possible from the standpoint of *freedom*. Freedom is what allows surpassing the mere causal succession of phenomena and situates the source in an agent. The

---

[7] Aristotle, *Ethica Eudemia*, ed. David Ross, trans. J. Solomon, *The Works of Aristotle*, vol. IX (Oxford: 1915), 1222 b 18-20.

[8] ———, *Ethica Nichomachea*, ed. David Ross, trans. David Ross, *The Works of Aristotle*, vol. IX (Oxford: 1915), 1113 b 20-21.

[9] Ibid., 1111 a 22-24.

[10] "Quodcumque igitur sic agit vel movetur a principio intrinseco, quod habet aliquam notitiam finis, habet in seipso principium sui actus non solum ut agat, sed etiam ut agat propter finem." Thomas Aquinas, *Opera omnia*, ed. Commissio Leonina (Paris: Librairie Philosophique J. Vein, 1882), Ia-IIæ, q. 6, a. 1, sol.

[11] It is not a merely descriptive judgment, but one with a specific valuation: it is an affirmation with ascriptive content. Cfr. Joachim Hruschka, "Imputation," in *Rechtfertigung und Entschuldigung. Rechtsvergleichende Perspektiven/ Justification and Excuse. Comparative Perspectives, I*, ed. Albin Eser and Walter Perron (Freiburg i.B.: Max-Planck-Institut für Auslandisches und Internationales Strafrecht, 1987), 123.

numerous causes follow their course back *ad infinitum*, while imputation determines a source, a starting point.

1.2. The stages of imputation: "action" and "reproach"

When events have been imputed to agents we speak of *actions* (or omissions).[12] These are attributed to their agents not only as their own, but also as reproachable or meritorious, or simply as due. Through the judgment of imputation, the process in which the subject is involved is considered action (or omission), meaning the subject is its source and what was done is something that acquires meaning based on rules or guidelines. This judgment is what imputation has as its object. Nevertheless, this judgment also refers to the bond between *that* deed and *its* agent. These are two different operations: the one considers the process as action or omission (already supposing attributing something to the agent) and the other attributes a quality of merit or demerit, as the case may be. In both operations judgments of imputation are reached, if they are attributions to the agent. The object, however, is different in each case.

More precisely, the attribution of a quality of merit or demerit to the subject presupposes that a comparison or measure of the action (or omission) has taken place in accordance with guidelines or rules of conduct. If it is an action or omission that the rule regards as due, it is not possible to impute merit or demerit to an agent, but only to impute the act as merely due "action" or a merely due "omission." The possibility of imputing merit or demerit, however, presupposes appreciating the difference between the deed and the rule. Not acting in accordance with the rule allows the attribution of demerit if one has acted with freedom, while if one acts above and beyond what the rule prescribes, the deed is meritorious.[13] The diversification of imputation into two judgments seems to make sense when there exists something more than the deed and the rule: the consequences of the deed, meaning sanctions and rewards. Since the attribution of a process as action (or omission) is distinguished from evaluation of this action in relation to the rule, it can be concluded that the deed is taken into consideration from two different points of view. The process in which the agent finds himself involved is first imputed as his

[12] Cfr. footnote 3, on the meaning of *action* and *deed*.

[13] These deal with supererogatory conducts, which will not be dealt with here. Cfr. Joachim Hruschka and Jan C. Joerden, "Supererogation: Vom deontologischen Sechseck zum deontologischen Zehneck," *Archiv für Rechts und Sozialphilosophie* 73 (1987): 93-123.

own action (or omission), and then it is imputed as either meritorious or demeritorious, leading to imposition of the consequences (sanctions and rewards).

The doctrine of imputation deals with two judgments, imputation of the deed (*imputatio facti*) and imputation of the law (*imputatio iuris*), aside from measuring the deed according to the law or application of the law to the deed (*applicatio legis ad factum*). It is not only an academic differentiation, but also a consequence of the diverse nature of the operations carried out by the imputing subject. It is necessary to differentiate between a deed as it is measured by the rule, and, as it is attributed to the agent. There are "deeds" that: a) are contrary to the rule (they do not meet what is required by the rule), and therefore imputed as demeritorius (save for when there are causes for the exclusion of that imputation, which will be dealt with later); or b) exceed what is required by the rule (they are supererogatory), and therefore imputed as meritorious; or c) coincide with what is required by the rule in question, for which neither an imputation of merit nor demerit follows, only an imputation of a due act (acting the way one is "supposed to" or compliance with the rule).

This differentiation was perceived in works as early as the eighteenth century. In 1740, Daries had already proceeded to differentiate *imputatio facti* and *imputatio iuris*. Furthermore, he proposed to differentiate from these two the so-called *applicatio legis ad factum*, which would mediate between both judgments of imputation, whose premise would be *imputatio facti*, and in turn serve as the premise for *imputatio iuris*. Thus Daries says *imputatio facti* and *imputatio iuris* are not diverse species of imputation,[14] but integral and necessary parts of the operation of imputation. Both have to concur in order to impute an action or an omission to its *auctor*, and to the latter as meritorious, demeritorious, or due. In turn, *imputatio iuris* is not possible without having previously imputed the *factum*, that is, without the *imputatio facti*. Daries also distinguishes between to whom the deed is imputed through the *imputatio facti* (named the *actor*), and who is imputing the law through the *imputatio iuris* (*iudex*.) Nevertheless, both operations are different from what is called *applicatio legis ad factum*, a function of the *iudex*, who then must judge the concordance of the deed to the *lex* following the *imputatio facti* and preceding the *imputatio iuris*. Towards the end of the eighteenth century, Kant asserts that action "stands

[14] "Notandum est, imputationem facti et imputationem iuris non esse diuersas imputationis species." J. G. Daries, *Institutiones Iurisprudentiae Universalis*, 4 ed. (Ienae: MDCCLI), § 218, cor. I, 117.

under laws,"[15] but focuses more on the *imputatio facti* than on the *imputatio iuris* or the *applicatio legis ad factum*.

1.3. The distinction between object of imputation and rules of imputation

As stated previously, it is necessary to differentiate imputation and evaluation of the imputed act, and therefore, between the rules of imputation and the object of imputation. The differentiation between the *object* (the "deed" and the quality of merit or demerit attributed to its author) and the *rules* of imputation is a milestone. The "deed" is considered to be *of* (*something proper or belonging to*) the actor, meaning it is attributed to him, and moreover the deed is measured according to the rules of conduct or the *lex*. These are two different operations:[16] imputation and measurement. Although in present, praxis the predominance of the idea of subsumption as a supposed paradigm of the work the judge undertakes, can lead one to think that law consists of looking for the solution to a case in precedents and statutes. This work is neither the only nor the main legal operation, for even before this operation, exist rules of imputation that are present alongside rules of conduct in our everyday lives. The rules of conduct would be nonsensical if they could neither be used as guidelines for conduct nor guidelines to measure what is done. This measurement operation in turn presupposes the attribution, through rules of imputation, of something like an action (or omission), and then as reproachable or not, meritorious or not. The rules of conduct, by defining prohibited, obligatory, and permitted conduct, give an actor guidelines for future conduct. These rules have a prospective character, shaping one's future actions. At the same time, these rules offer the imputing subject a gauge or scale of measurement, when confronted in retrospect by the object of the imputation: the deed. The rules have in this sense a retrospective character, and indicate when to attribute responsibility for what has been done or omitted.[17] Here the judgment of imputation comes into play. It affirms that what is done is an action (or omission) or that the agent is not only the source of the action (or omission) but is moreover considered rational as a subject governed by

[15] "Unter Gesetzen steht." Kant, *Die Metaphysik der Sitten*, 227 (21-24).

[16] Cfr. Joachim Hruschka, "Verhaltensregeln und Zurechnungsregeln," *Rechtstheorie* 22 (1991): 453; Hruschka, "Imputation," 137-9.

[17] Cfr. Hruschka, "Verhaltensregeln und Zurechnungsregeln," 450-1; ———, "Imputation," 138.

guidelines. Imputation opens to a peculiar process of communication: an "attribution of meaning." This process of attribution of meaning implies the specific meaning that the situation in which the agent is involved constitutes an expression of rules of conduct. Once the deed is imputed, it is subjected to rules of conduct used to "weigh," measure, and criticise it.[18]

This distinction is significant for highlighting that imputation is not an operation of mere comparison between what is done and the law, which is undertaken in the so-called *applicatio legis ad factum*. In judgments of imputation, insofar as they consist of attributing to the agent, something else is undertaken. In operations of imputation a connection is established between the two ends of the judgment of imputation (subject and deed). In the judgment of imputation of the deed (*imputatio facti*) this connection derives from the "identification" of the *causa libera* that constitutes the origin of a new deed. In order to say someone is *causa libera*, two criteria must be fulfilled, functioning as parallel or correspondent rules of imputation: the actor has to know the circumstances, and has to have control over his immediate surroundings. Therefore, a rule of imputation is that it is not possible to impute what the subject cannot avoid because it has its source in a different agent. Then the cause is not *libera* in its *radical* source origin, but simply a link in a chain of causes. The actor's knowledge of the circumstances is also necessary.

It has to be taken into account that on occasion, even in cases of absence of intention,[19] imputation is not excluded. This non-exclusion makes it possible to distinguish between the *consecutive* and *adversative* rules of imputation. The latter allow overcoming the impossibility of imputing when the subject has provoked his own non-imputation or absence of imputation.

Consecutive rules are those that link two ends in a logical conclusion: one of the ends is a consequence of the other. Imputation is conditioned because the deed must be done by a *causa libera*. In other words, what is understood by *causa libera* and its requirements can be used to reject

---

[18] German-rooted criminal law talks about commissions, omissions and justification, for the prospective character. For the retrospective character, offense definitions (*Tatbestände*), for both definitions of offenses of commission (*Begehungstatbestände*) and of omission (*Unterlassungstatbestände*) and justifications (*Rechtfertigungsgründe*), which refer to the conceptualisation of the conduct realised in light of its legal description.

[19] The reference to intention is used here to express that a subjective element is necessary to attribute responsibility for the conduct, as required in German law by the term "intent" (*Vorsatz*).

imputation if these requirements are not met. From time immemorial voluntary human action has been studied, as well as those assumptions indicating involuntariness, such as force and ignorance. As Aristotle states: "that which is done in ignorance, or though not done in ignorance is not in the agent's power, or is done under compulsion, is involuntary."[20]

Adversative rules are those that impute even without the elements upon which imputation is directly (consecutively) founded. Despite this lack, transgression without intention can be imputed as "mere *fault (culpa).*"[21] In this sense, the function of the rules of imputation is not limited to the functional role of establishing the connection between the two ends of the judgment of imputation: subject-deed (*imputatio facti*). Prior to Kant's doctrine, rules of this nature existed with a certain degree of elaboration. Pufendorf posed the possibility of imputation even in cases without intention.[22] The origin of these rules and structures of imputation is ancient, going as far back as Aristotle. One of the texts in which this question is clearly posed is found in Book III of the *Nichomachean Ethics*. Simple ignorance is distinguished from ignorance that has its cause in the agent. Ignorance that has its cause in the agent does not disrupt imputation. Ignorance (involuntariness) does not prevent the attribution of that exclusion of voluntariness to the agent if it were in his power to avoid the situation.[23] This elaboration continues with Thomas Aquinas for example, in the passage of his commentary *In decem libros ethicorum Aristotelis ad Nicomachum Expositio*, 1270-1272, Aristotle's doctrine is advanced further and significant differentiations are drawn.[24] This process has

[20] Aristotle, *Ethica Nichomachea*, 1135 a 32-35.

[21] "An *unintentional* transgression which can still be imputed to the agent is called a mere *fault* (*culpa*)." ("Eine *unvorsetzliche* Übertretung, die gleichwohl zugerechnet werden kann, heiβt bloβe *Verschuldung* (*culpa*).") Kant, *Die Metaphysik der Sitten*, 224 (4-7).

[22] Cfr. Joachim Hruschka, "Ordentliche und außerordentliche Zurechnung bei Pufendorf. Zur Geschichte und zur Bedeutung der Differenz von actio libera in se und actio libera in sua causa," *Zeitschrift für die gesamte Strafrechtswissenschaft* 96 (1984): 661-702.

[23] "For these [the legislators] punish and take vengeance on those who do wicked acts (unless they have acted under compulsion or as a result of ignorance for wich they are not themselves responsible) […] Indeed, we punish a man for his very ignorance, if he is thought responsible for the ignorance […]." Aristotle, *Ethica Nichomachea*, 1113 b 22 - 4 a 3.

[24] Cfr. Joachim Hruschka, "Conscientia erronea und ignorantia bei Thomas von Aquin," in *Festschrift für Hans Welzel zum 70. Geburtstag*, ed. Günter Stratenwerth et al. (Berlin – New York: Walter de Gruyter, 1974), 115-49. Cfr.

carried over all the way to present-day legislation, as clearly seen in penal codification, and even in academic doctrine, where the differentiations are seen when authors attribute the responsibility of the agent for his own non-imputation or absence of imputation (*actio libera in causa*, or controllable/avoidable error).

2. The systematic contributions of the doctrine of imputation

The foregoing historical exposition summarising three conceptual achievements or advances, can also be exposed systematically. To this end, it would serve in good stead first to highlight three differences: *i*) between imputation and application of the law; *ii*) first and second level imputation; and *iii*) ordinary and extraordinary imputation. It is also necessary to point out: *iv*) how imputation requires knowledge and that the source of what is caused can be situated in the subject to whom it is to be imputed. As noted above, these concepts are curiously related to one another. This interrelationship is precisely one of the greatest advantages of this model: it constitutes a minimum system that allows developments as it operates as an organisation of structures to which a variety of content can later be linked.

i) Imputation and application of a law have to be differentiated. Both operations should not be confused if the risk of substituting the operation of attributing responsibility with inadequate modes of proceeding is to be avoided. Both imputation and application of the law are judgments reached by the imputing subject. Imputation consists, however, of the attribution of a very concrete object: something like an action (or omission) and its reproach, while application of the law consists of evaluation of the imputed deed using the rule of conduct as the standard. The rule of conduct functions differently here from when it was directed at the actor, as now it serves to measure what has been done. At this point, the norms at play (prohibitions, obligations, and permissions) that operate prospectively are used retrospectively as a measure. Commissions, omissions, and justifications,[25] can then be discussed. Therefore, an action carried out contrary to what is required in a prohibitive norm fulfills the respective crime definition (of homicide, for example).

---

more references in Sanchez-Ostiz, *La noción de imputación ["The Notion of Imputation"]*, I.2.3.

[25] See footnote 18.

ii) It is necessary to differentiate between first- and second-level imputation. First-level imputation, or imputation of the deed (*imputatio facti*), is the judgment by virtue of which the process in which one finds oneself involved is seen as an action or an omission; and the subject involved in that process as its author. Second-level imputation, or imputation of the law (*imputatio iuris*), is the judgment by virtue of which a deed is attributed to the actor as his merit or demerit. The operation described as application of the law to the deed (*applicatio legis ad factum*) mediates between both judgments. The relation that exists between application of the law and first-level imputation is one of implication, such "application" of a law to a case presupposes that something could already have been imputed as a deed.[26] In turn, second-level imputation implies the law has been applied to the deed (*applicatio legis ad factum*). This consequence is also seen in relation to implication with the former operation.

The attribution of responsibility contained in every judgment of imputation supposes the possibility of setting limits to something in the world in which the subject is involved, and considering it *action* (or *omission*). Otherwise, the subject remains as mere nature. The subject's action or omission is that process in which the subject is involved, whose circumstances the subject knows and which he at least partially controls, i.e., a controllable process subjected to norms. This means that there is a deed if the process is present for the subject, who is then considered to be an agent (its author). "Present" here is taken to mean that the subject brings into the present moment what he can in this process. The actor's participation is possible thanks to the person's cognitive faculty, which perceives circumstances of the process in which he is involved. Moreover, this participation means that the person becomes an agent only when, upon controlling that process, he updates his knowledge (the possible anticipation of what could ensue from his act) and effectively exercises that control (or fails to exercise that control in the case of omission). These factors can be called simultaneity and reference.[27] *Simultaneity* means the

---

[26] Cfr. Hruschka, "Verhaltensregeln und Zurechnungsregeln," 453; ———, "Imputation," 126-8, 126 footnote 12. "... ex applicatione legis ad factum intelligitur, actionem esse talem, quae imputari possit." Christian Wolff, *Philosophia Practica Universalis, Pars Prima*, Francofurti et Lipsiae, 1738 ed. (Hildesheim – New York: Olms, 1971), § 598. (Translation, ibid., 127: "From the application of the law to the deed follows that the action is such that it can be imputed.")

[27] Cfr. Hruschka, *Strafrecht nach logisch-analytischer Methode*, 1-67.

representation and modification of the situation coincide at least for one relevant moment (the human process called action (or omission) occurs simultaneously when the subject's knowledge is *present at the time* of directing the process, at least partially.) Only then can the subject be considered the agent and the process an action (or omission). *Reference* means that external modification in which the subject is involved is the object of his representation or knowledge (the agent is such at the moment of carrying out his deed to the extent that his knowledge *influences the course of the process* that he is carrying out.) Only when the subject knows the potentiality of the accomplished process, and this process remains under his control, can we speak of an agent and an action (or omission).

iii) Imputation can also be ordinary or extraordinary. It is *ordinary* when the necessary elements concur. While, it is considered *extraordinary* when said elements do not concur, but in spite of this lack of concurrence the imputation to the actor is upheldby virtue of adversative rules (see 1.3). Extraordinary imputation cannot be based on an infraction of a rule, because the required elements for it to be considered a deed do not concur (there is no deed, so to speak, on the firstlevel of imputation), neither is the deed reproachable, because the required elements for its reproach do not concur (there is no reproachable deed on the second level of imputation). Nevertheless, extraordinary imputation is based on acting against what concerns the subject. The concerns[28] are presented as sources of guidelines for conduct that are not exactly rules of conduct but make these rules possible. The concept of "concern" requires a more detailed explication, which cannot be done here.

iv) In order to impute, it is necessary to verify that the subject knows the relevant circumstances and controls the process. A process (or a state of inactivity) wherein someone is involved is an action (or an omission) when it has its origin in the agent who knows the relevant circumstances of the case. The confirmation of a process as action (or omission) is precisely the result of judgment, called *imputatio facti* in the doctrine of

---

[28] Translated from the German *Obliegenheit*. It expresses that conduct is not only governed by duties and obligations, but also by norms whose content is related to duties. These are normative propositions that function as conditions of the possibility of duties and obligations, in such a way that the receiver of the concern enjoys freedom of action, as long as he can, when the time comes, properly fulfill that duty. These concerns are referred to by Hruschka in Ibid., 274-386; ———, "Ordentliche und außerordentliche Zurechnung bei Pufendorf," 661-702; ———, "Imputation," 140-57.

imputation. It is first-level imputation. The existence of an action (or omission) comes from verification of a process that has its source in the agent, and that agent's knowledge of the circumstances. Inversely, it is not possible to impute a process as *factum*, as action or omission, if ignorance of the circumstances intervenes or if the subject is not the source of the process. Instead, these are cases of physical or absolute necessity (*necessitas physica seu absoluta*). In the judgment of second-level imputation, or *imputatio iuris*, reproach is directed at the subject for having acted against what is required by the rule in question. In the same way as was pointed out for imputation of the deed (*imputatio facti*), it would not be possible to impute the action (or omission) as demeritorious (or meritorious) when, either the agent finds himself in a situation such as duress or necessity corresponds to the paradigm of compulsive (but not absolutely compelling) force (*vis compulsiva*), or they did not know the norm, ignorance of the law (*ignorantia iuris*).

The model of imputation just described presents diverse parallelisms, which have to be given close attention. A parallelism exists between two classes of ignorance: ignorance of the facts (*ignorantia facti*) and ignorance of the law (*ignorantia iuris*), relevant respectively to imputation of the deed (*imputatio facti*) and to imputation of the law (*imputatio iuris*), depending on whether something is being attributed as deed (action or omission) or the deed as demeritorious. A parallelism can also be seen between the assumptions of necessity (absolute or limited) (*necessitas absoluta* or *cum adiunctione*,) depending on whether what is excluded is the imputation of something as a deed, or the imputation of reproach for the deed. It can be seen how both conceptual pairs affect the two levels of imputation, respectively. They seem to be similar in a way, but at the same time different on each level. There are two modalities of necessity (*necessitas*), because there are two levels of imputation as there are two forms of ignorance (*ignorantia*). *Ignorantia* and *necessitas* both exclude imputation on the respective level, which exclusion does not, however, impede the possibility of extraordinary imputation. If imputation requires freedom in the agent, freedom disappears for any of these four causes of exclusion. The duality of forms of imputation (ordinary and extraordinary) underlies both levels.

The two levels of imputation, and their respective causes of exclusion, lead to a differentiation of two forms of freedom. The freedom that is required for first-level imputation is the minimum option for the subject to act according to the rules. Nothing more is required than having an option at that moment. On the other hand, the freedom that is required for second-level imputation is complete freedom based on option with acceptable motives, in acting "willfully." Freedom does not have the same meaning on both levels of imputation. It takes on full meaning when the agent not only *knows* what he is doing, but when he is also *conscious* of what he is doing (for instance, he knows that what he is doing is wrong, or right), that is, the agent acts and knows what his action means. In order to designate both aspects of freedom, the employment of the term *volition* is proposed for the former, and *willfulness* for the latter. *Volition* here denotes the mere act of the will by a person, without taking into consideration the acceptable motives behind the act. Once we allow for these motives however, freedom is better denoted with the term *willfulness*, to highlight the actor's commitment because the object of the act is understood as moral, in other words, once the agent has grasped the sense of good or bad, just or unjust, etc., of the deed.

3. Human rationality and imputation

The idea of imputation has been associated with that of a person: "A *person* is a subject whose actions can be *imputed* to him."[29] In effect, the previously explained parallelisms in the rules of imputation bring out an order and coherence that appeals to human rationality: the peculiar way of an agent's being. Hereafter, only the features of a concept of an agent-person as a rational subject are outlined. The person as agent can be described by three characteristics: permanence, practicality, and reflexiveness.[30]

Permanence means the person is situated in his action, not only at the moment of executing the act but also beyond the action itself. The actor is the agent of the action, as much at the moment of acting as after the action (in the sense that it is his act which is carried out by him.) This permanence is possible due to the immaterial character of the person: what is merely material does not transcend time, but is only at the moment it is perceived, while the person remains and transcends time. It can be said then that permanence is the transcendence of time: the *agent remains even after the action*. This permanence implies the immaterial character of the

29 "*Person* ist dasjenige Subject, dessen Handlungen einer *Zurechnung* fähig sind." Kant, *Die Metaphysik der Sitten*, 223 (24-25). On the other hand, for things there is no imputation: "A *thing* is that to which nothing can be imputed" ("*Sache* ist ein Ding, was keiner Zurechnung fähig ist.") ———, *Die Metaphysik der Sitten*, 223 (32).

30 This concept of person is discussed in Sanchez-Ostiz, *La noción de imputación ["The Notion of Imputation"]*, VIII.3.

person. The requirement of subjective elements—above all, intention—in law and ethics in order to impute responsibility can be understood as a consequence of permanence. The agent remains or endures past the action because the agent is endowed with an immaterial capacity not subjected to space or time, a capacity, which allows it to continue being the author of what was done. The process becomes a deed (an action or an omission) and endures as that deed, with a subject, beyond the concrete causal course realized. Knowing what is done is a necessary condition to be an author of what is done.

Practicality means that the agent cannot act except through rules and norms. That is, the action is an action as long as the agent intends to do something (impulse, something animal) that meets with a norm that abides within the subject himself (rule, something human and rational). To act then means *to realize human potentiality according to rules*. It is a conditioning derived from the agent's very constitution as a rational subject. This conditioning could be similar to the unconditional validity of the laws of logic,[31] in that, we like it or not, we can never cease to be moral subjects. On the other hand, what comes from a human subject but is not an object of rules of conduct, and is conditioned by his animality, does not constitute a human action although it comes from a human being. *Sleep*, as far as the subject is involved in sleep, is not a human action. *Going to sleep*, however, is, if the subject sets out to do it. Practicality is different from the human subject in that the subject is endowed with (practical) rationality. To speak of action, it is necessary that the subject can conjugate the "I act" and not simply employ the description "the things are affected," or "things happen." The "I act" means the agent subject makes whatever rules his or her own. Practicality therefore means that the person is an *agent insofar a he or she is guided by rules*.

Reflexiveness means the deed affects the very agent and remains in him. It can be said therefore that there are no merely transitive actions, rather, that all actions are reflexive, since all have repercussions on the agent and the first receiver of the action is the agent himself. In this sense, we do to ourselves whatever we do, insofar as the agent himself is the receiver of his action. So, even the most transitive of actions (*to give* something, for example) is reflexive (since it makes the agent a *giver* of things to others.) Hence, it can be said that as for "we do to ourselves whatever we do," it becomes possible to attribute to the agent the quality of merit or demerit for what is done. If the agent continues past the time of

---

[31] The comparison is from Joachim Hruschka, "Die Würde des Menschen bei Kant," *Archiv für Rechts und Sozialphilosophie* 88 (2002): 463-80, 469-71.

his deed (permanence), and the deed has repercussion on the agent himself (reflexiveness), then the deed is his. It belongs to the actor in a double sense: not only as far as the subject that lasts, but also as the agent accountable for actions (or omissions), for which he is imputed with merit or demerit. Actions done according to the norm are imputed in the sense that they indicate that at least the agent acted according to the norm.

From these three traits of the person as agent (permanence, practicality and reflexiveness) we can return to imputation and define it as: Imputation is a judgment by virtue of which the process in which the subject is involved is considered action (or omission), the actions (or omissions) are then evaluated according to the guidelines that govern these actions (or omissions), and are finally reproached or praised. Here we clearly see process/interrelation of the *imputatio facti* (judgment of imputation of the deeds the agent carries out), the *applicatio legis ad factum* (evaluation of the deeds according to the guidelines that govern these deeds), and the *imputatio iuris* (reproach or praise of the actions or omissions). The three traits of the person correspond to the three steps involved in all judgments of *complete* imputation.

Firstly, to be able to say that a person has acted, it is necessary to be able to affirm that the agent persists beyond his action. This affirmation is possible by virtue of the immaterial being of the person. The exigency of "subjective" elements (will, intention, knowledge, etc.) is a consequence of the agent's transcendence: in order to transcend the action the agent has to be conscious of his control, or at least possible control, over the physical laws in which he finds himself involved. Otherwise, the agent does not act; he cannot transcend time, as he is a mere object at the mercy of those same physical laws. It is a premise of the operation of *imputatio facti*.

Secondly, the premise of the *applicatio legis ad factum* is that the agent is governed by guidelines that are used later in the evaluation of the *factum*. This is the practicality of the person, that is, that the human agent is not only the agent because he is the origin of the process but also because in that process he intervenes as the bearer of practical rules. These rules govern his act and allow for the measure, evaluation, and criticism of his action.

Thirdly, imputing the deed (evaluated as inadequate according to the pertinent rule) to the agent as something demeritorious is possible as long as the action or omission remains in the agent beyond the deed's execution (reflexiveness.) It is precisely the imputation of the deed to the agent qualified as praiseworthy or reproachable that supposes a reflection on him of what he himself has done. That is to say, the reproach of guilt because of demerit, or of praise because of merit, presuppose that the deed is not only a mere external change but above all a change in the agent himself: the deed affects its agent subject.

The preceding exposition shows how the operation of the attribution of responsibility that we call imputation presents an internally coherent order and a consistent method of imputation. Rationality of the (imputing and imputed) person provides reasons explaining this consistency. Above and beyond specific national legislation, past and present, it is not venturous to think that human rationality provides a common ground that becomes evident in the rules of imputation.

Bibliography

Aristotle. *Ethica Eudemia*. Translated by J. Solomon. Edited by David Ross, *The Works of Aristotle*, vol. IX. Oxford, 1915.

—. *Ethica Nichomachea*. Translated by David Ross. Edited by David Ross, *The Works of Aristotle*, vol. IX. Oxford, 1915.

Daries, J. G. *Institutiones Iurisprudentiae Universalis*. 4 ed. Ienae, MDCCLI.

Hruschka, Joachim. "Conscientia erronea und ignorantia bei Thomas von Aquin." In *Festschrift für Hans Welzel zum 70. Geburtstag*, edited by Günter Stratenwerth et al., 115-49. Berlin – New York: Walter de Gruyter, 1974.

—. *Strukturen der Zurechnung*. Berlin – New York: Walter de Gruyter, 1976.

—. "Ordentliche und außerordentliche Zurechnung bei Pufendorf. Zur Geschichte und zur Bedeutung der Differenz von actio libera in se und actio libera in sua causa." *Zeitschrift für die gesamte Strafrechtswissenschaft* 96 (1984): 661-702.

—. "Imputation." In *Rechtfertigung und Entschuldigung. Rechtsvergleichende Perspektiven/Justification and Excuse. Comparative Perspectives, I*, edited by Albin Eser and Walter Perron, 120-74. Freiburg i.B.: Max-Planck-Institut für Auslandisches und Internationales Strafrecht, 1987.

—. *Strafrecht nach logisch-analytischer Methode*. 2 ed. Berlin – New York: Walter de Gruyter, 1988.

—. "Verhaltensregeln und Zurechnungsregeln." *Rechtstheorie* 22 (1991): 449-60.

—. "Rechtfertigungs- und Entschuldigungsgründe: Das Brett des Karneades bei Gentz und bei Kant." *Goltdammer's Archiv für Strafrecht* (1991): 1-10.

—. “Verhaltensregeln und Zurechnungsregeln.” *Rechtstheorie* 22 (1991): 449-60.

—. “Zurechnung.” In *Handwörterbuch zur deutschen Rechtsgeschichte*, edited by Adalbert Erler and Ekkehard Kaufman, 1803-6. Berlin: Schmidt, 1998.

—. “Regreßverbot, Anstiftungsbegriff und die Konsequenzen.” *Zeitschrift für die gesamte Strafrechtswissenschaft* 110 (1998): 581-610.

—. “Die Würde des Menschen bei Kant.” *Archiv für Rechts und Sozialphilosophie* 88 (2002): 463-80.

—. “Der Einfluß des Aristoteles und der Aristoteles-Rezeptionen auf die Bildung heutiger Rechtsbegriffe am Beispiel der ‘actio libera in causa’.” In *Festschrift für Christoph Link zum 70. Geburtstag*, edited by Heinrich de Wall and Michael German, 687-704. Tübingen: Mohr Siebeck, 2003.

—. *Imputación y Derecho penal. Estudios sobre la teoría de la imputación.* Pamplona: Aranzadi, 2005.

Hruschka, Joachim, and Jan C. Joerden. “Supererogation: Vom deontologischen Sechseck zum deontologischen Zehneck.” *Archiv für Rechts und Sozialphilosophie* 73 (1987): 93-123.

Kant, Immanuel. *Die Metaphysik der Sitten*. Edited by Akademie der Wissenschaften, *Kant's gesammelte Schriften*, vol. VI. Berlin, 1902 ff.

—. *Practical philosophy*. Translated by Mary J. Gregor. Edited by Mary J. Gregor. Cambridge: Cambridge University Press, 1996.

Sanchez-Ostiz, Pablo. *La noción de imputación [“The Notion of Imputation”]*, 2007, (in press).

Thomas Aquinas. *Opera omnia*. Edited by Commissio Leonina. Paris: Librairie Philosophique J. Vein, 1882.

Wolff, Christian. *Philosophia Practica Universalis, Pars Prima*. Francofurti et Lipsiae, 1738 ed. Hildesheim – New York: Olms, 1971.

CHAPTER TWENTY FOUR

PRACTICAL REASON, JUSTICE AND LAW (THE PRESENT RELEVANCE OF THE ARISTOTELEAN-THOMISTIC PERSPECTIVE)

DIEGO POOLE*

Introduction

In this work we deal with the first principles of natural law, considered as principles of acting, but noticing the great difference between the Grisez-Finnis theory and Aristotle's. Then we study the articulation of those principles in the structure of practical reasoning, noticing that practical reason does not consist in applying rules to the cases. In the third chapter we try to explain that the common good is an architectonic concept in view of which makes sense, not only the law itself, but also the same human existence. In the fourth chapter we explain the virtue of justice underlining the sense of aristotelic general justice. Last, we deal with the concept of law as analogical term, as the correct disposition of the parts towards the common good.

The image of "iusnaturalist essentialism" developed by Suarez—in alleged continuity with St. Thomas—has corrupted the genuine structure of practical reasoning as it was conceived by Aristotle and later developed faithfully by Aquinas. In a certain way, the distortion of the concept of natural law principles must be attributed to Suarez, especially in the way in which he loses sight of the different nature of the premises of both speculative and practical reasoning. The "naturalistic fallacy" criticism, that since Hume has been used against "classical iusnaturalism", could be pertinent and correct when applied to the theory of Suarez or to any iusnaturalism of rationalist style, yet, on the other hand, in the last three

* This work was written under under the auspices of the "I+D Comunidad de Madrid" (Project No. S2007/HUM-0403).

centuries it has been presented as if it were the only "classical theory of natural law".

Thanks largely to the studies on Aristotle done since Anscombe[1] and Nussbaum[2] that vindicate the specificity of practical reasoning as the Stagyrite conceived it, and thanks also to the neoclassical authors who are inspired by the moral philosophy of Grisez,[3] a whole line of reflection has been opened, which questions the conventional image of iusnaturalism that in fact now has little to do with the doctrines of the authors (especially Aristotle and St. Thomas) on whom those doctrines were theoretically based.[4]

In the area of the European moral philosophy those who are developing the specificity of practical reasoning with greater success are perhaps the Swiss professor Martin Rhonheimer and the Italian Giuseppe Abba.[5]

---

[1] Cf. G.E.M. Anscombe, *Intention* (Ithaca - New York: Cornell University Press, 1979). First published in 1957. And ———, "Modern Moral Philosophy," *Philosophy* 33, no. 134 (1958).

[2] Cf. Martha C. Nussbaum, *Aristotle's De Motu Animalium* (Princeton: Princeton University Press, 1985). First published in 1978; special attention should be paid to the fourth essay, 165-220.

[3] A key work that marks the beginning of this line of reflection is the work of Grisez, "The First Principle of Practical Reason. A Commentary on the *Summa theologiae*, 1-2, Question 94, Article 2." This article has been reedited in numerous publications. I have recently translated it into Spanish in *Persona y Derecho*, 52, (2005), 275-339. The translation is preceded by a magnificent introductory study written by Professor Eduardo Ortiz. In the same issue of *Persona y Derecho* I have published an extensive commentary on Grisez's theory about the first principle in contrast to St. Thomas (339-395).

[4] We have to notice that, in the case of the philosophers who are called "neoclassicists", although they propose a renewed study of Aristotle and Aquinas, they lack a faithful reflection of the thoughts of those authors.

[5] Of the works of Giuseppe Abbà we consider specially relevant for this subject the following: Giuseppe Abbà, *Lex et Virtus, Studi sull'evoluzione della morale di san Tommaso d'Aquino* (Roma: LAS, 1983). Abbà, *Quale impostazione per la filosofia morale?* Giuseppe Abbà, *Felicidad, vida buena y virtud* (Barcelona: Eiunsa, 1992). First edited in 1989. And the article ———, "Christian Moral Principles di Grisez e la Secunda Pars della Summa Thologiae," *Salesianum* 48 (1986): 637-80. Of Martin Rhonheimer the most significant work is, without a doubt, Rhonheimer, *Natural Law and Practical Reason*. That is an English translation of *Natur als Grundlage der Moral*, 1987 (there are also a Spanish and Italian version). There is an article where he presents in very clear synthesis his moral philosophy: Martin Rhonheimer, "Legge morale naturale: conoscenza morale and coscienza. The cognitiva struttura della legge naturale and verità della soggettività," *Ars*

However in the area of European legal philosophy we still face a great deal of work.

Here we try to present, with the new perspective of these philosophers, the classical thought of Aristotle and St. Thomas about the relationship between practical reason, justice and law.

A new interpretation of first principles and of the other principles of natural law

Principles of natural law are principles of human action. These principles of action constitute the premises of practical reasoning. Such premises are the aims or goods towards which practical reasoning is directed (in view of them, practical reasoning is constructed). If these premises are the ends of the action, they are not very general norms; only in view of such ends, and after the knowledge of them, we make the precepts, with which we describe those aims and we determine the way in which we obtain them. If they are called *principles*, it is because practical reasoning begins from them, because practical reasoning always begins with a desired end, which is the last in the acquisition. If principles of practical reasoning are the ends of the act, they will be as much more principles the more ultimate they are. And if it is absurd to think that man could have many *last* ends, for the same reason we cannot say that he has many "first principles" (all with the same degree of finality or ultimately, is understood). And it is absurd to think that man could have many final ends because, otherwise, it would be necessary to admit that man is a naturally *amorphous* being, because he could realize himself in any direction and in any way; but such an idea is counter to common experience. St. Thomas explains this by saying that the last end of a substance is its ultimate or final form, and that man reaches such an end by means of his morally good actions, because the fundamental criterion of morality of human action—as we will see later—will be determined *in the last instance* in view of the last end. We emphasized "*in the last instance*" because an approximate knowledge of the morality of our actions already comes to us by a certain congruency of each action with the appetitive dynamism proper to man.

Interpretandi 7 (2002): 47-78. —also it is gathered in the collective work published by Juan de Dios Vial and Elio Sgreccia, eds., *Natura and Dignità della persona umana a fondamento del diritto alla vita. Atti dell'ottava Assamblea Generale della Pontificia Accademia per la vita* (Roma: Libreria Editrice Vaticana, 2002), 125-58.

Normally, by its appetizing movement, each animal finds itself tending towards its own good. Irrational animals satisfy their appetites or instincts without knowing why they satisfy them, or at least without perceiving the internal hierarchy between their own appetites, and by all means, without being conscious that, when trying to obtain their own good, they enable other animals to effectively tend to their own as well. Man, like any animal, finds himself desiring goods that he himself does not choose to desire, but, unlike irrational animals, he can choose whether to satisfy them or not. Presupposed in any choice is the existence of an appetite in view of which one chooses one thing or another. And in the hierarchy of appetites there is an appetite that man cannot fail to choose: it is the appetite of happiness, fullness, unrestricted good, or however it is called. Nobody, in his right mind, can choose not to be happy. It is, therefore, in view of this appetite how we assess the right measure by which to satisfy the subordinated appetites. Man, thanks to suitable instruction and by means of the continuous exercise of correct actions, is used to his inferior appetites to desire in the right measure, so that all and each one of the appetites plays in favour of the appetite for happiness. Certainly all the appetites have an original direction towards their own corresponding good, but all the appetites have a natural correlation to each other, in such a way that the inferior appetites are at the service of (and integrated into) the superior appetites. For example, the nutritive appetite is at the service of (and integrated under) the most general appetite of preservation in the being, that, as well, is subordinated to a more general appetite of fullness or happiness (thanks to the fact that man flees passionately from death, he can perform other goods for which he lives, because the intelligent being is not contented with living to live, but to do something with his life). All this does not mean that man always considers, whenever he acts, this subordination and hierarchy of desired goods. It simply means that, when he stops to think, he can know this subordination of appetites, and can even leave some inferior appetite relatively unsatisfied in order to better fulfil a superior appetite. *The virtuous man is he who has so mastered his appetites, so that all in him desires according to the rational appetite of happiness*. For that reason, the virtuous man is a man who knows how to be happy; because he can maintain the rectitude of the appetites towards the best of his possibilities (vicious man lives under his possibilities).

The rank in the hierarchy of the appetites is not derived from its respective urgency, but by its greater or smaller finality (ultimateness). We have previously seen that in this hierarchy of appetites, there is an appetite that does not serve any other, and in whose service all the others exist. Man, in the way in which he develops intellectually, *identifies* this appetite better (certainly through the desired goods), although this fundamental appetite is present and is operative, by means of the other appetites, from the beginning of his life: everything that man does, since his coming into this world, he does because, consciously or unconsciously, he seeks happiness. Only with time man realizes that life has *a meaning*; that there exists a dominant appetite; he realizes that genuine human life is not a succession of disjointed satisfactions of appetites; he realizes that everything one desires, is such because it is able to be integrated in a unifying project, i.e., in view of an end desired by itself. In the measure in which man is maturing, he is integrating his appetites. The gluttonous boy, for example, has not applied the correct measure to his nutritive appetite, a measure that derives from the appetite of a superior good, as it is the appetite to conserve health or beauty. The gluttonous boy, and in general immature people, does not perceive the concatenation of the appetizing hierarchy by virtue of which the superior appetites establish the measure of the inferior ones. We could identify the fullness of maturity with a *suitable integration of all the appetites*, or what is the same, with the virtuous life itself.

But, why this reference to the appetites when we want to talk about the first principle and about the other principles of natural law? Because in the practical order, the first principle is the last desired end, and all the appetites exist in order to obtain (and to the service of) the last end. The goods desired naturally by man, will be principles of natural law as long as, in light of them, practical reasoning is articulated, and as long as such goods are also means (ends-means) to obtain other superior goods. The natural appetites are, for that reason, certain signs and *principia* of morality, but they are not the decisive criterion. If several "first principles", or similarly, several last ends, cannot exist, all those ends that are not the last end will be ends only in a sense that they are means for attaining the last end. And they will be means as much more valuable as long as they are more necessary for the attainment of the last end. Therefore, it seems that it is possible to set down an objective hierarchy between those ends-means, because of its greater or smaller necessity for the attainment of the last end, which is completely necessary. Perhaps with this perspective we could better interpret the list of "human goods" described by St. Thomas in art. 2 q.94, I-II of his *Summa Theologiae*, and we could suitably frame the theory of the "basic human goods" developed from Grisez (with the difference that we will consider the basic goods based on their greater or less necessity for the attainment of the last end).

A study of the articulation of such principles in the structure of practical reasoning

Can we conclude, based on what we just said, that a correct practical reasoning is, for that matter, a morally good reasoning? Not necessarily. Essential for a practical syllogism—a practical reasoning can consist of many practical syllogisms—it is the existence of a major premise that is an objective to obtain by means of action; an objective in view of which the means are *chosen,* means that are considered more apt to obtain that end. Each practical syllogism will be much better, the more it suitably disposes or orders the means by which one obtains the aim established by the major premise. The major premise is the propositional formulation of an appetizing act of, at least, an apparent good; and the conclusion of each practical syllogism is always a *decision,* by which the means considered more suitable to obtain the aim of the major premise are *chosen*. What is proper to practical reasoning is to dispose (*choosing, electing*) that one thing (an end) has to be done by means of another (the means chosen).[6] The fact that the material execution of the chosen act could be carried out by another person, regardless of who makes the practical reasoning, does not go against the practical nature of that reasoning, and therefore does not deprive responsibility from the agent who made that reasoning—this consideration is especially important for the philosophy of Law—. The major premise of each practical syllogism is, therefore, a desire of an object, and the conclusion (*election*) is also a desire of an object, because it is desired by virtue of the appetite of the aim that constitutes the practical major premise (Aristotle himself explains that every election is an appetite of a good within our reach). And although as the major premise of the practical syllogism, as their conclusion (decisions), can be formulated propositionally, they are not propositions, but, as we have said, they are appetitive acts controlled by reason.

In other words, we could say that the structure of practical reasoning, is a continuous game of knowledge and appetite, with the following structure: First syllogism: Appetite of a good F1 → Deliberation between diverse means to obtain F1→ Election of F2 to obtain F1 → Second Syllogism: Appetite of F2 → Deliberation between diverse means to obtain F2 → Election of F3 to obtain F2; and so on. All practical

6 To such an extent this is so in the doctrine of St. Thomas, that the acts of ordering and begging are also acts of the practical reason, because they suppose a certain arrangement in the sense that a man disposes that something has to be done by means of another. Cf. Aquinas, *S. Th.*, II-II q. 83, a. 1 c.

reasoning is made at heart in view of the first end: F1, before which all the other aims are means, and are desired because at heart one desires F1. Within each one of the practical syllogisms, election consists of the preference that we give to one possibility among those that are at our reach to obtain the respective end, which presupposes, in addition to an act of knowledge (by which we compare the diverse possibilities), an appetitive act, towards which we are more inclined to, among the other possibilities.

The moral qualification of practical reason is determined by the aptitude that such reasoning has of being integrated and assumed into that which we could call "the macro practical reasoning" of personal life as a whole (this thesis has nothing to do with the moral of the "fundamental option" according to which morality would be determined by a radical election of a good aim, with relative independence of the concrete daily actions; indeed what we defend is the opposite: that the morality of each action needs to be evaluated while considering its potential integration in a project of life as a whole). The question is then to determine if there is a unique objective that gives sense to all the actions that are directed towards it. Such an objective therefore would be the first principle of acting, that is, the first principle of practical reason. And if there is such a unique objective, in light of which the actions are evaluated, the decisive question will be to determine if that objective can be chosen freely by everyone, or if on the contrary, it is given to us by nature, and we only have to accept it. If we accept that reality, including the reality of human existence, is finalized, then man can *look for* (not *invent*) the *sense*, that is the end of his own existence, and, he can, by means of his choices, adapt himself to it, or reject it.[7] In an analogous way in which we use the expression *speculative truth* to refer to the adjustment of the mind to a reality that precedes us and ties us, we can also use the expression *moral truth* to refer to those human decisions in which we elect the means that *really* guide us towards the last end. Thus, from this perspective, moral

[7] To accept that the existence of man is naturally finalized, does not justify the obligatory nature of Nature, if we do not achieve the knowledge that the natural order responds to an omniscient project of an Absolute Being. The tendency, so many times renewed, to deny moral normativity of Nature is a reasonable attitude on the part of those who do not see in Nature more than an accidental product (non causal), on which everyone can impose the sense that each wants. A graphical example is that of the transvestite, for whom the slogan "I was born in a mistaken body" is very significant, in such a way that everyone has the identity that each *wants to have*, because there is no reason that justifies the dominion of a *blind* nature over the human will.

truth or falsity is not taken primarily from a supposed adjustment or not to the "essence", but from its greater or smaller aptitude to obtain the end. Therefore, what moral reflection needs is not to speak so much in terms of "essences", but rather of "ends". The knowledge of the essence follows the knowledge of the end, which is the decisive thing.[8]

Does this mean that it is not possible to reason practically if not in view of a first unifying principle of life as a whole? It is possible to reason practically, but without reference to a final end it is not possible to justify *completely* a moral reasoning. Before continuing, it is necessary to make a clear distinction between *the morality of a practical judgment* and *the speculative judgment on the morality of that practical judgment*. When we do a practical judgement, that is, when we *deliberate* and we choose something, we are acting morally and in a certain sense judging morally, but we are not necessarily making a judgment relative to the final end; this we begin to do when we reflect speculatively on the morality of a practical judgment. We have seen before that human appetites have a hierarchy, and that the appetite of inferior goods enables and facilitates the achievement of superior goods also desired, and also we have seen that in the measure in which a person develops his intelligence, he is more able to perceive that hierarchy of appetites, precisely because he is more able to appreciate superior goods (education consists basically in this). The actions, by which we procure the correlative goods of the different appetites, are morally good in the measure in which they are able to be integrated in the fundamental appetite of the last end. This does not mean that the decisions we make every day—which being free have moral transcendence—are preceded by an explicit reflection on the last end (already the classical authors distinguished between *real* intention and *virtual* intention). What this means is that when we stop to reflect on the morality of such actions, it is inevitable that we question ourselves about the aptitude of such actions to achieve the end that we consider last in our life. This is thus because the reflective moral judgment is a judgment that qualifies the person as person. When we compare the aptitude of the action to obtain a non-last end, like for example, the action of the cobbler who fixes shoes, we qualify it as bad or good, only in view of such aim (the end to fix the shoes well), and therefore is not a moral judgment. The moral judgment, which can also be applied to the same action, always has an ultimate *ratio*: Is he becoming a better person through this action of fixing shoes? Or said with other words: Is he coming closer to his last end by means of the

---

[8] Finnis states this very clearly in John Finnis, *Fundamentals of Ethics* (Oxford - New York: Clarendon Press, 1983).

action of fixing shoes? This is indeed a moral question. Perhaps with this example we can more clearly see that moral good or evil is not *primarily* determined by reference to some essence, but by reference to an end; and not by reference to just any end, but by reference to the last end. Not in vain is the immorality of a religious person usually more surprising, than that of an atheist, for the simple reason that we presume that the religious person usually calibrates his acts in reference to a last end, more so than the atheist.[9]

The "common good" as last end of human existence, and the "basic human goods" as means to obtain the last end[10]

According St. Thomas, the last end of man is the same coexistence or *communio* of men with each other and with God himself. The good quality of common living is not a simple means to obtain ulterior goods, but rather an end in and of itself. Therefore, the last end of man is not the mere individual accomplishment, where the community would only play an instrumental role for the attainment of this end. To say that man is naturally social, means that it is in the community where man realizes himself and, because of it, he maintains himself realized.

This common end is not a mere result that will only and completely take place in the future, all or nothing, but it is a progressive and participative end that begins in the earthly existence and could be progressively consolidated throughout the personal history of each man and throughout the history of humanity as a whole.[11]

---

[9] We think that this thesis means something very similar to the neoclassical idea, that states that the moral rationality is identified with *the fullness of practical rationality*, because the neoclassicists understand that the practical rationality is total when it structures all the elections of a life in view of a last end (indeed for that reason we can speak of *one* life). Germain Grisez, Joseph Boyle, and John Finnis, "Practical Principles, Moral Truth, and Ultimate Ends," *The American Journal of Jurisprudence* 32 (1987): 99-152.

[10] These considerations about the common good do not refer to what we could call "*judicial common good*". The *judicial common good* would be determined by the indispensable minimum of solidarity that could be demanded by the governor in the concrete historical community over which he governs.

[11] To what extent the political society and the Church could present inchoate this communitarian and unifying dynamism of human existence, is a subject to

This universal common good (understood as *communio*) could be illustrated with an image, that perhaps seems excessively poetic, but a better way of expressing it does not occur to us to refer to a reality that escapes from an analytical way of knowing. Common good would be like a cosmic symphony formed by all Creation, in which men would play the role of musicians with their respective instruments (the life that each one has been called to live), and where the rest of the *irrational* creatures would play an instrumental role at the service of men, like accompaniment or like elements of the same instruments of men. All the irrational beings, being directly moved by God by means of the eternal law, would participate *passively* in this orchestra. Men, however, would take part *actively* and responsibly with "the score" of natural law, intimated in their heart by means of the natural appetite of the last end (mediated by the appetite of the "basic human goods", which naturally are disposed to lead towards the last end). In this "cosmic symphony" each man would enjoy listening to his own instrument, but still would enjoy it more when realizes that the music of the whole orchestra is still better, of which each one takes part as musician and spectator at the same time. According to this, the individualist vision, the purely individual accomplishment, would be so irrational as if a musician, breaking the harmony, tried to prevail over the others by playing his violin louder (evidently, something he could do, but much less of what he could if integrated in the whole orchestra; and certainly, if he follows only his own, the others also lose). At the same time, this vision tries to justify the natural communal dimension of human existence, where mutual service is necessary to one another.[12]

This thesis represented by the image of the orchestra does not suppose a "cosmocentric" vision, distant from the idea of dignity of each person, because all the *material* nature is at the service of the human being, and because men are the only beings of the material world who deliberately participate in this cosmic symphony, that God composed, and continually directs, for them. The accomplishment of man is communitarian, necessarily supportive, shared in common, and it is only obtained when each one *personally* assumes the role that corresponds to him in the whole, *because the perfection of a part consists of being suitably disposed to the*

---

develop, that St. Thomas did not fully develop, and that goes beyond the limits of this work.

[12] Cf *S. Th*, I-II, q. 90, a. 2, s. and Thomas Aquinas, *Opera omnia iussu Leonis XIII P. M. edita: Compendium theologiae seu Brevis compilatio theologiae ad fratrem Raynaldum*, vol. 42 (Roma: Editori di San Tommaso, 1979), §148.

whole of which it is a part.[13] The core of this reflection, and maybe, the most shocking, for going against the individualism dominant thought, is the consideration of man *as part* of a whole. Certainly, St. Thomas explains that the last end of each being is the fullness of its form, and while it is not obtained, the being literally lives in tension (to be in tension is to be tending). But the fullness of someone who is essentially a part of a community *is to be well integrated in that community*, because, as we have just said, the perfection of a part consists of being suitably disposed to the whole of which it is a part. All the appetitive dynamism of man finds its sense in this natural tendency to the *communio*. Once man reaches it, all the appetites—man himself—will rest, because there will be nothing left to desire (man is moved by his appetites while he desires something that he yet does not have).[14]

Sometimes it would be better to talk about rectitude of the "appetitive dynamism" rather than rectitude of will, because all appetites are means with respect to the rational appetite that is the will. Sensitive appetites sometimes support the will, and others restrain it. When they support the will, we say that there is a "strong will", but this is so because of the correct disposition of the sensitive appetites. The dualist vision of the human being, which contemplates spiritual life (the activity of reason and will) as something independent from the material life, does not serve justice to the psychology of man, because common experience shows us that the inclination towards the last end is as if it were impressed in all parts of our body, including the most basic appetites. The moral effort consists precisely in achieving a harmonic conjunction of all the appetites based on the architectonic appetite of the last end. This conjunction is already given to us inchoated by Nature, and we have to complete it. But, if on one hand we underline the moral dimension of the sensitive appetites, on the other we also have to insist on the architectonic moral function of the last end: to construct a moral philosophy or a Natural Law theory without reference to the last end ("as if God did not exist"), seems to us as

[13] Thomas Aquinas writes in his *Summa Theolgiae* I-II, q. 92 a. 1 ad 3 "*bonitas cuiuslibet partis consideratur in proportione ad suum totum, unde et Augustinus dicit, in III Confess., quod turpis omnis pars est quae suo toti non congruit. Cum igitur quilibet homo sit pars civitatis, impossibile est quod aliquis homo sit bonus, nisi sit bene proportionatus bono communi, nec totum potest bene consistere nisi ex partibus sibi proportionatis.* (...)". With respect to the degree of virtue that citizens should have, St. Thomas does not say that they should have the integrity of the virtue, but only that degree of virtue necessary to maintain the community.

[14] Cf. Aquinas, *Compendium theologiae*, § 98.

limited as attempting to build a theory of vegetative life without realizing the influence of sunlight.

In our opinion, the so-called *basic human goods* (by Germain Grisez, John Finnis, Robert George...) could be understood like aids that facilitate man's walking towards the last end. For example, the inclination to the conservation of one's own self, with all that it supposes (nutrition, dress, health, etc.) is an inclination towards a reality that appears naturally *attractive*, but that does not give a *complete* reason by itself, because nobody wants to live simply to live. If it is desirable to live, it is for *something*. The same could be said of knowledge: nobody wants to know something simply to know something, because if that were true, the simple fact of knowing more data (for example to know the telephone directory by heart) would be a more valuable intellectual achievement than any other. Man wants to know something to become a better person. And something similar could be said of all of the *basic human goods*. Therefore, our thesis is that human goods are really such, as far as they serve man to obtain his last end. Moreover, the reference to the last end is indeed the reason for the goodness of all the human goods.

A reflection on the position that moral virtues occupy, and especially the virtue of justice in the process of practical knowledge

It is in view of this last end that all the appetitive movement is naturally disposed, including the most basic appetites. It is here where moral virtues (including justice) find their meaning, so far as each one contributes to adequately dispose man towards his last end. Although we analytically distinguish different virtues, all are *aspects of the same perfective process*, by which each man is suitably disposing himself, and in a certain way, progressively anticipating, his participation in the last end.

Many of the authors who, in supposed continuity with Aristotle and St. Thomas, have reflected on justice, have excessively emphasized the notion of *particular justice*, leaving a little to the side the notion of *general justice*; when it is that *general justice* is a key piece to understand all the aristotelian-thomist philosophy of virtues. Therefore, we think that it is worth spending a little time with the notion of *general justice*.

Since the realization of man is not obtained in solitary, but in community, it is necessary that man, by virtue, adequately disposes himself to the coexistence with others. And *the habit by which man adequately disposes himself to coexistence with others is justice.* In other words, if virtue is perfection of man by which he carries away the work began by Nature, and man is naturally a social being, justice, in so far as it perfects the social dimension of man, perfects man himself. And since man, due to his corporal nature, only communicates by means of external actions, signs and things (we do not *communicate* among ourselves telepathically), justice, while being an internal disposition, will *manifest* only on these external things through which people relate to each other.

If each man, thanks to the other moral virtues, tunes his sensitive *passions* so that they respond adequately to his own reason, by justice he tunes also his own *will, so that it could stably tend to the good of the neighbour*. This is a continuous process in which justice is like the last step of virtue; virtue that begins to form and to hold fast by temperance and fortitude, but that culminates in justice. In other words, the sensitive passions—disciplined by the other moral virtues—do not directly dispose man to his neighbour, however their effects, the outer operations, are ordenable to the neighbour, and this is obtained by means of the virtue of justice. When Aristotle says that general justice is the complete or perfect moral virtue, he is saying that the order impressed by reason in the appetites, is only a means for the adequate disposition of the will of man towards others. In other words, the order impressed in the sensitive appetites by the other moral virtues, is made in view of the exterior operations, and this order is maintained relatively unaltered in outer works thanks to the virtue of justice. In this sense, it is necessary to interpret the classic saying *Iustitia in se omnem virtutem complectitur*, because *the virtue of justice always presupposes the other virtues*.

Explained inversely, we can say that in the root of almost all injustice there is always an immorality of another species different from the injustice. For example, many murders are committed by a lack of control of wrath; most rapes are committed by a habitual inability to control the sexual instinct. Only those harmful voluntary actions committed against a fellow man, *not motivated by a sensitive passion*, are caused by pure injustice, and we properly call this “malice”, that is a perversion of the will itself.

Between the many consequences that could be derived from this consideration, we could emphasize that educating for justice presupposes educating the affection or appetites, teaching future citizens to live other virtues that apparently do not have social importance. This exposition that we defend also discredits part of the modern theories that differentiate between “public ethics” and “private ethics”, as if they were two completely independent spheres.

As a consequence of what we have just said, there is that the will of the debtor —justice, by definition, is the virtue of the debtor—has to be regulated by the good pertaining and convenient to the other (the creditor). Justice perfects the will perfecting the knowledge of truth and culminating the rectitude of the sensitive appetites (rectitude means the tendency—*mediately tendency* in the case of the sensitive appetites—of the appetites towards the true last end). In other words, general justice is the rectitude of the will, which presupposes: first, *to know* what the good is; and, second, that the sensitive appetites be attuned, because a passion contrary to reason can alter its judgment, diverting the will's focus, so that it is polarized in an unjust act.

Fortitude and temperance consist of a certain impression of the rational order in the sensitive appetites. These appetites are perfected by the order impressed on them by the right reason (*recta ratio*); that is, a reason that disposes every thing —including the moderation of the appetites— in order to achieve the natural last end. Prudence is the virtue by which one is use to choose promptly, joyfully and easily the most appropriate means to obtain the last end. The sensitive appetites are naturally needed of that adjustment made by reason, and as far as they are *perfected*, *moderated*—not suffocated—by moral virtue, are somehow domesticated, so that they are use to desire when they must and as they must, this is, according to the last end (as it is only caught by reason, we use the expression [according to] *recta ratio*). However, by justice—which presupposes order in the other appetites—man, as well as accustoming intelligence to discern the good of fellow man (reinforcing prudence), is getting his appetites used to collaborate to the natural will, which is naturally inclined to good, also to want the good of another as its own good. In other words, the virtue of justice is a virtue rooted in the will —general justice is the will rectitude itself—, by which man tends *to want* and *to enjoy* in the good of the fellow man, and this without being impeded, rather being accompanied, by the sensitive appetites. For that reason, the virtue of justice demands as necessary condition, but non sufficient, the existence of the other moral virtues, because nobody can become accustomed to wanting, without feeling, the good of his fellow man.

When we see the other as a part of the same community of us, we recognize to him the means or goods that are necessary to participate and subsist in this community. When the goods that each one really *needs* can only be achieved through the intervention of my will, then I find myself in the position of debtor. And when I have the habit of settling my debts, then I have got the virtue of justice.[15]

Summarizing the preceding paragraphs we could say: All the virtues are aspects of the same personal realization. The personal realization is only completed in coexistence. Justice manifests that the other virtues have taken root, because by justice transcends towards the others the adequate arrangement of all the appetites. Only when a person dominates his appetites, can he adequately dispose himself towards others. This suitable communication can be done by primarily taking care of the good of the whole, or by taking care, in first term, of some particular member of that whole. In the first case we speak of "legal justice", in the second, we speak of "particular justice". This particular justice can be verified as well in the *distributions of what is common* and in the *interchanges*, constituting two subspecies of justice, that are different by the way of measuring the right amount: "distributive justice" and "commutative justice". And it is common to all justice the contribution to the common good, directly or indirectly.[16]

All that has been said up to this point about justice is a moral discourse, which can come across strange to the philosophy of law, at least to the current European philosophy of law, or at least to a consideration of "merely" legal or political justice. It would be possible to disagree with this writing that the function of jurists or of politicians is much more modest. Certainly the politicians or the jurists have interest in the *acts of justice, done with or without virtue*, and, in addition, in just a few, only in

---

[15] The term *debtor* expresses, in this context, the moral necessity in which it is the free will of the debtor by the fact of being regulated by the good convenience to other, to the creditor. Cf. Abbà, *Felicidad, vida buena y virtud*, 193. First edited in Italian in 1989.

[16] The presentation of distributive justice as "justice of the governor" induces confusion (this is the case, for example of the German philosopher Joseph Pieper in his study on the virtue of Justice: *Die Gerechtigkeit*, 1954, collected in Spanish in a recollection of some of his works about the virtues, in the book Josef Pieper, *Las virtudes fundamentales* (Madrid: Rialp, 1990). We have to say that if there were a specific justice of the governor that it would be legal justice as specific justice (but neither it would be correct to attribute only to the governor legal justice). Whoever has to distribute goods that are common is the one who lives distributive justice. The origin of the erroneous interpretation of the thought of Aquinas—extended between many authors supposedly Thomists—is in the famous commentary by Cardinal Cayetano to II-II, q.61, a.1, where St. Thomas distinguishes between commutative justice and distributive justice. Cf. Finnis, *Natural Law and Natural Rights*, 185.

those that are considered necessary for the minimum social cohesion. But, if we admit that *all the moral dynamism is a centripetal movement of increasing solidarity*, to the positive law we could demand the determination of the minimum threshold of cohesion or indispensable solidarity, below which it is understood that life in community would be worthless (in Spanish we could say: *el derecho se justifica porque la convivencia vale la pena*). Certainly, the legal field is much more restricted than the moral one, but without knowing the moral science we would not know where the legal ends and where the merely moral begins (most of the legal obligations are also moral obligations); nor when the legal becomes immoral; and what is most important, so far as legal science (including legal philosophy) is not only science about *ius conditum*, but also about *ius condendum*, with out moral considerations, the legal science won't be able to vindicate, with extralegal arguments, new realities susceptible to legal regulation.

A reformulation of the analogical concept of law as a correct disposition of the parts towards the common good as end

For Aquinas, law in relation to man, has in general the function of helping him so that he may suitably dispose himself towards the common good. *Human law* orients man towards the *political common good.* If man is correctly disposed towards this good, we say that he is a *good citizen. Natural law,* however, orients man towards an end that is more ultimate than the political common good, which is the *universal common good.* If man is correctly disposed towards this end, we say that he is a *good person*).[17]

St. Thomas does not see law as an obstacle to the freedom of man, but rather as an instrument with an educational function of the human will in the search of the common good, that naturally desires. The participation of

[17] In *S. Th.*, I-II, q. 19 a. 10 c. Aquinas writes: "(...) Bonum autem totius universi est id quod est apprehensum a Deo, qui est universi factor et gubernator, unde quidquid vult, vult sub ratione boni communis, quod est sua bonitas, quae est bonum totius universi. [...]. Non est autem recta voluntas alicuius hominis volentis aliquod bonum particulare, nisi referat illud in bonum commune sicut in finem, cum etiam naturalis appetitus cuiuslibet partis ordinetur in bonum commune totius."

man in the good of the political community is only an intermediate step and an aid to better participate in *the common universal good.*

We have previously seen that human virtue is essentially a disposition towards the common good. We saw that this was thus because virtue is equivalent to personal perfection, and the perfection of something that is part of a whole, has to be appreciated by the relationship that it keeps with the whole of which it is a part. For that reason law, in general, is considered an external aid for personal accomplishment.

When St. Thomas says that "the law itself intends first and foremost to order towards the common good", he means that by the law individuals order or dispose themselves to the realization of the community formed by them themselves. The common good *is the same community well done*, *the quality of the living together, the worth of the coexistence*, and law helps to make that community, where each one finds their own realization. The community is the fruit of the law, because the law adequately disposes the parts in order to construct the community as a whole. And since the community conformed by the laws can be of a very diverse nature, diverse levels of common good can be distinguished, with their respective species of laws. What for Aristotle was the last end of man, the realization through the *political* common good, for Aquinas that will only be a particular end, the political coexistence, a mere stage of the *centripetal dynamism of the law in general*, that will reach its perfection in the kingdom of God, fully realized in the eternal life.[18]

In light of this finality of the law, that is essentially constituent of the community, the controversial thesis that *unjust law is not properly law,* is coherent with the thought of St. Thomas. And it is not *properly* law because it simply does not serve to conform the community, because the unjust law is a disturbing or disintegrating element of the community, because such is a negation of his final cause.[19] If an essential note of law consists in linking what is diverse, a law that destroys the community is not a law; it is precisely the negation of law: as poison is not a medicine, no matter how much it is sold in pharmacies, the unjust law is not properly a law, but its contradiction. Unjust law perhaps maintains its *efficient and material cause*, because it has been promulgated by its legitimate ruler, but if it lacks its *final cause*, it therefore lacks the most important.

As a consequence of this, we can say that a law that tends to disintegrate the community, to which it is destined, manifests the greater possible perversion of the "lawmaker" as such. If the best governor is the

[18] Cf. *S. Th.*, I-II, q. 90, a.2 c.

[19] Cf *S. Th.*, I-II, q. 96, a. 5 and a. 6.

one who unites his people more closely, in a harmonious and pacific coexistence, he who destroys this coexistence is the worst one of all.

At this point we can better understand that the philosophy of Aristotle and St. Thomas is very far from the individualism that considers happiness as a merely personal accomplishment. As we have seen, for St. Thomas, man reaches happiness in the measure in which he inserts himself in the coexistence with others, and suitably assumes the role that he plays in the community of which he is a part. Man in solitaire falls apart. If, as St. Thomas says, the part is ordered to the whole, as the imperfect to the perfect, the individual man is ordered to the perfect community to find in it his perfection, which is his happiness. Also when in his Nicomachean Ethics (book V) Aristotle speaks of "the legal things", he presents happiness and community united (political, in his case, because, for him, the political community is the perfect community; whereas for Aquinas the perfect community is the cosmic universal community, towards which the eternal law disposes).

When St. Thomas says that law belongs to reason, we have to understand that he opposes it to the appetite. All appetites have their natural proper goods, that man does not choose to have; including rational appetite or will, that tends towards its own good, a good without restriction, that nobody can fail to want. The appetite for fullness or happiness that determines the will, we do not choose: it is already "factory installed" in our own nature. In order to satisfy this rational appetite, we do everything what we chose to do. Reason tends to dispose, choosing the more adapted means, in order to obtain that desired happiness. For that reason law, in general, is mainly a work of prudence (prudence—said again—is the virtue by which one chose the most appropriate means to obtain the last end). If law obligates, it is not because there is a will ordering something, but because there is a good naturally convenient for man, that normally is naturally desired by will. For this reason, *the obligation of law has the same intensity of the degree of convenience of the good towards which the law disposes*.

If law is not only declarative, but also prescribes, it is because the goods to which law leads, present themselves appealing to the will as rational appetite. The obligation of the law derives from the kindness of the good, that appeals directly and by itself to the rational appetite.

The criticism of Hume, which derives the *ought* from the *is*, deriving prescriptive norms from descriptive statements, is an erroneous criticism if it is applied to Aquinas. St. Thomas does not derive the obligatory character of law from a speculative principle, but from a practical principle, this is, from a good that appeals directly and by itself to the human will, that is the human rational appetite.

While animals order themselves to the end by their instinct—rather animals *are ordered* by their instincts—, without knowing the end or even choosing the means, man orders himself to the end (to which he naturally tends) with the aid of law. St. Thomas explains that law is the appropriate way to govern the human person, because with his reason he can perceive the *ratio ordinis* of the law, and because he has dominion over his own actions. Because man is governed by means of law, and because he also governs other men through law, on one hand he makes his participation in the community commendable (he is not forced), and on the other hand he participates in the government of the world to which God associates him, granting him the dignity of being second cause in the disposition (in the ordering) of everything towards the last end, which is the universal common good. This governing of man by means of the law is of an order superior to the government by means of the natural inclinations that God puts in his creatures.

That law is the most conforming way to govern the human person, in accordance to his dignity, it is also manifested through the comparison with the government of man on irrational beings. All the unfolded activity in the use of irrational things subordinated to man, is reduced to the acts man performs with them:[20] if they are inert realities the reason is clear: for example, when one uses tools; and if they are irrational living beings, the motive resides in the automatism that occurs between the stimulus and the response when man provokes the appetites of the animal. For that reason man does not impose laws on irrational beings, no matter how much they are subjected to him, but he moves them by force, even though it seems that they obey freely. Human legislator, however, gives laws to the men of the community that he governs, when he imprints in their minds, with whatever mandate or indication, a rule in view of the conformation of the community that he directs. In this task, he is also participating, consciously or unconsciously, in the task of reunification, which disposes everything towards the universal common good.[21] For that reason, as we have seen, one will be a much better governor if he promotes more the unity of the members of the community that he governs, because authority's reason for being is to maintain the community united.

The common good is always relative to a certain community. For that reason whenever we speak of the "common good" we should specify to

[20] Cf. *S. Th.*, I-II, q. 1 a. 2.

[21] Cf *S. Th.*, I-II, q. 93, a. 5.

which community we are referring to (familiar, sportive, political, world-wide…). And for that reason the justice of law has to be evaluated in relation to the common good of the community for which it is dictated. *The definition of the common good of any community is the expression of the end of that community*, the expression of the reason of its constitution or existence.

Now, it is convenient to make a distinction that is not explicit in Aquinas, which if not noticed, could impede a suitable understanding of a good part of his thinking. When St. Thomas speaks about the common good of the political community, sometimes he refers to what we could call, with Rodríguez Luño, the "social integral common good" and, other times, he refers to the mere "political common good".[22] The former is more ample than the latter. The social integral common good comprehends all the goods that are presupposed by the common life of men. Man contributes to this common good by the acts of all his virtues, including those that at first sight only affect his private life (for example, acts of fortitude or chastity), and of course, all the social institutions such as family, religious communities, and the multitude of diverse associations that work within the political community also contribute to this common good. However, the "political common good"—what many interpreters of St. Thomas call "common good" without more specification—is that part of the social integral common good that can and must be promoted and protected by the State. According to this more restricted notion of common good, there would be vicious private behaviours that would not directly affect the political common good; and therefore would not have to be prohibited by the law, although they affect the social integral common good. If Aquinas recognizes that the moral category of the singular people always impact, *in some way*, the quality of coexistence between men (the social integral common good), he also recognizes that this influence admits degrees, and that the determination of the degree in which human law must intervene, is a relative question that depends on many factors: the level of education of the people, the increase of certain type of crime in the community, etc.

We could graphically represent this idea with two concentric circles, in which the radius length represents the intensity and number of relevant actions for the common good: the minor circle radius would mark the minimum demanded by human law, in view of the indispensable minimum cohesion of the community (determining therefore the *area* of the

[22] Cf. Antonio E. Rodríguez Luño, *Ética General* (Madrid: Eunsa, 2001), 269, note 17. First published in 1991).

"political common good"); and the one of greater radius would determine the "social integral common good", whose area would comprise all the moral behaviour of man. What lies within the competence of human legislator is to determine, according to the circumstances, the length of the radius of the first circle, by means of the regulation of the indispensable conducts of the citizens. These two circles would as well be within the circle of the common universal good to which God disposes all Creation.

Could we say that, for St. Thomas, the object of the rules of the human legislator should not surpass those acts of the virtue of justice? In a certain way, yes, because, as we have already seen, only by justice man adjusts his behaviour to the good of another person. We have seen that men communicate among themselves and conform the political community by means of exterior acts, and not simply with mere thought. The political community is only affected by people's good or bad desires when these desires are translated in exterior actions. For that reason only acts of justice are susceptible to legal regulation –but not all. *The acts of other virtues only interest the legislator in the measure in which they affect the order of social life.* For example, from the point of view of the educative legislation, it could be worth while to foster the order and temperance of the young people, to foster the courage of the soldiers, the diligence of the police in their investigations, or the chastity of the teachers in their relations with students... From this perspective we could situate difficult subjects of legal and political science, such as the treatment that should be given to pornography.[23]

Even though it is incumbent upon the legislator to stipulate the best possible way in which the citizen can contribute to the common good, it would be an error to ascribe to the legislator the exclusive responsibility for the maintenance and development of the community that he governs. This error presupposes an incompatible paternalism with personal and social responsibility that all people have. The governor is not the only one responsible for the common good. *Human law indicates the minimum threshold of solidarity, the minimum of contribution to the common good, which can be coercively demanded.* But the citizens, who are conscious of the shared-in-common dimension of their existence, assume responsibilities not demanded by human law, which doubtlessly contribute to the common good. Without this shared-in-common perspective of existence, which is developed independently from the law, the maintenance of any community would not be possible.

[23] Cf. *S. Th.*, I-II, q. 96, a. 3.

When one considers that law *in general* is essentially an aid to help man to more easily reach his end, it makes sense that the coercive character of law does not form part of its definition. This is made clear when St. Thomas distinguishes between two types of people upon whom law is imposed:

> "Of these, some are arrogant and proud, and by the law have to be repressed and tamed; and others are good, and by the law are instructed and helped in the realization of that which they intend".[24]

We think that the purpose of human law does not properly consist of making men moral, but rather, better citizens. Nevertheless, the fact that human law also contributes to making men moral, is a frequent and logical effect of it, but is not its own aim. Human law can have as an indirect effect the promotion of virtue in the measure in which it causes customs, which at the outset can be followed reluctantly for fear of punishment, but soon, once the practice is experienced, the acts could be realized with certain facility and even with joy.

When John Finnis explains, interpreting Aquinas, the convenience with which the civil law inculcates virtues, he writes:

> "The answer seems to be this. Human law must inculcate virtues because it will only work well as a guarantor of justice and peace if its subjects internalise its norms and requirements and—more important—adopt its purpose of promoting and preserving justice. The public good cannot be well preserved if people are untrustworthy, vengeful, willing to evade their taxes and other civic duties, biased in jury service, and so forth. So the preservation of public good needs people to have the *virtue*, the inner dispositions, of justice. (...) And if that is a legitimate purpose, then it must be at least a legitimate interest of government that citizens have other virtues too. *Practical reasonableness is essentially all of a piece*; those who violate or neglect its directiveness in 'private' choices are thereby weakened in their rational motives, and their dispositions, for following its directiveness in 'public', other-affecting choices".[25]

In any case, civil law and human governments must play a secondary role (or "subsidiary") in the virtuous development of the citizens. The primary role corresponds to families, religious institutions, private

---

[24] *S. Th.*, I-II, q. 98, a.6 c.

[25] John Finnis, *Aquinas: Moral, Political, and Legal Theory* (Oxford: Oxford University Press, 1998), 232, cursive ours.

associations, and other institutions that, working closely with the individuals, collaborate in the diffusion of the morality and promotion of virtue. “When families, religious associations, and other institutions of the civil society do not fulfil (or are incapable of carrying out) their mission, —writes Robert George—it will be difficult for laws to preserve the public morality. Ordinarily, at least, the role of the law is to support families, religious associations and the like. And, by all means, the law functions poorly when it displaces these institutions and it usurps its authority”.[26]

Works Cited

Abbà, Giuseppe. “Christian Moral Principles di Grisez e la Secunda Pars della Summa Thologiae.” *Salesianum* 48 (1986): 637-80.

—. *Felicidad, vida buena y virtud*. Barcelona: Eiunsa, 1992.

—. *Lex et Virtus, Studi sull'evoluzione della morale di san Tommaso d'Aquino*. Roma: LAS, 1983.

—. *Quale impostazione per la filosofia morale?* Roma: LAS, 1996.

Anscombe, G.E.M. *Intention*. Ithaca - New York: Cornell University Press, 1979.

—. “Modern Moral Philosophy.” *Philosophy* 33, no. 134 (1958): 1-19.

Aquinas, Thomas. *Opera omnia iussu Leonis XIII P. M. edita: Compendium theologiae seu Brevis compilatio theologiae ad fratrem Raynaldum*. Vol. 42. Roma: Editori di San Tommaso, 1979.

—. *Summa Theologica* Translated by the Fathers of the English Dominican Province. New York: Benzinger Bros., 1947.

Finnis, John. *Aquinas: Moral, Political, and Legal Theory* Oxford: Oxford University Press, 1998.

—. *Fundamentals of Ethics*. Oxford - New York: Clarendon Press, 1983.

—. *Natural Law and Natural Rights*. Oxford: Clarendon Press, 1980.

George, Robert P. *Making Men Moral. Civil Liberties and Public Morality*. Oxford: Clarendon Press, 1993.

—. *Para hacer mejores a los hombres*. Madrid: Eiunsa, 2002.

---

[26] Robert P. George, *Making Men Moral. Civil Liberties and Public Morality* (Oxford: Clarendon Press, 1993). Spanish edition ———, *Para hacer mejores a los hombres* (Madrid: Eiunsa, 2002). Paradoxically I have made the translation into English from the Epilogue of the Spanish version of Robert George's book *Making Men Moral*, whose epilogue does not appear in the English version, at least in that of 2002.

Grisez, Germain, Joseph Boyle, and John Finnis. “Practical Principles, Moral Truth, and Ultimate Ends.” *The American Journal of Jurisprudence* 32 (1987): 99-151.

Grisez, Germain G. “The First Principle of Practical Reason. A Commentary on the Summa theologiae, 1-2, Question 94, Article 2.” *Natural Law Forum* 10 (1965): 168-201.

Nussbaum, Martha C. *Aristotle's De Motu Animalium*. Princeton: Princeton University Press, 1985.

Pieper, Josef. *Las virtudes fundamentales*. Madrid: Rialp, 1990.

Rhonheimer, Martin. “Legge morale naturale: conoscenza morale and coscienza. The cognitiva struttura della legge naturale and verità della soggettività.” *Ars Interpretandi* 7 (2002): 47-78.

—. *Natural Law and Practical Reason: A Thomist View of Moral Autonomy*. New York: Fordham University Press, 2000.

Rodríguez Luño, Ángel. *Ética General*. Madrid: Eunsa, 2001.

Vial, Juan de Dios, and Elio Sgreccia, eds. *Natura and Dignità della persona umana a fondamento del diritto alla vita. Atti dell'ottava Assamblea Generale della Pontificia Accademia per la vita*. Roma: Libreria Editrice Vaticana, 2002.

CHAPTER TWENTY FIVE

EXIGIBILITY IN LEGAL OBLIGATIONS

CARIDAD VELARDE

The question of the obligatory nature of law is as old as legal thought and constitutes one of the field's most intractable problems. To borrow the image coined by Ihering: the risk of being stranded in the "Cape of Storms" of legal science, where many have been "shipwrecked," is well known. Thus, it should be made clear from the beginning that the purpose of this paper is not to resolve the quandary, but to address a specific point in an attempt to shed some light on it.[1] The point in question, as the title indicates, is the exigibility of certain human conduct as the hallmark of what is legal, and the key to its distinction with respect to the realm of morality.

The general problem of the obligatory nature of law was the subject of debate in legal philosophy circles at different times throughout the 20th century. One of the most emblematic debates was led by Radbruch at the beginning of the second half of the century, which was framed by reaction to a law that common consensus regarded, and continues to regard, as unjust. However, at least two other moments are of equal, or even greater, interest in this regard. The first coincides with the end of the 50's, when what many refer to as the "recovery of practical reason" movement was taking place, affecting not only the world of law but also encompassing the whole sphere of human action. The second did not present itself until the 80's, when representatives of legal thought on both sides of the

[1] That this issue has been dealt with on a continental level as well as on an Anglo-Saxon one, and in both has turned out to be very complex, ought to be taken into consideration. The way in which it has been dealt with in each is different because of the different starting points. Proof of this is the fact that Anglo-Saxon authors do not normally cite continental authors in the course of their arguments – or vice versa. One of the most noteworthy cases in this regard is Hart, who refers to Kelsen only to criticize him and link his thought directly to the tradition of Austin.

English Channel addressed the question of whether law is obligatory or not; if so, whether the obligatory nature generated by law is analogous to the binding force of moral obligation; and what the relationship between the two might be. While Joseph Raz openly declared his rejection of the existence of an obligation to obey law,[2] Robert Alexy held (in different terminological and argumentative keys) that its obligatory nature is a touchstone of law, a consequence of the possibility of speaking of practical reason and its translation into the legal field.[3]

There are two questions that must be answered with regard to the obligatory nature of law; they prompt the present study. The first question is if there is a moral obligation to obey law. An affirmative answer would imply prior acceptance of moral obligations, and a link between law and morality, which leads to the second question: whether the contents of law must conform to morality. This would appear to have little to do with the question of exigibility posed here. Nevertheless, it is hoped that the connection will become clear in the following discussion. To do so requires that what the notion of obligation implies in the legal and moral fields must first be established, which in turn involves ensuring that the term "obligation" has only one meaning, rather than being read [in different fields] in different ways.

The notion of 'obligation' and morality

Long before the 80's, and coinciding exactly with the recovery of practical reason movement referred to above, Hart responded to this question by drawing a line between the notion of obligation or legal duty and that of moral duty. His well-known thesis[4] is that the term "duty," proper to the field of law, is frequently and mistakenly translated into non-legal discourse, specifically into the realm of morals.

---

[2] "I shall argue that there is no obligation to obey the law even in a good society whose legal system is just". Joseph Raz, *The Authority of Law. Essays on Law and Morality* (Oxford: Clarendon Press, 1979), 233.

[3] Robert Alexy, *The Argument from Injustice. A Reply to Legal Positivism*, trans. S.L Paulson and B.L. Paulson (Oxford: Oxford University Press, 2002).

[4] Cfr. H. L. A. Hart, "Legal and Moral Obligation," in *Essays in Moral Philosophy*, ed. A. I. Melden (Seattle and London: University of Washington Press, 1958). On the same question, cf. Juan Carlos Bayón Mohino, *La normatividad del derecho: deber jurídico y razones para la acción* (Madrid: Centro de Estudios Constitucionales, 1995).

On this point, although his interests and conclusions differ, Hart would appear to be in agreement with the position adopted by E. Anscombe for whom the main problem of moral theory lies precisely in the use of the word "obligation."[5] The legalistic connotation of "obligation", and its consequent comparison to "being committed" or implication that someone "is required to," presupposes a subject who may lay claim to an action in accordance with a rule.[6] In Anscombe's view, this would imply a substitution of what is moral for what is legal, wherein the moral is affected and emptied, stripped of meaning if not of content. The root of the problem is the use of the same term to refer to essentially different realities, with the resulting need to add the qualifier "moral" or "legal." Paradoxically, this emptying of the autonomous content of morality generates a mentality in which failure to comply with a legal obligation is not immoral, and, at the same time, precludes the idea of moral absolutes, i.e., actions that are immoral whatever their end may be when they are performed. As has already been noted, the correspondence between these two positions is only superficial; in fact, they prompt opposing theses, in particular with regard to the relationship between morality and law.

From Anscombe's point of view, which I share, morality has more to do with reason than with adaptation to an external act of will; therefore, its contents can be known (at least in principle) by anybody. It is also related to the adaptation of means to the achievement of an end.

However, if Anscombe's proposal is followed literally, the argument below cannot be developed. Precisely because common language continues to function in these contexts, it is not possible to escape the notion of obligation; there is as yet no alternative to using the term "moral obligation," which, moreover, centuries of thought has endowed with its own meaning. Despite its questionable status, this vocabulary, which has borne considerable fruit in the history of legal thought, will be used, starting from a distinction between legal and moral obligations, and bearing in mind the fact that, with respect to moral obligation, conduct is guided by reason.

Judgments of duty are judgments on the reasonability of human actions. They translate into terms of correctness or incorrectness, which in

[5] Cfr. Anscombe, "Modern Moral Philosophy," 1-19.. Note that both Hart's and Anscombe's papers were published in 1958. The uneasiness of the moment would lead, ten years later, to the rebirth of the Practical Reason movement.

[6] This confusion is aggravated by the fact that religious connotations of this way of understanding morality make it difficult for it to survive the secularisation of Western societies.

turn are determined by different criteria depending on the area in question; each judgment is in direct relation to the end pursued (not to the individual end of the agent but to that of the overall "game" under consideration). Moreover, in each area, incorrectness has or can have consequences, even though these also differ from one area to another.

The notion of 'obligation' and law

From the legal perspective, a new series of questions emerges. One of them (though not necessarily the first) is if law can be reduced to a set of duties. Another question concerns what type of duty *legal* duty is. With regard to the latter, part of the question to be determined is whether duty and legal obligation are one and the same or if, on the contrary, a distinction may be drawn between the two, and if so, in what sense.

As for the second question, there is undoubtedly a terminological distinction that has to do with the etymology of the word "obligation." The age-old notion of obligation, whose origin is in fact legal, may be reduced to a specific aspect of the sphere of law relating to the autonomy of the will and private law. Here "obligations" refer to the commitments acquired by a responsible person.[7] The capacity to obligate (commit to present or future action) through contracts, promises, etc. is key to Western legal culture. Beyond the terms of this particular question, it makes no sense to distinguish between duty and obligation because all legal duty is obligatory except when it is not—in which case it is not a duty—. Obviously, in this apparent play on words, the term "obligatory" is taken in its moral sense.

The question may seem trivial, but it is significant and not merely so in theoretical terms, since the legitimacy of positive law and, ultimately, its obligatory nature, as well as the possibility that it may be obligatory to disobey the law,[8] depends on it. The law can certainly be studied from a normative point of view, but also from the perspective of entailed obligations. Having adopted this point of view, to differentiate legal obligations from other types of obligations, such as moral, religious, etc., may be a valuable exercise. The thesis of this paper, therefore, is that what

[7] The term, however, has been broadened to the extent of being independent of the capacity of persons, even to the point of being applicable to legal persons or persons who are not responsible for their acts.

[8] Cfr. John Finnis, "On the Incoherence of Legal Positivism," *Notre Dame Law Review* 75 (2000): 1597-611.

differentiates one obligation from another is none other than the exigibility of certain behaviours.

Many advocates of legal positivism, such as Kelsen, assume that the law is a set of duties (which Scandinavian realism would criticise as a form of metaphysics). On the other hand, authors such as Raz criticise any suggestion of an obligation to obey the law. Firstly, because in his radical separation of law from morality, the connection between law and rationality is based on the pursuit of social order that authority brings with it, and not so strictly on its content. This is where his position diverges in an absolute way from that held by Anscombe.

However, there is a further reason why Raz holds that an obligation to obey the law should not be spoken of and that is because not all norms have what he calls normative content:

> though (…) normativity is an important characteristic of the law, some laws are not norms; or more precisely, that, given the minimum content and minimum complexity of legal systems, and given an acceptable set of principles of individuation, there are in any legal system some laws which are not norms.[9]

On this point he is entirely in agreement with Hart's thesis. The truth is that this does not pose any special problem. In reality, distinguishing between parts of the legal system that do not properly contain duties but dispositions of any [other] type should not constitute a problem, as long as the principle that everything in the legal universe is orientated towards the notion of duty and obligatory contents is observed in the process. That is to say, even if there are normative dispositions that clarify points, constitute rules of interpretation, determine how institutions should work, or any other situation imaginable, none of this would make sense were it not for the functions of what Hart calls primary norms—which are, in the end, duties—.

Another question concerns whether or not legal norms constitute duties in a way analogous to the case of moral norms. In the realm of ethics, what is obligatory is such due to its conformity to the law of reason. In the realm of law, that obligatory nature is the consequence of the reasonability of a norm, whatever kind of norm it may be. The key to this discussion lies in whether reasonability is internal or external to law, but also in what should be regarded as external. The mere fact that it was dictated in

---

[9] Joseph Raz, *The Concept of a Legal System*, 2 ed. (Oxford: Clarendon Press, 1980), 168.

conformity to the system in force and by the competent authority is already a criterion of reasonability. In principle, it is not up to the citizen to judge whether it is the best possible norm to resolve a conflict. On the other hand, in the moral dimension of the norm in question, reasonability need not be the criterion that guides the citizen.

In order to talk in these terms, what "law" is must first be established. The assumption is that there are different ways of showing what law is in our life experience, one consequence of which is that the subject may be studied in different fields of inquiry.

According to Hart, the term "law" is used vaguely and ambiguously in ordinary language, comprising four fundamental meanings: the execution of justice; the set of norms or directive rules imposed by an authority and decided on in courts of justice; the powers, prerogatives and functions that correspond to each by virtue of his being a person; and lastly, legal science. These different meanings, says Hart, are related to one another by analogy. Given that the realities it encompasses are so different as to make expression in a single proposition impossible, it is not possible to offer a proper definition of law.[10] Nonetheless, what is common to the four meanings listed above can be discerned (and allows them to be spoken of as analogous);[11] this is the starting point for the discussion. On the other

[10] The following definition, which is really a description, is John Finnis's attempt to do so: "Rules made, in accordance with regulative legal rules, by a determinate and effective authority (itself identified and, standardly, constituted as an institution by legal rules) for a 'complete' community, and buttressed by sanctions in accordance with the rule-guided stipulations of adjudicative institutions, this ensemble of rules and institutions being directed to reasonably resolving any of the community's co-ordination problems (and to ratifying, tolerating, regulating or overriding co-ordination solutions from any other institutions or sources of norms) for the common good of that community, according to a manner and form itself adapted to that common good by features of specificity, minimization of arbitrariness, and maintenance of a quality or reciprocity between the subjects of the law both amongst themselves and in their relations with the lawful authorities". Finnis, *Natural Law and Natural Rights*, 276ff. In order to come up with this definition, Finnis attended to the implications of specific exigencies of practical reason from basic values to certain empirical characteristics of persons and their communities. As he himself declares, he neither aims to describe nor make a lexicographical approximation; in any case, his definition conforms to the existing reality at many points. On the other hand, he does not intend to adopt a concept that excludes everything that does not conform to it. For this reason he rejects the critique Raz made in *Practical Reason and Norms*. Cfr. Joseph Raz, *Practical Reason and Norms* (London: Hutchinson, 1975).

[11] Cfr. Hart, *The Concept of Law*, 15.

hand, law does not constitute a species within a broader genus—it is a *sui generis* reality—. My thesis is that the exigibility of behaviours referred to above constitutes the core of this reality.

Alexy, in a famous argument, attributes three elements to law: legality, effectiveness, and correctness of content.[12] His thesis is that the formal constituent of law entails these three elements. Hence, the following lengthy definition: "The law is a system of norms that lays claim to correctness, consists of the totality of the norms that belong to a constitution by and large socially efficacious and that are not themselves unjust in the extreme, as well as the totality of norms that are issued in accordance with this constitution, norms that manifest a minimum social efficacy or prospect of social efficacy and that are not themselves unjust in the extreme, and, finally comprises the principles and other normative arguments on which the process or procedure of law application is and/or must be based in order to satisfy the claim to correctness."[13] The predominant idea of this definition is that a critical attitude to positive law is possible from within; thus, such criticism cannot be dismissed as illegitimate, as coming from outside the system.

To return to the question of whether all law may be reduced to duties, in the context of the widespread criticism of the excessive importance attributed by man and modern thought to the notion of "rights" in detriment to the notion of "duties", it is true that law cannot be reduced to rights since they are not present in many legal relationships. It is unlikely that the obligation to pay taxes, for instance, can be read as the "right" of any individual. On the other hand, the inverse situation is indeed sustainable: every right brings with it a correlative duty. Except when the term "right" is used inappropriately, wherever there is a right there is a duty. Furthermore, if there is no duty, there can be no right, strictly speaking. Moreover, there are at least as many legal duties as there are rights—if not more—.

On the basis of Anscombe's observations cited above, the term "duty" may be said to belong more to the realm of law, and insofar as it is used in the moral sphere, it is used in an analogous sense. Thus, when the existence of a moral duty to obey a legal norm is spoken of, it may be interpreted as referring to a concept of duty different from that which properly constitutes the legal norm itself. Therefore, from this standpoint, legal duty and moral duty may be conceptually distinguished from one

[12] Cfr. Alexy, *The Argument from Injustice*, 14ff.

[13] Ibid., 127.

another.[14] Paradoxically, as history has shown, they may also be contradictory.

Distinction between legal obligations and other types of obligations

It may prove useful to continue to focus on the notion of legal obligation attended to by representatives of rationalist *iusnaturalism*. Pufendorf takes as his starting point the existence of duties the knowledge of which comes from three sources: the light of reason, civil laws, and the particular revelation of Divine Will. From the first flow the most common duties; from the second, duties in a particular state; and from the third, the duties of a Christian. Natural and civil law and moral theology, areas of interest which are not easy to separate,[15] also spring from these three sources. Thomasio also addresses this question, although his classification draws more on the content of duty than on the perspective of human knowledge of duty. So, three types of duties are distinguished: the legal, the moral, and those that are consequences of socially accepted uses.[16] Thomasio makes the following distinction: while morality is an internal question, which only affects the one carrying out the action and is not coercive, law is external, making reference to others and accompanied by a coercive mechanism. The so-called social uses are to be found between the former and the latter: unlike morality, but like law, they are external and affect others; however, unlike law, they are not coercive (coercive in the institutionalised sense, because the transgression of a fashion or custom can certainly lead to the exclusion from the group.)

The established consensus nowadays calls Thomasio's rationalist framework into question. Morality undoubtedly is internal not because the action it refers to is internal, but because it constitutes the internal dimension of that action. In other words, a single action may be immoral and illegal, depending on the point of view from which it is observed. Immoral content jeopardises the one who carries it out, as Plato pointed out in inimitable fashion; from the perspective of the one who suffers its effects, which is, ultimately, society as a whole, the same content may also

---

[14] Cfr. Luis Recaséns Siches, *Introducción al estudio del derecho*, 5 ed. (México D.F.: Porrúa, 1979), 128ff.

[15] Cfr. "Prologue", in Samuel Pufendorf, *De Officio Hominis et Civis juxta legem naturalem* (New York: Oxford University Press, 1927).

[16] Ch. Ch. Thomasius, *Fundamenta Iuris Naturae et Gentium* (1705), IV, LXXXIX.

be illegal. On the other hand, the internal dimension also matters to the realm of law. Proof of this is that in a [legal] system such as our own, importance is given not only to the consequences of acts, but also to their intentionality, which clearly pertains to the internal dimension.

Nevertheless, the keystone remains: now, as in Thomasio's time, the almost universal consensus is that what is backed by the coercive power of institutions is to be regarded as legal. It is for this reason that there are those who call international law into question, and cast even greater doubt on the resolutions of international organizations, which are at the mercy of a rudimentary or nonexistent coercive mechanism. At the same time, the individual capacity to create law by contractual means would be dependent on the law that protects and guarantees it. In spite of this, however, the thesis set out here is that the very content of exigible behaviours (perhaps, though not necessarily, as a consequence of the existence of law), rather than the direct or indirect origin of the law, is to be regarded as a determinant of what is legal.

Hart's approach corresponds in part with this line of reasoning, though not in the conclusion. For him, legal obligations are usually human artefacts, i.e., not only do we have them but we also create them, modify them, assume them, extinguish them, and so forth.[17] Legal duties are mainly created via the law, which in any modern society constitutes a complex operation. A person may also create or assume obligations on his own (bilateral or not). In any case, the difficulty lies in determining from where the force of obligation derives. It may be thought that the law confers a power from which that force derives; however, the word "power" is used incorrectly here because it does not mean the capacity to effect an observable physical change. The position of the emotivists is also well known. Hagerström says that to attribute this force to words (with Roman law formulae in mind, e.g.: "This slave is mine.") is to invoke magic. Although [this position] may provide an adequate explanation of historical events, it certainly does not explain what happens in the present day, nor does it suffice for legal acts such as the reading of a last will and testament, where the heirs must wait until after the demise of the testator.

Finally, Hart also regards as erroneous the argument that a moral obligation to obey the law may derive from the very existence of that law (in keeping with the Humean formulation). That someone understands the question in this way, he continues, may be explained in terms of a reaction to Kelsen's excessively geometric characterisation of the fundamental

[17] Hart, "Legal and Moral Obligation," 84.

norm,[18] but in fact there is no direct connection between the two positions. For example, there is no doubt that the generally-held understanding in England is that it is morally obligatory to follow the law, but this means neither that the obligation arises out of that conviction nor that the legal system cannot exist without it.

Taking this reasoning to its logical conclusion, however, implies a complete dissociation between law and morality. My argument here draws on the thesis that the notion "right" always implies a correlative obligation which, unlike moral or other types of obligation, is exigible. This is one of the strongest theses advanced by Raz in his critique of what he refers to as a morality based on rights.[19] While in legal terms, if there is no duty neither is there right properly speaking, for moral obligations it is possible not be exigible—or, rather, what makes them obligatory is not their exigibility—.

The difference between the thesis articulated here and that held by Raz centres, in the first place, on what should be regarded as exigible. This also involves a distinction with respect to the source of rights. In other words, obligations that go hand in hand with a right would be legal, although in the language of Hervada[20] they have yet to be formalised.[21]

It is possible to understand obligations as positive criteria (implying the presence of a social group in the idea of justice[22]) that have not yet been formalised. Understanding them in this way means they not only can they, but they must, orientate the legal system. Whether or not it is good that they orientate the system is not in question: they must do so if the system is to be legitimised.[23] The justice of a legal system, following Alexy, is not simply a moral consideration but a legal one. In other words, despite the fact that it may bring together unquestionable legal notes and a social configurative power identical to just law, unjust law is a contradiction in terms. On the other hand, the capacity of justice to integrate the legal system (that is, to close the existing gaps and act as a

---

[18] Ibid., 92.

[19] On this discussion, cfr, John Leslie Mackie, "Can There Be a Right-Based Moral Theory," in *Theories of Rights*, ed. Jeremy Waldron (Oxford: Oxford University Press, 1984), Joseph Raz, "Right Based Moralities," in *Theories of Rights*, ed. J.L. Mackie (Oxford: Oxford University Press, 1984).

[20] Hervada, *Introducción crítica al Derecho natural*, 176ff.

[21] In line with Anglo-Saxon tradition, Raz speaks of "moral rights".

[22] Cfr. Joseph Raz, "Rights and Politics," *Indiana Law Journal* 75, no. 1 (1995): 27-44.

[23] Cfr. Jürgen Habermas, "Human Rights and Popular Sovereignty: The Liberal and Republican Versions," *Ratio Iuris* 7, no. 1 (1994): 1-13.

hermeneutic criterion) would depend on its relation with law. In a way, this leads to theses such as that held by Dworkin in his attempt to integrate the legal system with the principles of a moral tradition. In his case, morality would be a component of law in the sense outlined here.

With regard to the content of what is exigible, what might appear to be simple is, again, only deceptively so. It is exigible to help an accident victim, but not to donate a kidney to her even if only one of the two we have is necessary for life. Intuitively, we know that kidney donation is not exigible, but the explanation of why it is not exigible is complicated. The question therefore may be: What do we owe others? This is the same as asking: What can we demand from one other? What determines what is exigible is not the vehicle, i.e., the law or a promise, but the content. On the other hand, in relation to the case of the law or the promise, the vehicle brings with it a form of content. What makes the law exigible is its content, but not its content alone, since other solutions to the same problem are probably conceivable. Endorsement of the obligation to respect traffic rules or the regulation of wireless telephone systems is a sufficient, legitimate orientating criterion for an activity. These activities may be regulated in another ways, though what is in force deserves respect because of the order and security generated.

The difficulty lies in determining what it is that makes a conduct exigible and deserving of protection by the system; that is, not only does morality operate as a negative limit (there are things which the law cannot infringe), but also as a positive one (the law must protect some things, though not others). A first order epistemological problem underlies this issue. What are the sources of exigible behaviours—the law, promises, and the vast range of obligations that might be referred to as natural, such as to the local community, family, etc., as well as the life situations in which the subject finds himself irrespective of his will—as illustrated by the examples of the obligation to help someone who has suffered an accident or needs help? Each of these factors' capacity to generate obligations is subject to many different reasons. The law, as has been stated above, creates a social order which is necessary although its content is improvable, or even substantially improvable; hence the presumption of the obligatory nature of any legal norm in the broad sense, i.e., of any general norm dictated by whoever wields legitimate authority. Then again, attributing the capacity to create legal obligations exclusively to the law is tantamount to legalistic reductionism.

With regard to the autonomy of the will's own capacity to create obligations, the origin of the force to obligate must be identified, which leads to the observation that it is not the promise itself that generates the right. Proof of this is that not everything to which one is obligated can be considered legal, not even in a pre-positive stage. On the contrary, the content of the promise in question must be [carefully] examined. The fulfilment of promises is one way in which personal responsibility may be exercised (it is only exigible for one who can promise, who knows what is promised, and who can fulfil the promise); however, it is not the promise in itself that protects, but (what may be referred to as) the institution invoked. This is clear in the case of promises referring to antisocial conduct, such as the commitment to loyalty within the Mafia. However, there may be promises whose content simply does not deserve institutional protection. For example, the commitment to play tennis every day stands in no need of institutional protection, whereas that of matrimonial fidelity does.

Political promises constitute a special case. Jurisprudence has dealt little with them to date,[24] and to do so here would fall beyond the remit of this discussion. To what extent are the obligations taken on by politicians exigible and, from this perspective, legal? Given that the responsibility (which is not solely political) of politicians depends on it, this question is especially significant.

As regards obligations generated by natural relationships (in essence, the family and local community), the difficulty lies not only in theoretical argumentation about whether or not such relationships generate rights and obligations,[25] but also in the existence and content of these relationships. Lipovetsky's appraisal of the situation in *Le Crépuscule du devoir*[26] (The Twilight of Duty) is very interesting in this regard. The French sociologist makes clear how, although the existence of parental duties towards children would appear to be universally recognised, the consensus does not necessarily hold when it comes to determining exactly what parents owe their children, especially when, as may happen nowadays, there is no certainty about what to be a "parent" means. Of the many questions posed by parent-child relationships, one of the simplest is whether or not children have a right to know the identity of their parents, which is complicated in this day and age by the possibility of a distinction between legal and biological parentage. Judges have to deal with ever more complex issues,

[24] Kevin Walton, "The Nature of Political Obligation," in *Australian Society for Legal Philosophy Annual Conference* (Canberra: March 2007).

[25] Cfr. Martha C. Nussbaum, "Patriotism and Cosmopolitanism," *The Boston Review* 19, no. 5 (1994).

[26] Gilles Lipovetsky, *Le Crépuscule du devoir. L'éthique indolore des nouveaux temps démocratiques* (Paris: Gallimard, 1992), 164ff.

from the alleged rights of children to have been aborted to, at the opposite extreme, whether or not the mother used a seat-belt or smoked, which actually permit children to sue mothers in court. Another very complex subject is the rights of parents, not only against but also in relation to children, which mainly involves discussion of whether or not it is possible to speak of a right to have children: "in the eyes of the majority, having a child is a legitimate right when the parents can raise the child in conditions considered, rightly or wrongly, satisfactory. However, there is no consensus on what is understood by a normal education or persons who can benefit from procreation techniques."[27]

On the possibility of finding reasonable criteria in this discussion

It is unlikely that what is "commonly accepted" constitutes a solid basis for the content of pre-formalised legal obligations. Undoubtedly, the question is closely tied to the position adopted with respect to the concept of law and its relation to justice, which in turn demands that close attention be paid to the legacy of long-established schools and systems of thought. Indeed, the argument between *iusnaturalists* and *iuspositivists* is as old as philosophical debate about law. This point should be borne in mind in any discussion of the value of an endless debate about these two positions, which, moreover, has often been written off as pointless. The debate is endless because, as should be obvious, its origin is lost in [the mists of] time; and it may be pointless because, as many have shown, more often than not it is a theoretical discussion that runs parallel to the real world, as much in legal as in political terms. To a certain extent, therefore, the debate serves more to cloud the issues involved than to clarify them.

In order to offer some clarification of the matter, though without the aim of resolving the issue, it would be good to determine what the debate is due to, which requires some reference to the reason for its futility. The answer to both questions is linked to the fact that it is a recurring debate.[28] It is well known that these types of debates are by their very nature irresolvable, and that their value lies in the discussion itself. The debates that address equality and difference or freedom and destiny in any form

---

[27] Ibid.

[28] In his speech at the opening of the academic year 1982-83 in Salamanca, J. Delgado Pinto uses as example of the debate's recurrence the writing of Geny in 1899 and in 1915, in relation with the irreducible natural law as one of the data that has to be a starting point for the scientific elaboration of positive Law.

are good cases in point. Nevertheless, although the debate is an age-old one, the last two centuries have witnessed a development prompted by the emergence of a system of law that, due to its own perfection, seems not to need, or is even incompatible with, any reference to natural law.[29] The incompatibility lies in the new system's principal achievement, which is legal security, that, as Delgado Pinto shows, following Kaufmann, generates a profound *horror iuris naturalis* in the professional of law.[30] Added to that, he continues, is the paradox that we are all born-*iusnaturalists* in a way, so that the caricature of the *iuspositivist* indifferent to justice is a thing of the past. The result is, in addition to those who hold to strict *iusnaturalist* or *iuspositivist* stances today (however difficult the definition of these positions may be), the emergence of a new attitude among many theorists of law who neither adhere to *iusnaturalist* theses nor wish to be regarded as positivists, and who claim to be uncomfortable in the face of a dilemma they say they do not share. One of the best examples in this regard is Alexy, who replaces the nomenclature referred to above with that of positivists and non-positivists.[31] To respect his wishes would involve not considering him to be a *iusnaturalist*, but this explanatory note reveals the problem to be a terminological one and shows that what causes confusion in the discussion is the choice of words. The worst aspect of natural law is probably its name. As a matter of fact, it is not necessary that the term be used for the discussion itself to take place.[32] Proof of this fact is obtained by inversion: that is, use of the same term does not necessarily imply support for the same position.[33] As Dworkin[34] points out, the problem is in large part due to the fact that identifying

---

[29] Cfr. Jesús Ballesteros, *Sobre el sentido del derecho* (Madrid: Tecnos, 1984), 19ff.

[30] "Since the last century and a half or more, (professional jurists) feel pleased deep down when they are able to carry out their task based on precise positive rules, while they detest having to venture into the open terrain of general validation guidelines, from legal principles, not to mention natural law." José Delgado Pinto, *De nuevo sobre el problema del Derecho natural* (Salamanca: Ediciones Universidad de Salamanca, 1982), 16.

[31] Cfr. Alexy, *The Argument from Injustice*, Foreword.

[32] Even if this may mean impoverishing the debate by abandoning a philosophical tradition that has borne considerable fruit.

[33] As MacCormick says, "'Natural Law' is a term so rich in ambiguities as to be rivaled only by 'positivism'". Neil MacCormick, "Natural Law reconsidered," *Oxford Journal of Legal Studies* 1 (1981): 99.

[34] Cfr. Ronald Dworkin, "Natural Law Revisited," *University of Florida Law Review* 34, no. 2 (1982): 165ff.

oneself as a *iusnaturalist* not only involves adopting an official category—in itself, a cumbersome move—but also leads one to spend far too much time explaining what being a *iusnaturalist* (or a *iuspositivist*,[35] as the case may be) actually means. This is, without doubt, an exercise in futility. Moreover, the debate may become even less fruitful than it already is if it devolves into a 'dialogue of the deaf' who [endlessly] repeat their own arguments without ever listening to what the other side has to say.[36]

The question that Alexy poses takes us further. What differentiates the *iuspositivists* (to use his terminology) from those who are not is the separation between law and morality. However, the negation of the notion of practical reason[37] is also common to positivism, or non-cognitivism or ethical emotivism as the case may be.[38] We must not lose sight of the fact that the notion of natural law arose in the context of moral thinking and prompted the development of a theory to explain the (moral) obligation to act against the law. The *raison d'être* of law is its role in establishing an order to conduct. The fact that it also has a capacity to condition lives in a way that can become injurious should also be borne in mind.

Works Cited

Alexy, Robert. *The Argument from Injustice. A Reply to Legal Positivism* Translated by S.L Paulson and B.L. Paulson. Oxford: Oxford University Press, 2002.

Anscombe, G.E.M. "Modern Moral Philosophy." *Philosophy* 33, no. 134 (1958): 1-19.

Ballesteros, Jesús. *Sobre el sentido del derecho*. Madrid: Tecnos, 1984.

[35] On the difficulties involved in defining iuspositivism, cfr. Uberto Scarpelli, *Cos'è il positivismo giuridico* (Milano: Edizioni di Comunità, 1965).

[36] An interesting issue in this regard is the ideological framework of both *iuspositivism* and *iusnaturalism*, which hinders mutual understanding of one another's reasons and, consequently, the opportunity to learn from one another. In this context, philosophers on the continent might find something to learn from in the modes of argument used in the analytical tradition, which focuses more on specific problems than on grand systems. Which, as a matter of fact, are quite different of the scholastic origins of the discussion as has been pointed out by Robert P. George, "Kelsen and Aquinas on 'the Natural-Law Doctrine'," *Notre Dame Law Review* 75 (2000): 1625-46.

[37] Cfr. also Andrés Ollero, *¿Tiene razón el derecho? Entre método científico y voluntad política* (Madrid: Congreso de los Diputados, 1996).

[38] Ibid., 131.

Bayón Mohino, Juan Carlos. *La normatividad del derecho: deber jurídico y razones para la acción*. Madrid: Centro de Estudios Constitucionales, 1995.

Delgado Pinto, José. *De nuevo sobre el problema del Derecho natural*. Salamanca: Ediciones Universidad de Salamanca, 1982.

Dworkin, Ronald. "Natural Law Revisited." *University of Florida Law Review* 34, no. 2 (1982): 165-88.

Finnis, John. *Natural Law and Natural Rights*. Oxford: Clarendon Press, 1980.

—. "On the Incoherence of Legal Positivism." *Notre Dame Law Review* 75 (2000): 1597-611.

George, Robert P. "Kelsen and Aquinas on 'the Natural-Law Doctrine'." *Notre Dame Law Review* 75 (2000): 1625-46.

Habermas, Jürgen. "Human Rights and Popular Sovereignty: The Liberal and Republican Versions." *Ratio Iuris* 7, no. 1 (1994): 1-13.

Hart, H. L. A. *The Concept of Law*. Oxford: Clarendon Press, 1967.

—. "Legal and Moral Obligation." In *Essays in Moral Philosophy*, edited by A. I. Melden. Seattle and London: University of Washington Press, 1958.

Hervada, Javier. *Introducción crítica al Derecho natural*. Pamplona: Eunsa, 2001.

Lipovetsky, Gilles. *Le Crépuscule du devoir. L'éthique indolore des nouveaux temps démocratiques*. Paris: Gallimard, 1992.

MacCormick, Neil. "Natural Law reconsidered." *Oxford Journal of Legal Studies* 1 (1981): 99-109.

Mackie, John Leslie. "Can There Be a Right-Based Moral Theory." In *Theories of Rights*, edited by Jeremy Waldron. Oxford: Oxford University Press, 1984.

Nussbaum, Martha C. "Patriotism and Cosmopolitanism." *The Boston Review* 19, no. 5 (1994).

Ollero, Andrés. *¿Tiene razón el derecho? Entre método científico y voluntad política*. Madrid: Congreso de los Diputados, 1996.

Pufendorf, Samuel. *De Officio Hominis et Civis juxta legem naturalem*. New York: Oxford University Press, 1927.

Raz, Joseph. *The Authority of Law. Essays on Law and Morality*. Oxford: Clarendon Press, 1979.

—. *The Concept of a Legal System*. 2 ed. Oxford: Clarendon Press, 1980.

—. *Practical Reason and Norms*. London: Hutchinson, 1975.

—. "Right Based Moralities." In *Theories of Rights*, edited by J.L. Mackie. Oxford: Oxford University Press, 1984.

—. "Rights and Politics." *Indiana Law Journal* 75, no. 1 (1995): 27-44.

Recaséns Siches, Luis. *Introducción al estudio del derecho*. 5 ed. México D.F.: Porrúa, 1979.

Scarpelli, Uberto. *Cos'è il positivismo giuridico*. Milano: Edizioni di Comunità, 1965.

Thomasius, Ch. *Fundamenta Iuris Naturae et Gentium*, 1705.

Walton, Kevin. "The Nature of Political Obligation." In *Australian Society for Legal Philosophy Annual Conference*. Canberra, March 2007.

BIBLIOGRAPHY

Selected bibliography on natural law

Abbà, Giuseppe. "Christian Moral Principles di Grisez e la Secunda Pars della Summa Thologiae." *Salesianum* 48 (1986): 637-80.

—. *Felicidad, vida buena y virtud*. Barcelona: Eiunsa, 1992.

—. *Lex et Virtus, Studi sull'evoluzione della morale di san Tommaso d'Aquino*. Roma: LAS, 1983.

—. *Quale impostazione per la filosofia morale?* Roma: LAS, 1996.

Aertsen, Jan A. "Natural Law in the Light of the Doctrine of Trascendentals." In *Lex et libertas: Freedom and Law According to St. Thomas Aquinas*, edited by L. J. Elders and K. Hedwig. Città del Vaticano: Editrice Vaticana, 1987.

—. *Nature and Creature: Thomas Aquinas way of Thought*. Leiden: Brill, 1988.

Anderson, Owen. "Is Contemporary Natural Law Theory a Beneficial Development? The Attempt to Study Natural Law and the Human Good Without Metaphysics." *New Blackfriars. A monthly review by the English Dominicans* 86, no. 2005 (September) (2005): 478.

Anscombe, G. E. M. "Modern Moral Philosophy." *Philosophy* 33 (1958): 1-19.

Armstrong, R. A. *Primary and Secondary Precepts in Thomistic Natural Law Teaching*. The Hague: Martinus Nijhoff, 1966.

Arnhart, Larry. "Thomistic Natural Law as a Darwinian Natural Right." *Social Philosophy and Policy Foundation* 18 (2001): 1-33.

Basso OP, Domingo. "Reflexiones sobre la ley natural." *Studium. Filosofía y Teología* 10, no. 20 (2007): 277-91.

Batscha, Zwi, ed. *Materialien zu Kant's Rechtsphilosophie*. Frankfurt a. M., 1976.

Bejczy, István P., ed. *Virtue Ethics in the Middle Ages. Commentaries on Aristotle's Nicomachean Ethics, 1200-1500*, Brill's Studies in Intellectual History, 160. Leiden and Boston (MA): Brill, 2007.

—. ed. *Virtue Ethics in the Middle Ages. Commentaries on Aristotle's Nicomachean Ethics, 1200-1500*, Brill's Studies in Intellectual History, 160. Leiden and Boston (MA): Brill, 2008.

Biggar, Nigel, and Rufus Black, eds. *The Revival of Natural Law: Philosophical, Theological, and Ethical Responses to the Finnis-Grisez School*. Aldershot: Ashgate, 2000.

Binmore, Ken. *Natural Justice*. Oxford: Oxford University Press, 2005.

Black, Rufus. *Christian moral realism: natural law, narrative, virtue, and the Gospel*. Oxford ; New York: Oxford University Press, 2000.

Bobbio, Norberto. "Hegel und die Naturrechtslehre." In *Materialen zu Hegels Rechtsphilosophie, vol. 2*, edited by Manfred Riedel. Frankfurt a. M., 1975.

Bormann, Franz-Josef. *Natur als Horizont sittlicher Praxis. Zur handlungstheoretischen Interpretation der Lehre vom natürlichen Sittengesetz bei Thomas von Aquin*. Stuttgart, Berlin, Bonn: Kohlhammer, 1999.

Boyd, Craig A. *A Shared Morality: a Narrative Defense of Natural Law Ethics*. Grand Rapids, MI: Brazos Press, 2007.

—. "Was Thomas Aquinas a Sociobiologist? Thomistic Natural Law, Rational Goods, and Sociobiology." *Zygon* 39, no. 3 (2004): 659-80.

Boyle, Joseph. "Fairness in Holdings: A Natural Law Account of Property and Welfare Rights." *Social Philosophy and Policy* 18, no. 1 (2001): 206-26.

—. "Natural Law and the Ethics of Traditions." In *Natural Law Theory. Contemporary Essays*, edited by Robert P. George, 3-30. Oxford: Clarendon Press, 1992.

—. "Natural Law and the Ethics of Traditions." In *Natural Law Theory. Contemporary Essays*, edited by Robert George, 3-30. Oxford: Clarendon Press, 1994.

—. "Natural Law, Ownership and the World's Natural Resources." *Journal of Value Inquiry* 23 (1989): 191-207.

—. "Radical Moral Disagreement in Contemporary Health Care: A Roman Catholic Perspective." *Journal of Medicine and Philosophy* 19, no. 2 (1994): 183-200.

—. "Sanctity of Life and Suicide: Tensions and Developments Within Common Morality." In *Suicide and Euthanasia*, edited by B. Brody, 221-50. Dordrecht: Kluwer, 1989.

Bradley, Gerald. "No Intentional Killing Whatsoever: the Case of Capital Punishment." In *Natural Law and Moral Inquiry. Ethics, Metaphysics, and Politics in the Work of Germain Grisez*, edited by Robert P. George, 155-73. Washington, D.C.: Georgetown University Press, 1998.

Brock, Stephen L. "Natural Inclination and the Intelligibility of the Good in Thomistic Natural Law." *Vera Lex* VI, no. 1-2 (2005): 57-78.

Brown, Oscar James. *Natural Rectitude and Divine Law in Aquinas. An Approach to an Integral Interpretation of the Thomistic Doctrine of Law*. Toronto: Pontifical Institute of Medieval Studies, 1981.
Buckle, Stephen. *Natural Law and the theory of Property: Grotius to Hume*. Oxford: Clarendon Press, 1991.
Butera, Guiseppe. "The Moral Status of the First Principle of Practical Reason in Thomas's Natural Law Theory." *The Thomist* 74, no. 4 (2008): 609-31.
Chalmeta, Gabriel. *Jacques Maritain : el elemento gnoseológico en la constitución de la ley moral natural*. Roma: Pontificia Universidad Urbaniana, 1989.
Chappell, Timothy. *Understanding Human Goods*. Edinburgh: Edinburgh University Press, 1995.
Cófreces, Evencio, and Ramón García de Haro. *Teología moral fundamental*. Pamplona: Eunsa, 1998.
Cogley, John, and Center for the Study of Democratic Institutions. *Natural law and Modern Society*. Cleveland: World Pub. Co., 1963.
Composta SDB, Dario. *Natura e Ragione. Studio sulle inclinazioni naturali in rapporto al diritto naturale*. Zürich: Pas-Verlag, 1971.
Cottier OP, Georges "Reflections on Marriage and the Family." *Nova et Vetera. The English Edition of the International Theological Journal* I, no. 1 (2003): 11-25.
Cottier OP, Georges M. "Loi naturelle et Décalogue." In *Doctor Communis, Proceedings of the Pontifical Academy of St. Thomas Aquinas "Persona, legge naturale, diritti umani in una societá complessa e globale / The Human Person, Natural Law, Human Rights in a Complex and Globalised World"*, edited by Pontificia Academia Sancti Thomae Aquinatis, 23-40. Vatican City: Pontificia Academia Sancti Thomae Aquinatis, 2007.
Cristina, L. H. Traina. *Feminist Ethics and Natural Law: The End of the Anathemas (Moral Traditions and Moral Arguments Series)*. Washington DC: Georgetown University Press, 2002.
Crowe, Michael Bertram. *The Changing Profile of the Natural Law*. Hague: Martinus Nijhoff, 1977.
—. "The Natural Law Before St. Thomas." *Irish Ecclesiastical Record* 76 (1951): 193-204.
Cruz, Alfredo. "Natural Law and Practical Philosophy: The Presence of a Theological Concept in Moral Knowledge." In *Contemporary Perspectives on Natural Law. Natural Law as a Limiting Concept*, edited by Ana Marta González, 161-74. Aldershot: Ashgate, 2008.

Cruz Cruz, Juan, ed. *La ley natural como fundamento moral y jurídico en Domingo de Soto*. Pamplona: Eunsa, 2007.

—. ed. *Ley natural y niveles antropológicos. Lecturas sobre Tomás de Aquino*. Vol. 203, Cuadernos de Anuario Filosófico. Serie Universitaria. Pamplona: Servicio de Publicaciones de la Universidad de Navarra, 2007.

—. "The Practical Reordering of Law in the Light of the Natural Law." *Anuario Filosófico* 41, no. 1 (2008): 155-79.

Cumberland, Richard. *A Treatise of the Laws of Nature*. Translated by John Maxwell. Edited by Jon Parkin. 1727 ed. Indianapolis, IN: Liberty Fund, 2005.

Davis, Scott. "Doing What Comes Naturally: Recent Work on Thomas Aquinas and the New Natural Law Theory." *Religion* 31 (2001): 407-33.

Di Blasi, Fulvio. *God and the Natural Law. A Rereading of Thomas Aquinas*. Translated by David Thunder. South Bend, Indiana: St. Augustine's Press, 2006.

—. "Law as Act of Reason and Command." *Nova et Vetera. The English Edition of the International Theological Journal* 4, no. 3 (2006): 515-28.

—. "Practical Syllogism, Proairesis, and the Virtues: Toward a Reconciliation of Virtue Ethics and Natural Law Ethics." *New Things & Old Things* 1 (2004): 21-41.

DiNoia OP, J. Augustine, and Romanus Cessario OP, eds. *Veritatis Splendor and the Renewal of Moral Theology*. Princeton, NJ - Huntington, IN - Chicago, Ill.: Scepter Publishers - Our Sunday Visitor - Midwest Theological Forum, 1999.

Dunn, John, and Ian Harris, eds. *Aquinas I*. Vol. IV, Great Political Thinkers 4. Cheltenham, UK - Lyme, US: Edward Elgar, 1997.

—. eds. *Aquinas II*. Vol. IV, Great Political Thinkers 4. Cheltenham, UK - Lyme, US: Edward Elgar, 1997.

Dworkin, Ronald. "Natural Law Revisited." *University of Florida Law Review* 34, no. 2 (1982): 165-88.

Elders, Leo. *The Ethics of St. Thomas Aquinas: Happiness, Natural Law and the Virtues*. Frankfurt am Main: Peter Lang Publ., 2005.

Elton, María. "Gnoseología de la ley natural." *Sapientia* 53 (1998): 175-94.

Filippi, Silvia. "The Resignification of the Natural Moral Law in Medieval Thought." *Anuario Filosófico* 41, no. 1 (2008): 13-40.

Finnis, John. *Aquinas: Moral, Political, and Legal Theory*. Oxford: Oxford University Press, 1998.

—. "Aristóteles, Santo Tomás y los absolutos morales." *Persona y Derecho* 23 (1993): 9-26.
—. *Fundamentals of Ethics*. Washington, D. C.: Georgetown University Press, 1983.
—. "Is Natural Law Theory Compatible with Limited Government?" In *Natural Law, Liberalism, and Morality*, edited by R. P. George, 10-18. Oxford: Oxford University Press, 1996.
—. "Liberalism and Natural Law Theory." *Mercer Law Review* 46 (1994): 687-704.
—. *Moral Absolutes. Tradition, Revision and Truth*. Washington D. C.: The Catholic University of America Press, 1991.
—. *Natural Law and Natural Rights*. Oxford: Clarendon Press, 1980.
—. "Natural Law and the Is-Ought Question: an Invitation to Professor Veatch." *Catholic Lawyer* 26 (1980-1981): 265-77.
—. *Natural Law. Vol I*. Aldershot: Dartmouth, 1991.
—. *Natural Law. Vol II*. Aldershot: Dartmouth, 1991.
—. "Natural Law: The Classical Tradition." In *The Oxford Handbook of Jurisprudence and Philosophy of Law*, edited by Jules Coleman and Scott Shapiro, 1-60. Oxford: Oxford University Press, 2002.
—. "Nature and Natural Law in Contemporary Philosophical and Theological Debates: Some Observations." In *The Nature and Dignity of the Human person as the Foundation of the Right to Life: the Challenges of the Contemporary Cultural Context (Proceedings of the Eighth Assembly of the Pontifical Academy for Life, Vatican City, 25-27 February 2002)*, edited by Juan de Dios Vial Correa and Elio Sgreccia, 81-109. Città del Vaticano: Libreria Editrice Vaticana, 2003.
—. "Public Good: The Specifically Political Common Good in Aquinas." In *Natural Law and Moral Inquiry. Ethics, Metaphysics, and Politics in the Work of Germain Grisez*, edited by R. P. George, 174-209. Washington, D. C.: Georgetown University Press, 1998.
Finnis, John, and Germain Grisez. "The Basic Principles of Natural Law: A Reply to Ralph McInerny." *The American Journal of Jurisprudence* 26 (1981): 21-31.
Flannery, Kevin L. *Acts amid Precepts: The Aristotelian Logical Structure of Thomas Aquinas's Moral Theory*. Washington D.C.: The Catholic University of America Press, 2001.
—. "The Conjugal Act and the Use of Prophylactics." *The National Catholic Bioethics Quarterly* 6, no. 4 (2006): 733-35.
—. "The Field of Moral Action according to Thomas Aquinas." *The Thomist* 69, no. 1 (2005): 1-30.

Flippen, Douglas. "Natural Law and Natural Inclinations." *The New Scholasticism* 60 (1986): 284-316.

Foot, Philippa. *Natural Goodness*. Oxford: Oxford University Press, 2000.

Frankel, Paul Ellen, Fred Dycus Jr. Miller Jr., and Jeffrey Paul. *Natural Law and Modern Moral Philosophy*.

Furton, Edward James, ed. *Live the Truth: The Moral Legacy of John Paul II in Catholic Health Care. Proceedings of the Twentieth Workshop for Bishops*. Philadelphia: National Catholic Bioethics Center, 2006.

—. "Restoring the Hierarchy of Values to Thomistic Natural Law." *The American Journal of Jurisprudence* 39 (1994): 373-97

García-Huidobro, Joaquín. "La is-ought question y el valor del argumento de la perversión de las facultades naturales." *Persona y Derecho* 29 (1993): 167-249.

—. *Razón práctica y derecho natural (el iusnaturalismo de Tomás de Aquino)*. Valparaíso: Edeval, 1993.

George, Robert P. *In Defense of Natural Law*. Oxford: Clarendon Press, 1999.

—. "Ley Natural y Naturaleza Humana." *Boletín Mexicano de Derecho Comparado* 37, no. 110 (2004): 597-610.

—. *Making Men Moral. Civil Liberties and Public Morality*. Oxford: Oxford University Press, 1993.

—. "Natural Law." *The American Journal of Jurisprudence* 52 (2007): 55-76.

—. ed. *Natural Law & Moral Inquiry. Ethics, Metaphysics, and Politics in the Work of Germain Grisez*. Washington D.C.: Georgetown University Press, 1998.

—. *Natural Law (The International Library of Essays in Law & Legal Theory Series)*, The International Library of Essays in Law & Legal Theory Series. Aldershot: Ashgate, 2003.

—. "Natural Law and Human Nature." In *Natural Law Theory. Contemporary Essays*, edited by Robert P. George. Oxford: Clarendon Press, 1992.

—. ed. *Natural Law Theory. Contemporary Essays*. Oxford: Clarendon Press, 1992.

—. ed. *Natural Law Theory. Contemporary Essays*. Oxford: Clarendon Press, 1994.

—. ed. *Natural Law, Liberalism and Morality: Contemporary Essays* Oxford: Clarendon Press, 1996.

Gierke, Otto von. *Natural Law and the Theory of Society, 1500–1800*. Cambridge: Cambridge University Press, 1958.

Golding, Martin P. "Aquinas and Some Contemporary Natural Law Theories." *Proceedings of the American Catholic Philosophical Association* 48 (1974): 238-47.

Gomez-Lobo, Alfonso. *Morality and the Human Goods: An Introduction to Natural Law Ethics*. Washington, D. C.: Georgetown University Press, 2002.

—. "Natural Law and Naturalism." *Proceedings of the American Catholic Philosophical Association* 69 (1984): 232-49.

González, Ana Marta. *Claves de ley natural*. Madrid: Rialp, 2006.

—. ed. *Contemporary Perspectives on Natural Law. Natural Law as a Limiting Concept*. Aldershot: Ashgate, 2008.

—. "*Depositum Gladius non debet restitui furioso:* Precepts, synderesis and virtues in Saint Thomas Aquinas." *The Thomist* 62, no. 2 (1999): 217-40.

—. *Moral, razón y naturaleza. Una investigación sobre Tomás de Aquino*. 2 ed. Pamplona: Eunsa, 2006.

—. "Natural Law as a Limiting Concept. A Reading of Thomas Aquinas." In *Contemporary Perspectives on Natural Law. Natural Law as a Limiting Concept*, edited by Ana Marta González. Aldershot: Ashgate, 2008.

Goyette, John. "Natural Law and the Metaphysics of Creation." In *St. Thomas Aquinas and the Natural Law Tradition*, edited by John Goyette, Mark S. Latkovic and Richard S. Myers, 74-77 (311). Washington, D.C.: Catholic University of America Press, 2004.

Goyette, John, Mark S. Latkovic, and Richard S. Myers. *St. Thomas Aquinas and the Natural Law Tradition: Contemporary Perspectives*. Washington D.C.: The Catholic University of America Press, 2004.

Grabill, Stephen J. *Rediscovering the Natural Law in Reformed Theological Ethics*. William B. Eerdmans Publishing Co.: Grand Rapids MI, Cambridge 2006.

Greene, Robert A. "Instinct of Nature: Natural Law, Synderesis, and the Moral Sense." *Journal of the History of Ideas* 58, no. 2 (1997): 173-98.

Grisez, Germain. *Contraception and the Natural Law*. Milwaukee: The Bruce Publishing Company, 1964.

—. "The First Principle of Practical Reason: A Commentary on the Summa Theologiae, 1-2, Question 94, Article 2." *Natural Law Forum* 10 (1965): 168-201.

—. "Natural Law, God, Religion and Human Fulfillment." *The American Journal of Jurisprudence* 46 (2001): 3-26.

—. "Toward a Consistent Natural law ethic of killing." *The American Journal of Jurisprudence* 15 (1970): 64-96.

—. *The Way of the Lord Jesus, Volume I: Christian Moral Principles*. Chicago: Franciscan Herald Press, 1983.

Grisez, Germain, and Joseph Boyle. "Response to Our Critics and Our Collaborators." In *Natural Law and Moral Inquiry, George, Robert P*, 213-37, 1998.

Grisez, Germain, Joseph Boyle, and John Finnis. "Practical Principles, Moral Truth, and Ultimate Ends." *The American Journal of Jurisprudence* 32 (1987): 99-151.

Grisez, Germain, and John Finnis. "The Basic Principles of Natural Law: a reply to Ralph McInerny." *The American Journal of Jurisprudence* 26 (1981): 21-32.

Grotius, Hugo. *The Law of War and Peace*. Translated by Louise R. Loomis. Roslyn, New York: Walter Black, 1949.

Guy Mansini OSB, Guy, and Lawrence J. Welch. "Revelation, Natural Law, and Homosexual Unions." *Nova et Vetera. The English Edition of the International Theological Journal* 2, no. 2 (2004): 337-66.

Haakonssen, Knud. "The Character and Obligation of Natural Law According to Richard Cumberland." In *English Philosophy in the Age of Locke*, edited by Michael A. Stewart. Oxford: Oxford University Press, 2000.

—. *Grotius, Pufendorf and Modern Natural Law*. Aldershot, Hants., Brookfield, Vt.: Ashgate/Dartmouth, 1998.

—. ed. *Natural Law and Moral Philosophy: From Grotius to the Scottish Enlightenment*. Cambridge: Cambridge University Press, 1996.

—. "Natural Law Theory." In *Encyclopedia of Ethics*: Garland, 1992.

—. *The Science of Legislator: the Natural Jurisprudence of David Hume and Adam Smith*. Cambridge: Cambridge University Press, 1981.

Hall, Pamela. *Narrative and the Natural Law: an Interpretation of Thomistic Ethics*. Notre Dame, IN: University of Notre Dame Press, 1998.

Hall, Richard B. "The Alterability of Natural Law." *The New Scholasticism* 55 (1981): 474-83.

Hallett, Garth. *Greater Good: The Case for Proportionalism*. Washington, D. C.: Georgetown University Press, 1995.

Hare, John E. *God's Call: Moral Realism, God's Commands, and Human Autonomy*. Grand Rapids: Eerdmans, 2001.

Hartung, Gerald *Die Naturrechtsdebatte. Geschichte der Obligatio vom 17. bis 20. Jahrhundert*. Freiburg, Munich: Alber, 1998.

Hervada, Javier. *Escritos de derecho natural*. 2 ed. Pamplona: Eunsa, 1993.

—. *Introducción crítica al Derecho natural*. Pamplona: Eunsa, 2001.

—. *Introducción crítica al derecho natural*. Pamplona: Eunsa, 1998.

—. *Natural Right and Natural Law. A Critical Introduction*. Translated by Alban d'Entremont. Pamplona: Servicio de Publicaciones de la Universidad de Navarra, 1987.

Hibbs, Thomas S. "Divine Ironie and the Natural Law Speculation and Edification in Aquinas." *International Philosophical Quarterly* 30 (1991): 419-29.

Hittinger, Russell. *A Critique of the New Natural Law Theory*. Notre Dame, Ind.: University of Notre Dame Press, 1987.

—. "Natural Law and the Human City." In *Contemporary Perspectives on Natural Law. Natural Law as a Limiting Concept*, edited by Ana Marta González, 29-42. London: Ashgate, 2008.

Höffe, Otfried, ed. *Immanuel Kant, Metaphysische Anfangsgründe der Rechtslehre*. Berlin: Akademie, 1999.

Hooker, Richard. *Of the Laws of Ecclesiastical Polity*. Edited by A. S. McGrade. Cambridge: Cambridge University Press, 1989.

Horowitz, M. C. "The Stoic Synthesis of the Idea of Natural Law in Man: Four Themes." *Journal of the History of Ideas* XXXI (1974): 3-16.

Inciarte, Fernando. *First principles, substance and action. Studies in Aristotle and Aristotelianism*. Edited by Lourdes Flamarique. Hildesheim, Georg Olms: Olms, 2005.

—. *Liberalismo y republicanismo. Ensayos de filosofía política*. Pamplona: Eunsa, 2001.

—. "Natura ad unum – ratio ad opposita. Zur Transformation des Aristotelismus bei Duns Scotus." In *Philosophie im Mittelalter. Entwicklungslinien und Paradigmen*, edited by J. P. Beckmann, L. Honnefelder, G. Schimpf and G. Wieland, 259-73. Hamburg: Felix Meiner, 1987.

Inglis, John, ed. *Thomas Aquinas*, International Library of Essays in the History of Social and Political Thought: Ashgate, 2006.

Irwin, Terence. "Ethics as an Inexact Science: Aristotle's Ambitions for Moral Theory." In *Moral Particularism*, edited by Brad Hooker and Margaret Little. Oxford: Oxford University Press, 2000.

Jacques, Francis. "Thomas d'Aquin et Emmanuel Kant: Loi naturelle et impératif catégorique. Et après?" In *Doctor Communis, Proceedings of the Pontifical Academy of St. Thomas Aquinas "Persona, legge naturale, diritti umani in una societá complessa e globale / The Human Person, Natural Law, Human Rights in a Complex and Globalised World"*, edited by Pontificia Academia Sancti Thomae Aquinatis, 93-128. Vatican City: Pontificia Academia Sancti Thomae Aquinatis, 2007.

John, Gardner. "Nearly Natural Law." *The American Journal of Jurisprudence* 52 (2007): 1-24.

Kaczor, Christopher Robert. *Proportionalism and the Natural Law Tradition*. Washington, D.C.: The Catholic University of America Press, 2002.

Kainz, Howard P. *Natural Law. An Introduction and Re-examination*. Chicago and La Salle, Illinois: Open Court, 2004.

Kesler, Charles Reeder, and Marco Tulio Cicerón. "Cicero and the natural law." Tesis Univ of Harvard, UMI,, 1991.

Kluxen, Wolfgang. *Lex naturalis bei Thomas von Aquin*. Bonn: Verlag Schöningh Paderborn 2001.

—. *Philosophische Ethik bei Thomas von Aquin*. Mainz: Matrias-Grünewald-Verlag, 1964.

Korkman, Peter. "Barbeyrac and Natural Law." Åbo Akademi University, 2001.

—. "Barbeyrac on Scepticism and on Grotian Modernity." *Grotiana* 20/21 (1999/2000): 77-106.

—. "Descartes, le droit naturel, et les fondements de la morale moderne." In *L'ésprit cartésien. Quatrième centenaire de la naissance de Descartes. Actes du XXVIe congrès de l'association des sociétés de philosophie de langue francaise (A.S.P.L.F.)*, edited by Bernard Bourgeois and Jacques Havet, 390-95. Paris: VRIN, 2000.

—. "Voluntarism and Moral Obligation – Barbeyrac's Defense of Pufendorf Revisited." In *Early Modern Natural Law Theories: Contexts and Strategies in the Early Enlightenment*, edited by Tim Hochstrasser and Peter Schröder, 195-225. London: Kluwer, 2003.

Kraut, Richard, ed. *The Blackwell Guide to Aristotle's Nicomachean Ethics*. Oxford UK - Malden MA: Blackwell Publishing, 2006.

Kries, Douglas. "On Leo Strauss' Understanding of the Natural Law Theory of Thomas Aquinas." *The Thomist* 57 (1993): 215-32.

Levering, Matthew. "Natural Law and Natural Inclinations: Rhonheimer, Pinckaers, McAleer." *The Thomist* 70, no. 2 (2006): 155-201.

Lisska, Anthony J. *Aquinas's Theory of Natural Law: An Analytic Reconstruction*. Oxford: Oxford University Press, 1996.

—. "On the Revival of Natural Law: Several Books from the Last Half-Decade." *American Catholic Philosophical Quarterly.* 81, no. 4 (2008): 613-38.

Llano, Alejandro. *El enigma de la representación*. Madrid: Síntesis, 1999.

Long, Steven A. "*Evangelium Vitae*, St. Thomas Aquinas, and the Death Penalty." *The Thomist* 63 (1999).

—. “On the Loss, and the Recovery, of Nature as a Theonomic Principle: Reflections on the Nature / Grace Controversy.” *Nova et Vetera. The English Edition of the International Theological Journal* 5, no. 1 (2007): 133-84.

—. “On the Loss, and the Recovery, of Nature as a Theonomic Principle: Reflections on the Nature / Grace Controversy.” *Nova et Vetera. The English Edition of the International Theological Journal* 5, no. 1 (2007): 133-84.

—. “On the Possibility of a Purely Natural End for Man.” *The Thomist* 64, no. 2 (2000): 211-37.

—. “Providence, Freedom, and Natural Law.” *Nova et Vetera. The English Edition of the International Theological Journal* 4, no. 3 (2006): 557-605.

—. “Reproductive Technologies and the Natural Law.” *The National Catholic Bioethics Quarterly* 2, no. 2 (2002): 221-28.

—. “Review: Natural Law and Practical Reason: A Thomist View of Moral Autonomy. By Martin Rhonheimer. Translated by Gerald Malsbary. Fordham University Press (2000).” *First Things* January (2001).

—. *The Teleological Grammar of the Moral Act*. Naples, FL: Sapientia Press of Ave Maria University 2007.

Lottin, Odon. *Le droit naturel chez S. Thomas d’Aquin et ses prédecesseurs*. Bruges, 1931.

MacCormick, Neil. “Natural Law reconsidered.” *Oxford Journal of Legal Studies* 1 (1981): 99-109.

MacIntyre, Alasdair. *First Principles, Final Ends and Contemporary Philosophical Issues*. Milwaukee: Marquette University Press, 1990.

MacKenzie, Iain M. *God’s Order and Natural Law. The Works of the Laudian Divines*, 2002.

Maritain, Jacques. *La loi naturelle ou loi non écrite*. Fribourg: Editions Universitaires, 1986.

—. *Nove lezioni sulla legge naturale*. Milano: Jaca Book, 1985.

—. *The rights of man and the natural law*. London: Geoffrey Bles, 1958.

Massini, Carlos Ignacio. “El primer principio del saber práctico: objeciones y respuestas.” *Sapientia* XLVI (1991): 171-78.

—. *La ley natural y su interpretación contemporánea*. Pamplona: Eunsa, 2006.

May, William E. “The Natural Law Doctrine of Francis Suarez.” *The New Scholasticism* 68 (1984): 409-23.

McInerny, Ralph. *Aquinas*. Cambridge: Polity Press, 2004.

—. *Aquinas on Human Action. A Theory of Practice*. Washington, D.C.: The Catholic University of America Press, 1992.

—. *Ethica Thomistica. The moral philosophy of Thomas Aquinas*. Washington, D.C.: The Catholic University of America Press, 1997.

—. "Portia's Lament: Reflections on Practical Reason." In *Natural Law and Moral Inquiry. Ethics, Metaphysics, and Politics in the Work of Germain Grisez*, edited by Robert George, 82-103. Washington D.C.: Georgetown University Press, 1998.

—. "The Principles of Natural Law." *American Journal of Jurisprudence* 25 (1980): 1-15.

—. "Thomistic Natural Law and Aristotelian Philosophy." In *St. Thomas Aquinas and the Natural Law Tradition: Contemporary Perspectives*, edited by John Goyette, Mark S. Latkovic and Richard S. Myers, 23-38. Washington D.C.: The Catholic University of America Press, 2004.

Mesa Posada, Carlos Augusto. *La ley natural en Santo Tomás: fundamentos metafísicos y propiedades* Chía (Colombia): Universidad de La Sabana, 1998.

Messner, Johannes. *Das Naturrecht. Handbuch der Gesselschaftsethik, Staatsethik und Wirtschaftsethik*. Berlin: Duncker und Humblot, 1984.

Molina, Enrique. *La moral entre la convicción y la utilidad. La evolución de la moral desde la manualística hasta el proporcionalismo y el pensamiento de Grisez-Finnis*. Pamplona: Eunsa, 1994.

Moore, Michael. "Good without God." In *Natural Law, Liberalism, and Morality*, edited by Robert P. George, 221-70. Oxford: Oxford University Press, 1996.

—. "Moral Reality." *Wisconsin Law Review* (1982): 1061-156.

Murphy Jr., William. "Veritatis Splendor and Traditionally Naturalistic Thomisms: The Object as Proximate End as Test Case." *Studia Moralia* 45, no. 2 (2007).

Murphy, Mark. *An Essay on Divine Authority*. Ithaca, NY: Cornell University Press, 2002.

—. "La epistemología de los primeros principios de la ley natural." In *Una ley de libertad para la vida del mundo. Actas del Congreso Internacional sobre Ley Natural*, edited by Juan José Pérez-Soba, Juan de Dios Larrú and Jaime Ballesteros, 111-24. Madrid: Collectanae Matritensia - 2007.

—. *Natural Law and Practical Rationality*. Cambridge: Cambridge University Press, 2001.

—. *Natural Law in Jurisprudence and Politics*. Cambridge: Cambridge University Press, 2006.

—. "The Natural Law Tradition in Ethics." *Standford Encyclopedia of Philosophy* (2002), http://plato.stanford.edu/entries/natural-law-ethics/.

—. "Natural Law, Consent, and Political Obligation." In *Natural Law and Modern Moral Philosophy*, edited by Paul Ellen Frankel, Fred D. Miller Jr. and Jeffrey Paul. Cambridge: Cambridge University Press, 2001.

—. "Natural Law, Impartialism, and Others' Good." *The Thomist* (1996).

—. *Philosophy of Law. The Fundamentals*: Blackwell, 2006.

—. "Self-evidence, human nature, and natural law." *American Catholic Philosophical Quarterly* LXIX (1995): 471-84.

Nelson, Daniel Mark. *The priority of prudence. Virtue and Natural Law in Thomas Aquinas and the implications for modern ethics*. Pennsylvania: The Pennsylvania University Press, 1992.

O'Connor, D. J. *Aquinas and natural law*. London, Melbourne, Toronto: MacMillan, 1967.

O'Reilly, Kevin. "The Vision of Virtue and Knowledge of the Natural Law in Thomas Aquinas." *Nova et Vetera. The English Edition of the International Theological Journal* 5, no. 1 (2007): 41-66.

Oderberg, David S. *Applied Ethics: A Non-Consequentialist Approach*. Oxford: Blackwell, 2000.

—. "The Metaphysical Foundations of Natural Law." In *Contemporary Perspectives on Natural Law: Natural Law as a Limiting Concept*, edited by Ana Marta González. Aldershot: Ashgate, 2008.

—. *Moral Theory: A Non-Consequentialist Approach*. Oxford: Blackwell, 2000.

Oderberg, David S., and Timothy Chappel, eds. *Human Values. New Essays on Ethics and Natural Law*. Houndmills, Basingstoke, Hampshire; New York: Palgrave Macmillan, 2004.

Oderberg, David S., and Jacqueline A. Laing, eds. *Human Lives: Critical Essays on Consequentialist Bioethics*. Houndmills: Macmillan Press, 1997.

Ottmann, Henning "Das Recht der Natur in Hegels Philosophie des Rechts." *Der Staat* 23 (1984): 1–15.

Pakaluk, Michael. "Is the Common Good of Political Society Limited and Instrumental?" *Review of Metaphysics* 55 (2001): 57-94.

Payer, Pierre J. "Prudence and the Principles of Natural Law: A Mediaeval Development." *Speculum* 54 (1979): 55–70.

Peretó, Ruben. "Natural Law in the High Middle Ages. The Case of Alcuin." *Anuario Filosófico* 41, no. 1 (2008): 55-68.

Perkams, Matthias. "Aquinas's Interpretation of the Aristotelian Virtue of Justice and his Doctrine of Natural Law." In *Virtue Ethics in the Middle Ages. Commentaries on Aristotele's Nichomachean Ethics, 1200-1500*, edited by István P. Bejczy, 131-50. Leiden - Boston: Brill, 2008.

Pontificia Academia Sancti Thomae Aquinatis. *Doctor Communis, Proceedings of the Pontifical Academy of St. Thomas Aquinas "Persona, legge naturale, diritti umani in una societá complessa e globale / The Human Person, Natural Law, Human Rights in a Complex and Globalised World"*. Vatican: Pontifical Academy of St. Thomas Aquinas, 2007.

Porter, Jean. *Natural and divine law: reclaiming the tradition for Christian ethics*, Saint Paul University series in ethics. Grand Rapids, MI: Wm. B. Eerdmans, 1999.

—. *Nature as reason: a Thomistic theory of the natural law*. Grand Rapids, Michigan - Cambridge: W.B. Eerdmans, 2005.

—. "What the Wise Person Knows: Natural Law and Virtue in Aquinas' Suma Theologiae." *Studies in Christian Ethics* 12 (1999): 57-69.

Pufendorf, Samuel. *The Political Writings of Samuel Pufendorf*. Translated by Michael J. Seidler. Oxford: Oxford University Press, 1994.

Rhonheimer, Martin. "The Cognitive Structure of the Natural Law and the Truth of Subjectivity." *The Thomist* 67, no. 1 (2003): 1-44.

—. "Contraception, Sexual Behavior, and Natural Law: Philosophical Foundation of the Norm of "Humanae Vitae"." In *"Humanae Vitae": 20 anni dopo. Atti del II Congresso Internazionale di Teologia Morale Roma (9-12 novembre 1988)*, edited by AA.VV., 73-113. Milano: ARES, 1989.

—. "The Contraceptive Choice, Condom Use, and Moral Arguments Based on Nature. A Reply to Christopher Oleson." *National Catholic Bioethics Quarterly* 7, no. 2 (2007): 273-91.

—. "Empfängnisverhütung, Sexualverhalten und Menschenbild." *Imago Hominis* 2 (1995): 145-53.

—. *Ética de la procreación*. Madrid: Rialp, 2004.

—. "Legge morale naturale: conoscenza morale and coscienza. The cognitiva struttura della legge naturale and verità della soggettività." *Ars Interpretandi* 7 (2002): 47-78.

—. *Ley natural y razón práctica. Una visión tomista de la autonomía moral*. Eunsa: Pamplona, 2000.

—. *Natur als Grundlage der Moral. Die personale Struktur des Naturgesetzes bei Thomas von Aquin, eine Auseinandersetzung mit autonomer und teleologischer Ethik*. Innsbruck: Tyrolia, 1987.

—. *Natural Law and Practical Reason: A Thomist View of Moral Autonomy*. New York: Fordham University Press, 2000.

—. "Natural Moral Law: Moral Knowledge and Conscience. The Cognitive Structure of the Natural Law and the Truth of Subjectivity." In *The Nature and Dignity of the Human person as the Foundation of the Right to Life (Proceedings of the Eighth Assembly of the Pontifical Academy for Life, 25-27 February 2002)*, edited by Juan de Dios Vial Correa and Elio Sgreccia, 123-59. Città del Vaticano: Libreria Editrice Vaticana, 2003.

—. "Nature as Reason: A Thomistic Theory of the Natural Law." *Studies in Christian Ethics* 19, no. 3 (2006): 357-78.

—. *The Perspective of the Acting Person: Essays in the Renewal of Thomistic Moral Philosophy*. Edited by William Murphy Jr. Washington DC: Catholic University Press, 2008.

—. "The *Political Ethos* of Constitutional Democracy and the Place of Natural Law in Public Reason: Rawls's 'Political Liberalism' Revisited." *American Journal of Jurisprudence* 50 (2005): 1-70.

—. "Practical Reason and the "Naturally Rational": On the Doctrine of the Natural Law as a Principle of Praxis in Thomas Aquinas." In *The Perspective of the Acting Person: Essays in the Renewal of Thomistic Moral Philosophy*, edited by William Murphy Jr., 95-128. Washington D.C.: The Catholic University of America Press, 2008.

—. *Praktische Vernunft und die Vernunftigkeit der Praxis. Handlungstheorie beit Thomas von Aquin in ihrer Entstehung aus dem Problemkontext der aristotelischen Ethik*. Berlin: Akademie, 1991.

Riley, Patrick. *Leibniz' Universal Jurisprudence. Justice as the Charity of the Wise*. Cambridge, MA: Harvard University Press, 1996.

Rommen, Heinrich. *The Natural Law. A Study in Legal and Social History and Philosophy*. St. Louis, London: Herder Book Company, 1948.

Santos, Modesto. *En defensa de la razón*. Pamplona: Eunsa, 2000.

Scherz, Luis Tomas. *Das Naturgesetz bei Thomas von Aquin un die "Tentatio Stoicorum". Heutige Auffassungen eines umstrittenen Begriffs*, Tübingen Studien zur Theologie und Philosophie, n° 24. Tübingen: Francke, 2006.

Schneewind, J. B. *The invention of autonomy*. Cambridge: Cambridge University Press, 1998.

—. "Kant and Natural Law Ethics." *Ethics* 104 (1993): 53-74.

Schneider, Hans–Peter. *Justitia Universalis. Quellenstudien zur Geschichte des 'Christlichen Naturrechts' bei Gottfried Wilhelm Leibniz*. Frankfurt a.M., 1967.

Schockenhoff, Eberhard. *Natural Law and Human Dignity: Universal Ethics in an Historical World.* Translated by Brian McNeil. Washington D.C.: The Catholic University of America Press, 2003.

Schütz, J. L. "'Ought'- Judgments: a descriptivist Analysis from a Thomistic Perspective." *The New Scholasticism* LXI (1987): 400-26.

—. "St Thomas Aquinas on Necessary Moral Principles." *The New Scholasticism* LXII (1988): 150-78.

Scully, Edgar. "The Political Limitations of Natural Law in Aquinas." In *The Medieval Tradition of Natural Law*, edited by Harold J. Johnson, 149-59. Michigan: Western Michigan University, 1987.

Seidl, H. "Sittliche Freiheit und Naturgesetz bei Thomas angesichts des modernen Gegensatzes von Autonomie und Heteronomie." In *Lex et Libertas. Freedom and law according to St Thomas Aquinas, Proceedings of the 4th Syumposium on St. Thomas Aquinas Philosophy*, edited by L. Elders and K. Hedwig, 113-24. Città del Vaticano, 1986.

Sève, René *Leibniz et l'école moderne du droit naturel*. Paris: PUF, 1989.

Simon, Yves R. *The Tradition of Natural Law: a Philosopher's Reflections*. Edited by Vukan Kuic. New York: Fordham University Press, 1965.

Simpson, Peter. "St. Thomas on the Naturalistic Fallacy." *The Thomist* 51 (1987): 51-69.

—. *Vices, Virtues, and Consequences. Essays on Moral and Political Philosophy*. Washington D. C.: The Catholic University of America Press, 2001.

Solum, Lawrence B. "Natural Justice." *The American Journal of Jurisprudence* 51 (2006): 65-105.

Soto Bruna, María Jesús, ed. *Metafísica y antropología en el siglo XII*. Pamplona: Eunsa, 2005.

Spaemann, Robert. *Das Natürliche und das Vernünftige. Essays zur Anthropologie*. München: Piper, 1987.

—. *Glück und Wohlwollen. Versuch über Ethik.* Stuttgart: Klett-Cotta, 1989.

—. "La naturaleza como instancia de apelación moral." In *El hombre: inmanencia y trascendencia*, edited by R. Alvira. Pamplona: Servicio de Publicaciones de la Universidad de Navarra, 1992.

Spaemann, Robert, and Reinhard Low. *Die Frage Wozu?: Geschichte und Wiederentdeckung des teleologischen Denkens* München: Piper, 1981.

Staley, Kevin M. "New Natural Law, Old Natural Law, or the same Natural Law." *The American Journal of Jurisprudence* 38 (1993): 109-35.

Strauss, Leo. "Natural Law." In *International Encyclopedia of the Social Sciences, vol. 11*, edited by David L. Sills, 80-85. New York: Macmillan, 1968.

—. *Natural Rights and History*. Chicago: Chicago University Press, 1953.

Striker, Gisela. "Origins of the Concept of Natural Law." *Proceedings of the Boston Area Colloquium in Ancient Philosophy* 2 (1986): 79-94.

Theron, Stephen. *Natural Law Reconsidered. The Ethics of Human Liberation*. Frankfurt am Main: Peter Lang, 2002.

Tierney, Brian. *The Idea of Natural Rights. Studies on Natural Rights, Natural Law and Church Law 1150-1626*. Atlanta: Scholars Press, 1997.

—. "Public Expediency and Natural Law: A Fourteenth Century Discussion on the Origins of Government and Property." In *Authority and Power: Studies on Medieval Law and Government Presented to Walter Ullmann on his Seventieth Birthday*, edited by B. Tierney and P. Lineham. Cambridge: Cambridge University Press, 1980.

—. *Rights, Laws and Infallibility in Medieval Thought*. Edited by Variorum, Variorum Collected Studies Series. Aldershot: Ashgate, 1997.

Triglio Jr., John. *Thomistic Renaissance - The Natural Law: The Reawakening of Scholasticism in Catholic Teaching as Evidenced by Pope John Paul II in Veritatis Splendor*. Boca Raton, Florida: Dissertation, 2004.

Trigo, Tomás. *El debate sobre la especificidad de la moral cristiana*. Pamplona: Eunsa, 2003.

Tuck, Richard. *Natural Rights Theories. Their origin and development*. Cambridge: Cambridge University Press, 1981.

Veatch, Henry Babcock. "Natural Law and the "Is"-"Ought" Question: Queries to Finnis and Grisez." In *Swimming Against the Current in Contemporary Philosophy. Occasional Essays and Papers*, 293-311. Washington D.C.: The Catholic University of America Press, 1990.

—. "Natural Law and the Is-Ought Question: Queries to Finnis and Grisez." In *Swimming Against the Current in Contemporary Philosophy* edited by Jude P. Dougherty, 293-311. Washington, D. C.: The Catholic University of America Press, 1981.

—. *Swimming Against the Current in Contemporary Philosophy. Occasional Essays and Papers*. Edited by Jude P. Daugherty, Studies in Philosophy and the History of Philosohy. Volume 20. Washington D.C.: The Catholic University of America Press, 1990.

Vial Correa, Juan de Dios, and Elio Sgreccia, eds. *The Nature and Dignity of the Human person as the Foundation of the Right to Life: the Challenges of the Contemporary Cultural Context (Proceedings of the Eighth Assembly of the Pontifical Academy for Life, Vatican City, 25-27 February 2002)*. Città del Vaticano: Libreria Editrice Vaticana, 2003.

Vigna, Carmelo. *Teorie della felicità*. Padova: Francisci, 1986.

Vigna, Carmelo, and Susy Zanardo, eds. *La regola d'oro come etica universale*. Milano: Vita e Pensiero, 2005.

Viola, Francesco. "Natural Law: Stability and Development of its contents." In *The Nature and Dignity of the Human person as the Foundation of the Right to Life: the Challenges of the Contemporary Cultural Context (Proceedings of the Eighth Assembly of the Pontifical Academy for Life, Vatican City, 25-27 February 2002)*, edited by Juan de Dios Vial Correa and Elio Sgreccia, 160-80. Città del Vaticano: Libreria Editrice Vaticana, 2003.

—. "Positive Law and Natural Law." *IVR Encyclopaedia of Jurisprudence, Legal Theory and Philosophy of Law*. *<http://www.ivr-enc.info/en/article.php?id=56>* (2005).

Waldstein, Wolfgang. "The Capacity of Human Mind to Know the Natural Law." In *The Nature and Dignity of the Human person as the Foundation of the Right to Life: the Challenges of the Contemporary Cultural Context (Proceedings of the Eighth Assembly of the Pontifical Academy for Life, Vatican City, 25-27 February 2002)*, edited by Juan de Dios Vial Correa and Elio Sgreccia. Città del Vaticano Libreria Editrice Vaticana, 2003.

Weinreb, Lloyd L. *Natural Law and Justice*. Cambridge, MA: Harvard University Press, 1987.

Westberg, Daniel. "The Relation between Positive and Natural Law in Aquinas." *Journal of Law and Religion* 11, no. 1 (1994-1995): 1-22.

—. *Right Practical Reason. Aristotle, Action and Prudence in Aquinas*. Oxford: Clarendon Press, 1994.

Westerman, Pauline C. *The disintegration of natural law theory: Aquinas to Finnis*. Leiden: Brill Academic Pub., 1998.

Widow, José Luis. "The Unity of the Natural Law and the Distinction of Precepts in Thomas Aquinas." *Anuario Filosófico* 41, no. 1 (2008): 99-120.

Wieland, Georg. "Secundum naturam vivere. Über das Verhaeltnis von Natur und Sittlichkeit." In *Natur im ethischen argument*, edited by Bernhard Fraling, 13-33. Freiburg, Schweiz: Universitaet-verlag, 1990.

Wolfe, Christopher. "Il Concetto di Diritto Naturale di Tommaso D'Aquino: Guida a un sano Liberalismo." In *Riscopire le radici e i valori comuni della civiltà occidentale: il concetto di legge in Tommaso d'Aquino*, edited by Fulvio Di Blasi. Soveria Mannelli: Rubbettino, 2007.

—. ed. *Liberalism at the Crossroads: An Introduction to Contemporary Liberal Political Theory and its Critics*. 2nd ed. Lanham, Md - Oxford Rowman & Littlefield, 2003.

—. *Natural Law Liberalism*. Cambridge: Cambridge University Press, 2006.

Zagar, Janko. *Acting on Principles. A Thomistic perspective in Making moral decisions*. Lanham, New York, London: University Press of America, 1984.

Zimmermann, A. "Erkennbarkeit des Natürlichen Gesetzes Gemäss Thomas von Aquin." In *Lex et Libertas. Freedom and law according to St Thomas Aquinas, Proceedings of the 4th Syumposium on St. Thomas Aquinas Philosophy*, edited by L. Elders and K. Hedwig, 56-66. Cittá del Vaticano, 1986.

Zuckert, Michael P. *Natural Rights and the new Republicanism*. New Jersey: Princeton University Press, 1994.

LIST OF CONTRIBUTORS

Angela Aparisi Miralles
Doctor of Law (University of Valencia). She is currently Lecturer and Director of the Department of Philosophy of Law and the Institute of Human Rights at the University of Navarra. She has served as a Deputy Judge on the Provincial Court of Valencia. Her publications include: *Los orígenes ideológicos de la Revolución Norteamericana*, *El Proyecto Genoma Humano. Reflexiones sobre sus relaciones con el Derecho*, and *Ética y Deontología para juristas*. Research interests: Philosophy of Law, Human Rights, Bioethics.

Ángel Beleña López
Doctor of Philosophy. He is Honorary Fellow in the Department of Moral and Political Philosophy II at the Universidad Complutense (Madrid). He has recently published *Obligación y consecuencialismo en los "moralistas británicos"* (2005), and *Sociopolítica del hecho religioso. Una introducción* (2007). His research interest is in the field of utilitarian and consequentialist philosophy.

Juan-Luis Caballero
B.A. in Sacred Scripture (Pontifical Biblical Institute, Rome) and Ph.D. in Biblical Theology. He is currently Professor of New Testament at the University of Navarra. The following biblical studies comprise a number of his contributions to the study of conscience and human behaviour: "Retorica y teología. La Carta a Filemón" (2005), "La 'verdad' en la Biblia" (2006), and "Creación y pecado en el pensamiento paulino. Juan Pablo II, lector de Rm 8,19-22" (forthcoming). His research interests include the New Testament, Rhetoric, Hermeneutics, and Pauline Theology.

Laura Estela Corso de Estrada
Doctor of Philosophy. She is currently Researcher and Professor at the Catholic University of Argentina and Researcher at the National Council of Scientific and Technical Research, Argentina. Her recent publications include: *Naturaleza y vida moral. Marco Tulio Cicerón y Tomás de Aquino* (2008), *Marco Tulio Cicerón. Sobre Las Leyes. Estudio preliminar y edición bilingüe anotada* (2008) and "Natura y ratio en la especulación

sobre el cosmos. Guillermo de Auxerre y Felipe el Canciller" (2008). Her main research interests are the sources of Stoic tradition in Mediaeval philosophy in the 12th and 13th centuries.

Agustín Ignacio Echavarría
He is currently Research Assistant and Assistant Lecturer in the Department of Philosophy at the University of Navarra. He has been DAAD Visiting scholar at Münster University. His recent publications include: "Harmony, Dissonance and the Permission of Evil in the Early Writings of Leibniz" (2006), "Existencia y optimidad en Leibniz: una encrucijada entre arbitrarismo y necesitarismo" (2006) and "Voluntad antecedente y voluntad consecuente: las aporías de una herencia escolástica en el sistema de Leibniz" (forthcoming). His research interests are in the areas of metaphysics and theodicy, with special interest in the problem of evil in authors such as Leibniz, Thomas Aquinas and Maritain.

María Elton Bulnes
Doctor of Philosophy and currently Professor at the University de los Andes (Santiago, Chile). She has been a Visiting Scholar at Glasgow University, Boston University and Cambridge University. She has published five books, among which are: *Amor y reflexión. El amor puro de Fénelon en el contexto del pensamiento moderno* (1989) and *La is-ought question. La crítica de T. Reid a la filosofía moral de D. Hume* (2000). Her main research interests are on Ethics and Modern Moral Philosophy.

Teresa Enríquez
B.A. in Philosophy and M.A. in the History of Thought. She is currently Professor at the Universidad Panamericana (Aguascalientes, Mexico). She has been Scholarship Researcher by the Mexican National Council for Science and Technology. Her research interests lie in moral philosophy and theory of action.

Joaquín García Huidobro
Doctor of Philosophy. He is currently Professor of Legal Philosophy at the Universidad de los Andes (Santiago, Chile). His recent publications include: *Filosofía y retórica del iusnaturalismo* (2002), and *Simpatía por la política* (2006). Research interests: ethics and political philosophy. He is a former DAAD and Humboldt Foundation scholar.

Raquel Lázaro
Doctor of Philosophy. She is currently Lecturer in the Department of Philosophy at the University of Navarra. She has been a Visiting Scholar in Glasgow and Paris. Her recent publications include: "Montaigne el escéptico: ¿un filósofo moderno o postmoderno?" (2005), "Adam Smith: Individuo, Organización Social y Participación" (2003) and *La sociedad comercial en Adam Smith : método, moral, religión* (2002). Her research interests are in the Scottish Enlightenment and 17th century French philosophy .

Encarna Llamas
PhD. in Philosophical Anthropology. She is currently Professor in the Department of Philosophy at the Catholic University of Valencia. She has been Fulbright Visiting Scholar at the Catholic University of America. Her publications include: *Charles Taylor: una antropología de la identidad* (2001), "La imaginación creadora" (2004), and "Intencionalidad como constitución en el conocimiento práctico" (2005). Research interests: phenomenology in philosophical anthropology, ethics and the social sciences.

Margarita Mauri Álvarez
Doctor of Philosophy. She is currently Professor of Ethics in the Faculty of Philosophy at the University of Barcelona. Her publications include: "Moral Knowledge in Aristotle's Ethics" (1992), *Les virtuts en el pensament contemporani* (1992), and *El conocimiento moral* (2005). Her research interest is in the field of moral philosophy.

Carlos I. Massini Correas
Doctor of Law and Doctor of Philosophy (2001). He is currently Professor of Philosophy of Law and Ethics at the University of Mendoza (Argentina) and of Practical Philosophy at Austral University (Buenos Aires). He has been Visiting Professor at many European and American universities; he is Academic Secretary of the University of Mendoza and a member of the Board of the Argentine Association of Philosophy of Law. His recent publications include: *Philosophy of Law* (2005), *La ley natural y su interpretación contemporánea* (2006), *La falacia de la "falacia naturalista"* (1995). His research interests are in the philosophy of law and ethics.

Ivone Moreira

Master in Philosophy. She is currently Reader at the Catholic University of Portugal. Her recent publications include: "A Virtude da Prudência no Pensamento Político de Edmund Burke" (2006), "Sociedade Política e Contrato Social – As Perspectivas de Locke e Burke" (2005), and "Conceito e Fins da Educação em Sérgio" (2004). Researchs interests: political and moral philosophy.

José Ignacio Murillo

Doctor of Philosophy. He is currently Lecturer in the Department of Philosophy and a Board Member of the Institute of Anthropology and Ethics at the University of Navarra. He has been a Visiting Research Scholar at the University of Munich, Catholic University of America, Oxford University and the University of Notre Dame. His publications include: *Operación, hábito y reflexión. El conocimiento como clave antropológica en Tomás de Aquino* (1999), and *El valor revelador de la muerte* (1999). His research interests are in philosophical anthropology.

Diego Poole

Doctor of Law (Universidad Complutense, Madrid). He is currently Professor in the School of Law at the Universidad Rey Juan Carlos (Madrid). He is the author of *El derecho de los juristas* (1998). His research interests are in the philosophy of law.

Pablo Sanchez-Ostiz

Doctor of Law and Doctor of Philosophy. He is currently Lecturer in Criminal Law and Criminal Justice Policy in the School of Law at the University of Navarra. He has been a Fellow of the Deutscher Akademischer Austausch Dienst (1996), and of the Humboldt Foundation since 2002. He is the author of *El delito contable tributario* (1995), and *¿Encubridores o cómplices?* (2004), and he was the Spanish editor of *Imputación y Derecho penal* (by Joachim Hruschka, 2005). His research interest relate to the theory of imputation, accessory liability, legal argumentation and 'white-collar' crime.

Juan Fernando Sellés

Doctor of Philosophy. He is currently Lecturer in the Department of Philosophy at the University of Navarre. He has been Visiting Professor at Notre Dame University. His recent publications include: *Propuestas antropológicas del siglo XX* (2004-2007), *Antropología para inconformes. Una antropologia abierta al futuro* (2006), and *El conocer personal.*

Estudio del entendimiento agente según Leonardo Polo (2003). His research interests are in the fields of philosophical anthropology and medieval philosophy.

Mario Šilar
He is currently Research Assistant and Assistant Lecturer in Ethics in the Department of Philosophy at the University of Navarra. He has been a Visiting Scholar at the University of Reading. His research interests are moral and social philosophy, natural law in Thomas Aquinas, the philosophy of law, and the relations between culture and philosophy. Select publications include: *Metodología de investigación y técnicas para la elaboración de tesis* (2006), and "Trascendentales, encuentro entre ética y religión" (2007).

Manfred Svensson
Doctor of Philosophy (University of Munich). He is currently Professor of Ethics at the University of los Andes (Santiago, Chile). His research interests include moral philosophy, St. Augustine and Melanchthon. He has translated Kierkegaard's *The Present Age* into Spanish (2001), and is the author of "Felipe Melanchthon y la teoría de la primera historiografía protestante" (2005) and of *Das Theorie-Praxis-Problem bei Augustin* (forthcoming).

José M. Torralba
PhD. in Philosophy. He is currently Lecturer in the Department of Philosophy at the University of Navarra. He has been a Visiting Scholar at the Universities of Oxford and Munich. Research interests: moral philosophy, theory of action and theory of judgment. He is the author of *Acción intencional y razomaniento práctico según G.E.M. Anscombe* (2005), and *La facultad del juicio en la filosofía práctica de Kant* (forthcoming), and the editor of *Two Hundred Years Later: Returns and Re-interpretations of Kant* (2005).

Tomás Trigo
Doctor of Theology and Philosophy (Pontifical University of the Holy Cross, Rome). He is currently Professor of Moral Theology in the Faculty of Theology at the University of Navarra. His recent publications include: *El debate sobre la especificidad de la moral cristiana* (2003), and *Moral de la persona* (2006). His research interests centre on moral theology and virtue ethics.

Julia Urabayen
Doctor of Philosophy. She is currently Professor in the Department of Philosophy at the University of Navarra, and Secretary of the Humanities Department and of the journal, *Anuario Filosófico*. Her recent publications include: *El pensamiento antropológico de Gabriel Marcel. Un canto al ser humano* (2001), *Las sendas del pensamiento hacia el misterio del ser. La filosofía concreta de Gabriel Marcel* (2001), and *Las raíces del humanismo de Emmanuel Levinas: el judaísmo y la fenomenología* (2005). Her main research interest is 20th century French Philosophy.

Caridad Velarde
Ph. D. in Law. She is currently Professor of Philosophy and Theory of Law at the University of Cádiz. She has been a Visiting Scholar at the Universities of Oxford, Toronto and New York. She is the author of *Hayek. Una teoría de la justicia, la moral y el derecho* (1994) and *Universalismo de derechos humanos. Análisis a la luz del debate anglosajón* (2003). Her research interests concern social reality in legal hermeneutics.

Héctor Zagal
Doctor of Philosophy. He is currently Lecturer in the Department of Philosophy at Universidad Panamericana (Mexico City). He has been a Visiting Scholar at the University of Notre Dame. His recent publications include: *Ethik für junge Menschen* (2000), *Horismós, syllogismós, asápheia en Aristóteles* (2002), and *Método y ciencia en Aristóteles* (2005).

María Idoya Zorroza
Doctor of Philosophy. She is currently working as a Research Specialist with the Special Research Group on "Classical Spanish Thought (14th–16th centuries): its Medieval Inspiration and Influence on Contemporary Philosophy" in the Department of Philosophy at the University of Navarra. She has translated and edited a number of books by Báñez, Aquinas, Francisco de Vitoria, and has published a number of papers on these topics. She is also a Visiting Professor at the University of Piura, Peru.

SUBJECT INDEX

NAME INDEX